The American Heritage®
Pocket Spanish Dictionary

Houghton Mifflin Harcourt
Boston • New York

Visit our website: www.hmhbooks.com

ISBN-13: 978-0-618-13216-4
ISBN-10: 0-618-13216-3

Manufactured in the United States of America

STAFF/PERSONAL

Editors/Redacción

Priscila Baldoví, Evelyn Boria Rivera, Helen Bronk,
Wade A. Ostrowski, David Pritchard, Hanna Schonthal

Production/Producción

Christopher Granniss, Christopher Leonesio

13 14 15 16 - DP - 14 13 12 11

GUIDE

Alphabetical order of entries reflects international rules of alphabetization. Therefore, *ch* and *ll* are no longer considered separate letters of the Spanish alphabet. However, it is convenient to think of *ch* and *ll* as unique for the purposes of pronunciation (see Spanish Pronunciation Guide, p. iv).

Irregular verbs are referenced to the Spanish Verb Table (pp. vi–viii) with a boldface section number (e.g., **dar §12**). The number corresponds to the appropriate model verb in the Table.

Common idioms and phrases are listed as run-on entries at the appropriate part of speech. The first run-on is introduced by a solid square (■). Additional run-ons follow in alphabetical order and are separated by bold bullets (•). Idioms involving the plural usage of the entry word are introduced by a solid square followed by the plural label (■ *pl*).

GUÍA

Todos los vocablos están escritos en orden alfabético. Los vocablos compuestos escritos en forma abierta (**air conditioner**), con guión (**father-in-law**) o en forma sólida (**businesswoman**) están escritos como si fueran sólidos.

Verbos irregulares se indican con una estrella después del vocablo (p.e., **give°**). El pretérito y el participio pasivo de estos verbos aparecen en la lista de Verbos Irregulares del Inglés (pp. ix–x).

Modismos y locuciones de interés general aparecen en la parte de la oración a la que correspondan, precedidos por un cuadrado en negrilla (■), y separados en forma alfabética por el símbolo (•). Las locuciones que se usan en su forma plural se indican con un cuadrado en negrilla seguido por el rótulo plural (■ *pl*).

ABBREVIATIONS/ABREVIATURAS

adj	adjective/adjetivo	*indef*	indefinite/indefinido
adv	adverb/adverbio	*interj*	interjection/interjección
art	article/artículo	*intr.*	intransitive/intransitivo
aux	auxiliary	JER.	jerga
COLL.	colloquial	*m, mpl*	masculine (plural)
conj	conjunction/conjunción	*pron*	pronoun/pronombre
contr	contraction/contracción	*reflex*	reflexive
def	definite/definido	*s, ssg, spl*	sustantivo (singular, plural)
f, fpl	feminine (plural)	SL.	slang
FAM.	familiar	*tr*	transitive/transitivo
FIG.	figurative		

(Other abbreviations, such as COMPUT. for "computers," are considered self-evident. / Otras abreviaturas, como COMPUT. para "computadoras," se consideran evidentes.)

SPANISH PRONUNCIATION GUIDE

Letter	Spanish Example	English Example	Description
a	pata	father	
b	boca	bib	At the beginning of a word
	rabo		Between vowels, closer to *v*
c	calco	cat	Before *a, o, u,* like *k*
	cedro	cedar	Before *e, i* like *s;* in much of Spain pronounced like *th* of *thick*
(ch)	chiste	church	
d	dar	die	At the beginning of a word
	cada		Between vowels, like *th* of *rather*
e	leche	café	
f	fácil	fat	
g	gente		Before *e, i,* like *h* of *ha!*
	guerra	guide	With *u* before *e, i,* a hard *g*
	gato	got	Before *a, o, u,* a hard *g*
h	honor		Always silent
i	silla	machine	
j	jugo		Like *h* in *ha!*
k	kilo	kite	
l	listo	list	
(ll)	llama		In Spain, like *lli* of *million;* elsewhere like Spanish consonant *y* (see below)
m	mamá	mum	
n	nona	none	
ñ	año		Like *ny* of *canyon*
o	solo	so	
p	papa	pipe	
q	quita	raquet	
r	caro		Like *dd* of *ladder*
(rr)	carro		Strongly trilled
s	soso	sass	
t	tonto	tight	
u	luto	lute	
	agüero	anguish	
v	vino		Identical to initial Spanish *b*
	lava		Identical to intervocalic Spanish *b*
w	wat		Pronounced either like English *v* or *w*
x	éxito	exit	Exception: in the words "México" and "mexicano" *x* is like Spanish *j*
	mixto		Before a consonant, may be pronounced *s*
y	y		Like *i* of *machine*
	yeso	yes	In River Plate, like *s* of *vision*
z	zona		Like *s* in *sass;* in much of Spain, like *th* of *thick*

GUÍA PARA LA PRONUNCIACIÓN INGLESA

letra	ejemplos y/o sonidos aproximados
a	pat (entre la *a* y la *e*); pay, mate (rey); care, hair (parecido a *ea* en *brea*, con la *r*); father (año); caught, paw (corre); swat (la)
b	bib (boca)
c	cat (casa); piece (sapo); church (chico); pick (casa)
d	deed, milled (dar); judge (entre la *y* inicial y la *ch*)
e	pet, feather (el); bee, me (mil); dear, mere (entre *ía* en *día* e *íe* en *fíe*, con la *r*); term (parecido a una *e* que tira a la *o*, con la *r*); few (ciudad)
f	fife (fama)
g	gag (gato); rough (fama)
h	hat (joya)
i	pit (entre la *i* y la *e*); piece (mil); pie, mice (aire); pier (entre *ía* en *día* e *íe* en *fíe*, con la *r*); firm (parecido a una *e* que tira a la *o*, con la *r*)
j	jump, major (entre la *y* inicial y la *ch*)
k	kid, make (casa)
l	lid, needle (luz)
m	mime (muy)
n	no, line, sudden (no); thing (inglés)
o	pot (la); toe, go, boat (solo); for (corre); noise, boy (oigo); took (parecido a la *u* en *yogur*, más breve); boot (uno); out, cow (auto); rough (parecido a una *o* que tira a la *a*)
p	pipe (pan); phase (fama)
q	quick (cuan); pique (casa)
r	roar (una *ere* con la lengua curvada hacia atrás)
s	saw, pass (sapo); ship, dish (una *che* suavizada, más como la *ese*); vision, pleasure (parecido a la *ll* de Argentina)
t	time, mate, stopped (tu); thin, path (parecido a la *ce* de Castilla); this, bathe (cada)
u	cut (parecido a una *o* que tira a la *a*); use (ciudad); urge (parecido a una *e* que tira a la *o*, con la r); suit (uno)
v	valve (una *efe* sonora)
w	with (cual); which (juez)
x	box, taxi (taxi); xylem (mismo)
y	yes (yo); by (aire)
z	zebra (mismo)

SPANISH VERB TABLE

The following list shows model conjugations for regular verbs and the most common irregular verbs. The tenses shown include the present indicative, imperfect, and preterit tenses and the past participle. Only tenses in which an irregular conjugation occurs are presented. Irregular forms are printed in bold type. Irregular verbs are referenced to the Table by means of section numbers; thus **despedir §32** follows the model conjugations given at §32 PEDIR in the Table.

§01 REGULAR VERBS

-AR Verbs: AMAR	-ER Verbs: VENDER	-IR Verbs: PARTIR
Present		
AM -o	VEND -o	PART -o
-as	-es	-es
-a	-e	-e
-amos	-emos	-imos
-áis	-éis	-ís
-an	-en	-en
Imperfect		
AM -aba	VEND -ía	PART -ía
-abas	-ías	-ías
-aba	-ía	-ía
-ábamos	-íamos	-íamos
-abais	-íais	-íais
-aban	-ían	-ían
Preterit		
AM -é	VEND -í	PART -í
-aste	-iste	-iste
-ó	-ió	-ió
-amos	-imos	-imos
-asteis	-isteis	-isteis
-aron	-ieron	-ieron
Past Participle		
amado	vendido	partido

IRREGULAR VERBS

§02 ALZAR Pret. **alcé,** alzaste, etc.

§03 ANDAR Pret. **anduve, anduviste, anduvo, anduvimos, anduvisteis, anduvieron**

§04 AVERGONZAR Pres. **avergüenzo, avergüenzas, avergüenza,** avergonzamos, avergonzáis, **avergüenzan** Pret. **avergoncé,** avergonzaste, etc.

§05 AVERIGUAR Pret. **averigüé,** averiguaste, etc.

§06 CABER Pres. **quepo,** cabes, etc. Pret. **cupe, cupiste, cupo, cupimos, cupisteis, cupieron**

§07 CAER Pres. **caigo,** caes, etc. Pret. caí, **caíste, cayó, caímos,** caísteis, **cayeron** Past Part. **caído**

§08 COLGAR Pres. **cuelgo, cuelgas, cuelga,** colgamos, colgáis, **cuelgan** Pret. **colgué,** colgaste, etc.

§09 CONOCER Pres. **conozco,** conoces, etc.

§10 CONSTRUIR Pres. **construyo, construyes, construye,** construimos, construís, **construyen** Pret. construí, construiste, **construyó,** construimos, construisteis, **construyeron**

§11 CONTAR Pres. **cuento, cuentas, cuenta,** contamos, contáis, **cuentan**

§12 DAR Pres. **doy,** das, etc. Pret. **di, diste, dio, dimos, disteis, dieron**

§13 DECIR Pres. **digo, dices, dice,** decimos, decís, **dicen** Past Part. **dicho**

§14 DEDUCIR Pres. **deduzco,** deduces, etc. Pret. **deduje, dedujiste, dedujo, dedujimos, dedujisteis, dedujeron**

§15 DISTINGUIR Pres. **distingo,** distingues, etc.

§16 DORMIR Pres. **duermo, duermes, duerme,** dormimos, dormís, **duermen** Pret. dormí, dormiste, **durmió,** dormimos, dormisteis, **durmieron**

§17 EMPEZAR Pres. **empiezo, empiezas, empieza,** empezamos, empezáis, **empiezan** Pret. **empecé,** empezaste, etc.

§18 ENVIAR Pres. **envío, envías, envía,** enviamos, enviáis, **envían**

§19 ERIGIR Pres. **erijo,** erijes, etc.

§20 ESCOGER Pres. **escojo,** escoges, etc.

§21 ESTAR Pres. **estoy, estás, está,** estamos, estáis, **están** Pret. **estuve, estuviste, estuvo, estuvimos, estuvisteis, estuvieron**

§22 FORZAR Pres. **fuerzo, fuerzas, fuerza,** forzamos, forzáis, **fuerzan** Pret. **forcé,** forzaste, etc.

§23 HABER Pres. **he, has, ha, hemos, habéis, han** Pret. **hube, hubiste, hubo, hubimos, hubisteis, hubieron**

§24 HACER Pres. **hago,** haces, etc. Pret. **hice, hiciste, hizo, hicimos, hicisteis, hicieron** Past Part. **hecho**

§25 IR Pres. **voy, vas, va, vamos, vais, van** Imp. **iba,** etc. Pret. **fui, fuiste, fue, fuimos, fuisteis, fueron**

§26 JUGAR Pres. **juego, juegas, juega,** jugamos, jugáis, **juegan** Pret. **jugué,** jugaste, etc.

§27 LEER Pret. leí, **leiste, leyó, leímos,** leísteis, **leyeron**

§28 LUCIR Pres. **luzco**, luces, etc.

§29 OÍR Pres. **oigo, oyes, oye, oímos,** oís, **oyen** Pret. oí, oíste, oyó, oímos, oísteis, **oyeron** Past Part. **oído**

§30 OLER Pres. **huelo, hueles, huele,** olemos, oléis, **huelen**

§31 PAGAR Pret. **pagué,** pagas, etc.

§32 PEDIR Pres. **pido, pides, pide,** pedimos, pedís, **piden** Pret. pedí, pediste, **pidió,** pedimos, pedisteis, **pidieron**

§33 PENSAR Pres. **pienso, piensas, piensa,** pensamos, pensáis, **piensan**

§34 PERDER Pres. **pierdo, pierdes, pierde,** perdemos, perdéis, **pierden**

§35 PLEGAR Pres. **pliego, pliegas, pliega,** plegamos, plegáis, pliegan Pret. **plegué,** plegaste, etc.

§36 PODER Pres. **puedo, puedes, puede,** podemos, podéis, **pueden** Pret. **pude, pudiste, pudo, pudimos, pudisteis, pudieron**

§37 PONER Pres. **pongo,** pones, etc. Pret. **puse, pusiste, puso, pusimos, pusisteis, pusieron** Past Part. **puesto**

§38 QUERER Pres. **quiero, quieres, quiere,** queremos, queréis, **quieren** Pret. **quise, quisiste, quiso, quisimos, quisisteis, quisieron**

§39 REÍR Pres. **río, ríes, ríe, reímos,** reís, **ríen** Pret. reí, **reíste, rió,** reímos, **reísteis, rieron** Past Part. **reído**

§40 SABER Pres. **sé,** sabes, etc. Pret. **supe, supiste, supo, supimos, supisteis, supieron**

§41 SALIR Pres. **salgo,** sales, etc.

§42 SEGUIR Pres. **sigo, sigues, sigue,** seguimos, seguís, **siguen** Pret. seguí, seguiste, **siguió,** seguimos, seguisteis, **siguieron**

§43 SENTIR Pres. **siento, sientes, siente,** sentimos, sentís, **sienten** Pret. sentí, sentiste, **sintió,** sentimos, sentisteis, **sintieron**

§44 SER Pres. **soy, eres, es, somos, sois, son** Imp. **era,** etc. Pret. **fui, fuiste, fue, fuimos, fuisteis, fueron**

§45 SITUAR Pres. **sitúo, sitúas, sitúa,** situamos, situáis, **sitúan**

§46 TENER Pres. **tengo, tienes, tiene,** tenemos, tenéis, **tienen** Pret. **tuve, tuviste, tuvo, tuvimos, tuvisteis, tuvieron**

§47 TOCAR Pret. **toqué,** tocaste, etc.

§48 TORCER Pres. **tuerzo, tuerces, tuerce,** torcemos, torcéis, **tuercen**

§49 TRAER Pres. **traigo,** traes, etc. Pret. **traje, trajiste, trajo, trajimos, trajisteis, trajeron** Past Part. **traído**

§50 VALER Pres. **valgo,** vales, etc.

§51 VENCER Pres. **venzo,** vences, etc.

§52 VENIR Pres. **vengo, vienes, viene,** venimos, venís, **vienen** Pret. **vine, viniste, vino, vinimos, vinisteis, vinieron**

§53 VER Pres. **veo,** ves, etc. Imp. **veía,** etc. Pret. **vi,** viste, **vio,** vimos, visteis, vieron Past Part. **visto**

§54 VOLVER Pres. **vuelvo, vuelves, vuelve,** volvemos, volvéis, **vuelven**

§55 IRREGULAR PAST PARTICIPLES
The following verbs are regular except for their past participles: abrir **abierto;** cubrir **cubierto;** escribir **escrito;** freír **frito;** imprimir **impreso;** romper **roto**

viii

VERBOS IRREGULARES DEL INGLÉS

La siguiente lista de verbos da el infinitivo, el pretérito y el participio pasivo de los verbos irregulares del inglés.

abide	abided *o* abode, abided *o* abode		**drive**	drove, driven
arise	arose, arisen		**dwell**	dwelled *o* dwelt, dwelled *o* dwelt
awake	awoke, awaked			
be	was, been		**eat**	ate, eaten
bear	bore, born *o* borne		**fall**	fell, fallen
beat	beat, beaten *o* beat		**feed**	fed, fed
begin	began, begun		**feel**	felt, felt
bend	bent, bent		**fight**	fought, fought
bet	bet *o* betted, bet *o* betted		**find**	found, found
bid	bade *o* bid, bidden *o* bid		**flee**	fled, fled
bind	bound, bound		**fling**	flung, flung
bite	bit, bitten		**fly**	flew, flown
bleed	bled, bled		**freeze**	froze, frozen
blend	blended *o* blent, blended *o* blent		**get**	got, got *o* gotten
			give	gave, given
bless	blessed *o* blest, blessed *o* blessed		**go**	went, gone
			grind	ground, ground
blow	blew, blown		**grow**	grew, grown
break	broke, broken		**hang**	hung, hung
breed	bred, bred		**have**	had, had
bring	brought, brought		**hear**	heard, heard
build	built, built		**hide**	hid, hidden *o* hid
burn	burned *o* burnt, burned *o* burnt		**hit**	hit, hit
			hold	held, held
buy	bought, bought		**hurt**	hurt, hurt
cast	cast, cast		**keep**	kept, kept
catch	caught, caught		**kneel**	knelt *o* kneeled, knelt *o* kneeled
choose	chose, chosen			
cling	clung, clung		**knit**	knit *o* knitted, knit *o* knitted
come	came, come		**know**	knew, known
cost	cost, cost		**lay**	laid, laid
creep	crept, crept		**lead**	led, led
crow	crowed *o* crew, crowed		**lean**	leaned *o* leant, leaned *o* leant
curse	cursed *o* curst, cursed *o* curst		**leap**	leaped *o* leapt, leaped *o* leapt
cut	cut, cut		**learn**	learned *o* learnt, learned *o* learnt
deal	dealt, dealt			
dig	dug, dug		**leave**	left, left
dive	dived *o* dove, dived		**lend**	lent, lent
do	did, done		**let**	let, let
draw	drew, drawn		**lie**	lay, lain
dream	dreamed *o* dreamt, dreamed *o* dreamt		**light**	lighted *o* lit, lighted *o* lit
			lose	lost, lost
drink	drank, drunk		**make**	made, made
			mean	meant, meant

meet	met, met	**spin**	spun, spun
mow	mowed, mowed *o* mown	**spit**	spat *o* spit, spat *o* spit
pay	paid, paid	**split**	split, split
prove	proved, proved *o* proven	**spoil**	spoiled *o* spoilt, spoiled *o* spoilt
put	put, put		
quit	quit *o* quitted, quit *o* quitted	**spread**	spread, spread
read	read, read	**spring**	sprang *o* sprung, sprung
rid	rid *o* ridded, rid *o* ridded	**stand**	stood, stood
ride	rode, ridden	**steal**	stole, stolen
ring	rang, rung	**stick**	stuck, stuck
rise	rose, risen	**sting**	stung, stung
run	ran, run	**stink**	stank *o* stunk, stunk
saw	sawed, sawed *o* sawn	**strew**	strewed, strewed *o* strewn
say	said, said	**stride**	strode, stridden
see	saw, seen	**strike**	struck, struck *o* stricken
seek	sought, sought	**string**	strung, strung
sell	sold, sold	**strive**	strove *o* strived, striven *o* strived
send	sent, sent		
set	set, set	**swear**	swore, sworn
sew	sewed, sewn *o* sewed	**sweat**	sweat *o* sweated, sweat *o* sweated
shake	shook, shaken		
shave	shaved, shaved *o* shaven	**sweep**	swept, swept
shed	shed, shed	**swell**	swelled, swelled *o* swollen
shine	shone *o* shined, shone *o* shined	**swim**	swam, swum
		swing	swung, swung
shoe	shod, shod *o* shodden	**take**	took, taken
shoot	shot, shot	**teach**	taught, taught
show	showed, shown *o* showed	**tear**	tore, torn
shrink	shrank *o* shrunk, shrunk *o* shrunken	**tell**	told, told
		think	thought, thought
shut	shut, shut	**thrive**	throve *o* thrived, thrived *o* thriven
sing	sang, sung		
sink	sank *o* sunk, sunk	**throw**	threw, thrown
sit	sat, sat	**thrust**	thrust, thrust
slay	slew, slain	**tread**	trod, trodden *o* trod
sleep	slept, slept	**wake**	woke *o* waked, waked *o* woken
slide	slid, slid	**wear**	wore, worn
sling	slung, slung	**weave**	wove *o* weaved, woven *o* weaved
slit	slit, slit		
smell	smelled *o* smelt, smelled *o* smelt	**weep**	wept, wept
		wet	wet *o* wetted, wet *o* wetted
sow	sowed, sown *o* sowed	**win**	won, won
speak	spoke, spoken	**wind**	wound, wound
speed	sped *o* speeded, sped *o* speeded	**wrap**	wrapt *o* wrapped, wrapt *o* wrapped
spend	spent, spent	**wring**	wrung, wrung
spill	spilled *o* spilt, spilled *o* spilt	**write**	wrote, written

x

Spanish/English

A

a ➤ *prep* to, into ∎ **a las dos** at two o'clock • **a pie** on foot • **a poco** after a while • **a 3 de Mayo** on May 3 • **mirar al sur** look to the south • **voy a la tienda** I'm going to the store • **llegó a Lima** she arrived in Lima.

abad ➤ *m* abbot.

abadesa ➤ *f* abbess.

abadía ➤ *f* abbey.

abajo ➤ *adv* down; (*en casa*) downstairs; (*posición*) below, underneath ∎ **hacia a.** downwards.

abandonar ➤ *tr* to abandon, desert; (*desertar*) to leave; (*renunciar*) to give up ➤ *reflex* (*entregarse a*) to abandon oneself to; (*descuidarse*) to become slovenly.

abandono ➤ *m* abandonment; (*descuido*) neglect; (*desenfrenamiento*) abandon.

abanico ➤ *m* fan.

abaratar ➤ *tr* to reduce (prices).

abarcar §47 ➤ *tr* (*contener*) to include, cover; (*abrazar*) to embrace; (*divisar*) to take in.

abarrotado, a ➤ *adj* full, crowded.

abarrotar ➤ *tr* (*llenar*) to fill up; (*exceso*) to overstock.

abarrotes ➤ *mpl* AMER. (*comestibles*) groceries.

abastecedor, a ➤ *mf* supplier.

abastecer §09 ➤ *tr* to supply, provide (*de* with).

abastecimiento ➤ *m* (*provisión*) supply; (*aprovisionamiento*) supplying.

abasto ➤ *m* supplying ∎ *pl* supplies, provisions.

abatido, a ➤ *adj* despondent.

abatir ➤ *tr* (*derribar*) to knock down, demolish; (*desanimar*) to depress.

abdicar §47 ➤ *tr & intr* to abdicate.

abdomen ➤ *m* abdomen.

abdominal ➤ *adj* abdominal.

abecedario ➤ *m* alphabet.

abedul ➤ *m* birch.

abeja ➤ *f* bee.

abejorro ➤ *m* bumblebee; (*pesado*) pest.

abertura ➤ *f* opening; (*hendidura*) crack; PHOTOG. aperture.

abeto ➤ *m* fir.

abierto, a ➤ *adj* open; (*raso*) open, clear; (*franco*) candid; (*sincero*) sincere.

abigarrado, a ➤ *adj* variegated, multicolored.

abismal ➤ *adj* abysmal.

abismo ➤ *m* abyss.

abjurar ➤ *tr* to abjure, renounce.

ablandamiento ➤ *m* softening.

ablandar ➤ *tr* to soften; (*suavizar*) to mollify; (*mitigar*) to mitigate ➤ *intr* (*la nieve*) to thaw ➤ *reflex* to soften.

abnegación ➤ *f* abnegation.

abnegar §35 ➤ *tr* to abnegate, renounce ➤ *reflex* to deny oneself.

abofetear ➤ *tr* to slap.

abogacía ➤ *f* law (profession).

abogado, a ➤ *mf* lawyer, attorney.

abolengo ➤ *m* ancestry, lineage; (*patrimonio*) inheritance.

abolición ➤ *f* abolition, repeal.

abolicionista ➤ *mf* abolitionist.

abolir ➤ *tr* to abolish, repeal.

abolladura ➤ *f* dent.

abollar ➤ *tr* to dent.

abominable ➤ *adj* abominable, detestable.

abominar ➤ *tr* to detest.

abonado, a ➤ *mf* subscriber, season ticket holder; (*viajero*) commuter.

abonar ➤ *tr* to vouch for, guarantee; AGR. to fertilize; (*pagar*) to pay ➤ *reflex* to subscribe.

abono ➤ *m* fertilizer; (*billete*) subscription; AMER. payment, installment.

abordar ➤ *tr* MARIT. to board; (*acercar*) to approach; (*emprender*) to tackle (a problem) ➤ *intr* MARIT. to dock.

aborigen ➤ *adj & mf* aboriginal.

aborrecer §09 ➤ *tr* to hate, abhor.

aborrecimiento ➤ *m* hatred, loathing.

abortar ➤ *tr & intr* to abort.

aborto ➤ *m* abortion.

abotonar ➤ *tr & reflex* to button (up) ➤ *intr* to bud.

abovedado ➤ *m* ARCHIT. vaulting.

abrasar ➤ *tr (quemar)* to burn; *(calentar)* to overheat. ➤*intr & reflex* to burn up.

abrazar §02 ➤ *tr* to embrace, hug; *(adoptar)* to adopt ➤ *reflex* to embrace (each other).

abrazo ➤ *m* embrace, hug.

abrelatas ➤ *m* can opener.

abrevadero ➤ *m* watering hole or trough.

abreviado, a ➤ *adj* brief, short; *(libros)* abridged.

abreviar ➤ *tr (reducir)* to abbreviate; *(libros)* to abridge; *(acelerar)* to shorten, hasten.

abreviatura ➤ *f* abbreviation; *(compendio)* compendium, résumé.

abrigar §31 ➤ *tr (proteger)* to shelter; *(cubrir)* to keep warm; *(sospechas)* to harbor ➤ *reflex* to wrap oneself up.

abrigo ➤ *m (protección)* shelter, cover; *(sobretodo)* overcoat.

abril ➤ *m* April.

abrir §55 ➤ *tr* to open; *(desplegar)* to spread out; *(empezar)* to begin; *(encabezar)* to lead, head.

abrochar ➤ *tr (con botones)* to button (up); *(con broches)* to fasten.

abrogar §31 ➤ *tr* to abrogate, repeal.

abrojo ➤ *m* thistle.

abrumador, a ➤ *adj* overwhelming.

abrumar ➤ *tr* to overwhelm, oppress ➤ *reflex* to become foggy.

abrupto, a ➤ *adj* abrupt; *(escarpado)* craggy.

absceso ➤ *m* abscess.

absolución ➤ *f* absolution.

absoluto, a ➤ *adj* absolute; *(sin mezcla)* pure (alcohol) • **en a.** absolutely not, not at all • **lo a.** the absolute ➤ *f (proposición)* absolute.

absolver §54 ➤ *tr* to absolve; LAW to acquit.

absorbente ➤ *adj* absorbent; FIG. absorbing.

absorber ➤ *tr* to absorb ➤ *reflex* to become absorbed or engrossed.

absorción ➤ *f* absorption.

abstemio, a ➤ *adj* abstemious, teetotaling ➤ *mf* teetotaler, non-drinker.

abstención ➤ *f* abstention.

abstenerse §46 ➤ *reflex* to abstain.

abstinencia ➤ *f* abstinence.

abstracto, a ➤ *adj & m* abstract.

abstraer §49 ➤ *tr* to abstract ➤ *reflex* to become withdrawn or lost in thought.

abstraído, a ➤ *adj (distraído)* absorbed; *(retirado)* withdrawn.

absurdidad ➤ *f* absurdity.

absurdo, a ➤ *adj* absurd, ridiculous ➤ *m* absurdity.

abuela ➤ *f* grandmother.

abuelo ➤ *m* grandfather ■ *pl* grandparents.

abultado, a ➤ *adj* large, bulky.

abultar ➤ *tr (engrosar)* to enlarge; *(hinchar)* to swell ➤ *intr* to be bulky.

abundancia ➤ *f* abundance.

abundante ➤ *adj* abundant, plentiful.

abundar ➤ *intr* to abound.

aburrido, a ➤ *adj (cansado)* bored; *(tedioso)* boring.

aburrir ➤ *tr* to bore ➤ *reflex* to become bored.

abusador, a ➤ *adj* AMER. abusive ➤ *mf* abuser.

abusar ➤ *intr* to go too far, exceed ■ **a. de** to abuse, misuse.

abuso ➤ *m* abuse, excess ■ **a. de alcohol** alcohol abuse • **a. sexual** sexual abuse.

acá ➤ *adv* here, over here ■ **a. y allá** here and there, everywhere • **más a.** closer.

acabado, a ➤ *adj* finished; *(perfecto)* complete, consummate ➤ *m* finish.

acabar ➤ *tr* to finish, complete; *(perfeccionar)* to put the finishing touches on; *(consumir)* to use up ➤ *intr* to end, stop ■ **a. de** to have just • **a. por** to end up ➤*reflex* to end, terminate ■ ¡**se acabó!** that's the end of that! • **se me acabó el tiempo** I ran out of time.

academia ➤ *f* academy.

académico, a ➤ *adj* academic ➤ *mf* academician.

acallar ➤ *tr* to hush, quiet.

acalorado, a ➤ *adj* heated, warm; *(enardecido)* heated, animated.

acalorar ➤ *tr* to warm up ➤ *reflex* to heat up; *(irritarse)* to get excited.

acampanado, a ➤ *adj* bell-shaped.

acampar ➤ *tr, intr, & reflex* to camp.

acantilado, a ➤ *adj* steep ➤ *m* cliff.

acaparar ➤ *tr* (*acumular*) to stockpile, hoard; (*monopolizar*) to monopolize.

acápite ➤ *m* S. AMER. (*párrafo*) paragraph; (*subtítulo*) subheading.

acariciar ➤ *tr* to caress; (*abrigar*) to cherish.

acarrear ➤ *tr* to cart, transport.

acaso ➤ *m* chance ➤ *adv* perhaps, maybe ■ **por si a.** just in case.

acatamiento ➤ *m* respect, reverence.

acatar ➤ *tr* (*respetar*) to respect; (*obedecer*) to observe, comply with.

acatarrarse ➤ *reflex* to catch a cold.

acaudalado, a ➤ *adj* wealthy, rich.

acceder ➤ *intr* to agree; (*al trono*) to accede.

acceso ➤ *m* (*entrada*) access, entry; (*accesibilidad*) accessibility.

accesorio, a ➤ *adj & m* accessory.

accidentado, a ➤ *adj* rough, uneven.

accidental ➤ *adj* accidental.

accidente ➤ *m* accident; (*del terreno*) roughness, unevenness ■ **por a.** by chance.

acción ➤ *f* action; (*hecho*) act, deed; (*efecto*) effect; (*judicial*) legal action, lawsuit; COM. share (of stock).

accionar ➤ *tr* to work, operate.

accionista ➤ *mf* shareholder, stockholder.

acechar ➤ *tr* to watch, spy on.

acecho ➤ *m* watching, spying.

aceitar ➤ *tr* to oil, lubricate.

aceite ➤ *m* oil ■ **a. vegetal** vegetable oil.

aceituna ➤ *f* olive.

acelerador ➤ *m* accelerator.

acelerar ➤ *tr* to speed up ➤ *intr* to hurry; (*motores*) to race.

acento ➤ *m* accent; (*signo*) accent mark; (*tono*) tone.

acentuar §45 ➤ *tr* to accent; (*hacer resaltar*) to accentuate ➤ *reflex* to stand out.

acepción ➤ *f* meaning.

aceptar ➤ *tr* to accept; (*admitir*) to believe in; (*aprobar*) to approve of.

acequia ➤ *f* irrigation ditch.

acera ➤ *f* sidewalk.

acerca de ➤ *prep* about, concerning.

acercar §47 ➤ *tr* to bring near ➤ *reflex*

to approach, draw near.

acero ➤ *m* steel; (*arma*) blade, sword.

acérrimo, a ➤ *adj* staunch, stalwart.

acertado, a ➤ *adj* correct, accurate.

acertar §33 ➤ *tr* (*adivinar*) to guess correctly; (*encontrar*) to find, hit upon ➤ *intr* (*tener razón*) to hit the mark, be correct.

acertijo ➤ *m* riddle.

acetato ➤ *m* acetate.

acetona ➤ *f* acetone.

achacar §47 ➤ *tr* to attribute, impute.

achaque ➤ *m* ailment, illness.

achicar §47 ➤ *tr* (*disminuir*) to reduce; (*humillar*) to humiliate; (*ropa*) to take in.

acicalado, a ➤ *adj* spruced up.

acicalar ➤ *tr & reflex* to dress or spruce up.

acidez ➤ *f* acidity.

ácido, a ➤ *adj* acid; (*agrio*) sour, tart ➤ *m* acid.

acierto ➤ *m* (*logro*) good shot, hit; (*éxito*) success; (*cordura*) good sense; (*habilidad*) skill.

aclaración ➤ *f* clarification.

aclarar ➤ *tr* to clarify; (*explicar*) to explain; (*aguar*) to thin; (*enjuagar*) to rinse ➤ *intr* (*clarear*) to clear up.

aclimatar ➤ *tr* to acclimatize, acclimate.

acné ➤ *f* acne.

acobardar ➤ *tr* to intimidate ➤ *reflex* to become intimidated.

acogedor, a ➤ *adj* (*cordial*) welcoming; (*cómodo*) inviting, cozy.

acoger §20 ➤ *tr* (*dar bienvenida*) to welcome; (*amparar*) to shelter ➤ *reflex* to take refuge ■ **a. a** to resort to.

acogida ➤ *f* reception, welcome.

acolchado, a ➤ *adj* padded, quilted ➤ *m* (*relleno*) padding; ARG. bedspread.

acometer ➤ *tr* to attack; (*intentar*) to undertake; (*dominar*) to overcome.

acometida ➤ *f* attack, assault.

acomodado, a ➤ *adj* (*rico*) well-off.

acomodador, a ➤ *mf* usher.

acomodar ➤ *tr* (*arreglar*) to arrange; (*adaptar*) to adapt; (*colocar*) to accommodate ➤ *intr* to suit ➤ *reflex*

AMER. to set oneself up.

acomodo ➤ *m* (*alojamiento*) lodgings.

acompañamiento ➤ *m* accompaniment; (*comitiva*) retinue.

acompañante, a ➤ *adj* accompanying ➤ *mf* companion; MUS. accompanist.

acompañar ➤ *tr* to accompany; (*agregar*) to enclose ▪ **a. en el sentimiento** to express one's condolences.

acondicionado, a ➤ *adj* conditioned ▪ **aire a.** air-conditioning.

acondicionador ➤ *m* conditioner ▪ **a. de aire** air conditioner.

acondicionar ➤ *tr* (*disponer*) to prepare; (*reparar*) to repair; (*el aire*) to air-condition.

aconsejar ➤ *tr* to advise, counsel.

acontecer §09 ➤ *intr* to happen, occur.

acontecimiento ➤ *m* event, occurrence.

acopiar ➤ *tr* to gather, collect.

acordado, a ➤ *adj* agreed (upon).

acordar §11 ➤ *tr* (*concordar*) to agree; (*decidir*) to decide; AMER. to grant ➤ *intr* to go together ➤ *reflex* (*recordar*) to remember; (*convenir*) to agree.

acorde ➤ *adj* in agreement ➤ *m* chord.

acordeón ➤ *m* accordion.

acorralar ➤ *tr* (*encerrar*) to pen; (*atrapar*) to corner.

acortar ➤ *tr* to shorten ➤ *reflex* to become shorter.

acosar ➤ *tr* (*perseguir*) to harass.

acostado, a ➤ *adj* in bed, lying down.

acostar §11 ➤ *tr* to put to bed ➤ *reflex* to go to bed.

acostumbrado, a ➤ *adj* accustomed *or* used (*a* to); (*habitual*) customary.

acostumbrar ➤ *tr & reflex* to accustom (oneself) ➤ *intr* to get accustomed.

acotar ➤ *tr* (*anotar*) to annotate; (*notar*) to remark; (*admitir*) to admit.

acre[1] ➤ *m* acre.

acre[2] ➤ *adj* acrid.

acrecentar §33 ➤ *tr* (*aumentar*) to increase; (*avanzar*) to promote.

acreditado, a ➤ *adj* accredited; (*ilustre*) reputable.

acreditar ➤ *tr* (*embajador*) to accredit; (*asegurar*) guarantee, vouch for.

acreedor, a ➤ *mf* creditor.

acribillar ➤ *tr* (*agujerear*) to riddle (*a*

with); (*molestar*) to hound.

acrílico, a ➤ *adj & mf* acrylic.

acróbata ➤ *mf* acrobat.

acta ➤ *f* (*informe*) record; (*minutas*) minutes.

actitud ➤ *f* attitude.

activar ➤ *tr* to activate; (*acelerar*) to expedite.

actividad ➤ *f* activity.

activo, a ➤ *adj* active ➤ *m* COM. assets.

acto ➤ *m* act; (*acción*) action.

actor ➤ *m* actor.

actriz ➤ *f* actress.

actuación ➤ *f* performance; (*acción*) action.

actual ➤ *adj* present-day, current.

actualidad ➤ *f* present (time); current situation ▪ **en la a.** nowadays ▪ *pl* news, current events.

actualizar §02 ➤ *tr* to modernize, update; COMPUT. to upgrade.

actualmente ➤ *adv* at present, nowadays.

actuar §45 ➤ *tr* to act.

acuarela ➤ *f* water color.

acuario ➤ *m* aquarium.

acuático, a ➤ *adj* aquatic.

acudir ➤ *intr* (*presentarse*) to go, come.

acueducto ➤ *m* aqueduct.

acuerdo ➤ *m* (*convenio*) agreement, accord ▪ **de a. con** in agreement *or* accordance with.

acumular ➤ *tr* to accumulate, gather.

acunar ➤ *tr* to rock, cradle.

acuñar ➤ *tr* (*monedas*) to coin, mint.

acupuntura ➤ *f* acupuncture.

acurrucarse §47 ➤ *reflex* to curl up.

acusación ➤ *f* accusation, charge.

acusado, a ➤ *adj & mf* accused.

acusar ➤ *tr* to accuse.

acústico, a ➤ *adj* acoustic(al) ➤ *f* acoustics.

adaptar ➤ *tr & reflex* to adapt (oneself).

adecuado, a ➤ *adj* (*apropiado*) appropriate, suitable; (*suficiente*) adequate, sufficient.

adelantado, a ➤ *adj* (*precoz*) precocious, advanced; (*reloj*) fast ▪ **por a.** in advance.

adelantar ➤ *tr* to advance, move forward; *(acelerar)* to speed up; *(aventajar)* to surpass; AUTO. to overtake, pass ➤ intr to advance; *(relojes)* to be fast; FIG. *(progresar)* to make progress ➤ reflex ■ a. a to get ahead of.

adelante ➤ adv forward, ahead ■ ¡a.! come in! • de aquí en a. from now on • más a. farther on.

adelanto ➤ m *(de paga)* advance; *(progreso)* progress.

adelgazar §02 ➤ intr to lose weight, become slim.

ademán ➤ m gesture.

además ➤ adv besides, in addition.

adentro ➤ adv within, inside.

adherir §43 ➤ intr & reflex *(pegarse)* to stick, adhere.

adhesivo, a ➤ adj & m adhesive.

adición ➤ f addition; AMER. bill, check.

adicional ➤ adj additional, added.

adicto, a ➤ adj addicted; *(dedicado)* fond, attached ➤ mf addict; *(partidario)* follower.

adiestrado, a ➤ adj trained.

adiestrar ➤ tr *(instruir)* to train, coach; *(guiar)* to guide, lead.

adinerado, a ➤ adj wealthy, affluent.

adiós ➤ interj & m goodbye.

aditivo, a ➤ adj & m additive.

adivinanza ➤ f riddle, puzzle.

adivinar ➤ tr to predict; *(conjeturar)* to guess; *(resolver)* to solve.

adivino, a ➤ mf fortuneteller.

adjetivo, a ➤ adj adjectival ➤ m adjective.

adjudicar §47 ➤ tr to award ➤ reflex to appropriate (for oneself).

adjunto, a ➤ adj attached, enclosed; *(persona)* assistant, adjunct ➤ mf associate.

administración ➤ f administration, management.

administrador, a ➤ mf administrator, manager.

administrar ➤ tr *(dirigir)* to manage; *(conferir)* to administer.

administrativo, a ➤ adj administrative.

admiración ➤ f admiration; *(sorpresa)* surprise, wonder.

admirar ➤ tr to admire ➤ reflex to marvel at.

admisión ➤ f admission.

admitir ➤ tr to admit.

adobar ➤ tr *(aderezar)* to marinate; *(preservar)* to pickle.

adobe ➤ m adobe.

adobo ➤ m marinade, seasoning.

adolecer §09 ➤ intr to fall ill.

adolescencia ➤ f adolescence, youth.

adolescente ➤ adj & mf adolescent, youth.

adonde ➤ conj where.

adónde ➤ adv where ■ ¿a. vas? where are you going?

adopción ➤ f adoption.

adoptar ➤ tr to adopt.

adoptivo, a ➤ adj adoptive, adopted.

adoquinado ➤ m pavement.

adoración ➤ f adoration, worship.

adorar ➤ tr & intr to adore, worship.

adormecer §09 ➤ tr to put to sleep ➤ reflex to doze off, get sleepy.

adormecido, a ➤ adj sleepy, drowsy; *(un miembro)* numb, asleep.

adornar ➤ tr to adorn; CUL. to garnish.

adorno ➤ m adornment, decoration.

adquirir ➤ tr to acquire, buy.

adquisición ➤ f acquisition, purchase.

adrede ➤ adv on purpose, deliberately.

aduana ➤ f customs.

aduanero, a ➤ adj customs ➤ m customs officer.

aducir §14 ➤ tr to adduce, cite.

adueñarse ➤ reflex to take over, take possession *(de* of).

adulteración ➤ f adulteration.

adulterar ➤ tr to adulterate ➤ intr to commit adultery.

adúltero, a ➤ mf adulterer.

adulto, a ➤ adj & mf adult.

adverbio ➤ m adverb.

adversario, a ➤ mf adversary, opponent.

adversidad ➤ f adversity, misfortune.

adverso, a ➤ adj *(desfavorable)* adverse.

advertencia ➤ f *(admonición)* warning; *(consejo)* advice; *(noticia)* notice.

advertir §43 ➤ tr *(fijar)* to notice; *(avisar)* to warn; *(aconsejar)* to advise.

adyacente ➤ adj adjacent.

aéreo, a ➤ adj air, aerial.

aerodinámico, a ➤ adj aerodynamic(al)

➤ *f* aerodynamics.
aeródromo ➤ *m* airdrome, aerodrome (G.B.).
aerolínea ➤ *f* airline.
aeromozo, a ➤ *mf* flight attendant.
aeronáutico, a ➤ *adj* aeronautic(al) ➤ *f* aeronautics.
aeropuerto ➤ *m* airport.
afable ➤ *adj* affable, genial.
afamado, a ➤ *adj* famous, renowned.
afán ➤ *m (fervor)* eagerness, zeal; *(anhelo)* urge.
afectación ➤ *f* affectation.
afectado, a ➤ *adj* affected; *(fingido)* feigned.
afectar ➤ *tr* to affect ➤ *reflex (impresionarse)* to be moved *or* affected.
afecto, a ➤ *adj* fond *(a* of).
afectuoso, a ➤ *adj* affectionate, loving.
afeitar ➤ *tr & reflex* to shave (oneself).
afeminado, a ➤ *adj* effeminate.
aferrar §33 ➤ *tr* to grasp ➤ *reflex* to cling *(a* to); *(insistir)* to persist *(a* in).
afianzar §02 ➤ *tr (garantizar)* to guarantee; *(asegurar)* to secure.
afición ➤ *f* inclination, liking *(a* for).
aficionado, a ➤ *adj* fond *(a* of); *(novicio)* amateur ➤ *mf* fan, enthusiast; *(novicio)* amateur.
afilado, a ➤ *adj* sharp.
afilador ➤ *m* sharpener.
afilar ➤ *tr* to sharpen.
afín ➤ *adj (próximo)* adjacent; *(parecido)* similar.
afinar ➤ *tr* to refine; MUS. to tune ➤ *intr* to be in tune.
afinidad ➤ *f* affinity.
afirmación ➤ *f* affirmation.
afirmar ➤ *tr* to affirm; *(afianzar)* to secure ➤ *reflex* to steady oneself.
afirmativo, a ➤ *adj & f* affirmative.
afligido, a ➤ *adj* distressed; *(por la muerte)* bereaved.
afligir §19 ➤ *tr* to trouble, distress ➤ *reflex* to be troubled *or* distressed *(con, de, por* by).
aflojar ➤ *tr* to loosen, slacken ➤ *intr (disminuir)* to diminish; *(decaer)* to grow lax, slack.
afluencia ➤ *f* flow; *(de gente)* crowding; *(abundancia)* affluence.

afluir §10 ➤ *intr (manar)* to flow; *(acudir)* to flock.
afónico, a ➤ *adj* hoarse.
afortunado, a ➤ *adj* fortunate, lucky.
afrenta ➤ *f* affront.
afrentar ➤ *tr* to affront.
África ➤ *f* Africa.
africano, a ➤ *mf* African.
afrontar ➤ *tr* to face (up to), confront.
afuera ➤ *adv* out, outside ➤ *fpl* outskirts.
agacharse ➤ *reflex* to crouch, squat.
agalla ➤ *f (de pez)* gill ■ *pl* COLL. guts, courage.
agarradera ➤ *f* AMER. handle, holder.
agarrar ➤ *tr (asir)* to grab, grasp; *(enfermedad)* to catch.
agasajar ➤ *tr* to entertain; *(regalar)* to lavish gifts on.
agasajo ➤ *m* entertainment; *(regalo)* present.
agencia ➤ *f* agency; *(oficina)* bureau.
agenda ➤ *f* notebook.
agente ➤ *mf* agent ■ **a. de bolsa** stockbroker, broker ■ **a. de policía** police officer.
ágil ➤ *adj* agile, nimble.
agilidad ➤ *f* agility, nimbleness.
agitación ➤ *f* agitation; *(alboroto)* excitement.
agitar ➤ *tr* to shake; *(alborotar)* to excite ➤ *reflex* to wave, flutter; *(perturbarse)* to be agitated; MARIT. to get rough *or* choppy.
agobiado, a ➤ *adj* bent over, stooped; *(fatigado)* exhausted, weary.
agobiar ➤ *tr (cargar)* to weigh down; *(cansar)* to weary; *(deprimir)* to depress.
agobio ➤ *m (carga)* burden; *(fatiga)* fatigue.
agonía ➤ *f* agony, anguish.
agonizar §02 ➤ *intr* to be at death's door; FIG. to be in agony.
agosto ➤ *m* August.
agotado, a ➤ *adj* exhausted; *(libros)* out-of-print; COM. sold-out.
agotador, a ➤ *adj* exhausting, tiring.
agotar ➤ *tr* to exhaust ➤ *reflex* to be used up; *(cansarse)* to be exhausted; *(libros)* to be out of print.

agraciar ➤ *tr* to embellish; *(favorecer)* to grace; *(premiar)* to award.

agradable ➤ *adj* agreeable, pleasant.

agradar ➤ *tr & intr* to please.

agradecer §09 ➤ *tr* to thank.

agradecido, a ➤ *adj* grateful, thankful ➤ *mf* grateful person.

agradecimiento ➤ *m* gratitude, thanks.

agrandar ➤ *tr* to enlarge; *(exagerar)* to exaggerate.

agrario, a ➤ *adj* agrarian, agricultural.

agravar ➤ *tr & reflex* to worsen.

agraviar ➤ *tr* to offend; *(perjudicar)* to harm ➤ *reflex* to take offense.

agravio ➤ *m* offense; *(perjuicio)* injury.

agredir ➤ *tr* to attack, assault.

agregar §31 ➤ *tr* to add, attach.

agriar ➤ *tr* to (make) sour ➤ *reflex* to become sour.

agrícola *or* **agricultor, a** ➤ *adj* agricultural, farming ➤ *mf* agriculturist, farmer.

agricultura ➤ *f* agriculture, farming.

agridulce ➤ *adj* bittersweet.

agrietar ➤ *tr & reflex* to crack, split.

agrio, a ➤ *adj* sour; *(áspero)* rude, disagreeable ➤ *m* sourness, acidity.

agrupación ➤ *f* *(grupo)* group; *(asociación)* association, union.

agrupar ➤ *tr & reflex* to group, cluster (together).

agua ➤ *f* water; *(lluvia)* rain ■ a. abajo, arriba downstream, upstream • a. corriente running water • a. oxigenada hydrogen peroxide.

aguacate ➤ *m* avocado.

aguacero ➤ *m* downpour.

aguanieve ➤ *f* sleet.

aguantar ➤ *tr* to endure, tolerate; *(sostener)* to hold up ➤ *reflex* to contain oneself.

aguar §05 ➤ *tr* to water down.

aguardar ➤ *tr* to wait for, await ➤ *intr* to wait.

aguarrás ➤ *m* turpentine.

agudeza ➤ *f* sharpness; *(ingenio)* wit.

agudo, a ➤ *adj* sharp; *(chillón)* shrill; MUS. high-pitched; GEOM., GRAM. acute.

agüero ➤ *m* prediction; *(señal)* omen.

aguijar ➤ *tr* to goad.

aguijón ➤ *m* sting; BOT. thorn.

águila ➤ *f* eagle.

aguja ➤ *f* needle; *(del reloj)* hand; ARCHIT. steeple ■ a. de gancho crochet hook.

agujerear ➤ *tr* to pierce, perforate.

agujero ➤ *m* hole.

aguzar §02 ➤ *tr* to sharpen ■ a. las orejas *or* los oídos to prick up one's ears.

ahí ➤ *adv* there ■ a. no más right over there • a. que hence • por a. thereabouts.

ahijado, a ➤ *mf* godchild ➤ *m* godson ➤ *f* goddaughter.

ahínco ➤ *m* eagerness, zeal.

ahogado, a ➤ *adj* stifling ■ *mf* drowned person.

ahogar §31 ➤ *tr* to drown; *(sofocar)* to choke; *(oprimir)* to oppress ➤ *reflex* to drown; *(sentir sofocación)* to choke.

ahondar ➤ *tr* to go deeper into ➤ *intr* to go deep.

ahora ➤ *adv* now; *(pronto)* soon; *(hace poco)* just now, a few moments ago ■ a. bien *or* pues well, now then • a. mismo right now • por a. for the time being.

ahorcar §47 ➤ *tr & reflex* to hang (oneself).

ahorrar ➤ *tr* to save.

ahorro ➤ *m* saving ■ *pl* savings.

ahuecar §47 ➤ *tr* to hollow out; *(mullir)* to fluff up; *(la voz)* to make deep.

ahumar ➤ *tr* CUL. to smoke, cure.

ahuyentar ➤ *tr* to drive *or* scare away.

airado, a ➤ *adj* angry, irate.

aire ➤ *m* air; *(viento)* wind; *(apariencia)* appearance; *(gracia)* grace; MUS. air, tune ■ a. acondicionado air conditioning • al a. libre in the open air • en el a. RAD., TELEV. on the air.

airear ➤ *tr* to ventilate, aerate.

aislado, a ➤ *adj* isolated; ELEC. insulated.

aislar ➤ *tr* to isolate; ELEC. to insulate.

ajar ➤ *tr* to crumple, wrinkle ➤ *reflex* to get crumpled *or* wrinkled.

ajedrez ➤ *m* chess; *(piezas)* chess set.

ajeno, a ➤ *adj* another's, someone else's; *(libre)* free, devoid; *(impropio)* inappropriate.

ajetreo ➤ *m* bustle, rush.

ají ➤ *m* red *or* green pepper.

ajo ➤ *m* garlic; *(diente)* garlic clove.

ajuar ➤ *m* trousseau.

ajustado, a ➤ *adj* tight.

ajustar ➤ *tr* to adjust, adapt; *(modificar)* to alter; *(reconciliar)* to reconcile; *(apretar)* to tighten.

ajuste ➤ *m* adjustment; *(modificación)* alteration, fitting.

ala ➤ *f* wing; *(del sombrero)* brim; *(de la hélice)* blade.

alabar ➤ *tr* to praise, laud ➤ *reflex* to boast, brag.

alambrado ➤ *m* wire fence.

alambre ➤ *m* wire ▪ a. de púas barbed wire.

alameda ➤ *f* poplar grove; *(paseo)* boulevard.

álamo ➤ *m* poplar.

alardear ➤ *intr* to boast, brag.

alargar §31 ➤ *tr* to lengthen; *(extender)* to extend, prolong; *(estirar)* to stretch (out).

alarido ➤ *m* yell, howl.

alarma ➤ *f* alarm ▪ dar la a. to sound the alarm.

alarmar ➤ *tr* to alarm; *(asustar)* to scare.

alba ➤ *f* dawn, daybreak; RELIG. alb.

albañil ➤ *mf* bricklayer, mason.

albañilería ➤ *f* masonry.

albaricoque ➤ *m* apricot.

alberca ➤ *f* *(tanque)* reservoir, tank; MEX. swimming pool.

albergar §31 ➤ *tr* to lodge, house.

albergue ➤ *m* *(alojamiento)* lodging; *(refugio)* shelter, refuge.

albóndiga ➤ *f* meatball.

albornoz ➤ *m* *(capa)* burnoose; *(bata)* bathrobe.

alborotado, a ➤ *adj* *(agitado)* excited; *(ruidoso)* rowdy; *(atolondrado)* rash; *(el mar)* rough.

alborotar ➤ *tr* *(agitar)* to agitate; *(incitar)* to incite; *(excitar)* to excite ➤ *intr* to make a racket.

alboroto ➤ *m* uproar; *(ruido)* racket.

alborozar §02 ➤ *tr* to delight ➤ *reflex* to be elated, rejoice.

alcachofa ➤ *f* artichoke.

alcalde ➤ *m* mayor.

alcaldía ➤ *f* mayor's office.

alcalino, a ➤ *adj* alkaline.

alcance ➤ *m* *(distancia)* reach; *(extensión)* range, scope ▪ al a. accessible, within reach (de to, of).

alcantarilla ➤ *f* *(cloaca)* sewer, drain.

alcanzar §02 ➤ *tr* to reach (up to); *(tomar)* to catch; *(conseguir)* to attain; *(comprender)* to grasp; *(igualar)* to catch up with.

alcaparra ➤ *f* caper.

alcázar ➤ *m* castle, fortress.

alce ➤ *m* elk, moose.

alcoba ➤ *f* bedroom.

alcohol ➤ *m* alcohol.

alcohólico, a ➤ *adj & mf* alcoholic.

alcornoque ➤ *m* cork oak.

aldea ➤ *f* village, hamlet.

alegación ➤ *f* allegation.

alegar §31 ➤ *tr* to allege.

alegoría ➤ *f* allegory.

alegórico, a ➤ *adj* allegorical.

alegrar ➤ *tr* to cheer; *(avivar)* to enliven ➤ *reflex* to rejoice, be happy.

alegre ➤ *adj* happy, glad; *(disposición)* cheerful; *(color)* bright; FIG. tipsy, high.

alegría ➤ *f* happiness, joy.

alejado, a ➤ *adj* distant, remote.

alejar ➤ *tr* to put farther away ➤ *reflex* to move away, withdraw.

alentador, a ➤ *adj* encouraging.

alentar §33 ➤ *intr* to breathe ➤ *tr* to encourage, inspire.

alergia ➤ *f* allergy.

alérgico, a ➤ *adj* allergic.

alero ➤ *m* eaves.

alerta ➤ *adv* on the alert ➤ *m* alert, warning.

alertar ➤ *tr* to alert, warn.

aleta ➤ *f* *(de pez)* fin; *(hélice)* blade.

alfabético, a ➤ *adj* alphabetical.

alfabeto ➤ *m* alphabet ▪ a. Morse Morse code.

alfarería ➤ *f* pottery.

alfarero, a ➤ *mf* potter, ceramist.

alférez ➤ *mf* second lieutenant.

alfil ➤ *m* bishop (in chess).

alfiler ➤ *m* pin ▪ a. de gancho AMER. safety pin.

alfombra ➤ *f* carpet; *(tapete)* rug, mat.

alfombrar ➤ *tr* to carpet.

alfombrilla ➤ *f* rug, mat, pad ▪ a. de ratón mouse pad.

alforja ➤ *f* knapsack; (*provisión*) supplies.

alforza ➤ *f* pleat, tuck.

alga ➤ *f* alga, seaweed.

algarabía ➤ *f* uproar, din.

álgebra ➤ *f* algebra.

algo ➤ *pron* something; (*in questions, negatives*) anything; (*cantidad*) some ▪ ¿hay a. para mí? is there anything for me?

algodón ➤ *m* cotton.

alguacil ➤ *m* sheriff.

alguien ➤ *pron* someone, somebody; (*in questions, negatives*) anyone, anybody ▪ ¿has visto a a.? have you seen anyone?

algún ➤ *adj contr of* alguno.

alguno, a ➤ *adj* some; (*in questions, negatives*) any ▪ no tengo duda a. I don't have any doubt ➤ *pron* someone ▪ *pl* some.

alhaja ➤ *f* jewel, gem.

aliado, a ➤ *adj* allied ➤ *mf* ally.

alianza ➤ *f* alliance.

aliar §18 ➤ *tr* to ally, join.

alicates ➤ *mpl* pliers, pincers.

aliciente ➤ *m* incentive.

alienar ➤ *tr* to alienate.

aliento ➤ *m* breath; (*valor*) courage.

aligerar ➤ *tr* to lighten; (*acelerar*) to quicken.

alimentación ➤ *f* feeding; (*comida*) food.

alimentar ➤ *tr* to feed, nourish.

alimento ➤ *m* food, nourishment ▪ *pl* alimony, support.

alinear ➤ *tr & reflex* to align, line up.

aliñar ➤ *tr* to straighten, tidy; CUL. to season.

alisar ➤ *tr* to smooth; (*el pelo*) to slick.

alistar ➤ *tr* to list ➤ *reflex* MIL. to enlist.

aliviar ➤ *tr* to alleviate, ease; (*aligerar*) to lighten ➤ *reflex* to get better.

alivio ➤ *m* alleviation; (*cese*) relief.

allá ➤ *adv* there, over there; (*en tiempo remoto*) way back ▪ más a. farther • más a. de beyond • por a. over there.

allanamiento ➤ *m* raid.

allanar ➤ *tr* (*nivelar*) to flatten; (*invadir*) to raid; (*superar*) to overcome.

allegado, a ➤ *mf* (*pariente*) relative, relation; (*partidario*) supporter.

allegar §31 ➤ *tr* to place near, gather ➤ *reflex* to approach.

allí ➤ *adv* there ▪ por a. (*sitio*) over there; (*camino*) that way.

alma ➤ *f* soul.

almacén ➤ *m* store, shop; (*depósito*) warehouse.

almacenamiento ➤ *m* storage.

almacenar ➤ *tr* to store, warehouse.

almanaque ➤ *m* calendar, almanac.

almeja ➤ *f* clam.

almendra ➤ *f* almond.

almendrado, a ➤ *adj* almond-shaped ➤ *m* (*pasta*) almond paste; (*macarrón*) macaroon.

almendro ➤ *m* almond tree.

almíbar ➤ *m* syrup.

almidón ➤ *m* starch.

almidonar ➤ *tr* to starch.

almirante ➤ *mf* admiral.

almohada ➤ *f* pillow.

almohadilla ➤ *f* small cushion.

almorranas ➤ *fpl* hemorrhoids, piles.

almorzar §22 ➤ *intr* to lunch, eat lunch.

almuerzo ➤ *m* lunch.

alojamiento ➤ *m* lodging(s); (*vivienda*) housing.

alojar ➤ *tr* to lodge; (*albergar*) to house ➤ *reflex* to lodge.

alondra ➤ *f* lark.

alpargata ➤ *f* espadrille.

alpinista ➤ *mf* mountain climber.

alpiste ➤ *m* birdseed; COLL. alcohol.

alquilar ➤ *tr* to rent, lease; (*personas*) to hire ▪ se alquila to let, for hire.

alquiler ➤ *m* renting, hiring; (*renta*) rent ▪ de a. for hire, for rent.

alquitrán ➤ *m* tar, pitch.

alrededor ➤ *adv* (*en torno*) around; (*cerca*) about ➤ *mpl* (*cercanías*) surroundings; (*afueras*) outskirts.

altanería ➤ *f* arrogance, haughtiness.

altanero, a ➤ *adj* (*pájaro*) high-flying; FIG. arrogant.

altavoz ➤ *m* loudspeaker.

alteración ➤ *f* alteration; (*alboroto*) disturbance; (*disputa*) altercation.

alterar ➤ *tr* to alter; *(perturbar)* to upset; *(enfadar)* to annoy ➤ *reflex (perturbarse)* to get upset.

alternar ➤ *tr & intr* to alternate ∎ a. con to mix *or* socialize with.

alternativa ➤ *f* alternative, choice.

alternativo, a *or* **alterno, a** ➤ *adj* alternating, alternate.

alteza ➤ *f* Highness; *(altura)* height.

altiplanicie ➤ *f or* **altiplano** ➤ *m* high plateau, altiplano.

altitud ➤ *f* altitude, height.

altivo, a ➤ *adj* haughty, proud.

alto, a ➤ *adj* high; *(estatura)* tall; *(piso)* upper; *(voz)* loud ∎ a. costura haute couture • altas horas late hours ➤ *m* height, elevation; MUS. alto; MIL. halt ∎ de lo a. from on high, from above ∎ *pl* AMER. upper floors ➤ *f* MED. discharge; *(ingreso)* entry ∎ dar de a. MIL. to admit; MED. to discharge ➤ *adv .(arriba)* up high, above; *(en voz fuerte)* aloud ➤ *interj* halt!, stop!

altoparlante ➤ *m* loudspeaker.

altura ➤ *f* height; *(altitud)* altitude ∎ *pl* the heavens • a estas a. at this point.

alubia ➤ *f* French *or* kidney bean.

alud ➤ *m* avalanche.

aludido, a ➤ *adj* abovementioned.

aludir ➤ *intr* to allude, refer (a to).

alumbrado, a ➤ *adj* lighted, lit ➤ *m* lighting.

alumbrar ➤ *tr* to light (up), illuminate ➤ *intr* to give light; *(dar a luz)* to give birth.

aluminio ➤ *m* aluminum.

alumno, a ➤ *mf* pupil, student.

alusión ➤ *f* allusion.

alza ➤ *f* rise, increase ∎ en a. on the rise.

alzamiento ➤ *m* POL. uprising.

alzar §02 ➤ *tr* to raise, lift (up); *(recoger)* to gather ➤ *reflex* to rise, get up; POL. to rebel.

ama ➤ *f (señora)* lady of the house, mistress; *(dueña)* proprietor ∎ a. de casa housewife.

amabilidad ➤ *f* kindness.

amable ➤ *adj* kind.

amado, a ➤ *adj & mf* beloved, dear (one).

amaestrar ➤ *tr* to train.

amainar ➤ *tr* MARIT. to lower ➤ *intr* to die down, let up.

amamantar ➤ *tr* to suckle, nurse.

amanecer §09 ➤ *intr* to dawn ➤ *m* dawn ∎ al a. at dawn.

amanerado, a ➤ *adj* mannered, affected.

amante ➤ *adj* fond, loving ➤ *mf* lover.

amapola ➤ *f* poppy.

amar ➤ *tr* to love.

amargado, a ➤ *adj* bitter, embittered.

amargar §31 ➤ *tr* to make bitter ➤ *intr & reflex* to become embittered.

amargo, a ➤ *adj* bitter.

amargura ➤ *f* bitterness.

amarillo, a ➤ *adj & m* yellow.

amarrar ➤ *tr* to tie (up), fasten; MARIT. to moor.

amateur ➤ *adj & mf* amateur.

amatista ➤ *f* MIN. amethyst.

amazona ➤ *f* MYTH. Amazon.

Amazonas ➤ *m* Amazon (River).

ambar ➤ *m* amber ∎ a. gris ambergris.

ambición ➤ *f* ambition.

ambiente ➤ *adj* surrounding, ambient ∎ el medio a. the environment ➤ *m* METEOROL., FIG. atmosphere.

ambigüedad ➤ *f* ambiguity.

ambiguo, a ➤ *adj* ambiguous.

ámbito ➤ *m* boundary, limit.

ambos, as ➤ *adj & indef pron* both.

ambulancia ➤ *f* ambulance.

ambulante ➤ *adj* traveling, itinerant.

ambular ➤ *intr* to stroll, amble.

amenaza ➤ *f* threat, menace.

amenazante, a *or* **amenazante** ➤ *adj* threatening.

amenazar §02 ➤ *tr & intr* to threaten.

amenidad ➤ *f* amenity, pleasantness.

ameno, a ➤ *adj* pleasant, agreeable.

América ➤ *f* America ∎ A. del Norte, del Sur North America, South America.

americano, a ➤ *adj & mf* American; *(norteamericano)* North American.

ametralladora ➤ *f* machine gun.

amianto ➤ *m* asbestos.

amigable ➤ *adj* amicable.

amígdala ➤ *f* tonsil.

amigdalitis ➤ *f* tonsilitis.

amigo, a ➤ *mf* friend ∎ a. íntimo *or* del

alma close friend ➤ *adj* friendly; FIG. fond of.

aminorar ➤ *tr* to reduce, diminish.

amistad ➤ *f* friendship ■ *pl* friends, acquaintances.

amistoso, a ➤ *adj* amicable, friendly.

amnistía ➤ *f* amnesty.

amo ➤ *m* master; *(dueño)* owner, proprietor.

amoldar ➤ *tr* to mold, model; FIG. to adapt.

amonestación ➤ *f* reprimand; *(advertencia)* warning.

amonestar ➤ *tr* to reprimand; *(advertir)* to warn.

amoniaco *or* **amoníaco** ➤ *m (gas)* ammonia.

amontonar ➤ *tr* to heap *or* pile (up); *(acumular)* to accumulate, gather.

amor ➤ *m* love; *(afecto)* affection; *(querido)* darling, beloved ■ **a. propio** pride.

amorío ➤ *m* fling, love affair.

amortiguador, a ➤ *adj (de golpes)* cushioning; *(de ruidos)* muffling ➤ *m* AUTO. shock absorber; *(parachoques)* bumper ■ **a. de luz** dimmer.

amortiguar §05 ➤ *tr (golpes)* to absorb; *(ruidos)* to muffle; *(luces)* to dim.

amortización ➤ *f* LAW amortization.

amortizar §02 ➤ *tr (un bono)* to redeem; *(una deuda)* to pay off.

amparar ➤ *tr* to protect ➤ *reflex* to protect oneself; *(acogerse)* to seek protection.

amparo ➤ *m* protection; *(defensa)* aid.

ampliar §18 ➤ *tr* to expand; *(aumentar)* to increase; *(ensanchar)* to widen; PHOTOG. to enlarge.

amplificación ➤ *f* amplification, magnification; PHOTOG. enlargement.

amplificador, a ➤ *adj* amplifying ➤ *m* ELEC., RAD. amplifier.

amplificar §47 ➤ *tr* to amplify; *(con microscopio)* to magnify; PHOTOG. to enlarge.

amplio, a ➤ *adj (espacioso)* spacious, roomy; *(extenso)* ample, broad; *(ancho)* full, wide.

amplitud ➤ *f (anchura)* fullness; *(extensión)* extent.

ampolla ➤ *f* blister.

amueblar ➤ *tr* to furnish.

amurallado, a ➤ *adj* walled.

anales ➤ *mpl* annals.

analfabeto, a ➤ *adj & mf* illiterate.

analgésico, a ➤ *adj & m* analgesic.

análisis ➤ *m* analysis ■ **a. de sangre** blood test.

analista ➤ *mf* analyst; *(historiador)* annalist.

analizar §02 ➤ *tr* to analyze, examine.

ananá(s) ➤ *m* pineapple.

anaquel ➤ *m* shelf.

anaranjado, a ➤ *adj & m (color)* orange.

anarquía ➤ *f* anarchy.

anarquista ➤ *mf* anarchist ➤ *adj* anarchistic.

anatomía ➤ *f* anatomy.

anca ➤ *f* rump, buttock.

ancho, a ➤ *adj* wide, broad; *(holgado)* loose, full ■ **de a.** wide ➤ *m* width, breadth ■ **a sus anchas** as one pleases.

anchoa ➤ *f* anchovy.

anchura ➤ *f* width, breadth; *(amplitud)* fullness.

anciano, a ➤ *adj* old, elderly ➤ *m* old *or* elderly man ➤ *f* old *or* elderly woman.

ancla ➤ *f* anchor.

anclar ➤ *intr* to anchor, drop anchor.

andamio ➤ *m* scaffold; *(tablado)* platform.

andar[1] §03 ➤ *intr* to walk; *(marchar)* to go, move ■ **¡anda!** get going!

andar[2] ➤ *m* pace, gait.

andén ➤ *m* station *or* railway platform.

andinista ➤ *mf* mountain climber.

andrajoso, a ➤ *adj* tattered, ragged.

anécdota ➤ *f* anecdote.

anejo, a ➤ *adj* attached, annexed.

anexar ➤ *tr* to join; *(documentos)* to enclose.

anexo, a ➤ *adj* joined; *(documento)* enclosed ➤ *m (suplemento)* annex.

anfitrión, ona ➤ *m* host ➤ *f* hostess.

ángel ➤ *m* angel ■ **a. de la guardia** guardian angel.

angélico, a *or* **angelical** ➤ *adj* angelic(al).

angosto, a ➤ *adj* narrow, tight.

anguila ➤ *f* eel.

ángulo ➤ *m* angle; *(esquina)* corner,

angle ■ de á. ancho PHOTOG. wide-angle • en á. at an angle.

angustia ➤ *f* anguish.

angustiar ➤ *tr* to (cause) anguish.

anhelar ➤ *intr* to yearn, long; *(jadear)* to gasp, pant ■ a. regresar to long to return ➤ *tr* to yearn or long for.

anhelo ➤ *m* yearning, longing.

anillo ➤ *m* ring.

ánima ➤ *f* soul, spirit.

animación ➤ *f* animation.

animado, a ➤ *adj* animated, lively; *(movido)* motivated; ZOOL. animate.

animal ➤ *adj & m* animal.

animar ➤ *tr* to animate; *(avivar)* to enliven; *(alentar)* to encourage.

ánimo ➤ *m* spirit; *(energía)* energy, vitality ■ ¡a.! courage!

anís ➤ *m* anise; *(licor)* anisette.

aniversario, a ➤ *adj & m* anniversary.

ano ➤ *m* anus.

anoche ➤ *adv* last night, yesterday evening.

anochecer §09 ➤ *intr* to get dark ➤ *m* nightfall, dusk.

anomalía ➤ *f* anomaly.

anómalo, a ➤ *adj* anomalous.

anonadar ➤ *tr* to overwhelm, dishearten.

anónimo, a ➤ *adj* anonymous.

anormal ➤ *adj* abnormal.

anotación ➤ *f* annotation.

anotar ➤ *tr (poner notas)* to annotate; *(apuntar)* to make note of.

ansia ➤ *f (inquietud)* anxiety; *(angustia)* anguish; *(anhelo)* yearning.

ansiar §18 ➤ *tr* to yearn or long for.

ansiedad ➤ *f* anxiety.

ansioso, a ➤ *adj (preocupado)* anxious; *(deseoso)* eager.

antagonista ➤ *adj* antagonist, antagonistic ➤ *mf* antagonist, rival.

antaño ➤ *adv* in days gone by.

ante¹ ➤ *m* ZOOL. elk.

ante² ➤ *prep (delante de)* before, in front of; *(considerando)* in view of, regarding.

anteanoche ➤ *adv* the night before last.

anteayer ➤ *adv* the day before yesterday.

antebrazo ➤ *m* forearm.

antecedente ➤ *adj* preceding ➤ *m*

antecedent ■ *pl* background.

antecesor, a ➤ *adj* former ➤ *mf* predecessor; *(antepasado)* ancestor.

antedicho, a ➤ *adj* aforesaid, aforementioned.

antelación ➤ *f* ■ con a. in advance • con a. a prior to.

antemano ➤ *adv* ■ de a. in advance.

antena ➤ *f* antenna.

anteojos ➤ *mpl (lentes)* glasses, eyeglasses; *(anteojeras)* blinders; INDUS., SPORT. goggles.

antepasado, a ➤ *adj* before last ➤ *mf* ancestor.

antepecho ➤ *m (baranda)* rail, railing.

anteponer §37 ➤ *tr* to put before.

anterior ➤ *adj* previous, before *(a* to); ANAT. front.

anterioridad ➤ *f* ■ con a. beforehand, in advance • con a. a prior to.

antes ➤ *adj & adv* before; *(antiguamente)* previously, formerly; *(más bien)* rather, sooner ■ a. de before, prior to • a. de ayer the day before yesterday • a. que before; *(en vez de)* rather than ➤ *conj* rather, on the contrary.

antesala ➤ *f* anteroom, vestibule.

antibiótico, a ➤ *adj & m* antibiotic.

anticipación ➤ *f* anticipation ■ con a. in advance.

anticipado, a ➤ *adj* advance, advanced ■ por a. in advance.

anticipar ➤ *tr (fecha)* to advance, move forward; S. AMER. to anticipate ➤ *reflex* to be or arrive early.

anticonceptivo, a ➤ *adj & m* contraceptive.

anticuado, a ➤ *adj* antiquated; *(pasado de moda)* old-fashioned.

anticuario, a ➤ *adj* antiquarian ➤ *m* antique dealer.

antídoto ➤ *m* antidote.

antifaz ➤ *m* mask.

antigüedad ➤ *f (vejez)* old age; *(época)* ancient times; *(en el empleo)* seniority ■ *pl* antiques.

antiguo, a ➤ *adj (viejo)* ancient, old; *(anterior)* former ■ a la a. in the old-fashioned way ➤ *m* old-timer ■ los antiguos the ancients.

antílope ➤ *m* antelope.

antipático, a ➤ *adj* disagreeable, unpleasant.

antiséptico, a ➤ *adj & m* antiseptic.

antisocial ➤ *adj* antisocial.

antítesis ➤ *f* antithesis.

antojarse ➤ *reflex* (*gustar*) to fancy, feel like; (*parecer*) to seem.

antojo ➤ *m* (*capricho*) whim; (*de comida*) craving; (*lunar*) birthmark.

antorcha ➤ *f* torch; FIG. guide.

antropología ➤ *f* anthropology.

antropólogo, a ➤ *mf* anthropologist.

anual ➤ *adj* annual, yearly.

anualidad ➤ *f* annual payment.

anuario ➤ *m* yearbook, annual.

anublar ➤ *tr* to cloud.

anudar ➤ *tr* (*hacer nudos*) to tie in knots; (*atar*) to tie together.

anulación ➤ *f* annulment, nullification.

anular ➤ *tr* to annul; (*desautorizar*) to remove from power.

anunciar ➤ *tr* to announce; COM. to advertise.

anuncio ➤ *m* announcement; (*cartel*) poster; (*señal*) sign; COM. advertisement.

anzuelo ➤ *m* fishhook; FIG. lure.

añadidura ➤ *f* addition.

añadir ➤ *tr* to add; (*aumentar*) to increase.

añejo, a ➤ *adj* aged, mature.

añicos ➤ *mpl* bits, pieces

añil ➤ *m* BOT. indigo; (*para lavado*) bluing.

año ➤ *m* year ■ a. bisiesto leap year • tener . . . años to be . . . years old.

añoranza ➤ *f* nostalgia.

añorar ➤ *tr & intr* to long, yearn (for).

apacentar §33 ➤ *tr & reflex* to graze, pasture.

apacible ➤ *adj* calm, gentle.

apaciguar §05 ➤ *tr* to appease.

apadrinar ➤ *tr* to sponsor; (*apoyar*) to support; (*a un niño*) to be godfather to.

apagado, a ➤ *adj* (*fuego, luz*) out; (*apocado*) shy; (*color*) dull, subdued.

apagar §31 ➤ *tr* (*fuego*) to put out; (*luz*) to turn out; (*cal*) to slake; (*ruido*) to silence; (*color*) to tone down.

apagón ➤ *m* blackout, power failure.

apalear ➤ *tr* to thrash; AGR. to winnow.

aparador ➤ *m* (*armario*) sideboard, cupboard; (*taller*) studio; (*escaparate*) window.

aparato ➤ *m* apparatus, device ■ a. de televisión television set.

aparcamiento ➤ *m* parking lot, garage.

aparcar §47 ➤ *tr & intr* to park.

aparear ➤ *tr* to match up, pair off.

aparecer §09 ➤ *intr & reflex* to appear.

aparejado, a ➤ *adj* apt, fit.

aparejar ➤ *tr* to prepare, make ready; (*los caballos*) to harness ➤ *reflex* to get ready.

aparejo ➤ *m* preparation; (*equipo*) gear, equipment; (*arreo*) harness; PAINT. priming.

aparentar ➤ *tr* (*fingir*) to pretend; (*parecer*) to seem.

aparición ➤ *f* appearance; (*fantasma*) apparition, specter.

apariencia ➤ *f* appearance ■ en a. apparently.

apartado, a ➤ *adj* remote, isolated ➤ *m* (*casilla postal*) post office box; (*párrafo*) paragraph, section.

apartamento ➤ *m* apartment, flat (G.B.).

apartar ➤ *tr* to separate; (*llevar aparte*) to take aside; (*alejar*) to put aside ➤ *reflex* to withdraw, move away.

aparte ➤ *adv* (*por separado*) apart, separate; (*a un lado*) aside, to one side.

apasionado, a ➤ *adj* enthusiastic, intense.

apasionante ➤ *adj* exciting, thrilling.

apatía ➤ *f* apathy, indifference.

apeadero ➤ *m* (*poyo*) mounting block; (*fonda*) inn; RAIL. way station.

apear ➤ *tr* to dismount ➤ *reflex* (*de un vehículo*) to get out of.

apegarse §31 ➤ *reflex* to become attached or fond (a to, of).

apego ➤ *m* attachment, fondness.

apelación ➤ *f* LAW appeal; (*recurso*) recourse.

apelar ➤ *intr* LAW to appeal.

apellidar ➤ *tr* to call, name ➤ *reflex* to be called or named.

apellido ➤ *m* last name, surname ■ a. de

soltera maiden name.

apenar ➤ *tr* to grieve, pain ➤ *reflex* to be grieved *or* pained.

apenas ➤ *adv* scarcely, hardly.

apéndice ➤ *m* appendage; ANAT. appendix.

apendicitis ➤ *f* appendicitis.

apercibir ➤ *tr* *(disponer)* to make ready; *(advertir)* to warn ➤ *reflex* to prepare oneself.

aperitivo ➤ *m* CUL. apéritif, appetizer.

apertura ➤ *f* opening.

apestar ➤ *tr* *(contaminar)* to infect (with the plague) ➤ *intr* to stink.

apetecer §09 ➤ *tr* to feel like, desire.

apetito ➤ *m* appetite ■ abrir, dar *or* despertar el a. to whet one's appetite.

ápice ➤ *m* *(cima)* apex, top, pinnacle; FIG. *(nonada)* iota, whit ■ no ceder un a. not to give an inch.

apicultor, a ➤ *mf* beekeeper.

apilar ➤ *tr* to pile *or* heap.

apiñar ➤ *tr & reflex* to cram, jam.

apio ➤ *m* celery.

apisonadora ➤ *f* steamroller.

apisonar ➤ *tr* *(tierra)* to pack down; *(carretera)* to steamroller.

aplacar §47 ➤ *tr* to appease, placate.

aplanar ➤ *tr* to level, flatten.

aplastar ➤ *tr* *(estrujar)* to crush; *(vencer)* to overwhelm.

aplaudir ➤ *tr* to applaud.

aplauso ➤ *m* applause, clapping.

aplazamiento ➤ *m* postponement.

aplazar §02 ➤ *tr* to postpone, put off.

aplicable ➤ *adj* applicable.

aplicado, a ➤ *adj* diligent.

aplicar §47 ➤ *tr* to apply.

aplomo ➤ *m* aplomb; *(verticalidad)* vertical alignment.

apodar ➤ *tr* to nickname.

apoderado, a ➤ *adj* empowered, authorized ➤ *mf* *(poderhabiente)* attorney, proxy; *(empresario)* manager, agent.

apoderar ➤ *tr* to grant power of attorney to ➤ *reflex* ■ a. de to take possession of.

apodo ➤ *m* nickname.

apogeo ➤ *m* apogee.

aporrear ➤ *tr* *(golpear)* to beat; *(instru-*

mento) to bang on; *(insistir)* to harp on.

aportar ➤ *tr* *(traer)* to bring; *(contribuir)* to contribute.

aporte ➤ *m* AMER. contribution, donation.

aposentar ➤ *tr & reflex* to lodge.

aposento ➤ *m* *(habitación)* room; *(hospedaje)* lodging, quarters.

apostar §11 ➤ *tr* *(jugar)* to wager; *(colocar)* to post, station.

apóstol ➤ *m* apostle.

apóstrofo ➤ *m* GRAM. apostrophe.

apoyar ➤ *tr* to lean, rest; *(ayudar)* to aid, support ➤ *intr* to lean, rest ➤ *reflex* ■ a. en to rest on, lean against; FIG. to rely on.

apoyo ➤ *m* support.

apreciación ➤ *f* *(valorización)* appraisal; *(aprecio)* appreciation.

apreciar ➤ *tr* COM. to appraise, assess; *(estimar)* to appreciate, esteem.

aprecio ➤ *m* COM. appraisal, valuation; *(estima)* esteem.

aprehender ➤ *tr* to apprehend, arrest; *(confiscar)* to seize.

apremiante ➤ *adj* pressing, urgent.

apremiar ➤ *tr* *(acelerar)* to press; *(oprimir)* to oppress; LAW to compel.

apremio ➤ *m* urgency; LAW judicial order.

aprender ➤ *tr* to learn *(a* to).

aprendiz, a ➤ *mf* apprentice.

aprendizaje ➤ *m* apprenticeship.

aprensión ➤ *f* *(miedo)* apprehension; *(sospecha)* suspicion.

aprensivo, a ➤ *adj* apprehensive.

apresar ➤ *tr* to capture; ZOOL. to grasp.

aprestar ➤ *tr* *(preparar)* to make ready.

apresto ➤ *m* preparation.

apresurar ➤ *tr* to hurry, hasten ➤ *reflex* to hurry, make haste *(a, por* to).

apretado, a ➤ *adj* *(comprimido)* cramped, tight.

apretar §33 ➤ *tr* *(nudo)* to tighten; *(tecla, pedal)* to press *(estrujar)* to squeeze; *(comprimir)* to compress ■ a. la mano to shake hands.

apretón ➤ *m* grip, squeeze ■ a. de manos handshake.

aprieto ➤ *m* jam, fix.

aprisa ➤ *adv* quickly, swiftly.

aprobado, a ➤ *adj* approved ➤ *m* passing grade.

aprobar §11 ➤ *tr* (*consentir*) to approve of; (*examen*) to pass.

apropiación ➤ *f* appropriation.

apropiado, a ➤ *adj* appropriate, suitable.

apropiar ➤ *tr* AMER., FIN. to earmark ➤ *reflex* to take possession (*de of*).

aprovechamiento ➤ *m* use, utilization.

aprovechar ➤ *intr* to be useful ➤ *tr* to make good use of ➤ *reflex* ∎ a. de to take advantage of.

aproximación ➤ *f* (*proximidad*) nearness; (*estimación*) approximation.

aproximadamente ➤ *adv* approximately.

aproximar ➤ *tr* to bring near ➤ *reflex* to draw near.

aptitud ➤ *f* aptitude ➤ *pl* gift, talent.

apto, a ➤ *adj* (*hábil*) able, competent; (*conveniente*) apt, fit.

apuntalar ➤ *tr* to prop up, shore up.

apuntar ➤ *tr* (*arma*) to aim, point; (*señalar*) to point to or at, indicate; (*tomar nota*) to make a note of; THEAT. to prompt.

apunte ➤ *m* (*nota*) note, notation; THEAT. (*persona*) prompter; (*señal*) cue.

apuñalar ➤ *tr* to stab, knife.

apurado, a ➤ *adj* AMER. in a hurry.

apurar ➤ *tr* AMER. to hurry, press; (*purificar*) to refine; (*agotar*) to use or finish up; (*enfadar*) to annoy.

apuro ➤ *m* hurry.

aquejar ➤ *tr* to afflict, distress.

aquel, lla ➤ *adj* that ∎ aquella mujer that woman (over there) ➤ *pl* those ∎ aquellos zapatos those shoes.

aquél, lla ➤ *pron* that one (over there); (*el primero*) the former ➤ *pl* those • dame aquellos give me those.

aquello ➤ *pron* that, that matter ∎ a. de that business about.

aquí ➤ *adv* (*en este lugar*) here; (*ahora*) now; (*entonces*) then, at that point ∎ por a. (*alrededor*) around here; (*por este lado*) this way.

aquietar ➤ *tr* to calm, soothe ➤ *reflex*

to calm down, become calm.

arada ➤ *f* plowing; (*tierra*) plowed land.

arado ➤ *m* plow; (*acción*) plowing.

arancel ➤ *m* tariff, duty.

araña ➤ *f* spider.

arañar ➤ *tr* (*rasgar*) to scratch, scrape.

arañazo ➤ *m* scratch.

arar ➤ *tr* to plow.

arbitraje ➤ *m* arbitration; COM. arbitrage.

arbitrar ➤ *tr* to arbitrate; SPORT. to referee ➤ *reflex* to get along, manage.

arbitrario, a ➤ *adj* arbitrary.

árbitro, a ➤ *mf* arbitrator; SPORT. referee, umpire.

árbol ➤ *m* tree.

arbolado, a ➤ *adj* wooded ➤ *m* grove.

arboleda ➤ *f* grove, wood.

arbusto ➤ *m* bush, shrub.

arca ➤ *f* (*cofre*) chest.

arcada ➤ *f* ARCHIT. arcade; (*de un puente*) span, arch ➤ *pl* retching, heaves.

arcaico, a ➤ *adj* archaic, old-fashioned.

arce ➤ *m* maple (tree).

archipiélago ➤ *m* archipelago.

archivador, a ➤ *mf* filing clerk ➤ *m* filing cabinet.

archivar ➤ *tr* to file, put into a file.

archivo ➤ *m* archives; (*de oficina*) files; COMPUT. file.

arcilla ➤ *f* clay.

arco ➤ *m* GEOM. arc; ARCHIT., ANAT. arch; ARM., MUS. bow ∎ a. iris rainbow.

arder ➤ *intr* to burn.

ardid ➤ *m* ruse, scheme.

ardiente ➤ *adj* burning, ardent.

ardilla ➤ *f* squirrel ∎ a. listada chipmunk, ground squirrel.

ardor ➤ *m* heat; FIG. zeal.

arduo, a ➤ *adj* arduous, difficult.

área ➤ *f* area.

arena ➤ *f* sand; (*redondel*) ring; (*campo de batalla*) battlefield ∎ arenas movedizas quicksand.

arenal ➤ *m* sandy ground; (*arenas movedizas*) quicksand.

arenga ➤ *f* harangue; FIG. sermon.

arenisco, a ➤ *adj* sandy ➤ *f* sandstone.

arenoso, a ➤ *adj* sandy.

arenque ➤ *m* herring.

arete ➤ *m (aro)* hoop, ring; *(pendiente)* earring.

argamasa ➤ *f* mortar, plaster.

argentino, a ➤ *adj & mf* Argentine, Argentinian.

argentinismo ➤ *m* Argentine word or expression.

argolla ➤ *f* ring; S. AMER. wedding ring.

argot ➤ *m* slang, jargon.

argüir ➤ *intr* to argue; *(deducir)* to deduce; *(probar)* to prove.

argumento ➤ *m (razonamiento)* line of reasoning; *(trama)* plot; *(sumario)* summary.

aria ➤ *f* aria.

aridez ➤ *f* aridity, aridness.

árido, a ➤ *adj* arid, dry.

arisco, a ➤ *adj* unfriendly.

aristocracia ➤ *f* aristocracy.

aristócrata ➤ *mf* aristocrat.

aristocrático, a ➤ *adj* aristocratic.

aritmética ➤ *f* arithmetic.

arma ➤ *f* weapon, arm ■ a. de fuego firearm.

armadura ➤ *f* MIL. armor; *(armazón)* frame, framework.

armamento ➤ *m* armament; *(armas)* weapons.

armar ➤ *tr (dar armas)* to arm; *(aprestar)* to prime; *(montar)* to assemble; FIG. to create.

armario ➤ *m* closet, wardrobe.

armazón ➤ *m or f* framework, frame.

armería ➤ *f* military museum.

armisticio ➤ *m* armistice.

armonía ➤ *f* harmony.

armónico, a ➤ *adj & m* harmonic ➤ *f* harmonica.

armonioso, a ➤ *adj* harmonious.

armonizar §02 ➤ *tr & intr* to harmonize.

aro ➤ *m* hoop, ring.

aroma ➤ *m* aroma, scent; *(del vino)* bouquet.

aromático, a ➤ *adj* aromatic.

aromatizar §02 ➤ *tr* to perfume; CUL. to flavor.

arpa ➤ *f* harp.

arpía ➤ *f* harpy.

arpón ➤ *m* harpoon; ARCHIT. clamp.

arqueada ➤ *f* MUS. bowing.

arquear ➤ *tr (curvar)* to curve; MARIT. to gauge.

arqueo ➤ *m (acción)* curve; COM. audit ■ a. bruto MARIT. gross tonnage.

arqueología ➤ *f* archaeology.

arqueólogo, a ➤ *mf* archaeologist.

arquitecto, a ➤ *mf* architect.

arquitectura ➤ *f* architecture.

arraigar §31 ➤ *intr* BOT. to take root.

arrancar §47 ➤ *tr (de raíz)* to pull up; *(con violencia)* to pull or yank out.

arranque ➤ *m (acción)* uprooting; *(toma)* seizure; *(arrebato)* outburst; AUTO. starter.

arrasar ➤ *tr* to level.

arrastrar ➤ *tr* to pull, drag; *(los pies)* to drag, shuffle.

arrastre ➤ *m* dragging.

arrebatado, a ➤ *adj (impetuoso)* impetuous; *(sonrojado)* flushed.

arrebatar ➤ *tr (arrancar)* to snatch; FIG. *(conmover)* to move, stir.

arrebato ➤ *m (arranque)* fit, seizure; *(furor)* rage.

arrecife ➤ *m* reef.

arreglado, a ➤ *adj* orderly, neat.

arreglar ➤ *tr (ordenar)* to put in order; *(acomodar)* to tidy up; *(reparar)* to repair; MUS. to arrange.

arreglo ➤ *m* arrangement; *(orden)* order; *(compostura)* repair.

arremeter ➤ *tr* to attack.

arrendador, a ➤ *mf (propietario)* landlord; *(inquilino)* tenant.

arrendamiento ➤ *m (acción)* rental; *(alquiler)* rent.

arrendar §33 ➤ *tr* to rent.

arrendatario, a ➤ *adj* renting ➤ *mf* tenant.

arrepentimiento ➤ *m* repentance.

arrepentirse §43 ➤ *reflex* to repent; FIG. to regret.

arrestar ➤ *tr* to arrest, detain.

arresto ➤ *m* arrest; *(reclusión)* imprisonment; *(audacia)* boldness.

arriar §18 ➤ *tr* MARIT. to lower; *(aflojar)* to slacken.

arriba ➤ *adv* above; *(en casa)* upstairs ■ de a. from above ■ de a. abajo from top to bottom; *(desde el principio al fin)* from beginning to end • **para a.** upwards, up.

arribar ➤ *intr* to arrive ∎ **a. a** to manage to.

arriesgado, a ➤ *adj (peligroso)* risky; *(audaz)* daring.

arriesgar §31 ➤ *tr* to risk, venture.

arrimar ➤ *tr* to bring *or* draw near.

arrinconar ➤ *tr* to put in a corner, put aside; *(perseguir)* to corner.

arrobamiento ➤ *m* ecstasy, rapture.

arrobar ➤ *tr* to enrapture ➤ *reflex (extasiarse)* to be enraptured.

arrodillar ➤ *tr* to make (someone) kneel ➤ *reflex* to kneel (down).

arrogancia ➤ *f* arrogance.

arrogante ➤ *adj* arrogant.

arrojar ➤ *tr* to hurl, fling; *(emitir)* to emit; *(vomitar)* to throw up.

arrojo ➤ *m (atrevimiento)* boldness; *(resolución)* resoluteness.

arrollar ➤ *tr (envolver)* to roll up; *(llevar)* to sweep *or* carry away.

arropar ➤ *tr (cubrir)* to wrap with clothes; *(acostar)* to tuck in (to bed).

arroyo ➤ *m* brook; *(cuneta)* gutter.

arroz ➤ *m* rice ∎ **a. con leche** rice pudding.

arruga ➤ *f (en la piel)* wrinkle; *(en la ropa)* crease; GEOL. fold.

arrugado, a ➤ *adj* wrinkled.

arrugar §31 ➤ *tr* to wrinkle; *(hacer arrugas)* to crease; *(papel)* to crumple.

arruinar ➤ *tr* to ruin; FIG. to destroy.

arrullar ➤ *tr* to coo; *(adormecer)* to lull to sleep.

arsénico ➤ *m* arsenic.

arte ➤ *m or f* art; *(habilidad)* art, skill ∎ **bellas artes** fine arts.

arteria ➤ *f* artery.

artesanía ➤ *f (habilidad)* craftsmanship; *(producto)* crafts.

artesano, a ➤ *mf* artisan, craftsman ➤ *f* craftswoman.

ártico, a ➤ *adj & m* Arctic.

articulación ➤ *f* ANAT., MECH. joint; *(pronunciación)* enunciation.

articular¹ ➤ *adj* ANAT. articular, of the joints.

articular² ➤ *tr (palabra)* to enunciate.

artículo ➤ *m* article; *(cosa)* item, thing; *(escrito)* essay.

artificial ➤ *adj* artificial.

artificio ➤ *m (habilidad)* ability; *(aparato)* device; *(ardid)* trick.

artillería ➤ *f* artillery.

artilugio ➤ *m (aparato)* contraption; *(trampa)* gimmick.

artimaña ➤ *f (trampa)* trick; *(astucia)* cunning.

artista ➤ *mf* artist; *(actor, actriz)* actor, actress.

artístico, a ➤ *adj* artistic.

artritis ➤ *f* MED. arthritis.

arzobispo ➤ *m* archbishop.

as ➤ *m* ace.

asa ➤ *f* handle.

asado ➤ *m (carne)* roasted meat; AMER. barbecued meat; *(comida)* cookout, barbecue.

asalariado, a ➤ *adj* salaried ➤ *mf* salaried worker.

asaltar ➤ *tr (atacar)* to assault; *(sobrevenir)* to overtake.

asalto ➤ *m (ataque)* assault; *(en el boxeo)* round.

asamblea ➤ *f (reunión)* meeting; *(congreso)* conference.

asar ➤ *tr* to roast ∎ **a. al horno** to bake • **a. a la parrilla** to broil.

ascendencia ➤ *f* ancestry.

ascender §34 ➤ *intr* to rise; *(de categoría)* to be promoted.

ascendiente ➤ *adj* ascending.

ascensión ➤ *f* ascension, rise.

ascenso ➤ *m (adelanto)* promotion; *(subida)* ascent, rise.

ascensor ➤ *m* elevator, lift (G.B.).

ascético, a ➤ *adj* ascetic ➤ *f* asceticism.

asco ➤ *m* disgust, revulsion.

ascua ➤ *f* ember.

aseado, a ➤ *adj (limpio)* clean; *(ordenado)* neat, tidy.

asear ➤ *tr (lavar)* to wash; *(limpiar)* to clean; *(ordenar)* to tidy (up).

asedio ➤ *m* siege.

asegurado, a ➤ *adj* insured ➤ *mf* insured (person), policyholder.

asegurar ➤ *tr (afirmar)* to secure; *(garantizar)* to guarantee; *(tranquilizar)* to assure; COM. to insure.

asentado, a ➤ *adj* (*juicioso*) judicious; (*estable*) stable.

asentar §33 ➤ *tr* (*anotar*) to record; (*fundar*) to found; (*colocar*) to place; (*afirmar*) to affirm; (*aplanar*) to level.

asentir §43 ➤ *intr* to assent, agree.

aseo ➤ *m* (*limpieza*) cleanliness; (*orden*) neatness, tidiness.

asequible ➤ *adj* (*accesible*) accessible; (*posible*) feasible.

aserradero ➤ *m* sawmill.

aserrar §33 ➤ *tr* to saw.

aserrín ➤ *m* sawdust.

asesinar ➤ *tr* to murder; POL. to assassinate.

asesinato ➤ *m* murder; POL. assassination.

asesino, a ➤ *mf* murderer; POL. assassin.

asesor, a ➤ *adj* advising, advisory ➤ *mf* adviser, counselor.

asesorar ➤ *tr* to advise ➤ *reflex* to seek advice.

asestar ➤ *tr* (*arma*) to aim; (*golpe*) to deal.

aseverar ➤ *tr* to assert.

asfalto ➤ *m* asphalt.

asfixiar ➤ *tr* to asphyxiate ➤ *reflex* to suffocate.

así ➤ *adv* (*de esta manera*) so, this way; (*de esa manera*) that way, like that; (*tanto*) so, in such a way ▪ **a. a.** so-so, fair • **a. como** as soon as ➤ *conj* (*en consecuencia*) therefore, thus; (*aunque*) even if, even though ➤ *adj* such.

Asia ➤ *f* Asia.

asiático, a ➤ *adj & mf* Asian.

asiduo, a ➤ *adj* assiduous.

asiento ➤ *m* seat; (*silla*) chair; (*sitio*) site.

asignación ➤ *f* (*distribución*) allotment; (*cita*) appointment.

asignar ➤ *tr* (*señalar*) to assign; (*nombrar*) to appoint.

asignatura ➤ *f* EDUC. subject, course ▪ **aprobar una a.** to pass a course.

asilo ➤ *m* asylum; (*refugio*) shelter.

asimilar ➤ *tr* to assimilate.

asimismo ➤ *adj* (*igualmente*) likewise, in like manner; (*también*) also, too.

asir ➤ *tr & intr* to grasp.

asistencia ➤ *f* (*concurrencia*) attendance; (*ayuda*) aid.

asistente, a ➤ *adj* assisting ➤ *mf* (*ayudante*) assistant.

asistir ➤ *intr* to attend ➤ *tr* (*acompañar*) to accompany; (*ayudar*) to aid; (*cuidar*) to nurse.

asma ➤ *f* asthma.

asno ➤ *m* donkey; FIG. jackass.

asociación ➤ *f* association ▪ **a. gremial** trade union • **a. sindical** labor union.

asociado, a ➤ *adj* associated ➤ *mf* associate.

asociar ➤ *tr* (*ligar*) to connect; (*combinar*) to combine ➤ *reflex* to become partners.

asolador, a ➤ *adj* ravaging.

asolar §11 ➤ *tr* to ravage.

asomar ➤ *intr* to appear ➤ *tr* to show ➤ *reflex* to appear; (*de una ventana*) to look or lean out.

asombrar ➤ *tr* to amaze, astonish ➤ *reflex* to be amazed or astonished.

asombro ➤ *m* amazement; (*maravilla*) marvel.

asombroso, a ➤ *adj* amazing, astonishing.

aspa ➤ *f* (*cruz*) X-shaped cross; (*devanadera*) spool; (*de molinos*) blade.

aspecto ➤ *m* aspect.

aspereza ➤ *f* (*escabrosidad*) ruggedness; (*brusquedad*) gruffness.

áspero, a ➤ *adj* (*rugoso*) rough; (*escabroso*) rugged; (*brusco*) gruff.

aspiradora ➤ *f* vacuum cleaner.

aspirina ➤ *f* aspirin.

asquear ➤ *tr* to disgust ➤ *intr* to be disgusting.

asqueroso, a ➤ *adj* (*repugnante*) repulsive; (*sucio*) filthy.

asta ➤ *f* (*lanza*) spear; (*de lanza*) shaft; (*de bandera*) flagpole; (*cuerno*) horn, antler.

asterisco ➤ *m* asterisk.

asteroide ➤ *m* asteroid ➤ *adj* asteroidal.

astilla ➤ *f* splinter ▪ **hacer astillas** to splinter.

astringente ➤ *adj & m* astringent.

astringir §19 ➤ *tr* to contract.

astro ➤ *m* star.

astrólogo, a ➤ *mf* astrologist ➤ *adj* astrological.

astronauta ➤ *mf* astronaut.
astronomía ➤ *f* astronomy.
astrónomo, a ➤ *mf* astronomer.
astucia ➤ *f* astuteness; *(ardid)* trick.
astuto, a ➤ *adj (listo)* astute, clever; *(mañoso)* crafty, shrewd.
asumir ➤ *tr* to assume, take on.
asunción ➤ *f* assumption.
asunto ➤ *m (tópico)* topic; *(tema)* subject matter; *(argumento)* plot.
asustadizo, a ➤ *adj* easily frightened, skittish.
asustar ➤ *tr* to frighten, scare ➤ *reflex* to be frightened *or* scared *(de, por, con* by).
atacar §47 ➤ *tr* to attack.
atajo ➤ *m* short cut.
ataque ➤ *m* attack ■ a. aéreo air raid.
atar ➤ *tr* to tie, fasten.
atascadero ➤ *m* bog.
atascamiento ➤ *m* obstruction.
atascar §47 ➤ *tr (obstruir)* to clog; *(impedir)* to hamper.
atasco ➤ *m* obstruction; FIG. obstacle.
ataúd ➤ *m* coffin, casket.
ataviar §18 ➤ *tr* to adorn, deck out.
atemorizar §02 ➤ *tr* to frighten.
atención ➤ *f* attention ■ llamar la a. *(atraer)* to catch the eye • prestar a. to pay attention ■ *pl* courtesies.
atender §34 ➤ *tr (hacer caso de)* to pay attention to; COM. to wait on ➤ *intr* to pay attention.
atentado ➤ *m* crime; *(ataque)* attempt.
atento, a ➤ *adj (observador)* attentive; *(cortés)* considerate ■ a. a in view of.
aterrar ➤ *tr* to terrify.
aterrizaje ➤ *m* landing.
aterrizar §02 ➤ *intr* to land.
aterrorizador, a ➤ *adj* terrifying.
aterrorizar §02 ➤ *tr* to terrorize.
ático ➤ *m* attic.
atizar §02 ➤ *tr (el fuego)* to poke, stir.
atlas ➤ *m* atlas.
atleta ➤ *mf* athlete.
atlético, a ➤ *adj* athletic.
atmósfera ➤ *f* atmosphere.
atolondrado, a ➤ *adj* reckless.
atómico, a ➤ *adj* atomic.
atomizador ➤ *m* atomizer, sprayer.
átomo ➤ *m* atom.

atónito, a ➤ *adj* astonished, amazed.
atontar ➤ *tr (embrutecer)* to stun; *(aturdir)* to confuse.
atormentar ➤ *tr* to torment; *(torturar)* to torture; *reflex* to worry.
atornillar ➤ *tr* to screw in *or* on.
atracadero ➤ *m* pier, dock.
atracar §47 ➤ *tr (asaltar)* to hold up; COLL. *(hartar)* to stuff, cram ➤ *intr* MARIT. to dock ➤ *reflex* to stuff *or* gorge oneself.
atracción ➤ *f* attraction.
atraco ➤ *m* holdup, robbery.
atractivo, a ➤ *adj* attractive.
atraer §49 ➤ *tr* to attract, draw.
atragantarse ➤ *reflex* COLL. to get tongue-tied ■ a. con to choke on.
atrancar §47 ➤ *tr (cerrar)* to bolt ➤ *reflex* to get stuck.
atranco *or* **atranque** ➤ *m* obstruction; FIG. jam.
atrapar ➤ *tr* COLL. to catch, trap.
atrás ➤ *adv* back, behind; *(antes)* back, ago ■ ¡a.! get back! • dar marcha a. AUTO. to back up • ir hacia a. to go backward.
atrasado, a ➤ *adj (reloj)* slow; *(persona)* late; *(país)* underdeveloped.
atrasar ➤ *tr* to delay; *(reloj)* to set back ➤ *intr* to be slow ➤ *reflex* to be late.
atraso ➤ *m* delay; *(retraso)* tardiness ■ *pl* arrears.
atravesar §33 ➤ *tr (pasar)* to cross (over); *(traspasar)* to pierce ➤ *reflex (obstruir)* to block.
atreverse ➤ *reflex* to dare *(a* to).
atrevido, a ➤ *adj (osado)* bold; *(descarado)* impudent.
atribuir ➤ *tr* to credit; *(imputar)* to grant.
atributo ➤ *m* attribute.
atrio ➤ *m (patio)* atrium; *(entrada)* vestibule.
atrocidad ➤ *f* atrocity; FIG. enormity.
atrofiado, a ➤ *adj* atrophied, atrophic.
atropellar ➤ *tr (derribar)* to run over; *(agraviar)* to bully; *(hacer precipitadamente)* to rush through.
atropello ➤ *m* assault; FIG. abuse.
atroz ➤ *adj* atrocious; FIG. enormous.
atuendo ➤ *m* attire.

atún ➤ *m* tuna (fish).

aturdido, a ➤ *adj (estupefacto)* stunned; *(turbado)* confused.

aturdir ➤ *tr (atontar)* to stun; *(turbar)* to confuse.

audacia ➤ *f* audacity.

audaz ➤ *adj* audacious.

audición ➤ *f (facultad)* hearing; *(programa)* program; THEAT. audition.

audiencia ➤ *f* audience.

audífono ➤ *m* hearing aid; *(auricular)* earphone.

audiovisual ➤ *adj* audio-visual.

auditorio, a ➤ *m (público)* audience; *(sala)* auditorium.

auge ➤ *m (apogeo)* peak; COM. boom, expansion; ASTRON. apogee.

augurio ➤ *m* augury, omen.

aula ➤ *f* classroom, lecture hall.

aullido or **aúllo** ➤ *m* howl, wail ■ dar aullidos to howl, wail.

aumentar ➤ *tr* to increase; RAD. to amplify; *(salario)* to raise ➤ *intr* to increase.

aumento ➤ *m* increase; RAD. amplification; *(de sueldo)* raise.

aun ➤ *adv* even ■ a. así even so.

aún ➤ *adv* still, yet ■ a. no not yet • más a. furthermore.

aunque ➤ *conj (si bien)* although, even though; *(a pesar de)* even if.

aureola ➤ *f* RELIG. halo; ASTRON. aureole.

auricular ➤ *m* TELEC. earpiece ■ *pl* earphones.

aurora ➤ *f* dawn.

ausencia ➤ *f* absence.

ausentarse ➤ *reflex (alejarse)* to leave.

ausente ➤ *adj* absent ➤ *mf* absentee.

austero, a ➤ *adj* austere.

austral ➤ *adj* austral, southern.

Australia ➤ *f* Australia.

australiano, a ➤ *adj & mf* Australian.

auténtico, a ➤ *adj* authentic, genuine.

auto¹ ➤ *m* LAW judicial decree or ruling; ■ *pl* LAW case file.

auto² ➤ *m* COLL. car, auto.

autobiografía ➤ *f* autobiography.

autobiográfico, a ➤ *adj* autobiographical.

autobús ➤ *m* bus.

autoedición ➤ *f* desktop publishing.

autógrafo ➤ *m* autograph.

automático, a ➤ *adj* automatic.

automóvil ➤ *m* automobile, car.

automovilista ➤ *mf* driver, motorist.

autonomía ➤ *f* autonomy.

autopista ➤ *f* expressway, superhighway.

autopsia ➤ *f* autopsy.

autor, a ➤ *mf* author, writer.

autoridad ➤ *f* authority; *(oficial)* official.

autoritario, a ➤ *adj* authoritarian.

autorizado, a ➤ *adj* authorized.

autorizar §02 ➤ *tr* to authorize.

autorretrato ➤ *m* self-portrait.

autosuficiencia ➤ *f* self-sufficiency.

auxiliar¹ ➤ *adj* auxiliary ➤ *mf (subalterno)* assistant ➤ *m* GRAM. auxiliary.

auxiliar² ➤ *tr* to assist, aid.

auxilio ➤ *m* assistance, aid ■ primeros auxilios first aid.

avalancha ➤ *f* avalanche.

avance¹ ➤ *m* advance.

avance² ➤ *m* preview.

avanzado, a ➤ *adj* advanced.

avanzar §02 ➤ *tr* to advance.

avaricia ➤ *f* avarice, greed.

avaro, a ➤ *adj (tacaño)* miserly; *(codicioso)* greedy ➤ *mf (tacaño)* miser.

ave ➤ *f* bird.

avellano, a ➤ *adj* hazel ➤ *m* hazel (tree) ➤ *f* hazelnut.

avena ➤ *f* oat, oats.

avenida ➤ *f* avenue.

avenirse §52 ➤ *reflex* to come to an agreement.

aventajar ➤ *tr (superar)* to surpass; *(ganar)* to beat; *(llevar ventaja)* to be ahead of.

aventura ➤ *f* adventure; *(riesgo)* risk.

aventurarse ➤ *reflex* to take a risk.

aventurero, a ➤ *adj* adventurous ➤ *m* adventurer ➤ *f* adventuress.

avergonzar §04 ➤ *tr* to shame ➤ *reflex* to be ashamed *(de* to, *por* of).

avería ➤ *f (rotura)* breakdown.

averiar §18 ➤ *tr (estropear)* to damage ➤ *reflex* to become damaged; *(descom-*

ponerse) to break (down).

averiguar §05 ➤ *tr* to find out, ascertain; *(investigar)* to investigate; *(verificar)* to verify.

avestruz ➤ *m* ostrich.

aviación ➤ *f* aviation; MIL. air force.

aviador, a ➤ *mf* pilot, aviator.

avidez ➤ *f* avidity; *(codicia)* greed.

ávido, a ➤ *adj* avid, eager; *(codicioso)* greedy.

avinagrado, a ➤ *adj* sour.

avión ➤ *m* airplane, plane ■ **por a.** by air mail.

avioneta ➤ *f* light airplane.

avisar ➤ *tr (informar)* to inform; *(advertir)* to warn.

aviso ➤ *m (notificación)* notice; *(advertencia)* warning.

avispa ➤ *f* wasp.

avivar ➤ *tr (un fuego)* to stoke; *(encender)* to arouse ➤ *intr & reflex* to revive, liven up.

axila ➤ *f* BOT. axil; ANAT. axilla, armpit.

¡ay! ➤ *interj* oh!, ouch! *(dolor)* ow!, ouch!

ayer ➤ *adv* yesterday; *(en el pasado)* formerly, in the past ➤ *m* yesterday, past.

ayuda ➤ *f (auxilio)* help, aid.

ayudante, a ➤ *mf* assistant, aide.

ayudar ➤ *tr* to help, aid.

ayunar ➤ *intr* to fast.

ayuno ➤ *m* fast ■ **en a.** *(sin comer)* fasting ➤ *m* fast, fasting.

ayuntamiento ➤ *m (corporación)* city council; *(edificio)* city hall.

azada ➤ *f* hoe.

azafata ➤ *f* AVIA. flight attendant.

azafrán ➤ *m* saffron.

azahar ➤ *f* orange, lemon, *or* citron blossom.

azar ➤ *m (casualidad)* chance ■ **al a.** at random • **por a.** by chance.

azorar ➤ *tr* to confuse ➤ *reflex* to become confused *or* bewildered.

azotaina ➤ *f* COLL. flogging.

azotar ➤ *tr* to flog; FIG. to beat upon.

azote ➤ *m* spanking.

azotea ➤ *f (tejado)* terraced roof.

azúcar ➤ *m or f* sugar.

azucarado, a ➤ *adj* sweet.

azucarera ➤ *f* sugar bowl.

azucena ➤ *f* white lily.

azul ➤ *adj & m* blue ■ **a. celeste** sky blue • **a. marino** navy blue • **a. turquí** indigo.

azulejo ➤ *m* glazed tile.

B

baba ➤ *f* spittle.

babero ➤ *m* bib.

babor ➤ *m* MARIT. port.

baboso, a ➤ *adj* drooling; C. AMER. foolish ➤ *mf* drooler ➤ *f* ZOOL. slug.

bacalao ➤ *m* codfish.

bache ➤ *m* pothole; AER. air pocket.

bachillerato ➤ *m* studies required to enter a university, equivalent to a high school diploma.

bacteria ➤ *f* bacterium.

bahía ➤ *f* bay.

bailador, a ➤ *mf* dancer.

bailar ➤ *intr* to dance.

bailarín, ina ➤ *mf* dancer ➤ *m* ballet dancer ➤ *f* ballerina.

baile ➤ *m* dance.

baja ➤ *f* drop; MIL. loss ■ **dar de b.** to expel; MIL. *(un soldado)* to discharge.

bajada ➤ *f* drop; *(camino)* sloped path.

bajamar ➤ *f* low tide.

bajar ➤ *intr* to descend; *(apearse)* to get off; *(disminuir)* to drop ➤ *tr* to lower; *(llevar abajo)* to bring *or* take down; *(ir abajo)* to go down; COMPUT. to download.

bajo ➤ *m (voz)* bass ➤ *pl (piso)* ground floor ➤ *adv (abajo)* below; *(en voz baja)* low ➤ *prep* under, beneath.

bajo, a ➤ *adj* low; *(persona)* short; *(inclinado)* downcast; *(poco vivo)* pale.

bajón ➤ *m* drop, slump; MUS. bassoon.

bala ➤ *f* bullet; *(de cañón)* cannonball; *(de carabina)* shot; *(fardo)* bale.

balada ➤ *f* ballad(e).

balance ➤ *m* balance ■ **b. comercial** balance of trade • **b. pendiente** balance due.

balanza ➤ *f* scales ■ **b. comercial** *or* **mercantil** ECON. balance of trade.

balazo ➤ *m (golpe)* shot; *(herida)* bullet wound.

balbucir ➤ *intr* to stammer.

balcón ➤ *m* balcony.

balde¹ ➤ *m* pail ■ como un b. de agua fría like a ton of bricks.

balde² ➤ *adv* ■ de b. *(gratuitamente)* free; *(sin motivo)* without reason • en b. in vain.

baldosa ➤ *f* floor tile.

balín ➤ *m* pellet, shot ■ *pl* buckshot.

ballena ➤ *f* whale; *(de un corsé)* stay.

ballet ➤ *m* ballet.

balneario, a ➤ *adj* bathing ➤ *m* spa.

balón ➤ *m* soccer ball, football (G.B.).

baloncesto ➤ *m* basketball.

balonmano ➤ *m* handball.

balonvolea ➤ *m* volleyball.

balota ➤ *f* ballot.

balsa ➤ *f* *(charca)* pool; *(embarcación)* raft.

bálsamo ➤ *m* balsam.

bambú ➤ *m* bamboo.

banana ➤ *f* banana.

banca ➤ *f* bench; COM. banking.

bancarrota ➤ *f* bankruptcy.

banco ➤ *m* bench; COM. bank ■ b. de ahorros savings bank • b. de arena sandbar • b. de datos data bank • b. de nieve snowbank.

banda¹ ➤ *f* *(faja)* band; *(cinta)* ribbon ■ b. sonora *or* de sonido soundtrack • b. transportadora conveyor belt.

banda² ➤ *f* MIL. troop, band; *(pandilla)* gang; MUS. band.

bandada ➤ *f* group; *(de aves)* flock.

bandeja ➤ *f* tray.

bandera ➤ *f* flag.

banderín ➤ *m* pennant.

bandido, a ➤ *m* bandit; COLL. rascal.

bandolero ➤ *m* bandit.

banjo ➤ *m* banjo.

banquero, a ➤ *mf* banker.

banqueta ➤ *f* stool; *(para los pies)* footstool.

banquete ➤ *m* banquet.

bañador, a ➤ *adj* bathing ➤ *mf* AMER. bather ➤ *m* bathing suit.

bañar ➤ *tr* to bathe ➤ *reflex* to bathe, take a bath.

bañera ➤ *f* bathtub.

bañista ➤ *mf* swimmer.

baño ➤ *m* *(ducha)* bath; *(bañera)* bathtub; *(cuarto de baño)* bathroom ■ b. de María double boiler ■ *pl* spa.

baptisterio ➤ *m* baptistry.

bar ➤ *m* barroom, bar.

baraja ➤ *f* deck (of cards).

baranda ➤ *f* banister; *(de billar)* cushion.

barandilla ➤ *f* banister, handrail.

baratija ➤ *f* trinket, bauble ■ *pl* junk.

barato, a ➤ *adj & adv* cheap(ly), inexpensive(ly).

barba ➤ *f* *(barbilla)* chin; *(pelo)* beard.

barbacoa ➤ *f* barbecue; AMER. makeshift cot.

barbaridad ➤ *f* barbarity; *(necedad)* foolish act, nonsense.

barbería ➤ *f* barbershop.

barbero ➤ *m* barber.

barbilla ➤ *f* chin.

barbudo, a ➤ *adj* heavily bearded.

barca ➤ *f* small boat.

barcaza ➤ *f* launch.

barco ➤ *m* boat, ship ■ b. de carga freighter.

barítono ➤ *m* baritone.

barlovento ➤ *m* windward.

barniz ➤ *m* varnish, lacquer.

barómetro ➤ *m* barometer.

barquillo ➤ *m* CUL. rolled wafer; *(helado)* ice-cream cone.

barra ➤ *f* bar; *(barandilla)* railing; *(mostrador)* counter; *(de arena)* sandbar ■ b. de tareas COMPUT. taskbar.

barraca ➤ *f* hut, cabin; AMER. warehouse.

barranco ➤ *m or* **barranca** ➤ *f* ravine, gorge.

barrendero, a ➤ *mf* street sweeper.

barreno ➤ *m* *(instrumento)* large drill, auger; MIN. blasting hole.

barrer ➤ *tr* to sweep.

barrera ➤ *f* barrier ■ b. de peaje tollgate.

barricada ➤ *f* barricade, barrier.

barriga ➤ *f* abdomen, stomach, belly.

barril ➤ *m* barrel, keg; *(jarro)* jug.

barrio ➤ *m* neighborhood ■ barrios bajos slums.

barro ➤ *m* *(lodo)* mud; *(arcilla)* clay.

barroco, a ➤ *adj* baroque; *(extravagante)* ornate, elaborate.

bártulos ➤ *mpl* household goods, belongings.

barullo ➤ *m* COLL. racket, rowdiness.

basar ➤ *tr* to base, support ➤ *reflex* to be based.

base ➤ *f* base; FIG. basis, foundation.

básico, a ➤ *adj* basic.

bastante ➤ *adj* enough, sufficient ➤ *adv* enough, sufficiently; *(muy)* rather, quite.

bastar ➤ *intr* to be enough, suffice ■ ¡basta! that's enough of that! ➤ *reflex* to be self-sufficient.

bastidor ➤ *m* frame, framework; THEAT. wing; AUTO. chassis ■ entre bastidores FIG. behind the scenes; THEAT. off-stage.

basto, a ➤ *adj* coarse, rough ➤ *m* *(albarda)* packsaddle ➤ *f* SEW. basting.

bastón ➤ *m* cane, walking stick.

basura ➤ *f* garbage, trash.

basurero ➤ *m* garbage collector; *(cubo)* garbage *or* trash can; *(basural)* dump.

bata ➤ *f* housecoat, robe; *(de trabajo)* frock, smock.

batalla ➤ *f* battle.

batallón ➤ *m* battalion.

batata ➤ *f* sweet potato, yam.

bate ➤ *m* SPORT. bat.

bateador, a ➤ *mf* SPORT. batter, hitter.

batear ➤ *tr* SPORT. to bat, hit.

batería ➤ *f* battery; MUS. drums, percussion ■ b. de cocina kitchen utensils.

batido ➤ *m (bebida)* shake.

batidora ➤ *f* CUL. whisk; ELEC. blender.

batir ➤ *tr* to beat, hit; *(revolver)* to beat, mix; *(agitar)* to beat, flap.

batuta ➤ *f* MUS. baton.

baúl ➤ *m* trunk; *(cofre)* coffer, chest.

bautismo ➤ *m* baptism, christening.

bautisterio ➤ *m* baptistry, baptistery.

bautizar §02 ➤ *tr* to baptize, christen.

bautizo ➤ *m* baptism, christening.

bazar ➤ *m* bazaar, marketplace.

bazo ➤ *m* ANAT. spleen.

beato, a ➤ *adj (beatificado)* beatified; *(piadoso)* pious.

bebé ➤ *m* baby.

beber ➤ *tr* to drink.

bebida ➤ *f* drink, beverage.

beca ➤ *f* grant, scholarship.

becario, a ➤ *mf* scholarship student.

becerro, a ➤ *m* yearling bull.

bechamel ➤ *f* white *or* béchamel sauce.

bedel ➤ *m* EDUC. proctor.

béisbol ➤ *m* baseball.

belén ➤ *m* crèche, nativity scene.

bélico, a ➤ *adj* bellicose, warlike.

belleza ➤ *f* beauty.

bello, a ➤ *adj* beautiful, lovely.

bellota ➤ *f* acorn.

bemol ➤ *m & adj* MUS. flat.

bencina ➤ *f* benzine.

bendecir ➤ *tr* to bless.

bendición ➤ *f* blessing.

bendito, a ➤ *adj* blessed.

beneficencia ➤ *f* welfare, public assistance.

beneficiar ➤ *tr* to benefit ➤ *intr* to be of benefit ➤ *reflex* to profit *(de* by, from).

beneficiario, a ➤ *mf* beneficiary.

beneficio ➤ *m* benefit, advantage; *(ganancia)* profit, gain.

beneficioso, a ➤ *adj* beneficial.

benéfico, a ➤ *adj* beneficent, charitable.

benevolencia ➤ *f* benevolence.

benigno, a ➤ *adj* benign.

berenjena ➤ *f* eggplant.

bermuda ➤ *f* Bermuda grass ■ *pl* Bermuda shorts.

berrinche ➤ *m* COLL. rage, tantrum.

berro ➤ *m* watercress.

besar ➤ *tr* to kiss.

beso ➤ *m* kiss.

bestia ➤ *f* beast.

besugo ➤ *m* sea bream; COLL. idiot.

betún ➤ *m* shoe polish.

biberón ➤ *m* baby bottle.

biblia ➤ *f* Bible.

bibliografía ➤ *f* bibliography.

biblioteca ➤ *f* library; AMER. bookcase.

bicarbonato ➤ *m* bicarbonate ■ b. de sodio *or* de sosa CUL. baking soda.

bicentenario ➤ *m* bicentennial.

biceps ➤ *m* biceps.

bicho ➤ *m* bug, insect.

bicicleta ➤ *f* bicycle.

bien ➤ *m* good, goodness; *(provecho)* good, benefit ■ hacer (el) b. to do good ■ *pl* property, goods • b. inmuebles *or* raíces real estate ➤ *adv* well; *(justamente)* right, correctly; *(de buena gana)* willingly; *(sin dificultad)* easily; *(bastante)* very; *(sí)* okay ■ más b. rather • o b. or else, otherwise • por b.

willingly • **pues b.** then, well now • **y b.** well then.

bienestar ➤ *m* well-being, comfort.

bienvenida ➤ *f* welcome, greetings.

bife ➤ *m* AMER. steak, beefsteak.

bifocal ➤ *adj* bifocal.

biftec ➤ *m* steak, beefsteak.

bifurcación ➤ *f* bifurcation, branch; *(de un camino)* fork; RAIL. junction.

bigote ➤ *m* mustache ▪ *pl* whiskers.

bilateral ➤ *adj* bilateral.

bilingüe ➤ *adj* bilingual.

bilis ➤ *f* bile.

billar ➤ *m* billiards.

billete ➤ *m* ticket; *(papel moneda)* bill.

billetera ➤ *f* wallet, billfold.

billón ➤ *m* [10¹²] trillion (U.S.), billion (G.B.).

bimotor ➤ *adj & m* AVIA. twin-engine (plane).

binario, a ➤ *adj* binary.

binocular ➤ *adj* binocular.

biografía ➤ *f* biography.

biología ➤ *f* biology.

biológico, a ➤ *adj* biologic(al).

biólogo, a ➤ *mf* biologist.

biombo ➤ *m* folding screen.

biopsia ➤ *f* biopsy.

biosfera ➤ *f* biosphere.

birlocha ➤ *f* kite (toy).

birrete ➤ *m* RELIG. biretta; *(bonete)* cap.

bisabuelo, a ➤ *mf* great-grandparent.

bisagra ➤ *f* hinge.

bisiesto ➤ *adj & m* leap (year).

bisnieto, a ➤ *mf* great-grandchild.

bisonte ➤ *m* bison.

bisté *or* **bistec** ➤ *m* beefsteak.

bisutería ➤ *f* costume jewelry.

bitio ➤ *m* COMPUT. bit.

bizantino, a ➤ *adj & mf* Byzantine.

bizco, a ➤ *adj & mf* cross-eyed.

bizcocho ➤ *m* sponge cake.

biznieto, a ➤ *m* var. of **bisnieto**.

blanco, a ➤ *adj* white; *(claro)* fair, light ▪ *mf* white (person) ▪ *m* white; *(tiro)* target; *(centro)* center; *(espacio)* blank space, blank ▪ **dar en el b.** to hit the nail on the head.

blando, a ➤ *adj* soft; *(tierno)* tender.

blanquear ➤ *tr* to whiten; *(dar cal)* to whitewash; *(ropa)* to bleach.

blasfemia ➤ *f* blasphemy.

blasón ➤ *m* heraldry; *(escudo)* coat of arms.

blindado, a ➤ *adj* armored, armor-plated.

bloc ➤ *m* writing pad *or* tablet.

bloque ➤ *m* block; *(grupo)* bloc, coalition; *(papel)* pad, notepad.

bloquear ➤ *tr* MIL. to blockade; *(impedir)* to block, obstruct; *(obstruir)* to jam.

blusa ➤ *f* blouse.

blusón ➤ *m* loose blouse, smock.

boa ➤ *f* ZOOL. boa (constrictor).

bobada ➤ *f* foolish act *or* remark.

bobina ➤ *f* spool, reel; SEW. bobbin.

bobo, a ➤ *adj* silly, foolish ▪ *mf* fool.

boca ➤ *f* mouth; ZOOL. pincer ▪ **b. abajo,** arriba face down, up • **¡cállate la b.!** COLL. be quiet!, shut up!

bocacalle ➤ *f* intersection.

bocadillo ➤ *m* sandwich.

bocado ➤ *m* mouthful, bite.

bocanada ➤ *f* swallow, swig; *(de humo)* puff; *(de aire)* gust, rush.

boceto ➤ *m* sketch, draft.

bocha ➤ *f* wooden ball.

bochinche ➤ *m* COLL. uproar, commotion.

bochorno ➤ *m* *(vergüenza)* embarrassment, shame; *(calor)* suffocating heat.

bocina ➤ *f* horn; MARIT. foghorn.

boda ➤ *f* wedding, marriage.

bodega ➤ *f* wine cellar; *(taberna)* tavern, bar; AMER. grocery store.

bodegón ➤ *m* *(taberna)* tavern, bar; ARTS still life.

bofetada ➤ *f* slap; *(afrenta)* insult.

bohemio, a ➤ *adj & mf* bohemian.

bohío ➤ *m* AMER. hut, shack.

boicotear ➤ *tr* to boycott.

boina ➤ *f* beret, cap.

boite ➤ *f* nightclub.

bola ➤ *f* ball; *(canica)* marble; *(mentira)* lie, fib ▪ **b. de nieve** snowball.

bolera ➤ *f* bowling alley.

bolero ➤ *m* MUS. bolero.

boletería ➤ *f* AMER. ticket *or* box office.

boletín ➤ *m* bulletin.

boleto ➤ *m* AMER. ticket.

bolígrafo ➤ *m* ballpoint pen.

boliviano, a ➤ *adj* Bolivian ➤ *mf* Bolivian ➤ *m* BOL., FIN. boliviano.

bolívar ➤ *m* VEN., FIN. bolivar.

bollo ➤ *m* bun, roll; *(hueco)* dent.

bolos ➤ *mpl* bowling, ninepins.

bolsa ➤ *f (saco)* sack, bag; FIN. stock market ■ b. de comercio commodity exchange.

bolsillo ➤ *m* pocket; *(dinero)* purse, money.

bolso ➤ *m* purse, pocketbook.

bomba ➤ *f* MIL. bomb, shell; TECH. pump; *(sorpresa)* bombshell, stunning news ■ pasarlo b. to have a ball.

bombardear ➤ *tr* to bombard, bomb.

bombardeo ➤ *m* bombardment.

bombero, a ➤ *mf* fireman, firefighter.

bombilla ➤ *f* light bulb.

bombo ➤ *m* bass drum.

bombón ➤ *m* bonbon, chocolate.

bonachón, ona ➤ *adj & mf* COLL. good-natured (person).

bondad ➤ *f* goodness, kindness.

bondadoso, a ➤ *adj* good, kind.

boniato ➤ *m* sweet potato.

bonito, a ➤ *adj (lindo)* pretty, nice-looking ➤ *m* tuna, bonito.

bono ➤ *m (vale)* voucher; COM. *(fianza)* bond.

boquera ➤ *f* lip sore, mouth ulcer.

boquerón ➤ *m* anchovy.

boquete ➤ *m (agujero)* hole.

boquiabierto, a ➤ *adj* open-mouthed, gaping; *(atónito)* amazed, astonished.

boquilla ➤ *f* MUS. mouthpiece; *(del cigarillo)* cigarette holder; *(filtro)* filter tip.

borbotear ➤ *intr* to boil, bubble.

bordado ➤ *m* embroidery.

bordar ➤ *tr* to embroider.

borde ➤ *m* border, edge; *(canto)* brim, rim.

bordear ➤ *tr* to border; *(ir por el borde)* to skirt, go around.

bordillo ➤ *m* curb.

boreal ➤ *adj* boreal, northern.

borgoña ➤ *f* Burgundy (wine).

borla ➤ *f* tassel.

borrachera ➤ *f (ebriedad)* drunkenness; *(parranda)* binge, spree.

borracho, a ➤ *adj* drunk; CUL. rum-soaked ➤ *mf* drunk, drunkard.

borrador ➤ *m (escrito)* rough draft; *(papel)* scratch pad; *(de borrar)* eraser.

borrar ➤ *tr* to erase.

borrasca ➤ *f* storm, tempest.

borrego, a ➤ *mf* lamb.

borrico ➤ *m* ass, donkey.

borroso, a ➤ *adj* blurred, fuzzy.

bosque ➤ *m* woods, forest; FIG. confusion.

bosquejo ➤ *m* sketch, outline, draft.

bostezar §02 ➤ *intr* to yawn.

bostezo ➤ *m* yawn.

bota ➤ *f* boot; *(odre)* wineskin; *(tonel)* wooden cask.

botánico, a ➤ *adj* botanical ➤ *mf* botanist ➤ *f* botany.

botar ➤ *tr* to fling, hurl; AMER. *(tirar)* to throw away; *(malgastar)* to waste, squander ➤ *intr* to bounce.

bote ➤ *m (brinco)* prance; *(rebote)* bounce; *(pote)* pot, jar; *(lata)* tin can; *(barco)* rowboat.

botella ➤ *f* bottle.

botica ➤ *f* pharmacy, drugstore.

botijo ➤ *m* earthenware jug.

botín ➤ *m* booty, spoils.

botiquín ➤ *m* medicine chest or cabinet; *(estuche)* first-aid kit.

botón ➤ *m* button.

botones ➤ *mpl* bellboy, bellhop.

bóveda ➤ *f* vault; *(techo)* dome, cupola; *(cripta)* crypt ■ b. celeste firmament, heavens.

boxeador, a ➤ *mf* boxer.

boxeo ➤ *m* boxing.

boya ➤ *f* buoy.

bozal ➤ *m* muzzle.

bracero ➤ *m* laborer, worker.

braga ➤ *f (pañal)* diapers ■ *pl (calzón femenino)* panties.

bragueta ➤ *f* fly (of pants).

brasa ➤ *f* live or hot coal.

brasero ➤ *m* brazier.

brasileño, a ➤ *adj & mf* Brazilian.

bravo, a ➤ *adj* brave, valiant; *(feroz)* ferocious, wild; *(enojado)* angry, furious ■ ¡b.! bravo!, well done!

brazada ➤ *f* breaststroke.

brazalete ➤ *m* bracelet.

brazo ➤ *m* arm ■ *pl (jornaleros)* hands, laborers.

brecha ➤ *f* gap, opening.
brécol ➤ *m* broccoli.
breve ➤ *adj* brief, short ▪ **en b.** *(pronto)* shortly, soon.
bribón, ona ➤ *adj & mf (pícaro)* roguish (person).
bridge ➤ *m (naipes)* bridge; DENT. bridge, bridgework.
brigada ➤ *f* brigade; *(división)* squad, unit; *(equipo)* gang, team.
brillante ➤ *adj* brilliant.
brillar ➤ *intr* to shine.
brillo ➤ *m (lustre)* brilliance, shine; *(gloria)* distinction, glory ▪ **dar** *or* **sacar b.** to shine.
brincar §47 ➤ *intr* to jump, leap about.
brindar ➤ *intr* to toast, drink a toast.
brindis ➤ *m* toast.
brío ➤ *m* strength, vigor; *(garbo)* grace, charm.
brisa ➤ *f* breeze, light wind.
británico, a ➤ *adj & mf* British (person).
brocado, a ➤ *adj & m* brocade.
brocha ➤ *f* paintbrush; *(de afeitar)* shaving brush.
broche ➤ *m* clasp, hook and eye; *(prendedor)* brooch.
bróculi ➤ *m* broccoli.
broma ➤ *f* joke, prank; *(diversión)* fun, jest ▪ **b. pesada** practical joke, prank • **ni en b.** not on your life.
bromear ➤ *intr* to joke, jest.
bronce ➤ *m* bronze.
bronceado, a ➤ *adj (tostado)* tanned ➤ *m (piel tostada)* suntan.
bronceador ➤ *m* suntan lotion.
broncear ➤ *tr (piel)* to tan, suntan ➤ *reflex* to get a tan, suntan.
bronquitis ➤ *f* bronchitis.
brotar ➤ *intr* BOT. to bud, sprout; *(agua)* to spring, flow; *(estallar)* to break out, spring up.
bruja ➤ *f* witch, sorceress.
brújula ➤ *f* compass; *(norma)* standard, norm.
bruma ➤ *f* fog, mist.
bruñido, a ➤ *adj* burnished, polished.
brusco, a ➤ *adj* brusque.
brutalidad ➤ *f* brutality; *(incapacidad)*

stupidity, foolishness; *(gran cantidad)* loads, slew.
bruto, a ➤ *adj* brutish, boorish; *(necio)* stupid, ignorant; *(diamante)* rough, uncut; COM. gross.
bucear ➤ *intr* to swim under water.
buceo ➤ *m* underwater swimming; *(exploración)* exploration, searching.
bucólico, a ➤ *adj* bucolic, pastoral.
buen ➤ *adj contr of* **bueno.**
bueno, a ➤ *adj* good; *(bondadoso)* kind, benevolent; *(útil)* fit, appropriate; *(sano)* well, healthy; *(bonachón)* innocent, naive ▪ **buenas noches, tardes** good night, afternoon • **buenos días** good morning ➤ *adv* all right, okay ➤ *m* ▪ **lo b.** (the) good.
buey ➤ *m* ox, bullock.
búfalo, a ➤ *mf (buey salvaje)* buffalo; *(bisonte)* bison.
bufanda ➤ *f* scarf, muffler.
bufete ➤ *m* lawyer's office.
buhardilla ➤ *f (ventana)* dormer; *(desván)* attic, garret.
búho ➤ *m* horned owl; *(recluso)* hermit.
buitre ➤ *m* vulture, buzzard.
bujía ➤ *f (vela)* candle; ELEC. spark plug.
bulbo ➤ *m* bulb.
bullicio ➤ *m* bustle, hubbub.
bullicioso, a ➤ *adj* bustling.
bulto ➤ *m (forma)* form, shape; *(fardo)* package, bundle; MED. swelling, lump.
buñuelo ➤ *m* fried dough, fritter.
buque ➤ *m* ship, vessel.
burbuja ➤ *f* bubble.
burdel ➤ *m* brothel.
burguesía ➤ *f* bourgeoisie, middle class.
burla ➤ *f* jeer, taunt.
burlarse ➤ *reflex* to make fun, joke ▪ **b. de** to make fun of, ridicule.
burocracia ➤ *f* bureaucracy.
burra ➤ *f* donkey, jenny; COLL. *(ignorante)* dunce.
burro ➤ *m* donkey, jackass; *(ignorante)* dunce.
bursátil ➤ *adj* stock, stock market.
busca ➤ *f* search ▪ **ir en** *or* **a la b. de** to go in search of.

buscador, a ➤ *mf* searcher ➤ *m* COMPUT. search engine.

buscar §47 ➤ *tr* to search *or* look for, seek.

búsqueda ➤ *f* search.

busto ➤ *m* ANAT. chest, bust; SCULP. bust.

butaca ➤ *f* armchair, easy chair; THEAT. orchestra *or* box seat.

butano ➤ *m* butane.

buzo ➤ *m* (deep-sea) diver; (*prenda*) overalls, jumpsuit.

buzón ➤ *m* mailbox, letter box.

C

cabalgar §31 ➤ *intr* to ride horseback.

caballa ➤ *f* mackerel.

caballería ➤ *f* (*animal*) mount, steed; MIL. cavalry.

caballeriza ➤ *f* stable; (*criados*) stablehands.

caballero ➤ *m* knight; (*señor*) gentleman ■ armar c. to knight.

caballete ➤ *m* easel.

caballo ➤ *m* horse; (*en ajedrez*) knight ■ a c. on horseback • c. de montar *or* de silla saddle horse • montar a c. to go horseback riding ■ *pl* horsepower.

cabaña ➤ *f* hut, cabin.

cabaret ➤ *m* night club, cabaret.

cabecera ➤ *f* (*lugar principal*) head; (*de una cama*) headboard ■ médico de c. attending physician.

cabecilla ➤ *mf* ringleader.

cabellera ➤ *f* head of hair.

cabello ➤ *m* hair.

caber §06 ➤ *intr* (*tener lugar*) to fit; (*corresponder*) to fall to; (*ser posible*) to be possible ■ cabe decir one might say • no cabe duda there is no doubt • no cabe más FIG. that's the limit.

cabeza ➤ *f* head; (*jefe*) chief ■ a la c. de at the head of; (*en control*) in charge of • subirse a la c. to go to one's head.

cabida ➤ *f* capacity.

cabildo ➤ *m* town council.

cabina ➤ *f* booth.

cable ➤ *m* cable.

cablevisión ➤ *f* cable television.

cabo ➤ *m* end; (*pedazo*) stub, bit; GEOG. cape; MARIT. cable; MIL. corporal ■ al c. de at the end of • atar cabos to put two and two together • llevar a c. to carry out.

cabra ➤ *f* goat.

cabritilla ➤ *f* lambskin, kid.

cacahuete ➤ *m* peanut.

cacao ➤ *m* cacao; CUL. cocoa.

cacatúa ➤ *f* cockatoo.

cacería ➤ *f* (*caza*) hunting; (*partida*) hunting party.

cacerola ➤ *f* casserole, pot.

cachalote ➤ *m* sperm whale.

cacharro ➤ *m* (*vasija*) crock; COLL. (*trasto*) piece of junk; (*máquina*) wreck; (*coche*) jalopy ■ *pl* junk.

cachemira ➤ *f* cashmere.

cachete ➤ *m* (*mejilla*) cheek; (*cacheтáда*) slap.

cachivache ➤ *m* piece of junk.

cacho ➤ *m* (*pedazo*) piece.

cachorro, a ➤ *mf* (*perro*) puppy; (*de otros mamíferos*) cub.

cacique ➤ *mf* COLL. (*jefe*) political boss; (*déspota*) tyrant.

caco ➤ *m* burglar.

cactus *or* **cacto** ➤ *m* cactus.

cada ➤ *adj* each, every ■ c. cual *or* uno each one, everyone • ¿c. cuánto? how often? • c. vez más more and more • c. vez menos less and less • c. vez peor worse and worse • c. vez que whenever.

cadáver ➤ *m* corpse, cadaver.

cadena ➤ *f* chain ■ c. de emisoras network • c. de montañas mountain range • c. perpetua life imprisonment.

cadera ➤ *f* hip, hip joint.

caducar §47 ➤ *intr* to lapse, expire.

caducidad ➤ *f* expiration.

caer §07 ➤ *intr* to fall; (*derrumbarse*) to fall down, collapse; (*los precios*) to drop; (*el sol*) to set; (*comprender*) to see; COMPUT. to crash ■ al c. la noche at nightfall • c. bien (*prenda*) to suit; (*persona*) to make a good impression on; (*alimento*) to agree with • c. mal (*prenda*) to fit poorly; (*persona*) to displease; (*alimento*) to upset one's stomach ➤ *reflex* to fall; (*de las manos*) to drop, fall.

café ➤ *m* coffee; (*cafetería*) café.

cafetal ➤ *m* coffee plantation.

cafetera ➤ *f* CUL. coffeepot ■ c. de filtro percolator.

cafetería ➤ *f* coffee shop, café.

caída ➤ *f* fall; *(de la temperatura)* drop; *(tumbo)* tumble; *(ruina)* downfall.

caimán ➤ *m* alligator.

cairel ➤ *m* hairpiece; *(fleco)* fringe.

caja ➤ *f* box; *(de madera)* chest; *(ataúd)* coffin; *(ventanilla)* cashier's window ■ c. de ahorros savings bank • c. de cambios *or* velocidades AUTO. transmission • c. de fusibles ELEC. fuse box • c. de seguridad safe-deposit box • c. fuerte safe.

cajero, a ➤ *mf* teller, cashier ■ c. automático automated teller machine.

cajón ➤ *m (caja grande)* case; *(gaveta)* drawer.

cal ➤ *f* MIN. lime.

calabaza ➤ *f* squash, pumpkin.

calabozo ➤ *m (cárcel)* underground prison; *(celda)* jail cell.

calamar ➤ *m* squid.

calambre ➤ *m* cramp, spasm.

calamidad ➤ *f* misfortune.

calar ➤ *tr (mojar)* to drench; *(penetrar)* to penetrate ➤ *reflex (mojarse)* to get drenched; *(ponerse)* to put on.

calavera ➤ *f* skull.

calcar §47 ➤ *tr* to trace; FIG. to copy.

calcetín ➤ *m* sock.

calcio ➤ *m* calcium.

calco ➤ *m* tracing; FIG. copy.

calcomanía ➤ *f* decal, transfer.

calculadora ➤ *f* calculator.

calcular ➤ *tr (computar)* to calculate; *(proyectar)* to estimate.

cálculo ➤ *m (proceso)* calculation; *(suposición)* estimate; MED. stone, calculus; MATH. calculus.

caldera ➤ *f* MECH. boiler.

caldero ➤ *m* small caldron.

caldo ➤ *m* broth.

calefacción ➤ *f* heat, heating.

calendario ➤ *m* calendar; *(programa)* schedule.

calentador ➤ *m* heater; *(para agua)* water heater.

calentar §33 ➤ *tr* to warm *or* heat (up); ➤ *reflex* to warm oneself up.

calentura ➤ *f* fever.

calidad ➤ *f* quality.

cálido, a ➤ *adj* warm.

cal(e)idoscopio ➤ *m* kaleidoscope.

caliente ➤ *adj* hot, warm; FIG. heated.

calificar §47 ➤ *tr* EDUC. to grade.

calificativo ➤ *m* qualifier.

caligrafía ➤ *f* calligraphy.

cáliz ➤ *m* chalice.

callar ➤ *intr* to be *or* become silent ➤ *tr (silenciar)* to silence, hush ➤ *reflex (guardar silencio)* to be quiet *or* silent; *(quedarse callado)* to keep quiet ■ ¡cállate! be quiet!

calle ➤ *f* street.

callejón ➤ *m* alley ■ c. sin salida blind alley.

callo ➤ *m* corn ■ *pl* tripe.

callosidad ➤ *f* callosity, callus.

calmante ➤ *adj & m* sedative.

calmar ➤ *tr* to soothe, calm (down) ➤ *intr* to calm (down), abate ➤ *reflex* to calm down.

calma ➤ *f* calm ■ con c. calmly.

caló ➤ *m* Gypsy dialect; *(jerga)* slang.

calor ➤ *m* warmth, heat ■ hacer c. *(tiempo)* to be hot *or* warm • tener c. *(persona)* to be hot *or* warm.

caloría ➤ *f* calorie.

calumnia ➤ *f* calumny, slander.

caluroso, a ➤ *adj* warm, hot; FIG. warm, enthusiastic.

calvario ➤ *m* calvary; RELIG. Calvary.

calvo, a ➤ *adj* bald ➤ *mf* bald person ➤ *f* bald spot.

calzada ➤ *f* highway, road.

calzado ➤ *m* footwear.

calzador ➤ *m* shoehorn.

calzar §02 ➤ *tr* to put (shoes) on; *(rueda)* to wedge ■ ¿qué número calza? what size shoe do you take? ➤ *reflex* to put on shoes.

calzón ➤ *m or* **calzones** ➤ *mpl* pants, trousers.

calzoncillos ➤ *mpl* underwear, boxers.

cama ➤ *f* bed ■ c. gemela twin bed • c. matrimonial double bed.

cámara ➤ *f (sala)* hall; *(junta)* chamber; AUTO. inner tube; PHOTOG. camera ■ c. cinematográfica movie camera • c. lenta slow motion.

camarada ➤ *mf* comrade.

camarero, a ➤ *mf* waiter, waitress.

camarín ➤ *m* THEAT. dressing room.

camarón ➤ *m* shrimp, prawn.

camarote ➤ *m* MARIT. cabin, berth.

cambiar ➤ *tr* to change; (*alterar*) to alter; (*reemplazar*) to replace; COM. to exchange, change ▪ *intr* to change ▪ c. de casa to move • c. de color to change color • c. de ropa to change clothes ➤ *reflex* to change.

cambio ➤ *m* change; (*alteración*) alteration; COM. rate of exchange ▪ a c. de in exchange for • c. automático automatic transmission • c. de marchas or velocidades gearshift • casa de c. foreign exchange office.

camello ➤ *m* camel.

camerino ➤ *m* THEAT. dressing room.

camilla ➤ *f* MED. stretcher.

caminar ➤ *intr & tr* to walk.

caminata ➤ *f* walk, hike.

camino ➤ *m* road; (*senda*) path, trail; (*vía*) route ▪ abrir c. to make way • a medio c. halfway • c. a towards • en c. on the way • en c. de FIG. on the way to.

camión ➤ *m* truck, lorry (G.B.); MEX. bus ▪ c. de bomberos fire engine • c. de mudanzas moving van.

camionero, a ➤ *mf* truck driver.

camioneta ➤ *f* van.

camisa ➤ *f* shirt ▪ c. de fuerza straitjacket • en mangas de c. in shirtsleeves.

camiseta ➤ *f* T-shirt; (*ropa interior*) undershirt; SPORT. jersey.

camisón ➤ *m* nightgown.

camote AMER. ➤ *m* sweet potato.

campamento ➤ *m* camp ▪ c. de verano summer camp.

campana ➤ *f* bell.

campanada ➤ *f* stroke, ring (of a bell).

campanario ➤ *m* bell tower, belfry.

campanilla ➤ *f* hand bell; (*timbre*) doorbell.

campaña ➤ *f* (*llanura*) plain; MIL., POL. campaign ▪ hacer c. to campaign • tienda de c. tent.

campeón, ona ➤ *mf* champion.

campeonato ➤ *m* championship.

campesino, a ➤ *adj* rustic ➤ *mf* peasant.

campo ➤ *m* country, countryside; (*plantío*) field; MIL., SPORT. field ▪ a c. traviesa cross-country • casa de c. country house • c. de golf golf course.

camposanto ➤ *m* cemetery, graveyard.

camuflar ➤ *tr* to camouflage.

can ➤ *m* dog.

cana ➤ *f* gray hair.

canadiense ➤ *adj & mf* Canadian.

canal ➤ *m* canal; (*estrecho*) strait, channel; (*de puerto*) navigation channel; TELEV. channel.

canalización ➤ *f* ELEC. wiring.

canalla COLL. ➤ *m* scoundrel ➤ *f* riffraff.

canalón ➤ *m* gutter, drainpipe.

canapé ➤ *m* sofa; CUL. canapé.

canastilla ➤ *f* small basket; (*de bebé*) layette.

canasto ➤ *m* basket.

cancelar ➤ *tr* to cancel; (*saldar*) to pay off.

cáncer ➤ *m* cancer.

canceroso, a ➤ *adj* cancerous.

cancha ➤ *f* playing field; (*de tenis*) court; AMER. open ground.

canciller ➤ *mf* chancellor.

canción ➤ *f* song ▪ c. de cuna lullaby.

candado ➤ *m* padlock.

candela ➤ *f* candle.

candelabro ➤ *m* candelabrum.

candidato, a ➤ *mf* candidate.

candidatura ➤ *f* candidacy.

candoroso, a ➤ *adj* frank, candid; (*ingenuo*) naive.

canela ➤ *f* cinnamon.

canelones ➤ *mpl* canneloni (pasta).

cangrejo ➤ *m* crab ▪ c. de río crayfish.

canguro ➤ *m* kangaroo.

caníbal ➤ *adj* cannibalistic ➤ *mf* cannibal.

canica ➤ *f* marble ➤ *pl* (game of) marbles.

canícula ➤ *f* dog days, midsummer heat.

canoa ➤ *f* canoe; (*bote*) rowboat.

canoso, a ➤ *adj* gray-haired.

cansado, a ➤ *adj* (*fatigado*) tired; (*agotado*) worn-out.

cansancio ➤ *m* tiredness ▪ muerto de c. dog-tired.

cansar ➤ *tr* to tire, make tired; *(aburrir)* to bore; *(fastidiar)* to annoy ▪ **c. la vista** to strain one's eyes ➤ *reflex* to become *or* get tired ➤ *intr* to be tiring; *(aburrir)* to be boring.

cantante ➤ *mf* singer, vocalist.

cantar ➤ *tr & intr* to sing.

cántaro ➤ *m* jug ▪ **llover a cántaros** COLL. to rain cats and dogs.

cantera ➤ *f* quarry, pit.

cántico ➤ *m* canticle; FIG. song.

cantidad ➤ *f* quantity; *(suma)* sum.

cantimplora ➤ *f* canteen.

canto[1] ➤ *m* song; *(arte)* singing.

canto[2] ➤ *m* *(extremo)* edge; *(borde)* border ▪ **de c.** on end, on edge.

canturrear ➤ *intr* COLL. to sing softly.

caña ➤ *f* reed; *(de azúcar)* cane; *(tallo)* stalk ▪ **c. de pescar** fishing rod.

cañaveral ➤ *m* cane thicket; *(plantación)* sugar-cane plantation.

cañería ➤ *f* pipe; *(tubería)* pipeline.

caño ➤ *m* pipe, tube.

cañón ➤ *m* MIL. cannon; ARM. barrel; GEOG. canyon, gorge.

cañonazo ➤ *m* cannon shot.

caoba ➤ *f* mahogany.

caos ➤ *m* chaos.

caótico, a ➤ *adj* chaotic.

capa ➤ *f* *(manto)* cape; *(de pintura)* coat; *(cubierta)* covering; GEOL. layer.

capacidad ➤ *f* capacity.

caparazón ➤ *m* shell, carapace.

capataz ➤ *mf* foreman/woman.

capaz ➤ *adj* capable.

capilla ➤ *f* chapel.

capital ➤ *adj* capital; *(esencial)* vital ➤ *m* FIN. capital; *(el que produce intereses)* principal ➤ *f* capital, capital city.

capitalista ➤ *adj & mf* capitalist.

capitán, ana ➤ *m* captain.

capitel ➤ *m* capital (of a column).

capitolio ➤ *m* capitol.

capitulación ➤ *f* capitulation.

capítulo ➤ *m* chapter; *(reunión)* assembly.

capó ➤ *m* AUTO. hood, bonnet (G.B.).

capote ➤ *m* cape ▪ **c. de montar** riding cape.

capricho ➤ *m* whim; *(antojo)* fancy.

caprichoso, a ➤ *adj* whimsical; *(inconstante)* fickle.

cápsula ➤ *f* capsule.

captar ➤ *tr* to attract, win.

captura ➤ *f* capture.

capturar ➤ *tr* to capture.

capucha ➤ *f* hood.

capullo ➤ *m* *(brote)* bud; *(de larva)* cocoon ▪ **c. de rosa** rosebud.

caqui ➤ *m* BOT. persimmon; *(tela y color)* khaki.

cara ➤ *f* face; *(superficie)* surface; *(frente)* front; *(aspecto)* appearance ▪ **hacer c.** to confront.

caracol ➤ *m* snail; *(espiral)* spiral.

caracola ➤ *f* conch.

carácter ➤ *m* character; *(índole)* nature; *(rasgo)* trait.

característico, a ➤ *adj & f* characteristic.

caracterizar §02 ➤ *tr* to characterize; THEAT. to portray (a role) expressively.

¡caramba! ➤ *interj* *(asombro)* good heavens!; *(enfado)* damn it!

carámbano ➤ *m* icicle.

caramelo ➤ *m* caramel; *(dulce)* candy.

caravana ➤ *f* caravan.

carbón ➤ *m* coal; *(de leña)* charcoal; *(lápiz)* carbon pencil.

carboncillo ➤ *m* ARTS charcoal pencil.

carbono ➤ *m* carbon.

carburador ➤ *m* carburetor.

carburante ➤ *m* fuel.

carcajada ➤ *f* loud laughter ▪ **reír a carcajadas** to split one's sides laughing.

cárcel ➤ *f* *(prisión)* jail; TECH. clamp.

carcelero, a ➤ *mf* jailer ➤ *adj* jail.

cardenal ➤ *m* RELIG., ORNITH. cardinal; COLL. *(mancha)* bruise, welt.

cardíaco, a *or* **cardíaco, a** ➤ *adj* cardiac ▪ **ataque c.** heart attack.

cardinal ➤ *adj* cardinal.

cardiograma ➤ *m* electrocardiogram.

cardiólogo, a ➤ *mf* cardiologist.

cardo ➤ *m* thistle.

cardume(n) ➤ *m* school (of fish).

carecer §09 ➤ *intr* ▪ **c. de** to lack.

carencia ➤ *f* lack; MED. deficiency.

carente ➤ *adj* lacking (in), devoid of.

carestía ➤ *f* scarcity.

careta ➤ *f* mask ▪ **c. antigás** gas mask.

carey ➤ *m* sea turtle; *(caparazón)* tortoiseshell.

carga ➤ *f* load; *(acción)* loading; *(flete)* cargo; *(peso)* burden; ELEC. charge ▪ **llevar la c. de** to be responsible for.

cargado, a ➤ *adj* laden; *(sabor)* strong; *(atmósfera)* heavy; ELEC. charged ▪ **c. de años** old, ancient • **c. de espaldas** round-shouldered.

cargamento ➤ *m* load, cargo.

cargar §31 ➤ *tr* to load; *(llenar)* to fill; *(imputar)* to ascribe; *(con obligaciones)* to burden; *(con impuestos)* to impose; COLL. *(importunar)* to pester; ELEC., MIL. to charge; AMER. to carry ▪ **c. en cuenta** COM. to charge to one's account ➤ *intr* to load ▪ **c. con** to carry; FIG. to shoulder ➤ *reflex* COLL. *(molestarse)* to become annoyed; METEOROL. to cloud over.

cargo ➤ *m* *(peso)* load; *(dignidad)* position; *(acusación)* charge; COM. debit ▪ **a c. de** in charge of • **hacerse c. de** to take charge of.

caribe *or* **caribeño, a** ➤ *adj* Caribbean.

caricatura ➤ *f* caricature.

caricia ➤ *f* caress ▪ **hacer caricias a** to caress, fondle.

caridad ➤ *f* charity.

caries ➤ *f* MED. caries, decay.

cariño ➤ *m* affection; *(amor)* love.

cariñoso, a ➤ *adj* affectionate, loving.

caritativo, a ➤ *adj* charitable.

carnaval ➤ *m* carnival.

carne ➤ *f* flesh; CUL. meat; BOT. pulp ▪ **c. asada al horno** roast (of meat) • **c. asada a la parrilla** broiled meat • **c. de gallina** COLL. goose bumps. • **c. picada** chopped meat, ground meat.

carnero ➤ *m* sheep; *(macho)* ram; CUL. mutton.

carnet *or* **carné** ➤ *m* card.

carnicería ➤ *f* butcher shop; FIG. carnage, butchery.

carnicero, a ➤ *mf* butcher.

caro, a ➤ *adj* *(costoso)* expensive; *(amado)* dear ➤ *adv* at a high price.

carpa ➤ *f* AMER. tent; *(toldo)* awning.

carpeta ➤ *f* folder.

carpintería ➤ *f* *(oficio)* carpentry; *(taller)* carpenter shop.

carpintero, a ➤ *mf* carpenter ➤ *m* ORNITH. woodpecker.

carraspear ➤ *intr* to clear one's throat.

carraspeo ➤ *m* hoarseness.

carrera ➤ *f* race; *(pista)* racetrack; *(profesión)* career; *(hilera)* row; ARCHIT. beam ▪ **c. a pie** footrace • **c. de relevos** relay race ▪ *pl* races.

carrete ➤ *m* *(bobina)* bobbin; *(de la caña de pescar)* reel.

carretera ➤ *f* highway, road ▪ **c. de circunvalación** bypass • **c. de cuatro vías** four-lane highway • **c. de vía libre** expressway.

carretilla ➤ *f* *(carro pequeño)* cart; *(de una rueda)* wheelbarrow.

carril *(de tránsito)* lane; RAIL. rail.

carrillo ➤ *m* jowl ▪ **comer a dos carrillos** to stuff oneself.

carrito ➤ *m* cart ▪ **c. de compras** shopping cart.

carro ➤ *m* *(vehículo)* cart; AMER. *(automóvil)* car; *(de máquina)* carriage ▪ **c. blindado** armored car.

carrocería ➤ *f* AUTO. body.

carruaje ➤ *m* carriage.

carrusel ➤ *m* carousel, merry-go-round.

carta ➤ *f* letter; *(naipe)* playing card; *(de derechos)* charter; *(documento)* document ▪ **a la c.** a la carte • **c. aérea** airmail letter.

cartel ➤ *m* poster, bill; FIN. cartel.

cartelera ➤ *f* billboard; *(de un periódico)* entertainment section.

cartera ➤ *f* *(de hombre)* billfold, wallet; *(de mujer)* pocketbook; *(portadocumentos)* briefcase; *(de bolsillo)* pocket flap; *(ministerio)* cabinet post.

cartero, a ➤ *mf* mail carrier.

cartón ➤ *m* *(papel)* cardboard; *(caja)* cardboard box; *(de cigarrillos)* carton.

cartucho ➤ *m* *(cono)* paper cone; *(bolsa)* paper bag.

cartulina ➤ *f* pasteboard.

casa ➤ *f* house; *(residencia)* home; COM. firm ▪ **c. de la moneda** mint • **c. editorial** publishing house • **en c.** at home • **estar de c.** to be casually dressed.

casado, a ➤ *adj & mf* married (person)

■ **recién casados** newlyweds.

casamiento ➤ *m* marriage, wedding.

casar ➤ *intr* to marry ➤ *tr* to marry (off) ➤ *reflex* to get married.

cascabel ➤ *m* small bell ■ **serpiente de c.** rattlesnake.

cascada ➤ *f* waterfall.

cascanueces ➤ *m* nutcracker.

cascar §47 ➤ *tr & reflex* to crack.

cáscara ➤ *f* shell; *(de fruta)* skin; *(de queso, fruta)* rind; *(de cereal)* husk.

cascarón ➤ *m* eggshell.

casco ➤ *m* MIL. helmet; *(tonel)* barrel; MARIT. hull; ZOOL. hoof.

caserío ➤ *m (pueblo)* hamlet; *(cortijo)* country house *or* estate.

casero, a ➤ *adj (de la casa)* domestic; *(de la familia)* family; *(hecho en casa)* homemade; *(hogareño)* home-loving ■ **cocina c.** home cooking ➤ *mf (dueño)* owner, landlord ➤ *f* landlady.

caserón ➤ *m* COLL. large ramshackle house.

caseta ➤ *f* cottage; *(casilla)* booth.

casete ➤ *f* cassette, tape cartridge.

casi ➤ *adv* almost, nearly ■ **c. c.** COLL. very nearly • **c. nada** next to nothing • **c. nunca** hardly ever.

casino ➤ *m* casino.

caso ➤ *m* case; *(acontecimiento)* event; *(circunstancia)* circumstance ■ **en c. de** in the event of • **en c. de que** in case • **en todo c.** in any case • **hacer** *or* **venir al c.** COLL. to be relevant • **hacer c. a** to heed • **hacer c. de** to pay attention to.

caspa ➤ *f* dandruff.

castaña ➤ *f (fruta)* chestnut.

castañeta ➤ *f* castanet.

castaño, a ➤ *adj* chestnut, brown ➤ *m (árbol)* chestnut tree.

castellano ➤ *m* Spanish.

castigar §31 ➤ *tr* to punish; *(mortificar)* to discipline; SPORT. to penalize.

castigo ➤ *m* punishment; *(mortificación)* self-denial; SPORT. penalty.

castillo ➤ *m* castle.

casual ➤ *adj* chance, coincidental.

casualidad ➤ *f* chance ■ **de c.** by chance • **por c.** by any chance.

casualmente ➤ *adv* by chance *or* accident.

cataclismo ➤ *m* cataclysm, upheaval.

catacumbas ➤ *fpl* catacombs.

catador, a ➤ *mf* taster, sampler.

catalogar §31 ➤ *tr* to catalog(ue), list.

catálogo ➤ *m* catalog(ue).

catar ➤ *tr* to sample, taste.

catarata ➤ *f* waterfall; MED. cataract.

catarro ➤ *m* cold, catarrh.

catástrofe ➤ *f* catastrophe.

cátedra ➤ *f (rango)* professorship; *(asiento)* professor's chair.

catedral ➤ *f* cathedral.

catedrático, a ➤ *mf* university professor.

categoría ➤ *f* category; *(clase)* type.

católico, a ➤ *adj & mf* Catholic.

catorce ➤ *adj & m* fourteen.

cauce ➤ *m* riverbed; *(acequia)* ditch.

caucho ➤ *m* rubber.

caudal ➤ *adj* ZOOL. caudal; *(río)* deep ➤ *m (del río)* volume; *(riqueza)* wealth.

caudillo ➤ *m* leader; AMER. political boss.

causa ➤ *f* cause; *(motivo)* reason; LAW lawsuit.

causante ➤ *adj* causative ➤ *mf* originator.

causar ➤ *tr* to cause; *(ira)* to provoke.

cautela ➤ *f* caution.

cautivar ➤ *tr (aprisionar)* to capture; *(fascinar)* to captivate.

cautiverio ➤ *m or* **cautividad** ➤ *f* captivity.

cautivo, a ➤ *adj & mf* captive.

cavar ➤ *tr* to dig.

caverna ➤ *f* cavern, cave.

cavidad ➤ *f* cavity.

cavilar ➤ *intr* to ponder, ruminate.

cayo ➤ *m* MARIT. key, islet.

caza ➤ *f (cacería)* hunt; *(animales)* game ➤ *f* de c. to go hunting.

cazador, a ➤ *adj* hunting; ZOOL. predatory ➤ *mf* hunter.

cazar §02 ➤ *tr* to hunt.

cazo ➤ *m* CUL. *(cucharón)* ladle; *(cacerola)* saucepan.

cazuela ➤ *f* casserole; *(guisado)* stew.

cebado, a ➤ *adj* AMER., ZOOL. fattened ➤ *f* BOT. barley.

cebiche ➤ *m* AMER. marinated raw fish.

cebo ➤ *m (alimento)* feed; *(detonador)*

charge; *(del anzuelo)* bait.

cebolla ➤ *f* onion; *(bulbo)* bulb.

cebra ➤ *f* zebra.

ceder ➤ *tr* to cede; *(transferir)* to transfer; SPORT. to pass ➤ *intr* to cede; *(rendirse)* to yield, give in *or* up; *(disminuirse)* to abate.

cédula ➤ *f* document ▪ c. de identidad identification card *or* papers.

cegar §35 ➤ *tr* to blind ➤ *reflex* FIG. to be blinded.

ceguera *or* **ceguedad** ➤ *f* blindness.

ceja ➤ *f* eyebrow.

celada ➤ *f* ambush; FIG. trap.

celador, a ➤ *mf (en la escuela)* monitor; *(de prisión)* guard.

celda ➤ *f (del cárcel, monasterio)* cell.

celebración ➤ *f* celebration; *(aclamación)* praise.

celebrar ➤ *tr* to celebrate; *(alabar)* to praise; *(venerar)* to venerate; *(una reunión)* to hold; *(un acuerdo)* to reach ➤ *reflex (cumpleaños)* to be *or* fall on; *(una reunión)* to take place.

célebre ➤ *adj* celebrated, famous.

celebridad ➤ *f* celebrity.

celeste ➤ *adj* sky-blue ▪ cuerpo c. heavenly body ➤ *m* sky blue.

célibe ➤ *adj & mf* celibate.

celo ➤ *m (cuidado)* diligence; *(entusiasmo)* zeal; *(envidia)* jealousy ➤ *pl* jealousy ▪ dar c. to make jealous ▪ tener c. to be jealous.

celoso, a ➤ *adj* jealous.

célula ➤ *f* BIOL., ELEC., POL. cell.

celular ➤ *adj* cellular ➤ *m* cell phone.

celulitis ➤ *f* cellulitis.

celuloso, a ➤ *adj* cellulous, cellular ➤ *f* cellulose.

cementerio ➤ *m* cemetery.

cemento ➤ *m* cement; *(hormigón)* concrete.

cena ➤ *f* dinner, supper.

cenar ➤ *intr* to have dinner *or* supper.

cenicero ➤ *m* ashtray.

cenit ➤ *m* zenith.

censo ➤ *m* census; *(lista)* roll; *(arrendamiento)* rental ▪ levantar el c. to take a census.

censura ➤ *f* censure; *(de expresión, arte)* censorship.

censurar ➤ *tr* to censor; *(criticar)* to criticize.

centavo, a ➤ *adj* hundredth ➤ *m* cent.

centellear *or* **centellar** ➤ *intr (fulgurar)* to sparkle; *(destellar)* to twinkle; *(chispear)* to flicker.

centena ➤ *f* (one) hundred.

centenar ➤ *m* (one) hundred.

centenario, a ➤ *adj & m* centennial.

centeno ➤ *m* rye.

centésimo, a ➤ *adj & m* hundredth.

centígrado, a ➤ *adj* centigrade.

centigramo ➤ *m* centigram.

centilitro ➤ *m* centiliter.

centímetro ➤ *m* centimeter.

céntimo, a ➤ *adj* hundredth ➤ *m* cent.

centinela ➤ *mf* sentinel, sentry; FIG. lookout.

central ➤ *adj* central ➤ *f (oficina)* headquarters; ELEC. power plant ▪ c. de correos main post office.

centrar ➤ *tr* to center; *(determinar)* to find the center of; *(enfocar)* to focus; FIG. to aim.

céntrico, a ➤ *adj* central, centric.

centro ➤ *m* center; *(medio)* middle; *(núcleo)* core; *(ciudad)* downtown ▪ c. comercial shopping center.

centroamericano, a ➤ *adj & mf* Central American.

ceño ➤ *m* frown ▪ arrugar *or* fruncir el c. to frown.

cepa ➤ *f (de la vid)* rootstalk; *(vid)* vine.

cepillar ➤ *tr (limpiar)* to brush.

cepillo ➤ *m* brush ▪ c. de dientes toothbrush ▪ c. para el pelo hairbrush.

cera ➤ *f* wax; *(de los oídos)* earwax; *(de lustrar)* polish.

cerámico, a ➤ *adj* ceramic ➤ *f* ceramics.

cerca ➤ *adv* nearby, close by ▪ c. de *(cercano a)* near, close to; *(alrededor de)* about ▪ de c. closely ➤ *f* fence.

cercano, a ➤ *adj (próximo)* close; *(vecino)* neighboring; FIG. impending.

cercar §47 ➤ *tr (con cerca)* to fence in; *(rodear)* to surround; MIL. to besiege.

cerco ➤ *m* circle; *(borde)* edge; *(seto)* hedge; *(cercado)* enclosure.

cerdo ➤ *m* pig ▪ carne de c. pork.

cereal ➤ *adj & m* cereal ▪ *pl* cereals, grain.

cerebro ➤ *m* brain; FIG. brains.

ceremonia ➤ *f* ceremony.

cereza ➤ *f* cherry (fruit).

cerezo ➤ *m* cherry (tree).

cerilla ➤ *f (fósforo)* match.

cero ➤ *m* zero.

cerrado, a ➤ *adj* closed ▪ a puerta c. behind closed doors.

cerradura ➤ *f* lock.

cerrar §33 ➤ *tr* to close (up), shut; *(con cerrojo)* to bolt; *(paquete, abertura)* to seal (up); *(negocio)* to close down; *(llave)* to turn off; *(camino, acceso)* to block off; *(cuenta bancaria)* to close out ▪ c. con llave to lock ➤ *intr* to close, shut.

cerro ➤ *m* hill.

cerrojo ➤ *m* bolt, latch.

certamen ➤ *m* contest, competition.

certificado, a ➤ *adj* certified; *(cartas)* registered ▪ *m* certificate.

cervecería ➤ *f (fábrica)* brewery; *(taberna)* bar, pub.

cerveza ➤ *f* beer, ale ▪ c. de barril draft beer ▪ c. negra dark beer.

cesar ➤ *intr* to end, stop ➤ *tr* to fire, dismiss ▪ sin c. unceasingly.

cese ➤ *m* cessation; *(de un empleado)* dismissal ▪ c. de fuego cease-fire.

césped ➤ *m* lawn, grass.

cesta ➤ *f* basket.

cesto ➤ *m* basket ▪ c. de or para papeles wastepaper basket.

chacra ➤ *f* AMER. farm.

chal ➤ *m* shawl.

chaleco ➤ *m* vest ▪ c. salvavidas life jacket.

chalet ➤ *m* chalet; *(de playa)* beach house; *(de lujo)* villa.

champán ➤ *m* champagne.

champiñón ➤ *m* mushroom.

champú ➤ *m* shampoo.

chance ➤ *m* chance.

chancleta ➤ *f (zapatilla)* slipper.

chancho ➤ *m* pig, hog.

chantaje ➤ *m* blackmail.

chapa ➤ *f (de metal)* sheet; *(de madera)* panel; *(tapa)* bottletop.

chapado, a ➤ *adj (de metal)* plated; *(de madera)* veneered.

chaparrón ➤ *m* downpour; FIG. shower.

chapotear ➤ *intr* to splash.

chapucería ➤ *f* COLL. sloppy job.

chapuza ➤ *f* COLL. botched job.

chapuzón ➤ *m* dip, swim; *(zambullida)* dive ▪ darse un c. to go for a swim.

chaqué ➤ *m* morning coat.

chaqueta ➤ *f* jacket ▪ c. de fumar smoking jacket ▪ c. salvavidas life jacket.

chaquetón ➤ *m* overcoat.

charca ➤ *f* pond, pool.

charco ➤ *m* puddle, pool.

charla ➤ *f (conversación)* chat; *(conferencia)* talk ▪ sala de c. chat room.

charlar ➤ *intr* COLL. *(parlotear)* to chatter; *(hablar)* to chat.

charlatán, ana ➤ *adj (parlanchín)* talkative; *(chismoso)* gossipy ➤ *mf (parlanchín)* chatterbox; *(murmurador)* gossip; *(curandero)* quack.

charol ➤ *m (barniz)* lacquer; *(cuero)* patent leather.

chasco ➤ *m (burla)* trick; *(decepción)* disappointment.

chasis ➤ *m* chassis.

chasquido ➤ *m* crack, snap.

chatarra ➤ *f* scrap iron.

chato, a ➤ *adj (de nariz)* flat-nosed; *(la nariz)* flat.

chauvinista ➤ *adj* chauvinistic ➤ *m* chauvinist.

chaval, a ➤ *adj* young ➤ *m* youngster, lad ➤ *f* young girl, lass.

cheque ➤ *m* check, cheque (G.B.) ▪ c. de viajero traveler's check.

chequeo ➤ *m* AMER. inspection, check; MED. checkup.

chic ➤ *adj* chic, stylish.

chicano, a ➤ *adj & mf* Mexican-American, Chicano, Chicana.

chicle ➤ *m (de mascar)* chewing gum; *(gomorresina)* chicle.

chico, a ➤ *adj* small, little ➤ *m* boy ➤ *f* girl.

chícharo ➤ *m* pea.

chicharra ➤ *f* cicada.

chicharrón ➤ *m* fried pork rind.

chichón ➤ *m* bump (on the head).

chiflado, a ➤ *adj* COLL. *(loco)* nuts;

(enamorado) in love.

chile ➤ *m* AMER. pepper, chili.

chileno, a ➤ *adj & mf* Chilean.

chillar ➤ *intr* to shriek; *(chirriar)* to squeak; *(destacarse)* to be loud.

chillido ➤ *m* shriek; *(chirrido)* squeak.

chillón, ona ➤ *adj* COLL. *(gritón)* shrieking; *(estridente)* loud ➤ *mf* screamer.

chimenea ➤ *f* chimney; *(hogar)* fire-place, hearth.

chincheta ➤ *f* thumbtack.

chiquillada ➤ *f* childish act.

chiquillo, a ➤ *adj* small ➤ *mf* child.

chirriar §18 ➤ *intr* *(rueda)* to squeak; *(pájaro)* to screech; *(al freír)* to sizzle.

chirrido ➤ *m (ruido)* screeching; COLL. *(grito)* shriek; *(al freír)* sizzle.

chisme ➤ *m (murmuración)* gossip; COLL. *(baratija)* trinket.

chismear ➤ *intr* to gossip.

chismoso, a ➤ *adj* gossipy ➤ *mf* gossip-monger.

chispa ➤ *f* or **chispazo** ➤ *m* spark.

chispear ➤ *intr* to spark; *(lloviznar)* to drizzle; *(brillar)* to be brilliant.

chisporrotear ➤ *intr* to spark, crackle.

chiste ➤ *m* joke.

chistoso, a ➤ *adj* funny.

chivo, a ➤ *mf* ZOOL. kid.

chocante ➤ *adj* offensive.

chocar §47 ➤ *intr (topar)* to crash; *(pelear)* to clash; COLL. *(disgustar)* to offend ■ c. de frente to hit one's head on.

chochear ➤ *intr* to be senile.

chocho, a ➤ *adj (caduco)* senile; COLL. *(lelo)* doting.

chocolate ➤ *adj* chocolate ➤ *m* chocolate; *(bebida)* hot chocolate, cocoa.

chófer or **chofer** ➤ *mf* chauffeur.

chopo ➤ *m* black poplar.

choque ➤ *m (colisión)* collision; *(impacto)* impact; *(pelea)* clash.

chorrear ➤ *intr (fluir)* to gush; *(gotear)* to trickle ➤ *tr (derramar)* to pour.

chorro ➤ *m (de líquido)* spout; *(de luz)* flood ■ a c. abundantly.

chubasco ➤ *m* squall, downpour.

chuchería ➤ *f* trinket.

chucho, a ➤ *m* COLL. dog.

chuleta ➤ *f (carne)* cutlet.

chupado, a ➤ *adj* COLL. emaciated.

chupar ➤ *tr* to suck; *(absorber)* to soak up.

chupete ➤ *m (de niños)* pacifier.

churrasco ➤ *m* AMER. grilled or broiled steak.

churrete ➤ *m* stain.

churro ➤ *m* CUL. fritter.

ciática ➤ *adj* sciatic ➤ *f* sciatica.

ciberespacio ➤ *m* cyberspace.

cibernética ➤ *f* cybernetics.

cicatriz ➤ *f* scar.

cicatrizar §02 ➤ *tr & intr* to heal.

ciclista ➤ *adj* cycling ➤ *mf* cyclist.

ciclo ➤ *m* cycle.

ciclomotor ➤ *m* moped, motorbike.

ciclón ➤ *m* cyclone.

ciego, a ➤ *adj & mf* blind (person) ■ *pl* a ciegas blindly • andar a ciegas to grope one's way.

cielo ➤ *m* sky; *(paraíso)* heaven ■ c. raso ceiling.

ciempiés ➤ *m* centipede.

cien ➤ *adj* contr of **ciento**.

ciénaga ➤ *f* swamp, marsh.

ciencia ➤ *f* science; *(erudición)* knowledge ■ a or de c. cierto for certain.

cieno ➤ *m* muck.

científico, a ➤ *adj* scientific ➤ *mf* scientist.

ciento ➤ *adj & m* one hundred, a hundred ■ c. por c. one hundred per cent • por c. per cent.

cierre ➤ *m (acción)* closing; *(clausura)* shut down ■ c. patronal R.P. lockout.

cierto, a ➤ *adj* certain; *(determinado)* definite; *(verdadero)* true; *(alguno)* some ➤ *adv* certainly ■ lo c. es que the fact is that • por c. *(a propósito)* incidentally; *(ciertamente)* certainly.

ciervo ➤ *m* deer, stag.

cifra ➤ *f (número)* digit; *(cantidad)* quantity; *(total)* sum (total).

cigarra ➤ *f* cicada.

cigarrillo ➤ *m* cigarette.

cigarro ➤ *m* cigar.

cigüeña ➤ *f* stork.

cilantro ➤ *m* coriander.

cilindro ➤ *m* cylinder; *(rodillo)* roller.

cima ➤ *f* summit; FIG. pinnacle.

cimiento ➤ *mpl* CONSTR. foundation; FIG. basis.

cincel ➤ *m* chisel.

cinco ➤ *adj & m* five ∎ **las c.** five o'clock.

cincuenta ➤ *adj & m* fifty.

cine ➤ *m* cinema; PHOTOG., TECH. cinematography; COLL. *(espectáculo)* movies; *(teatro)* movie theater.

cínico, a ➤ *adj* cynical ➤ *mf* cynic.

cinta ➤ *f* ribbon; *(película)* film ∎ **c. adhesiva** adhesive tape • **c. magnetofónica** recording tape • **c. métrica** tape measure.

cintura ➤ *f* waist, waistline.

cinturón ➤ *m* belt ∎ **c. de seguridad** seat or safety belt.

ciprés ➤ *m* cypress.

circo ➤ *m* circus; GEOL. cirque.

circuito ➤ *m* circuit ∎ **corto c.** short circuit.

circulación ➤ *f* circulation; *(transmisión)* dissemination; *(tráfico)* traffic.

circular[1] ➤ *adj* circular ➤ *f* circular, flier.

circular[2] ➤ *intr & tr* to circulate.

círculo ➤ *m* circle; *(circunferencia)* circumference.

circuncisión ➤ *f* circumcision.

circunferencia ➤ *f* circumference.

circunflejo, a ➤ *adj & m* circumflex.

circunstancia ➤ *f* circumstance.

cirio ➤ *m* church candle.

ciruela ➤ *f* plum ∎ **c. pasa** prune.

ciruelo ➤ *m* plum tree.

cirugía ➤ *f* surgery ∎ **c. plástica** or **estética** plastic or cosmetic surgery.

cirujano, a ➤ *mf* surgeon.

cisne ➤ *m* swan; R.P. powder puff.

cisterna ➤ *f* cistern, reservoir.

cita ➤ *f* *(entrevista)* appointment; meeting; *(con novio, amigo)* date; *(referencia)* quote.

citar ➤ *tr* to cite; LAW to summon.

cítrico, a ➤ *adj* citric; BOT. citrus ➤ *mpl* citrus fruits.

ciudad ➤ *f* city.

ciudadanía ➤ *f* citizenship.

ciudadano, a ➤ *adj* civic, city ➤ *mf* citizen.

ciudadela ➤ *f* citadel, fortress.

cívico, a ➤ *adj* civic.

civil ➤ *adj* civil ➤ *mf* civilian.

civilización ➤ *f* civilization.

civilizado, a ➤ *adj* civilized, refined.

civismo ➤ *m* civic-mindedness.

clamoroso, a ➤ *adj* clamorous.

clan ➤ *m* clan.

clandestino, a ➤ *adj* clandestine.

claraboya ➤ *f* skylight.

clarear ➤ *tr & intr* to dawn.

clarete ➤ *adj & m* claret (wine).

claridad ➤ *f* clarity; *(luz)* brightness; *(nitidez)* clearness ∎ **con c.** clearly.

clarinete ➤ *m* clarinet; *(músico)* clarinetist.

claro, a ➤ *adj* clear; *(luminoso)* bright; *(aguado)* thin ∎ **verde c.** light green ➤ *adv* plainly ∎ **¡c.!** or **¡c. que sí!** of course!, sure! ➤ *m* *(espacio)* clearing ∎ **c. de luna** moonlight • **poner** or **sacar en c.** to clarify, explain ➤ *f* white (of egg).

claroscuro ➤ *m* chiaroscuro.

clase ➤ *f* class; *(lección)* lesson; *(aula)* classroom ∎ **c. turista** coach • **toda c. de** all kinds of.

clásico, a ➤ *adj* classic, classical ➤ *mf* classic author ➤ *m* *(obra)* classic.

clasificación ➤ *f* classification.

clasificar §47 ➤ *tr* to classify; *(archivar)* to file ➤ *reflex* SPORT. to qualify.

claustro ➤ *m* cloister; EDUC. faculty.

cláusula ➤ *f* clause.

clausura ➤ *f* *(abadía)* cloister; *(estado)* monastic life; *(conclusión)* closing ceremony; AMER. *(cierre)* closing; EDUC. commencement.

clavar ➤ *tr* to nail; *(hincar)* to drive.

clave ➤ *f* *(cifra)* code; *(esencia)* key; *(acceso)* password.

clavel ➤ *m* carnation.

clavícula ➤ *f* clavicle, collarbone.

clavo ➤ *m* nail; BOT. clove ∎ **dar en el c.** COLL. to hit the nail on the head.

clemencia ➤ *f* clemency.

clérigo ➤ *m* clergyman.

clero ➤ *m* clergy.

cliché ➤ *m* cliché; PHOTO. negative.

cliente ➤ *mf* client, customer.

clima ➤ *m* climate.

climatizar §02 ➤ *tr* to air-condition.

clínica ➤ *f* private hospital.

cloaca ➤ *f* sewer.

cloro ➤ *m* chlorine.

cloroformo ➤ *m* chloroform.

club ➤ *m* club.

coacción ➤ *f* coercion; LAW duress.

coalición ➤ *f* coalition.

coartada ➤ *f* alibi.

cobarde ➤ *adj* cowardly ➤ *mf* coward.

cobertizo ➤ *m* (*protección*) shelter; (*barraca*) shed; AUTO. carport.

cobertor ➤ *m* (*colcha*) bedspread; (*de plumas*) comforter; (*manta*) blanket.

cobija ➤ *f* blanket.

cobijar ➤ *tr* to cover (up).

cobra ➤ *f* cobra.

cobrador, a ➤ *mf* (*recaudador*) bill or tax collector; (*perro*) retriever.

cobrar ➤ *tr* (*recibir*) to collect; (*recuperar*) to retrieve; (*precios*) to charge; (*un cheque*) to cash.

cobre ➤ *m* copper; AMER. cent.

cobro ➤ *m* collection, collecting; (*de un cheque*) cashing.

cocaína ➤ *f* cocaine.

cocción ➤ *f* cooking; (*hervor*) boiling; (*en un horno*) baking.

cocer §48 ➤ *tr* to cook; (*hervir*) to boil; (*en un horno*) to bake ➤ *intr* to boil.

coche ➤ *m* car (*carruaje*) carriage ■ c. cama sleeper, sleeping car.

cochino, a ➤ *mf* pig; COLL. (*persona*) swine ➤ *adj* filthy; COLL. (*ruin*) rotten.

cocina ➤ *f* (*cuarto*) kitchen; (*aparato*) stove, range; (*estilo*) cuisine.

cocinar ➤ *tr & intr* to cook.

cocinero, a ➤ *mf* cook, chef.

coco ➤ *m* coconut.

cocodrilo ➤ *m* crocodile.

cocotero ➤ *m* coconut palm.

cóctel ➤ *m* (*bebida*) cocktail; (*reunión*) cocktail party.

codazo ➤ *m* jab, poke (with one's elbow) ■ dar un c. to jab, poke.

codicia ➤ *f* greed.

codicioso, a ➤ *adj & mf* greedy (person).

código ➤ *m* code ■ c. postal zip code.

codo ➤ *m* elbow ➤ *pl* hablar por los c. to be a chatterbox.

coetáneo, a ➤ *adj & mf* contemporary.

coexistir ➤ *intr* to coexist.

cofre ➤ *m* (*arca*) chest; (*caja*) box.

coger §20 ➤ *tr* to grab, grasp; (*recoger*) to gather up; (*sorprender*) to catch by surprise; (*enfermedad*) to catch; (*entender*) to understand.

cogote ➤ *m* back of the neck.

cohabitar ➤ *intr* to live together, cohabit.

coherente ➤ *adj* coherent.

cohete ➤ *m* rocket.

cohibir ➤ *tr* (*inhibir*) to inhibit ➤ *reflex* to be or feel inhibited.

coincidencia ➤ *f* coincidence.

coincidir ➤ *intr* to coincide; (*concordar*) to agree.

cojear ➤ *intr* to limp; (*una mesa*) to wobble.

cojera ➤ *f* limp, lameness.

cojín ➤ *m* cushion.

cojinete MECH. bearing.

cojo, a ➤ *adj & mf* lame (person).

col ➤ *f* cabbage ■ c. de Bruselas Brussels sprouts • c. rizada kale.

cola[1] ➤ *f* tail; (*de vestido*) train; (*fila*) line, queue (G.B.); (*parte final*) rear ■ a la c. last • c. de caballo BOT. horsetail; (*pelo*) ponytail • hacer c. to line up.

cola[2] ➤ *f* glue, gum.

colaboración ➤ *f* collaboration.

colaborador, a ➤ *adj* collaborating; LIT. contributing ➤ *mf* collaborator; LIT. contributor.

colaborar ➤ *intr* to collaborate; LIT. to contribute.

colada ➤ *f* whitening.

colador ➤ *m* strainer; RELIG. collator.

colapso ➤ *m* collapse ■ c. nervioso nervous breakdown.

colar §11 ➤ *tr* to strain; COLL. to pass or foist (off) ➤ *reflex* to sneak in.

colcha ➤ *f* bedspread.

colchón ➤ *m* mattress.

colchoneta ➤ *f* light mattress.

colección ➤ *f* collection; LIT. anthology.

coleccionar ➤ *tr* to collect.

colectivo, a ➤ *adj* collective; (*mutuo*) joint ➤ *m* GRAM. collective (noun); ARG., BOL., PERU small bus.

colega ➤ *mf* colleague, associate.

colegial ➤ *adj* school.

colegial, a ➤ *mf* schoolboy, schoolgirl.
colegio ➤ *m* (*primario*) elementary school; (*secundario*) high school; (*asociación*) college, association.
cólera ➤ *f* choler; FIG. anger ▪ **dar c. to** infuriate ▪ *m* MED. cholera.
colesterol ➤ *m* cholesterol.
colgante ➤ *adj* hanging ▪ *m* pendant.
colgar §08 ➤ *tr* to hang (up) ➤ *intr* to hang; (*caer*) to hang down; COMPUT. to crash.
colibrí ➤ *m* hummingbird.
cólico, a ➤ *adj* colonic ▪ *m* colic.
coliflor ➤ *f* cauliflower.
colina ➤ *f* hill.
colirio ➤ *m* eyewash.
coliseo ➤ *m* coliseum, colosseum.
colisión ➤ *f* collision; FIG. conflict.
collado ➤ *m* (*cerro*) hill; (*entre montañas*) mountain pass.
collar ➤ *m* (*adorno*) necklace; (*de animal*) collar.
colmado, a ➤ *adj* (*lleno*) full, filled; (*cucharada*) heaping.
colmena ➤ *f* beehive, hive.
colmillo ➤ *m* canine tooth, eyetooth; ZOOL. (*del elefante*) tusk; (*del perro*) fang.
colmo ➤ *m* (*exceso*) overflow; (*cumbre*) height; (*límite*) limit.
colocación ➤ *f* (*acción*) placing; (*lugar*) place; (*empleo*) position.
colocar §47 ➤ *tr* to place, position; (*dinero*) to invest.
colombiano, a ➤ *adj & mf* Colombian.
colonia ➤ *f* colony; (*perfume*) cologne.
colonial ➤ *adj* colonial.
colonizar §02 ➤ *tr* to colonize, settle.
coloquio ➤ *m* (*conversación*) talk; (*conferencia*) seminar.
color ➤ *m* color; (*aspecto*) aspect ▪ **a c.** in color ▪ **de c.** colored ▪ *pl* **ponerse de** mil c. COLL. to flush.
colorado, a ➤ *adj* red ▪ **ponerse c.** to blush ➤ *m* red.
colorante ➤ *adj* coloring ➤ *m* colorant.
colorear ➤ *tr* to color.
colorete ➤ *m* rouge.
colorido ➤ *m* (*acción*) coloring; (*colores*) coloration; (*color*) color.
columna ➤ *f* column, pillar ▪ **c. verte-**

bral spine, spinal column.
columpio ➤ *m* swing.
coma¹ ➤ *f* comma.
coma² ➤ *m* MED. coma.
comadrona ➤ *f* midwife.
comandancia ➤ *f* headquarters.
comandante ➤ *mf* commanding officer, commander; (*grado*) major ▪ **c. en** jefe *or* general commander-in-chief.
comarca ➤ *f* region, district.
combate ➤ *m* combat ▪ **ganar por fuera** de c. SPORT. to win by a knockout.
combatir ➤ *intr* to battle ➤ *tr* (*luchar* contra*) to fight.
combinación ➤ *f* combination; (*prenda*) slip.
combinar ➤ *tr* to combine; (*arreglar*) to arrange, work out.
combustible ➤ *adj* combustible ➤ *m* fuel ▪ **c. fósil** fossil fuel.
comedia ➤ *f* comedy.
comedor ➤ *m* dining room ▪ **coche c.** dining car.
comentador, a ➤ *mf* commentator.
comentar ➤ *tr* to comment on.
comentario ➤ *m* commentary ▪ **sin c.** no comment.
comenzar §17 ➤ *tr & intr* to begin, start ▪ **c. a** to begin to ▪ **c. con** to begin with ▪ **c. por** to begin with *or* by.
comer ➤ *tr & intr* to eat ▪ **dar de c.** to feed ➤ *reflex* to eat up; FIG. to squander.
comercial ➤ *adj* commercial ▪ **centro c.** shopping center.
comerciante ➤ *mf* merchant.
comerciar ➤ *intr* to trade, deal.
comercio ➤ *m* (*negocio*) business; (*tienda*) store.
comestible ➤ *adj* edible ➤ *m* foodstuff ▪ *pl* groceries.
cometa ➤ *m* comet ➤ *f* (*juguete*) kite.
cometer ➤ *tr* (*un crimen*) to commit; (*un error*) to make.
comezón ➤ *f* itch.
cómico, a ➤ *adj* comical, funny ➤ *m* comic actor ➤ *f* comic actress.
comida ➤ *f* (*almuerzo, cena*) food, meal; (*almuerzo*) lunch.
comienzo ➤ *m* beginning, start ▪ **dar c.** to begin, start.

comillas ➤ *fpl* quotation marks ∎ entre c. in quotes.

comisaría ➤ *f* police station.

comisión ➤ *f* commission; *(encargo)* assignment.

comité ➤ *m* committee.

comitiva ➤ *f* retinue, party.

como ➤ *adv* as; *(de tal modo)* like; *(casi)* about, approximately ∎ c. quiera que no matter how • c. sea one way or the other ➤ *conj (puesto que)* as, since; *(si)* if; *(así que)* as; *(por ejemplo)* such as, like ∎ **así c.** as soon as • **c. que** or si as if.

cómo ➤ *adv (en qué condiciones)* how; *(por qué)* why, how come ∎ **¿a c.?** how much? • ∎**¡c. no!** AMER. of course!

cómoda ➤ *f* chest of drawers, bureau.

comodidad ➤ *f (confort)* comfortableness; *(conveniencia)* convenience.

cómodo, a ➤ *adj (confortable)* comfortable; *(útil)* convenient.

compacto, a ➤ *adj (apretado)* compact; *(denso)* tight.

compadecer §09 ➤ *tr & reflex* to sympathize (with), feel sorry (for).

compañero, a ➤ *mf* companion ∎ c. de clase classmate • c. de cuarto roommate.

compañía ➤ *f* company.

comparación ➤ *f* comparison; LIT. simile ∎ en c. con in comparison with *or* to • sin c. beyond compare.

comparar ➤ *tr (relacionar)* to compare; *(cotejar)* to collate, check.

compartim(i)ento ➤ *m* compartment.

compartir ➤ *tr* to share.

compás ➤ *m* compass; MUS. rhythm.

compasión ➤ *f* compassion, pity.

compatible ➤ *adj* compatible.

compatriota ➤ *mf* compatriot.

compensación ➤ *f* compensation.

compensar ➤ *tr* to compensate; *(recompensar)* to indemnify.

competencia ➤ *f* competition; *(rivalidad)* rivalry; *(aptitud)* competence.

competición ➤ *f* competition; *(rivalidad)* rivalry.

competir §32 ➤ *intr* to compete.

compinche ➤ *mf* COLL. pal, chum; *(cómplice)* accomplice.

complacer ➤ *tr* to please, gratify ➤ *reflex* ∎ c. en *or* de to delight in, take pleasure in.

complejo, a ➤ *adj & m* complex.

complemento ➤ *m* complement; GRAM. object.

completar ➤ *tr* to complete; *(acabar)* to finish.

completo, a ➤ *adj* complete; *(acabado)* finished; *(lleno)* full ∎ por c. completely.

complicado, a ➤ *adj* complicated.

complicar §47 ➤ *tr* to complicate; *(embrollar)* to entangle ➤ *reflex* to become complicated.

cómplice ➤ *mf* accomplice.

complot ➤ *m* plot; *(intriga)* scheme.

componer §37 ➤ *tr* to compose; *(reparar)* to fix ➤ *intr* to compose ➤ *reflex* to be made up *(de* of).

comportamiento ➤ *m* behavior, conduct.

comportar ➤ *reflex* to behave ∎ c. mal to misbehave.

composición ➤ *f* composition.

compra ➤ *f (acción)* purchasing; *(adquisición)* purchase ∎ pl hacer c. to shop • ir de c. to go shopping.

comprar ➤ *tr* to buy, purchase.

comprender ➤ *tr* to understand; *(contener)* to include.

comprensible ➤ *adj* comprehensible.

comprensión ➤ *f* understanding.

comprensivo, a ➤ *adj* comprehensive.

compresión ➤ *f* compression.

comprimir ➤ *tr* to compress.

comprobante ➤ *m* proof, COM. voucher ∎ c. de venta sales slip.

comprobar §11 ➤ *tr (cotejar)* to check; *(verificar)* to verify.

comprometer ➤ *tr (poner en peligro)* to endanger; *(poner en apuros)* to compromise; *(salud)* to impair ➤ *reflex (obligarse)* to commit oneself; *(ponerse en peligro)* to compromise oneself; *(novios)* to get engaged.

compromiso ➤ *m* obligation; *(apuro)* jam; *(convenio)* agreement; *(novios)* engagement.

computadora ➤ *f* computer ∎ c. portátil laptop computer.

computar ➤ *tr* to compute, calculate.
común ➤ *adj* common; *(usual)* customary, usual; *(compartido)* shared, joint; *(vulgar)* common, vulgar; FIN. common, public ■ por lo c. generally.
comunicación ➤ *f* communication; TELEC. connection ■ medios de c. mass media.
comunicar §47 ➤ *tr* to communicate; *(transmitir)* to transmit ➤ *intr (tener paso)* to adjoin ➤ *reflex* to communicate; *(tener paso)* to be connected.
comunidad ➤ *f* community.
comunión ➤ *f* communion; *(comunicación)* fellowship.
con ➤ *prep* with ■ c. que so then • c. tal (de) que provided that • c. todo nevertheless.
concebir §32 ➤ *tr* to imagine, conceive of; *(comprender)* to understand ➤ *intr* to conceive, become pregnant.
conceder ➤ *tr (otorgar)* to grant; *(admitir)* to concede.
concejal, a ➤ *mf (town)* councilor ➤ *m* councilman ➤ *f* councilwoman.
concentración ➤ *f* concentration.
concentrar ➤ *tr & reflex* to concentrate.
concepción ➤ *f* conception.
concepto ➤ *m* concept, idea ■ bajo ningun c. under no circumstances • en or por c. de as, by way of.
concertar §33 ➤ *tr* to arrange, coordinate.
concesionario, a ➤ *adj* concessionary ➤ *mf* concessionaire, licensee.
concha ➤ *f* ZOOL. shell; *(molusco)* shellfish, mollusk; *(carey)* tortoise shell.
conciencia ➤ *f* conscience; *(integridad)* conscientiousness; *(conocimiento)* consciousness ■ a c. conscientiously • en c. in good conscience.
concienzudo, a ➤ *adj* conscientious.
concierto ➤ *m* concert; *(ajuste)* agreement; MUS. harmony; *(obra)* concerto.
concluir §10 ➤ *tr* to conclude, finish; *(deducir)* to deduce ➤ *intr* to finish, end.
conclusión ➤ *f* conclusion, end; *(deducción)* deduction; *(decisión)* decision.
concretar ➤ *tr* to summarize; *(precisar)* to specify ➤ *reflex* to limit oneself.

concreto, a ➤ *adj* concrete ■ en c. in short ➤ *m* AMER. concrete.
concurrencia ➤ *f* audience, crowd; *(simultaneidad)* concurrence.
concurrido, a ➤ *adj (animado)* busy, crowded; *(popular)* well-attended; *(frecuentado)* frequented.
concursante ➤ *mf* competitor, contestant.
concurso ➤ *m* competition, contest ■ c. hípico horse show.
condado ➤ *m (dignidad)* earldom; *(territorio)* county.
condena ➤ *f* LAW *(juicio)* sentence.
condenar ➤ *tr* to condemn, sentence; *(declarar culpable)* to convict.
condensación ➤ *f* condensation.
condensar ➤ *tr (reducir)* to condense; *(abreviar)* to shorten.
condición ➤ *f* condition; *(estado)* state ■ a c. de que on the condition that ■ *pl (circunstancias)* circumstances • c. convenidas COM. terms agreed upon • estar en c. de to be fit for.
condimento ➤ *m* condiment, seasoning.
condominio ➤ *m* condominium.
condón ➤ *m* condom.
conducir §14 ➤ *tr (guiar)* to lead; AUTO. to drive ➤ *intr* to lead; AUTO. to drive.
conducta ➤ *f* conduct.
conducto ➤ *m* conduit.
conductor, a ➤ *mf* AUTO. driver.
conectado, a ➤ *adj* connected; COMPUT. on-line.
conectar ➤ *tr* to connect; *(enchufar)* to plug in ➤ *reflex* COMPUT. to log in or on.
conejo ➤ *m* rabbit.
conexión ➤ *f* connection.
confección ➤ *f* manufacture; *(ropa hecha)* ready-to-wear clothing.
conferencia ➤ *f* conference; *(discurso)* lecture.
confesar §33 ➤ *tr* to confess; *(admitir)* to admit ➤ *reflex* to confess.
confesión ➤ *f* confession.
confianza ➤ *f* confidence; *(seguridad)* self-confidence; *(familiaridad)* closeness ■ de c. *(confiable)* reliable • tener c. con alguien to be on close terms with someone.

confiar §18 ➤ *intr* to trust, feel confident; (*contar con*) to count, rely (*en* on) ➤ *tr* (*encargar*) to entrust; (*un secreto*) to confide ➤ *reflex* to trust.

confidencial ➤ *adj* confidential.

confirmar ➤ *tr* to confirm; (*corroborar*) to endorse.

confiscar §47 ➤ *tr* to confiscate.

confitería ➤ *f* candy store.

confitura ➤ *f* CUL. jam, preserve.

conflicto ➤ *m* conflict; (*lucha*) struggle.

confluir §10 ➤ *intr* to converge.

conformar ➤ *tr* (*adaptar*) to conform, adapt ➤ *intr* to agree (*con, en* with, on) ➤ *reflex* to resign oneself.

conforme ➤ *adj* ■ c. a consistent with • c. con resigned to • c. en in agreement on ➤ *adv* as soon as ■ c. a in accordance with.

confort ➤ *m* comfort.

confortable ➤ *adj* comfortable.

confrontación ➤ *f* confrontation.

confrontar ➤ *tr* to confront.

confundido, a ➤ *adj* confused.

confundir ➤ *tr* to confuse; (*desconcertar*) to perplex ➤ *reflex* to be or get mixed up; (*en una multitud*) to mingle.

confusión ➤ *f* confusion.

confuso, a ➤ *adj* jumbled, mixed up.

congelador ➤ *m* freezer.

congelar ➤ *tr* to freeze ➤ *reflex* to become frozen.

congestión ➤ *f* congestion.

congoja ➤ *f* anguish; (*pena*) grief.

congreso ➤ *m* congress, meeting; POL. Congress (of the United States).

conjugación ➤ *f* conjugation.

conjugar §31 GRAM. to conjugate.

conjunción ➤ *f* conjunction.

conjunto ➤ *m* whole; (*agregado*) collection; (*vestido*) outfit; (*de muebles*) suite (of furniture); MECH. unit; MUS. band ■ en c. altogether.

conmemoración ➤ *f* commemoration.

conmigo ➤ *pron* with me.

conmoción ➤ *f* commotion; (*sacudimiento*) shock; (*tumulto*) upheaval ■ c. cerebral concussion.

conmovedor, a ➤ *adj* moving, touching.

conmover §54 ➤ *tr* (*emocionar*) to move, touch; (*sacudir*) to shake ➤ *reflex* to be moved or touched.

conmutar ➤ *tr* to trade; LAW to commute.

cono ➤ *m* cone.

conocedor, a ➤ *adj* knowledgeable, informed ➤ *mf* connoisseur.

conocer §09 ➤ *tr* to know, be acquainted with; (*tener contacto*) to meet; (*reconocer*) to recognize; (*un tema*) to know about ■ c. de nombre to know by name • c. de vista to know by sight.

conocido, a ➤ *adj* well-known, famous ➤ *mf* acquaintance.

conocimiento ➤ *m* knowledge; (*entendimiento*) understanding; MED. consciousness.

conquista ➤ *f* conquest.

conquistador, a ➤ *adj* conquering ➤ *mf* conqueror.

conquistar ➤ *tr* to conquer; (*conseguir*) to win.

consagrar ➤ *tr* to consecrate ➤ *reflex* to devote or dedicate oneself (*a* to).

consciente ➤ *adj* (*enterado*) aware; MED. conscious.

consecuencia ➤ *f* consequence; (*deducción*) deduction ■ a or como c. de as a result or consequence of • en c. accordingly • por c. consequently, therefore.

consecutivo, a ➤ *adj* consecutive.

conseguir §42 ➤ *tr* to obtain; (*llegar a hacer*) to attain; (*lograr*) to manage.

consejero, a ➤ *mf* (*guía*) counselor; (*de un consejo*) councilor.

consejo ➤ *m* advice; POL. council ■ c. de ministros cabinet.

consenso ➤ *m* consensus.

consentido, a ➤ *adj* spoiled, pampered.

consentimiento ➤ *m* consent.

consentir §43 ➤ *tr* (*autorizar*) to consent to; (*permitir*) to allow ■ c. a or con to be indulgent with.

conserje ➤ *mf* (*custodio*) concierge; (*portero*) porter.

conserjería ➤ *f* concierge's office; (*de un hotel*) reception desk.

conserva ➤ *f* (*confitura*) jam, preserve;

(alimentos) preserved food ■ **conservas alimenticias** canned goods • **en c.** canned.

conservador, a conservative; *(prudente)* prudent ➤ *mf* conservative.

conservar ➤ *tr* to conserve; *(preservar)* preserve; *(guardar)* to keep; *(cuidar)* to keep up; CUL. to can ➤ *reflex (permanecer)* to survive; *(cuidarse)* to take care of oneself; *(guardar para sí)* to keep for oneself; CUL. to keep, stay fresh.

conservatorio ➤ *m* conservatory.

considerado, a ➤ *adj (respetuoso)* considerate; *(respetado)* respected.

considerar ➤ *tr* to consider; *(reflexionar)* to take into consideration; *(estimar)* to regard.

consigna ➤ *f (slogan)* watchword; *(depósito)* checkroom.

consignar ➤ *tr* to consign.

consigo ➤ *pron* with him, her, them, you.

consiguiente ➤ *adj* consequent, resulting ■ **por c.** consequently, therefore.

consistente ➤ *adj* consistent.

consistir ➤ *intr* to consist *(en* of, in).

consola ➤ *f* console table; COMPUT. workstation.

consolar §11 ➤ *tr & reflex* to console (oneself).

consomé ➤ *m* consommé.

consonante ➤ *adj & f* consonant.

consorcio ➤ *m* consortium.

consorte ➤ *mf* consort.

conspiración ➤ *f* conspiracy.

conspirar ➤ *intr* to conspire.

constante ➤ *adj* constant; *(perseverante)* persevering ➤ *f* constant.

constar ➤ *intr (ser cierto)* to be clear or evident; *(quedar registrado)* to be on record; *(consistir)* to consist *(de* of) ■ **que conste que** let it be clearly known that.

constatar ➤ *tr* to verify, confirm.

constelación ➤ *f* constellation.

consternar ➤ *tr* to consternate ➤ *reflex* to be dismayed.

constipado, a ➤ *adj* congested, stopped up ➤ *m* MED. cold, head cold.

constitución ➤ *f* constitution.

constituir §10 ➤ *tr* to constitute ➤ *reflex* to be established.

construcción ➤ *f* construction; *(edificio)* building.

constructor, a ➤ *mf* builder.

construir §10 ➤ *tr* to construct, build.

consuelo ➤ *m* consolation, solace.

cónsul ➤ *mf* consul.

consulado ➤ *m* consulate.

consulta ➤ *f* consultation; *(opinión)* opinion, advice.

consultar ➤ *intr* to consult, discuss *(con* with) ➤ *tr* to consult.

consultorio ➤ *m (oficina)* office; MED. doctor's office.

consumidor, a ➤ *adj & mf* consumer.

consumir ➤ *tr* to consume; *(gastar)* use up; *(destruir)* to destroy ➤ *reflex* to be consumed or used (up).

consumo ➤ *m* consumption ■ **bienes de c.** consumer goods.

contabilidad ➤ *f (teneduría de libros)* bookkeeping; *(profesión)* accounting.

contable ➤ *adj* countable.

contacto ➤ *m* contact ■ **lentes** or **lentillas de c.** contact lenses • **ponerse en c.** to get in touch.

contado, a ➤ *adj* rare ■ **al c.** (in) cash.

contador, a ➤ *mf (de libros)* accountant; TECH. meter.

contagiar ➤ *tr* MED. to contaminate; FIG. to corrupt ➤ *reflex* MED. to become infected.

contagioso, a ➤ *adj* contagious, catching.

contaminación ➤ *f* contamination; *(del aire, agua)* pollution.

contar §11 ➤ *tr* to count; *(referir)* to tell, relate ➤ *intr* to count ■ **c. con** *(confiar)* to count or rely on.

contemplar ➤ *tr & intr* to contemplate.

contemporáneo, a ➤ *adj & mf* contemporary.

contender §34 ➤ *intr* to contend; *(competir)* to compete; *(disputar)* to dispute.

contendiente ➤ *mf* contender, competitor.

contener §46 ➤ *tr* to contain; *(impedir)* to hold back ➤ *reflex* to control oneself.

contenido, a ➤ *adj* contained, controlled ■ *m* content(s).

contentar ➤ *tr* to content, satisfy ➤ *reflex* to be content.

contento, a ➤ *adj* happy, pleased; *(satisfecho)* satisfied, content ➤ *m* happiness; *(satisfacción)* contentment.

contestación ➤ *f* answer.

contestar ➤ *tr* to answer.

contienda ➤ *f (pelea)* battle; *(disputa)* argument.

contigo ➤ *pron* with you.

contiguo, a ➤ *adj* contiguous, adjacent.

continente ➤ *adj & m* continent.

continuación ➤ *f* continuation ■ a c. next, following.

continuar §45 ➤ *tr* to continue, keep on ➤ *intr* to continue, go on *(con* with).

continuo, a ➤ *adj* continuous; *(constante)* constant.

contra ➤ *prep* against ■ en c. de against ➤ *m* ■ el pro y el c. the pros and cons.

contrabando ➤ *m (mercancía)* contraband; *(acción)* smuggling.

contracción ➤ *f* contraction.

contracepción ➤ *f* contraception.

contraceptivo, a ➤ *adj & m* contraceptive.

contradecir ➤ *tr* to contradict ➤ *reflex* to contradict oneself.

contradicción ➤ *f* contradiction.

contraer §49 ➤ *tr* to contract; *(enfermedad)* to catch • c. matrimonio to get married.

contrapeso ➤ *m* counterbalance.

contraproducente ➤ *adj* counterproductive.

contrariedad ➤ *f (obstáculo)* obstacle; *(desazón)* annoyance; *(contratiempo)* setback; *(percance)* mishap.

contrario, a ➤ *adj* opposite; *(adverso)* adverse ■ al c. to the contrary • al c. de contrary to • todo lo c. quite the opposite ➤ *mf* opponent, adversary ➤ *f* ■ llevar la c. COLL. to contradict.

contrarrestar ➤ *tr* to counteract, offset; *(resistir)* to resist, oppose.

contrastar ➤ *intr* to contrast, differ ➤ *tr* to verify.

contraste ➤ *m* contrast.

contratar ➤ *tr* to contract for;

(emplear) to hire.

contratiempo ➤ *m* setback; MUS. syncopation.

contratista ➤ *mf* contractor ■ c. de obras building contractor.

contrato ➤ *m* contract.

contribución ➤ *f* contribution; *(impuesto)* tax.

contribuidor, a ➤ *adj* contributory, contributing ➤ *mf* contributor.

contribuir §10 ➤ *tr & intr* to contribute.

contribuyente ➤ *mf* contributor; *(que paga impuestos)* taxpayer.

contrincante ➤ *mf* rival, opponent.

control ➤ *m* control; *(inspección)* check; *(lugar)* checkpoint.

controlador, a ➤ *mf* controller; COMPUT. driver ■ c. aéreo air-traffic controller.

controlar ➤ *tr* to control; *(inspeccionar)* to inspect; *(comprobar)* to check; COM. to audit.

controversia ➤ *f* controversy, dispute.

contusión ➤ *f* bruise, contusion.

convalecencia ➤ *f* convalescence.

convalidar ➤ *tr* to confirm, ratify.

convencer §51 ➤ *tr* to convince ➤ *reflex* to be or become convinced.

convenido ➤ *adv* agreed.

conveniencia ➤ *f* convenience.

conveniente ➤ *adj* convenient; *(oportuno)* suitable.

convenio ➤ *m* agreement; *(pacto)* pact.

convenir §52 ➤ *intr (acordar)* to concur; *(corresponder)* to be fitting; *(venir bien)* to suit.

convento ➤ *m* convent; *(monasterio)* monastery.

conversación ➤ *f* conversation.

conversar ➤ *intr* to converse, talk.

conversión ➤ *f* conversion.

convertible ➤ *adj* convertible ➤ *m* AUTO. convertible.

convertir §43 ➤ *tr (cambiar)* to change, turn ➤ *reflex* to convert, be converted ■ c. en to turn into.

convicción ➤ *f* conviction.

convidado, a ➤ *adj* invited ➤ *mf* guest.

convidar ➤ *tr* to invite.

convite ➤ *m (invitación)* invitation;

(banquete) banquet, feast.

convivencia ➤ *f* living together; *(coexistencia)* coexistence.

convivir ➤ *intr* to live together.

convocar §47 ➤ *tr* to convoke, summon.

convocatoria ➤ *f* summons, notice.

convulsión ➤ *f* convulsion; *(modificación)* FIG. upheaval; GEOL. *(temblor)* tremor.

conyugal ➤ *adj* conjugal, connubial.

cónyuge ➤ *mf* spouse ■ *pl* husband and wife.

coñac ➤ *m* cognac, brandy.

cooperación ➤ *f* cooperation.

cooperar ➤ *intr* to cooperate.

cooperativo, a ➤ *adj & f* cooperative.

coordenada ➤ *f* MATH. coordinate.

coordinación ➤ *f* coordination.

coordinar ➤ *tr* to coordinate.

copa ➤ *f* glass, goblet; *(trago)* drink; *(de árbol)* treetop; *(de sombrero)* crown; SPORT. cup ■ **tomarse una c.** to have a drink *or* cocktail.

copia ➤ *f* copy; *(duplicado)* duplicate.

copiadora ➤ *f* photocopier.

copiar ➤ *tr* to copy.

copla ➤ *f* ballad; *(estrofa)* stanza.

copo ➤ *m (de nieve)* snowflake.

coquetear ➤ *intr* to flirt.

coqueto, a ➤ *adj* flirtatious; *(agradable)* charming.

coraje ➤ *m (valor)* courage; *(ira)* anger.

coral[1] ➤ *m* coral.

coral[2] ➤ *adj* choral ➤ *m* chorale.

corazón ➤ *m* heart ■ **de c.** sincerely.

corbata ➤ *f* tie, necktie.

corcho ➤ *m* cork; *(de la pesca)* float.

cordel ➤ *m* cord, thin rope.

cordero ➤ *m* lamb; *(piel)* lambskin.

cordial ➤ *adj* cordial, warm.

cordón ➤ *m (cuerda)* cord; *(cinta)* cordon; *(de zapatos)* shoelace.

cornada ➤ *f (golpe)* butt (with a horn); *(herida)* goring.

corneta ➤ *f* bugle; MIL. cornet.

cornisa ➤ *f* cornice.

coro ➤ *m* chorus, choir ■ **a c.** in unison.

corona ➤ *f* crown; *(de laureles)* wreath; *(aureola)* halo; ASTRON. corona.

coronación ➤ *f* crowning, coronation.

coronel ➤ *mf* colonel.

coronilla ➤ *f* ANAT. crown ■ **estar hasta la c.** COLL. to be fed up.

corporación ➤ *f* corporation.

corral ➤ *m* corral; *(redil)* pen.

correa ➤ *f (de cuero)* strap; *(cinturón)* belt; TECH. belt.

corrección ➤ *f* correction; *(modificación)* adjustment; *(urbanidad)* propriety.

corredizo, a ➤ *adj (puerta)* sliding; *(nudo)* slip, running.

corredor, a ➤ *adj* running ➤ *mf* runner ➤ *m (pasillo)* corridor; COM. agent.

corregir ➤ *tr* to correct; *(castigar)* to punish ➤ *reflex* to mend one's ways.

correo ➤ *m* mail; *(buzón)* mailbox; *(oficina)* post office ■ **c. aéreo** air mail • **c. basura** COMPUT. junk mail, spam • **c. de voz** voice mail • **c. electrónico** COMPUT. e-mail • **echar al c.** to mail • **por c.** by mail ■ *pl (servicio)* mail service; *(oficina)* post office.

correr ➤ *intr* to run; *(en una carrera)* to race; *(aguas)* to flow; *(viento)* to blow; *(camino)* to run; *(horas)* to pass; *(rumor)* to circulate ➤ *tr* to race; *(riesgo)* to run; *(cortinas)* to draw; *(cerrojo)* to slide; *(aventuras)* to meet with ➤ *reflex (deslizarse)* to slide; *(moverse)* to slide over.

correspondencia ➤ *f* correspondence, mail.

corresponder ➤ *intr* to correspond, match; *(reciprocar)* to return; *(tocar)* to be one's turn; *(pertenecer)* to belong ➤ *reflex (escribir)* to correspond.

correspondiente ➤ *adj* corresponding ➤ *mf* correspondent.

corresponsal ➤ *adj & mf* correspondent.

corrida ➤ *f* race, run ■ **c. de toros** bullfight.

corriente ➤ *adj* running; *(actual)* current; *(usual)* usual; *(ordinario)* ordinary; *(moderno)* up-to-date ■ **poner al c.** to bring up-to-date • **tener al c.** to keep informed ➤ *f* current ■ **c. alterna, directa** alternating, direct current.

corro ➤ *m* circle, ring.

corromper ➤ *tr* to corrupt; *(pudrir)* to decay.

corrupción ➤ *f* corruption.

cortacésped ➤ *m* lawnmower.

cortacircuitos ➤ *m* circuit breaker.

cortado, a ➤ *adj (estilo)* disjointed; COLL. *(sin palabras)* speechless ➤ *m* coffee with milk.

cortar ➤ *tr* to cut; *(recortar)* to trim; *(carne, aves)* to carve; *(un árbol)* to cut down, fell; *(atravesar)* to cut through; *(omitir)* to cut out; *(interrumpir)* to cut off ➤ *reflex* to become flustered; *(la piel)* to chap; *(la leche)* to curdle.

cortaúñas ➤ *m* nail clipper.

corte[1] ➤ *m* cutting; *(filo)* (cutting) edge; SEW. cutting (out); *(estilo)* cut ■ c. de pelo haircut • c. y confección dressmaking.

corte[2] ➤ *f* (royal) court.

cortés ➤ *adj* courteous, polite.

cortesía ➤ *f* courtesy.

corteza ➤ *f (de árbol)* bark; *(del pan)* crust; *(de queso, tocino)* rind.

cortijo ➤ *m* farm, grange.

cortina ➤ *f* curtain.

corto, a ➤ *adj* short; *(breve)* brief; *(escaso)* short.

cortocircuito ➤ *m* short circuit.

cosa ➤ *f* thing; *(asunto)* business ■ como si tal c. COLL. as if such a thing had never happened • no es gran c. it's nothing great ¿ que c.? COLL. what did you say?

cosecha ➤ *f* harvest; *(temporada)* harvest time; FIG. crop.

cosechar ➤ *tr* to harvest; *(frutas, flores)* to pick ➤ *intr* to harvest.

coser ➤ *tr* to sew.

cosmético, a ➤ *adj & m* cosmetic.

cosmonauta ➤ *mf* cosmonaut.

cosmos ➤ *m* cosmos, universe.

cosquillas ➤ *fpl* ticklishness ■ hacer c. to tickle.

costa ➤ *f (costo)* cost; *(orilla)* shore.

costado ➤ *m* side, flank.

costar §11 ➤ *intr* to cost ■ c. barato to be cheap *or* inexpensive • c. caro to be expensive • c. trabajo to take a lot to • me cuesta creerlo I find it hard to believe.

costarriqueño, a ➤ *adj & mf* Costa Rican.

coste ➤ *m* cost.

costear ➤ *tr* to finance; MARIT. to coast.

costero, a ➤ *adj* coastal ➤ *f* shore.

costilla ➤ *f* ANAT. rib; *(chuleta)* cutlet, chop.

costo ➤ *m* cost.

costra ➤ *f* crust; MED. scab.

costumbre ➤ *f* custom; *(hábito)* habit ■ de c. usual, usually.

costura ➤ *f* needlework; *(unión)* seam ■ alta c. high fashion.

costurera ➤ *f* seamstress.

costurero ➤ *m* sewing basket.

cotidiano, a ➤ *adj* daily, everyday.

cotización ➤ *f* COM. quotation, price.

cotizar §02 ➤ *tr* COM. to quote; price.

coto ➤ *m (terreno)* reserved area; *(mojón)* boundary marker ■ c. de caza game preserve.

coz ➤ *f* backward kick; ARM. recoil; *(culata)* butt ■ dar *or* pegar coces to kick.

cráneo ➤ *m* cranium, skull.

cráter ➤ *m* crater.

creación ➤ *f* creation.

crear ➤ *tr* to create.

crecer §09 ➤ *intr* to grow; *(un río)* to swell; *(la luna)* to wax.

crecimiento ➤ *m (acción)* growth; *(aumento)* increase.

credencial ➤ *adj* accrediting ➤ *f* credential.

crédito ➤ *m* COM. credit; *(asenso)* credence ■ abrir *or* dar c. a to give *or* extend credit to • a c. on credit.

creer §27 ➤ *tr* to believe; *(imaginar)* to think ■ c. que sí to think so ➤ *intr* to believe ■ ver es c. seeing is believing ➤ *reflex* to consider *or* regard oneself.

crema ➤ *f* cream; *(natillas)* custard.

cremallera ➤ *f* zipper.

crematorio, a ➤ *adj & m* crematory.

cremoso, a ➤ *adj* creamy.

crepé §27 ➤ *m (tela fina)* crepe, crêpe.

crepúsculo ➤ *m* twilight.

cresta ➤ *f* crest; *(cima)* summit ■ c. de gallo cockscomb.

cría ➤ *f* raising; *(animal)* offspring; *(camada)* litter.

criado, a ➤ *adj* bred, brought up ➤ *m* servant ➤ *f* maid.

crianza ➤ *f* nurturing; ZOOL. raising.

criar §18 ➤ *tr* (*nutrir*) to nurse; (*animales*) to raise; (*niños*) to bring up.

criatura ➤ *f* (*niño*) infant; (*cosa creada*) creature.

criba ➤ *f* screen, sieve.

crimen ➤ *m* crime; FIG. shame.

criminal ➤ *adj* & *mf* criminal.

crin ➤ *f* horsehair.

crío ➤ *m* COLL. (*de pecho*) infant; (*niño*) kid.

criollo, a ➤ *adj* & *mf* native, Creole.

crisis ➤ *f* crisis; (*escasez*) shortage ■ c. nerviosa nervous breakdown.

cristal ➤ *m* crystal; (*vidrio*) glass.

cristiano, a ➤ *adj* & *mf* Christian.

criterio ➤ *m* (*regla*) criterion; (*juicio*) judgment; (*opinión*) opinion.

crítico, a ➤ *adj* critical; (*crucial*) crucial ➤ *mf* critic ➤ *f* criticism.

cromosoma ➤ *m* chromosome.

crónico, a ➤ *adj* chronic ➤ *f* (*historia*) chronicle; (*artículo*) article.

cronología ➤ *f* chronology.

cronológico, a ➤ *adj* chronologic(al).

cronómetro ➤ *m* chronometer.

croqueta ➤ *f* CUL. croquette.

croquis ➤ *m* sketch.

cruce ➤ *m* (*acción*) crossing; (*punto*) intersection.

crucero ➤ *m* cruise; ARCHIT. transept; MIL. cruiser.

crucifijo ➤ *m* crucifix.

crucigrama ➤ *m* crossword puzzle.

crudo, a ➤ *adj* raw; (*verde*) green; (*petróleo*) crude; (*clima*) harsh ➤ *m* crude oil.

cruel ➤ *adj* cruel.

crueldad ➤ *f* cruelty.

crujir ➤ *intr* (*hoja, tela*) to rustle; (*puerta, madera*) to creak; (*huesos*) to crack; (*grava*) to crunch.

cruz ➤ *f* cross; (*reverso*) tails.

cruzado, a ➤ *adj* crossed; BIOL., ZOOL. hybrid.

cruzar §02 ➤ *tr* to cross ➤ *reflex* to cross one another; (*pasarse*) to pass ■ c. de brazos to do nothing.

cuaderno ➤ *m* notebook.

cuadra ➤ *f* stable; (*de casas*) block.

cuadrado, a ➤ *adj* & *m* square.

cuadrícula ➤ *f* grid.

cuadrilla ➤ *f* (*de obreros*) crew; (*de malhechores*) gang; TAUR. team assisting a bullfighter.

cuadro ➤ *m* square; ARTS painting.

cual ➤ *rel pron* ■ al c. (*persona*) to whom; (*cosa*) to which ■ c. (*persona*) who; (*cosa*) which ▪ por lo c. whereby, because of which.

cuál ➤ *adj* which ➤ *rel pron* which (one) ➤ *indef pron* some ➤ *adv* how.

cualidad ➤ *f* quality, characteristic.

cualquier ➤ *adj contr of* **cualquiera**.

cualquiera ➤ *adj* (just) any, any ordinary ➤ *indef pron* any(one), anybody ■ un (hombre) c. a nobody ➤ *rel pron* (*persona*) whoever; (*cosa*) whatever; (*nadie*) nobody.

cuán ➤ *adv* how ▪ c. tonto how silly.

cuando ➤ *adv* when, since ▪ de c. en c. from time to time ➤ *conj* when; (*aunque*) although, even if; (*puesto que*) since; (*si*) if ▪ c. quiera whenever ➤ *prep* (*durante*) at the time of ▪ c. niño as a child.

cuándo ➤ *adv* when ▪ ¿c. llegó el tren? when did the train arrive?

cuanto[1] ➤ *m* PHYS. quantum.

cuanto[2] ➤ *adv* as much as; (*todo el tiempo que*) as long as ▪ c. antes as soon as possible • c. más even more so • en c. as soon as • en c. a as to, as for.

cuánto ➤ *adv* how ▪ ¡c. me alegro! how happy I am! • ¡c. cuesta la carne! how expensive beef is!

cuanto, a ➤ *adj* as much as ▪ c. más . . . (tanto) más the more . . . the more • c. menos the less • cuantos as many • unos cuantos a few, some ➤ *pron* all that, everything, as much as ▪ unos cuantos some, a few.

cuánto, a ➤ *adj* how much ▪ ¿cada c. tiempo? how often? • cuántos, cuántas how many ➤ *pron* how much ▪ cuántos, cuántas how many.

cuarenta ➤ *adj* & *m* forty.

cuartel ➤ *m* MIL. barracks.

cuarto, a ➤ *adj* fourth ➤ *m* (*habitación*) room; (*cantidad*) fourth, quarter ▪ c.

de baño bathroom.

cuatro ➤ *adj & m* four ■ **las c.** four o'clock.

cuatrocientos, as ➤ *adj & m* four hundred.

cuba ➤ *f (tonel)* cask; *(tina)* vat.

cubano, a ➤ *adj & mf* Cuban.

cubierto, a ➤ *m (comida)* meal (at a fixed price) ➤ *f* cover; MARIT. deck ■ **bajo c.** under cover.

cubo ➤ *m* cube; *(balde)* bucket; *(tina)* vat; *(de rueda)* hub.

cubrir §55 ➤ *tr* to cover (up); *(esconder)* to conceal ➤ *reflex* to cover oneself.

cucaracha ➤ *f* cockroach.

cuchara ➤ *f* spoon ■ **c. sopera** *or* **de sopa** soupspoon, tablespoon.

cucharada ➤ *f* spoonful.

cucharón ➤ *m* ladle; TECH. scoop.

cuchichear ➤ *intr* to whisper.

cuchilla ➤ *f (cuchillo)* knife; *(hoja)* blade; *(de afeitar)* razor blade.

cuchillo ➤ *m* knife.

cuco ➤ *m* cuckoo.

cuello ➤ *m* neck ■ **c. alto** turtleneck.

cuenca ➤ *f* valley; *(hoya)* river basin.

cuenco ➤ *m* earthenware bowl.

cuenta ➤ *f (de restaurante)* check; *(bolita)* bead; COM. account; *(explicación)* account; *(cargo)* responsibility ■ **c. bancaria** *or* **de banco** bank account • **c. corriente** checking account • **c. de ahorros** savings account • **darse c. de** to realize • **perder la c. de** to lose track of • **trabajar por su c.** to be self-employed ■ *pl* accounts ■ **llevar las c.** to keep the books • **pedir c. a** to call to account.

cuentagotas ➤ *m* eyedropper.

cuentakilómetros ➤ *m* odometer.

cuento ➤ *m* story, tale; LIT. short story ■ **c. de hadas** fairy tale.

cuerda ➤ *f (cordón)* cord, string; *(del reloj)* watch spring; MUS. string ■ **dar c. a un reloj** to wind a watch ■ *pl* **c. vocales** ANAT. vocal cords.

cuerdo, a ➤ *adj & mf* sane, sensible (person).

cuerno ➤ *m* ZOOL., MUS. horn.

cuero ➤ *m (piel)* hide; *(de zapatos)* leather ■ **c. charolado** patent leather • **en cueros** naked.

cuerpo ➤ *m* body; *(torso)* torso; *(figura)* figure ■ **c. celeste** heavenly body • **c. diplomático** diplomatic corps.

cuervo ➤ *m* crow, raven.

cuesta ➤ *f* slope, hill ■ **c. abajo** downhill • **c. arriba** uphill.

cuestión ➤ *f (asunto)* question, matter; *(duda)* dispute.

cuestionario ➤ *m (encuesta)* questionnaire; *(examen)* test questions.

cueva ➤ *f* cave.

cuidado ➤ *m* care; *(cautela)* caution; *(miedo)* concern ■ **con c.** carefully • **c. con** beware of • **tener c.** to be careful.

cuidadoso, a ➤ *adj* careful, cautious.

cuidar ➤ *tr & intr* ■ **c. (de)** to take care of ➤ *reflex* to take care of oneself ■ **c. de** *(preocuparse)* to care about; *(protegerse)* to be careful about.

culebra ➤ *f* snake.

culpa ➤ *f* blame, guilt; *(falta)* fault ■ **por c. de** through the fault of • **echar la c. a uno** to blame someone • **tener la c.** to be to blame.

culpabilidad ➤ *f* guilt.

culpable ➤ *adj* guilty; *(acusado)* accused ■ **confesarse c.** to plead guilty ■ **declarar c.** to find guilty ➤ *mf* culprit.

cultivar ➤ *tr* to cultivate.

cultivo ➤ *m* cultivation; *(cosecha)* crop.

culto, a ➤ *adj (civilizado)* cultured; *(instruido)* learned ➤ *m (secta)* cult; *(homenaje)* worship; *(rito)* ritual.

cultura ➤ *f* culture.

cumbre ➤ *f* summit; FIG. pinnacle.

cumpleaños ➤ *m* birthday.

cumplir ➤ *tr (llevar a cabo)* to carry out; *(la palabra)* to keep; *(la ley)* to obey ■ **hoy cumple diez años** today she is ten years old ➤ *intr* ■ **c. con** *(promesa)* to fulfill; *(obligaciones)* to fulfill one's obligations to ➤ *reflex (realizarse)* to be fulfilled; COM. to fall due.

cuna ➤ *f* cradle; *(lugar de nacimiento)* birthplace ■ **canción de c.** lullaby.

cuneta ➤ *f (de un foso)* ditch; *(de una calle)* gutter.

cuñado, a ➤ *mf* brother/sister-in-law.

cuota ➤ *f* quota, share; *(pago)* fee, dues ▪ **c. de admisión** admission fee.

cupón ➤ *m* coupon.

cúpula ➤ *f* dome, cupola.

cura¹ ➤ *m* RELIG. priest.

cura² ➤ *f* MED. cure.

curar ➤ *intr* ▪ **c. de** MED. to recover from ➤ *tr* MED. to cure; *(tratar)* to treat; FIG. to soothe.

curiosidad ➤ *f* curiosity; *(cosa)* curio.

curioso, a ➤ *adj* curious; *(limpio)* neat; *(cuidadoso)* careful; *(excepcional)* odd ➤ *mf* curious person; *(entremetido)* busybody.

curriculum vitae ➤ *m* resumé.

cursar ➤ *tr* *(estudiar)* to study; *(dar curso a)* to attend to.

cursi ➤ *adj* *(presumido)* pretentious; *(de mal gusto)* tasteless.

cursillo ➤ *m* *(curso)* short course; *(conferencias)* series of lectures.

curso ➤ *m* course; FIN. circulation ▪ **c. acelerado** crash course • **tener c. legal** to be legal tender.

cursor ➤ *m* cursor.

curtir ➤ *tr* *(adobar)* to tan ➤ *reflex* to become weather-beaten.

curva ➤ *f* curve; *(recodo)* curve, bend ▪ **c. cerrada** sharp curve.

custodia ➤ *f* custody; *(cuidado)* care.

custodiar ➤ *tr* to take care of; *(vigilar)* to watch over; *(proteger)* to protect.

cutícula ➤ *f* cuticle.

cutis ➤ *m* skin, complexion.

cuyo, a ➤ *rel pron* whose; *(personas)* of whom; *(cosas)* of which.

D

dado, a ➤ *adj* given ➤ *m* die ▪ *pl* dice.

dalia ➤ *f* dahlia.

dama ➤ *f* lady; *(de la reina)* lady-in-waiting ▪ *pl* checkers, draughts (G.B.).

damnificado, a ➤ *adj* damaged ➤ *mf* victim.

danza ➤ *f* dance.

danzarín, ina ➤ *mf* dancer.

daño ➤ *m* damage, harm ▪ **hacer d.** to be painful; *(perjudicar)* to harm, injure.

dar §12 ➤ *tr* to give; *(conferir)* to grant; *(proponer)* to propose, offer; *(sacri-*

ficar) to give up; *(repartir)* to deal; *(producir)* to produce, bear; *(soltar)* to give off, emit; *(imponer)* to impose; *(sonar)* to strike; THEAT. to show; *(comunicar)* to express, convey ▪ **d. a luz** to give birth • **darle ganas de** to feel like, have a mind to • **d. gusto a** to please, make happy • **d. una vuelta, paseo** to take a stroll ➤ *intr* *(ocurrir)* to arise, occur ▪ **d. a** to overlook, face • ¡**dale!** *(¡apúrate!)* hurry up!; *(¡adelante!)* keep it up! • **d. con** *(encontrar)* to find, hit on; *(encontrarse)* to meet, run into; *(chocar)* to hit • **d. igual** or **lo mismo** to be all the same ➤ *reflex* to give oneself up, surrender; *(suceder)* to arise, occur ▪ **d. cuenta de** to realize • **d. las manos** or **la mano** to shake hands • **d. por** to consider oneself • **d. prisa** to hurry.

dardo ➤ *m* dart, arrow.

data ➤ *f* date; COM. data, items.

datar ➤ *tr* to date; COM. to enter, credit ➤ *intr* to date, begin.

dato ➤ *m* fact, datum; *(documento)* document ▪ *pl* data, information.

de ➤ *prep* of, from ▪ **a las tres de la tarde** at three in the afternoon • **de rodillas** on one's knees • **hablar de** to talk about • **lejos de aquí** far from here • **los ojos del niño** the child's eyes • **más de diez** more than ten • **soy de Chile** I'm from Chile • **tiritar del frío** to shiver with cold.

debajo ➤ *adv* underneath, below ▪ *(por)* **d. de** under, underneath, beneath.

debate ➤ *m* debate, discussion.

debatir ➤ *tr* to debate, discuss; *(combatir)* to fight, struggle.

debe ➤ *m* COM. debit.

deber¹ ➤ *tr* to owe; *(hay que)* to ought to ▪ **d. de** to be probable ➤ *reflex* to be due to.

deber² ➤ *m* duty, obligation; *(faena)* chore; *(deuda)* debt ▪ *pl* AMER. homework.

debidamente ➤ *adv* properly, duly.

debido, a ➤ *adj* due; *(apropiado)* fitting.

débil ➤ *adj* weak.

debilidad ➤ *f* weakness.

debutar ➤ *intr* to begin; THEAT. to debut.

década ➤ *f* decade.

decadencia ➤ *f* decadence, decline.

decaimiento ➤ *m* decadence, decline; *(debilidad)* weakness; *(desaliento)* discouragement.

decano ➤ *m* EDUC. dean.

decatlón ➤ *m* decathlon.

decena ➤ *f* group of ten; MUS. tenth.

decente ➤ *adj* decent.

decepción ➤ *f* deception; *(desengaño)* disenchantment, disappointment.

decidido, a ➤ *adj* determined, resolute.

decidir ➤ *tr, intr & reflex* to decide.

decimal ➤ *adj & m* decimal.

décimo, a ➤ *adj & m* tenth.

decir §13 ➤ *tr* to say; *(relatar)* to tell; *(hablar)* to speak; *(nombrar)* to call, name ■ es d. that is (to say) • ¡no me digas! you don't say!, really! • querer d. to mean.

decisión ➤ *f* decision; *(firmeza)* determination; LAW verdict, ruling.

decisivo, a ➤ *adj* decisive, conclusive.

declamar ➤ *tr & intr* to declaim, recite.

declaración ➤ *f* declaration, statement; LAW deposition; *(de cartas)* bid, call.

declaradamente ➤ *adv* manifestly, openly.

declarante ➤ *adj* declaring ➤ *mf* LAW declarant, witness.

declarar ➤ *tr & intr* to declare.

decoración ➤ *f* decoration; THEAT. scenery.

decorar ➤ *tr* to decorate; *(memorizar)* to memorize, learn by heart.

decorativo, a ➤ *adj* decorative.

decreto ➤ *m* decree, order.

dedal ➤ *m* thimble.

dedicar §47 ➤ *tr & reflex* to dedicate (oneself).

dedo ➤ *m* finger; *(del pie)* toe; *(porción)* bit, smidgen ■ d. meñique little finger, pinky • d. pulgar or gordo thumb; *(del pie)* big toe.

deducir §14 ➤ *tr* to deduce, conclude; *(rebajar)* to deduct, subtract.

defecar §47 ➤ *tr & intr* to defecate.

defecto ➤ *m* defect, flaw; *(falta)* absence, lack ■ ser por d. COMPUT. to default.

defectuoso, a ➤ *adj* defective, faulty.

defender §34 ➤ *tr* to defend ➤ *intr & reflex* to defend or protect oneself; *(arreglárselas)* to manage, get by.

defensa ➤ *f* defense ■ d. propia or legítima self-defense.

defensivo, a ➤ *adj* defensive ➤ *m* defense, safeguard ➤ *f* defensive.

deficiente ➤ *adj* deficient, lacking.

definición ➤ *f* definition; *(determinación)* determination, decision.

definir ➤ *tr* to define; *(determinar)* to determine, decide.

definitivamente ➤ *adv* definitely.

deformar ➤ *tr* to deform ➤ *reflex* to be or become deformed.

defraudar ➤ *tr* to defraud, cheat.

degenerado, a ➤ *adj & mf* degenerate.

degradante ➤ *adj* degrading, debasing.

degustación ➤ *f* tasting, sampling.

dejar ➤ *tr* to leave; *(consentir)* to let, allow; *(desamparar)* to abandon, desert ■ ¡deja! or ¡déjalo! never mind! • d. caer to drop, let go of ➤ *intr* ■ d. de to stop, leave off ➤ *reflex (descuidarse)* to let oneself go, become sloppy.

del ➤ *contr* of **de** and **el.**

delantal ➤ *m* apron.

delante ➤ *adv (con prioridad)* in front, ahead; *(enfrente)* facing, opposite ■ d. de in front of.

delatar ➤ *tr* to denounce, inform on; *(revelar)* to reveal, expose.

delegación ➤ *f* delegation; *(oficina)* office, branch.

delegado, a ➤ *mf* delegate.

deletrear ➤ *tr (pronunciar)* to spell (out); *(descifrar)* to decipher.

delfín ➤ *m* dolphin.

delgado, a ➤ *adj (esbelto)* slender, slim; *(flaco)* thin ■ ponerse d. to lose weight.

deliberado, a ➤ *adj* deliberate, intentional.

delicadeza ➤ *f* delicacy; *(discreción)* tact.

delicado, a ➤ *adj* delicate; *(quebradizo)* fragile.

delicioso, a ➤ *adj (agradable)* delightful; *(sabroso)* delicious.

delincuente ➤ *adj & mf* delinquent.

delirar ➤ *intr* to be delirious.

delirio ➤ *m* delirium; *(manía)* mania, frenzy.

delito ➤ *m* offense, crime.

demanda ➤ *f* demand; *(petición)* appeal, request; *(pregunta)* question, inquiry; *(empresa)* enterprise; *(empeño)* perseverance; ELEC. load; LAW *(escrito)* writ; *(acción)* lawsuit.

demandar ➤ *tr (pedir)* to request, ask for; LAW to sue, file suit against.

demás ➤ *adj* other, rest of the ▪ lo d. the rest • **por d.** *(en demasía)* excessively, too much; *(inútilmente)* in vain • **por lo d.** otherwise, other than that.

demasiado, a ➤ *adj* too much or many ➤ *adv* too, too much.

demencia ➤ *f* dementia.

democracia ➤ *f* democracy.

demócrata ➤ *mf* democrat.

democrático, a ➤ *adj* democratic.

demográfico, a ➤ *adj* demographic.

demoler §54 ➤ *tr* to demolish, destroy.

demonio ➤ *m* demon, devil.

demora ➤ *f* delay, wait.

demorar ➤ *tr* to delay, hold up ➤ *intr* to linger, stay ➤ *reflex* to take a long time, delay.

demostrar §11 ➤ *tr* to demonstrate, show.

denegar §35 ➤ *tr (rechazar)* to refuse, reject; *(negar)* to deny.

denigrar ➤ *tr* to denigrate, disparage.

denominación ➤ *f* denomination.

denominador ➤ *m* denominator.

denominar ➤ *tr* to denominate, name.

denotar ➤ *tr* to denote.

densidad ➤ *f* density.

denso, a ➤ *adj* dense, thick; *(sólido)* heavy, solid; *(oscuro)* dark, black.

dentadura ➤ *f* (set of) teeth.

dental ➤ *adj* dental.

dentífrico ➤ *m* toothpaste.

dentista ➤ *mf* dentist.

dentro ➤ *adv* inside, within; *(de un edificio)* inside, indoors ▪ **d. de poco** shortly, soon • **por d.** inwardly, (on the) inside.

denuncia ➤ *f* accusation, denunciation; *(declaración)* declaration, report.

denunciar ➤ *tr* to accuse, denounce; *(pronosticar)* to foretell; *(declarar)* to declare, announce.

departamento ➤ *m* department, section; *(distrito)* province, district; *(compartimiento)* compartment; *(piso)* apartment, flat (G.B.).

depender ➤ *intr* to depend *(de* on).

dependiente, a ➤ *adj* dependent ➤ *mf (empleado)* employee; *(de tienda)* clerk, salesperson.

depilar ➤ *tr* to depilate.

deponer §37 ➤ *tr (apartar)* to lay or put aside; *(privar)* to depose; LAW to testify, provide testimony for.

deportar ➤ *tr* to deport, exile.

deporte ➤ *m* sport.

deportista ➤ *adj* sporting, sporty; COLL. *(aficionado)* fond of sports ➤ *mf* sports fan, sportsman/woman.

deportivo, a ➤ *adj* sporting, sports; *(aficionado)* fond of sports.

depositar ➤ *tr* to deposit; *(encomendar)* to place ➤ *reflex* to settle.

depósito ➤ *m* deposit; *(almacén)* warehouse; *(cisterna)* cistern, tank; MIL. depot, dump.

depresión ➤ *f* depression.

deprimente ➤ *adj* depressing.

deprimir ➤ *tr* to depress ➤ *reflex* to get depressed.

derecho, a ➤ *adj* right, right-hand; *(vertical)* upright, straight ➤ *f (lado derecho)* right or right-hand side; *(diestra)* right hand; POL. right; right wing ▪ **a la d.** to or on the right ➤ *m* right; LAW. privilege ▪ **de d.** LAW de jure, by right ▪ **tener d.** to have a right to ▪ *pl (impuestos)* duties, taxes; *(honorarios)* fees, charges • **d. de autor** royalties ➤ *adv* straight, right ▪ **todo d.** straight ahead.

derivación ➤ *f* derivation; ELEC. *(pérdida)* loss of current; *(circuito)* bypass, shunt.

derivar ➤ *tr* to derive ➤ *intr* to derive, be derived.

dermatología ➤ *f* dermatology.

dermatólogo, a ➤ *mf* dermatologist.

derramar ➤ *tr* to spill, pour out; *(sangre)* to shed; *(diseminar)* to spread, scatter ➤ *reflex* to overflow, spill over.

derretir §32 ➤ *tr* to dissolve; *(hielo)* to melt ➤ *reflex* to fall madly in love.

derribar ➤ *tr* to knock down; *(subvertir)* to overthrow, topple.

derrocar §47 ➤ *tr* to throw down; *(arruinar)* to demolish; *(subvertir)* to overthrow.

derrochar ➤ *tr* to squander, waste.

derroche ➤ *m* squandering, waste.

derrota ➤ *f* defeat, rout.

derrotar ➤ *tr* to defeat, beat.

derruir §10 ➤ *tr* to knock down, demolish.

derrumbar ➤ *tr (despeñar)* to hurl down; *(demoler)* to knock down, demolish ➤ *reflex (caerse)* to collapse, fall; AMER. to fail.

desabrigar §31 ➤ *tr* to uncover, expose.

desabrochar ➤ *tr* to undo, unfasten.

desacertado, a ➤ *adj* mistaken.

desacierto ➤ *m* error, mistake.

desacreditar ➤ *tr* to discredit, disgrace.

desactivar ➤ *tr* to deactivate.

desacuerdo ➤ *m* disagreement; *(error)* error, mistake; *(olvido)* forgetfulness.

desafiar §18 ➤ *tr* to challenge, dare; *(competir)* to oppose, compete with.

desafinar ➤ *intr* MUS. to be out of tune.

desafío ➤ *m* challenge, defiance.

desafortunado, a ➤ *adj* unfortunate.

desagradable ➤ *adj* disagreeable.

desagradar ➤ *tr* to displease, offend.

desagradecido, a ➤ *adj & mf* ungrateful (person).

desagrado ➤ *m* displeasure, discontent.

desagüe ➤ *m* drainage; *(desaguadero)* drain.

desahogado, a ➤ *adj (descarado)* brazen, fresh; *(despejado)* clear, open; *(espacioso)* roomy, spacious; *(acomodado)* relaxing, easy.

desahogar §31 ➤ *tr* to alleviate, ease; *(dar rienda suelta)* to vent ➤ *reflex* to let off steam; *(confiarse)* to confide; *(descansar)* to relax, take it easy.

desahogo ➤ *m* relief, alleviation; *(descanso)* rest, respite; *(expansión)* space, room; *(libertad)* freedom; *(comodidad)* comfort, ease.

desahuciar ➤ *tr* to remove all hope

from; *(un inquilino)* to evict.

desaire ➤ *m (falta de gracia)* gracelessness; *(desprecio)* slight, snub.

desajuste ➤ *m* maladjustment; *(avería)* breakdown, failure.

desalentar §33 ➤ *tr* to leave breathless; *(desanimar)* to discourage ➤ *reflex* to become discouraged.

desaliento ➤ *m* discouragement.

desaliñado, a ➤ *adj* slovenly, untidy.

desaliño ➤ *m (descompostura)* slovenliness, untidiness.

desalmado, a ➤ *adj* heartless, cruel.

desalojar ➤ *tr* to remove, expel; *(desplazar)* to dislodge, displace; *(abandonar)* to abandon, evacuate ➤ *intr* to leave.

desangrar ➤ *tr* to bleed (a patient) ➤ *reflex* to bleed profusely.

desanimado, a ➤ *adj* downhearted; *(poco animado)* dull, lifeless.

desanimar ➤ *tr* to discourage, depress ➤ *reflex* to become discouraged.

desánimo ➤ *m* discouragement, dejection.

desapacible ➤ *adj* unpleasant, disagreeable.

desaparecer §09 ➤ *tr* to make disappear ➤ *intr & reflex* to disappear.

desaparición ➤ *f* disappearance, vanishing.

desarmar ➤ *tr, intr & reflex* to disarm.

desarme ➤ *m* disarmament; *(desmontaje)* dismantling.

desarraigado, a ➤ *adj* uprooted, rootless.

desarreglar ➤ *tr* to make untidy, mess (up); *(quebrar)* to break ➤ *reflex* to break (down).

desarrollado, a ➤ *adj* developed.

desarrollar ➤ *tr & reflex* to unroll, unfold; *(extender)* to develop, expand.

desarrollo ➤ *m* unrolling, unfolding; *(extensión)* development, expansion.

desarticular ➤ *tr (desmontar)* to disassemble, take apart.

desasir ➤ *tr* to release, let go ➤ *reflex* to yield, give up.

desasosiego ➤ *m* uneasiness, restlessness.

desastre ➤ *m* disaster, catastrophe.

desatar ➤ *tr* to untie, undo; *(soltar)* to unleash, let go; *(aclarar)* to unravel, solve ➤ *reflex* to come untied *or* undone; *(soltarse)* to break loose.

desatino ➤ *m* nonsense, foolishness.

desatrancar §47 ➤ *tr (la puerta)* to unbolt; *(desatrampar)* to clear, unblock.

desautorizar §02 ➤ *tr* to deprive of authority; *(desmentir)* to deny; *(prohibir)* to prohibit.

desavenencia ➤ *f* discord, enmity.

desayunar ➤ *intr & reflex* to have breakfast, breakfast.

desayuno ➤ *m* breakfast.

desbarajuste ➤ *m* confusion, disorder.

desbaratar ➤ *tr* to ruin, wreck; *(malgastar)* to squander, waste ➤ *intr* to talk *or* act wildly.

desbordamiento ➤ *m* overflowing, running over; *(de cólera)* outburst.

desbordar ➤ *intr & reflex (derramarse)* to overflow, run over; *(rebosar)* to burst *or* brim with.

descabellado, a ➤ *adj* wild, crazy.

descafeinado, a ➤ *adj & m* decaffeinated (coffee).

descalabrar ➤ *tr* to injure, wound ➤ *reflex* to injure one's head.

descalabro ➤ *m* setback; MIL. defeat.

descalificar §47 ➤ *tr* to disqualify.

descalzar §02 ➤ *tr* to take off ➤ *reflex* to take off one's shoes.

descalzo, a ➤ *adj* barefoot(ed), shoeless; *(pobre)* destitute, poor.

descampado, a ➤ *adj* open, clear ➤ *m* open field.

descansado, a ➤ *adj (tranquilo)* restful, tranquil; *(refrescado)* rested, relaxed.

descansar ➤ *intr* to rest, take a rest; *(calmarse)* to relax ➤ *tr* to rest, give rest to; *(apoyar)* to rest *or* lean (something) on ➤ *reflex* to rest, take a rest.

descanso ➤ *m* rest; *(alivio)* relief; *(período)* break; SPORT. half time; THEAT. intermission.

descapotable ➤ *adj & m* AUTO. convertible.

descarado, a ➤ *adj & mf* shameless (person).

descarga ➤ *f* unloading; ARM. discharge, firing; ELEC. discharge.

descargar §31 ➤ *tr* to unload; *(disparar)* to discharge, shoot; ELEC. to discharge; *(liberar)* to release, free; *(aliviar)* to ease, relieve; COMPUT. to download ➤ *intr* to flow, empty ➤ *reflex (dimitir)* to resign, quit; *(eximirse)* to unburden oneself; *(exonerarse)* to clear oneself.

descargo ➤ *m* unloading; COM. entry; *(excusa)* excuse; *(dispensa)* release.

descaro ➤ *m* shamelessness.

descarriar §18 ➤ *tr* to misdirect, send the wrong way; *(apartar de la razón)* to lead astray ➤ *reflex* to stray, get lost.

descarrilamiento ➤ *m* RAIL. derailment; *(descarrío)* act of going astray.

descarrilar ➤ *intr* to jump the track; *(una persona)* to get off the track.

descartar ➤ *tr* to discard, put aside ➤ *reflex* to discard ■ d. de to excuse oneself from.

descendencia ➤ *f (hijos)* descendants, offspring; *(linaje)* descent, origin.

descender §34 ➤ *intr* to descend, go down; *(proceder)* to be descended from; *(un líquido)* to run *or* flow down; *(de nivel)* to drop, fall ➤ *tr (bajar)* to descend, go down; *(bajar una cosa)* to lower, bring down.

descendiente ➤ *adj* descending ➤ *mf* descendant, offspring.

descenso ➤ *m* descent, going down; *(de nivel)* fall, drop.

descifrar ➤ *tr* to decipher, decode.

descolgar §08 ➤ *tr (quitar)* to take down; *(bajar)* to let down; *(teléfono)* to pick up ➤ *reflex* to come down; *(presentarse)* to show up, drop in.

descolorido, a ➤ *adj* discolored; *(pálido)* pallid, colorless.

descomponer §37 ➤ *tr (desordenar)* to disarrange, mess up; *(podrir)* to decompose; MECH. to break; *(trastornar)* to upset, disturb ➤ *reflex (corromperse)* to decompose; MECH. to break down; *(indisponerse)* to feel sick; *(irritarse)* to get upset.

descomposición ➤ *f* decomposition, decay; *(desarreglo)* disorder, disarrangement.

descompuesto, a ➤ *adj* decomposed; *(desarreglado)* messy; MECH. out of order, broken; *(perturbado)* upset.

descomunal ➤ *adj (enorme)* enormous, huge; *(extraordinario)* extraordinary.

desconcertante ➤ *adj* disconcerting.

desconcertar §33 ➤ *tr* to disconcert, upset; *(desordenar)* to disarrange, disrupt; MED. to dislocate ➤ *reflex* to be disconcerted; *(desavenirse)* to fall out, disagree; *(descomedirse)* to go off the deep end; MED. to become dislocated.

desconectar ➤ *tr* to disconnect ➤ *reflex* to become disconnected; COMPUT. to log out or off.

desconfiado, a ➤ *adj & mf* distrustful, suspicious (person).

desconfianza ➤ *f* distrust, mistrust.

desconfiar §18 ➤ *intr* to distrust, mistrust.

descongelar ➤ *tr* to thaw, defrost.

desconocer §09 ➤ *tr* not to know; *(no reconocer)* not to recognize; *(negar)* to deny, disavow; *(desentenderse)* to ignore.

desconocido, a ➤ *adj* unknown; *(extraño)* strange, unfamiliar ➤ *mf (extraño)* stranger.

desconsolado, a ➤ *adj* disconsolate.

desconsuelo ➤ *m* grief, distress.

descontar §11 ➤ *tr (quitar)* to deduct; *(rebajar)* to discount; *(dar por cierto)* to take for granted.

descontento, a ➤ *adj* discontented, dissatisfied ➤ *m* discontent, dissatisfaction.

descorchar ➤ *tr* to uncork.

descorrer ➤ *tr (cortinas)* to draw back, open ➤ *intr & reflex* to flow.

descortesía ➤ *f* discourtesy, rudeness.

descoser ➤ *tr* SEW. to unstitch, rip ➤ *reflex* SEW. to come unstitched, rip.

descosido, a ➤ *adj* SEW. unstitched, ripped; *(indiscreto)* indiscreet, talkative.

descrédito ➤ *m* discredit, disrepute.

describir §55 ➤ *tr* to describe; *(trazar)* to trace, describe.

descripción ➤ *f* description.

descubierto, a ➤ *adj* uncovered,

exposed; *(yermo)* bare, barren; *(sin sombrero)* bareheaded ■ **al d.** COM. short; FIG. openly, in the open • **estar en d.** COM. to be overdrawn ➤ *m* COM. deficit, shortage.

descubrimiento ➤ *m* discovery; *(revelación)* disclosure, revelation.

descubrir §55 ➤ *tr* to discover; *(revelar)* to reveal, uncover.

descuento ➤ *m* discount, reduction.

descuidado, a ➤ *adj (negligente)* careless; *(desaliñado)* untidy, slovenly; *(abandonado)* neglected ➤ *mf* careless person; *(desaliñado)* slob.

descuidar ➤ *tr* to neglect, forget ➤ *reflex* to be careless; *(desaliñarse)* to neglect oneself, be sloppy.

descuido ➤ *m* carelessness, neglect; *(desaliño)* untidiness.

desde ➤ *prep* from, since ■ **d. hace un año** for a year • **d. luego** of course • **d. que** since.

desdén ➤ *m* disdain, scorn.

desdeñar ➤ *tr* to disdain, scorn ➤ *reflex* to be disdainful ■ **d.** de not to deign to.

desdichado, a ➤ *adj (desgraciado)* unfortunate, pitiful; *(infeliz)* unhappy, wretched ➤ *mf* wretch.

desdoblar ➤ *tr* to unfold, spread out; *(separar)* to split, break down.

desear ➤ *tr* to wish, desire.

desechar ➤ *tr* to reject, decline; *(apartar)* to get rid of.

desembarcar §47 ➤ *tr* to disembark, unload ➤ *intr* to disembark, go ashore.

desembarco ➤ *m* landing, disembarkation.

desembarque ➤ *m (de mercancías)* debarkation, unloading; *(de pasajeros)* landing.

desembocadura ➤ *f* outlet.

desembocar §47 ➤ *intr (río)* to flow, run; *(calle)* to lead to, run.

desempaquetar ➤ *tr* to unpack, unwrap.

desempatar ➤ *tr* to break a tie between.

desempeñar ➤ *tr (rescatar)* to recover, redeem; *(pagar)* to get out of debt; *(cumplir)* to fulfill, carry out; *(sacar de apuro)* to get (someone) out of trouble; THEAT. to play (a part).

desempeño ➤ *m (rescate)* redemption, redeeming; *(de deudas)* freeing from debt; *(cumplimiento)* fulfillment; THEAT. performance.

desempleado, a ➤ *adj & mf* unemployed (person).

desempleo ➤ *m* unemployment.

desencadenamiento ➤ *m* unchaining; *(de sucesos)* unfolding.

desencadenar ➤ *tr* to unchain, unfetter; *(incitar)* to start, incite ➤ *reflex* to break loose.

desencanto ➤ *m* disenchantment.

desenchufar ➤ *tr* to unplug, disconnect.

desenclavijar ➤ *tr* to disconnect, loosen.

desenfadado, a ➤ *adj* confident, self-assured; *(despreocupado)* carefree, uninhibited.

desenfado ➤ *m* confidence, self-assurance; *(facilidad)* ease, naturalness.

desenfreno ➤ *m* wantonness, licentiousness.

desenganchar ➤ *tr* to unhook, unfasten.

desengañar ➤ *tr* to disillusion ➤ *reflex* to become disillusioned.

desengaño ➤ *m* disillusionment; *(comprensión)* enlightenment.

desengrasar ➤ *tr* to remove the grease from ➤ *intr* to lose weight.

desenlace ➤ *m* untying, unfastening; LIT. denouement, ending; *(resultado)* result, outcome.

desenmascarar ➤ *tr* to unmask, expose.

desenredar ➤ *tr* to disentangle, unravel; *(poner en orden)* to put in order, straighten out ➤ *reflex* to extricate oneself.

desenrollar ➤ *tr* to unroll, unwind.

desentenderse §34 ➤ *reflex* to pretend not to know ■ d. de to have nothing to do with.

desentrañar ➤ *tr* to eviscerate; *(solucionar)* to get to the bottom of ➤ *reflex* to give one's all.

desenvolver §54 ➤ *tr* to unroll, unwrap; *(aclarar)* to unravel, disentangle

➤ *reflex* to come unrolled *or* unwrapped.

desenvuelto, a ➤ *adj (confiado)* natural, confident; *(elocuente)* eloquent; *(desvergonzado)* forward, brazen.

deseo ➤ *m* desire, wish.

desequilibrado, a ➤ *adj & mf* unbalanced (person).

desequilibrio ➤ *m* imbalance.

desértico, a ➤ *adj* desert-like, barren.

desesperación ➤ *f* despair, desperation.

desesperado, a ➤ *adj & mf* hopeless, desperate (person).

desesperar ➤ *tr* to drive to despair, discourage; *(irritar)* to exasperate ➤ *intr & reflex* to lose hope, despair.

desfachatez ➤ *f* cheek, nerve.

desfallecer §09 ➤ *tr* to weaken ➤*intr* to faint.

desfallecido, a ➤ *adj* faint, dizzy.

desfavorable ➤ *adj* unfavorable, adverse.

desfigurar ➤ *tr (afear)* to disfigure; *(deformar)* to deform, misshape; *(desvirtuar)* to distort, misrepresent.

desfiladero ➤ *m* defile, narrow pass.

desfilar ➤ *intr* to parade, march.

desfile ➤ *m* march, procession; MIL. parade.

desganado, a ➤ *adj* without appetite, not hungry; *(sin entusiasmo)* unenthusiastic.

desgastar ➤ *tr* to wear down; *(debilitar)* to weaken ➤ *reflex* to become weak.

desgaste ➤ *m* erosion; *(daño)* damage, wear; *(debilitación)* weakening, debilitation.

desgracia ➤ *f* misfortune, adversity; *(accidente)* mishap, setback; *(pérdida de favor)* disgrace, disfavor; *(desagrado)* displeasure ■ por d. unfortunately.

desgraciadamente ➤ *adv* unfortunately.

desgraciado, a ➤ *adj & mf* unfortunate (person); *(infeliz)* unhappy (person); *(desagradable)* unpleasant (person); *(sinvergüenza)* despicable (person).

desgravar ➤ *tr* to reduce taxes *or* duties.

deshabitado, a ➤ *adj* uninhabited.

deshacer §24 ➤ *tr* to undo; (*destruir*) to destroy, ruin; (*dividir*) to cut up; (*desarmar*) to take apart; (*disolver*) to melt, dissolve; (*desconcertar*) to break; (*desempacar*) to unpack ➤ *reflex* (*descomponerse*) to fall apart, break; (*desaparecer*) to vanish; (*extenuarse*) to weaken ∎ **d.** to get rid of.

deshecho, a ➤ *adj* undone; (*cansado*) tired, worn out.

deshidratar ➤ *tr* to dehydrate ➤ *reflex* to become dehydrated.

deshonesto, a ➤ *adj* dishonest; (*indecente*) indecent, improper.

deshora ➤ *f* inconvenient time.

deshuesar ➤ *tr* (*carne*) to debone; (*fruta*) to remove the pit from.

desierto, a ➤ *adj* deserted, uninhabited; (*desolado*) desolate, bleak ➤ *m* desert.

designar ➤ *tr* to design, plan; (*nombrar*) to designate, appoint; (*señalar*) to point out.

desigual ➤ *adj* unequal; (*quebrado*) uneven; (*diferente*) different.

desigualdad ➤ *f* inequality, disparity; (*aspereza*) roughness, ruggedness.

desilusión ➤ *f* disillusionment.

desilusionar ➤ *tr* to disillusion ➤ *reflex* to become disillusioned.

desinfectante ➤ *adj & m* disinfectant.

desinfectar ➤ *tr* to disinfect.

desinflamar ➤ *tr* to reduce inflammation in.

desinflar ➤ *tr* to deflate, let air out of.

desintegrar ➤ *tr* to disintegrate; PHYS. to split.

desinteresado, a ➤ *adj* disinterested, impartial; (*generoso*) altruistic, unselfish.

desistir ➤ *intr* to desist (*de* from); (*de un derecho*) to waive a right.

deslenguado, a ➤ *adj* foul-mouthed, coarse.

deslizar §02 ➤ *tr & intr* to slide, slip ➤ *reflex* (*resbalarse*) to slide; (*caerse*) to slip (and fall).

deslumbrante or **deslumbrador, a** ➤ *adj* (*brillante*) dazzling, brilliant; (*asombrante*) overwhelming.

deslumbrar ➤ *tr* (*cegar*) to dazzle, blind; (*confundir*) to overwhelm, bewilder.

desmandar ➤ *tr* to countermand ➤ *reflex* to go too far, get out of hand.

desmantelar ➤ *tr* (*derribar*) to knock down, dismantle; (*una casa*) to vacate, abandon.

desmayarse ➤ *reflex* to faint, swoon.

desmayo ➤ *m* (*síncope*) faint, swoon; (*desánimo*) downheartedness; BOT. weeping willow.

desmejorar ➤ *tr* to impair, damage ➤ *intr & reflex* to deteriorate, get worse.

desmemoriado, a ➤ *adj & mf* forgetful, absent-minded (person).

desmentida ➤ *f* (*negación*) denial; (*contradicción*) contradiction.

desmentir §43 ➤ *tr* to contradict; (*refutar*) to refute, disprove.

desmenuzar §02 ➤ *tr* to crumble, break into pieces; (*examinar*) to scrutinize.

desmesurado, a ➤ *adj* (*desmedido*) excessive, inordinate; (*sin límite*) boundless, limitless.

desmontar ➤ *tr* dismantle, disassemble; (*árboles*) to fell, cut down; (*terreno*) to level ➤ *intr & reflex* to dismount.

desmoralizar §02 ➤ *tr* to demoralize; (*corromper*) to corrupt.

desnatar ➤ *tr* to skim the cream off.

desnivel ➤ *m* unevenness; (*depresión*) depression, drop; (*diferencia*) difference, disparity.

desnudar ➤ *tr* to strip, undress; (*descubrir*) to lay bare, uncover ➤ *reflex* to strip.

desnudo, a ➤ *adj* undressed; (*en cueros*) naked, nude; (*despojado*) stripped, bare ➤ *m* ARTS nude.

desnutrición ➤ *f* malnutrition.

desobedecer §09 ➤ *tr* to disobey.

desobediencia ➤ *f* disobedience.

desobediente ➤ *adj & mf* disobedient (person).

desodorante ➤ *adj* deodorizing ➤ *m* deodorant.

desolación ➤ *f* desolation.

desolar §11 ➤ *tr* to desolate ➤ *reflex* to be grieved, be distressed.

desorden ➤ *m* disorder, disarray; (*lío*) muddle, mess; (*conducta*) unruliness.

desordenado, a ► *adj* disorderly; *(falta de aseo)* slovenly, untidy.

desordenar ► *tr* to disorder; *(causar confusión)* to throw into confusion; *(desasear)* to make messy ► *reflex* to become disorderly.

desorientar ► *tr* to disorient; *(confundir)* to confuse ► *reflex* to be disoriented; *(confundirse)* to become confused.

despabilado, a ► *adj (despierto)* alert, wide-awake; *(listo)* clever, sharp.

despachar ► *tr* to complete, conclude; *(resolver)* to resolve, settle; *(enviar)* to dispatch, send; *(despedir)* to fire, dismiss ► *intr (darse prisa)* to hurry up; *(hablar)* to speak one's mind; COM. to do business ► *reflex* AMER. *(darse prisa)* to hurry up ■ d. de to get rid of.

despacho ► *m* dispatch; *(oficina)* office, bureau.

despacio ► *adv* slow, slowly; AMER. in a low voice, quietly.

desparramar ► *tr* to spread; *(derramar)* to spill, splash ► *reflex* to scatter, spread.

despavorido, a ► *adj* terrified, afraid.

despectivo, a ► *adj* disparaging, pejorative.

despedida ► *f (adiós)* goodbye, farewell; *(despacho)* dismissal, firing.

despedir §32 ► *tr (decir adiós)* to say goodbye; *(despachar)* to dismiss, fire ► *reflex* to say goodbye *(de* to).

despegable ► *adj* detachable.

despegar §31 ► *tr* to unstick; *(separar)* to detach; *(quitar)* to remove ► *intr* AVIA. to take off ► *reflex* to become unglued; *(separarse)* to become detached.

despegue ► *m* takeoff.

despeinar ► *tr* to mess, tousle (a hairdo).

despejar ► *tr* to clear up, sort out ► *reflex* METEOROL. to clear up; *(divertirse)* to enjoy oneself.

despensa ► *f* larder, pantry; *(provisiones)* provisions, supplies; *(oficio)* stewardship.

despeñar ► *tr* to hurl, throw ► *reflex* *(precipitarse)* to hurl or throw oneself; *(entregarse)* to give oneself up.

desperdiciar ► *tr* to waste, squander; *(no aprovecharse de)* not to take advantage of, miss.

desperdicio ► *m* waste, squandering; *(residuo)* waste, remains.

desperezarse §02 ► *reflex* to stretch.

desperfecto ► *m* flaw, blemish; *(deterioro)* wear and tear.

despertador, a ► *adj* awakening, arousing ► *m* alarm clock; *(aviso)* warning.

despertar §33 ► *tr* to wake up ► *intr* to wake up, awaken; *(ser más listo)* to wise up ► *reflex* to wake up, awaken.

despiadado, a ► *adj* pitiless, merciless.

despido ► *m* dismissal, firing.

despierto, a ► *adj* awake; *(despabilado)* alert, wide-awake; *(listo)* clever.

despilfarrar ► *tr* to squander, waste ► *reflex* to squander a fortune.

despistado, a ► *adj & mf* absent-minded (person).

despistar ► *tr* to lead astray ► *reflex* to be disoriented, lose one's bearings.

desplazamiento ► *m* displacement.

desplazar §02 ► *tr* to displace; *(trasladar)* to move, shift.

desplegar §35 ► *tr* to unfold, spread out; *(aclarar)* to explain; *(mostrar)* to display, show ► *reflex* to unfold, spread out.

despliegue ► *m* display, show.

despojar ► *tr* to deprive, dispossess; *(quitar)* to strip; *(robar)* to rob ► *reflex (renunciar)* to give up, relinquish.

desposarse ► *reflex (persona)* to get engaged or married *(con* to); *(pareja)* to get engaged or to marry.

déspota ► *mf* despot, tyrant.

despreciar ► *tr* to disdain, scorn.

desprecio ► *m* disdain, scorn; *(desaire)* slight, snub.

desprender ► *tr* to unfasten, detach; *(soltar)* to loosen; *(emitir)* to emit, give off ► *reflex* to become detached; *(ser emitido)* to issue, emanate ■ d. de to give up, part with.

despreocupado, a ► *adj* unconcerned, nonchalant.

desprestigiar ► *tr* to ruin (someone's) reputation; *(desacreditar)* to discredit, disparage.

desprevenido, a ► *adj* unprepared, off guard.

después ► *adv (más tarde)* afterward, later; *(entonces)* next, then ■ d. de *(que)* after.

destacar §47 ► *tr* to emphasize, highlight; MIL. to detail, assign ► *intr & reflex* to stand out, be outstanding.

destapar ► *tr* to open, uncover; *(una botella)* to uncork, uncap.

destartalado, a ► *adj* ramshackle, dilapidated.

destello ► *m* flash (of light); *(centelleo)* sparkle, glitter ■ *pl* signs, indications.

desteñir ► *tr & intr* to fade, discolor.

destilar ► *tr* to distill.

destilería ► *f* distillery.

destinar ► *tr* to destine, intend; *(asignar)* to assign, appoint ► *reflex* to intend to go into.

destino ► *m* destiny, fate; *(destinación)* destination; *(empleo)* job, position.

destituir §10 ► *tr (revocar)* to dismiss; *(privar)* to deprive.

destornillador ► *m* screwdriver.

destreza ► *f* skill, dexterity.

destrozar §02 ► *tr* to smash, break into pieces; *(arruinar)* to destroy.

destrucción ► *f* destruction.

destruir §10 ► *tr* to destroy, ruin.

desuso ► *m* disuse, obsolescence.

desvalijar ► *tr* to rob, plunder.

desván ► *m* attic, garret.

desvanecer §09 ► *tr* to make vanish *or* disappear ► *reflex (desmayarse)* to become dizzy, faint.

desvarío ► *m* delirium, madness; *(disparate)* raving, nonsense; *(capricho)* whim.

desvelar ► *tr & reflex* to stay awake, go without sleep.

desventaja ► *f* disadvantage, drawback.

desventura ► *f* misfortune, bad luck.

desvergonzado, a ► *adj & mf* impudent, shameless (person).

desvestir §32 ► *tr & reflex* to undress.

desviar §18 ► *tr* to divert, deflect

► *reflex* to turn off; *(hacer un rodeo)* to take a detour; *(apartarse)* to deviate.

desvío ► *m* detour, diversion.

detallar ► *tr* to detail; *(especificar)* to specify, itemize.

detalle ► *m* detail; *(gesto)* gesture, kind thought.

detallista ► *adj* retail ► *mf* COM. retailer; *(considerado)* thoughtful person.

detectar ► *tr* to detect.

detective ► *mf* detective.

detector, a ► *m* detector ■ d. de metales metal detector ► *adj* detecting.

detener §46 ► *tr* to stop, halt; *(retrasar)* to delay, detain; *(arrestar)* to arrest ► *reflex* to stop; *(retardarse)* to linger.

detenido, a ► *adj (preso)* detained, in custody ► *mf* person under arrest.

detergente ► *adj & m* detergent.

deterioración ► *f* deterioration.

deteriorar ► *tr* to deteriorate; *(estropear)* to damage, spoil; *(desgastar)* to wear (out) ► *reflex (dañarse)* to damage, harm; *(desgastarse)* to wear out.

determinado, a ► *adj* determined, resolute; *(preciso)* specific, particular.

determinar ► *tr* to determine; *(convencer)* to convince, decide ► *reflex* to decide, make up one's mind.

detestar ► *tr* to detest, hate.

detrás ► *adv* behind ■ d. de behind, in back of • por d. behind one's back.

deuda ► *f* debt.

deudo, a ► *mf* relative.

deudor, a ► *adj* debit; *(que debe)* indebted ► *mf* debtor.

devaluación ► *f* devaluation.

devaluar §45 ► *tr* to devaluate.

devastar ► *tr* to devastate, destroy.

devoción ► *f* devotion; *(piedad)* piety.

devolución ► *f* return; *(restauración)* restoration; COM. refund.

devolver §54 ► *tr* to return, give back; *(restaurar)* to restore; COM. to refund ► *reflex* AMER. to return.

devorar ► *tr* to devour, eat up.

devoto, a ► *adj* devout, pious; *(aficionado)* devoted ► *mf* devout person; *(aficionado)* devotee, enthusiast.

día ➤ *m* day; *(no noche)* daytime, daylight ■ **al d.** per day, a day; *(al corriente)* up to date • **al otro d.** on the following day, the next day • **de d.** by day • **d. de fiesta** holiday • **hoy (en) d.** nowadays, these days ■ *pl* **¡buenos d.!** good morning • **ocho d.** a week • **quince d.** two weeks, fortnight • **todos los d.** every day, daily.

diabético, a ➤ *adj & mf* diabetic.

diablo ➤ *m* devil, demon.

diafragma ➤ *m* diaphragm.

diagnosis ➤ *f* diagnosis.

diagonal ➤ *adj & f* diagonal.

diálogo ➤ *m* dialogue.

diamante ➤ *m* diamond.

diámetro ➤ *m* diameter.

diapositiva ➤ *f* slide, transparency.

diariamente ➤ *adv* daily, every day.

diario, a ➤ *adj* daily ➤ *m* daily (paper); *(relación)* diary, journal ➤ *adv* daily ■ **a d.** daily, every day • **de d.** *(diariamente)* daily, every day; *(ordinario)* everyday.

diarrea ➤ *f* diarrhea.

dibujante ➤ *adj* drawing, sketching ➤ *mf* drawer, sketcher; *(de dibujos animados)* cartoonist; TECH. draftsman.

dibujar ➤ *tr* to draw; *(describir)* to describe, depict.

dibujo ➤ *m* drawing, sketch ■ *pl* **d. animados** cartoons.

dicción ➤ *f* diction.

diccionario ➤ *m* dictionary.

dicha ➤ *f* happiness; *(suerte)* good fortune ■ **a o por d.** fortunately, happily.

dicho, a ➤ *adj* said, aforementioned ■ **d. y hecho** no sooner said than done • **mejor d.** rather, more accurately ➤ *m* *(refrán)* saying, proverb ■ *pl* marriage vows.

dichoso, a ➤ *adj* *(feliz)* happy, contented; *(afortunado)* lucky, fortunate.

diciembre ➤ *m* December.

dictador, a ➤ *mf* dictator.

dictar ➤ *tr* to dictate; *(sentencia)* to pronounce; AMER. *(una clase)* to give, teach.

didáctico, a ➤ *adj* didactic.

diecinueve ➤ *adj & m* nineteen.

dieciocho ➤ *adj & m* eighteen.

dieciséis ➤ *adj & m* sixteen.

diecisiete ➤ *adj & m* seventeen.

diente ➤ *m* tooth; ZOOL. fang; *(de un tenedor)* prong; BOT. clove ■ **d. de león** dandelion.

diestro, a ➤ *adj* deft, dexterous; *(derecho)* right ➤ *f* right hand.

dieta ➤ *f* diet.

dietético, a ➤ *adj* dietetic, dietary ➤ *mf* dietician.

diez ➤ *adj & m* ten ■ **las d.** ten o'clock.

diferencia ➤ *f* difference ■ **a d. de** unlike.

diferenciar ➤ *tr* to differentiate, distinguish ➤ *intr* to differ.

diferente ➤ *adj* different ■ **diferentes** various, several ➤ *adv* differently.

difícil ➤ *adj* difficult.

dificultad ➤ *f* difficulty, obstacle.

difundir ➤ *tr* to diffuse; *(derramar)* to spread, scatter ➤ *reflex* to spread out.

difunto, a ➤ *adj* deceased, dead ➤ *mf* dead person; *(cadáver)* corpse.

difusión ➤ *f* diffusion; *(radio)* broadcasting.

difuso, a ➤ *adj* diffuse; *(ancho)* wide, extended; *(vago)* vague, hazy.

digerir ➤ *tr* to digest.

digestión ➤ *f* digestion.

digital ➤ *adj* digital.

dígito ➤ *m* digit.

dignidad ➤ *f* dignity; *(rango)* rank.

digno, a ➤ *adj* worthy; *(apropiado)* proper, fitting; *(mesurado)* dignified.

dilatar ➤ *tr* to dilate, expand; *(retrasar)* to delay; *(propagar)* to spread ➤ *reflex* to dilate, expand.

dilema ➤ *m* dilemma.

diligencia ➤ *f* diligence; *(prisa)* speed, briskness; *(recado)* errand, task; LAW proceeding.

diluir §10 ➤ *tr* to dilute; *(disolver)* to dissolve.

diluviar ➤ *intr* to pour down, rain hard.

dimensión ➤ *f* dimension.

diminutivo, a ➤ *adj & m* diminutive.

diminuto, a ➤ *adj* diminutive, little.

dimisión ➤ *f* resignation (from office).

dinámico, a ➤ *adj* dynamic ➤ *f* dynamics.

dinamita ➤ *f* dynamite.

dinamo *or* **dínamo** ➤ *f* dynamo.

dinero ➤ *m* money; *(caudal)* wealth, fortune.

dinosaurio ➤ *m* dinosaur.

dios ➤ *m* god ∎ **D.** God • ¡D. mío! my God!, oh my! • por D. for God's sake.

diploma ➤ *m* diploma, certificate.

diplomacia ➤ *f* diplomacy.

diplomado, a ➤ *adj* having a diploma ➤ *mf* graduate.

diplomático, a ➤ *adj* diplomatic ➤ *mf* diplomat ➤ *f* diplomacy.

diptongo ➤ *m* diphthong.

dique ➤ *m* dike, sea wall; *(restricción)* check, restriction.

dirección ➤ *f* direction; *(junta)* board of directors; *(cargo)* directorship; *(señas)* address; AUTO., TECH. steering ∎ d. general headquarters.

directo, a ➤ *adj* direct; *(derecho)* straight ➤ *f* AUTO. high gear.

director, a ➤ *adj* directing ➤ *mf* director; *(de escuela)* principal; MUS. conductor.

dirigir §19 ➤ *tr* to direct; *(administrar)* to manage; *(una carta)* to address; *(guiar)* to guide; AUTO. to drive, steer; MUS. to conduct ➤ *reflex* to go, make one's way; *(hablar)* to address, speak.

discapacitado, a ➤ *adj & mf* disabled, handicapped (person).

disciplina ➤ *f* discipline; *(doctrina)* doctrine.

discípulo, a ➤ *mf* disciple; *(alumno)* student.

disco ➤ *m* disk, disc; *(para escuchar)* record; *(para el tránsito)* traffic signal; SPORT. discus; COMPUT. diskette ∎ d. compacto compact disk • d. rígido *or* duro COMPUT. hard disk.

discoteca ➤ *f* discotheque.

discreción ➤ *f* discretion, tact.

discrepancia ➤ *f* discrepancy.

discreto, a ➤ *adj* discreet; *(ingenioso)* witty, clever; MATH., PHYS. discrete.

disculpa ➤ *f* *(por una ofensa)* apology; *(excusa)* excuse.

disculpar ➤ *tr* to excuse, pardon ➤ *reflex* to apologize *(con* to; *de, por* for).

discurrir ➤ *intr* to roam; *(reflexionar)* to reflect; *(hablar)* to discourse; *(fluir)* to flow, run.

discurso ➤ *m* speech, discourse; *(facultad)* reasoning; *(transcurso)* passage, course.

discusión ➤ *f* discussion; *(disputa)* dispute, argument.

discutir ➤ *tr* to discuss, debate ➤ *intr* *(debatir)* to discuss, talk about; *(disputar)* to argue.

diseñar ➤ *tr* to design; *(dibujar)* to draw, sketch.

diseño ➤ *m* design; *(dibujo)* drawing, sketch.

disfraz ➤ *m* disguise; *(máscara)* mask.

disfrazar §02 ➤ *tr & reflex* to disguise (oneself).

disfrutar ➤ *tr* *(gozar)* to enjoy; *(aprovechar)* to make the most of ➤ *intr* to enjoy oneself ∎ d. de to enjoy.

disgustado, a ➤ *adj* annoyed, displeased.

disgustar ➤ *tr* to annoy, displease ➤ *reflex (desagradarse)* to be annoyed *or* displeased; *(desazonarse)* to fall out.

disgusto ➤ *m* *(desagrado)* annoyance, displeasure; *(contienda)* quarrel, disagreement.

disimular ➤ *tr* to conceal, hide; *(fingir)* to feign, pretend.

disipar ➤ *tr* to dissipate; *(derrochar)* to squander, waste; *(una duda)* to dispel ➤ *reflex (desaparecer)* to disappear, vanish; *(dispersarse)* to scatter.

dislocar §47 ➤ *tr & reflex* to dislocate.

disminuir §10 ➤ *tr, intr & reflex* to diminish.

disolver §54 ➤ *tr & reflex* to dissolve.

disparar ➤ *tr* to fire, shoot; *(echar)* to throw, hurl ➤ *intr* to fire, shoot; *(disparatar)* to act foolishly ➤ *reflex (una arma)* to go off, fire.

disparate ➤ *m* absurd *or* nonsensical thing ∎ *pl* nonsense.

dispensar ➤ *tr* to dispense, give out; *(eximir)* to exempt; *(perdonar)* to forgive, excuse.

dispensario ➤ *m* dispensary, clinic.

dispersar ➤ *tr & reflex* to disperse, scatter; *(dividir)* to divide.

disponer §37 ➤ *tr* to arrange, place; *(preparar)* to prepare ➤ *intr* ∎ **d. de** *(poseer)* to have at one's disposal; *(utilizar)* to make use of; *(deshacerse de)* to dispose of ➤ *reflex* to prepare, get ready.

disponible ➤ *adj* available, on hand.

disposición ➤ *f* disposition; *(posesión)* disposal; LAW *(precepto)* provision; *(orden)* decree, order ∎ **estar en d.** to be ready to • **última d.** last will and testament ∎ *pl* measures.

dispositivo ➤ *m* device, mechanism.

disputa ➤ *f* dispute.

disquete ➤ *m* diskette, floppy disk.

distancia ➤ *f* distance; *(diferencia)* difference ∎ **a (la) d.** at or from a distance • **a larga d.** long-distance.

distante ➤ *adj* distant.

distinguido, a ➤ *adj* distinguished.

distinguir §15 ➤ *tr* to distinguish; *(preferir)* to favor; *(honrar)* to pay tribute to, honor ➤ *intr* to distinguish, discriminate ➤ *reflex (ser distinto)* to be distinguished, differ; *(sobresalir)* to distinguish oneself, excel.

distinto, a ➤ *adj (diferente)* distinct, different; *(claro)* distinct.

distracción ➤ *f* distraction; *(error)* slip, oversight.

distraer §49 ➤ *tr* to distract; *(entretener)* to amuse, entertain ➤ *intr* to be entertaining ➤ *reflex (entretenerse)* to amuse oneself; *(descuidarse)* to be distracted.

distraído, a ➤ *adj (divertido)* entertaining; *(desatento)* absent-minded.

distribuidor, a ➤ *adj* distributing, distributive ➤ *mf* distributor.

distribuir §10 ➤ *tr* to distribute.

distrito ➤ *m* district, zone.

disturbar *tr* to disturb.

disturbio ➤ *m* disturbance, trouble.

disuadir *tr* to dissuade, discourage.

diván ➤ *m* divan, couch.

diverso, a ➤ *adj* diverse ∎ *pl* several, various.

divertido, a ➤ *adj* amusing, entertaining.

divertir §43 ➤ *tr* to amuse, entertain;

(distraer) to divert, distract ➤ *reflex* to amuse oneself, have a good time; *(distraerse)* to be distracted.

dividendo ➤ *m* dividend.

dividir ➤ *tr* to divide ➤ *reflex* to divide; *(separarse)* to separate.

divisa ➤ *f* emblem, insignia; COM. currency.

divisar ➤ *tr* to discern, make out.

división ➤ *f* division.

divisor, a ➤ *adj* dividing ➤ *m* divider; MATH. divisor, denominator.

divorciado, a ➤ *adj* divorced ➤ *m* divorcé ➤ *f* divorcée.

divorciar ➤ *tr* to divorce; *(separar)* to separate, divide ➤ *reflex* to divorce, get divorced.

divorcio ➤ *m* divorce; *(separación)* separation, division.

divulgar §31 ➤ *tr* to divulge, disclose; *(popularizar)* to popularize ➤ *reflex* to be divulged.

dobladillo ➤ *m* hem.

dobladura ➤ *f* fold, crease.

doblar ➤ *tr* to double; *(encorvar)* to bend; CINEM. to dub ∎ **d. la esquina** to turn the corner.

doble ➤ *adj* double; *(grueso)* thick, heavy; *(disimulado)* two-faced ➤ *m* double; *(pliegue)* fold, crease; *(copia)* copy ∎ **al d.** doubly ➤ *mf (actor)* double, stand-in ➤ *adv* doubly.

doce ➤ *adj & m* twelve ∎ **las d.** twelve o'clock.

docena ➤ *f* dozen.

docente ➤ *adj* teaching, educational.

dócil ➤ *adj* docile; *(dúctil)* ductile.

doctor, a ➤ *mf* doctor; *(maestro)* teacher, professor.

doctorado ➤ *m* doctorate.

documentación ➤ *f* documentation.

documental ➤ *adj & m* documentary.

documento ➤ *m* document; *(prueba)* proof, evidence ∎ **d. justificativo** voucher, certificate.

dólar ➤ *m* dollar.

doler §54 ➤ *intr* to hurt ➤ *reflex* to repent; *(sentir)* to regret; *(compadecerse)* to sympathize, be sorry.

dolor ➤ *m* pain, ache; *(congoja)* sorrow, distress; *(arrepentimiento)* regret.

domar ➤ *tr* to tame, domesticate; *(vencer)* to subdue, master.

doméstico, a ➤ *adj* domestic ➤ *mf* domestic, household servant.

domicilio ➤ *m* domicile, residence ■ d. social head office, corporate headquarters.

dominar ➤ *tr* to dominate; *(someter)* to subdue, control; *(saber a fondo)* to know well, master ➤ *intr* to dominate, stand out ➤ *reflex* to control or restrain oneself.

domingo ➤ *m* Sunday.

dominicano, a ➤ *adj & mf* Dominican.

dominio ➤ *m* dominion, domain; *(superioridad)* dominance; *(maestría)* mastery, command.

dominó ➤ *m* dominoes.

don¹ ➤ *m (regalo)* gift, present; *(gracia)* gift, talent, knack.

don² ➤ *m* Don (title of respect used before a man's first name).

donar ➤ *tr* to donate, give.

donativo ➤ *m* donation, gift.

donde ➤ *adv* where ■ d. no otherwise • en d. in which • por d. whereby ➤ *prep* S. AMER. to or at the house of.

dónde ➤ *adv* when ■ ¿a d.? where? • ¿de d.? from where? • ¿por d.? why?

dondequiera ➤ *adv* anywhere ■ d. que wherever • por d. everywhere, all over the place.

doña ➤ *f* Mrs., Madame (title of respect used before a woman's first name).

dorado, a ➤ *adj* golden; *(cubierto de oro)* gilt, gilded ➤ *m* gilding.

dormilón, ona ➤ *adj* sleepy ➤ *mf* sleepyhead ➤ *f* easy chair.

dormir §16 ➤ *intr* to sleep ➤ *reflex* to fall asleep ➤ *tr* to put to sleep ■ d. la siesta to take a nap.

dormitorio ➤ *m* bedroom; *(residencia)* dormitory.

dorso ➤ *m* back.

dos ➤ *adj & m* two ■ las d. two o'clock • los or las d. both.

doscientos, as ➤ *adj & m* two hundred.

dosis ➤ *f* dose; FIG. portion, quantity.

dragón ➤ *m* dragon; BOT. snapdragon; MIL. dragoon.

drama ➤ *m* drama.

dramático, a ➤ *adj* dramatic ➤ *mf* dramatist, playwright; *(actor)* actor ➤ *f* actress; *(arte dramático)* drama.

drástico, a ➤ *adj* drastic.

droga ➤ *f* drug.

drogadicto, a ➤ *mf* drug addict.

drogar §31 ➤ *tr* to drug, dope.

droguería ➤ *f* drugstore, pharmacy; *(comercio)* drug trade.

ducha ➤ *f (baño)* shower; MED. douche.

duda ➤ *f* doubt, uncertainty ■ no cabe or no hay d. (there is) no doubt • poner en d. to question, doubt.

dudar ➤ *tr & intr* to doubt.

dueña ➤ *f* owner; *(ama)* landlady.

dueño ➤ *m* owner; *(amo)* landlord.

dulce ➤ *adj* sweet; *(dúctil)* soft, ductile; *(agua)* fresh ➤ *m* candy, sweet.

duna ➤ *f* dune.

duodécimo, a ➤ *adj & m* twelfth.

duplicar §47 ➤ *tr* to duplicate, copy; *(doblar)* to double.

duración ➤ *f* duration.

durante ➤ *prep* during.

durar ➤ *intr* to last, endure; *(quedar)* to remain.

durazno ➤ *m* peach.

dureza ➤ *f* hardness; *(dificultad)* difficulty; *(severidad)* severity, *(obstinación)* obstinacy, stubbornness.

duro, a ➤ *adj* hard; *(fuerte)* tough, strong; *(resistente)* resistant, resilient; *(obstinado)* stubborn, obstinate; *(áspero)* harsh ➤ *adv* hard.

E

e ➤ *conj* and (before *i-* and *hi-*).

ebanista ➤ *mf* cabinetmaker, woodworker.

ébano ➤ *m* ebony.

echar ➤ *tr* to throw, cast, toss; *(expulsar)* to expel; *(empleado)* to fire; *(desechar)* to throw out or away; *(emitir)* to emit, give off; *(verter)* to pour; *(añadir)* to add, put in; BOT. to sprout; *(aplicar)* to apply; *(imponer)* to impose, give; LAW to condemn, sentence; *(llave)* to turn; *(cerrojo)* to shoot; *(publicar)* to publish; *(drama)* to put on, present; *(discurso)* to give,

deliver; *(presentar)* to bring, present ■
e. a perder to spoil, ruin • e. de menos
a to miss ➤ *intr* to grow, sprout ■
e. por *(una carrera)* to choose, go into;
(ir) to go ➤ *reflex* to throw oneself;
(tenderse) to lie down, stretch out ■
e. a to begin, start.

echarpe ➤ *m* stole, shawl.

eclesiástico, a ➤ *adj & m* ecclesiastic.

eclipse ➤ *m* eclipse.

eco ➤ *m* echo ■ tener e. to catch on, be
popular.

ecología ➤ *f* ecology.

economía ➤ *f* economy; *(ciencia)* economics; *(parsimonia)* thrift, frugality.

económico, a ➤ *adj* economic(al).

economista ➤ *mf* economist.

economizar §02 ➤ *tr* to economize on.

ecosistema ➤ *m* ecosystem.

ecuación ➤ *f* equation.

ecuador ➤ *m* equator.

ecuánime ➤ *adj* even-tempered, level-
headed.

ecuatorial ➤ *adj* equatorial.

ecuatoriano, a ➤ *adj & mf* Ecuadorian.

ecuestre ➤ *adj* equestrian.

edad ➤ *f* age; *(período)* time; *(época)*
era, epoch ■ E. Media Middle Ages •
mayor de e. of age • menor de e.
underage • ¿qué e. tienes? how old are
you?

edición ➤ *f* publication; *(conjunto de
libros o periódicos)* edition; *(conjunto
de revistas)* issue.

edicto ➤ *m* edict, proclamation.

edificio ➤ *m* building, edifice; FIG.
structure, fabric.

editar ➤ *tr* to publish.

editor, a ➤ *adj* publishing ➤ *mf* publisher; *(redactor)* editor.

editorial ➤ *adj* publishing ➤ *m* editorial ➤ *f* publishing house.

educación ➤ *f* education, training.

educado, a ➤ *adj* educated, trained;
(cortés) well-mannered, polite.

educar §47 ➤ *tr* to educate, teach;
(criar) to raise, bring up; *(desarrollar)*
to develop, train.

efectivamente ➤ *adv* really, in fact; *(por
supuesto)* indeed, certainly.

efectivo, a ➤ *adj* effective; *(verdadero)*

real, actual; *(permanente)* permanent
➤ *m* (hard) cash ■ en e. in cash.

efecto ➤ *m* effect, result; *(fin)* end, purpose; *(impresión)* impression, impact;
(rotación) spin ■ en e. *(efectivamente)*
in effect, in fact; *(en conclusión)*
indeed, precisely • efectos de resultado *or* de residuo* COMPUT. output • e.
útil MECH. output • tener e. *(efec-
tuarse)* to take effect; *(ocurrir)* to take
place ■ *pl* effects, property; *(mercancía)* goods, merchandise; FIN. assets,
securities.

efectuar §45 ➤ *tr* to effect, bring about
➤ *reflex* to take effect.

eficacia ➤ *f* efficacy, effectiveness.

eficaz ➤ *adj* efficacious, effective.

eficiente ➤ *adj* efficient, effective.

efusivo, a ➤ *adj* effusive.

egoísta ➤ *adj & mf* egoistic (person).

egresar ➤ *intr* AMER. to graduate.

eje ➤ *m* axis; FIG. crux, main point;
MECH., TECH. shaft, axle.

ejecutar ➤ *tr* to execute; COMPUT. *(un
programa)* to run.

ejecutivo, a ➤ *adj & mf* executive.

ejemplar ➤ *adj* exemplary ➤ *m* example; PRINT. copy; *(número)* number,
issue; SCI. specimen.

ejemplo ➤ *m* example ■ por e. for
example, for instance.

ejercer §51 ➤ *tr* to exercise; *(una profesión)* to practice.

ejercicio ➤ *m* exercise; *(desempeño)*
practice; *(prueba)* examination ■ e.
económico fiscal year.

ejercitar ➤ *tr* *(una profesión)* to practice; *(adiestrar)* to train, drill ➤ *reflex*
to train, drill.

ejército ➤ *m* MIL. army; FIG. army, flock.

el ➤ *def art* the ➤ *pron* the one ■ el que
the one that; *(él)* he who.

él ➤ *pron* he, him, it ■ de él his • él
mismo he himself • para él for him ■
pl ellos they, them • de ellos theirs •
ellos mismos they themselves.

elaborar ➤ *tr* *(fabricar)* to manufacture; *(crear)* to make, create; *(preparar)* to prepare, work out.

elasticidad ➤ *f* elasticity.

elástico, a ➤ *adj* elastic; *(flexible)* flexible ➤ *m* elastic, rubber band ■ *pl* suspenders.

elección ➤ *f* election; *(selección)* selection, choice.

electorado ➤ *m* electorate.

electricidad ➤ *f* electricity.

electricista ➤ *adj* electrical ➤ *mf* electrician.

eléctrico, a ➤ *adj* electric(al); FIG. lightning-fast.

electrocutar ➤ *tr* to electrocute.

electrónico, a ➤ *adj* electronic ➤ *f* electronics.

elefante, a ➤ *mf* elephant.

elegancia ➤ *f* elegance, polish.

elegante ➤ *adj* elegant, stylish.

elegir ➤ *tr* to choose, select; POL. to elect.

elemental ➤ *adj* elemental; *(obvio)* elementary, obvious; *(fundamental)* fundamental, essential.

elemento ➤ *m* element; *(miembro)* member; ELEC. cell ■ *pl* rudiments, basic principles; *(recursos)* resources, means; *(lluvia, etc.)* elements.

elevación ➤ *f* elevation; *(construcción)* erection, building; FIG. promotion; *(enajenamiento)* rapture, ecstasy; MATH. raising.

elevado, a ➤ *adj* tall, high; *(sublime)* elevated, lofty.

elevador ➤ *m* AMER. elevator.

elevar ➤ *tr* to elevate; *(ennoblecer)* to ennoble ➤ *para e.* for her ■ *pl* MATH. to raise.

eliminar ➤ *tr* to eliminate.

ella ➤ *pron* she, her, it ■ de e. hers • e. misma she herself • para e. for her ■ *pl* ellas they, them • de ellas theirs • ellas mismas they themselves.

ello ➤ *pron* it.

ellos, ellas ➤ *pron* they, them.

elocuente ➤ *adj* eloquent.

elogiar ➤ *tr* to eulogize, praise.

eludir ➤ *tr* to elude, avoid.

embajada ➤ *f* embassy; *(cargo)* ambassadorship.

embajador, a ➤ *mf* ambassador.

embalaje ➤ *m* packing, crating; *(materia)* packing material.

embalar ➤ *tr* to pack, crate; *(motor)* to rev ➤ *intr* to race, sprint.

embalse ➤ *m* dam.

embarazada ➤ *adj* pregnant ➤ *f* pregnant woman.

embarazo ➤ *m* *(preñez)* pregnancy; *(dificultad)* difficulty.

embarazoso, a ➤ *adj* troublesome.

embarcación ➤ *f* boat, vessel; *(embarco)* embarkation; *(viaje)* voyage.

embarcadero ➤ *m* pier; *(muelle)* wharf, dock; AMER. loading platform.

embarcar §47 ➤ *tr* to embark; *(poner a bordo)* to load, ship aboard ➤ *reflex* to embark; *(enredarse)* to get involved in, engage in.

embarque ➤ *m* loading, shipment.

embestir §32 ➤ *tr & intr* to attack.

emblema ➤ *m* emblem, symbol.

émbolo ➤ *m* piston.

embolsar ➤ *tr* to pocket, collect.

emborrachar ➤ *tr* to intoxicate; *(adormecer)* to make drowsy ➤ *reflex* to get drunk.

emboscada ➤ *f* ambush.

embotellamiento ➤ *m* bottling; *(de la circulación)* traffic jam, bottleneck.

embotellar ➤ *tr* to bottle; *(obstruir)* to jam, block.

embrague ➤ *m* AUTO. clutch.

embriagar §31 ➤ *tr* to intoxicate ➤ *reflex* to get drunk.

embrollar ➤ *tr* to confuse, embroil.

embrollo ➤ *m* confusion, tangle; *(embuste)* trick, fraud.

embrujo ➤ *m* spell, charm.

embudo ➤ *m* funnel; *(trampa)* trick, fraud.

embuste ➤ *m* hoax, fraud; *(mentira)* lie.

embustero, a ➤ *adj* lying, deceitful ➤ *mf* liar, cheat.

embutido ➤ *m* ARTS inlay, marquetry; CUL. sausage.

emergencia ➤ *f* *(surgimiento)* emergence; *(accidente)* emergency.

emigrante ➤ *adj* emigrating, migrating ➤ *mf* emigrant, émigré.

emigrar ➤ *intr* to emigrate; ZOOL. to migrate.

emisión ➤ *f* emission; TELEC. transmission, broadcast; COM. issuance, issue.

emisor, a ➤ *adj* TELEC. broadcasting;

COM. issuing ➤ *mf* issuer ➤ *m* TELEC. *(aparato)* transmitter ➤ *f (estación)* broadcasting station.

emitir ➤ *tr* to emit; *(poner en circulación)* to issue; *(expresar)* to utter ➤ *intr* to broadcast, transmit.

emoción ➤ *f* emotion, feeling.

emocionante ➤ *adj* moving, thrilling.

emocionar ➤ *tr* to move, affect ➤ *reflex* to be moved *or* affected.

empacar §47 ➤ *tr & intr* to pack.

empacho ➤ *m* indigestion.

empalmar ➤ *tr (unir)* to connect, join ➤ *intr & reflex* to meet, join.

empalme ➤ *m* join, joint; RAIL., AUTO. junction; PHOTOG. splice.

empanada ➤ *f* CUL. turnover.

empañar ➤ *tr (con pañales)* to diaper, swaddle; *(obscurecer)* to blur, mist.

empapar ➤ *tr* to soak; *(absorber)* to absorb, soak up ➤ *reflex* to get soaked.

empapelar ➤ *tr* to wrap in paper; *(forrar)* to paper, wallpaper.

empaquetar ➤ *tr* to pack, wrap.

empaste ➤ *m (de diente)* filling; *(de libros)* bookbinding.

empatar ➤ *tr* to tie; equal; *(estorbar)* to impede, hold up ➤ *intr* to tie, be equal ➤ *reflex* to result in a tie *or* draw.

empate ➤ *m* tie, draw; AMER. *(estorbo)* obstacle; *(unión)* joint, connection.

empedrado, a ➤ *adj* dappled, spotted ➤ *m* cobblestones.

empeine ➤ *m (del vientre)* groin; *(del pie)* instep; MED. impetigo.

empeñar ➤ *tr* to pawn ➤ *reflex (entramparse)* to go into debt; *(insistir)* to insist, persist ■ e. en to be bent on *or* determined to.

empeño ➤ *m* pawn, pledge; *(constancia)* insistence, tenacity.

empeorar ➤ *tr* to make worse ➤ *intr & reflex* to worsen, deteriorate.

emperador ➤ *m* emperor.

emperatriz ➤ *f* empress.

empezar §17 ➤ *tr & intr* to begin *(a* to, *por* by) ■ al e. at the beginning *or* start • para e. to begin with, first.

empleado, a ➤ *mf* employee.

emplear ➤ *tr* to employ; *(invertir)* to invest ➤ *reflex* to get a job, become employed.

empleo ➤ *m* job, occupation; *(uso)* use.

emplomar ➤ *tr (diente)* to fill.

empobrecer §09 ➤ *tr* to impoverish ➤ *intr & reflex* to become poor *or* impoverished.

empobrecimiento ➤ *m* impoverishment.

emporio ➤ *m* emporium, market; *(lugar famoso)* capital, center; AMER. department store.

emprendedor, a ➤ *adj* enterprising.

emprender ➤ *tr* to begin, set about ■ emprenderla con to quarrel with.

empresa ➤ *f* enterprise; *(sociedad)* company, firm; *(dirección)* management.

empresarial ➤ *adj* managerial, management.

empresario, a ➤ *mf* manager, director.

empujar ➤ *tr* to push.

empujón ➤ *m* push, shove.

emulsión ➤ *f* emulsion.

en ➤ *prep* in, into ■ en aquel momento at that time • en avión by plane • en la mesa on the table • estar en casa to be at home.

enaguas ➤ *fpl* petticoat, underskirt.

enamorado, a ➤ *adj* enamored, in love *(de* with, of) ➤ *mf* lover.

enamorarse ➤ *reflex* to fall in love *(de* with); *(aficionarse)* to become enamored *(de* of).

enano, a ➤ *adj* small, minute ➤ *mf* dwarf.

enarbolar ➤ *tr* to raise, hoist.

encabezamiento ➤ *m* caption, headline; *(de una carta)* heading; *(registro)* census list.

encabezar §02 ➤ *tr* to head.

encajar ➤ *tr* to fit, insert; *(forzar)* to force ➤ *intr* to fit (well) ➤ *reflex* to squeeze in.

encaje ➤ *m* lace; *(inserción)* insertion, fit.

encallar ➤ *intr* MARIT. to run aground.

encaminar ➤ *tr* to guide, guide ➤ *reflex* to make for, set out for.

encantado, a ➤ *adj* delighted, charmed; *(casa)* haunted.

encantador, a ➤ *adj* enchanting, charming ➤ *mf* charmer ➤ *m* sorcerer ➤ *f* sorceress.

encantar ➤ *tr* to enchant; charm; *(hechizar)* to bewitch, cast a spell on.

encanto, ➤ *m* enchantment, bewitchment; *(magia)* magic ∎ *pl* charms.

encapricharse ➤ *reflex* to take it into one's head, take a fancy *(por, con* to).

encaramar ➤ *tr (levantar)* to lift, raise ➤ *reflex* to climb up; AMER. to blush.

encarar ➤ *intr, tr & reflex* to face, confront.

encarcelar ➤ *tr* to incarcerate, imprison; CARP. to clamp.

encargado, a ➤ *adj* in charge ➤ *mf* person in charge.

encargar §31 ➤ *tr* to put in charge; *(pedir)* to advise; *(ordenar)* to order ➤ *reflex* to take charge.

encargo ➤ *m* errand, task; *(trabajo)* assignment, job; *(empleo)* post.

encariñarse ➤ *reflex* to become fond *(con* of).

encarnado, a ➤ *adj & m* red.

encarnar ➤ *tr* to personify, embody.

encauzar §02 ➤ *tr* to channel, direct.

encender §34 ➤ *tr* to light; *(incendiar)* to set on fire; *(luz)* to turn on ➤ *reflex* to catch on fire.

encendido, a ➤ *adj* lit, switched on; *(hecho ascua)* red, red-hot ➤ *m* AUTO. ignition.

encerado, a ➤ *adj (pulido)* waxed, polished ➤ *m (pizarra)* blackboard.

encerrar §33 ➤ *tr* to enclose, confine; *(incluir)* to hold, contain; *(implicar)* to involve, entail ➤ *reflex* to go into seclusion.

enchufar ➤ *tr* ELEC. to connect, plug in; *(acoplar tubos)* to fit together, couple.

enchufe ➤ *m* ELEC., TECH. connection; *(hembra)* socket; *(macho)* plug.

encía ➤ *f* ANAT. gum, gingiva.

enciclopedia ➤ *f* encyclop(a)edia.

encima ➤ *adv (sobre)* on top; *(además)* in addition, besides ∎ **e.** de above • por **e.** superficially • por **e.** de in spite of.

encinta ➤ *adj* pregnant.

encintar ➤ *tr* to adorn with ribbon.

enclenque ➤ *adj & mf* weak, sickly (person).

encoger §20 ➤ *tr* to contract, draw in; *(reducir)* to shrink ➤ *intr & reflex* to contract; *(reducirse)* to shrink ∎ **e.** de hombros to shrug one's shoulders.

encolar ➤ *tr* to glue, stick.

encolerizar §02 ➤ *tr* to anger, enrage ➤ *reflex* to become angry or enraged.

encono ➤ *m* rancor, ill will.

encontrar §11 ➤ *tr* to find; *(topar)* to meet, encounter ➤ *intr & reflex* to meet; *(estar)* to be, be located; *(sentirse)* to find oneself ∎ **e.** con to meet, run into.

encrucijada ➤ *f* crossroads, intersection.

encuadernar ➤ *tr* to bind.

encubrir §55 ➤ *tr* to hide, conceal.

encuentro ➤ *m* meeting, encounter; SPORT. match, game.

encuesta ➤ *f* investigation, inquiry; *(sondeo)* survey, poll.

endeble ➤ *adj* weak, flimsy.

endémico, a ➤ *adj* endemic.

enderezar §02 ➤ *tr* to straighten; *(poner vertical)* to set or stand up straight; *(enmendar)* to correct, rectify.

endeudarse ➤ *reflex* to fall into debt; FIG. to become indebted.

endiablado, a ➤ *adj* diabolical; *(feísimo)* hideous, repulsive.

endibia ➤ *f* endive.

endosar ➤ *tr (un cheque)* to endorse; *(encajar)* to palm off.

endovenoso, a ➤ *adj* intravenous.

endulzar §02 ➤ *tr* to sweeten; *(suavizar)* to soften, ease.

endurecer §09 ➤ *tr & reflex* to harden; *(robustecer)* to toughen (up).

enemigo, a ➤ *mf* enemy, adversary ➤ *f* enmity.

enemistar ➤ *tr* to antagonize ➤ *reflex* to become enemies.

energía ➤ *f* energy; *(vigor)* vitality, vigor; *(eficacia)* efficacy, effectiveness; *(ánimo)* spirit.

enérgico, a ➤ *adj* energetic.

enero ➤ *m* January.

enfadar ➤ *tr* to anger, annoy ➤ *reflex* to

get angry or annoyed.

enfado ➤ *m* annoyance, anger.

énfasis ➤ *m* emphasis.

enfermar ➤ *intr* to get sick, become sick ➤ *tr* to make ill; *(debilitar)* to weaken.

enfermedad ➤ *f* illness, sickness.

enfermería ➤ *f* infirmary.

enfermero, a ➤ *mf* nurse.

enfermizo, a ➤ *adj* sickly, unhealthy.

enfermo, a ➤ *adj & mf* sick (person).

enfocar §47 ➤ *tr* to focus.

enfrentar ➤ *tr* to bring or put face to face ➤ *intr* to face ➤ *reflex* to confront, face.

enfrente ➤ *adv* facing, opposite; *(delante)* in front.

enfriar §18 ➤ *tr & intr* to cool ➤ *reflex* to be cold; MED. to catch a cold.

enfurecer §09 ➤ *tr* to madden, infuriate ➤ *reflex* to become furious, lose one's temper.

enganchar ➤ *tr* to hook; *(colgar)* to hang (up); FIG. to persuade; MIL. to recruit ➤ *reflex* to get caught up; MIL. to enlist.

engañar ➤ *tr* to deceive, trick ➤ *intr* to be deceptive or misleading ➤ *reflex* to deceive oneself; *(equivocarse)* to be wrong.

engaño ➤ *m (equivocación)* error, mistake; *(trampa)* deception, trick.

engañoso, a ➤ *adj* deceptive, tricky; *(deshonesto)* dishonest, deceitful; *(mentiroso)* misleading, wrong.

engastar ➤ *tr* JEWEL. to set, mount.

engendrar ➤ *tr* to engender.

englobar ➤ *tr* to include, comprise.

engordar ➤ *tr* to fatten ➤ *intr* to get fat.

engorro ➤ *m* obstacle, impediment.

engranaje ➤ *m* MECH. gear; *(acción)* meshing; COLL. connection, link.

engrasar ➤ *tr* to grease; *(aceitar)* to oil.

engreído, a ➤ *adj* conceited, arrogant; AMER. spoiled.

engrudo ➤ *m* paste.

engullir ➤ *tr* to gulp down, gobble.

enhorabuena ➤ *f* congratulations.

enigma ➤ *m* enigma, riddle.

enjabonar ➤ *tr* to soap, wash with soap; *(adular)* to flatter; *(reprender)* to scold.

enjambre ➤ *m* swarm.

enjaular ➤ *tr* to cage, put in a cage.

enjuagar §31 ➤ *tr & reflex* to rinse.

enjugar §31 ➤ *tr* to dry ➤ *reflex* to wipe, dry ■ **e. las lágrimas** to dry one's tears.

enjuiciar ➤ *tr (juzgar)* to judge; *(sujetar a juicio)* to indict, prosecute.

enlace ➤ *m* connection, link; *(casamiento)* marriage, matrimony; COMPUT. hyperlink, link.

enlazar §02 ➤ *tr* to lace, interlace; *(trabar)* to link, connect ➤ *intr* RAIL. to connect.

enloquecer §09 ➤ *tr* to drive mad or insane; *(excitar)* to excite, drive crazy ➤ *intr & reflex* to go insane.

enmarañar ➤ *tr* to entangle, snarl; *(confundir)* to muddle, confuse ➤ *reflex* to become tangled.

enmarcar §47 ➤ *tr* to frame.

enmascarado, a ➤ *adj & mf* masked (person).

enmascarar ➤ *tr* to mask; *(disfrazar)* to conceal, disguise.

enmendar §33 ➤ *tr* to correct, amend.

enmienda ➤ *f* amendment; *(reparo)* reparation, compensation.

enmohecer §09 ➤ *tr & reflex* to make moldy; *(metales)* to rust.

enmudecer §09 ➤ *tr* to silence, hush ➤ *intr* to be silent, keep quiet.

ennegrecer §09 ➤ *tr* to blacken or darken ➤ *reflex* to turn black or dark.

enojar ➤ *tr* to anger, make angry ➤ *reflex* to get angry.

enojoso, a ➤ *adj* bothersome, annoying.

enorgullecer §09 ➤ *tr* to make proud ➤ *reflex* to be proud.

enorme ➤ *adj* enormous, huge.

enrarecer §09 ➤ *intr & reflex* to become rare or scarce.

enredadera ➤ *adj* climbing, trailing ➤ *f* climbing plant, creeper.

enredar ➤ *tr* to tangle up, snarl; *(embrollar)* to confuse; *(comprometer)* to involve ➤ *intr* to get into mischief ➤ *reflex* to get tangled up; *(complicarse)* to become confused; *(comprometerse)* to become involved.

enriquecer §09 ➤ *tr* to enrich, make wealthy ➤ *intr & reflex* to get rich.

enrojecer §09 ➤ *intr* to blush, turn red.

enrollar ➤ *tr* to roll *or* wind up ➤ *intr* COMPUT. to scroll ➤ *reflex* to be rolled *or* wound up; COLL. to get involved.

enroscar §47 ➤ *tr* to coil, twist; *(atornillar)* to screw in.

ensalada ➤ *f* salad; FIG. hodgepodge.

ensanchar ➤ *tr* to widen, expand ➤ *intr & reflex* to get conceited; *(engrandecerse)* to expand.

ensanche ➤ *m* extension, expansion; *(barrio)* suburban development.

ensangrentar §33 ➤ *tr* to stain with blood ➤ *reflex* to become bloodstained; FIG. to become furious.

ensayar ➤ *tr* to test, try out; THEAT. to rehearse, practice; *(adiestrar)* to train, teach; *(intentar)* to try *or* attempt ➤ *reflex* to practice, rehearse.

ensayo ➤ *m* test, trial; *(ejercicio)* exercise, practice; *(intento)* attempt; LIT. essay; METAL. assay; THEAT. rehearsal.

enseguida ➤ *adv* immediately, at once.

ensenada ➤ *f* cove, inlet.

enseñanza ➤ *f* teaching; *(instrucción)* training; *(educación)* education; *(lección)* lesson.

enseñar ➤ *tr* to teach; *(indicar)* to indicate, point out; *(mostrar)* to show.

enseres ➤ *mpl* ▪ e. domésticos household goods.

ensimismarse ➤ *reflex* to be absorbed in thought; AMER. to become vain.

ensombrecerse §09 ➤ *reflex* to darken, get dark; FIG. to become sad *or* gloomy.

ensordecedor, a ➤ *adj* deafening.

ensuciar ➤ *tr* to dirty, soil; *(estropear)* to make a mess of, mess up ➤ *reflex* to become dirty *or* soiled.

ensueño ➤ *m* dream; *(fantasía)* fantasy, illusion.

entablar ➤ *tr* to board (up); *(empezar)* to begin, start; LAW to bring, file ▪ e. amistad to become friends.

ente ➤ *m* entity, being; COM. firm, company.

entender §34 ➤ *tr* to understand, comprehend; *(creer)* to believe, think ➤ *intr* ▪ e. en *or* de to be good at • e.

mal to misunderstand ➤ *reflex* to be understood; *(interpretarse)* to be meant; *(ponerse de acuerdo)* to come to an agreement; *(llevarse bien)* to get along; *(tener relaciones amorosas)* to have an affair ➤ *m* opinion.

entendimiento ➤ *m* understanding, comprehension; *(juicio)* judgment, sense.

enterar ➤ *tr* to inform, make aware ➤ *reflex* to find out, become aware.

entereza ➤ *f* integrity, uprightness.

enternecer §09 ➤ *tr* to soften, make tender ➤ *reflex* *(conmoverse)* to be touched *or* moved.

entero, a ➤ *adj* entire, complete; MATH. whole ▪ por e. entirely, completely.

enterrar §33 ➤ *tr* to bury.

entidad ➤ *f* entity; *(organización)* organization.

entierro ➤ *m* burial; *(funerales)* funeral; *(sepulcro)* tomb, grave.

entonar ➤ *tr* to intone; MED. to tone up.

entonces ➤ *adv* *(en aquel momento)* then, at that time; *(en tal caso)* then, in that case ▪ desde e. since then, from then on • en aquel e. *or* por e. around that time • hasta e. till then.

entornar ➤ *tr* to half-close, leave ajar.

entorpecer §09 ➤ *tr* to make torpid *or* slow; FIG. to dull, deaden.

entrada ➤ *f* entry, entrance; *(vestíbulo)* vestibule, entrance hall; *(ingreso)* admission; *(desembolso)* deposit, down payment; CUL. entrée; COMPUT., ELEC., input.

entrañable ➤ *adj* intimate, close; *(querido)* beloved, dear.

entrar ➤ *intr* to enter, come in; *(ser admitido)* to be admitted; *(ingresar)* to join; *(encajar)* to go, fit; *(desaguar)* to flow; *(formar parte)* to be part; *(ser contado)* to be counted; *(emplearse)* to go, be used; *(empezar)* to begin; COMPUT. to log in *or* on ▪ e. en to enter, go in ➤ *tr* *(meter)* to bring *or* put inside; COMPUT. to input.

entre ➤ *prep* between; *(en el número de)* among ▪ e. tanto meanwhile.

entreabierto, a ➤ *adj* half-open, ajar.

entrecejo ➤ *m* ANAT. space between the

eyebrows; *(ceño)* frown.

entrega ➤ *f* delivery; *(rendición)* handing over.

entregar §31 ➤ *tr (dar)* to deliver; *(poner en manos)* to hand over *or* in ➤ *reflex (rendirse)* to surrender, submit.

entrelazar §02 ➤ *tr* to interlace, interweave.

entremés ➤ *m* appetizer.

entremeter ➤ *tr* to insert, put *or* place in between ➤ *reflex (injerirse)* to meddle, interfere.

entremetido, a ➤ *adj* meddlesome, interfering ➤ *mf* meddler, busybody.

entrenador, a ➤ *mf* trainer, coach.

entrenamiento ➤ *m* training, coaching.

entrenar ➤ *tr & reflex* to train.

entresuelo ➤ *m* mezzanine.

entretanto ➤ *adv* meanwhile, in the meantime ➤ *m* meantime, meanwhile.

entretener §46 ➤ *tr* to entertain, amuse; *(detener)* to detain, delay ➤ *reflex (detenerse)* to dally, dawdle; *(divertirse)* to be entertained *or* amused.

entretenido, a ➤ *adj* amusing, entertaining.

entretenimiento ➤ *m* amusement, entertainment; *(detenimiento)* detainment, delay.

entretiempo ➤ *m* between-season.

entrevista ➤ *f* meeting, conference; JOURN. interview.

entrevistar ➤ *tr* to interview ➤ *reflex* to hold an interview *or* a meeting.

entristecer §09 ➤ *tr* to sadden, grieve ➤ *reflex* to become sad *or* grieved.

entumecer §09 ➤ *tr* to (make) numb ➤ *reflex* to go or become numb; *(hincharse)* to swell.

enturbiar ➤ *tr* to cloud ➤ *reflex* to become clouded *or* cloudy.

entusiasmar ➤ *tr* to enthuse ➤ *reflex* to become enthusiastic.

entusiasmo ➤ *m* enthusiasm.

enumerar ➤ *tr* to enumerate.

envasar ➤ *tr* to pack, package; *(embotellar)* to bottle.

envase ➤ *m* packing, packaging; *(paquete)* package; *(botella)* bottle.

envejecer §09 ➤ *tr* to age, make old ➤ *intr & reflex* to grow old, age.

envenenar ➤ *tr* to poison.

envergadura ➤ *f* wingspan, wingspread; FIG. importance, significance.

enviar §18 ➤ *tr* to send, dispatch; *(transmitir)* to convey, transmit.

envidia ➤ *f* envy.

envidiar ➤ *tr* to envy, be envious of.

envidioso, a ➤ *adj & mf* envious (person).

envío ➤ *m* dispatch; *(paquete)* package; *(dinero)* remittance; *(mercancías)* shipment, consignment.

envoltorio ➤ *m* bundle; *(cubierta)* wrapper.

envolver §54 ➤ *tr (cubrir)* to envelop, cover; *(empaquetar)* to pack, wrap up.

enyesar ➤ *tr* to plaster; MED. to set in plaster, put a cast on.

epidemia ➤ *f* epidemic.

epilepsia ➤ *f* epilepsy.

episodio ➤ *m* episode.

época ➤ *f* epoch, era; *(período)* time, period; GEOL. age ■ en aquella é. at that time.

equilibrio ➤ *m* equilibrium.

equilibrista ➤ *mf* tightrope walker.

equipaje ➤ *m* luggage, baggage; MARIT. crew.

equipar ➤ *tr* to equip, outfit.

equipo ➤ *m (acción)* outfitting; *(equipamiento)* equipment, gear; SPORT. team; *(de trabajadores)* shift, crew.

equitación ➤ *f* riding, equitation.

equitativo, a ➤ *adj* equitable, fair.

equivalente ➤ *adj & m* equivalent.

equivocación ➤ *f* error, mistake.

equivocado, a ➤ *adj* wrong, mistaken.

equivocar §47 ➤ *tr* to mistake ➤ *intr* to equivocate, lie ➤ *reflex* to be mistaken.

equívoco, a ➤ *adj* equivocal, ambiguous ➤ *m* ambiguity; *(malentendido)* misunderstanding.

era ➤ *f* era, age; *(período)* period, time.

erguir §19 ➤ *tr* to raise, lift up ➤ *reflex* to straighten up.

erigir §19 ➤ *tr* to erect, build; *(fundar)* to found, establish.

erizar §02 ➤ *tr* to make stand on end, set on end ➤ *reflex* to stand on end.

erosión ➤ f erosion.
erradicar §47 ➤ tr to eradicate.
errante ➤ adj errant, wandering.
errar ➤ tr to miss; (faltar) to fail (someone) ➤ intr to wander, roam; (equivocarse) to make a mistake.
errata ➤ f erratum.
erróneo, a ➤ adj erroneous, mistaken.
error ➤ m error, mistake.
eructar ➤ intr to burp, belch.
eructo ➤ m burp, belch.
erudito, a ➤ adj & mf erudite.
erupción ➤ f eruption.
esbelto, a ➤ adj slender, svelte.
escabeche ➤ m (adobo) marinade; (pescado) marinated fish salad.
escabullirse ➤ reflex to escape.
escala ➤ f (gal; (escalera de mano) ladder; MARIT. port of call, AVIA. stop.
escalar ➤ tr to scale, climb ➤ intr MIL., POL. to escalate.
escaldar ➤ tr to scald, burn.
escalera ➤ f stairs, staircase; (escalerilla) ladder; (de naipes) straight ∎ e. mecánica or automática escalator.
escalerilla ➤ f stepladder.
escalfar ➤ tr to poach.
escalofrío ➤ m (de miedo) shiver, shudder; (de fiebre) chill, shiver.
escalón ➤ m step, stair.
escalonar ➤ tr (colocar) to space out; (horas) to stagger; AGR. to terrace.
escama ➤ f scale.
escamotear ➤ tr to make disappear; COLL. (robar) to steal.
escampar ➤ tr & intr to clear (up).
escandalizar §02 ➤ tr to scandalize, shock ➤ reflex to be shocked.
escándalo ➤ m scandal ∎ armar un e. to make a scene.
escanear ➤ tr COMPUT. (foto) to scan.
escáner ➤ m COMPUT. scanner.
escapada ➤ f escape, flight.
escapar ➤ intr & reflex to escape.
escaparate ➤ m shop or display window; AMER. (ropero) wardrobe, closet.
escape ➤ m escape, flight; AUTO. exhaust (pipe).
escarabajo ➤ m scarab, black beetle.
escarbadientes ➤ m toothpick.
escarbar ➤ tr (rascar) to scrape,

scratch; (los dientes) to pick.
escarcha ➤ f frost.
escarlata ➤ adj & f scarlet.
escarlatina ➤ f scarlet fever.
escarmentar §33 ➤ tr to chastise, teach a lesson to ➤ intr to learn one's lesson.
escarmiento ➤ m (aviso) warning, lesson; (castigo) punishment.
escarola ➤ f escarole.
escarpado, a ➤ adj (pendiente) steep, sheer; (escabroso) craggy, rugged.
escasear ➤ intr to become or be scarce.
escasez ➤ f scarcity, lack.
escaso, a ➤ adj scarce, limited.
escena ➤ f scene; THEAT. stage ∎ poner en e. to stage, present.
escenario ➤ m stage, scene.
escéptico, a ➤ adj skeptical ➤ mf skeptic.
esclarecer §09 ➤ tr to illuminate, light up; (elucidar) to clarify.
esclavo, a ➤ adj enslaved ➤ mf slave.
esclusa ➤ f lock, sluice; (compuerta) floodgate.
escoba ➤ f broom.
escocer §48 ➤ intr to sting, smart.
escoger §20 ➤ tr to choose, select.
escolar ➤ adj scholastic, school ➤ mf pupil, student.
escolta ➤ f escort.
escoltar ➤ tr to escort.
escollo ➤ m reef, rock; FIG. stumbling block.
escombro ➤ m rubble, debris; MIN. slag.
esconder ➤ tr & reflex to hide, conceal.
escondidas ➤ fpl ∎ a e. secretly, covertly.
escondite ➤ m hiding place; (juego) hide-and-seek.
escondrijo ➤ m hiding place.
escopeta ➤ f shotgun, rifle.
escorpión ➤ m scorpion.
escote ➤ m neck, neckline.
escotilla ➤ f hatch(way).
escozor ➤ m smarting; (pena) grief, sorrow.
escribir §55 ➤ tr & intr to write ∎ e. a máquina to type.
escrito, a ➤ adj written ➤ m document, writing ∎ por e. in writing.
escritor, a ➤ mf writer.

escritorio ➤ *m* desk; (*despacho*) office, study.

escritura ➤ *f* writing; (*sistema de signos*) script; LAW document.

escrúpulo ➤ *m* scruple.

escrupuloso, a ➤ *adj* scrupulous.

escrutinio ➤ *m* scrutiny, examination.

escuadra ➤ *f* carpenter's square; MIL. squad, squadron.

escuálido, a ➤ *adj* squalid, filthy.

escuchar ➤ *tr* to listen to.

escudo ➤ *m* shield; HER. coat of arms, escutcheon.

escuela ➤ *f* school ■ e. primaria, secundaria elementary, high school.

escueto, a ➤ *adj* concise, direct; (*libre*) free, unencumbered.

escultor, a ➤ *mf* sculptor.

escultura ➤ *f* sculpture, carving.

escupir ➤ *tr* to spit; COLL. (*pagar*) to cough up, fork over or out; (*confesar*) to spill, give ➤ *intr* to spit.

escurridizo, a ➤ *adj* slippery.

escurridor ➤ *m* colander.

escurrir ➤ *tr* to drain; (*hacer que chorrea*) to wring (out) ➤ *intr* to drip, trickle; (*deslizar*) to slip, slide ➤ *reflex* to slip out, escape.

ese, esa ➤ *adj* that ■ *pl* those.

ése, ésa ➤ *pron* that one; (*el primero*) the former; (*allí*) there ■ *pl* those.

esencia ➤ *f* essence ■ quinta e. quintessence.

esencial ➤ *adj* essential.

esfera ➤ *f* sphere; (*del reloj*) dial, face.

esforzar §22 ➤ *tr* to strengthen; (*dar ánimo*) to encourage ➤ *reflex* to strive.

esfuerzo ➤ *m* effort, exertion.

esfumarse ➤ *reflex* to disappear, vanish.

esguince ➤ *m* sprain, twist.

eslabón ➤ *m* link.

esmalte ➤ *m* enamel.

esmeralda ➤ *f* emerald.

esmerarse ➤ *reflex* to be painstaking, take great care.

esmoquin ➤ *m* dinner jacket, tuxedo.

esnob ➤ *mf* snob.

eso ➤ *pron* that ■ a e. de about, around • e. es that's it • e. mismo exactly, the same • por e. therefore, that's why.

espacial ➤ *adj* spatial; (*del espacio*) space ■ nave e. spaceship.

espacio ■ *m* space.

espacioso, a ➤ *adj* spacious, roomy; (*lento*) slow, deliberate.

espada ➤ *f* sword; (*naipe*) spade ■ entre la e. y la pared between a rock and a hard place.

espagueti ➤ *m* spaghetti.

espalda ➤ *f* back ■ dar or volver la e. to turn one's back ■ *pl* back ■ de e. from behind.

espantapájaros ➤ *m* scarecrow.

espantar ➤ *tr* to frighten, scare ➤ *reflex* to be frightened or scared.

espantoso, a ➤ *adj* frightening, scary.

español, a ➤ *adj* Spanish ➤ *m* (*idioma*) Spanish ➤ *mf* Spaniard.

esparadrapo ➤ *m* adhesive tape.

esparcir ➤ *tr* to scatter, spread ➤ *reflex* to scatter, be scattered.

espárrago ➤ *m* asparagus.

espátula ➤ *f* CUL. spatula; ORNITH. spoonbill.

especia ➤ *f* spice.

especial ➤ *adj* special ■ en e. especially.

especialidad ➤ *f* specialty.

especialista ➤ *adj & mf* specialist.

especializar §02 ➤ *tr, intr & reflex* to specialize.

especialmente ➤ *adv* especially.

especie ➤ *f* species; (*tipo*) type, kind; (*asunto*) matter, affair.

especificar §47 ➤ *tr* to specify.

específico, a ➤ *adj & m* specific.

espectacular ➤ *adj* spectacular.

espectáculo, ➤ *m* spectacle.

espectador, a ➤ *mf* spectator, onlooker.

espectro ➤ *m* PHYS. spectrum; (*fantasma*) ghost, spook; (*horror*) specter.

especulación ➤ *f* speculation.

especulador, a ➤ *mf* speculator.

espejismo ➤ *m* mirage.

espejo ➤ *m* mirror; (*modelo*) model, example.

espeluznante ➤ *adj* COLL. hair-raising.

espera ➤ *f* wait; LAW respite.

esperanza ➤ *f* hope.

esperar ➤ *tr* to hope (for); (*aguardar*) to wait for; (*confiar en*) to expect; (*ser inminente*) to await ➤ *intr* to wait.

esperma ➤ *f* sperm, semen.

espesar ➤ *tr* to thicken ➤ *reflex* to grow *or* become thicker.

espeso, a ➤ *adj* thick; *(sucio)* dirty, unkempt.

espesor ➤ *m* thickness; *(densidad)* density.

espía ➤ *mf* spy ➤ *f* MARIT. warping.

espiar §18 ➤ *tr & intr* to spy (on).

espiga ➤ *f* BOT. spike, ear; CARP. tenon; *(clavija)* peg, pin.

espigado, a ➤ *adj* spiky.

espina ➤ *f* thorn; *(de pez)* fishbone; ANAT. spine; *(pesar)* grief, sorrow.

espinaca ➤ *f* spinach.

espinazo ➤ *m* ANAT. spine, backbone; ARCHIT. keystone.

espinilla ➤ *f* shinbone; *(granillo)* blackhead.

espionaje ➤ *m* espionage, spying.

espiral ➤ *adj* spiral, winding ➤ *m* balance spring, hairspring; MED. coil ➤ *f* spiral.

espirar ➤ *tr & intr* to exhale, breathe out.

espíritu ➤ *m* spirit; *(alma)* soul ■ e. de cuerpo esprit de corps.

espiritual ➤ *adj & m* spiritual.

espléndido, a ➤ *adj* splendid; *(generoso)* generous.

esplendor ➤ *m* splendor.

esponja ➤ *f* sponge.

esponjoso, a ➤ *adj* spongy.

espontáneo, a ➤ *adj* spontaneous.

esposa ➤ *f* wife, spouse ■ *pl* handcuffs.

esposar ➤ *tr* to handcuff.

esposo ➤ *m* husband, spouse.

espuela ➤ *f* spur.

espuma ➤ *f* foam; *(de un líquido)* froth, spume; *(de jabón)* lather.

espumoso, a ➤ *adj* frothy, foamy.

esqueleto ➤ *m* skeleton.

esquema ➤ *m* scheme, outline.

esquemático, a ➤ *adj* schematic.

esquí ➤ *m* ski; *(deporte)* skiing.

esquiador, a ➤ *mf* skier.

esquiar §18 ➤ *intr* to ski.

esquina ➤ *f* corner ■ a la vuelta de la e. just around the corner • doblar la e. to turn the corner.

esquivar ➤ *tr* to avoid, evade; *(un golpe)* to dodge ➤ *reflex* to withdraw, shy away.

estabilidad ➤ *f* stability.

estabilizar §02 ➤ *tr* to stabilize, make stable.

estable ➤ *adj* stable.

establecedor, a ➤ *adj* establishing, founding ➤ *mf* establisher, founder.

establecer §09 ➤ *tr* to establish, found ➤ *reflex* to establish oneself.

establecimiento ➤ *m* establishment.

establo ➤ *m* stable.

estaca ➤ *f* stake, post; CARP. spike, nail.

estación ➤ *f* *(estado)* position; *(tiempo)* season; RAIL., TELEC. station.

estacionamiento ➤ *m* stationing, positioning; AUTO. parking place *or* space.

estacionar ➤ *tr* to station, place; AUTO. to park ➤ *reflex* to park.

estacionario, a ➤ *adj* stationary.

estadio ➤ *m* stadium; *(fase)* phase, stage.

estadista ➤ *mf* statesman/woman; *(estadístico)* statistician.

estado ➤ *m* state; *(condición)* condition ■ e. civil marital status.

estafa ➤ *f* swindle, hoax.

estafar ➤ *tr* to swindle, cheat.

estafeta ➤ *f* mail, post; *(de correo)* post office.

estalactita ➤ *f* stalactite.

estalagmita ➤ *f* stalagmite.

estallar ➤ *intr* to burst, explode; *(sobrevenir)* to break out.

estallido ➤ *m* explosion; FIG. outbreak, outburst.

estampado, a ➤ *adj* TEX. stamped ➤ *m* printing, engraving.

estampilla ➤ *f* stamp, seal; AMER. postage stamp.

estancar §47 ➤ *tr* to dam up, stem ➤ *reflex* to stagnate.

estancia ➤ *f* *(mansión)* country house, estate; *(estadía)* stay; AMER. ranch.

estanque ➤ *m* *(charca)* pond, pool; *(depósito)* tank, reservoir.

estante ➤ *m* shelving, shelf.

estantería ➤ *f* shelving, shelves.

estaño ➤ *m* tin.

estar §21 ➤ *intr* to be ¡cómo estás? how are you? • e. bien, mal to be well,

ill • e. de más to be superfluous • e. en
(entender) to understand; (consistir
en) to depend on • e. para to be about
to • e. por (favorecer) to be for, be in
favor of • e. por irse to be about to go.
estatal ➤ adj state, of the state.
estatua ➤ f statue; COLL. cold fish.
estatura ➤ f stature.
estatuto ➤ m statute, law; (regla) rule.
este ➤ adj eastern, easterly ➤ m east.
este, a ➤ adj this ■ pl these.
éste, a ➤ pron this one; (el segundo) the
latter; (aquí) here ■ pl these.
estela ➤ f AVIA. trail; MARIT. wake.
estepa ➤ f steppe.
estera ➤ f matting.
estéreo ➤ adj & f stereo.
estereofónico, a ➤ adj stereophonic,
stereo.
estereotipo ➤ m stereotype.
estéril ➤ adj sterile, infertile.
esterlina ➤ adj sterling.
esternón ➤ m sternum, breastbone.
estero ➤ m estuary; AMER. (pantano)
marsh, swamp.
estético, a ➤ adj aesthetic ➤ m aesthetic, aesthete ➤ f aesthetics.
estilar ➤ intr & reflex to be customary;
(estar de moda) to be in fashion.
estilo ➤ m style ■ por el e. like that.
estilográfica ➤ f fountain pen.
estima ➤ f esteem, respect.
estimación ➤ f esteem, respect; COM.
appraisal, valuation.
estimar ➤ tr to esteem, hold in esteem;
COM. to appraise; (juzgar) to consider,
deem ➤ reflex to be esteemed.
estimulante ➤ adj stimulating ➤ m
stimulant.
estimular ➤ tr to stimulate; (incitar) to
urge on; (la curiosidad) to arouse.
estímulo ➤ m stimulus.
estío ➤ m summer.
estirar ➤ tr to stretch; (extender) to
extend ➤ reflex to stretch oneself.
estival ➤ adj summer.
esto ➤ pron this; (asunto) this business
or matter ■ por e. for this reason.
estocada ➤ f thrust, stab.
estofado, a ➤ adj stewed; (acolchado)
quilted ➤ m stew; SEW. quilting.

estómago ➤ m stomach.
estorbar ➤ tr to obstruct, block; (difi-
cultar) to hinder, hamper.
estorbo ➤ m obstruction, obstacle;
(molestia) bother, annoyance.
estornudar ➤ intr to sneeze.
estornudo ➤ m sneeze.
estragón ➤ m tarragon.
estrangular ➤ tr to strangle.
estratagema ➤ f stratagem.
estratégico, a ➤ adj strategic.
estraza ➤ f rag.
estrechamiento ➤ m narrowing, tight-
ening.
estrechar ➤ tr (reducir) to narrow;
(apretar) to tighten; (sisar) to take in ■
e. la mano a to shake hands with
➤ reflex to narrow; (apretarse) to
tighten; (ceñirse) to squeeze together;
(amistarse) to become close.
estrechez ➤ f narrowness; (pobreza)
poverty, need; (austeridad) austerity ■
pl (apuros) dire straits.
estrecho, a ➤ adj narrow; (apretado)
tight; (íntimo) close, intimate; (rígido)
rigid, severe ➤ m strait, channel.
estrella ➤ f star; (asterisco) asterisk ■ e.
de mar starfish.
estrellar ➤ tr & reflex COLL. (romper) to
smash, crash.
estremecer §09 ➤ tr to shake; FIG. to
shock, disturb ➤ reflex to shake, tremble.
estrenar ➤ tr to use or wear for the first
time; CINEM., THEAT. to première, open
➤ reflex to première, debut.
estreno ➤ m opening, debut; CINEM.,
THEAT. première.
estreñimiento ➤ m constipation.
estrépito ➤ m uproar, din.
estribillo ➤ m POET. refrain; MUS. chorus.
estribo ➤ m stirrup; (de carruaje) foot-
board ■ perder los estribos to lose
one's head.
estribor ➤ m starboard.
estricto, a ➤ adj strict.
estropajo ➤ m dishcloth, rag.
estropear ➤ tr to damage, ruin; (maltratar) to mistreat, mishandle.
estructura ➤ f structure.

estruendo ➤ *m* clamor, uproar.

estrujar ➤ *tr* to squeeze, crush.

estuche ➤ *m* case, box; *(vaina)* sheath.

estudiante ➤ *mf* student, pupil.

estudiar ➤ *tr & intr* to study.

estudio ➤ *m* study; *(cuarto)* study, studio.

estudioso, a ➤ *adj & mf* studious (person).

estufa ➤ *f* stove, heater.

estupefaciente ➤ *adj* stupefying, astonishing ➤ *m* narcotic, stupefacient.

estupefacto, a ➤ *adj* stupefied, astonished.

estupendo, a ➤ *adj* stupendous, tremendous.

estupidez ➤ *f* stupidity, idiocy.

estúpido, a ➤ *adj* stupid, dumb ➤ *mf* idiot, dumbbell.

etapa ➤ *f* phase, stage.

etcétera ➤ *adv* et cetera.

eternidad ➤ *f* eternity.

eterno, a ➤ *adj* eternal.

ético, a ➤ *adj* ethical, moral ➤ *m* moralist ➤ *f* ethics.

etiqueta ➤ *f* etiquette, ceremony; *(rótulo)* tag, label ∎ de e. formal.

étnico, a ➤ *adj* ethnic.

eucalipto ➤ *m* eucalyptus.

eufórico, a ➤ *adj* euphoric, jubilant.

Europa ➤ *f* Europe.

europeo, a ➤ *adj & mf* European.

eutanasia ➤ *f* euthanasia.

evacuación ➤ *f* evacuation.

evacuar ➤ *tr* to evacuate.

evadir ➤ *tr* to evade, avoid ➤ *reflex* to escape, sneak away.

evaluar §45 ➤ *tr* to evaluate, assess.

evangelio ➤ *m* gospel.

evaporación ➤ *f* evaporation.

evaporar ➤ *tr & reflex* to evaporate.

evasión ➤ *f* escape; *(evasiva)* evasion.

evasivo, a ➤ *adj* evasive ➤ *f* evasion.

evento ➤ *m* chance event, contingency.

eventual ➤ *adj* unexpected, incidental.

evidencia ➤ *f* proof, evidence.

evidente ➤ *adj* evident, clear.

evitar ➤ *tr* to avoid.

evolución ➤ *f* evolution.

evolucionar ➤ *intr* to evolve.

exacerbar ➤ *tr* to exacerbate, aggravate.

exactitud ➤ *f* exactitude, exactness; *(puntualidad)* punctuality.

exacto, a ➤ *adj* exact, precise; *(puntual)* punctual.

exageración ➤ *f* exaggeration.

exagerado, a ➤ *adj* exaggerated.

exagerar ➤ *tr* to exaggerate.

exaltar ➤ *tr* to exalt, glorify ➤ *reflex* to get worked up.

examen ➤ *m* examination, test; *(interrogación)* interrogation.

examinar ➤ *tr* to examine ➤ *reflex* to take an exam.

exasperar ➤ *tr* to exasperate ➤ *reflex* to become exasperated.

excavación ➤ *f* excavation.

excavar ➤ *tr* to excavate, dig.

excedente ➤ *adj* excessive; *(sobrante)* excess, surplus ➤ *m* excess, surplus.

exceder ➤ *tr* to exceed, surpass ➤ *reflex* *(sobrepasarse)* to go too far.

excelencia ➤ *f* excellence.

excelente ➤ *adj* excellent.

excéntrico, a ➤ *adj* eccentric.

excepción ➤ *f* exception ∎ a or con e. de except for.

excepcional ➤ *adj* exceptional.

excepto ➤ *prep* except, excepting.

exceptuar §45 ➤ *tr* to exclude, exempt ➤ *reflex* to be excluded or exempted.

excesivo, a ➤ *adj* excessive.

exceso ➤ *m* excess; COM. surplus.

excitación ➤ *f* excitement.

excitante ➤ *adj* stimulating ➤ *m* stimulant.

excitar ➤ *tr* to excite ➤ *reflex* to become excited.

exclamación ➤ *f* exclamation; *(signo ortográfico)* exclamation point.

exclamar ➤ *intr* to exclaim.

excluir §10 ➤ *tr* to exclude; *(expulsar)* to throw out, expel.

exclusive ➤ *adv* exclusively; *(no incluyendo)* exclusive of, not including.

exclusivo, a ➤ *adj* exclusive ➤ *f* *(repulsa)* rejection; *(privilegio)* exclusive or sole right.

excursión ➤ *f* excursion.

excursionista ➤ *mf* sightseer.

excusa ➤ *f* excuse ∎ a e. secretly.

excusar ➤ *tr* to excuse ➤ *reflex* to

excuse oneself ■ e. de to refuse.
exento, a ➤ *adj* exempt, free.
exhalar ➤ *tr* to exhale.
exhaustivo, a ➤ *adj* exhaustive.
exhausto, a ➤ *adj* exhausted.
exhibición ➤ *f* exhibition, exhibit.
exhibir ➤ *tr* to exhibit, display ➤ *reflex* to show up, to show oneself.
exigencia ➤ *f* exigency, demand.
exigente ➤ *adj* demanding.
exigir §19 ➤ *tr* to demand, require.
exil(i)ado, a ➤ *adj* exiled, in exile ➤ *mf* exile.
exil(i)ar ➤ *tr* to exile, banish.
exilio ➤ *m* exile, banishment.
existencia ➤ *f* existence ■ *pl* stock, goods.
existente ➤ *adj* existent; COM. in stock.
existir ➤ *intr* to exist, be in existence.
éxito ➤ *m* success; *(resultado)* result, outcome ■ tener é. to be successful.
exitoso, a ➤ *adj* AMER. successful.
éxodo ➤ *m* exodus.
exorbitante ➤ *adj* exorbitant, excessive.
exótico, a ➤ *adj* exotic.
expandir ➤ *tr & reflex* to expand.
expansión ➤ *f* expansion; *(recreo)* relaxation, recreation; *(franqueza)* expansiveness.
expectación ➤ *f* expectation.
expectativo, a ➤ *adj* expectant, hopeful ➤ *f* expectation, anticipation.
expedición ➤ *f* expedition; *(prontitud)* speed, dispatch; COM. shipping, shipment.
expediente ➤ *adj* expedient ➤ *m* expedient; *(archivo)* file, dossier, record.
expedir §32 ➤ *tr (enviar)* to send, ship; *(despachar)* to expedite, dispatch; *(dictar)* to issue.
expensas ➤ *fpl* expenses, costs.
experiencia ➤ *f* experience; CHEM., PHYS. experiment.
experimentado, a ➤ *adj* experienced.
experimental ➤ *adj* experimental.
experimentar ➤ *tr* to try out, test; *(sentir en sí)* to experience, undergo.
experimento ➤ *m* experiment.
experto, a ➤ *adj & mf* expert.
expirar ➤ *intr* to expire.
explanada ➤ *f* esplanade.

explicación ➤ *f* explanation.
explicar §47 ➤ *tr* to explain; *(enseñar)* to teach ➤ *reflex* to explain oneself; *(comprender)* to understand.
exploración ➤ *f* exploration.
explorador, a ➤ *adj* exploratory ➤ *mf* explorer ➤ *m* COMPUT. browser.
explorar ➤ *tr & intr* to explore.
explosión ➤ *f* explosion.
explosivo, a ➤ *adj & m* explosive.
explotación ➤ *f* exploitation; *(operación)* running; *(cultivo)* cultivation.
explotar ➤ *tr* to exploit; *(operar)* to run, operate; *(cultivar)* to cultivate ■ *intr* to go off, explode.
exponer §37 ➤ *tr* to expose; *(explicar)* to propound, explain; *(exhibir)* to exhibit ➤ *reflex* to expose oneself.
exportación ➤ *f* exportation; *(mercancías)* exports; *(artículo)* export.
exportador, a ➤ *adj* exporting ➤ *mf* exporter.
exportar ➤ *tr & intr* to export.
exposición ➤ *f* exhibition, show; *(explicación)* explanation; *(orientación)* exposure.
expresamente ➤ *adv* clearly, explicitly; *(de propósito)* specifically.
expresar ➤ *tr & reflex* to express (oneself).
expresión ➤ *f* expression.
expreso, a ➤ *adj* express ➤ *m (tren)* express train; *(correo)* express mail.
exprimidor ➤ *m* squeezer, juicer.
exprimir ➤ *tr* to squeeze.
expulsar ➤ *tr* to expel, drive out.
exquisito, a ➤ *adj* exquisite.
extender §34 ➤ *tr* to extend, enlarge; *(desdoblar)* to spread out, spread ➤ *reflex* to stretch, extend.
extensión ➤ *f* extension; *(amplitud)* expanse, stretch; *(dimensión)* extent.
extenso, a ➤ *adj* extensive, ample, vast.
extenuado, a ➤ *adj* debilitated, weakened.
extenuar §45 ➤ *tr* to debilitate, weaken.
exterior ➤ *adj* exterior, outer; *(extranjero)* foreign ➤ *m* exterior, outside.
exterminar ➤ *tr* to exterminate.
externo, a ➤ *adj* external, outward.
extinguir §15 ➤ *tr* to extinguish, put

out ➤ *reflex* to fade, go out.
extinto, a ➤ *adj* extinguished; *(desaparecido)* extinct.
extorsión ➤ *f* extortion; *(molestia)* harm, trouble.
extorsionar ➤ *tr* to extort.
extra ➤ *adj* extra ➤ *prep* ▪ e. de COLL. besides, in addition to ➤ *mf* CINEM., THEAT. extra ➤ *m* gratuity; *(gasto)* extra charge.
extracto ➤ *m* extract; *(compendio)* summary.
extraer §49 ➤ *tr* to extract.
extranjero, a ➤ *adj* alien, foreign ➤ *mf* foreigner, alien ➤ *m* abroad.
extrañar ➤ *tr* to find strange, not to be used to; AMER. to miss ➤ *reflex* to be surprised or astonished.
extraño, a ➤ *adj* foreign, alien; *(raro)* strange, odd; *(que no tiene que ver)* extraneous ➤ *mf* foreigner.
extraoficial ➤ *adj* unofficial.
extraordinario, a ➤ *adj* extraordinary ➤ *m* *(correo urgente)* special delivery; *(periódico)* special edition.
extravagancia ➤ *f* extravagance.
extravagante ➤ *adj* extravagant ➤ *mf* eccentric.
extraviar §18 ➤ *tr* *(desviar)* to lead astray, misguide; *(perder)* to misplace, lose ➤ *reflex* to get lost.
extremidad ➤ *f* *(punta)* end, tip; *(parte extrema)* extremity ➤ *pl* extremities.
extremo, a ➤ *adj* *(último)* last, ultimate; *(intenso)* extreme, greatest, utmost; *(distante)* farthest ➤ *m* extreme.
extrovertido, a ➤ *adj* extroverted, extraverted ➤ *mf* extrovert, extravert.
exuberancia ➤ *f* exuberance, abundance.

F

fábrica ➤ *f* factory, plant.
fabricación ➤ *f* manufacture.
fabricante ➤ *mf* manufacturer.
fabricar §47 ➤ *tr* to manufacture, make.
fábula ➤ *f* fable; *(invención)* lie, fiction.
fabuloso, a ➤ *adj* fabled, imaginary; *(extraordinario)* fabulous.
facción ➤ *f* faction, party ▪ *pl (rasgo)*

features, facial features.
fácil ➤ *adj* easy; *(probable)* likely, probable; *(dócil)* easygoing ➤ *adv* easily.
facilidad ➤ *f* facility, ease ▪ *pl* terms.
facilitar ➤ *tr* to facilitate, make easy; *(proporcionar)* to supply, furnish.
facsímile ➤ *m* facsimile.
factoría ➤ *f* AMER. plant, factory.
factura ➤ *f* COM. invoice, bill.
facturación ➤ *f* billing, invoicing.
facturar ➤ *tr* to invoice, bill.
facultad ➤ *f* faculty; *(derecho)* power, right; *(licencia)* license, permission; EDUC. school, college, faculty.
faena ➤ *f* task, chore; *(mental)* mental task; COLL. *(trastada)* dirty trick.
faisán ➤ *m* pheasant.
faja ➤ *f* *(corsé)* girdle, corset; ;*(tira de papel)* wrapper; AMER. belt, waistband.
fajo ➤ *m* bundle, sheaf; *(de billetes)* wad, roll.
falda ➤ *f* skirt; *(ala de sombrero)* brim, flap; *(de un monte)* foot; *(regazo)* lap.
falla ➤ *f* defect, fault; GEOG., MIN. fault.
fallar ➤ *tr* to fail, disappoint ➤ *intr* to fail; COMPUT. to crash.
fallecer §09 ➤ *intr* to die, expire.
fallo ➤ *m* *(sentencia)* ruling, judgment; *(falta)* error, fault ▪ f. de sistema COMPUT. crash.
falsificar §47 ➤ *tr* to falsify; *(copiar)* to counterfeit, forge.
falso, a ➤ *adj* false; *(falsificado)* counterfeit, fake.
falta ➤ *f* lack, shortage; *(ausencia)* absence; *(defecto)* flaw; *(infracción)* misdemeanor; *(culpa)* fault; *(error)* error ▪ a f. de for want of • hacer f. *(faltar)* to need, be lacking; *(ser necesario)* to be necessary • sin f. without fail.
faltar ➤ *intr* *(hacer falta)* to be lacking; *(estar ausente)* to be missing *(de* from); *(no responder)* to fail to function; *(ofender)* to insult ▪ f. a *(la clase)* to miss, be absent from; *(un deber)* to fail in; *(una promesa)* to break • f. mucho para to be a long way off • faltan diez minutos para las ocho it is ten minutes to eight • f. poco para not to be long before • nos falta dinero we need money.

fama ➤ *f* fame, reputation.

familia ➤ *f* family.

familiar ➤ *adj (relativo a la familia)* familial, family; *(llano)* casual; *(conocido)* familiar ➤ *mf* family member; *(amigo íntimo)* intimate friend.

famoso, a ➤ *adj* famous; COLL. excellent.

fanático, a ➤ *adj* fanatic(al) ➤ *mf* fanatic; *(entusiasta)* fan.

fango ➤ *m* mud, mire.

fantasía ➤ *f* fantasy ▪ de f. fancy.

fantasma ➤ *m* ghost, apparition; *(visión)* vision, illusion; *(persona seria)* stuffed shirt.

fantástico, a ➤ *adj* fantastic.

fardo ➤ *m* large bundle *or* parcel.

farmacéutico, a ➤ *adj* pharmaceutical ➤ *mf* pharmacist, druggist.

farmacia ➤ *f* pharmacy.

faro ➤ *m (torre)* lighthouse; *(señal)* beacon; AUTO. headlight.

farol ➤ *m* lantern; *(luz pública)* street lamp.

farola ➤ *f (farol)* streetlight, street lamp; *(faro)* beacon.

fascinación ➤ *f* fascination.

fascinante ➤ *adj* fascinating.

fascinar ➤ *tr* to fascinate; *(engañar)* to deceive.

fascista ➤ *adj & mf* fascist, Fascist.

fase ➤ *f* phase; TECH. stage.

fastidiar ➤ *tr* to annoy; *(cansar)* to tire, bore ➤ *reflex* to get annoyed.

fast(u)oso, a ➤ *adj* lavish, splendid.

fatal ➤ *adj* fatal; *(funesto)* unfortunate.

fatiga ➤ *f* fatigue.

fatigar §31 ➤ *tr* to fatigue; *(molestar)* to annoy ➤ *reflex* to get tired.

fauna ➤ *f* fauna, animal life.

favor ➤ *m* favor; *(amparo)* protection ▪ a f. de in favor of, in behalf of ▪ de f. complimentary, free ▪ por f. please.

favorable ➤ *adj* favorable.

favorecer §09 ➤ *tr* to favor, support ➤ *reflex* to help one another ▪ f. de to avail oneself of.

favorito, a ➤ *adj & mf* favorite.

fe ➤ *f* faith; *(creencia)* credence; *(confianza)* trust, confidence.

fealdad ➤ *f* ugliness, foulness.

febrero ➤ *m* February.

fecha ➤ *f* date ▪ hasta la f. so far, to date.

fechar ➤ *tr* to date.

federal ➤ *adj & mf* federal.

felicidad ➤ *f* felicity, happiness; *(suerte feliz)* good luck ▪ *pl (enhorabuena)* congratulations; *(deseos amistosos)* best *or* warm wishes.

felicitar ➤ *tr* to congratulate.

feliz ➤ *adj* happy; *(acertado)* felicitous, apt; *(oportuno)* lucky.

felpa ➤ *f* plush.

felpudo, a ➤ *adj* plush, velvety ➤ *m* mat.

femenino, a ➤ *adj & m* feminine.

feminista ➤ *adj & mf* feminist.

fémur ➤ *m* femur, thighbone.

fenomenal ➤ *adj* phenomenal.

fenómeno ➤ *m* phenomenon.

feo, a ➤ *adj* ugly ➤ *adv* AMER. awful.

féretro ➤ *m (ataúd)* coffin; *(andas)* bier.

feria ➤ *f (mercado)* market; *(exposición)* fair; *(día de fiesta)* holiday.

fermentar ➤ *tr & intr* to ferment.

ferocidad ➤ *f* ferocity.

feroz ➤ *adj* ferocious, fierce.

ferretería ➤ *f* foundry; *(comercio)* hardware store; *(quincalla)* hardware.

ferrocarril ➤ *m* railroad, railway.

ferroviario, a ➤ *adj* railroad.

fértil ➤ *adj* fertile.

fertilidad ➤ *f* fertility.

fertilizante ➤ *adj* fertilizing ➤ *m* fertilizer.

fertilizar §02 ➤ *tr* to fertilize.

festejar ➤ *tr* to entertain; *(celebrar)* to celebrate.

festejo ➤ *m* entertainment, feast; AMER. celebration, party.

festín ➤ *m* banquet, feast.

festival ➤ *m* festival.

festivo, a ➤ *adj* festive; *(agudo)* witty, humorous.

feto ➤ *m* fetus.

fiable ➤ *adj* reliable, dependable.

fiador, a ➤ *mf* guarantor.

fiambre ➤ *adj* CUL. (served) cold ➤ *m* cold cut.

fianza ➤ *f* guaranty; *(depósito)* deposit.

fibra ➤ *f* fiber; *(de madera)* grain; MIN. vein.

ficción ➤ *f* fiction.

ficha ➤ *f (en los juegos)* counter, chip; *(dominó)* domino; *(disco de metal)* token; *(tarjeta)* index card.

fichar ➤ *tr* to keep on an index card; *(en bares, restaurantes)* to keep on a tab; *(en fábricas)* to punch (a clock) in *or* out; *(en dominó)* to play.

fichero ➤ *m* file (cabinet); COMPUT. file.

ficticio, a ➤ *adj* fictitious.

fidelidad ➤ *f* fidelity; *(exactitud)* accuracy.

fideo ➤ *m* noodle.

fiebre ➤ *f* fever.

fiel ➤ *adj* faithful, loyal; *(exacto)* exact, accurate; *(honrado)* trustworthy.

fieltro ➤ *m* felt; *(sombrero)* felt hat.

fierro AMER. ➤ *m* brand, mark ■ *pl* tools.

fiesta ➤ *f* party, celebration; *(feriado)* holiday; RELIG. feast, holy day.

figura ➤ *f* figure; *(actor)* character; *(mudanza)* dance step; MUS. note.

figurar ➤ *tr* to represent, depict; *(fingir)* to feign, simulate ➤ *intr* to figure, take part ➤ *reflex* to imagine, figure ■ ¡figúrate! just imagine!

fijador, a ➤ *adj* fixative ➤ *m (para el pelo)* hair spray; PHOTOG. fixative.

fijamente ➤ *adv* firmly, assuredly; *(atentamente)* fixedly, steadfastly.

fijar ➤ *tr* to fix, fasten; *(establecer)* to establish ➤ *reflex* to settle, become fixed; *(atender)* to pay attention ■ ¡fíjate! just imagine!

fijo, a ➤ *adj* fixed; *(permanente)* permanent; *(estable)* stable, steady; *(de colores)* fast, indelible ➤ *f (bisagra)* large hinge; CONSTR. trowel.

fila ➤ *f (hilera)* file; *(cola)* line, queue (G.B.); *(línea)* row, tier; MIL. rank.

filántropo, a ➤ *mf* philanthropist.

filarmónico, a ➤ *adj* philharmonic.

filete ➤ *m* CUL. fillet; TECH. thread.

filial ➤ *adj* filial; COM. subsidiary, branch ➤ *f* COM. *(sucursal)* branch (office); *(subdivisión)* subsidiary.

film *or* **filme** ➤ *m* film, movie.

filmar ➤ *tr* to film, shoot.

filo ➤ *m* (cutting) edge ■ al f. de la medianoche at the stroke of midnight • dar (un) f. *(afilar)* to sharpen.

filosofía ➤ *f* philosophy.

filósofo, a ➤ *adj* philosophic(al) ➤ *mf* philosopher.

filtración ➤ *f* filtration.

filtrar ➤ *tr & intr* to filter ➤ *reflex (pasarse)* to filter, pass through; *(disminuirse)* to dwindle.

filtro ➤ *m* filter.

fin ➤ *m* end; *(meta)* aim ■ a f. de in order to • a f. de cuentas in the final analysis • a f. de que so that • a fines de at the end of • al *or* por f. at last, finally • al f. y al cabo after all, when all is said and done • en f. finally; *(en resumen)* in short • f. de semana weekend.

final ➤ *adj* final, last ➤ *m (fin)* end, ending; MUS. finale ➤ *f* SPORT. final ■ al f. in *or* at the end.

finalizar §02 ➤ *tr* to finish, conclude ➤ *intr* to (come to an) end.

financiación ➤ *f or* **financiamiento** ➤ *m* financing.

financiar ➤ *tr* to finance.

financiero, a ➤ *adj* financial ➤ *mf* financier.

finca ➤ *f* property, real estate; AMER. farm.

fingir §19 ➤ *tr* to pretend, feign.

fino, a ➤ *adj* fine; *(precioso)* precious; *(cortés)* refined, elegant; *(delicado)* delicate.

firma ➤ *f* signature; *(acción)* signing; COM. firm, company.

firmamento ➤ *m* firmament, heavens.

firmar ➤ *tr & reflex* to sign.

firme ➤ *adj* firm; *(constante)* steadfast, staunch ➤ *m* foundation, bed ➤ *adv* firmly, steadily.

firmeza ➤ *f* firmness.

fiscal ➤ *adj* fiscal ➤ *mf (tesorero)* treasurer; *(abogado)* district attorney.

fisco ➤ *m* public treasury.

físico, a ➤ *adj* physical ➤ *mf* physicist ➤ *m* physique; *(apariencia)* looks, appearance ➤ *f* physics.

fisiología ➤ *f* physiology.

fisioterapia ➤ *f* physiotherapy.

flaco, a ➤ *adj* thin, lean; *(sin fuerza)* weak.

flamenco, a ➤ *adj* flamenco ➤ *m* ORNITH. flamingo.

flan ➤ *m* flan, caramel custard.

flanco ➤ *m* side, flank.

flaquear ➤ *intr* to weaken.

flauta ➤ *f* flute ➤ *mf* flautist, flutist.

fleco ➤ *m* fringe; *(borde desgastado)* frayed edge; *(flequillo)* bangs.

flecha ➤ *f* arrow.

flechazo ➤ *m* arrow shot *or* wound.

flema ➤ *f* phlegm.

flemático, a ➤ *adj* phlegmatic(al).

flequillo ➤ *m* bangs.

fletar ➤ *tr* *(alquilar)* to charter; *(embarcar)* to load; AMER. to hire, rent.

flexible ➤ *adj* flexible ➤ *m* electric cord.

flexión ➤ *f* flexion; GRAM. inflection.

flirtear ➤ *intr* to flirt.

flojera ➤ *f* laziness, carelessness.

flojo, a ➤ *adj* *(suelto)* loose, slack; *(débil)* weak; *(holgazán)* lazy, shiftless ➤ *mf* idler, loafer.

flor ➤ *f* flower ■ en f. in bloom.

flora ➤ *f* flora.

florecer §09 ➤ *intr* to flower, bloom; *(prosperar)* to flourish.

florero ➤ *m* (flower) vase.

flota ➤ *f* fleet; AER. squadron.

flotador, a ➤ *adj* floating, buoyant ➤ *m* float; MARIT. outrigger.

flotar ➤ *intr* to float.

flote ➤ *m* ■ a f. afloat.

flotilla ➤ *f* flotilla.

fluctuar §45 ➤ *intr* to fluctuate; *(dudar)* to vacillate, waver.

fluido, a ➤ *adj* fluid; *(inseguro)* in flux ➤ *m* fluid; ELEC. current.

fluir §10 ➤ *intr* to flow; *(brotar)* to gush, stream.

flujo ➤ *m* flow, flux.

flúor ➤ *m* fluorine.

fluorescente ➤ *adj* fluorescent.

fluvial ➤ *adj* fluvial, river.

fobia ➤ *f* phobia.

foca ➤ *f* seal.

foco ➤ *m* focus; *(fuente)* source; *(reflector)* spotlight.

fogata ➤ *f* bonfire.

fogón ➤ *m* stove, range; AMER. bonfire.

folio ➤ *m* page, leaf.

folklórico, a ➤ *adj* folk, folkloric.

follaje ➤ *m* foliage.

folletín ➤ *m* serial.

folleto ➤ *m* pamphlet, brochure.

fomentar ➤ *tr* to foment, stir up; *(promover)* to promote, foster.

fomento ➤ *m* promotion, development.

fonda ➤ *f* *(posada)* inn; *(restaurante)* restaurant; AMER. tavern, bar.

fondear ➤ *tr* to sound, fathom; *(examinar)* to investigate, probe ➤ *intr* MARIT. to drop anchor.

fondo ➤ *m* *(base)* bottom; *(hondura)* depth, bed; *(parte más lejos)* rear, back; *(campo)* background; *(residuo)* residue; *(lo principal)* essence; *(reserva)* store, reservoir ■ a f. completely, thoroughly • echar a f. to sink • irse a f. to sink, founder • sin f. bottomless ■ *pl* funds, capital • f. disponibles ready cash.

fonético, a ➤ *adj* phonetic ➤ *f* phonetics.

forastero, a ➤ *adj* foreign, alien ➤ *mf* stranger, outsider.

forcejar ➤ *intr* to struggle, resist.

forcejeo ➤ *m* struggle, struggling.

forense ➤ *adj* forensic.

forestal ➤ *adj* forest, of a forest.

forjar ➤ *tr* to forge, hammer; *(fabricar)* to make, form.

forma ➤ *f* form; *(dimensiones)* shape; *(silueta)* figure, outline; *(molde)* mold, pattern; *(documento)* form, questionnaire; *(manera)* way, method ■ de f. que so that, in such a way that.

formación ➤ *f* formation; *(educación)* upbringing, training.

formal ➤ *adj* formal.

formalidad ➤ *f* formality.

formalizar §02 ➤ *tr* to formalize.

formar ➤ *tr* to form; *(moldear)* to shape; *(criar)* to bring up, rear ➤ *intr* MIL. to fall in ➤ *reflex* to take form; *(desarrollarse)* to develop.

formatear ➤ *tr* to format.

formato ➤ *m* format; *(tamaño)* size.

formidable ➤ *adj* formidable.

fórmula ➤ *f* formula; MED. prescription; CUL. recipe.

formular ➤ *tr* to formulate ➤ *adj* formulaic.

formulario ➤ *m* form, blank.

forrar ➤ *tr* (*coser*) to line; (*cubrir*) to cover ➤ *reflex* AMER., COLL. to get rich.

forro ➤ *m* lining; (*cubierta*) cover, covering.

fortalecer §09 ➤ *tr* to fortify.

fortaleza ➤ *f* (*vigor*) strength, vigor; (*virtud*) fortitude; (*fortín*) fortress.

fortificar §09 ➤ *tr* to fortify.

fortuna §02 ➤ *f* fortune ■ **por f.** fortunately.

forzado, a ➤ *adj* forced.

forzar §22 ➤ *tr* to force; (*capturar*) to take by force.

forzoso, a ➤ *adj* unavoidable, inevitable.

fosa ➤ *f* grave, tomb ■ **fosas nasales** nostrils.

fósforo ➤ *m* phosphorus; (*cerilla*) match.

fósil ➤ *m* fossil ➤ *adj* fossil, fossilized; COLL. (*antiguo*) old, outdated.

fosilizarse §02 ➤ *reflex* to fossilize.

foso ➤ *m* pit, ditch; THEAT. pit; MIL. moat.

foto ➤ *f* photo, picture ■ **sacar fotos** to take pictures.

fotocopia ➤ *f* photocopy.

fotocopiar ➤ *tr* to photocopy.

fotografía ➤ *f* photography; (*retrato*) photograph, picture; (*taller*) photography studio.

fotografiar §18 ➤ *tr* to photograph.

fotógrafo, a ➤ *mf* photographer.

frac ➤ *m* tails, formal coat.

fracasar ➤ *intr* to fail.

fracaso ➤ *m* failure.

fracción ➤ *f* fraction.

fraccionar ➤ *tr* to divide, break (into parts); CHEM. to fractionate.

fractura ➤ *f* fracture, break.

fragancia ➤ *f* fragrance, perfume.

frágil ➤ *adj* fragile; (*fugaz*) fleeting.

fragmento ➤ *m* fragment; (*trozo*) passage, excerpt.

fraile ➤ *m* friar, monk.

frambuesa ➤ *f* raspberry.

franco, a ➤ *adj* frank; (*liberal*) generous; (*exento*) exempt ➤ *m* FIN. franc.

franela ➤ *f* TEX. flannel; AMER. undershirt.

franja ➤ *f* fringe, border; (*banda*) strip, band.

franqueza ➤ *f* frankness, candor; (*exención*) freedom, exemption; (*generosidad*) generosity.

frasco ➤ *m* small bottle; (*redoma*) flask, vial.

frase ➤ *f* sentence, phrase ■ **f. hecha** set expression.

fraterno, a ➤ *adj* fraternal.

fraude ➤ *m* fraud.

frazada ➤ *f* blanket.

frecuencia ➤ *f* frequency.

frecuentar ➤ *tr* to frequent.

frecuente ➤ *adj* frequent; (*común*) common, habitual.

fregadero ➤ *m* kitchen sink.

fregar §35 ➤ *tr* to scour, scrub; (*lavar*) to wash; AMER., COLL. to annoy ➤ *reflex* AMER. to become annoyed.

fregón, ona ➤ *adj* AMER. annoying ➤ *mf* AMER. pest, annoyance ➤ *f* mop.

freír §39 ➤ *tr* to fry.

frenar ➤ *tr* to brake, apply the brake to; (*hábito, vicio*) to curb, check.

frenazo ➤ *m* sudden braking.

frenético, a ➤ *adj* frenetic, frenzied; (*colérico*) mad, furious.

freno ➤ *m* EQUIT. bit; MECH. brake.

frente ➤ *f* forehead, brow; (*rostro*) face ➤ *m* front; (*fachada*) face, façade; MIL., METEOROL. front ■ **al** or **en f.** in front, opposite • **al f. de** at the head of, in charge of • **f. a** facing, opposite.

fresa ➤ *adj & f* strawberry.

fresco, a ➤ *adj* cool; (*nuevo*) fresh; (*descarado*) fresh, impudent ➤ *m* cool, coolness; (*aire*) fresh air; ARTS fresco.

frescura ➤ *f* freshness, coolness; (*chanza*) fresh remark.

fríamente ➤ *adv* coldly, cooly.

fricción ➤ *f* friction; (*masaje*) massage.

frígido, a ➤ *adj* frigid.

frigorífico ➤ *m* refrigerator.

frijol *or* **frijol** ➤ *m* bean.

frío, a ➤ *adj* cold; *(sin gracia)* insipid ■ *m* cold, coldness ■ **hacer f.** *(tiempo)* to be cold • **tener f.** *(persona)* to be cold.

friolero, a ➤ *adj* sensitive to the cold ➤ *f* trifle, bauble.

frívolo, a ➤ *adj* frivolous.

frontera ➤ *f* border, frontier.

frontón ➤ *m* handball court; ARCHIT. pediment, gable.

frotar ➤ *tr & reflex* to rub (together).

fruncir ➤ *tr* SEW. to gather; *(labios)* to purse; *(frente)* to wrinkle.

frustrado, a ➤ *adj* frustrated, thwarted.

frustrar ➤ *tr* to frustrate, thwart ➤ *reflex (fracasar)* to fail, come to nothing; *(privarse)* to be frustrated.

fruta ➤ *f* fruit; FIG., COLL. fruit, result.

frutería ➤ *f* fruit store or stand.

fruto ➤ *m* fruit.

fuego ➤ *m* fire; *(llama)* flame, heat; *(hogar)* hearth, home; *(fósforo)* light ■ **a f. lento** little by little; CUL. on a low flame • **fuegos artificiales** fireworks.

fuente ➤ *f* *(manantial)* spring; *(aparato)* fountain, water fountain; *(plato)* platter, serving dish; *(origen)* source, origin.

fuera ➤ *adv* outside, out ■ **¡f.!** get out! • **f. de** outside of; *(además de)* besides, except for • **f. de que** aside from the fact that • **f. de sí** beside oneself • **por f.** on the outside.

fuerte ➤ *adj* strong; *(fortificado)* fortified; *(intenso)* powerful, forceful; *(con voz alta)* loud ■ *m* fort, fortress; *(talento)* forte, strong point ➤ *adv* hard; *(en voz alta)* loudly.

fuerza ➤ *f* force, strength; *(poder)* power ■ **a f. de** by dint of • **a la f. or por f.** by force, forcibly; *(forzosamente)* necessarily.

fuga ➤ *f* flight, escape; *(ardor)* ardor; *(escape)* leak, leakage; MUS. fugue.

fugarse §31 ➤ *reflex* to flee, run away; *(salirse)* to leak (out).

fulgir §19 ➤ *intr* to shine, sparkle.

fumador, a ➤ *adj* smoking ➤ *mf* smoker.

fumar ➤ *intr & tr* to smoke.

funcionar ➤ *intr* to work, run.

funcionario, a ➤ *mf* civil servant, official.

funda ➤ *f* cover, case.

fundación ➤ *f* foundation.

fundamental ➤ *adj* fundamental.

fundar ➤ *tr* to found, establish; *(apoyar)* to base, rest ➤ *reflex* FIG. to be founded or based.

fundir ➤ *tr* METAL. to melt, smelt; *(moldear)* to cast, mold; *(bombilla)* to burn out ➤ *reflex* to merge, fuse; AMER. to go bankrupt.

funeral ➤ *adj & m* funeral.

furgoneta ➤ *f* van, truck.

furia ➤ *f* fury.

furioso, a ➤ *adj* furious; *(grande)* tremendous.

furor ➤ *m* fury, rage.

furtivo, a ➤ *adj* furtive, stealthy.

fusible ➤ *adj* fusible ■ *m* fuse.

fusil ➤ *m* rifle, gun.

fusilar ➤ *tr* to shoot.

fusión ➤ *f* melting, fusion; COM. merger.

fusionar ➤ *intr* to merge.

fútbol or **futbol** ➤ *m* soccer, football (G.B.) ■ **f. americano** football.

futbolista ➤ *mf* soccer player, footballer (G.B.).

futuro, a ➤ *adj & m* future ➤ *m* future.

G

gabán ➤ *m* overcoat, topcoat.

gabardina ➤ *f* gabardine; *(sobretodo)* raincoat.

gabinete ➤ *m* *(cuarto)* study, office; *(laboratorio)* laboratory; POL. cabinet.

gacho, a ➤ *adj* *(inclinado)* bowed, bent; *(flojo)* drooping, floppy ➤ *f* mush, paste ■ *pl* porridge.

gafas ➤ *fpl* (eye)glasses ■ **g. de esquí, seguridad** ski, safety goggles.

gaita ➤ *f* MUS. bagpipe; *(organillo)* hurdy-gurdy.

gajo ➤ *m* *(de naranja)* section.

gala ➤ *f* *(vestido)* full dress; *(gracia)* elegance; *(regalos)* wedding gifts.

galán ➤ *m* handsome man; *(pretendiente)* suitor; THEAT. leading man.

galante ➤ *adj* gallant; *(amatorio)* flirtatious.

galápago ➤ *m* ZOOL. freshwater tortoise; METAL. ingot; EQUIT. English saddle.

galardón ➤ *m* award, prize.

galardonar ➤ *tr* to award.

galería ➤ *f* gallery.

gallardía ➤ *f* elegance, grace.

gallardo, a ➤ *adj* elegant, graceful.

galleta ➤ *f* cookie, biscuit (G.B.); *(salada)* cracker.

gallina ➤ *f* hen, chicken.

gallinero ➤ *m* chicken coop, henhouse.

gallo ➤ *m* cock, rooster.

galón ➤ *m* gallon.

galopar *or* **galopear** ➤ *intr* to gallop.

galope ➤ *m* gallop.

gama ➤ *f* gamut.

gamba ➤ *f* prawn.

gamuza ➤ *f* chamois.

gana ➤ *f* *(deseo)* desire, longing; *(apetito)* appetite ■ darle ganas *or* darle la g. de to feel like • de buena, mala g. willingly, unwillingly ■ *pl* tener g. de to want to, feel like.

ganado ➤ *m* livestock; AMER. cattle.

ganador, a ➤ *adj* winning, victorious ➤ *mf* winner.

ganancia ➤ *f* profit, gain.

ganar ➤ *tr* *(lograr)* to gain; *(llevarse)* to win, get; *(recibir)* to earn.

ganchillo ➤ *m* *(aguja)* crochet needle; *(labor)* crochet.

gancho ➤ *m* hook; AMER. hairpin.

ganga ➤ *f* bargain.

ganso, a ➤ *m* gander ➤ *f* goose.

garabato ➤ *m* *(gancho)* hook; *(letra)* scribble, scrawl.

garaje ➤ *m* garage.

garantía ➤ *f* guarantee.

garantizar §02 ➤ *tr* to guarantee.

garbanzo ➤ *m* chickpea.

garfio ➤ *m* grappling iron, grapple.

garganta ➤ *f* throat; *(del pie)* instep; *(desfiladero)* gorge.

garra ➤ *f* claw, talon.

garrafa ➤ *f* carafe, decanter.

garrapata ➤ *f* tick, mite; *(caballo)* nag.

garrotazo ➤ *m* blow.

garrote ➤ *m* *(palo)* club; *(tormento)* garrote.

garza ➤ *f* heron.

gas ➤ *m* gas.

gasa ➤ *f* gauze; *(de luto)* crepe.

gasolina ➤ *f* gasoline, gas.

gasolinera ➤ *f* gas station.

gastar ➤ *tr* *(pagar)* to spend; *(consumir)* to consume, exhaust; *(echar a perder)* to wear out; *(malgastar)* to waste ➤ *intr* to spend ➤ *reflex* *(consumirse)* to be used up, to wear out.

gasto ➤ *m* expenditure, expense.

gastronomía ➤ *f* gastronomy.

gatear ➤ *intr* to walk on all fours.

gatillo ➤ *m* trigger.

gato, a ➤ *mf* cat ➤ *m* TECH., ELEC. jack ■ a gatas on all fours.

gaucho, a ➤ *adj & m* gaucho.

gaveta ➤ *f* drawer.

gavilla ➤ *f* *(cereales)* sheaf of grain; *(gente)* gang, band.

gaviota ➤ *f* seagull, gull.

gaznate ➤ *m* throat, windpipe.

gazpacho ➤ *m* gazpacho.

géiser ➤ *m* geyser.

gelatina ➤ *f* gelatin.

gemelo, a ➤ *adj & mf* twin ➤ *mpl* *(anteojos)* binoculars; *(de camisa)* cuff links • g. de teatro opera glasses.

gemido ➤ *m* moan, groan.

gemir §32 ➤ *intr* to moan, groan.

gen *or* **gene** ➤ *m* gene.

generación ➤ *f* generation.

general ➤ *adj* general ■ en g. *or* por lo g. generally, in general ➤ *mf* general.

generalizar §02 ➤ *tr* to generalize.

generar ➤ *tr* to generate, produce.

género ➤ *m* type, kind; AMER. fabric, material; BIOL. genus.

generosidad ➤ *f* generosity.

generoso, a ➤ *adj* generous.

genético, a ➤ *adj* genetic ➤ *f* genetics.

genial ➤ *adj* brilliant, inspired.

genio ➤ *m* *(carácter)* temperament, disposition; *(talento)* genius ■ de mal g. bad-tempered.

gente ➤ *f* people; *(nación)* folk.

gentío ➤ *m* crowd, mob.

gentuza ➤ *f* riffraff, rabble.

genuino, a ➤ *adj* genuine.

geografía ➤ *f* geography.

geología ➤ *f* geology.

geometría ➤ *f* geometry.

geranio ➤ *m* geranium.

gerencia ➤ *f* management.

gerente ➤ *mf* manager, director.

germen ➤ *m* germ.

gerundio ➤ *m* GRAM. *(del español)* present participle; *(del latín)* gerund.

gestación ➤ *f* gestation.

gesticular ➤ *intr* to gesture, gesticulate; *(hacer muecas)* to grimace, make faces.

gestión ➤ *f (dirección)* administration, management; *(trámite)* step, measure.

gesto ➤ *m* gesture, gesticulation.

giganta ➤ *f* giant, giantess.

gigante ➤ *adj* giant, gigantic ➤ *m* giant.

gigantesco, a ➤ *adj* gigantic, huge.

gimnasia ➤ *f* gymnastics.

gimnasio ➤ *m* gymnasium, gym.

gimnasta ➤ *mf* gymnast.

gimnástica ➤ *f* gymnastics.

ginecólogo, a ➤ *mf* gynecologist.

gira ➤ *f* trip, outing; *(viaje)* tour.

girar ➤ *intr (dar vueltas)* to revolve, rotate; *(alrededor de un eje)* to gyrate; *(torcer)* to turn; COM. to draw.

girasol ➤ *m* BOT. sunflower.

giratorio, a ➤ *adj* turning, rotating.

giro ➤ *m* turn; *(frase)* turn of phrase; COM. draft ▪ g. postal money order.

gitano, a ➤ *adj & mf* Gypsy.

glaciar ➤ *m* glacier ➤ *adj* glacial.

glándula ➤ *f* gland.

glicerina ➤ *f* glycerine.

global ➤ *adj* global; COM. total.

globo ➤ *m* globe; *(de goma)* balloon.

gloria ➤ *f* glory; *(honor)* fame; *(cielo)* heaven.

glorieta ➤ *f* plaza, square; *(cenador)* arbor.

glosario ➤ *m* glossary.

glotón, ona ➤ *adj* gluttonous ➤ *mf* glutton.

glucosa ➤ *f* glucose.

gobernación ➤ *f* government ▪ Ministerio de la G. Ministry of the Interior.

gobernador, a ➤ *mf* governor.

gobernante ➤ *adj* ruling, governing ➤ *mf* ruler, leader.

gobernar §33 ➤ *tr* to govern.

gobierno ➤ *m* government.

gol ➤ *m* goal ▪ marcar *or* meter un g. to make *or* score a goal.

golf ➤ *m* golf ▪ campo de g. golf course.

golfo ➤ *m* GEOG. gulf; *(bahía)* bay.

golfo, a ➤ *mf* urchin.

golondrina ➤ *f* swallow.

golosina ➤ *f* sweet, delicacy.

goloso, a ➤ *mf* sweet-toothed.

golpe ➤ *m* blow, hit; *(sacudida)* bump; COMPUT. hit ▪ de g. suddenly • g. de estado coup d'état.

golpear ➤ *tr & intr* to beat, strike.

goma ➤ *f (caucho)* rubber; *(pegamento)* glue; *(elástico)* rubber band ▪ g. de borrar eraser.

góndola ➤ *f* gondola.

gordo, a ➤ *adj (obeso)* fat, plump; *(abultado)* big; *(grasa)* fatty, greasy.

gordura ➤ *f (grasa)* fat, grease; *(corpulencia)* obesity, fatness.

gorila ➤ *m* gorilla.

gorjear ➤ *intr* to warble, trill.

gorjeo ➤ *m* warble, trill.

gorra ➤ *f* cap; *(de bebé)* bonnet.

gorrear ➤ *intr* AMER. to freeload.

gorrión ➤ *m* sparrow.

gorro ➤ *m* cap; *(de niños)* bonnet.

gota ➤ *f* drop; MED. gout ▪ g. a g. bit by bit, little by little.

gotear ➤ *intr* to drip, trickle.

goteo ➤ *m* dripping, trickling.

gotera ➤ *f* leak.

gótico, a ➤ *adj & mf* Gothic.

gozar §02 ➤ *tr & intr* to enjoy, take pleasure in.

gozne ➤ *m* hinge.

grabación ➤ *f* recording.

grabado ➤ *m (arte, obra)* engraving; *(ilustración)* print, illustration ▪ g. en madera woodcut.

grabador, a ➤ *mf* engraver ➤ *f* tape recorder ▪ g. de video VCR.

grabar ➤ *tr* to engrave; *(registrar sonidos)* to record, tape; COMPUT. to save.

gracia ➤ *f (donaire)* charm, grace; *(agudeza)* witty remark, joke ▪ tener g. to be funny ▪ *pl* thank you, thanks • dar g. to give thanks.

gracioso, a ➤ *adj (encantador)* charming; *(divertido)* amusing, funny.

grada ➤ *f* step, stair; *(asientos)* tier.

grado ➤ *m (calidad)* grade, quality; *(nivel)* degree; *(título académico)* degree, academic title.

graduación ➤ f graduation.
graduado, a ➤ mf graduate.
gradual ➤ adj gradual.
graduar §45 ➤ tr & reflex to graduate.
gráfico, a ➤ adj graphic ➤ m o f graph, chart ■ mpl graphics.
gragea ➤ f sugar-coated pill.
gramática ➤ f grammar.
gramo ➤ m gram, gramme (G.B.).
gran ➤ adj contr of **grande**.
granada ➤ f pomegranate; MIL. grenade, shell.
granate ➤ adj maroon ➤ m garnet.
grande ➤ adj large, big; (considerable) great ■ en g. on a grand scale.
granel ➤ m ■ a g. in bulk, loose.
granero ➤ m granary.
granito ➤ m granite; MED. small pimple.
granizada ➤ f hailstorm.
granizado ➤ m iced drink.
granizo ➤ m hail.
granja ➤ f farm.
granjero, a ➤ mf farmer.
grano ➤ m (semilla) grain, seed; (fruto) grain, cereal; MED. pimple.
granuja ➤ m COLL. (pícaro) rogue, scoundrel; (pilluelo) street urchin.
grapa ➤ f (para los papeles) staple.
grapadora ➤ f stapler.
grasiento, a ➤ adj greasy.
graso, a ➤ adj fatty, greasy.
gratis ➤ adv gratis, free.
gratitud ➤ f gratitude.
gratuito, a ➤ adj free (of charge).
grava ➤ f gravel.
gravar ➤ tr to levy, impose.
grave ➤ adj (serio) grave, serious; (bajo) deep, low.
gravedad ➤ f gravity, seriousness; PHYS. gravity.
gremio ➤ m (sindicato) union, trade union; (asociación) association, society; HIST. guild.
greña ➤ f shock or mop of hair.
greñudo, a ➤ adj disheveled.
gresca ➤ f uproar, hubbub.
grey ➤ f (rebaño) flock, herd; (fieles) congregation.
grieta ➤ f crack, crevice.
grifo ➤ m tap, spigot.

grillete ➤ m fetter, shackle.
grillo ➤ m cricket.
gringo, a ➤ adj foreign; (de E.U.) Yankee ➤ mf foreigner; (de E.U.) Yankee.
gripe ➤ f grippe, flu.
gris ➤ adj gray.
grisáceo, a ➤ adj grayish.
gritar ➤ intr to shout, scream.
grito ➤ m shout, scream.
grosella ➤ f currant ■ g. silvestre gooseberry.
grosería ➤ f (tosquedad) coarseness; (indecencia) vulgarity.
grosero, a ➤ adj coarse, crude.
grosor ➤ m thickness.
grotesco, a ➤ adj grotesque.
grúa ➤ f (máquina) crane, derrick; (camión de auxilio) tow truck.
grueso, a ➤ adj (corpulento) stout, fat; (de grosor) thick ➤ m (espesor) thickness; (parte principal) bulk.
grumo ➤ m (de líquido) lump.
gruñido ➤ m grunt; (de un perro) growl.
gruñir ➤ intr to grunt; (un perro) to growl; (refunfuñar) to grumble.
gruñón, ona ➤ adj COLL. grouchy, grumpy.
grupo ➤ m group.
gruta ➤ f grotto, cavern.
guaba ➤ f guava.
guacho, a ➤ adj S. AMER. orphaned.
guagua ➤ f S. AMER. baby; CARIB. bus.
guante ➤ m glove.
guantera ➤ f glove compartment.
guapo, a ➤ adj good-looking, attractive.
guarda ➤ mf guard, custodian.
guardabarros ➤ mpl fender, mudguard.
guardabosque(s) ➤ mf forest ranger.
guardacostas ➤ m coast guard cutter.
guardaespaldas ➤ mf bodyguard.
guardameta ➤ mf goalkeeper, goalie.
guardar ➤ tr (proteger) to protect; (animales) to keep, tend; (conservar) to save, put away; COMPUT. to save.
guardarropa ➤ m cloakroom, checkroom; (ropero) wardrobe, closet.
guardería ➤ f daycare center, nursery.
guardia ➤ f (tropas) guard; (defensa)

defense, protection ➤ *mf (centinela)* guard; *(policía)* policeman/woman.

guardián, ana ➤ *mf* guardian, custodian; *(vigilante)* watchman.

guardilla ➤ *f* attic, garret.

guasa ➤ *f* joke, jest.

guatemalteco, a ➤ *adj & mf* Guatemalan.

guayaba ➤ *f* BOT. guava; *(jalea)* guava jelly.

guayabera ➤ *f* AMER. lightweight shirt.

guerra ➤ *f* war; *(ciencia)* warfare ■ hacer la g. to wage war • Primera, Segunda Guerra Mundial First, Second World War.

guerrero, a ➤ *adj* warring, fighting ➤ *mf* warrior, fighter.

guerrilla ➤ *f* MIL. guerrilla warfare; *(partida)* band of guerrillas.

guerrillero, a ➤ *mf* guerilla.

guía ➤ *mf* guide; *(consejero)* adviser; *(libro)* guide, directory.

guiar §18 ➤ *tr* to guide, lead; *(conducir)* to drive.

guijarro ➤ *m* pebble.

guinda ➤ *f* sour cherry.

guindilla ➤ *f* red pepper.

guiñar ➤ *tr* to wink.

guiño ➤ *m* wink.

guión ➤ *m* CINEM., THEAT. script; GRAM. hyphen.

guirnalda ➤ *f* garland, wreath.

guisado ➤ *m* stew.

guisante ➤ *m* pea.

guisar ➤ *tr* to cook; *(estofar)* to stew.

guiso ➤ *m* stew; *(plato)* cooked dish.

guita ➤ *f* twine.

guitarra ➤ *f* guitar.

guitarrista ➤ *mf* guitarist.

gula ➤ *f* gluttony.

gusano ➤ *m* worm; *(oruga)* caterpillar.

gustar ➤ *tr (probar)* to taste, sample; *(experimentar)* to test, try ➤ *intr* to please, be pleasing ■ me gustan los mariscos I like seafood • ¿te gustaría conocerla? would you like to meet her?

gusto ➤ *m* taste; *(sabor)* flavor; *(placer)* pleasure ■ a g. comfortable; *(a voluntad)* at will; CUL. to taste • con mucho g. with pleasure.

gustoso, a ➤ *adj* tasty, savory.

H

haba ➤ *f* fava bean.

haber[1] ➤ *m* COM. credit ■ *pl* assets, property.

haber[2] §23 ➤ *aux* to have ■ h. de to have to, must ➤ *impers* ■ hace ago • hay there is, there are • hay que it is necessary • no hay de qué don't mention it, you're welcome • ¿qué hay? what's up? ➤ *tr (poseer)* to have.

hábil ➤ *adj* capable; *(diestro)* skillful.

habilidad ➤ *f (capacidad)* capability; *(ingeniosidad)* skill.

habitación ➤ *f (cuarto)* room; *(domicilio)* dwelling, residence.

habitante ➤ *mf* inhabitant.

habitar ➤ *tr* to inhabit, live in.

hábito ➤ *m* habit.

habituar §45 ➤ *tr* to habituate ➤ *reflex* to become accustomed *(a* to).

hablador, a ➤ *adj* talkative.

hablar ➤ *intr & tr* to speak, talk ■ ¡ni h! out of the question!

hacer §24 ➤ *tr* to make; *(efectuar)* to do; *(causar)* to cause ■ h. cara o frente a to face • h. caso de *or* a to pay attention to • h. falta *(faltar)* to be needed; *(echar de menos)* to be missed • h. saber to let know • h. una maleta to pack a suitcase • h. una pregunta to ask a question • h. una visita to pay a visit ➤ *impers* ■ desde hace for • hace frío it is cold • hace mucho long ago • hace poco a little while ago ➤ *reflex* to become; *(convertirse)* to turn into.

hacha ➤ *f* ax, axe.

hachís ➤ *m* hashish.

hacia ➤ *prep* toward; *(alrededor de)* about, around ■ h. abajo downward • h. acá here, this way • h. adelante forward • h. arriba upward • h. atrás backward.

hacienda ➤ *f* ranch.

hada ➤ *f* fairy ■ cuento de hadas fairy tale.

halagar §31 ➤ *tr* to flatter.

halago ➤ *m* flattery.

halcón ➤ *m* falcon, hawk.

hallar ➤ *tr (por casualidad)* to come across; *(encontrar)* to find; *(averiguar)* to find out ➤ *reflex (encontrarse)* to be, find oneself.

hallazgo ➤ *m* discovery.

hamaca ➤ *f* hammock.

hambre ➤ *f* hunger; *(de una nación)* famine ■ **tener h.** to be hungry.

hamburguesa ➤ *f* hamburger.

harina ➤ *f* flour.

hartar ➤ *tr (saciar el apetito)* to stuff; *(satisfacer)* to satisfy; *(fastidiar)* to annoy; *(cansar)* to tire.

harto, a ➤ *adj (cansado)* fed up ■ *adv (bastante)* enough; *(muy)* very.

hasta ➤ *prep* until ■ **fueron h. el río** they went as far as the river • **h. la vista** *or* **h. luego** see you, so long • **h. que** until ➤ *adv* even ■ **h. los vecinos lo vieron** even the neighbors saw it.

hebilla ➤ *f* buckle, clasp.

hebra ➤ *f (hilo)* thread; *(fibra)* fiber.

hechicería ➤ *f (brujería)* witchcraft; *(hechizo)* spell.

hechizo ➤ *m (sortilegio)* spell; *(encanto)* charm.

hecho, a ➤ *adj* done; *(ropa)* ready-made ■ **h. y derecho** in every respect ➤ *m (acto)* act, action; *(hazaña)* deed; *(suceso)* event; *(realidad)* fact; *(asunto)* point ■ **de h.** *(en realidad)* as a matter of fact.

hedor ➤ *m* stench, stink.

heladería ➤ *f* ice-cream parlor.

helado, a ➤ *adj* frozen; *(muy frío)* freezing ➤ *m* ice cream; *(sorbete)* sherbet.

helar §33 ➤ *tr & reflex* to freeze.

hélice ➤ *f* helix; AVIA. propeller; ZOOL. snail.

helicóptero ➤ *m* helicopter.

hembra ➤ *f* woman; *(animal)* female.

hemisferio ➤ *m* hemisphere.

hemorragia ➤ *f* hemorrhage.

hendidura ➤ *f* crack.

heno ➤ *m* hay.

hepatitis ➤ *f* hepatitis.

herbolario ➤ *m* herbalist's shop.

heredar ➤ *tr* to inherit.

heredero, a ➤ *m* heir ➤ *f* heiress.

herencia ➤ *f (patrimonio)* inheritance; *(tradición)* heritage; BIOL. heredity.

herido, a ➤ *adj* wounded ➤ *mf (persona)* wounded *or* injured person.

herir §43 ➤ *tr* to wound.

hermanastro, a ➤ *mf* stepbrother/sister.

hermano, a ➤ *m* brother ■ **h. gemelo** twin brother • **primo h.** first cousin ➤ *f* sister ■ **h. gemela** twin sister • **prima h.** first cousin.

hermético, a ➤ *adj* airtight.

hermoso, a ➤ *adj* beautiful.

hermosura ➤ *f* beauty.

héroe ➤ *m* hero.

heroína ➤ *f* heroine; *(droga)* heroin.

herradura ➤ *f* horseshoe.

herramienta ➤ *f* tool.

hervir §43 ➤ *intr* to boil.

heterogéneo, a ➤ *adj* heterogeneous.

híbrido, a ➤ *adj & mf* hybrid.

hidratar ➤ *tr* to hydrate.

hidráulica ➤ *f* hydraulics.

hidroavión ➤ *m* hydroplane.

hidroeléctrico, a ➤ *adj* hydroelectric.

hidrógeno ➤ *m* hydrogen.

hidroplano ➤ *m* MARIT. hydrofoil; AVIA. seaplane.

hiedra ➤ *f* ivy.

hielo ➤ *m* ice.

hiena ➤ *f* hyena.

hierba ➤ *f* grass; *(medicinal)* herb; COLL. marijuana ■ **mala h.** weed.

hierbabuena ➤ *f* mint.

hierro ➤ *m* iron; *(marca)* brand ■ **h. forjado** wrought iron.

hígado ➤ *m* liver.

higiénico, a ➤ *adj* hygienic.

higo ➤ *m* fig.

higuera ➤ *f* fig tree.

hijastro, a ➤ *mf* stepchild, stepson/daughter.

hijo, a ➤ *m* son ➤ *f* daughter ■ *pl* children.

hilera ➤ *f* row, file.

hilo ➤ *m (hebra)* thread; *(tejido)* linen.

himno ➤ *m* hymn ■ **h. nacional** national anthem.

hincapié ➤ *m* planting one's feet ■ **hacer h. en** COLL. to insist on, stress.

hincar §47 ➤ *tr (clavar)* to sink, drive (in) ➤ *reflex* to sink into *or* down.

hincha ➤ *f* grudge ➤ *m* COLL. fan, supporter.

hinchado, a ➤ *adj* swollen.

hinchar ➤ *tr (aumentar)* to swell; *(inflar)* to inflate, blow up ➤ *reflex* MED. to swell.

hinchazón ➤ *f* MED. swelling.

hinojo ➤ *m* fennel.

hiperenlace ➤ *m* hyperlink, link.

hipertensión ➤ *f* hypertension, high blood pressure.

hipertexto ➤ *m* hypertext.

hípico, a ➤ *adj* horse, equine.

hipnosis ➤ *f* hypnosis.

hipnotizar §02 ➤ *tr* to hypnotize.

hipo ➤ *m* hiccup.

hipocresía ➤ *f* hypocrisy.

hipócrita ➤ *adj* hypocritical ➤ *mf* hypocrite.

hipopótamo ➤ *m* hippopotamus.

hipoteca ➤ *f* mortgage.

hipotecar §47 ➤ *tr* to mortgage; *(comprometer)* to compromise.

hipótesis ➤ *f* hypothesis.

hirviente ➤ *adj* boiling.

hispano, a ➤ *adj & mf* Hispanic.

hispanohablante ➤ *adj & mf* Spanish-speaking (person).

histeria ➤ *f* hysteria.

histérico, a ➤ *adj (alterado)* hysteric(al).

historia ➤ *f* history; *(cuento)* story.

historiador, a ➤ *mf* historian.

historial ➤ *m* file, dossier.

histórico, a ➤ *adj* historic(al).

historieta ➤ *f* story, anecdote ■ *pl* h. ilustradas *or* cómicas comic strips.

hocico ➤ *m* ZOOL. muzzle, snout.

hogar ➤ *m (de una chimenea)* hearth, fireplace; *(casa)* home.

hoguera ➤ *f* bonfire.

hoja ➤ *f* leaf; *(pétalo)* petal; *(de papel)* sheet; *(documento)* form; *(cuchilla)* blade ■ h. de cálculo spreadsheet.

hojalata ➤ *f* tin.

hojaldre ➤ *mf* puff pastry.

hojarasca ➤ *f* dead *or* fallen leaves.

hojear ➤ *tr* to skim *or* leaf (through); COMPUT. *(una lista)* to browse.

¡hola! ➤ *interj* hello!, hi!

holgado, a ➤ *adj (ancho)* big, loose; *(vida)* comfortable, well-off.

holgazán, ana ➤ *adj* lazy.

hollín ➤ *m* soot.

hombre ➤ *m* man; *(humanidad)* mankind; *(esposo)* husband ■ h. de negocios businessman.

hombrera ➤ *f* shoulder pad.

hombro ➤ *m* shoulder ■ a hombros piggyback • encogerse de hombros to shrug.

homenaje ➤ *m* homage.

homicidio ➤ *m* homicide.

homogéneo, a ➤ *adj* homogeneous.

homosexual ➤ *adj & mf* homosexual.

hondo, a ➤ *adj* deep.

hondureño, a ➤ *adj & mf* Honduran.

honestidad ➤ *f* honesty.

honesto, a ➤ *adj (honrado)* honest; *(decente)* decent; *(pudoroso)* modest.

hongo ➤ *m* mushroom; MED. fungus; *(sombrero)* derby, bowler (hat).

honor ➤ *m* honor ■ hacer h. a to honor.

honorario, a ➤ *adj* honorary ➤ *m* honorarium ■ *pl* fees.

honra ➤ *f* honor, self-respect; *(buena fama)* reputation ■ *pl* last respects.

honradez ➤ *f* honesty, integrity.

honrado, a ➤ *adj* honest, honorable.

honrar ➤ *tr* to honor, respect.

hora ➤ *f* hour; *(momento)* time ■ a la h. on time, punctually ¿a qué h.? at what time?, when? • a última h. at the last minute; *(por la noche)* last thing at night • h. punta rush hour • por h. per hour • ¿qué h. es? what time is it? ■ *pl* h. de oficina office hours.

horario ➤ *m* schedule, timetable.

horca ➤ *f* gallows; AGR. pitchfork.

horcajadas ➤ *adv* ■ a h. astride, straddling.

horizontal ➤ *adj & f* horizontal.

horizonte ➤ *m* horizon.

hormiga ➤ *f* ant.

hormigón ➤ *m* concrete.

hormiguero ➤ *m* ENTOM. anthill.

hormona ➤ *f* hormone.

hornada ➤ *f* CUL. batch (of baked goods).

hornear ➤ *intr & tr* to bake.

horno ➤ *m* oven; TECH. furnace; CERAM. kiln ■ h. microondas microwave oven.

horóscopo ➤ *m* horoscope.

horquilla ➤ *f* hairpin, hair clip.

horrible ➤ *adj* horrible.

horror ➤ *m* horror; *(temor)* terror.
horrorizar §02 ➤ *tr* to horrify ➤ *reflex* to be horrified.
horroroso, a ➤ *adj* horrible; COLL. *(feo)* hideous; *(muy malo)* terrible.
hortaliza ➤ *f* vegetable.
hortensia ➤ *f* hydrangea.
horticultura ➤ *f* horticulture.
hosco, a ➤ *adj (áspero)* gruff, surly.
hospedaje ➤ *m* lodging.
hospedar ➤ *tr* to lodge, put up ➤ *reflex* to lodge or stay *(en at)*.
hospicio ➤ *m* orphanage.
hospital ➤ *m* hospital.
hospitalario, a ➤ *adj* hospitable.
hospitalidad ➤ *f* hospitality.
hospitalizar §02 ➤ *tr* to hospitalize.
hostelería ➤ *f* hotel management; *(industria)* hotel business.
hostil ➤ *adj* hostile.
hotel ➤ *m* hotel.
hotelero, a ➤ *adj* hotel ➤ *mf (dueño)* hotelkeeper, hotel owner.
hoy ➤ *adv (en este día)* today; *(en el tiempo presente)* nowadays ■ de or desde h. en adelante from now on • h. *(en)* día nowadays.
hoyo ➤ *m* hole.
hoz ➤ *f* sickle.
hucha ➤ *f (alcancía)* piggy bank; *(arca)* chest; *(ahorros)* savings.
hueco, a ➤ *adj* hollow ➤ *m (cavidad)* hollow; *(espacio)* space.
huelga ➤ *f (paro)* strike ■ declararse en h. to go on strike.
huelguista ➤ *mf* striker.
huella ➤ *f (del pie)* footprint; *(de un animal)* track, print ■ h. digital or dactilar fingerprint.
huérfano, a ➤ *adj* orphan(ed) ➤ *mf* orphan.
huerta ➤ *f (sembrado)* large vegetable garden; *(de árboles)* orchard; SP. *(regadío)* irrigated land.
huerto ➤ *m (jardín)* vegetable garden; *(de árboles)* orchard.
hueso ➤ *m* ANAT. bone; BOT. pit, stone.
huésped, a ➤ *mf (invitado)* guest; BIOL. host ➤ *m (invitante)* host ➤ *f* hostess.
huevo ➤ *m* egg ■ h. duro hard-boiled egg • huevos revueltos scrambled eggs.

huida ➤ *f* escape.
huir §10 ➤ *intr* to escape, run away ■ h. de flee from ➤ *reflex* to run away, flee.
hule ➤ *m* rubber; *(tela)* oilcloth.
hulla ➤ *f* coal.
humanidad ➤ *f* humanity; *(género)* mankind.
humanitario, a ➤ *adj* humanitarian.
humano, a ➤ *adj* human; *(benévolo)* humane ➤ *m* human (being).
humear ➤ *intr (echar humo)* to smoke; *(echar vapor)* to steam ➤ *tr* AMER. to fumigate.
humedad ➤ *f* humidity; *(calidad de húmedo)* dampness, moisture.
humedecer §09 ➤ *tr* to humidify; *(mojar)* to dampen, moisten.
húmedo, a ➤ *adj* humid; *(mojado)* damp, moist.
humildad ➤ *f* humility.
humilde ➤ *adj* humble, meek; *(bajo)* lowly; *(de poco monto)* modest, poor.
humillar ➤ *tr (rebajar)* to humble; *(avergonzar)* humiliate.
humo ➤ *m* smoke.
humor ➤ *m* humor; *(talante)* mood, humor; *(agudeza)* humor, wit.
hundimiento ➤ *m (naufragio)* sinking; *(derrumbe)* cave-in; *(ruina)* ruin.
hundir ➤ *tr (sumergir)* to sink; *(clavar)* to plunge ➤ *reflex (sumergirse)* to sink; *(caer)* to fall down, collapse.
huracán ➤ *m* hurricane.
huraño, a ➤ *adj* unsociable.
hurgar §31 ➤ *tr* to poke or rummage around in.
hurtar ➤ *tr* to steal.
hurto ➤ *m* theft, robbery.

I

icono ➤ *m* icon.
ida ➤ *f (acción)* going; *(viaje)* trip ■ i. y vuelta round trip.
idea ➤ *f* idea; *(concepto)* concept; *(noción)* notion ■ cambiar de i. to change one's mind.
ideal ➤ *adj* ideal.
idealista ➤ *adj & mf* idealist.
idear ➤ *tr* to think up, plan.
idéntico, a ➤ *adj* identical.

identidad ➤ *f* identity.
identificación ➤ *f* identification.
identificar §47 ➤ *tr* to identify ➤ *reflex* to identify (oneself) with.
ideología ➤ *f* ideology.
idilio ➤ *m* idyll.
idioma ➤ *m* language, tongue.
idiota ➤ *adj* foolish, idiotic ➤ *mf* idiot, imbecile.
idolatría ➤ *f* idolatry.
ídolo ➤ *m* idol.
idóneo, a ➤ *adj (apto)* capable, apt; *(conveniente)* suitable, fit.
iglesia ➤ *f* church.
ignorancia ➤ *f* ignorance.
ignorante ➤ *adj* ignorant, uneducated ➤ *mf* ignoramus.
ignorar ➤ *tr* to be ignorant of, not to know.
igual ➤ *adj* equal; *(parejo)* even, level ■ **darle a uno i.** to be the same to one ➤ *m* MATH. equal sign ➤ *mf* equal ■ **al i. que** just like • **i. que** the same as.
igualar ➤ *tr* to equalize, make equal ➤ *intr* ■ **i. a** or **con** to be equal to.
igualdad ➤ *f* equality.
igualmente ➤ *adv* equally; *(en la misma manera)* the same, likewise.
ilegal ➤ *adj & mf* illegal (person).
ilegible ➤ *adj* illegible.
ilegítimo, a ➤ *adj* illegitimate.
ileso, a ➤ *adj* unhurt, unscathed.
ilícito, a ➤ *adj* illicit.
iluminación ➤ *f* illumination; *(alumbrado)* lighting.
iluminar ➤ *tr* to illuminate; *(alumbrar)* to light.
ilusión ➤ *f* illusion; *(esperanza)* hope ■ **hacerse la i. de que** to imagine that.
ilusionar ➤ *tr* to build up (someone's) hopes; *(engañar)* to deceive ➤ *reflex* to get one's hopes up.
ilustración ➤ *f* illustration; *(grabado)* picture.
ilustrar ➤ *tr* to illustrate.
ilustre ➤ *adj* illustrious, distinguished.
imagen ➤ *f* image.
imaginación ➤ *f* imagination.
imaginar ➤ *tr* to imagine.
imán ➤ *m* magnet.
imbécil ➤ *adj & mf* imbecile.

imitación ➤ *f* imitation.
imitar ➤ *tr* to imitate, mimic.
impacientar ➤ *tr* to make (someone) lose patience ➤ *reflex* to lose one's patience.
impaciente ➤ *adj* impatient, restless.
impacto ➤ *m* impact; *(choque)* shock.
impar ➤ *adj* odd, uneven.
imparcial ➤ *adj* impartial.
impasible ➤ *adj* impassive.
impecable ➤ *adj* impeccable.
impedido, a ➤ *adj & mf* disabled (person).
impedimento ➤ *m* impediment.
impedir §32 ➤ *tr* to prevent, obstruct.
impenetrable ➤ *adj* impenetrable.
imperativo, a ➤ *adj & m* imperative.
imperdible ➤ *m* safety pin.
imperfecto, a ➤ *adj* imperfect.
imperial ➤ *adj* imperial.
imperio ➤ *m* empire; *(autoridad)* authority; *(duración)* reign.
impermeable ➤ *adj* impermeable, waterproof ➤ *m* raincoat, mackintosh (G.B.).
impersonal ➤ *adj* impersonal.
impertinencia ➤ *f* impertinence.
impertinente ➤ *adj* impertinent.
ímpetu ➤ *m* impetus; *(violencia)* violence; *(energía)* energy; *(fogosidad)* impetuosity.
impetuoso, a ➤ *adj* violent; *(fogoso)* impetuous.
implacable ➤ *adj* implacable.
implantar ➤ *tr* to implant.
implicar §47 ➤ *tr* to implicate; *(significar)* to imply, mean ➤ *reflex* to become involved.
implícito, a ➤ *adj* implicit.
implorar ➤ *tr* to implore.
imponente ➤ *adj* imposing.
imponer §37 ➤ *tr (ordenar)* to impose; *(infundir)* to inspire, instill ➤ *reflex* ■ **i. a** to dominate.
importación ➤ *f* import.
importador, a ➤ *mf* importer.
importancia ➤ *f* importance.
importante ➤ *adj* important.
importar ➤ *intr* to be important, matter ➤ *tr* to cost; COM. to import.
importe ➤ *m* amount, cost.

imposibilitar ➤ *tr* to make impossible.

imposible ➤ *adj* impossible.

impostor, a ➤ *mf* impostor.

impotencia ➤ *f* impotence.

imprenta ➤ *f (arte)* printing; *(establecimiento)* printing house.

imprescindible ➤ *adj* indispensable.

impresión ➤ *f* impression; *(edición)* printing; *(obra)* edition.

impresionante ➤ *adj* impressive.

impresionar ➤ *tr* to make an impression on, impress ➤ *reflex* to be moved.

impresionista ➤ *adj & mf* impressionist.

impreso, a ➤ *adj* printed.

impresora ➤ *f* COMPUT. printer.

imprevisible ➤ *adj* unpredictable.

imprevisto, a ➤ *adj* unforeseen, unexpected.

imprimir §55 ➤ *tr* to print.

impropio, a ➤ *adj* inappropriate.

improvisar ➤ *tr* to improvise.

imprudencia ➤ *f* imprudence.

impuesto ➤ *m* tax, duty ∎ i. a las rentas income tax • i. a las ventas sales tax.

impulsar ➤ *tr* to impel, drive.

impulso ➤ *m* impulse.

impureza ➤ *f* impurity.

inacabable ➤ *adj* interminable, endless.

inaccesible ➤ *adj* inaccessible.

inaceptable ➤ *adj* unacceptable.

inactivo, a ➤ *adj* inactive.

inadecuado, a ➤ *adj* unsuitable, inadequate.

inagotable ➤ *adj* inexhaustible, endless.

inaguantable ➤ *adj* unbearable, insufferable.

inalámbrico, a ➤ *adj* wireless.

inanimado, a ➤ *adj* inanimate, lifeless.

inauguración ➤ *f* inauguration.

inaugurar ➤ *tr* to inaugurate, open.

incalculable ➤ *adj* incalculable.

incansable ➤ *adj* untiring, tireless.

incapacitado, a ➤ *adj* incapacitated; *(discapacitado)* disabled, handicapped.

incapacitar ➤ *tr* to incapacitate.

incapaz ➤ *adj* incapable.

incendiar ➤ *tr* to set on fire, set fire to

➤ *reflex* to catch fire.

incendio ➤ *m* fire.

incentivo ➤ *m* incentive.

incertidumbre ➤ *f* uncertainty, doubt.

incinerar ➤ *tr* to incinerate, cremate.

incipiente ➤ *adj* incipient.

incitar ➤ *tr* to incite, instigate.

inclinación ➤ *f* inclination; *(del cuerpo)* bowing; *(pendiente)* slope, slant.

inclinar ➤ *tr (la cabeza)* to bow, lower; *(torcer)* to slant, tilt ➤ *reflex (doblarse)* to bow; *(parecerse)* to resemble; *(estar dispuesto)* to be or feel inclined.

incluir §10 ➤ *tr* to include; *(encerrar)* to enclose; *(comprender)* to comprise.

incluso ➤ *adv (inclusivamente)* inclusively; *(aun más)* even.

incógnito, a ➤ *adj* unknown ∎ de i. incognito ➤ *f* MATH. unknown quantity.

incoherente ➤ *adj* incoherent.

incoloro, a ➤ *adj* colorless.

incombustible ➤ *adj* incombustible, fireproof.

incomible ➤ *adj* inedible.

incomodidad ➤ *f* discomfort; *(molestia)* inconvenience.

incómodo, a ➤ *adj* uncomfortable.

incomparable ➤ *adj* incomparable.

incompatible ➤ *adj* incompatible.

incompetente ➤ *adj* incompetent.

incompleto, a ➤ *adj* incomplete, unfinished.

incomprensible ➤ *adj* incomprehensible.

incomunicado, a ➤ *adj* isolated, cut off; CRIMIN. incommunicado.

inconcebible ➤ *adj* inconceivable.

incondicional ➤ *adj* unconditional.

inconfundible ➤ *adj* unmistakable.

incongruente ➤ *adj* incongruous.

inconsciente ➤ *adj* unconscious; unaware; *(irreflexivo)* thoughtless ➤ *m* unconscious.

inconsecuente ➤ *adj* inconsistent.

inconsistente ➤ *adj* inconsistent.

inconsolable ➤ *adj* inconsolable.

incontable ➤ *adj* countless.

incontrolable ➤ *adj* uncontrollable.

inconveniente ➤ *adj* inconvenient;

(inapropiado) inappropriate ➤ *m (obstáculo)* obstacle; *(objeción)* objection; *(desventaja)* drawback ∎ **tener i.** to mind, object.
incorporación ➤ *f* incorporation.
incorporar ➤ *tr* to incorporate ➤ *reflex* to sit up; *(unirse a)* to join.
incorrecto, a ➤ *adj* incorrect.
incorregible ➤ *adj* incorrigible.
incrédulo, a ➤ *adj* incredulous.
increíble ➤ *adj* incredible, unbelievable.
incrementar ➤ *tr* to increase, augment.
inculto, a ➤ *adj* uncultured, uneducated.
incurable ➤ *adj* incurable.
incurrir ➤ *intr* ∎ **i. en** *(error, crimen)* to commit; *(deuda, ira)* incur.
indagar §31 ➤ *tr* to investigate, inquire into.
indecente ➤ *adj* indecent.
indecisión ➤ *f* indecision.
indeciso, a ➤ *adj (irresoluto)* undecided; *(incierto)* indecisive.
indefenso, a ➤ *adj* defenseless.
indefinido, a ➤ *adj* undefined; *(indeterminado)* indefinite.
indemnización ➤ *f* indemnity.
independencia ➤ *f* independence.
independiente ➤ *adj & mf* independent ➤ *adv* independently.
indescifrable ➤ *adj* undecipherable.
indescriptible ➤ *adj* indescribable.
indeseable ➤ *adj & mf* undesirable.
indeterminado, a ➤ *adj* indeterminate; *(indeciso)* indecisive, irresolute.
indicación ➤ *f* indication; *(señal)* sign; *(sugerencia)* suggestion; *(instrucción)* direction, instruction.
indicador, a ➤ *adj* indicating ➤ *m* indicator.
indicar §47 ➤ *tr* to indicate.
indicativo, a ➤ *adj & m* indicative.
índice ➤ *m* index; *(general)* table of contents; *(de biblioteca)* catalogue; *(dedo)* index finger.
indicio ➤ *m* indication, sign ∎ *pl* clues.
indiferencia ➤ *f* indifference.
indiferente ➤ *adj* indifferent.
indígena ➤ *adj & mf* native.
indigestión ➤ *f* indigestion.

indignación ➤ *f* indignation.
indignar ➤ *tr* to anger, infuriate ➤ *reflex* to become indignant.
índigo ➤ *m* indigo.
indio, a ➤ *adj & mf* Indian.
indirecto, a ➤ *adj* indirect ➤ *f* hint.
indiscreto, a ➤ *adj* indiscreet.
indiscutible ➤ *adj* indisputable.
indispensable ➤ *adj* indispensable.
indisponer §37 ➤ *tr* to set against ➤ *reflex (enfermarse)* to become indisposed; *(malquistarse)* to fall out.
indisposición ➤ *f* indisposition.
indispuesto, a ➤ *adj* indisposed.
individual ➤ *adj* individual; *(habitación)* single.
individuo, a ➤ *adj & m* individual.
indivisible ➤ *adj* indivisible.
índole ➤ *f (naturaleza)* nature, character; *(tipo)* type, kind.
inducir §14 ➤ *tr* to induce.
indudable ➤ *adj* indubitable, certain.
indulgente ➤ *adj* indulgent.
indultar ➤ *tr (perdonar)* to pardon; *(exonerar)* to exempt.
indumentaria ➤ *f* clothing, garments.
industria ➤ *f* industry.
industrial ➤ *adj* industrial ➤ *m* industrialist.
industrializar §02 ➤ *tr* to industrialize.
ineficaz ➤ *adj* ineffective, inefficacious.
ineptitud ➤ *f* ineptitude.
inepto, a ➤ *adj & mf* inept (person).
inerte ➤ *adj* inert.
inesperado, a ➤ *adj* unexpected.
inestable ➤ *adj* unstable.
inevitable ➤ *adj* inevitable.
inexacto, a ➤ *adj* inexact, inaccurate.
inexistente ➤ *adj* nonexistent.
inexplicable ➤ *adj* inexplicable.
inexplorado, a ➤ *adj* unexplored.
infalible ➤ *adj (inequívoco)* infallible; *(inevitable)* inevitable.
infancia ➤ *f* infancy.
infantería ➤ *f* infantry.
infantil ➤ *adj* infantile; *(aniñado)* childish.
infarto ➤ *m* infarct, infarction.
infección ➤ *f* infection.
infectar ➤ *tr* to infect ➤ *reflex* to become infected.

infeliz ➤ *adj* unhappy; *(desgraciado)* unfortunate; *(miserable)* wretched.

inferior ➤ *adj (de abajo)* lower; *(menor)* inferior; *(menos)* less.

infestar ➤ *tr* to infest.

infidelidad ➤ *f* infidelity.

infierno ➤ *m* hell.

infinidad ➤ *f* infinity.

infinitivo, a ➤ *adj & m* infinitive.

infinito, a ➤ *adj & m* infinite.

inflación ➤ *f* inflation.

inflamación ➤ *f* inflammation.

inflamar ➤ *tr* to set on fire; *(las pasiones)* to inflame ➤ *reflex* to catch fire.

inflar ➤ *tr* to inflate.

inflexible ➤ *adj* inflexible, rigid.

influencia ➤ *f* influence.

influir §10 ➤ *intr* to have influence.

información ➤ *f* information; *(datos)* data.

informal ➤ *adj* informal; *(de poco fiar)* unreliable.

informalidad ➤ *f* informality; *(falta de seriedad)* irresponsibility.

informar ➤ *tr* to inform, tell *(de* of, *sobre* about) ➤ *reflex* to find out.

informática ➤ *f* computer science.

informe ➤ *m* report ■ *pl* information.

infortunio ➤ *m* misfortune, bad luck.

infracción ➤ *f* infraction.

infraestructura ➤ *f* infrastructure.

infringir §19 ➤ *tr* to infringe, violate.

infundir ➤ *tr* to instill, arouse.

infusión ➤ *f* infusion.

ingeniería ➤ *f* engineering.

ingeniero, a ➤ *mf* engineer.

ingenio ➤ *m (habilidad)* ingenuity; *(talento)* talent; *(agudeza)* wit.

ingenioso, a ➤ *adj* ingenious.

ingenuo, a ➤ *adj & mf* naive (person).

ingle ➤ *f* groin.

inglés, a ➤ *adj* English ➤ *m (idioma)* English ➤ *mf* Englishman/woman.

ingratitud ➤ *f* ingratitude.

ingrato, a ➤ *adj* ungrateful; *(que no satisface)* thankless.

ingrediente ➤ *m* ingredient.

ingresar ➤ *intr* to enter, go in; *(hacerse miembro)* to join ➤ *tr* to deposit.

ingreso ➤ *m (acción)* entrance; *(entrada)* entryway; *(de dinero)* income ■ *pl* earnings.

inhabilidad ➤ *f (falta de maña)* unskillfulness; *(impedimento)* handicap.

inhalar ➤ *tr* to inhale.

inhumano, a ➤ *adj* inhuman, cruel.

inicial ➤ *adj & f* initial.

iniciar ➤ *tr* to initiate; *(admitir)* to introduce; COMPUT. to boot.

iniciativa ➤ *f* initiative.

inicio ➤ *m* beginning.

injerir §43 ➤ *tr* to insert ➤ *reflex* to interfere, meddle.

injuria ➤ *f* insult; *(daño)* injury.

injuriar ➤ *tr (ofender)* to insult; *(dañar)* to injure.

injusticia ➤ *f* injustice.

injustificable ➤ *adj* unjustifiable.

injusto, a ➤ *adj* unjust.

inmaculado, a ➤ *adj* immaculate.

inmaduro, a ➤ *adj (fruta)* unripe, green; *(persona)* immature.

inmediato, a ➤ *adj* next to, adjoining ■ de i. immediately, at once.

inmenso, a ➤ *adj* immense.

inmigración ➤ *f* immigration.

inmigrante ➤ *adj & mf* immigrant.

inmigrar ➤ *intr* to immigrate.

inminente ➤ *adj* imminent.

inmobiliario, a ➤ *adj* real estate.

inmoral ➤ *adj* immoral.

inmortal ➤ *adj* immortal.

inmóvil ➤ *adj* immobile.

inmovilizar §02 ➤ *tr* to immobilize.

inmueble ➤ *adj* ■ bienes inmuebles real estate ➤ *m* building.

inmunización ➤ *f* immunization.

inmunizar §02 ➤ *tr* to immunize.

inmutable ➤ *adj* immutable.

innato, a ➤ *adj* innate.

innecesario, a ➤ *adj* unnecessary.

innegable ➤ *adj* undeniable.

innovación ➤ *f* innovation.

innumerable ➤ *adj* innumerable.

inocencia ➤ *f* innocence.

inocente ➤ *adj & mf* innocent.

inoculación ➤ *f* inoculation.

inolvidable ➤ *adj* unforgettable.

inoportuno, a ➤ *adj* inopportune.

inoxidable ➤ *adj* rustproof ■ acero i. stainless steel.

inquietante ➤ *adj* worrying, disturbing.

inquieto, a ➤ *adj (intranquilo)* restless; *(desasosegado)* worried, anxious.

inquilino, a ➤ *mf* tenant.

inquisitivo, a ➤ *adj* inquisitive.

insaciable ➤ *adj* insatiable.

insatisfecho, a ➤ *adj (deseo)* unsatisfied; *(persona)* dissatisfied.

inscribir §55 ➤ *tr (grabar)* to engrave; *(matricular)* to register; *(anotar)* to record ➤ *reflex* to register, enroll.

inscripción ➤ *f* inscription; *(anotación)* record; *(matriculación)* enrollment.

insecticida ➤ *m* insecticide.

insecto ➤ *m* insect.

inseguro, a ➤ *adj* insecure.

insensato, a ➤ *adj* foolish, senseless ■ *mf* fool, dolt.

insensible ➤ *adj (que no siente)* insensible; *(sin compasión)* unfeeling.

inseparable ➤ *adj* inseparable.

insertar ➤ *tr* to insert.

insignia ➤ *f* badge, emblem.

insignificante ➤ *adj* insignificant.

insinuar §45 ➤ *tr* to insinuate ➤ *reflex* to ingratiate oneself.

insistir ➤ *intr* to insist *(en* on).

insolación ➤ *f* MED. sunstroke.

insolencia ➤ *f* insolence.

insolente ➤ *adj* insolent.

insólito, a ➤ *adj* unusual, uncommon.

insomnio ➤ *m* insomnia, sleeplessness.

insoportable ➤ *adj* unbearable.

inspección ➤ *f* inspection.

inspeccionar ➤ *tr* to inspect, examine.

inspector, a ➤ *mf* inspector.

inspiración ➤ *f* inspiration; *(de aire)* inhalation.

inspirar ➤ *tr* to inhale; *(infundir sentimientos)* to inspire ➤ *reflex* to be inspired *(en* by).

instalación ➤ *f* installation; *(equipo)* equipment ■ **i. sanitaria** plumbing.

instalar ➤ *tr* to install ➤ *reflex* to establish oneself.

instancia ➤ *f* instance ■ **a i. de** at the request of.

instantáneo, a ➤ *adj* instantaneous.

instante ➤ *m* instant, moment ■ **al i.** immediately.

instaurar ➤ *tr* to establish.

instigar §31 ➤ *tr* to incite.

instintivo, a ➤ *adj* instinctive.

instinto ➤ *m* instinct.

institución ➤ *f* institution.

instituir §10 ➤ *tr* to institute.

instituto ➤ *m* institute; *(escuela)* school.

instrucción ➤ *f* instruction ■ *pl* directions.

instructor, a ➤ *mf* instructor.

instruir §10 ➤ *tr* to instruct, teach.

instrumental ➤ *adj* instrumental ➤ *m* instruments.

instrumento ➤ *m* instrument.

insubordinar ➤ *tr* to incite to rebellion ➤ *reflex* to rebel.

insuficiente ➤ *adj* insufficient.

insulina ➤ *f* insulin.

insultar ➤ *tr* to insult.

insulto ➤ *m* insult.

insurrección ➤ *f* insurrection.

intacto, a ➤ *adj* intact.

integral ➤ *adj & f* integral.

integrar ➤ *tr* to integrate.

integridad ➤ *f* integrity.

íntegro, a ➤ *adj* whole, complete.

intelectual ➤ *adj & mf* intellectual.

inteligencia ➤ *f* intelligence.

inteligente ➤ *adj* intelligent.

inteligible ➤ *adj* intelligible.

intemperie ➤ *f* bad weather ■ **a la i.** outdoors.

intención ➤ *f* intention; *(voluntad)* wish.

intensidad ➤ *f* intensity, strength.

intensificar §47 ➤ *tr* to intensify.

intenso, a ➤ *adj* intense.

intentar ➤ *tr (tener intención)* to intend, plan; *(ensayar)* to try, attempt.

intento ➤ *m (propósito)* intent; *(tentativa)* attempt, try.

interacción ➤ *f* interaction.

intercambio ➤ *m* exchange.

interceder ➤ *tr* to intercede.

interceptar ➤ *tr* to intercept.

interés ➤ *m* interest ■ *pl* possessions.

interesante ➤ *adj* interesting.

interesar ➤ *tr* to interest ➤ *intr* to be of interest ➤ *reflex* to be *or* become interested *(en, por* in).

interferencia ➤ *f* interference.

interior ➤ *adj* interior, inner; *(nacional)* domestic, internal ➤ *m (parte interna)* interior, inside.
interjección ➤ *f* interjection.
intermediario, a ➤ *adj* intermediate ➤ *mf* intermediary.
intermedio, a ➤ *adj* intermediate ➤ *m* interval; THEAT. intermission.
interminable ➤ *adj* interminable.
intermitente ➤ *adj* intermittent.
internacional ➤ *adj* international.
internado, a ➤ *adj* institutionalized ➤ *m* boarding school.
internar ➤ *tr* to hospitalize; *(encerrar)* to confine ➤ *reflex* to penetrate.
Internet ➤ *m* Internet.
interno, a ➤ *adj* internal ➤ *mf* boarding student; *(médico)* internist.
interpretación ➤ *f* interpretation.
interpretar ➤ *tr* to interpret; MUS. to perform.
intérprete ➤ *mf (traductor)* interpreter; *(cantante)* singer.
interrogación ➤ *f* interrogation; GRAM. question mark.
interrogar §31 ➤ *tr* to interrogate, question.
interrumpir ➤ *tr* to interrupt.
interruptor ➤ *m* ELEC. switch.
intervalo ➤ *m* interval.
intervenir §52 ➤ *intr* to intervene ➤ *tr (las cuentas)* to audit.
intestino ➤ *m* intestine.
intimidar ➤ *tr* to intimidate.
íntimo, a ➤ *adj (interior)* intimate; *(privado)* private.
intoxicación ➤ *f* intoxication.
intranquilo, a ➤ *adj* uneasy.
intransitivo, a ➤ *adj* intransitive.
intriga ➤ *f* intrigue.
intrigar §31 ➤ *intr & tr* to intrigue.
introducir §14 ➤ *tr (insertar)* to insert; *(presentar)* to introduce.
introvertido, a ➤ *adj* introverted ➤ *mf* introvert.
intruso, a ➤ *adj* intrusive, meddlesome ➤ *mf* intruder.
intuición ➤ *f* intuition.
intuir §10 ➤ *tr* to intuit, sense.
inundación ➤ *f* flood.
inundar ➤ *tr* to flood.

inusitado, a ➤ *adj* unusual, uncommon.
inútil ➤ *adj* useless; *(vano)* vain.
inválido, a ➤ *adj* invalid, disabled; *(nulo)* invalid, null ➤ *mf* invalid, disabled person.
invariable ➤ *adj* invariable.
invasión ➤ *f* invasion.
invasor, a ➤ *adj* invading ➤ *mf* invader.
invencible ➤ *adj* invincible.
invención ➤ *f* invention.
inventar ➤ *tr* to invent; *(forjar)* to make up.
inventario ➤ *f* inventory.
invento ➤ *m* invention; *(creación)* creation.
invernadero ➤ *m* greenhouse.
invernar §33 ➤ *intr* to hibernate.
inversión ➤ *f* inversion; FIN. investment.
inverso, a ➤ *adj* inverse, inverted.
invertir §43 ➤ *tr* to invert; COM., FIN. to invest.
investigación ➤ *f* investigation; *(estudio)* research, study.
investigar §31 ➤ *tr* to investigate; *(estudiar)* to research, study.
invierno ➤ *m* winter.
invisible ➤ *adj* invisible.
invitación ➤ *f* invitation.
invitado, a ➤ *mf* guest.
invitar ➤ *tr* to invite.
involuntario, a ➤ *adj* involuntary.
inyección ➤ *f* injection.
ir §25 ➤ *intr* to go; *(moverse)* to move; *(caminar)* to walk; *(viajar)* to travel; *(extenderse)* to extend; *(quedar bien)* to suit, become ∎ ¿cómo le va? how is it going? • i. de compras to go shopping • i. de mal en peor to go from bad to worse • i. de paseo to go for a walk • i. de viaje to go on a trip • ¡vaya! *(sorpresa)* you don't say! ➤ *reflex* to go away, leave ∎ i. abajo to topple, collapse • vámonos let's go.
ira ➤ *f (cólera)* anger; *(furia)* fury.
irascible ➤ *adj* irascible.
iris ➤ *m* ANAT. iris ∎ arco i. rainbow.
ironía ➤ *f* irony.
irónico, a ➤ *adj* ironic(al).

irracional ➤ *adj* irrational.
irreal ➤ *adj* unreal.
irregular ➤ *adj* irregular.
irresistible ➤ *adj* irresistible.
irresponsable ➤ *adj* irresponsible.
irritar ➤ *tr* to irritate.
irrumpir ➤ *intr* to burst (*en* into).
isla ➤ *f* island.
islámico, a ➤ *adj* Islamic.
itinerario, a ➤ *adj & m* itinerary.
izquierdo, a ➤ *adj* left ➤ *f (mano)* left
hand; *(lado)* left ■ **a la i.** *(dirección)*
left, to the left; *(sitio)* on the left • **por
la i.** on the left.

J

jabalí ➤ *m* wild boar.
jabón ➤ *m* soap.
jabonera ➤ *f* soap dish.
jacinto ➤ *m* BOT. hyacinth.
jactarse ➤ *reflex* to boast (*de* about).
jadear ➤ *intr* to pant, gasp.
jalea ➤ *f* jelly.
jaleo ➤ *m* riotous fun, uproar.
jamás ➤ *adv (nunca)* never; *(alguna
vez)* ever ■ **nunca j.** never again.
jamón ➤ *m* ham ■ **j. serrano** cured
ham.
jaque ➤ *m* check ■ **j. mate** checkmate.
jaqueca ➤ *f* migraine headache.
jarabe ➤ *m* syrup.
jardín ➤ *m* garden ■ **j. de infancia** *or*
infantes kindergarten.
jardinera ➤ *f* flower stand *or* box.
jardinero, a ➤ *mf* gardener.
jarra ➤ *f* *or* **jarro** ➤ *m* jug, pitcher.
jarrón ➤ *m* urn, vase.
jaula ➤ *f* cage; *(embalaje)* crate; *(para
niños)* playpen.
jazmín ➤ *m* jasmine ■ **j. del Cabo** gar-
denia.
jefatura ➤ *f (dirección)* management;
(oficina) headquarters.
jefe, a ➤ *mf* boss, chief; *(gerente)* manager; *(líder)* leader.
jején ➤ *m* gnat.
jengibre ➤ *m* ginger.
jerez ➤ *m* sherry.
jerga ➤ *f* jargon; *(galimatías)* gibber-
ish.
jeringa ➤ *f* syringe.

jeroglífico, a ➤ *adj* hieroglyphic ➤ *m*
hieroglyph.
jilguero ➤ *m* goldfinch, linnet.
jinete ➤ *mf* horseman/woman.
jira ➤ *f* excursion.
jirafa ➤ *f* giraffe.
jirón ➤ *m* shred, tatter.
jornada ➤ *f* journey, trip; *(día de trabajo)* workday ■ **de media j.** part-time.
jornal ➤ *m* day's wage.
jornalero, a ➤ *mf* day laborer.
jorobado, a ➤ *adj* hunchbacked ➤ *mf*
hunchback.
joven ➤ *adj* young, youthful ➤ *mf*
young person, youth.
joya ➤ *f* jewel ■ *pl* jewelry • **j. de fantasía** costume jewelry.
joyería ➤ *f* jewelry store.
joyero, a ➤ *mf* jeweler, jeweller (G.B.)
➤ *m (caja)* jewelry box.
jubilado, a ➤ *adj & mf* retired (person).
jubilar ➤ *tr & reflex* to retire.
judío, a ➤ *adj* Jewish ➤ *mf* Jew ➤ *f* BOT.
bean ■ **j. verde** green bean.
juego ➤ *m* play, game; *(deporte)* sport;
(vicio) gambling; *(en naipes)* hand;
(de loza, cristal) set ■ **hacer j.** to match
• **j. de damas** checkers.
juerga ➤ *f* fun ■ **ir de j.** to live it up.
jueves ➤ *m* Thursday.
juez ➤ *mf* judge ■ **j. de línea** SPORT.
linesman.
jugada ➤ *f* play, move.
jugador, a ➤ *mf (en los juegos)* player;
(en el azar) gambler.
jugar §26 ➤ *intr* to play ➤ *tr* to play;
(apostar) to wager ➤ *reflex* to risk.
jugo ➤ *m* juice.
juguete ➤ *m* toy.
juicio ➤ *m* judgment; *(opinión)* opinion; LAW *(pleito)* trial.
julio ➤ *m* July.
junco ➤ *m* BOT. rush.
junio ➤ *m* June.
junior ➤ *m* junior.
juntar ➤ *tr (unir)* to join; *(reunir)* to
assemble ➤ *reflex (reunirse)* to gather;
(asociarse) to get together.
junto, a ➤ *adj (cercano)* close ➤ *adv*
together ■ **j. a** close to, near • **j. con**
along with, together with • **todo j.** at

the same time, all together ➤ f *(de personas)* board; *(reunión)* meeting, session; *(unión)* union.
jurado ➤ m jury; *(miembro)* juror.
juramento ➤ m oath.
jurar ➤ tr to swear.
justicia ➤ f justice.
justificar §47 ➤ tr to justify ➤ *reflex (explicarse)* to explain oneself.
justo, a ➤ adj just, fair; *(exacto)* exact, precise; *(apretado)* tight ➤ mf just person.
juvenil ➤ adj young, youthful.
juventud ➤ f *(edad)* youth.
juzgado ➤ m *(tribunal)* court.
juzgar §31 ➤ tr to judge ▪ a j. por judging by or from.

K

karate ➤ m karate.
kilo ➤ m kilo, kilogram.
kilogramo ➤ m kilogram.
kilómetro ➤ m kilometer.
kiwi ➤ m kiwi.

L

la ➤ def art the ➤ pron her, you, it.
laberinto ➤ m labyrinth.
labio ➤ m lip.
labor ➤ f *(trabajo)* work; *(faena)* task, job; *(bordado)* embroidery.
laborable ➤ adj work, working.
laboral ➤ adj *(del trabajo)* labor; *(técnico)* technical.
laboratorio ➤ m laboratory.
laca ➤ f lacquer; *(pelo)* hair spray ▪ l. de uñas nail polish.
ladear ➤ tr to bend, tilt.
ladera ➤ f slope.
lado ➤ m side ▪ al l. near, close at hand ▪ al l. de beside, next to • por otro l. on the other hand • por un l. on the one hand.
ladrar ➤ intr to bark.
ladrillo ➤ m brick.
ladrón, ona ➤ mf thief, robber.
lagartija ➤ f small lizard.
lagarto ➤ m lizard.
lago ➤ m lake.
lágrima ➤ f tear.
laguna ➤ f lagoon.

lamentar ➤ tr *(sentir)* to regret ➤ *reflex* to grieve, lament.
lamer ➤ tr to lick.
lámina ➤ f lamina, plate.
lámpara ➤ f lamp.
lana ➤ f wool.
lancha ➤ f boat ▪ l. motora motorboat • l. salvavidas lifeboat.
langosta ➤ f ENTOM. locust; ZOOL. lobster.
langostino ➤ m crayfish.
lanza ➤ f lance, spear.
lanzar §02 ➤ tr *(arrojar)* to throw; *(un proyectil)* to launch ➤ *reflex* to throw oneself.
lápiz ➤ m pencil ▪ l. de labios lipstick.
largo, a ➤ adj long ▪ a la l. in the long run • a lo l. lengthwise; *(por)* along; *(a través)* throughout ➤ m length ▪ tener diez pies de l. to be ten feet long ➤ *interj* get out! ▪ ¡l. de aqui! get out of here!
las ➤ def art the ➤ pron them.
láser ➤ m laser ▪ rayo l. laser beam.
lástima ➤ f pity ▪ es una l. que it's a shame that • ¡qué l.! what a shame!
lata ➤ f tin plate; *(envase)* tin can.
lateral ➤ adj lateral, side.
latido ➤ m *(del corazón)* beat, throb.
látigo ➤ m whip.
latino, a ➤ adj & mf *(latinoamericano)* Latino.
latinoamericano, a ➤ adj & mf Latin American.
latir ➤ intr *(el corazón)* to beat, throb.
latitud ➤ f GEOG. latitude.
latón ➤ m brass.
laurel ➤ m laurel, bay.
lava ➤ f lava.
lavable ➤ adj washable.
lavabo ➤ m *(lavamanos)* sink, wash basin; *(cuarto)* bathroom.
lavado ➤ m *(acción)* washing, wash ▪ l. en seco dry cleaning.
lavador, a ➤ mf washer ➤ f washing machine ▪ l. de platos dishwasher.
lavanda ➤ f lavender.
lavandería ➤ f laundry, laundromat.
lavaplatos ➤ m dishwasher.
lavar ➤ tr to wash.
lazo ➤ m *(nudo)* knot.

le ➤ *pron* him, you; to him, her, it, *or* you; for him, her, it, *or* you; from him, her, it, *or* you.

leal ➤ *adj* loyal, faithful.

lección ➤ *f* lesson.

leche ➤ *f* milk ▪ l. desnatada skim milk.

lechón ➤ *m* suckling pig.

lechuga ➤ *f* lettuce.

lechuza ➤ *f* owl.

lector, a ➤ *adj* reading ➤ *mf* reader.

lectura ➤ *f* (*acción*) reading.

leer §27 ➤ *tr* to read.

legal ➤ *adj* legal.

legislación ➤ *f* legislation.

legítimo, a ➤ *adj* legitimate; (*cierto*) genuine.

legumbre ➤ *f* legume; CUL. vegetable.

lejano, a ➤ *adj* distant, remote.

lejía ➤ *f* bleach.

lejos ➤ *adv* far (away) ▪ a lo l. in the distance, far away • desde l. from afar, from a distance • l. de far from.

lema ➤ *m* motto.

lencería ➤ *f* (*ropa blanca*) lingerie; (*géneros*) linen goods.

lengua ➤ *f* tongue; (*idioma*) language.

lenguado ➤ *m* sole, flounder.

lenguaje ➤ *m* language, speech.

lente ➤ *m or f* lens ▪ l. de contacto contact lens ▪ *pl* eyeglasses, glasses.

lenteja ➤ *f* lentil.

lentilla ➤ *f* contact lens.

lento, a ➤ *adj* slow.

leña ➤ *f* firewood.

leño ➤ *m* log.

león ➤ *m* lion.

leona ➤ *f* lioness.

leopardo ➤ *m* leopard.

leotardo ➤ *m* leotard.

les ➤ *pron* to them *or* you; for them *or* you; from them *or* you.

lesión ➤ *f* lesion, injury.

lesionar ➤ *tr* to wound, injure.

letal ➤ *adj* lethal.

letargo ➤ *m* lethargy.

letra ➤ *f* letter; (*modo de escribir*) handwriting; MUS. lyrics ▪ l. de cambio bill of exchange • l. mayúscula capital letter • l. minúscula lower-case letter ▪ *pl* letters, learning.

letrero ➤ *m* sign; (*etiqueta*) label.

levadura ➤ *f* yeast ▪ l. de cerveza brewer's yeast • l. en polvo baking powder.

levantamiento ➤ *m* (*acción*) raising, lifting; (*motín*) uprising.

levantar ➤ *tr* to raise, lift ➤ *reflex* to rise; (*ponerse de pie*) to stand up; (*de la cama*) to get out of bed.

ley ➤ *f* law, statute; (*regla*) rule.

leyenda ➤ *f* (*fábula*) legend; (*texto*) legend, caption.

liar §18 ➤ *tr* (*atar*) to tie, bind; (*envolver*) to wrap (up) ➤ *reflex* (*mezclarse*) to be mixed up in.

liberación ➤ *f* liberation.

liberal ➤ *adj* liberal; (*generoso*) generous ➤ *mf* liberal.

liberar ➤ *tr* to free, liberate.

libertad ➤ *f* liberty, freedom.

libra ➤ *f* pound.

librar ➤ *tr* (*salvar*) to free, deliver; (*eximir*) to exempt, release ➤ *reflex* to avoid, escape.

libre ➤ *adj* free.

librecambio ➤ *m* free trade.

librería ➤ *f* (*tienda*) bookstore; (*armario*) bookcase, bookshelf.

libreta ➤ *f* notebook.

libro ➤ *m* book ▪ l. de texto textbook.

licencia ➤ *f* license, permit; (*permiso*) permission.

licenciado, a ➤ *mf* EDUC. university graduate, bachelor; AMER. lawyer.

licenciatura ➤ *f* (*título*) bachelor's degree; (*estudios*) degree program.

licor ➤ *m* liquor, spirits.

licuadora ➤ *f* mixer, blender.

líder ➤ *mf* leader, chief.

lidia ➤ *f* fight, battle.

lidiar ➤ *tr* (*torear*) to fight (bulls).

liebre ➤ *f* hare.

liga ➤ *f* league.

ligar §31 ➤ *tr* (*atar*) to tie, bind; (*unir*) to join.

ligereza ➤ *f* (*liviandad*) lightness; (*rapidez*) quickness, swiftness.

ligero, a ➤ *adj* (*leve*) light; (*rápido*) quick, swift; (*ágil*) agile, nimble.

lija ➤ *f* sandpaper.

lijar ➤ *tr* to sand.

lima ➤ *f* file ▪ l. para las uñas nail file.

limitar ➤ *tr* to limit; *(delimitar)* to delimit; *(restringir)* to restrict ➤ *reflex* to limit oneself.

límite ➤ *m* limit; *(frontera)* boundary ∎ **fecha l.** deadline.

limón ➤ *m (fruto)* lemon.

limonada ➤ *f* lemonade.

limonero ➤ *m* lemon tree.

limpiaparabrisas ➤ *m* windshield wiper.

limpiar ➤ *tr* to clean, cleanse.

limpieza ➤ *f (calidad)* cleanliness; *(acción)* cleaning, cleansing.

limpio, a ➤ *adj (sin mancha)* clean, spotless ➤ *adv* fair.

lindar ➤ *intr* to border (on), be adjacent (to).

lindo, a ➤ *adj* pretty, lovely ∎ **de lo l.** much, a lot.

línea ➤ *f* line ∎ **l. aérea** airline.

lingüístico, a ➤ *adj* linguistic ➤ *f* linguistics.

lino ➤ *m* linen.

linterna ➤ *f* lantern; *(de bolsillo)* flashlight.

lío ➤ *m (bulto)* bundle, package; COLL. *(embrollo)* jam, mess ∎ **armar un l.** to make a fuss or racket.

liquidación ➤ *f (un negocio)* liquidation; *(venta)* clearance sale.

liquidar ➤ *tr* to sell off, liquidate.

líquido, a ➤ *adj* liquid; *(sin gravamen)* net ➤ *m* liquid.

lirio ➤ *m* iris; *(azucena)* lily.

liso, a ➤ *adj (parejo)* smooth, even; *(llano)* flat.

lista ➤ *f* list; *(raya)* stripe.

listado, a ➤ *adj* striped.

listo, a ➤ *adj (inteligente)* smart, clever; *(preparado)* ready.

litera ➤ *f* MARIT., RAIL. berth, bunk; *(cama)* bunk bed.

literatura ➤ *f* literature.

litigio ➤ *m* lawsuit.

litoral ➤ *adj & m* littoral, coast.

litro ➤ *m* liter.

llaga ➤ *f* wound, sore.

llama ➤ *f* flame ∎ **en llamas** in flames.

llamada ➤ *f* call; TELEC. telephone call.

llamar ➤ *tr* to call ∎ **l. por teléfono** to telephone, phone ➤ *intr* to ring a doorbell; *(tocar a la puerta)* to knock at the door; *(por teléfono)* to call, telephone ➤ *reflex* to be called *or* named.

llano, a ➤ *adj (liso)* flat, even; *(sencillo)* natural, simple.

llanta ➤ *f (de rueda)* rim; AMER. tire.

llanto ➤ *m* crying, weeping.

llanura ➤ *f* GEOG. plain.

llave ➤ *f* key; *(grifo)* tap, faucet; ELEC. switch; MECH. wrench ∎ **l. inglesa** monkey wrench.

llavero ➤ *m* key ring.

llegada ➤ *f* arrival; SPORT. finish.

llegar §31 ➤ *intr (venir)* to arrive ∎ **l. a** to arrive at, reach.

llenar ➤ *tr* to fill (up); *(cumplir)* to fulfill, meet ➤ *intr* ASTRON. to be full ➤ *reflex* to fill up.

lleno, a ➤ *adj* full, filled.

llevar ➤ *tr (transportar)* to carry, take; *(vestir)* to wear; *(pasar)* to have spent, have been ➤ *intr* to lead ➤ *reflex (sacar)* to take away, carry off ∎ **l. bien, mal** to get along well, badly.

llorar ➤ *intr* to cry, weep.

llover §54 ➤ *intr* to rain.

llovizna ➤ *f* drizzle.

lluvia ➤ *f* rain.

lluvioso, a ➤ *adj* rainy, wet.

lo ➤ *def art* the . . . thing, the . . . part ∎ **lo de** the matter of, the business of ∎ **lo que** what, which ➤ *pron* it, him.

lobo, a ➤ *m* wolf ➤ *f* wolf, she-wolf.

local ➤ *adj* local ➤ *m* premises.

localidad ➤ *f (población)* district; *(local)* locale, site; THEAT. seat.

localizar §02 ➤ *tr* to localize; *(encontrar)* to locate.

loción ➤ *f* lotion.

loco, a ➤ *adj* mad, crazy ∎ **volverse l.** to go crazy ➤ *mf* crazy person.

locomotora ➤ *f* locomotive.

locura ➤ *f* madness, insanity.

locutor, a ➤ *mf* radio announcer.

lodo ➤ *m* mud.

lógico, a ➤ *adj* logical.

lograr ➤ *tr (obtener)* to get, obtain; *(realizar)* to achieve ➤ *reflex* to succeed, be successful.

lombriz ➤ *f* worm, earthworm.

lomo ➤ *m* ANAT., CUL. loin; ZOOL. back.

longaniza ➤ *f* pork sausage.

longitud ➤ *f* length; GEOG. longitude.

lonja ➤ *f* (*tira*) slice; COM. (*edificio*) marketplace, exchange.

loro ➤ *m* parrot.

los ➤ *def art* the ➤ *pron* them.

losa ➤ *f* slab, stone.

lote ➤ *m* lot, share.

lotería ➤ *f* lottery ▪ l. casera bingo.

loza ➤ *f* (*barro vidriado*) glazed pottery; (*platos*) china.

lubricante ➤ *m* lubricant.

lucha ➤ *f* struggle, conflict; SPORT. wrestling.

luchar ➤ *intr* to fight; SPORT. to wrestle.

lucir §28 ➤ *intr* to shine ➤ *tr* to show off, display ➤ *reflex* (*vestir bien*) to dress up; (*distinguirse*) to shine.

luego ➤ *adv* (*después*) then, afterward; (*más tarde*) later, later on ▪ desde l. of course, naturally ▪ hasta l. so long ➤ *conj* therefore.

lugar ➤ *m* (*sitio*) place ▪ en l. de instead of ▪ en primer l. in the first place, first.

lujo ➤ *m* luxury.

lujuria ➤ *f* lust.

lumbre ➤ *f* fire; FIG. brilliance.

luminoso, a ➤ *adj* luminous.

luna ➤ *f* moon; (*espejo*) mirror ▪ estar en la l. to be daydreaming ▪ l. de miel honeymoon.

lunar ➤ *m* mole, beauty mark.

lunes ➤ *m* Monday.

lupa ➤ *f* magnifying glass.

lustre ➤ *m* luster, shine.

luto ➤ *m* mourning.

luz ➤ *f* light ▪ dar a l. to give birth ▪ sacar a l. (*descubrirse*) to come to light ▪ *pl* enlightenment, learning.

M

macarrón ➤ *m* macaroon ▪ *pl* macaroni.

maceta ➤ *f* flowerpot.

machacar §47 ➤ *tr* to crush, pound.

machete ➤ *m* machete.

macho ➤ *adj* male; (*viril*) manly, virile ➤ *m* (*animal*) male; COLL. he-man.

macizo, a ➤ *adj* solid ➤ *m* GEOL. massif.

madeja ➤ *f* skein (of wool); (*pelo*) mop.

madera ➤ *f* wood; (*de construcción*) lumber ▪ de m. wooden, of wood.

madrastra ➤ *f* stepmother.

madre ➤ *f* mother ▪ ¡m. mía! my goodness! ▪ m. patria mother country.

madrina ➤ *f* (*de bautismo*) godmother; (*de boda*) bridesmaid.

madrugada ➤ *f* dawn ▪ de m. at daybreak, very early.

madrugador, a ➤ *adj* early-rising ➤ *mf* early riser.

madrugar §31 ➤ *intr* to get up early.

madurar ➤ *tr* AGR to ripen, mature.

maduro, a ➤ *adj* AGR ripe; (*juicioso*) wise; (*entrado en años*) mature.

maestría ➤ *f* (*habilidad*) mastery, skill; (*título avanzado*) Master's degree.

maestro, a ➤ *adj* masterly ➤ *m* (*profesor*) teacher; (*artesano*) master; MUS. maestro ➤ *f* (*profesora*) teacher.

magia ➤ *f* magic.

mágico, a ➤ *adj* magic(al) ➤ *f* magic.

magistrado, a ➤ *mf* magistrate.

magnético, a ➤ *adj* magnetic.

magnetófono ➤ *m* tape recorder.

magnífico, a ➤ *adj* magnificent.

mago ➤ *m* magician, wizard ▪ los Reyes Magos the Magi.

magullar ➤ *tr* to bruise, batter.

maicena ➤ *f* cornstarch.

maíz ➤ *m* corn, maize.

majestad ➤ *f* majesty.

majo, a ➤ *adj* SP. (*bonito*) pretty, (*simpático*) nice, sweet.

mal[1] ➤ *adj contr of* **malo** ➤ *m* (*vicio*) evil; (*daño*) harm; (*enfermedad*) illness ▪ hacer m. to harm, hurt ▪ m. de mar seasickness.

mal[2] ➤ *adv* (*pobremente*) badly; (*difícilmente*) hardly ▪ de m. en peor from bad to worse ▪ menos m. just as well.

malabarista ➤ *mf* juggler.

malcontento, a ➤ *adj* discontented, unhappy ➤ *mf* malcontent.

malcriado, a ➤ *adj* rude, ill-bred.

maldad ➤ *f* wickedness, evil.

maldecido, a ➤ *adj* evil, wicked.

maldecir ➤ *tr* to curse.

maldición ➤ *f* curse, damnation.

maldito, a ➤ *adj* damned.

malecón ➤ *m* sea wall, jetty.

maleducado, a ➤ *adj* bad-mannered.

malentendido ➤ *m* misunderstanding.

malestar ➤ *m* malaise, indisposition; *(inquietud)* uneasiness.

maleta ➤ *f* suitcase ■ **hacer la m.** to pack one's bag.

maletero ➤ *m* station porter; AUTO. trunk.

maletín ➤ *m* small suitcase, briefcase.

maleza ➤ *f* BOT. weeds, underbrush.

malgastar ➤ *tr* to waste, misspend.

malhablado, a ➤ *adj* foul-mouthed, vulgar.

malhechor, a ➤ *mf* wrongdoer.

malhumor ➤ *m* bad temper.

malicia ➤ *f* malice, wickedness.

malicioso, a ➤ *adj* malicious; *(astuto)* sly.

malla ➤ *f* *(de red)* mesh, netting; AMER. *(traje de baño)* swimsuit.

malo, a ➤ *adj* bad; *(perverso)* evil; *(dañino)* harmful; *(desagradable)* unpleasant; *(enfermo)* sick, ill ■ **a (las) malas** on bad terms • **lo m. es que** the trouble is. . . • **ponerse m.** to become sick • **por las malas** by force.

malpensado, a ➤ *adj & mf* evil-minded or malicious (person).

malta ➤ *f* malt.

maltratar ➤ *tr* to mistreat.

mamá ➤ *f* mama, mommy.

mamar ➤ *tr* to suckle, nurse.

mamífero ➤ *m* mammal.

mampara ➤ *f* screen, partition.

manada ➤ *f* *(hato)* flock, herd; *(de lobos)* pack.

manantial ➤ *m* spring.

mancha ➤ *f* stain, spot.

manchar ➤ *tr* to stain, spot.

manco, a ➤ *adj & mf* one-handed or one-armed (person).

mandado ➤ *m* *(orden)* order; *(encargo)* task, assignment; *(recado)* errand.

mandar ➤ *tr* to order, command; *(enviar)* to send ➤ *intr* to be in charge.

mandarina ➤ *f* mandarin orange, tangerine.

mandato ➤ *m* order, command.

mandíbula ➤ *f* jaw.

mando ➤ *m* *(autoridad)* authority; *(dirección)* command; MECH. control ■

estar al m. to be in command • **tablero de mandos** instrument panel.

manecilla ➤ *f* *(del reloj)* hand.

manejable ➤ *adj* manageable.

manejar ➤ *tr* to handle; *(empresa)* to run, manage; *(automóvil)* to drive ➤ *reflex* to get or move around.

manejo ➤ *m* *(uso)* handling; *(funcionamiento)* running, operation ■ **instrucciones de m.** directions.

manera ➤ *f* manner; *(modo)* way; *(tipo)* type; *(estilo)* style ■ **de alguna m.** somehow, in some way • **de cualquier m.** anyhow • **de ninguna m.** by no means, in no way • **de otra m.** otherwise • **de tal m.** in such a way • **de todas maneras** at any rate, anyway.

manga ➤ *f* sleeve; *(manguera)* hose.

mango[1] ➤ *m* handle.

mango[2] ➤ *m* mango (tree and fruit).

manguera ➤ *f* garden hose.

maní ➤ *m* peanut.

manía ➤ *f* mania; *(capricho)* craze, fad.

maniático, a ➤ *adj* maniacal ➤ *mf* maniac.

manicomio ➤ *m* mental health facility.

manifestación ➤ *f* manifestation; POL. demonstration..

manifestar §33 ➤ *tr* *(expresar)* to declare; *(anunciar)* to show, reveal ➤ *intr* to be evident; POL. to demonstrate.

manija ➤ *f* handle.

manilla ➤ *f* bracelet; *(manija)* handle.

manillar ➤ *m* handlebars (of a bicycle).

maniobra ➤ *f* maneuver, stratagem.

manipular ➤ *tr* to manipulate; *(manejar)* to handle.

maniquí ➤ *m* mannequin.

manivela ➤ *f* crank.

manjar ➤ *m* dish.

mano[1] ➤ *f* hand; *(pata)* forefoot, front paw; *(lado)* side ■ **a m.** by hand; *(cerca)* at hand, on hand • **dar la m. a** to shake hands with • **de primera m.** firsthand • **de segunda m.** secondhand • **m. de obra** labor.

manojo ➤ *m* bundle, bunch.

mansión ➤ *f* mansion, residence.

manso, a ➤ *adj* tame.

manta ➤ *f* blanket.

manteca ➤ f (*grasa*) fat; (*de cerdo*) lard; (*de vaca*) butter.

mantel ➤ m tablecloth.

mantener §46 ➤ tr to maintain, support; (*conservar*) to keep; (*continuar*) to keep up; (*afirmar*) to affirm ■ reflex (*alimentarse*) to feed oneself; (*sustentarse*) to support oneself.

mantenimiento ➤ m maintenance; (*sustento*) sustenance, food.

mantequilla ➤ f butter.

manto ➤ m cloak.

mantón ➤ m shawl.

manual ➤ adj & m manual.

manubrio ➤ m crank; (*manija*) handle.

manufactura ➤ f manufacture.

manufacturar ➤ tr to manufacture.

manuscrito ➤ m manuscript.

manzana ➤ f apple; (*cuadra*) block.

manzano ➤ m apple tree.

maña ➤ f (*habilidad*) skill, dexterity; (*astucia*) craftiness, guile.

mañana ➤ f morning ■ a la m. siguiente the next morning • ayer por la m. yesterday morning • de or en or por la m. in the morning ■ adv tomorrow; (*en el futuro*) in the future ■ a partir de m. starting tomorrow, as of tomorrow • hasta m. see you tomorrow • m. por la m. tomorrow morning • pasado m. the day after tomorrow.

mañoso, a ➤ adj skillful.

mapa ➤ m map, chart.

maquillaje ➤ m makeup, cosmetics.

maquillar ➤ tr to put makeup on.

máquina ➤ f machine; (*cámara*) camera ■ hecho a m. machine-made • m. de escribir typewriter • m. de lavar washing machine • m. registradora S. AMER. cash register.

maquinaria ➤ f (*conjunto*) machinery; (*mecanismo*) mechanism.

maquinilla ➤ f small machine or device ■ m. de afeitar safety razor.

mar ➤ m or f sea ■ alta m. high seas.

maravilla ➤ f wonder, marvel.

maravilloso, a ➤ adj marvelous, wonderful.

marca ➤ f mark; (*tipo*) make, brand; COM. trademark; SPORT. record ■ m. registrada (registered) trademark.

marcar §47 ➤ tr (*poner marca*) to mark; (*el pelo*) to set; (*un número de teléfono*) to dial; SPORT. to score.

marcha ➤ f march; (*funcionamiento*) operation, running; FIG. progress, course ■ a toda m. at full speed • m. atrás AUTO. reverse • poner(se) en m. to start (off).

marchar ➤ intr (*ir*) to go; (*andar*) to walk; (*progresar*) to go, proceed; MIL. to march ■ reflex to go (away), leave.

marco ➤ m (*cerco*) frame; FIN. mark.

marea ➤ f tide ■ m. alta high tide • m. baja low tide.

marearse ➤ reflex to become nauseated or seasick.

marejada ➤ f (*del mar*) swell.

mareo ➤ m nausea; MARIT. seasickness; (*en vehículos*) motion sickness.

margarina ➤ f margarine.

margarita ➤ f BOT. daisy.

margen ➤ m margin, border; COM. margin.

marginar ➤ tr to leave out.

marido ➤ m husband, spouse.

marinero ➤ m sailor, mariner.

marino, a ➤ adj marine ■ azul m. navy blue ■ m. marine, sailor.

mariposa ➤ f butterfly.

marisco ➤ m shellfish, crustacean.

marítimo, a ➤ adj maritime, sea.

mármol ➤ m marble.

marrano, a ➤ adj dirty, filthy ➤ m ZOOL. pig, hog; COLL. (*sucio*) slob.

marrón ➤ adj brown.

martes ➤ m Tuesday.

martillo ➤ m hammer.

mártir ➤ mf martyr.

marzo ➤ m March.

más ➤ adv more, most ■ a m. y mejor a lot, really • de m. too much, extra • durar m. to last longer • m. allá further • m. bien rather • m. de more than • m. que more than; (*sino*) but, except • ni m. ni menos no more, no less • no m. only, no more • no m. que only • por m. que no matter how much ➤ m plus sign ■ ➤ prep plus.

masa ➤ f mass; (*volumen*) volume, bulk; (*pasta*) dough.

masaje ➤ m massage.

mascar §47 ➤ *tr* to chew.

máscara ➤ *f* mask.

masculino, a ➤ *adj & m* masculine.

masticar §47 ➤ *tr* to chew.

mástil ➤ *m* mast.

mata ➤ *f* bush, shrub.

matador, a ➤ *mf* bullfighter, matador.

matar ➤ *tr* to kill.

mate[1] ➤ *adj* (*sin brillo*) matte; (*apagado*) dull.

mate[2] ➤ *m* (*ajedrez*) mate; (*bebida*) S. AMER. maté, tea.

matemática ➤ *fpl* mathematics.

materia ➤ *f* matter; (*material*) material, substance; EDUC. subject ■ m. prima raw material.

material ➤ *adj* material ➤ *m* materials.

maternal ➤ *adj* maternal.

maternidad ➤ *f* maternity.

materno, a ➤ *adj* maternal.

matinal ➤ *adj* morning, matinal.

matrícula ➤ *f* (*inscripción*) registration, matriculation; (*gente matriculada*) roll; AUTO. registration.

matricular ➤ *tr & reflex* to register, matriculate.

matrimonio ➤ *m* marriage, matrimony; COLL. (*marido y mujer*) married couple ■ fuera del m. out of wedlock • m. civil civil marriage • partida de m. marriage certificate.

matrona ➤ *f* midwife.

maullar ➤ *intr* to meow, mew.

máximo, a ➤ *adj* maximum, greatest ➤ *m* maximum ■ al m. to the maximum • como m. at the most • hacer el m. to do one's utmost.

mayo ➤ *m* May.

mayonesa ➤ *f* mayonnaise.

mayor ➤ *adj* (*más grande*) bigger, larger; (*el más grande*) biggest, largest; (*importante*) greater; (*el más importante*) greatest; (*de más edad*) older, elder; (*entrado en años*) elderly; (*el más viejo*) oldest, eldest; (*adulto*) adult; (*principal*) main ■ al por m. COM. wholesale • m. de edad of age.

mayoría ➤ *f* majority ■ en la m. de los casos in most cases • m. de edad legal age.

mayúscula ➤ *f* capital letter.

mazmorra ➤ *f* dungeon.

mazo ➤ *m* mallet; (*manojo*) bunch.

mazorca ➤ *f* ear (of corn).

me ➤ *pron* me; to, for, *or* from me; myself.

mecánico, a ➤ *adj* mechanical ➤ *mf* mechanic ➤ *f* mechanics.

mecanismo ➤ *m* mechanism.

mecedora ➤ *f* rocking chair, rocker.

mecer §51 ➤ *tr & reflex* to rock.

mechón ➤ *m* (*de pelo*) lock, tuft.

medalla ➤ *f* medal.

media ➤ *f* (*de mujer*) stocking; (*de hombre*) sock ■ las dos y m. half past two ➤ *mpl* the media.

mediador, a ➤ *mf* mediator.

mediano, a ➤ *adj* medium.

medianoche ➤ *f* midnight.

mediante ➤ *adv* through, by means of.

medicamento ➤ *m* medicine, medication.

medicina ➤ *f* medicine.

médico, a ➤ *adj* medical ➤ *mf* doctor, physician.

medida ➤ *f* measure, measurement ■ a m. que as, while • en menor m. to a lesser extent • hecho a la m. made-to-order • sin m. in excess.

medieval ➤ *adj* medieval.

medio, a ➤ *adj* half; (*mediano*) middle, medium; (*central*) middle, midway; (*regular*) average ■ m. hermano, a half brother, sister • m. luna half-moon • m. pasaje half fare ➤ *m* (*centro*) middle, center; (*medida*) measure; (*moderación*) middle ground • en m. de in the middle of • m. ambiente environment • ➤ *adv* half, partially ■ a medias halfway.

mediocre ➤ *adj* mediocre.

mediodía ➤ *m* midday, noon.

medir §32 ➤ *tr* to measure.

meditar ➤ *tr & intr* to meditate.

medula *or* **médula** ➤ *f* marrow.

mejilla ➤ *f* cheek.

mejillón ➤ *m* mussel.

mejor ➤ *adj* better, best ■ lo m. posible as well as possible ➤ *adv* (*más bien*) better; (*antes*) rather ■ a lo m. maybe, perhaps • en el m. de los casos at best • m. dicho rather, more specifically •

tanto m. so much the better.

mejora ➤ *f* (*adelanto*) improvement, betterment; (*aumento*) increase.

mejorar ➤ *tr* to improve, make better; (*aumentar*) to raise ➤ *intr & reflex* to improve, get better; (*el tiempo*) to clear up.

melancolía ➤ *f* melancholy.

melancólico, a ➤ *adj* melancholy.

melena ➤ *f* (*cabello*) long hair, mop (of hair); (*de león*) mane.

melifluo, a ➤ *adj* mellifluous.

melocotón ➤ *m* peach.

melodía ➤ *f* melody, tune.

melón ➤ *m* melon; FIG. idiot, fool.

membrana ➤ *f* membrane.

membrillo ➤ *m* (*fruta*) quince; (*dulce*) quince jam or jelly.

memoria ➤ *f* memory; COM. (*informe*) financial report or statement ■ **de m. by heart** • **venir a la m.** to come to mind ■ *pl* (*libro*) memoirs.

mención ➤ *f* mention.

mencionar ➤ *tr* to mention.

mendigo, a ➤ *mf* beggar, mendicant.

mendrugo ➤ *m* crust, crumb.

menear ➤ *tr & reflex* (*mover*) to move; (*agitar*) to shake, wag; (*oscilar*) to sway, swing.

menguar §05 ➤ *intr* to diminish, decrease.

menor ➤ *adj* less, lesser; (*mínimo*) least; (*más joven*) younger; (*el más joven*) youngest ■ **al por m.** COM. retail • **m. de edad** minor, under age ➤ *mf* minor, juvenile ■ **tribunal de menores** juvenile court.

menos ➤ *adv* less, least; (*número*) fewer ■ **al m.** at least • **a m. que unless** • **cada vez m.** less and less • **cuanto m. . . . m.** the less . . . the less • **de m.** short • **echar a alguien de m.** to miss someone • **más o m.** more or less • **lo m.** the least • **m. de** less than • **m. que** less than • **ni más ni m.** exactly • **por lo m. at least** ➤ *m* minus sign ➤ *conj* but, except ➤ *prep* minus.

menosprecio ➤ *m* contempt.

mensaje ➤ *m* message.

mensajero, a ➤ *adj & mf* messenger.

mensual ➤ *adj* monthly.

menta ➤ *f* mint.

mental ➤ *adj* mental.

mente ➤ *f* mind.

mentir §43 ➤ *intr* to lie, tell lies.

mentira ➤ *f* lie, falsehood.

menú ➤ *m* menu, bill of fare.

menudo, a ➤ *adj* small, little ■ **a m.** often, frequently ➤ *mpl* CUL. giblets.

mercadeo ➤ *m* marketing.

mercado ➤ *m* market; (*sitio*) marketplace.

mercancía ➤ *f* (*artículo*) piece of merchandise, article; (*existencias*) merchandise, goods.

mercantil ➤ *adj* mercantile, commercial.

merecer §09 ➤ *tr* to deserve ■ **m. la pena** to be worthwhile, be worth the trouble ➤ *reflex* to be deserving or worthy.

merendar §33 ➤ *tr* to snack on ➤ *intr* to have a snack.

meridional ➤ *adj* southern.

merienda ➤ *f* snack.

mérito ➤ *m* merit.

merluza ➤ *f* hake.

mermelada ➤ *f* jam, marmalade.

mes ➤ *m* month ■ **al** or **por m.** by the month.

mesa ➤ *f* table ■ **poner la m.** to set the table.

meseta ➤ *f* GEOG. plateau.

mesón ➤ *m* inn, tavern.

meta ➤ *f* (*fin*) goal, objective; (*de carrera*) finish.

metal ➤ *m* metal.

metálico, a ➤ *adj* metallic ➤ *m* cash, currency.

meteorología ➤ *f* meteorology.

meter ➤ *tr* to insert, put (in, inside); (*implicar*) to involve, get into ➤ *reflex* (*entrar*) to get into, enter; (*entremeterse*) to intervene, butt in; (*enredarse*) to get mixed up in ■ **m. con** to annoy • **m. en todo** to meddle.

método ➤ *m* method.

métrico, a ➤ *adj* metric ■ **cinta m.** tape measure.

metro[1] ➤ *m* (*medida*) meter.

metro[2] ➤ *m* subway.

mexicano, a ➤ *adj & mf* Mexican.

mezcla ➤ *f (acción)* mixing; *(combinación)* mixture, combination.

mezclar ➤ *tr & reflex* to mix, blend.

mezquino, a ➤ *adj (pobre)* poor, wretched; *(avaro)* stingy, miserly.

mezquita ➤ *f* mosque.

mí ➤ *pron* me ■ **me toca a mí** it's my turn.

mi, mis ➤ *adj* my.

microbio ➤ *m* microbe.

microbús ➤ *m* microbus, minibus.

micrófono ➤ *m* microphone.

microonda ➤ *f* microwave.

microscopio ➤ *m* microscope ■ **m. electrónico** electron microscope.

miedo ➤ *m (temor)* fear, dread; *(aprensión)* apprehension • **que da** *or* **mete m.** frightening, fearsome • **tener m.** (a *or* de) to be afraid (of), fear • **tener m.** (de) que to be afraid that.

miedoso, a ➤ *adj* fearful.

miel ➤ *f* honey.

miembro ➤ *m* member.

mientras ➤ *adv* ■ **m. más** the more • **m. tanto** meanwhile, in the meantime ➤ *conj (pero)* while, whereas; *(durante)* while, as long as ■ **m. que** while.

miércoles ➤ *m* Wednesday ■ **m. de ceniza** RELIG. Ash Wednesday.

miga ➤ *f* crumb.

mil ➤ *adj* thousand ■ **m. millones** billion, milliard (G.B.).

milagro ➤ *m* miracle.

milésimo, a ➤ *adj & m* thousandth.

militar ➤ *adj* military ➤ *mf* soldier.

milla ➤ *f* mile.

millar ➤ *m* thousand.

millón ➤ *m* million.

millonario, a ➤ *adj & mf* millionaire.

mimar ➤ *tr* to spoil.

mimbre ➤ *m* wicker.

mina ➤ *f* mine; *(de lápiz)* pencil lead.

minarete ➤ *m* minaret.

mineral ➤ *adj & m* mineral.

minero, a ➤ *adj* mining ➤ *m* miner.

miniatura ➤ *f* miniature.

minicomputadora ➤ *f* minicomputer.

mínimo, a ➤ *adj* minimum, least; *(minucioso)* minimal ➤ *m* minimum.

ministerio ➤ *m* ministry; *(cuerpo de ministros)* cabinet ■ **M. de Relaciones Exteriores** State Department.

ministro ➤ *mf* minister ■ **M. de Relaciones Exteriores** Secretary of State • **primer m.** POL. prime minister.

minoría *or* **minoridad** ➤ *f* minority.

minúsculo, a ➤ *adj* minuscule, tiny ➤ *f* small *or* lowercase letter.

minuto ➤ *m* minute ■ **al m.** at once.

mío, a ➤ *adj* mine, my; *(querido)* my dear ➤ *pron* mine ■ **lo m.** my affair, my business • **los míos** my people.

miope ➤ *adj* myopic, nearsighted.

mirada ➤ *f (acción)* look, glance; *(apariencia)* look, expression ■ **echar una m. a** to cast a glance at.

mirar ➤ *tr* to look at; *(observar)* to watch, observe ➤ *intr* to look; *(observar)* to watch; *(dar a)* to look out on, overlook ➤ *reflex* to look at oneself; *(a otro)* to look at one another.

mirasol ➤ *m* sunflower.

misa ➤ *f* Mass.

miserable ➤ *adj (pobre)* poor, wretched; *(tacaño)* stingy, miserly; *(lastimoso)* miserable.

miseria ➤ *f* misery, suffering; *(pobreza)* poverty; *(avaricia)* miserliness.

misión ➤ *f* mission.

misionero, a ➤ *adj & mf* missionary.

mismo, a ➤ *adj (idéntico)* same; *(exacto)* very • **ahora m.** right now • **así m.** *(de esta manera)* in the same way, likewise; *(también)* also • **lo m.** the same thing • **por lo m.** for that (very) reason • **yo m.** I myself.

misterio ➤ *m* mystery.

mitad ➤ *f* half; *(medio)* middle ■ **a** *or* **en la m. de** in the middle of • **por la m.** in half, in two.

mítico, a ➤ *adj* mythic(al).

mito ➤ *m* myth; *(leyenda)* legend.

mixto, a ➤ *adj* mixed.

mobiliario, a ➤ *m* furniture, furnishings.

mochila ➤ *f* backpack, knapsack.

mocoso, a ➤ *mf* snotty kid, brat.

moda ➤ *f* style, fashion ■ **a la m.** *or* **de m.** fashionable, in fashion • **desfile de modas** fashion show • **pasado de m.** old-fashioned.

modelo ➤ *adj & m* model ➤ *mf* fashion model.

módem ➤ *m* COMPUT. modem.

moderado, a ➤ *adj & mf* moderate.

modernista ➤ *adj & mf* modernist.

modernizar §02 ➤ *tr* to modernize.

moderno, a ➤ *adj* modern.

modesto, a ➤ *adj* modest.

modificar §47 ➤ *tr* to modify.

modista ➤ *mf* dressmaker.

modo ➤ *m* manner, way ▪ de m. que so that • de ningún m. by no means • de todos modos anyway • m. de ser character, way of being ▪ *pl* manners.

moho ➤ *m* mold, mildew.

mohoso, a ➤ *adj* moldy, mildewed.

mojar ➤ *tr* to wet, make wet; (*empapar*) to drench, soak; (*bañar*) to dip ➤ *reflex* to get wet.

molde ➤ *m* mold; (*forma*) pattern, model.

moler §54 ➤ *tr* to grind.

molestar ➤ *tr* to bother, annoy ➤ *reflex* to bother, take the trouble ▪ no se moleste don't bother.

molestia ➤ *f* (*fastidio*) bother, annoyance; (*malestar*) discomfort ▪ si no es m. if it isn't too much trouble.

molesto, a ➤ *adj* bothersome, annoying; (*enojado*) bothered, annoyed.

molino ➤ *m* mill ▪ m. de viento windmill.

momentáneo, a ➤ *adj* momentary.

momento ➤ *m* moment; (*ocasión*) occasion, time ▪ a partir de este m. from this moment (on) • de un m. a otro at any moment • dentro de un m. in a moment.

monasterio ➤ *m* monastery.

moneda ➤ *f* coin ▪ m. corriente currency.

monedero ➤ *m* change purse.

monetario, a ➤ *adj* monetary.

monitor, a ➤ *mf* trainer, coach ➤ *m* COMPUT. monitor.

monja ➤ *f* nun.

monje ➤ *m* monk.

mono, a ➤ *adj* COLL. cute, darling ➤ *mf* monkey.

monopolio ➤ *m* monopoly.

monótono, a ➤ *adj* monotonous.

monstruo ➤ *m* monster.

montaje ➤ *m* assembly, installation.

montaña ➤ *f* mountain ▪ m. rusa roller coaster.

montañoso, a ➤ *adj* mountainous.

montar ➤ *intr* (*subir a caballo*) to mount ▪ m. a caballo to ride horseback • m. en (*bicicleta*) to ride (a bicycle) ➤ *tr* to mount; (*armar*) to assemble, set up; (*establecer*) to set up.

monte ➤ *m* mount, mountain.

montón ➤ *m* pile, heap.

montura ➤ *f* (*caballo, etc.*) mount.

monumento ➤ *m* monument.

moño ➤ *m* (*pelo*) bun, chignon.

morado, a ➤ *adj* purple.

moral ➤ *adj* moral ➤ *f* (*ética*) morals, ethics; (*ánimo*) morale, spirits.

morcilla ➤ *f* CUL. blood pudding.

mordaz ➤ *adj* mordant.

morder §54 ➤ *tr* to bite.

mordisco ➤ *m* nibble, bite.

moreno, a ➤ *adj* (*pardo*) brown; (*tostado*) brown-skinned, dark-skinned; (*pelo*) brown ➤ *mf* (*negro*) Black; (*de pelo castaño*) brunette.

morir §16 ➤ *intr* to die; (*lumbre*) to die, go out ▪ m. ahogado to drown • m. de frío to freeze to death • m. de risa to die laughing ➤ *reflex* to die ▪ m. de aburrimiento to be bored to death • m. por (*estar loco por*) to be crazy about; (*querer*) to be dying to.

morro ➤ *m* snout, nose.

mortal ➤ *adj* mortal; (*penoso*) dreadful, awful ➤ *m* mortal.

mosca ➤ *f* fly.

mosquito ➤ *m* mosquito.

mostaza ➤ *f* mustard.

mostrar §11 ➤ *tr* (*enseñar*) to show; (*explicar*) to demonstrate, show; (*indicar*) to point out ➤ *reflex* (*darse a conocer*) to show oneself.

mote[1] ➤ *m* nickname.

mote[2] ➤ *m* AMER. stewed corn.

motín ➤ *m* insurrection, riot.

motivo ➤ *m* motive, cause.

moto ➤ *f* COLL. moped, motorcycle.

motocicleta ➤ *f* motorcycle.

motociclista ➤ *mf* motorcyclist.

motor, a ➤ *adj* motor ➤ *m* motor,

engine ■ m. de reacción *or* de chorro
jet engine • m. de vapor steam engine
• m. diesel diesel.
motorista ➤ *mf* motorist.
mover §54 ➤ *tr* to move; MECH. to drive,
power ➤ *reflex* to move.
movimiento ➤ *m* movement, motion;
MECH. motion; COM. activity ■ **poner
en m.** to put in motion.
mozo, a ➤ *adj* young ➤ *m* boy;
(camarero) waiter; *(en hotel, etc.)* porter ■ **buen m.** AMER. handsome ➤ *f*
girl.
muchacho, a ➤ *mf* child, youngster
➤ *m* boy ➤ *f* girl.
muchedumbre ➤ *f* multitude, crowd.
mucho, a ➤ *adj* much, a lot of ■ **hace m.
frío** it's very cold ■ *pl* many, a lot of
➤ *pron* a lot ■ *pl* many ➤ *adv* a lot,
much ■ **hace mucho** for a long time •
m. después much later • **ni m. menos**
not by a long shot • **por m. que no**
matter how much • **tener en m.** to
hold in high regard.
mudanza ➤ *f (traslado)* move, moving
■ **estar de m.** to be moving.
mudar ➤ *tr (cambiar)* to change;
(trasladar) to move ➤ *reflex* to move.
mudo, a ➤ *adj* mute, dumb.
mueble ➤ *m* piece of furniture ■ *pl* furniture.
muela ➤ *f* ANAT. molar ■ **m. de juicio**
wisdom tooth.
muelle[1] ➤ *m* MECH. spring.
muelle[2] ➤ *m* pier, dock.
muérdago ➤ *m* mistletoe.
muerte ➤ *f* death ■ **de m.** seriously,
fatally.
muerto, a ➤ *adj* dead ■ **m. de dying of**
➤ *mf* dead person; *(cadáver)* corpse ■
hacerse el m. COLL. to play dead.
muestra ➤ *f (ejemplo)* sample, specimen; *(señal)* sign, indication; *(modelo)* model, guide.
mugre ➤ *f* filth, grime.
mujer ➤ *f* woman; *(esposa)* wife ■ **m. de
la limpieza** cleaning woman • **m. de
(su) casa** housewife.
mulato, a ➤ *adj & mf* mulatto.
muleta ➤ *f* crutch; FIG. support.
mulo, a ➤ *mf* mule.

multa ➤ *f* fine; AUTO. parking ticket.
multinacional ➤ *adj* multinational.
múltiple ➤ *adj* multiple.
multiplicación ➤ *f* multiplication.
multiplicar §47 ➤ *tr & reflex* to multiply.
multiprocesador ➤ *adj & m* COMPUT.
multiprocessor.
multitud ➤ *f* multitude.
mundial ➤ *adj* world; *(universal)*
worldwide ■ **guerra m.** world war ➤ *m*
world championship ■ **m. de fútbol**
world soccer championship.
mundo ➤ *m* world; *(tierra)* earth.
municipalidad ➤ *f* municipality.
municipio ➤ *m (ayuntamiento)* town
council; *(pueblo)* township, district.
muñeca ➤ *f* wrist; *(juguete)* doll.
muñeco ➤ *m (juguete)* doll; *(marioneta)* puppet.
muralla ➤ *f* wall, rampart.
murmullo ➤ *m* murmur.
murmurar ➤ *intr* to whisper; *(hojas)* to
rustle; *(quejar)* to grumble; COLL.
(chismear) to gossip.
muro ➤ *m* wall.
músculo ➤ *m* muscle.
museo ➤ *m* museum.
musgo ➤ *m* moss.
musical ➤ *adj & m* musical.
músico, a ➤ *mf* musician.
muslo ➤ *m* thigh; *(de pollo)* drumstick.
mutilar ➤ *tr* to mutilate.
mutuo, a ➤ *adj* mutual.
muy ➤ *adv* very ■ **m. señor mío** Dear
Sir • **ser m. de su casa** COLL. to be a
homebody.

N

nabo ➤ *m* turnip.
nácar ➤ *m* nacre, mother-of-pearl.
nacer §09 ➤ *intr* to be born; *(los astros)*
to rise; *(brotar)* to rise, start to flow ■
al n. at birth.
nación ➤ *f* nation; *(pueblo)* people.
nacional ➤ *adj* national, domestic.
nacionalidad ➤ *f* nationality.
nada ➤ *pron* nothing, not anything ■
antes de n. first, before anything else •
de n. you're welcome ■ **n. de no, none** •
n. menos no less, nothing less • **ni n.**

COLL. or anything ➤ in no way, not at all ➤ *f* nothingness, nothing; *(cosa mínima)* the slightest thing.

nadar ➤ *intr* to swim.

nadie ➤ *pron* nobody, no one ➤ *m* a nobody ■ **no ser n.** to be a nobody.

nafta ➤ *f* naphtha; AMER. gasoline.

naipe ➤ *m* card, playing card.

nalga ➤ *f* buttock.

nana ➤ *f* COLL. *(abuela)* granny; *(arrullo)* lullaby; AMER. nanny.

naranja ➤ *f* orange ➤ *m* orange (color).

naranjada ➤ *f* orangeade.

naranjo ➤ *m* orange tree.

nariz ➤ *f* nose.

narrar ➤ *tr* to narrate, relate.

nata ➤ *f* cream.

natación ➤ *f* swimming.

natillas ➤ *fpl* custard.

natural ➤ *adj* natural ■ **al n.** naturally, without adornment.

naturaleza ➤ *f* nature.

naturalidad ➤ *f* naturalness.

naturalizar §02 ➤ *tr* to naturalize, nationalize.

naufragar §31 ➤ *intr* MARIT. to be shipwrecked.

naufragio ➤ *m* MARIT. shipwreck.

náusea ➤ *f* nausea; *(repugnancia)* disgust ■ **dar náuseas** to disgust, nauseate • **sentir náuseas** to feel sick.

navaja ➤ *f* jackknife, penknife ■ **n. de afeitar** razor.

nave ➤ *f* ship, vessel; ARCHIT. nave.

navegación ➤ *f* navigation.

navegador, a ➤ *mf* navigator ➤ *m* COMPUT. browser.

navegar §31 ➤ *intr* to navigate; *(por barco)* to sail; COMPUT. to browse.

Navidad ➤ *f* Christmas, Nativity ■ **¡Feliz N.!** Merry Christmas!

navío ➤ *m* ship, vessel.

neblina ➤ *f* mist, fog.

necesario, a ➤ *adj* necessary; *(esencial)* essential.

necesidad ➤ *f* necessity, need.

necesitar ➤ *tr* to need, want.

necio, a ➤ *adj* ignorant, foolish ➤ *mf* fool, simpleton.

nectarina ➤ *f* nectarine.

negación ➤ *f* negation, denial.

negar §35 ➤ *tr* to deny; *(rehusar)* to refuse ➤ *reflex* *(rehusar)* to refuse; *(privarse)* to deny oneself.

negativo, a ➤ *adj* negative ➤ *f* negation, denial ➤ *m* PHOTOG. negative.

negligencia ➤ *f* negligence.

negligente ➤ *adj* negligent.

negociación ➤ *f* negotiation.

negociar ➤ *intr* *(tratar)* to negotiate, discuss; *(comerciar)* to deal, do business *(con, en* in) ➤ *tr* to negotiate.

negocio ➤ *m* *(comercio)* business; *(transacción)* transaction, deal; *(utilidad)* profit, return; *(asunto)* affair, concern; R.P. shop, store ■ **persona de negocios** business person • **encargado de negocios** chargé d'affaires.

negro, a ➤ *adj* black; *(oscuro)* dark, black ■ **ponerse n.** to get angry ➤ *mf* Black person; AMER. *(querido)* dear, darling ➤ *m* *(color)* black.

nene, a ➤ *mf* COLL. baby, infant.

neolítico, a ➤ *adj* Neolithic.

nervio ➤ *m* nerve; *(tendón)* tendon, sinew; BOT. rib, vein.

nervioso, a ➤ *adj* nervous ■ **ponerse n.** to get nervous.

neto, a ➤ *adj* COM. net.

neumático, a ➤ *adj* pneumatic ➤ *m* tire.

neumonía ➤ *f* pneumonia.

neurosis ➤ *f* neurosis.

neurótico, a ➤ *adj & mf* neurotic.

neutral ➤ *adj & mf* neutral.

neutro, a ➤ *adj* neutral.

nevado, a ➤ *adj* snowy, snow-covered; FIG. snow-white ➤ *f* snowfall.

nevar §33 ➤ *intr* to snow.

nevera ➤ *f* refrigerator.

ni ➤ *conj* neither, nor ■ **ni . . . ni** neither . . . nor • **ni me vió** she didn't even see me • **ni que** not even if.

nicaragüense ➤ *adj & mf* Nicaraguan.

nido ➤ *m* nest.

niebla ➤ *f* fog, mist; *(nube)* cloud.

nieto, a ➤ *mf* grandchild, grandson/daughter ■ *pl* grandchildren.

nieve ➤ *f* snow.

ningún ➤ *adj contr* of **ninguno** ■ **de n. modo** in no way.

ninguno, a ➤ *adj* none, no, not any ■ **de n. manera** in no way, by no means • **en n. parte** nowhere ➤ *pron* none, not any; *(nadie)* no one, nobody.

niñero, a ➤ *adj* fond of children ➤ *f* nursemaid, nanny, babysitter.

niño, a ➤ *adj* young ➤ *mf* child ➤ *m* boy ■ **de n.** as a child • **desde n.** from childhood ■ *pl* children ➤ *f* girl; *(del ojo)* pupil (of the eye).

nitrógeno ➤ *m* nitrogen.

nivel ➤ *m* level, height ■ **n. de vida** standard of living • **n. del mar** sea level.

no ➤ *adv* no • **¿cómo no?** of course, why not? • **no bebedor** nondrinker • **no bien** no sooner • **no más** no more, only; AMER., COLL. feel free to • **no obstante** nevertheless • **no sea que** in case, lest • **no vengo** I'm not coming ➤ *m* no.

noble ➤ *adj (aristocrático)* noble, aristocratic; *(elevado)* noble, honorable ➤ *mf* nobleman/woman.

noche ➤ *f* night, evening ■ **buenas noches** good evening, good night • **de la n. a la mañana** suddenly, overnight • **de n.** or **por la n.** at night, in the evening • **esta n.** tonight.

Nochebuena ➤ *f* Christmas Eve.

noción ➤ *f* notion, idea.

nocturno, a ➤ *adj* nocturnal, nightly; *(triste)* sad, melancholy.

nombrar ➤ *tr* to name, mention by name.

nombre ➤ *m* name; GRAM. noun ■ **de n. by name** • **n. y apellido** full name.

nordeste or **noreste** ➤ *m* northeast.

norma ➤ *f (modelo)* norm; *(regla)* rule.

normal ➤ *adj* normal, standard.

normalizar §02 ➤ *tr* to normalize; INDUS. to standardize.

noroeste ➤ *m* northwest.

norte ➤ *adj* northern, northerly ➤ *m* north.

Norteamérica ➤ *f* North America.

norteamericano, a ➤ *adj* & *mf* North American.

nos ➤ *pron* us; to, for, or from us ■ **n. vimos** we saw each other.

nosotros, as ➤ *pron* we, us.

nostalgia ➤ *f* nostalgia, homesickness.

nota ➤ *f* note, notation; *(reparo)*

notice, heed; EDUC. grade, mark.

notable ➤ *adj* notable, noteworthy; *(superior)* outstanding, striking.

notar ➤ *tr* to note, point out; *(observar)* to notice ➤ *reflex* to see, notice.

notario, a ➤ *mf* notary, notary public.

noticia ➤ *f* news item ■ *pl* news ■ **n. de última hora** the latest news.

noticiero ➤ *m* news report.

notificar §47 ➤ *tr* to notify, inform.

novato, a ➤ *mf* COLL. beginner, novice.

novecientos, as ➤ *adj* & *m* nine hundred.

novedad ➤ *f* novelty, innovation; *(cambio)* change; *(noticia)* recent event.

novela ➤ *f* novel ■ **n. policíaca** detective story.

novelista ➤ *mf* novelist.

noveno, a ➤ *adj* & *m* ninth.

noventa ➤ *adj* & *m* ninety.

noviembre ➤ *m* November.

novillo, a ➤ *m* young bull ➤ *f* heifer, young cow.

novio, a ➤ *m* boyfriend; *(prometido)* fiancé; *(recién casado)* groom ■ *pl (casados)* newlyweds; *(prometidos)* engaged couple ➤ *f* girlfriend; *(prometida)* fiancée; *(recién casada)* bride.

nube ➤ *f* cloud.

nublado, a ➤ *adj* cloudy, overcast.

nublar ➤ *tr* to cloud, darken ➤ *reflex* to become cloudy or overcast.

nuca ➤ *f* nape (of the neck).

nuclear ➤ *adj* nuclear.

núcleo ➤ *m* nucleus; ELEC. core; BOT. kernel, pit; *(esencial)* core, essence.

nudillo ➤ *m* knuckle.

nudista ➤ *mf* nudist.

nudo ➤ *m* knot.

nuera ➤ *f* daughter-in-law.

nuestro, a ➤ *adj* our ➤ *pron* ours, of ours ■ **el n. es rojo** ours is red.

nueve ➤ *adj* & *m* nine ■ **las n.** nine o'clock.

nuevo, a ➤ *adj* new.

nuez ➤ *f* walnut; ANAT. Adam's apple

numeral ➤ *adj* numeral.

numerar ➤ *tr (foliar)* to number; *(contar)* to count, enumerate.

numérico, a ➤ *adj* numerical.

número ➤ *m* number; *(ejemplar)* issue, copy; *(medida)* size.

numeroso, a ➤ *adj* numerous.

nunca ➤ *adv* never, not ever ▪ **más que n.** more than ever • **n. jamás** *or* **n. más** never again.

nutrición ➤ *f* nutrition.

nutrir ➤ *tr* to nourish, feed.

nutritivo, a ➤ *adj* nutritious, nutritive.

Ñ

ñame ➤ *m* yam.

ñoñería *or* **ñoñez** ➤ *f* foolishness, simplemindedness.

ñoño, a ➤ *adj & mf* COLL. *(apocado)* bashful (person); *(soso)* dull (person).

O

o ➤ *conj* or ▪ **o . . . o** either . . . or • **o sea** that is to say.

oasis ➤ *m* oasis.

obedecer §09 ➤ *tr* to obey.

obediente ➤ *adj* obedient.

obeso, a ➤ *adj* obese.

obispo ➤ *m* bishop.

objetivo, a ➤ *adj & m* objective.

objeto ➤ *m* object, aim.

oblicuo, a ➤ *adj* oblique, slanting.

obligación ➤ *f* obligation.

obligar §31 ➤ *tr* to oblige, obligate; *(compeler)* to force, compel.

obligatorio, a ➤ *adj* obligatory.

oblongo, a ➤ *adj* oblong.

obra ➤ *f* work; *(acto)* act; *(construcción)* construction site ▪ **o. maestra** masterpiece • **obras públicas** public works.

obrar ➤ *tr (madera, etc.)* to work ➤ *intr* to act, proceed.

obrero, a ➤ *adj* working ▪ **sindicato o. labor** union ➤ *mf* worker.

obsceno, a ➤ *adj* obscene.

obscuro ➤ *adj var of* oscuro.

obsequio ➤ *m* gift, present.

observador, a ➤ *adj* observant ➤ *mf* observer.

observar ➤ *tr* to observe; *(espiar)* to watch; *(notar)* to notice; *(comentar)* to remark.

observatorio ➤ *m* observatory.

obsesión ➤ *f* obsession.

obstáculo ➤ *m* obstacle.

obstante ➤ *adj* ▪ **no o.** nevertheless.

obstinado, a ➤ *adj* obstinate.

obstinarse ➤ *reflex* to be *or* become obstinate.

obstruir §10 ➤ *tr* to obstruct.

obtener §46 ➤ *tr* to obtain, get.

obvio, a ➤ *adj* obvious.

ocasión ➤ *f* occasion; *(oportunidad)* opportunity; *(circunstancia)* circumstance ▪ **en ocasiones** sometimes.

ocasionar ➤ *tr* to cause.

occidental ➤ *adj* western.

occidente ➤ *m* west, occident.

océano ➤ *m* ocean; FIG. ocean, sea.

ochenta ➤ *adj & m* eighty.

ocho ➤ *adj & m* eight ▪ **las o.** eight o'clock.

ocio ➤ *m (inactividad)* idleness, inactivity; *(tiempo libre)* leisure, free time.

octavo, a ➤ *adj & m* eighth.

octubre ➤ *m* October.

oculista ➤ *mf* optometrist.

ocultar ➤ *tr* to hide, conceal *(de* from).

ocupación ➤ *f* occupation.

ocupado, a ➤ *adj (teléfono, línea)* busy; *(territorio)* occupied; *(seat)* taken.

ocupante ➤ *adj* occupying ➤ *mf* occupant.

ocupar ➤ *tr* to occupy; *(emplear)* to employ, give work to ➤ *reflex* to occupy oneself; *(atender a)* to attend, pay attention *(de* to).

ocurrencia ➤ *f* witticism.

ocurrir ➤ *intr* to occur, happen ➤ *reflex* to occur to, strike.

odiar ➤ *tr* to hate, loathe.

odio ➤ *m* hatred, loathing.

odontología ➤ *f* dentistry.

oeste ➤ *adj* western, westerly ➤ *m* west.

ofender ➤ *tr* to offend, insult ➤ *reflex* to take offense.

ofensa ➤ *f* offense.

ofensivo, a ➤ *adj & f* offensive.

oferta ➤ *f* offer; COM. bid.

oficial ➤ *adj* official ➤ *mf* official, officer; *(obrero)* skilled worker.

oficina ➤ *f* office ▪ **horas de o.** business hours.

oficinista ➤ *mf* clerk, office worker.

oficio ➤ *m* (*ocupación*) labor, work; (*artesanía*) trade, craft.

ofrecer §09 ➤ *tr* to offer ➤ *reflex* to offer oneself, volunteer.

ofrecimiento ➤ *m* offer, offering.

oftalmólogo, a ➤ *mf* ophthalmologist.

oído ➤ *m* hearing, sense of hearing; ANAT. ear.

oír §29 ➤ *tr* to hear ■ ¡oye! *or* ¡oiga! (*para llamar la atención*) listen!; (*para reprender*) look here!

ojal ➤ *m* buttonhole.

¡ojalá! ➤ *interj* would to God!, if only ■ o. que . . . I hope that. . . .

ojeada ➤ *f* glance, glimpse.

ojear ➤ *tr* to look at.

ojera ➤ *f* dark circle (under the eyes).

ojo ➤ *m* eye; (*agujero*) hole; (*de la cerradura*) keyhole ■ abrir los ojos to be on the alert • ¡ojo! look out!

ola ➤ *f* wave.

oleaje ➤ *m* (*olas*) surf, waves; (*marejada*) swell.

óleo ➤ *m* oil ■ pintura al ó. oil painting.

oleoducto ➤ *m* oil pipeline.

oler §30 ➤ *tr* to smell ➤ *intr* (*tener olor*) to smell ■ o. a to smell of or like.

olfato ➤ *m* sense of smell.

olímpico, a ➤ *adj* Olympian, Olympic ■ juegos olímpicos Olympic Games.

oliva ➤ *adj & f* olive.

olivo ➤ *m* olive tree; (*color*) olive.

olla ➤ *f* (*vasija*) pot, kettle; (*cocido*) stew ■ o. de presión pressure cooker.

olor ➤ *m* smell.

oloroso, a ➤ *adj* perfumed, fragrant.

olvidar ➤ *tr & reflex* (*no recordar*) to forget; (*dejar*) to leave (behind) ■ olvidarse de to forget to.

ombligo ➤ *m* navel.

omisión ➤ *f* omission.

omitir ➤ *tr* to omit.

omóplato ➤ *m* shoulder blade.

once ➤ *adj & m* eleven ■ las o. eleven o'clock.

onda ➤ *f* wave.

ondulado, a ➤ *adj* wavy.

ondular ➤ *intr* to wave, undulate.

onza ➤ *f* ounce.

opaco, a ➤ *adj* opaque.

opcional ➤ *adj* optional.

ópera ➤ *f* opera.

operación ➤ *f* operation; FIN. transaction.

operador, a ➤ *adj* operating ➤ *mf* operator.

operar ➤ *intr* to operate; COM. to deal, do business ➤ *tr* to operate on.

opinar ➤ *intr* (*formar opinión*) to think, have an opinion; (*expresar la opinión*) to express an opinion.

opinión ➤ *f* opinion.

oponerse §37 ➤ *reflex* ■ o. a to oppose, object to; (*ser contrario*) to be in opposition to.

oporto ➤ *m* port (wine).

oportunidad ➤ *f* opportunity.

oportuno, a ➤ *adj* opportune, timely.

oposición ➤ *f* opposition.

opresión ➤ *f* oppression.

oprimir ➤ *tr* (*tiranizar*) to oppress, tyrannize; (*apretar*) to press, squeeze.

optativo, a ➤ *adj* optional.

óptico, a ➤ *adj* optical ➤ *m* optician.

optimista ➤ *adj* optimistic ➤ *mf* optimist.

óptimo, a ➤ *adj* optimal, best.

opuesto, a ➤ *adj* (*enfrente*) opposite; (*contrario*) opposing, contrary.

opulencia ➤ *f* opulence.

oración ➤ *f* RELIG. prayer; GRAM. (*frase*) sentence; (*cláusula*) clause.

orador, a ➤ *mf* orator.

oral ➤ *adj* oral.

orar ➤ *intr* to pray.

orden ➤ *m* (*disposición*) order ■ o. del día agenda • poner en o. to put in order ➤ *f* (*mandato*) order ■ a la o. de at the order of • a sus ordenes at your service.

ordenado, a ➤ *adj* orderly, methodical.

ordenador, a ➤ *m or f* computer.

ordenar ➤ *tr* put in order; (*arreglar*) to arrange; (*mandar*) to order.

ordeñar ➤ *tr* to milk.

ordinal ➤ *adj & m* ordinal.

ordinario, a ➤ *adj* ordinary, common.

oreja ➤ *f* ear.

orfanato ➤ *m* orphanage.

orfebrería ➤ *f* gold or silver work.

orgánico, a ➤ *adj* organic.

organismo ➤ *m* organism; (*organi-*

zación) organization, institution.

organización ➤ f organization.

organizar §02 ➤ tr to organize ➤ reflex to be organized.

órgano ➤ m organ.

orgullo ➤ m (arrogancia) arrogance, conceit; (sentimiento legítimo) pride.

orgulloso, a ➤ adj proud.

orientación ➤ f orientation; (colocación) positioning; (consejo) guidance, direction.

oriental ➤ adj oriental, eastern ➤ mf Oriental.

orientar ➤ tr to position; (un edificio) to orient; (encaminar) to guide.

oriente ➤ m east, orient.

orificio ➤ m orifice, opening.

origen ➤ m origin.

original ➤ adj & m original.

orilla ➤ f (borde) border, edge; (del mar) shore; (de un río) bank.

orinar ➤ intr to urinate.

orla TEX. border, hem.

ornamento ➤ m ornament, adornment; ARCHIT. ornamentation.

oro ➤ m gold ∎ chapado de o. goldplated.

orquesta ➤ f orchestra.

ortodoxo, a ➤ adj orthodox.

ortografía ➤ f orthography.

ortopédico, a ➤ adj orthopedic.

oruga ➤ f ENTOM. caterpillar.

os ➤ pron you; to, for, or from you.

osadía ➤ f boldness, audacity.

oscilar ➤ intr to oscillate.

oscurecer §09 ➤ tr to darken ➤ intr to be getting dark ➤ reflex (nublarse) to become cloudy or overcast.

oscuridad ➤ f darkness.

oscuro, a ➤ adj dark; (desconocido) obscure; (nebuloso) cloudy, overcast.

oso ➤ m bear ∎ o. gris grizzly bear.

ostentación ➤ f ostentation.

ostra ➤ f oyster.

otoño ➤ m autumn, fall.

otorgar §31 ➤ tr to grant, give.

otro, a ➤ adj other, another ∎ o. vez again ∎ por o. parte on the other hand ➤ pron another one ∎ unos a otros each other, one another ∎ pl others.

ovación ➤ f ovation.

oval or **ovalado, a** ➤ adj oval.

oveja ➤ f ewe, female sheep.

ovillo ➤ m (de hilo) ball.

ovni ➤ m UFO.

oxidar ➤ tr & reflex to oxidize, rust.

óxido ➤ m oxide.

oxígeno ➤ m oxygen.

ozono ➤ m ozone.

P

pabellón ➤ m (bandera) flag, banner; (edificio) pavilion.

paciencia ➤ f patience.

paciente ➤ adj & mf patient.

pacificar §47 ➤ tr to pacify.

pacifista ➤ adj & mf pacifist.

pactar ➤ tr to agree to ➤ intr to come to an agreement, make a pact.

pacto ➤ m pact, agreement.

padecer §09 ➤ tr & intr to suffer ∎ p. del corazón to have heart trouble.

padrastro ➤ m stepfather; (pellejo) hangnail.

padre ➤ m father ∎ pl parents.

padrenuestro ➤ m Lord's Prayer.

padrino ➤ m (de niño) godfather; (de boda) best man ∎ pl godparents.

padrón ➤ m census.

paella ➤ f dish of rice with meat or chicken.

paga ➤ f (acción) payment; (sueldo) wages.

pagar §31 ➤ tr & intr to pay; (recompensar) to repay ∎ p. a crédito or a plazos to pay in installments • p. por adelantado to pay in advance.

pagaré ➤ m promissory note, IOU.

página ➤ f page.

pago ➤ m (entrega) payment; (recompensa) repayment, recompense.

país ➤ m country, nation.

paisaje ➤ m landscape.

paja ➤ f straw.

pájaro ➤ m bird.

pala ➤ f (herramienta) shovel, spade; (del remo) blade.

palabra ➤ f word; (promesa) word, promise ∎ bajo p. on one's word of honor • cumplir or mantener su p. uno to keep one's word.

palabrota ➤ f COLL. swearword.

palacio ➤ *m* palace ∎ **p. de justicia** courthouse.

paladear ➤ *tr* to savor, relish.

palanca ➤ *f* lever ∎ **p. de cambio** gearshift.

palco ➤ *m* THEAT. box.

paleta ➤ *f* small shovel; *(del pintor)* palette; *(del albañil)* trowel.

palidecer §09 ➤ *intr* to turn pale.

palidez ➤ *f* paleness, pallor.

pálido, a ➤ *adj* pale.

palillo ➤ *m (mondadientes)* toothpick; *(de tambor)* drumstick.

paliza ➤ *f* beating, thrashing.

palma ➤ *f (de la mano)* palm; *(palmera)* palm (tree).

palmada ➤ *f* slap, pat ∎ **dar palmadas** to clap.

palmera ➤ *f* palm tree.

palmo ➤ *m* span ∎ **p. a p.** little by little, inch by inch.

palo ➤ *m (vara)* stick, pole; *(mango)* stick, handle ∎ **palos de golf** golf clubs.

paloma ➤ *f* dove, pigeon.

palomita ➤ *f* popcorn.

palpar ➤ *tr* to touch, feel.

palpitar ➤ *intr* to palpitate.

palurdo, a ➤ *adj* boorish ➤ *mf* boor.

pampa ➤ *f* pampa, plain.

pan ➤ *m* bread ∎ **p. integral** wholewheat bread.

pana ➤ *f* corduroy.

panadería ➤ *f* bakery.

panal ➤ *m* honeycomb.

pandilla ➤ *f* gang, band.

panecillo ➤ *m* roll, bun.

panfleto ➤ *m* pamphlet.

pánico, a ➤ *adj & m* panic.

panorama ➤ *m* panorama.

pantalla ➤ *f* CINEM., COMPUT. screen; *(de lámpara)* lamp shade.

pantalón *or* **pantalones** ➤ *m(pl)* pants ∎ **p. corto** shorts ∎ **p. vaquero** jeans.

pantano ➤ *m* marsh.

panteón ➤ *m* pantheon.

pantera ➤ *f* panther.

pantorrilla ➤ *f* ANAT. calf.

pantufla ➤ *f* slipper.

pañal ➤ *m* diaper.

paño ➤ *m (tela)* cloth; *(trapo)* rag.

pañuelo ➤ *m* handkerchief; *(pañoleta)* scarf.

papa[1] ➤ *m* Pope.

papa[2] ➤ *f* AMER. potato.

papá ➤ *m* papa, daddy.

papagayo ➤ *m* parrot.

papaya ➤ *f* papaya.

papel ➤ *m* paper; *(hoja)* piece of paper; THEAT. role ∎ **p. de cartas** stationery • **p. de seda** tissue paper • **p. higiénico** toilet paper ∎ *pl* papers, documents.

papelería ➤ *f* stationery store.

papera ➤ *pl* mumps.

papilla ➤ *f* soft food, pap.

paquete ➤ *m (bulto)* package; *(caja)* pack, packet.

par ➤ *adj (igual)* equal; MATH. even ➤ *m (dos)* couple; *(zapatos, etc.)* pair; MATH. even number ∎ **al p. de** on the same level as • **a pares** *or* **en pares** in pairs, by twos • **de p. en p.** wide.

para ➤ *prep* for, to; *(con el propósito de)* in order to ∎ **estoy p. salir** I'm about to leave • **p. mañana** for *or* by tomorrow • **p. que** so that • **¿p. qué?** why?, for what? • **p. siempre** forever • **un cuarto p. las once** a quarter to eleven.

parabrisas ➤ *m* windshield.

paracaídas ➤ *f* parachute.

parachoques ➤ *m* bumper, fender.

paradero ➤ *m* whereabouts.

parado, a ➤ *adj (inmóvil)* stationary; *(detenido)* stopped; *(inactivo)* idle; *(sin empleo)* unemployed; AMER. standing ∎ **salir bien, mal p.** to come off well, badly ➤ *f* stop; *(suspensión)* halt ∎ **p. de taxis** taxi stand.

parador ➤ *m* inn, roadhouse.

paraguas ➤ *m* umbrella.

paraguayo, a ➤ *adj & mf* Paraguayan.

paraíso ➤ *m* paradise.

paralelo ➤ *adj & m* parallel.

parálisis ➤ *f* paralysis ∎ **p. cerebral** cerebral palsy.

paralizar §02 ➤ *tr* to paralyze ➤ *reflex* to become paralyzed.

parámetro ➤ *m* parameter.

parapeto ➤ *m* parapet.

parar ➤ *intr (cesar)* to stop ∎ **ir a p.** to end up • **p. en** to end up, result in ∎ **sin p.** nonstop ➤ *tr (detener)* to stop

➤ *reflex (detenerse)* to stop; AMER. to stand up ■ p. a to stop, pause (to).

parásito, a ➤ *adj* parasitic ➤ *m* parasite.

parcela ➤ *f* parcel, plot.

parche ➤ *m* patch.

parcial ➤ *adj* partial.

pardo, a ➤ *adj* brown.

parecer¹ ➤ *m* opinion.

parecer² **§09** ➤ *intr* to seem; *(semejarse)* to resemble, seem like ■ al p. apparently • así parece so it seems ➤ *reflex* to look alike ■ p. a to look like.

parecido, a ➤ *adj* similar ■ ser p. a to resemble, be like ➤ *m* similarity.

pared ➤ *f* wall.

parentesco ➤ *m* kinship; *(lazo)* tie.

paréntesis ➤ *m* parenthesis ■ entre p. in parentheses.

pariente, a ➤ *mf* relative, relation.

parir ➤ *intr & tr* to give birth (to).

parlamento ➤ *m* parliament.

paro ➤ *m* stoppage, standstill; COM. unemployment ■ p. laboral strike.

parpadear ➤ *intr (párpados)* to blink; *(luz)* to flicker.

párpado ➤ *m* eyelid.

parque ➤ *m* park; AUTO. parking lot ■ p. de atracciones amusement park.

parquear ➤ *tr* AMER. to park.

parra ➤ *f* grapevine.

párrafo ➤ *m* paragraph.

parrilla ➤ *f* grill.

parrillada ➤ *f* CUL. grilled seafood.

párroco ➤ *m* parish priest.

parroquia ➤ *f* parish.

parte ➤ *f* part; *(porción)* portion; *(cantidad asignada)* share; *(sitio)* place, spot ■ de p. de on behalf of • ¿de p. de quién? who's calling? • en alguna p. somewhere • en cualquier p. anywhere • en gran p. for the most part • en ninguna p. nowhere • en or por todas partes everywhere • la mayor p. the majority • p. por p. bit by bit • por mi p. as far as I am concerned • por otra p. on the other hand.

participación ➤ *f* participation.

participar ➤ *tr* to inform ➤ *intr* to participate, take part ■ p. en to share in.

participio ➤ *m* participle.

particular ➤ *adj (privado)* private; *(especial)* particular, special ➤ *mf* individual; *(asunto)* matter, point.

partidario, a ➤ *adj & mf* partisan.

partido, a ➤ *adj* divided ➤ *m* POL. party; SPORT. game ■ sacar p. de to benefit from • ➤ *f* departure ■ p. de matrimonio marriage certificate.

partir ➤ *tr (dividir)* to divide, split; *(romper)* to break, crack open ➤ *intr* to leave ■ a p. de as of, starting from.

parto ➤ *m* childbirth, delivery.

pasa ➤ *f* raisin ■ p. de Corinto currant.

pasadizo ➤ *m* passage.

pasado, a ➤ *adj* past, gone by; *(anterior)* last ■ p. de moda old-fashioned • p. mañana day after tomorrow ➤ *m* past.

pasaje ➤ *m* passage.

pasajero, a ➤ *adj* passing, fleeting ➤ *mf* passenger, traveler.

pasamano ➤ *m* handrail.

pasaporte ➤ *m* passport.

pasar ➤ *tr* to pass, hand; *(atravesar)* to cross; *(ir más allá)* to go beyond; *(disfrutar)* to spend, pass; *(sufrir)* to suffer, undergo; *(aprobar)* to pass ■ p. lista to call roll • pasarla bien, mal to have a good, bad time ➤ *intr* to pass, go by; *(entrar)* to come in; *(ocurrir)* to happen, occur ■ p. de *(exceder)* to exceed, surpass; *(edad)* to be over • p. de moda to go out of fashion • p. por to stop by ➤ *reflex (olvidarse)* to forget; *(deslizar)* to run; *(excederse)* to go too far.

pasarela ➤ *f (puentecillo)* footbridge; *(de desfile de modas)* runway.

pasatiempo ➤ *m* pastime.

Pascua ➤ *f* Easter ■ pl Christmastime.

pasear ➤ *intr* to go for a walk ➤ *tr* to take for a walk.

paseo ➤ *m (caminata)* stroll; *(a caballo, coche)* ride; *(avenida)* avenue ■ dar un p. *(andar)* to go for a walk; *(en coche)* to go for a ride.

pasillo ➤ *m* corridor, hall(way).

pasión ➤ *f* passion.

pasivo, a ➤ *adj* passive.

paso ➤ *m* step; EQUIT. gait; *(camino)* passage; GEOG. pass; *(pisada)* footstep; *(en el baile)* step ■ abrir p. a to make way for • **aflojar el p.** to slow down • **apretar el p.** to go faster • **a pocos pasos** at a short distance • **ceder el p.** to step aside • **p. de peatones** crosswalk • **p. por p.** step by step.

pasta ➤ *f* paste ■ **p. de dientes** toothpaste ■ *pl* noodles, pasta.

pastel ➤ *m* CUL. *(dulce)* cake; *(de carne, queso)* pie.

pastelería ➤ *f* pastry shop.

pastilla ➤ *f* *(de jabón)* bar, cake; MED. lozenge, drop; *(de menta)* mint.

pastor ➤ *m* pastor; *(ovejero)* shepherd.

pata ➤ *f* ZOOL. *(pie)* paw, foot; *(pierna)* leg ■ **meter la p.** to put one's foot in it ■ **tener mala p.** to be unlucky.

patada ➤ *f* kick.

patalear ➤ *intr* *(pisar)* to stamp, stomp.

patata ➤ *f* potato.

patente ➤ *adj & f* patent.

paternal ➤ *adj* paternal.

patín ➤ *m* skate ■ **p. de hielo** ice skate • **p. de ruedas** roller skate.

patinaje ➤ *m* skating ■ **p. sobre hielo** ice skating • **p. sobre ruedas** roller skating.

patinar ➤ *intr* to skate; *(un vehículo)* to skid; *(resbalar voluntariamente)* to slide; *(resbalar sin querer)* to slip.

patinazo ➤ *m* skid.

patio ➤ *m* patio, courtyard.

pato ➤ *m* duck.

patria ➤ *f* homeland ■ **madre p.** motherland.

patrimonio ➤ *m* patrimony, heritage.

patriota ➤ *mf* patriot.

patriótico, a ➤ *adj* patriotic.

patrocinar ➤ *tr* to sponsor, patronize.

patrón, ona ➤ *mf* RELIG. patron saint; *(jefe)* boss ■ *m* *(modelo)* pattern; *(unidad)* standard.

patrono, a ➤ *mf* *(jefe)* boss; *(empresario)* employer.

patrulla ➤ *f* squad, patrol.

paulatino, a ➤ *adj* gradual.

pausa ➤ *f* pause, break.

pavimento ➤ *m* pavement.

pavo ➤ *m* turkey ■ **p. real** peacock.

pavor ➤ *m* fright, terror.

payaso ➤ *m* clown, buffoon.

paz ➤ *f* peace; *(calma)* peacefulness.

peaje ➤ *m* toll.

peatón, ona ➤ *mf* pedestrian.

peca ➤ *f* freckle.

pecado ➤ *m* sin.

pecar ➤ *intr* to sin.

pecera ➤ *f* fishbowl, aquarium.

pecho ➤ *m* chest; *(busto)* breast; *(seno)* bosom, breast.

pechuga ➤ *f* *(del ave)* breast.

peculiar ➤ *adj* peculiar.

pedagogía ➤ *f* pedagogy.

pedal ➤ *m* *(foot)* pedal.

pedazo ➤ *m* piece ■ **a pedazos** in pieces.

pediatra ➤ *mf* pediatrician.

pediatría ➤ *f* pediatrics.

pedido ➤ *m* order, request ■ **hacer un p.** to place an order.

pedir §32 ➤ *tr* to ask, request; *(demandar)* to demand; *(mendigar)* to beg; *(comida, etc.)* to order ■ **p. prestado** to borrow.

pega ➤ *f* gluing, sticking; FIG. snag.

pegajoso, a ➤ *adj* adhesive, sticky.

pegamento ➤ *m* glue, adhesive.

pegar §31 ➤ *tr* to glue; *(golpear)* to hit ■ **no p. un ojo** not to sleep a wink • **p. un susto** to frighten ➤ *intr* *(adherir)* to adhere, stick; *(golpear)* to hit; *(armonizar)* to go together ➤ *reflex* CUL. *(quemarse)* to stick to the pan.

peinado ➤ *m* hair style.

peinar ➤ *tr* to comb ➤ *reflex* to comb one's hair.

peine ➤ *m* comb.

pelado, a ➤ *adj* *(con el pelo cortado)* shorn; *(frutos)* peeled; *(pobre)* broke ➤ *m* haircut; *(esquileo)* shearing; *(pobre)* pauper ■ **p. crew cut.**

pelar ➤ *tr* *(pelo)* to cut; *(fruto)* to peel.

peldaño ➤ *m* step, stair; *(de escala)* rung.

pelea ➤ *f* fight.

pelear ➤ *intr* to fight, quarrel.

peletería ➤ *f* fur shop; *(pieles)* furs.

película ➤ *f* film; CINEM. movie, film ■ **de p.** COLL. fabulous.

peligro ➤ *m* danger.

peligroso, a ➤ *adj* dangerous.

pelirrojo, a ➤ *adj* red-haired, red-headed ➤ *mf* redhead.

pellejo ➤ *m* *(de animal)* hide; *(piel)*

skin ■ jugarse el p. to risk one's neck.
pellizcar ➤ *tr* to pinch.
pellizco ➤ *m* pinch.
pelmazo ➤ *mf* COLL. bore.
pelo ➤ *m (cabello)* hair; ZOOL. *(piel)* fur, coat; *(del tejido)* nap ■ por los pelos by the skin of one's teeth • tomar a alguien el p. to pull someone's leg.
pelota ➤ *f* ball.
peluca ➤ *f* wig.
peluche ➤ *f* plush.
peludo, a ➤ *adj* hairy, shaggy.
peluquería ➤ *f (para hombres)* barber shop; *(para mujeres)* beauty parlor.
peluquero, a ➤ *mf* hairdresser; *(para hombres)* barber.
pena ➤ *f (castigo)* punishment; *(aflicción)* sorrow ■ dar p. to grieve • p. de muerte death penalty • ¡qué p.! what a shame! • valer la p. to be worthwhile.
pendiente ➤ *adj (colgante)* hanging; *(sin solucionar)* pending ➤ *m (arete)* earring ➤ *f (cuesta)* slope.
penetrante ➤ *adj (que penetra)* penetrating; *(inteligencia)* acute; *(voz, mirada)* piercing; *(frío)* biting.
penetrar ➤ *tr & intr* to penetrate.
penicilina ➤ *f* penicillin.
península ➤ *f* peninsula.
pensamiento ➤ *m* thought; *(idea)* idea.
pensar §33 ➤ *tr (considerar)* to think about, consider; *(creer)* to think, believe; *(planear)* to intend ➤ *intr* to think ■ p. en *or* sobre to think about.
pensativo, a ➤ *adj* pensive.
pensión ➤ *f (en un hotel)* room and board; *(de retiro)* pension; *(casa)* boarding house.
penúltimo, a ➤ *adj & mf* penultimate.
penumbra ➤ *f* shadow; PHYS. penumbra.
peña ➤ *f (roca)* boulder; *(círculo)* group.
peñón ➤ *m* craggy rock.
peón ➤ *m* unskilled laborer; *(de ajedrez)* pawn.
peor ➤ *adj* worse, worst ■ cada vez p. worse and worse ➤ *adv* worse ■ p. que p. *or* tanto p. worse still ➤ *mf* worse, worst ■ lo p. the worst thing.
pepino ➤ *m* cucumber.

pequeño, a ➤ *adj* small; *(corto)* short; *(joven)* young ➤ *mf* child ■ de p. as a child.
pera ➤ *f* pear.
percance ➤ *m* mishap.
percha ➤ *f* hanger, coat hanger.
percibir ➤ *tr (distinguir)* to perceive, sense; *(cobrar)* to collect, receive.
percusión ➤ *f* percussion.
perder §34 ➤ *tr* to lose; *(desperdiciar)* to miss ■ echar a p. to spoil • p. de vista to lose sight of ➤ *intr* to lose ➤ *reflex* to lose, mislay; *(desorientarse)* to get lost; *(dejar de ser útil)* to go to waste; *(arruinarse)* to go astray ■ p. de vista to disappear.
pérdida ➤ *f* loss, waste ■ pérdidas y ganancias profit and loss.
perdiz ➤ *f* partridge.
perdón ➤ *m* pardon ■ ¡p.! sorry!
perdonar ➤ *tr* to pardon, forgive; *(la vida)* to spare.
perecer §09 ➤ *intr* to perish, die.
peregrinación ➤ *f* pilgrimage.
peregrino, a ➤ *mf* pilgrim.
perejil ➤ *m* parsley.
perenne ➤ *adj* perennial.
pereza ➤ *f* laziness.
perezoso, a ➤ *adj & mf* lazy (person).
perfección ➤ *f* perfection.
perfeccionar ➤ *tr (hacer perfecto)* to make perfect; *(mejorar)* to improve.
perfeccionista ➤ *adj & mf* perfectionist.
perfectamente ➤ *adv* perfectly ■ ¡p.! right!
perfecto, a ➤ *adj* perfect.
perfil ➤ *m* profile; *(contorno)* outline ■ de p. in profile.
perforar ➤ *tr* to perforate.
perfumar ➤ *tr* to perfume.
perfume ➤ *m* perfume; *(aroma)* fragrance.
pericia ➤ *f* skill, expertise.
periferia ➤ *f* periphery.
periódico, a ➤ *adj* periodic(al) ➤ *m* newspaper.
periodismo ➤ *m* journalism.
periodista ➤ *mf* journalist.
periquito ➤ *m* parakeet.
perjudicar §47 ➤ *tr* to damage, harm.

perjudicial ➤ *adj* harmful, detrimental.
perjuicio ➤ *m (material)* damage; *(moral)* injury; FIN. loss.
perla ➤ *f* pearl.
permanecer §09 ➤ *intr* to stay, remain.
permanente ➤ *adj* permanent ➤ *f* permanent wave.
permiso ➤ *m* permission; *(documento)* permit ■ con (su) p. excuse me • p. de conducir driver's license.
permitir ➤ *tr* to permit, let ■ permítame allow me ➤ *reflex* to be permitted *or* allowed.
pero ➤ *conj* but.
perpendicular ➤ *adj & f* perpendicular.
perpetuo, a ➤ *adj* perpetual.
perplejo, a ➤ *adj* perplexed.
perro, a ➤ *mf* dog ➤ *f* bitch.
persecución ➤ *f (tormento)* persecution; *(seguimiento)* pursuit, chase.
perseguir §42 ➤ *tr (seguir)* to pursue, chase; *(acosar)* to persecute.
persiana ➤ *f* blind, shade.
persistir ➤ *intr* to persist.
persona ➤ *f* person ■ por p. per person, each.
personaje ➤ *m* celebrity; LIT. character.
personal ➤ *adj* personal ➤ *m* personnel, staff.
perspectiva ➤ *f* perspective; *(vista)* view.
perspicaz ➤ *adj* sharp, keen; *(sagaz)* shrewd.
persuadir ➤ *tr* to persuade.
persuasión ➤ *f* persuasion.
pertenecer §09 ➤ *intr* to belong *(a* to).
pertinaz ➤ *adj* obstinate, tenacious.
perturbación ➤ *f* disturbance.
peruano, a ➤ *adj & mf* Peruvian.
perverso, a ➤ *adj* wicked.
pervertir §43 ➤ *tr* to pervert.
pesa ➤ *f* weight ■ *pl* dumbbells, weights.
pesadilla ➤ *f* nightmare.
pesado, a ➤ *adj* heavy; *(molesto)* annoying; *(fatigante)* tedious.
pésame ➤ *m* condolence ■ dar el p. to express condolences.
pesar[1] ➤ *m (pena)* sorrow; *(arrepentimiento)* regret ■ a p. de in spite of, despite • a p. de uno against one's will.

pesar[2] ➤ *tr* to weigh; FIG. to weigh, consider ➤ *intr (tener peso)* to weigh; *(ser pesado)* to weigh a lot; *(ser importante)* to carry weight ■ pese a quien le pese say what they will.
pesca ➤ *f* fishing.
pescadería ➤ *f* fish market.
pescado ➤ *m* CUL. fish.
pescador, a ➤ *mf* fisherman/woman.
pescar §47 ➤ *tr* to fish (for).
pescuezo ➤ *m (de animal)* neck.
peseta ➤ *f* FIN. peseta.
pesimista ➤ *adj* pessimistic ➤ *mf* pessimist.
pésimo, a ➤ *adj* very bad, terrible.
peso ➤ *m* weight; FIN. peso.
pestaña ➤ *f* eyelash.
peste ➤ *f* plague; *(olor)* stench.
pétalo ➤ *m* petal.
petición ➤ *f* petition.
petróleo ➤ *m* petroleum, oil.
petrolero ➤ *m* oil tanker.
pez ➤ *m* ZOOL. fish.
pezón ➤ *m* nipple.
pezuña ➤ *f* hoof.
piadoso, a ➤ *adj* pious.
pianista ➤ *mf* pianist.
piano ➤ *m* piano.
picadillo ➤ *m* chopped meat.
picador ➤ *m* TAUR. picador.
picadura ➤ *f* bite.
picante ➤ *adj* spicy; *(chiste)* risqué.
picaporte ➤ *m (barrita)* latch; *(aldaba)* doorknocker.
picar §47 ➤ *tr (morder)* to bite; *(comer)* to nibble; *(quemar)* to sting; *(cortar)* to mince; *(estimular)* to arouse, pique ➤ *intr (escocer)* to itch; *(morder)* to sting; *(calentar)* to be hot ➤ *reflex (fruto)* to rot; *(vino)* to turn sour; *(irritarse)* to get annoyed.
picarón, ona ➤ *adj* COLL. mischievous ➤ *mf* COLL. rascal.
pico ➤ *m (de aves)* beak; *(punta)* tip; *(herramienta)* pick; *(cima)* peak ■ veinte dólares y p. twenty-odd dollars • son las ocho y p. it is a little after eight.
pie ➤ *m* foot; *(base)* base, stand ■ al p. de la letra to the letter • a p. on foot • de p. upright.

piedad ➤ f piety; (*lástima*) pity.

piedra ➤ f (*peña*) stone, rock; (*granizo*) hailstone.

piel ➤ f skin; (*con pelo*) fur, pelt; (*cuero*) leather; BOT. peel ▪ de p. (*de cuero*) leather; (*abrigo*) fur (coat) ▪ p. de gallina goose bumps.

pienso ➤ m fodder.

pierna ➤ f leg.

pieza ➤ f piece; (*de maquinaria*) part; (*habitación*) room ▪ de una p. solid • p. de repuesto spare part.

pijama or **piyama** ➤ m pajamas.

pila ➤ f (*recipiente*) basin; (*de cocina*) sink; (*montón*) pile; ELEC. battery ▪ nombre de p. Christian name.

píldora ➤ f pill.

pillar ➤ tr to catch, get caught.

pilotar or **pilotear** ➤ tr to pilot.

piloto ➤ mf pilot; AUTO. driver ➤ m (*llama*) pilot light ➤ adj pilot, model.

pimentón ➤ m paprika.

pimienta ➤ f (*especia*) pepper ▪ p. negra black pepper.

pimiento ➤ m BOT. (bell) pepper; (*pimentón*) paprika ▪ p. verde green pepper.

pinar ➤ m pine grove.

pincel ➤ m brush.

pinchar ➤ tr to puncture; FIG. to annoy.

pinchazo ➤ m puncture.

pingüino ➤ m penguin.

pino ➤ m pine (tree).

pintar ➤ tr to paint; (*describir*) to depict ➤ intr to paint ➤ reflex to put on make-up.

pinto, a ➤ adj speckled ➤ f (*mancha*) spot; COLL. (*aspecto*) look; (*medida*) pint ▪ tener p. de COLL. to look like.

pintor, a ➤ mf painter.

pintoresco, a ➤ adj picturesque.

pintura ➤ f painting; (*color*) paint.

pinza ➤ f (*de langosta*) claw ▪ pl (*tenacillas*) tweezers; (*tenazas*) tongs.

piña ➤ f (*del pino*) pine cone; (*ananás*) pineapple.

piñón ➤ m pine nut.

piojo ➤ m louse.

pionero, a ➤ mf & adj pioneer.

pipa¹ ➤ f (*para fumar*) pipe.

pipa² ➤ f pip, seed.

pirámide ➤ f pyramid.

piraña ➤ f AMER. piranha.

pirata ➤ mf & adj pirate; COMPUT. hacker ▪ p. aéreo hijacker.

pisada ➤ f (*acción*) step, footstep; (*huella*) footprint.

pisapapeles ➤ m paperweight.

pisar ➤ tr to step or walk on.

piscina ➤ f swimming pool.

piso ➤ m (*suelo*) ground; (*de una habitación*) floor; (*planta*) floor, story.

pisotear ➤ tr to trample.

pisotón ➤ m ▪ dar un p. to step on someone's foot.

pista ➤ f (*huella*) trail; SPORT. racetrack; AER. runway; (*indicio*) clue.

pistacho ➤ m pistachio (nut).

pistola ➤ f pistol.

pitar ➤ intr to blow a whistle, whistle.

pitillo ➤ m cigarette.

pito ➤ m whistle.

pizarra ➤ f (*troca*) slate; (*pizarrón*) blackboard ▪ p. electrónica COMPUT. bulletin board.

pizca ➤ f pinch ▪ ni p. not (at all).

placa ➤ f (*lámina*, *chapa*) plate; COMPUT. chip ▪ p. de circuitos COMPUT. circuit board • p. de matrícula license plate.

placer ➤ m pleasure.

plaga ➤ f plague; BOT. blight.

plagio ➤ m plagiarism.

plan ➤ m plan; (*proyecto*) project; (*programa*) program ▪ p. de estudios curriculum, course of study.

plana ➤ f (*página*) page ▪ de primera p. front-page (news).

plancha ➤ f (*lámina*) sheet; (*utensilio*) iron ▪ a la p. grilled.

planchar ➤ tr to iron (clothes).

planeador ➤ m glider.

planeta ➤ m planet.

planetario, a ➤ adj planetary ➤ m planetarium.

planicie ➤ f GEOG. plain.

planificación ➤ f planning.

planilla ➤ f AMER. (*formulario*) form.

plano, a ➤ adj (*llano*) level, even; (*chato*) flat ➤ m map chart.

planta ➤ f plant; (*del pie*) sole; (*piso*) floor ▪ p. baja ground floor, first floor.

plantar ➤ *tr* to plant, sow; *(colocar)* to put ■ *reflex* to stand firm.

plantear ➤ *tr* to expound; *(planear)* to outline; *(proponer)* to propose.

plantilla ➤ *f* insole.

plástico, a ➤ *adj & m* plastic.

plata ➤ *f* silver; AMER. money.

plataforma ➤ *f* platform.

plátano ➤ *m* banana; *(grande)* plantain.

platea ➤ *f* orchestra seat *or* section.

platillo ➤ *m* saucer ■ p. volador flying saucer.

plato ➤ *m* plate, dish; CUL. course.

playa ➤ *f* beach.

plaza ➤ *f* plaza, square; *(mercado)* marketplace; *(sitio)* place; *(empleo)* position ■ p. de toros bullring.

plazo ➤ *m* *(término)* term, period; *(pago)* installment ■ a corto p. short-term • a largo p. long-term • comprar a plazos to buy on credit.

plegable ➤ *adj* folding.

plegar §35 ➤ *tr* to pleat; *(doblar)* to fold.

pleito ➤ *m* lawsuit; *(disputa)* quarrel.

pleno, a ➤ *adj* full ■ en p. día in broad daylight ➤ *m* joint session.

pliegue ➤ *m* fold; SEW. pleat.

plomero ➤ *m* AMER. plumber.

plomo ➤ *m* lead; ELEC. fuse ■ a p. plumb.

pluma ➤ *f* feather; *(estilográfica)* pen.

población ➤ *f* population; *(lugar)* locality; *(ciudad)* city; *(pueblo)* town.

poblado ➤ *m* *(habitantes)* population; *(ciudad)* city; *(pueblo)* town.

pobre ➤ *adj* poor; *(necesitado)* needy ➤ *mf* poor person, pauper.

pobreza ➤ *f* poverty; *(escasez)* lack.

pocillo ➤ *m* cup.

poco, a ➤ *adj* little ■ p. tiempo short while ■ *pl* few • pocas veces not very often, rarely ➤ *m* little ■ dentro de p. soon • un p. de a little, some ■ *pl* few ➤ *adv* *(con escasez)* little, not much; *(en corta duración)* not long; *(no muy)* not very • falta p. para it will not be long before • hace p. a short time ago • p. a p. little by little • p. después a little after • por p. almost.

poder[1] ➤ *m* power.

poder[2] §36 ➤ *tr* to be able to ➤ *intr* to be able ■ puede que . . . it is possible that . . . • ¿puedes ir? can you go?

poderoso, a ➤ *adj* powerful.

podrido, a ➤ *adj* rotten.

podrir ➤ *tr & reflex* to rot, putrefy.

poema ➤ *m* poem.

poesía ➤ *f* poetry.

poeta ➤ *mf* poet.

polea ➤ *f* pulley.

polémico, a ➤ *adj* polemic(al).

polen ➤ *m* pollen.

policía ➤ *f* police (force) ➤ *m* policeman ➤ *f* policewoman.

polilla ➤ *f* moth.

politécnico, a ➤ *adj* polytechnic.

político, a ➤ *adj* political; *(de parentesco)* -in-law ➤ *mf* politician ➤ *f* politics; *(modo de obrar)* policy.

póliza ➤ *f* *(de seguros)* insurance policy; *(contrato)* contract; *(sello)* stamp.

pollo ➤ *m* chicken; *(cría)* chick.

polo ➤ *m* pole ■ p. sur South Pole • p. norte North Pole.

polución ➤ *f* pollution.

polvo ➤ *m* dust; *(substancia pulverizada)* powder ■ en. p. powdered.

polvoriento, a ➤ *adj* dusty.

pomelo ➤ *m* grapefruit.

pómulo ➤ *m* cheekbone.

ponche ➤ *m* punch.

ponchera ➤ *f* punch bowl.

poner §37 ➤ *tr* to put, place; *(disponer)* to set; *(instalar)* to set up; *(nombrar)* to give; ORNIT. to lay (an egg); THEAT. to put on; *(imponer)* to levy; *(causar)* to cause to be, put ■ p. al día to bring up to date • p. en venta to put up for sale • p. la mesa to set the table • p. por escrito to put in writing ➤ *reflex* *(colocarse)* to put or place oneself; *(vestirse)* to put on; ASTRON. to set; *(dedicarse)* to apply oneself ■ p. a to begin to • p. de acuerdo to reach an agreement • p. de pie to stand up • p. en camino to set out.

poniente ➤ *m* west.

popa ➤ *f* stern.

popular ➤ *adj* popular, well-liked; *(música)* folk.

popularidad ➤ *f* popularity.

póquer ➤ *m* poker.

por ➤ *prep* for, by ■ caminar p. la calle to walk along the street • entrar p. to enter through • enviar p. to send by • escrito p. written by • extenderse p. to extend throughout • hacerlo p. necesidad to do it out of necessity • pasar p. el café to pass by the cafe • p. acá or aquí around here • p. ahí or allí around there • p. ciento per cent • p. cierto indeed • p. completo completely • p. correo by mail • p. desgracia unfortunately • ¡p. Dios! for Heaven's sake! • p. eso therefore • p. la noche at night • p. la tarde in the afternoon • p. lo bajo softly • p. lo menos at least • p. lo tanto therefore • p. medio de through • p. otra parte *or* p. lo demás on the other hand • ¿p. qué? why? • p. si acaso in case • p. sí mismo by oneself • p. supuesto of course • p. todos lados everywhere • p. valor de in the amount of.

porcelana ➤ *f* porcelain.

porcentaje ➤ *m* percentage.

porción ➤ *f* portion.

pormenor ➤ *m* detail, particular.

pornográfico, a ➤ *adj* pornographic.

poro ➤ *m* interstice; BIOL. pore.

porque ➤ *conj* because.

porqué ➤ *m* reason (*de* for), cause.

porquería ➤ *f* filth; (*basura*) garbage.

porra ➤ *f* club.

porrazo ➤ *m* (*golpe*) blow; (*choque*) bump.

portaaviones ➤ *m* aircraft carrier.

portada ➤ *f* title page; (*tapa*) cover.

portaequipajes ➤ *m* AUTO. trunk; (*rejilla*) luggage rack.

portal ➤ *m* entrance hall; (*porche*) porch.

portarse ➤ *reflex* to behave.

portátil ➤ *adj* portable ➤ *m* laptop (computer).

portavoz ➤ *mf* spokesman/woman.

portazo ➤ *m* (*de puerta*) slam ■ dar un p. to slam the door.

portería ➤ *f* concierge's office; SPORT. goal.

portero, a ➤ *mf* concierge; (*de vivienda*)

janitor; SPORT. goalkeeper.

pórtico ➤ *m* portico.

porvenir ➤ *m* future.

posada ➤ *f* inn.

posar ➤ *intr* to pose ➤ *reflex (las aves)* to perch ➤ *tr* to put, lay.

posdata ➤ *f* postscript.

poseer §31 ➤ *tr* to possess.

posesión ➤ *f* possession.

posibilidad ➤ *f* possibility ■ *pl* chances.

posible ➤ *adj* possible ■ hacer (todo) lo p. to do everything possible • lo antes p. as soon as possible.

posición ➤ *f* position.

positivo, a ➤ *adj* positive.

posponer §37 ➤ *tr* (*poner detrás*) to put behind; (*diferir*) to postpone.

postal ➤ *adj* postal ■ giro p. money order ➤ *f* postcard.

poste ➤ *m* post ■ p. indicador signpost.

posterior ➤ *adj* (*ulterior*) subsequent (*a* to), later; (*trasero*) rear, back.

posteriormente ➤ *adv* later (on).

postigo ➤ *m* (*contraventana*) shutter; (*de ciudad*) side gate.

postizo, a ➤ *adj* false; (*de quitapón*) detachable ■ brazo p. artificial arm.

postre ➤ *m* dessert.

póstumo, a ➤ *adj* posthumous.

postura ➤ *f* posture; (*posición*) position.

potable ➤ *adj* potable, drinkable.

potaje ➤ *m* stew.

potencia ➤ *f* power ■ p. mundial world power.

potente ➤ *adj* powerful.

potro ➤ *m* colt; SPORT. horse.

pozo ➤ *m* well; (*hoyo*) pit.

practicar §47 ➤ *tr* to practice; (*hacer*) to perform, carry out.

práctico, a ➤ *adj* practical; (*conveniente*) useful ➤ *m* MARIT. pilot ➤ *f* practice; (*experiencia*) experience.

prado ➤ *m* meadow.

pragmático, a ➤ *adj* pragmatic.

preámbulo ➤ *m* (*prólogo*) preamble; (*rodeo*) digression.

precario, a ➤ *adj* precarious.

precaución ➤ *f* precaution; (*prudencia*) caution ■ por p. as a precaution.

precavido, a ➤ *adj* cautious.

precedente ➤ *adj* preceding ➤ *m* precedent ■ sentar un p. to set a precedent.

precepto ➤ *m* precept.

precio ➤ *m* price, cost.

precioso, a ➤ *adj* (*de valor*) precious, valuable; (*lindo*) lovely.

precipicio ➤ *m* precipice, cliff.

precipitación ➤ *f* precipitation.

precipitar ➤ *tr* (*lanzar*) to hurl; (*apresurar*) to hasten ➤ *reflex* (*lanzarse*) to rush headlong.

precisamente ➤ *adv* precisely.

precisar ➤ *tr* (*explicar*) to explain; (*fijar*) to set; (*necesitar*) to need.

precisión ➤ *f* precision.

preciso, a ➤ *adj* necessary; (*fijo*) precise; (*exacto*) exact; (*claro*) distinct.

precoz ➤ *adj* precocious.

predecir ➤ *tr* to predict.

predicado ➤ *m* GRAM., LOG. predicate.

predicar §47 ➤ *tr* to preach.

predicción ➤ *f* prediction.

predilecto, a ➤ *adj* favorite.

predisponer §37 ➤ *tr* to predispose.

predominar ➤ *intr* to prevail.

preescolar ➤ *adj* preschool.

preferencia ➤ *f* preference.

preferible ➤ *adj* preferable.

preferir §43 ➤ *tr* to prefer.

prefijo ➤ *m* prefix; TELEC. area code.

pregunta ➤ *f* question ■ hacer una p. to ask a question.

preguntar ➤ *tr* to ask ■ p. por (*noticias*) to inquire about; (*persona*) to ask for ➤ *reflex* to wonder.

prehistórico, a ➤ *adj* prehistoric.

prejuicio ➤ *m* prejudice.

preliminar ➤ *adj & m* preliminary.

prematuro, a ➤ *adj* premature.

premeditado, a ➤ *adj* premeditated.

premiar ➤ *tr* (*recompensar*) to reward; (*en certamen*) to award a prize to.

premio ➤ *m* (*recompensa*) reward; (*en certamen*) prize; COM., FIN. premium.

prenatal ➤ *adj* prenatal.

prenda ➤ *f* article of clothing.

prendedor ➤ *m* clasp; JEWEL. pin.

prender ➤ *tr* (*clavar*) to fasten; AMER. (*con fuego*) to light; (*un aparato*) to turn *or* switch on ■ p. fuego a to set fire to ➤ *intr* (*planta*) to take root; (*fuego*)

to catch fire; (*vacuna*) to take (effect).

prensa ➤ *f* press.

preñado, a ➤ *adj* pregnant.

preocupación ➤ *f* preoccupation; (*ansiedad*) worry, anxiety.

preocupar ➤ *tr* to preoccupy; (*inquietar*) to worry ➤ *reflex* to worry (*con, de, por* about); (*cuidarse*) to take care.

preparación ➤ *f* preparation.

preparar ➤ *tr & reflex* to prepare (oneself).

preposición ➤ *f* preposition.

prepotente ➤ *adj* arrogant.

presa ➤ *f* (*en la caza*) prey; (*dique*) dam.

presagiar ➤ *tr* to presage.

presagio ➤ *m* (*señal*) omen; (*adivinación*) premonition.

prescindir ➤ *intr* to do without.

presencia ➤ *f* presence.

presenciar ➤ *tr* to witness.

presentación ➤ *f* presentation; (*exhibición*) exhibition.

presentar ➤ *tr* to present; (*mostrar*) to show; (*introducir*) to introduce ➤ *reflex* (*mostrarse*) to present oneself; (*venir*) to show up; (*dar el nombre*) to introduce oneself.

presente ➤ *adj* present ■ tener p. to keep in mind ➤ *m* GRAM. present.

presentimiento ➤ *m* premonition.

preservar ➤ *tr* to preserve.

preservativo ➤ *m* condom.

presidente, a ➤ *mf* president; (*de reunión*) chairman/woman.

presidio ➤ *m* prison.

presidir ➤ *tr* (*dirigir*) to preside over; (*predominar*) to dominate.

presión ➤ *f* pressure ■ olla a p. pressure cooker • p. arterial blood pressure.

presionar ➤ *tr* (*apretar*) to press; (*hacer presión*) to put pressure on.

preso, a ➤ *mf* prisoner.

préstamo ➤ *m* loan.

prestar ➤ *tr* to lend ■ p. atención to pay attention ➤ *reflex* (*consentir*) to consent; (*ser apto para*) to lend itself (*a, para* to); (*ofrecerse*) to offer.

prestigio ➤ *m* prestige.

presumido, a ➤ *adj* conceited.

presumir ➤ *tr* to presume ➤ *intr* ■ p. de

to think *or* fancy oneself.

presuntuoso, a ➤ *adj & mf* presumptuous *or* conceited (person).

presupuesto ➤ *m* budget estimate.

pretender ➤ *tr (intentar)* to try, attempt; *(a una mujer)* to court.

pretendiente, a ➤ *mf (al trono)* claimant ■ *m* suitor.

pretensión ➤ *f* claim; AMER. pretention; *(vanidad)* pretentiousness.

pretérito, a ➤ *adj & m* past.

pretexto ➤ *m* pretext.

prevenir §52 ➤ *tr (impedir)* to prevent; *(avisar)* to forewarn.

previo, a ➤ *adj* previous, prior.

previsto, a ➤ *adj* foreseen.

primario, a ➤ *adj* primary.

primavera ➤ *f (estación)* spring.

primer ➤ *adj contr of* **primero.**

primero, a ➤ *adj* first; *(fundamental)* basic ■ **de primera** first-class • **en primer lugar** first of all ➤ *mf* first; *(el mejor)* best ➤ *adv* first.

primitivo, a ➤ *adj & mf* primitive.

primo, a ➤ *mf* cousin • **p. hermano** *or* carnal first cousin.

primogénito, a ➤ *adj & mf* first-born.

primoroso, a ➤ *adj* beautiful, exquisite.

princesa ➤ *f* princess.

principal ➤ *adj* principal, main.

príncipe ➤ *m* prince.

principio ➤ *m* beginning; *(fundamento)* principle ■ **a p.** *or* **principios de** at the beginning of • **al p.** at first.

pringar §31 ➤ *tr (ensuciar)* to get grease on; *(empapar)* to dip in fat.

prioridad ➤ *f* priority.

prisa ➤ *f (apuro)* haste; *(velocidad)* speed; *(urgencia)* urgency ■ **a** *or* **de p.** quickly • **andar** *or* **estar de p.** to be in a hurry • **dar** *or* **meter p.** a alguien to rush someone • **darse p.** to hasten, hurry (up) • **tener p.** to be in a hurry *(por, en* to).

prisión ➤ *f* prison.

prisionero, a ➤ *mf* prisoner.

prismáticos ➤ *mpl* binoculars.

privado, a ➤ *adj* private ■ **vida p.** privacy.

privar ➤ *tr* to deprive ➤ *reflex* to abstain *(de* from).

privilegio ➤ *m* privilege.

pro ➤ *mf* profit, benefit ■ **en p. de** pro, in favor of • **el p. y el contra** pro and con.

proa ➤ *f* prow, bow.

probabilidad ➤ *f* probability.

probable ➤ *adj* probable.

probador ➤ *m* fitting room.

probar §11 ➤ *tr (ensayar)* to test; *(ropa)* to try on; *(comida)* to taste ➤ *intr* to try ➤ *reflex* to try on.

probeta ➤ *f* test tube.

problema ➤ *m* problem.

proceder ➤ *intr (originarse)* to originate *(de* in); *(ir con orden)* to proceed; *(portarse)* to behave; *(continuar)* to go on *or* ahead with.

procedimiento ➤ *m* procedure.

procesamiento ➤ *m* COMPUT. processing ■ **p. de texto** word processing.

procesar ➤ *tr* LAW to prosecute; COMPUT. to process.

procesión ➤ *f* procession.

proceso ➤ *m* process; LAW *(causa)* trial.

proclamar ➤ *tr & reflex* to proclaim (oneself).

procurador, a ➤ *mf (apoderado)* proxy; *(abogado)* attorney.

procurar ➤ *tr (intentar)* to endeavor; *(obtener)* to obtain ➤ *reflex* to obtain.

prodigio ➤ *m (persona)* prodigy; *(fenómeno)* wonder.

prodigioso, a ➤ *adj* marvelous.

producción ➤ *f* production ■ **p. en serie** mass production.

producir §14 ➤ *tr* to produce; *(ocasionar)* to cause; FIN. to yield ➤ *reflex* to take place.

productividad ➤ *f* productivity.

productivo, a ➤ *adj* productive; *(lucrativo)* lucrative.

producto ➤ *m* product; COM. *(beneficio)* profit.

productor, a ➤ *adj* productive, producing ➤ *mf* producer.

proeza ➤ *f* feat.

profano, a ➤ *adj* profane.

profesión ➤ *f* profession.

profesional ➤ *adj & mf* professional.

profesor, a ➤ *mf (de escuela)* teacher; *(de universidad)* professor.

profesorado ➤ *m* faculty.

profetizar §02 ➤ *tr* to prophesy.

profundidad ➤ *f* depth ■ **dos metros de p.** two meters deep.

profundo, a ➤ *adj (hondo)* deep; *(intenso)* profound.

progenitor ➤ *m* progenitor ■ *pl* ancestors; *(padres)* parents.

programa ➤ *m* program ■ **p. de estudios** curriculum.

programación ➤ *f* programming.

programador, a ➤ *mf* programmer.

programar ➤ *tr* to plan; COMPUT. to program.

progresar ➤ *intr* to progress.

progresivo, a ➤ *adj* progressive.

progreso ➤ *m* progress.

prohibido, a ➤ *adj* prohibited.

prohibir ➤ *tr* to prohibit, forbid ■ **se prohibe fumar** no smoking.

prole ➤ *f* progeny.

proliferar ➤ *intr* to proliferate.

prólogo ➤ *m* prologue.

prolongado, a ➤ *adj* prolonged.

prolongar §31 ➤ *tr* to prolong; *(alargar)* to lengthen ➤ *reflex* to extend; *(durar más tiempo)* to last longer.

promedio ➤ *m* average ■ **por p.** on average.

promesa ➤ *f* promise.

prometer ➤ *tr* to promise ➤ *intr* to be promising ➤ *reflex* to promise oneself, expect; *(novios)* to become engaged.

prometido, a ➤ *m* fiancé ➤ *f* fiancée.

prominente ➤ *adj* prominent.

promoción ➤ *f* promotion.

promocionar ➤ *tr* to promote.

promover §54 ➤ *tr* to promote; *(fomentar)* to foster; *(provocar)* to cause.

pronombre ➤ *m* pronoun.

pronosticar §47 ➤ *tr* to predict.

pronóstico ➤ *m* prediction ■ **p. del tiempo** weather forecast.

pronto, a ➤ *adj (veloz)* quick; *(diligente)* prompt ➤ *adv (velozmente)* quickly ■ **de p.** suddenly.

pronunciación ➤ *f* pronunciation.

pronunciar ➤ *tr* to pronounce; *(discurso)* to deliver.

propaganda ➤ *f* propaganda; COM. advertising ■ **hacer p.** to advertise.

propagar §31 ➤ *tr & reflex* to propagate; *(difundir)* to spread.

propenso, a ➤ *adj* prone *(a* to).

propiamente ➤ *adv* ■ **p. dicho** strictly speaking.

propicio, a ➤ *adj* propitious.

propiedad ➤ *f* property; *(posesión)* ownership; *(heredad)* estate ■ **p. intelectual** copyright.

propietario, a ➤ *mf* owner, proprietor.

propina ➤ *f* tip, gratuity.

propio, a ➤ *adj* own; selfsame; *(conveniente)* proper, suitable; *(característico)* typical.

proponer §37 ➤ *tr (sugerir)* to propose; *(presentar)* to nominate ➤ *reflex* to intend to do.

proporción ➤ *f* proportion.

proporcional ➤ *adj* proportional.

proporcionar ➤ *tr* to provide.

proposición ➤ *f* proposition; *(propuesta)* proposal.

propósito ➤ *m (intención)* intention; *(objetivo)* purpose ■ **a p.** *(por cierto)* by the way; *(adrede)* deliberately.

propuesta ➤ *f* proposal.

propulsión ➤ *f* propulsion ■ **p. delantera** front wheel drive.

prórroga ➤ *f* extension.

prorrumpir ➤ *intr* to burst *(en* into).

prosa ➤ *f* prose.

proseguir §42 ➤ *tr & intr* to pursue, carry on with.

prospecto ➤ *m* prospectus, brochure.

prosperar ➤ *intr* to prosper.

prosperidad ➤ *f* prosperity.

próspero, a ➤ *adj* prosperous.

prostituta ➤ *f* prostitute.

protagonista ➤ *mf* protagonist.

protección ➤ *f* protection.

protector, a ➤ *adj* protective ➤ *mf* protector; *(patrocinador)* patron.

proteger §20 ➤ *tr* to protect.

proteína ➤ *f* protein.

protesta ➤ *f* protest.

protestante ➤ *adj & mf* Protestant.

protestar ➤ *tr & intr* to protest.

protocolo ➤ *m* protocol.

provecho ➤ *m (beneficio)* benefit; *(ganancia)* profit ■ **¡buen p.!** COLL. enjoy your meal!

proveedor, a ➤ *mf* supplier.
proveer §27 ➤ *tr* to provide (*de* with).
proveniente ➤ *adj* proceeding (*de* from).
provenir §52 ➤ *intr* to come (*en* from).
proverbio ➤ *m* proverb.
providencial ➤ *adj* providential.
provincia ➤ *f* province.
provisión ➤ *fpl* supplies.
provisional ➤ *adj* temporary.
provocar §47 ➤ *tr* (*incitar*) to provoke; (*irritar*) to annoy; (*despertar*) to rouse; (*causar*) to cause.
provocativo, a ➤ *adj* inviting, tempting.
próximamente ➤ *adv* soon, before long.
proximidad ➤ *f* proximity.
próximo, a ➤ *adj* (*cercano*) near; (*siguiente*) next.
proyección ➤ *f* projection; CINEM. screening.
proyectar ➤ *tr* (*planear*) to plan; (*sombra*) to cast; CINEM. to show.
proyectil ➤ *m* projectile, missile.
proyecto ➤ *m* project.
proyector ➤ *m* CINEM. projector.
prudencia ➤ *f* prudence.
prudente ➤ *adj* prudent.
prueba ➤ *f* (*razón*) proof, evidence; (*examen*) test ■ a p. de agua, balas waterproof, bulletproof.
psicoanálisis ➤ *m or f* psychoanalysis.
psicología ➤ *f* psychology.
psicólogo, a ➤ *mf* psychologist.
psicópata ➤ *mf* psychopath.
psicosis ➤ *f* psychosis.
psicoterapia ➤ *f* psychotherapy.
psiquíatra *or* **psiquiatra** ➤ *mf* psychiatrist.
psiquiatría ➤ *f* psychiatry.
púa ➤ *f* BOT. thorn; ZOOL. quill.
pubertad ➤ *f* puberty.
publicación ➤ *f* publication.
publicar §47 ➤ *tr* to publish.
publicidad ➤ *f* publicity; (*anuncio*) advertisement ■ agencia de p. advertising agency.
público, a ➤ *adj* public ➤ *m* public; (*auditorio*) audience.
puchero ➤ *m* CUL. stew.
pudín ➤ *m* pudding.

pudor ➤ *m* (*recato*) modesty, shyness; (*vergüenza*) shame.
pudrir ➤ *tr & reflex* to rot.
pueblo ➤ *m* (*población*) town; (*nación*) people, nation.
puente ➤ *m* bridge ■ p. aéreo airlift.
puerco, a ➤ *adj* filthy ➤ *m* ZOOL. pig, hog ➤ *f* ZOOL. sow.
pueril ➤ *adj* childish.
puerta ➤ *f* door; (*armazón*) gate.
puerto ➤ *m* port, harbor.
puertorriqueño, a ➤ *adj & mf* Puerto Rican.
pues ➤ *conj* since, as ■ ¡p. claro! of course! • ¡p. qué? so what?
puesto, a ➤ *adj* dressed ➤ *m* (*sitio*) place; (*de venta*) stall; (*cargo*) position ■ p. que since, as ➤ *f* ASTRON. setting ■ p. del sol sunset • p. en escena staging.
pugilista ➤ *mf* boxer.
pulcritud ➤ *f* neatness.
pulcro, a ➤ *adj* neat.
pulga ➤ *f* flea.
pulgada ➤ *f* inch.
pulgar ➤ *adj & m* thumb.
pulir ➤ *tr* to polish.
pulmón ➤ *m* lung.
pulpa ➤ *f* pulp.
púlpito ➤ *m* pulpit.
pulpo ➤ *m* octopus.
pulsar ➤ *tr* to push ➤ *intr* to beat; COMPUT. to click.
pulsera ➤ *f* bracelet; (*de reloj*) watch band.
pulso ➤ *m* (*latido*) pulse; (*seguridad*) steady hand.
puma ➤ *m* puma, mountain lion.
pundonor ➤ *m* honor, integrity.
punta ➤ *f* point; (*extremidad*) tip; (*clavo*) small nail ■ sacar p. a to sharpen.
puntapié ➤ *m* kick ■ echar a puntapiés to kick out.
puntería ➤ *f* MIL. aim.
puntiagudo, a ➤ *adj* sharp, pointed.
puntilla ➤ *f* tack, brad; SEW. lace trim.
puntilloso, a ➤ *adj* punctilious.
punto ➤ *m* point; (*señal pequeña*) dot; (*sitio*) spot; (*de oración*) period, full stop; (*puntada*) stitch ■ dos puntos colon • en p. on the dot, sharp • p. de

vista point of view, viewpoint • **p. final** period • **p. y coma** semicolon.
puntuación ➤ *f* punctuation; *(calificación)* grade, mark.
puntual ➤ *adj* prompt.
puñado ➤ *m* handful.
puñal ➤ *m* dagger.
puñalada ➤ *f* stab.
puñetazo ➤ *m* punch ■ *pl* a p. with one's fists.
puño ➤ *m* fist; SEW. cuff.
pupa ➤ *f (en los labios)* cold sore.
pupila ➤ *f* ANAT. pupil.
pupitre ➤ *m* desk.
puré ➤ *m* CUL. purée.
pureza ➤ *f* purity.
purga ➤ *f* laxative.
purificar §47 ➤ *tr* to purify.
puro, a ➤ *adj* pure ➤ *m* cigar.
púrpura ➤ *f* purple.
puta ➤ *f* prostitute, whore.
pútrido, a ➤ *adj* putrid.

Q

que ➤ *rel pron* that, which; who, whom ■ **el** *or* **la q.** he *or* she who, the one that • **las q.** *or* **los q.** those who, the ones that • **lo q.** which, what ➤ *conj* that; *(porque)* because; *(si)* whether ■ **a q.** I bet that • **hay mucho q. hacer** there is a lot to do • **más q.** more than • **yo q. tú** if I were you.
qué ➤ *adj* which, what ➤ *pron* what ➤ *adv* how ■ **¡a mí q.!** so what! • **no hay de q.** you're welcome • **¿para q.?** what for? • **¿por q.?** why? • **¿q. pasa?** what's the matter? • **¿q. tal?** how goes it? • **¡q. va!** nonsense!, come on! • **un no sé q.** a certain something • **¿y q.?** so what?
quebrada ➤ *f* ravine; AMER. stream.
quebradizo, a ➤ *adj* brittle, fragile.
quebrado, a ➤ *adj* broken; COM. bankrupt.
quebrar §33 ➤ *tr* to break ➤ *intr* COM. to go bankrupt ➤ *reflex* to be broken.
quedar ➤ *intr* to remain, stay; *(estar)* to be; *(restar)* to be left; MATH. to leave ■ **q. bien, mal** to come out well, badly; *(ropa)* to look good, bad • **q. en** to agree ➤ *reflex* to stay; *(estar)* to be;

(ponerse) to become ■ **q. con** to keep • **q. sin** to run out of.
quehaceres ➤ *mpl* chores.
queja ➤ *f* moan, groan; *(protesta)* complaint.
quejarse ➤ *reflex* to moan; *(lamentarse)* to whine, complain *(de* about).
quema ➤ *f* burning; *(incendio)* fire.
quemadura ➤ *f* burn.
quemar ➤ *tr* to burn ➤ *intr* to be burning hot ➤ *reflex* to burn oneself.
querella ➤ *f* dispute, quarrel; LAW complaint.
querer[1] ➤ *m* love, affection.
querer[2] §38 ➤ *tr* to want; *(amar)* to love ■ **cuando quiera** at any time • **no q.** to refuse • **sin q.** unintentionally • ➤ *intr* to look as if it is going to.
querido, a ➤ *adj* dear, beloved ➤ *mf* darling, dear.
quesadilla ➤ *f* cheese-filled tortilla.
queso ➤ *m* cheese.
quiebra ➤ *f* COM. bankruptcy.
quien ➤ *pron* who, whom; whoever, he *or* she who.
quién ➤ *pron* who, whom ■ **de q.** *or* **de quiénes** whose.
quienquiera ➤ *pron* whoever, whomever.
quieto, a ➤ *adj* *(inmóvil)* motionless, still; *(sosegado)* quiet.
quietud ➤ *f* calm, tranquillity.
quilla ➤ *f* keel.
quilo ➤ *m* kilo, kilogram.
química ➤ *f* chemistry.
químico, a ➤ *adj* chemical ➤ *mf* chemist.
quimioterapia ➤ *f* chemotherapy.
quince ➤ *adj & m* fifteen.
quinto, a ➤ *adj & m* fifth ➤ *f* country house.
quiosco ➤ *m* kiosk.
quirófano ➤ *m* operating room.
quirúrgico, a ➤ *adj* surgical.
quitaesmalte ➤ *m* nail polish remover.
quitamanchas ➤ *m* stain remover.
quitanieves ➤ *m* snowplow.
quitar ➤ *tr (apartar)* to take away; *(hurtar)* to rob of; *(restar)* to subtract; *(abrogar)* to repeal; *(prohibir)* to forbid ■ **q. la mesa** to clear the table

➤ *reflex* to take off; *(mancha)* to come out ■ **q. de encima** to get rid of.

quizá(s) ➤ *adv* maybe, perhaps.

R

rábano ➤ *m* radish.

rabia ➤ *f* fury, rage; MED. rabies ■ **dar r.** to infuriate.

rabiar ➤ *intr* to be furious.

rabillo ➤ *m* stem.

rabino ➤ *m* rabbi.

rabioso, a ➤ *adj* furious; MED. rabid.

rabo ➤ *m* tail.

racha ➤ *f* gust; *(suerte)* run (of luck).

racial ➤ *adj* racial.

ración ➤ *f* ration; *(porción)* serving.

racional ➤ *adj* rational.

racionar ➤ *tr* to ration.

rada ➤ *f* MARIT. roads; GEOG. bay, inlet.

radar ➤ *m* radar.

radiación ➤ *f* radiation.

radiactividad ➤ *f* radioactivity.

radiactivo, a ➤ *adj* radioactive.

radiador ➤ *m* radiator.

radiante ➤ *adj* radiant.

radical ➤ *adj & mf* radical.

radicar §47 ➤ *intr* to reside.

radio¹ ➤ *m* MATH. radius; *(rayo)* spoke.

radio² ➤ *m or f* radio.

radiocasete ➤ *m* boom box, tape player.

radiografía ➤ *f* radiography; *(imagen)* x-ray.

radioyente ➤ *mf* radio listener.

ráfaga ➤ *f* gust (of wind).

raído, a ➤ *adj* worn, threadbare.

raíz ➤ *f* root; FIG. origin ■ **bienes raíces** real estate • **r. cuadrada** square root.

raja ➤ *f* crack; *(de melón, etc.)* slice.

rajar ➤ *tr* to crack ➤ *reflex* to crack; COLL. *(acobardarse)* to chicken out.

rallador ➤ *m* grater.

rallar ➤ *tr* to grate.

ralo, a ➤ *adj* thin.

rama ➤ *f* branch ■ **en r.** raw.

ramillete ➤ *m* bouquet.

ramo ➤ *m (ramillete)* bouquet; *(subdivisión)* branch ■ **Domingo de Ramos** Palm Sunday.

rampa ➤ *f* ramp.

rana ➤ *f* frog.

rancho ➤ *m* AMER. ranch, farm; *(comida)* mess.

rancio, a ➤ *adj* rancid.

rango ➤ *m* rank; AMER. pomp.

ranura ➤ *f* groove.

rapar ➤ *tr (el pelo)* to crop.

rapaz, a ➤ *mf* youngster ➤ *adj* rapacious.

rape ➤ *m* ■ **al r.** close-cropped.

rapidez ➤ *f* speed.

rápido, a ➤ *adj* fast, quick ➤ *m (tren)* express train; *(en un río)* rapids ➤ *adv* quickly.

raptar ➤ *tr* to abduct, kidnap.

rapto ➤ *m* kidnaping; *(éxtasis)* rapture.

raqueta ➤ *f* racket; *(para nieve)* snowshoe.

raro, a ➤ *adj* rare, uncommon; *(extraño)* odd ■ **rara vez** rarely.

ras ➤ *m* ■ **a r. de** level with.

rascacielos ➤ *m* skyscraper.

rascar §47 ➤ *tr (con la uña)* to scratch ➤ *reflex* to scratch oneself.

rasgar §31 ➤ *tr* to tear, rip.

rasgo ➤ *m (trazo)* stroke; *(carácter)* trait, feature ■ *pl* features.

rasguñar ➤ *tr* to scratch.

rasguño ➤ *m* scratch.

raso, a ➤ *adj (llano)* flat; *(el cielo)* clear ■ **cielo r.** ceiling ➤ *m* satin.

raspar ➤ *tr* to scrape (off).

rastrear ➤ *tr* to trail.

rastrillar ➤ *tr* AGR. to rake.

rastrillo ➤ *m* rake.

rastro ➤ *m (pista)* trail; *(señal)* trace.

rasurar ➤ *tr* to shave.

rata ➤ *f* rat.

ratero, a ➤ *mf* thief, pickpocket.

ratificar §47 ➤ *tr* to ratify.

rato ➤ *m* while ■ **a cada r.** all the time • **al poco r.** shortly after • **de r. en r.** from time to time • **un buen r.** quite some time.

ratón ➤ *m* ZOOL., COMPUT. mouse.

ratonero ➤ *m* mousetrap.

raudo, a ➤ *adj* swift.

raya ➤ *f (lista)* stripe; *(línea)* line; *(en el pelo)* part; *(pliegue)* crease; GRAM., TELEC. dash ■ **a rayas** striped.

rayar ➤ *tr* to draw lines on ➤ *intr (lindar)* to be next to; *(amanecer)* to dawn; (arañar) to scratch.

rayo ➤ *m* ray; (de rueda) spoke; (relámpago) lightning.

rayón ➤ *m* rayon.

raza ➤ *f* race; (de animales) breed.

razón ➤ *f* reason; (cómputo) rate ▪ dar la r. a alguien to side with someone ▪ tener r. to be right.

razonable ➤ *adj* reasonable.

razonar ➤ *intr* to reason ➤ *tr* to give reasons for.

reacción ➤ *f* reaction.

reaccionar ➤ *intr* to react.

reajuste ➤ *m* readjustment.

real¹ ➤ *adj* real.

real² ➤ *adj* royal.

realidad ➤ *f* reality ▪ en r. actually • r. virtual virtual reality.

realizar §02 ➤ *tr* to realize; (ejecutar) to accomplish ➤ *reflex* to come true.

reanimar ➤ *tr* to revive ➤ *reflex* to recover.

reanudar ➤ *tr* to resume ➤ *reflex* to begin again.

rebaja ➤ *f* (acción) reduction; (descuento) discount.

rebajar ➤ *tr* (reducir) to reduce; (bajar) to lower; (humillar) to humiliate ➤ *reflex* to degrade oneself.

rebanada ➤ *f* slice (of bread).

rebaño ➤ *m* herd.

rebasar ➤ *tr* to surpass ➤ *intr* to overflow.

rebelarse ➤ *reflex* to rebel.

rebelde ➤ *adj* rebellious ➤ *mf* rebel.

rebeldía ➤ *f* rebelliousness.

rebelión ➤ *f* rebellion.

rebosar ➤ *intr & reflex* to overflow (de with).

rebotar ➤ *intr* (pelota) to bounce.

rebozo ➤ *m* shawl.

rebuscado, a ➤ *adj* pedantic, affected.

rebuznar ➤ *intr* to bray.

recado ➤ *m* (mensaje) message; (mandado) errand.

recaída ➤ *f* relapse.

recalcar §47 ➤ *tr* (insistir) to stress.

recalentar §33 ➤ *tr* to reheat.

recambio ➤ *m* spare part.

recapacitar ➤ *tr* to reconsider.

recargado, a ➤ *adj* overloaded; FIG.

overdone; ELEC. recharged.

recargar §31 ➤ *tr* to overload; FIG. to overdecorate; ELEC. to recharge.

recatado, a ➤ *adj* modest.

recaudador, a ➤ *mf* tax collector.

recaudar ➤ *tr* to collect.

recelar ➤ *tr* to suspect.

receloso, a ➤ *adj* suspicious.

recepción ➤ *f* reception; (en un hotel) front desk.

recepcionista ➤ *mf* receptionist.

receptor, a ➤ *m* receiver.

receta ➤ *f* MED. prescription; CUL. recipe.

recetar ➤ *tr* to prescribe.

rechazar §02 ➤ *tr* to reject.

rechinar ➤ *intr* (hacer ruido) to grate; (los dientes) to grind.

recibimiento ➤ *m* reception; (vestíbulo) (entrance) hall.

recibir ➤ *tr & intr* to receive ➤ *reflex* ▪ r. de to graduate as.

recibo ➤ *m* receipt ▪ acusar r. de to acknowledge receipt of.

reciclaje ➤ *m* recycling.

reciclar ➤ *tr* to recycle.

recién ➤ *adv* recently ▪ r. nacido newborn.

reciente ➤ *adj* recent; (moderno) modern.

recientemente ➤ *adv* recently.

recinto ➤ *m* place.

recio, a ➤ *adj* (vigoroso) strong; (abultado) bulky; (lluvia) heavy.

recipiente ➤ *m* container.

recíproco, a ➤ *adj* reciprocal.

recital ➤ *m* MUS. recital; LIT. reading.

recitar ➤ *tr* to recite.

reclamación ➤ *f* (petición) claim; (protesta) complaint.

reclamar ➤ *tr* (pedir) to claim; (exigir) to demand ➤ *intr* to protest.

reclinar ➤ *tr* to lean *or* rest on ➤ *reflex* to recline.

recluir §10 ➤ *tr* to seclude.

recluso, a ➤ *adj* (encerrado) secluded; (preso) imprisoned ➤ *mf* prisoner.

recluta ➤ *f* recruitment ➤ *mf* recruit.

recobrar ➤ *tr & reflex* to recover.

recodo ➤ *m* bend.

recoger §20 ➤ *tr* (volver a coger) to pick

up; *(juntar)* to gather; *(coleccionar)* to save; AGR. to harvest.

recomendación ➤ *f* recommendation.

recomendar §33 ➤ *tr* to recommend.

recompensa ➤ *f* reward.

reconciliar ➤ *tr & reflex* to reconcile.

reconocer §09 ➤ *tr* to recognize; *(identificar)* to identify; *(agradecer)* to appreciate; *(examinar)* to examine.

reconocimiento ➤ *m* recognition; *(gratitud)* gratitude; *(examinación)* examination; MED. checkup.

reconstrucción ➤ *f* reconstruction, CONSTR. rebuilding.

reconstruir §10 ➤ *tr* to reconstruct; CONSTR. to rebuild.

recopilación ➤ *f* compilation.

recopilar ➤ *tr* to compile.

récord ➤ *m & adj* record.

recordar §11 ➤ *tr* to remember; *(avisar)* to remind ➤ *intr* to remember ➤ *reflex* ▪ r. que to remind oneself that.

recorrer ➤ *tr* to travel (through).

recorrido ➤ *m* *(viaje)* journey; *(trayecto)* path; *(de cartero)* route.

recortar ➤ *tr* to cut out.

recorte ➤ *m* newspaper clipping.

recostar §11 ➤ *tr* to lean (on) ➤ *reflex* to lie down.

recreo ➤ *m* *(acción)* recreation; *(en escuela)* recess ▪ de r. pleasure.

recriminar ➤ *intr & reflex* to recriminate (each other).

rectángulo ➤ *adj* rectangular ➤ *m* rectangle.

rectificar §47 ➤ *tr* *(enderezar)* to straighten; *(corregir)* to rectify.

recto, a ➤ *adj* *(derecho)* straight; GEOM. right ➤ *adv* straight.

rector, a ➤ *mf* *(de universidad)* president ➤ *m* *(cura)* priest.

recuento ➤ *m* count, recount.

recuerdo ➤ *m* *(memoria)* memory; *(regalo)* souvenir ▪ *pl* regards.

recuperación ➤ *f* recovery.

recuperar ➤ *tr* *(recobrar)* to recover; *(reconquistar)* to win back; *(el tiempo)* to make up for ➤ *reflex* to recover.

recurrir ➤ *intr* to turn *or* appeal (to); *(volver)* to return *or* revert (to).

recurso ➤ *m* recourse ▪ *pl* resources.

red ➤ *f* net; *(de tiendas)* chain; *(conspiración)* network ▪ R. Internet, Net.

redacción ➤ *f* writing; *(oficina)* editorial office; *(personal)* editorial staff.

redactar ➤ *tr* to draft; *(revisar)* to edit.

redactor, a ➤ *mf* writer; *(revisor)* editor ▪ r. jefe editor in chief.

redondel ➤ *m* circle; TAUR. arena.

redondo, a ➤ *adj* round ▪ a la r. around.

reducción ➤ *f* reduction.

reducir §14 ➤ *tr* to reduce; *(sujetar)* to subjugate ➤ *reflex* to be reduced; *(venir a ser)* to boil down (a to).

redundante ➤ *adj* redundant.

reelegir §37 ➤ *tr* to reelect.

reembolsar ➤ *tr* to reimburse.

reembolso ➤ *m* reimbursement ▪ enviar contra r. to send C.O.D.

reemplazar §02 ➤ *tr* to replace.

referencia ➤ *f* reference.

referir §43 ➤ *tr* to refer; *(contar)* to relate, tell ➤ *reflex* to refer (a to).

refinar ➤ *tr* to refine.

refinería ➤ *f* refinery.

reflector, a ➤ *adj* reflecting ➤ *m* spotlight.

reflejar ➤ *tr* to reflect ➤ *reflex* to be reflected.

reflejo ➤ *m* reflection; PHYSIOL. reflex; *(brillo)* gleam.

reflexionar ➤ *intr & tr* to reflect *(en, sobre* on).

reflexivo, a ➤ *adj* reflective; GRAM. reflexive.

reforestación ➤ *f* AMER. reforestation.

reforma ➤ *f* reform; *(modificación)* alteration.

reformar ➤ *tr* to reform; *(mejorar)* to improve; *(restaurar)* to renovate; *(modificar)* to alter ➤ *reflex* to reform.

reforzar §22 ➤ *tr* to reinforce.

refrán ➤ *m* saying.

refrescante ➤ *adj* refreshing.

refrescar §47 ➤ *tr* to refresh ➤ *intr & reflex* to become cool; *(tomar fuerzas)* to refresh (oneself).

refresco ➤ *m* *(alimento)* refreshment; *(bebida)* soft drink.

refrigeración ➤ *f* refrigeration; *(de aire)* air conditioning.

refrigerador ➤ *m* refrigerator.
refrigerar ➤ *tr* to refrigerate.
refuerzo ➤ *m* reinforcement.
refugiar ➤ *tr* to give refuge ➤ *reflex* to take refuge.
refugio ➤ *m* refuge.
refunfuñar ➤ *intr* to grumble.
regadera ➤ *f* watering can.
regalar ➤ *tr* (*dar*) to give (as a present); (*donar*) to give away.
regaliz ➤ *m* licorice.
regalo ➤ *m* present, gift.
regañadientes ∎ a r. COLL. grudgingly.
regañar ➤ *intr* to quarrel, argue ➤ *tr* COLL. to scold.
regar §35 ➤ *tr* to water; FIG. to strew.
regata ➤ *f* regatta.
regatear ➤ *tr & intr* to bargain (for).
regateo ➤ *m* haggling.
regazo ➤ *m* lap.
regeneración ➤ *f* regeneration.
régimen ➤ *m* regime; MED. diet.
regio, a ➤ *adj* royal; FIG. magnificent.
región ➤ *f* region.
regional ➤ *adj* regional.
registrar ➤ *tr* (*inspeccionar*) to examine; (*en un registro*) to register; (*rebuscar*) to search ➤ *reflex* to register.
registro ➤ *m* register; (*búsqueda*) search; (*oficina*) registry.
regla ➤ *f* (*para trazar*) ruler; (*norma*) rule; (*modelo*) model; (*menstruación*) period ∎ poner algo en r. to put or set something straight.
reglamentario, a ➤ *adj* prescribed.
reglamento ➤ *m* (*reglas*) rules.
regocijar ➤ *tr* to delight ➤ *reflex* to be delighted.
regocijo ➤ *m* joy.
regresar ➤ *tr, intr & reflex* to return.
regresión ➤ *f* regression.
regreso ➤ *m* return ∎ estar de r. to be back.
regular¹ ➤ *adj* regular; (*aceptable*) fairly good; (*mediano*) average ➤ *adv* so-so.
regular² ➤ *tr* to regulate, control.
regularidad ➤ *f* regularity.
rehabilitación ➤ *f* rehabilitation.
rehabilitar ➤ *tr* to rehabilitate.
rehacer §24 ➤ *tr* to redo, remake.

rehén ➤ *mf* hostage.
rehogar §31 ➤ *tr* CUL. to brown.
rehuir §10 ➤ *tr* to avoid ➤ *reflex* to flee or shrink from.
rehusar ➤ *tr* to refuse.
reimprimir §55 ➤ *tr* to reprint.
reina ➤ *f* queen.
reinar ➤ *tr* to reign.
reincidencia ➤ *f* relapse; CRIMIN. recidivism.
reincidir ➤ *intr* to relapse.
reiniciar ➤ *tr* COMPUT. to reboot.
reino ➤ *m* kingdom.
reír §39 ➤ *intr & reflex* to laugh (at).
reiterar ➤ *tr* to reiterate.
reja ➤ *f* (*de ventana*) grating.
rejilla ➤ *f* grille; (*de un horno*) fire grate; RAIL. luggage rack.
relación ➤ *f* relation; (*conexión*) connection; (*relato*) account, report ∎ con or en r. a in relation to.
relacionado, a ➤ *adj* related (con to).
relacionar ➤ *tr* to relate ➤ *reflex* to be related; (*amigos*) to make friends.
relajación ➤ *f* relaxation.
relajar ➤ *tr & reflex* to relax.
relámpago ➤ *m* lightning; FIG. flash.
relatar ➤ *tr* to narrate.
relato ➤ *m* narration; (*cuento*) story.
relegar §31 ➤ *tr* to relegate.
relevar ➤ *tr* to relieve (de from).
relevo ➤ *m* relief; SPORT. relay.
religión ➤ *f* religion.
religioso, a ➤ *adj* religious ➤ *m* monk ➤ *f* nun.
relinchar ➤ *intr* to neigh.
reliquia ➤ *f* relic.
rellano ➤ *m* landing.
rellenar ➤ *tr* to refill; (*completamente*) to fill up; CUL. to stuff.
relleno, a ➤ *adj* stuffed ➤ *m* stuffing.
reloj ➤ *m* clock; (*de pulsera*) watch.
relojería ➤ *f* jewelry store.
reluciente ➤ *adj* shining.
relucir §28 ➤ *intr* to shine.
remache ➤ *m* rivet.
remangar §31 ➤ *tr* to roll or tuck up.
remar ➤ *intr* to row.
rematar ➤ *tr* to finish (off).
remate ➤ *m* conclusion; (*toque final*) finishing touch; (*subasta*) auction.

remediar ► *tr* to remedy.

remedio ► *m* remedy ∎ **como último r.** as a last resort • **no haber (más) r.** to be unavoidable • **no tener r.** to be hopeless.

remendar §33 ► *tr* to mend.

remesa ► *f* consignment.

remiendo ► *m* mending; SEW. patch.

remilgado, a ► *adj* affected.

remitente ► *mf* sender.

remitir ► *tr* to send; *(dinero)* to remit.

remo ► *m* oar; *(de canoa)* paddle.

remolcador ► *m* AUTO. tow truck; MARIT. tugboat.

remolcar §47 ► *tr* to tow.

remolino ► *m* *(de agua)* whirlpool; *(de aire)* whirlwind.

remolque ► *m* *(acción)* towing; *(vehículo)* tow truck.

remordimiento ► *m* remorse.

remoto, a ► *adj* remote.

remover §54 ► *tr* to move; *(quitar)* to remove; *(mezclar)* to stir ► *reflex* to shake.

remuneración ► *f* remuneration.

remunerar ► *tr* to remunerate.

renacimiento ► *m* revival ∎ **R. Renaissance.**

renacuajo ► *m* tadpole.

rencilla ► *f* quarrel.

rencor ► *m* rancor.

rencoroso, a ► *adj* resentful.

rendido, a ► *adj* exhausted.

rendija ► *f* crack.

rendir §32 ► *tr* to yield; *(dar fruto)* to bear; *(cansar)* to tire out ► *intr* to yield ► *reflex* to surrender, give up.

renglón ► *m* line (of text).

renombre ► *m* renown.

renovación ► *f* *(extensión)* renewal; *(restauración)* renovation.

renovar §11 ► *tr* *(extender)* to renew; *(restaurar)* to renovate.

renta ► *f* *(ingresos)* income; *(interés)* interest; *(alquiler)* rent.

rentable ► *adj* profitable.

renunciar ► *tr* to renounce; *(a un puesto)* to resign; *(no aceptar)* to reject.

reñido, a ► *adj* *(enemistado)* at odds; *(difícil)* hard-fought.

reñir ► *intr* to quarrel ► *tr* *(regañar)* to scold.

reo, a ► *mf* LAW defendant.

reparación ► *f* repair.

reparar ► *tr* to repair; *(remediar)* to redress.

reparo ► *m* objection, criticism; *(duda)* misgiving.

repartidor, a ► *mf* distributor.

repartir ► *tr* *(dividir)* to divide; *(distribuir)* to distribute.

reparto ► *m* *(distribución)* distribution; *(entrega)* delivery.

repasar ► *tr* to review.

repaso ► *m* review.

repelente ► *adj* repellent.

repeler ► *tr* to repel; *(rechazar)* to reject.

repente ► *m* start ∎ **de r.** suddenly.

repentino, a ► *adj* sudden.

repercutir ► *intr* to reverberate ∎ **r. en** to have repercussions on.

repertorio ► *m* repertory, repertoire.

repetición ► *f* repetition.

repetir §32 ► *tr & intr* to repeat.

repicar §47 ► *intr* to ring out, peal.

repisa ► *f* shelf.

replegar §35 ► *tr* to fold over ► *reflex* MIL. to retreat.

repleto, a ► *adj* full.

réplica ► *f* retort; *(copia)* replica.

replicar §47 ► *intr* to retort, reply.

repollo ► *m* cabbage.

reponer §37 ► *tr* to replace; THEAT. to revive ► *reflex* to recover.

reportaje ► *m* *(artículo)* report; *(de noticias)* news coverage.

reportero, a ► *mf* reporter.

reposar ► *intr* to rest.

reposo ► *m* repose.

repostería ► *f* pastry shop, bakery.

reprender ► *tr* to reprimand.

represa ► *f* dam.

represalia ► *f* reprisal.

representación ► *f* representation; THEAT. performance.

representante ► *mf* representative.

representar ► *tr* to represent; *(aparentar)* to appear to be; THEAT. to perform ► *intr* to picture.

represión ► *f* repression.

reprimenda ➤ *f* reprimand.
reprimir ➤ *tr & reflex* to repress (oneself).
reprochar ➤ *tr* to reproach.
reproducción ➤ *f* reproduction.
reproducir §14 ➤ *tr & reflex* to reproduce.
reptil ➤ *m* reptile.
república ➤ *f* republic.
repuesto ➤ *m* spare (part) ■ **de r.** spare.
repugnante ➤ *adj* repugnant.
repugnar ➤ *intr* to detest.
repulsivo, a ➤ *adj* repulsive.
reputación ➤ *f* reputation.
requesón ➤ *m* cottage cheese.
requisar ➤ *tr* to requisition.
requisito ➤ *m* requirement.
res ➤ *f* animal ■ **r. vacuna** cow, bull.
resaca ➤ *f* MARIT. undertow; FIG. hangover.
resaltar ➤ *intr* to jut out; FIG. to stand out ■ **hacer r.** to stress, emphasize.
resbaladizo, a ➤ *adj* slippery.
resbalar ➤ *intr* to slip; AUTO. to skid.
resbalón ➤ *m* slip.
rescatar ➤ *tr* to recover; *(cautivos)* to ransom; *(salvar)* to rescue.
rescate ➤ *m* rescue; *(dinero)* ransom.
rescoldo ➤ *m* embers.
resentimiento ➤ *m* resentment.
reserva ➤ *f* reserve; *(excepción, territorio)* reservation.
reservación ➤ *f* reservation.
reservado, a ➤ *adj* reserved.
reservar ➤ *tr* to reserve ➤ *reflex* to save one's strength *or* oneself.
resfriado ➤ *m* cold.
resfriar §18 ➤ *tr* to cool ➤ *reflex* to catch a cold.
residencia ➤ *f* residence.
residencial ➤ *adj* residential.
residir ➤ *intr* to reside.
resignar ➤ *tr & reflex* to resign (oneself).
resina ➤ *f* resin.
resistencia ➤ *f* resistance.
resistir ➤ *intr* to resist; *(durar)* to endure ➤ *tr* to resist; *(aguantar)* to bear ➤ *reflex* to resist; *(luchar)* to fight; *(negarse)* to refuse (*a* to).
resolución ➤ *f* resolution.

resolver §54 ➤ *tr* to solve ➤ *reflex* to resolve itself.
resonar §11 ➤ *intr* to resound.
resoplar ➤ *intr* to puff.
resorte ➤ *m* MECH. spring; FIG. resort.
respaldo ➤ *m* back, backing.
respecto ➤ *m* respect ■ **al r.** about the matter • **r. a** *or* **de** with respect to.
respetar ➤ *tr* to respect.
respeto ➤ *m* respect.
respetuoso, a ➤ *adj* respectful.
respiración ➤ *f* respiration, breathing.
respirar ➤ *intr* to breathe.
resplandecer §09 ➤ *intr* to shine.
resplandor ➤ *m* brightness; *(brillo)* shine; *(esplendor)* splendor.
responder ➤ *tr* to answer ➤ *intr (contestar)* to answer; *(replicar)* to answer back; *(reaccionar)* to respond.
responsabilidad ➤ *f* responsibility.
responsable ➤ *adj* responsible.
respuesta ➤ *f* answer.
resta ➤ *f* subtraction.
restablecer §09 ➤ *tr* to reestablish ➤ *reflex* to recover.
restante ➤ *adj* remaining.
restar ➤ *tr* MATH. to subtract; *(quitar)* to take away.
restaurante ➤ *m* restaurant.
restaurar ➤ *tr* to restore.
resto ➤ *m* remainder ■ *pl* leftovers.
restricción ➤ *f* restriction.
restringir §19 ➤ *tr* to restrict ➤ *reflex* to cut down on.
resucitar ➤ *tr* to resuscitate; *(memoria)* to revive ➤ *intr* to be resuscitated.
resuelto, a ➤ *adj* determined.
resultado ➤ *m* result, outcome.
resultar ➤ *intr* to turn out *(que* that).
resumen ➤ *m* summary ■ **en r.** in short.
resumir ➤ *tr* to summarize.
retar ➤ *tr* to challenge.
retazo ➤ *m (de tela)* remnant.
retener §46 ➤ *tr* to retain; *(deducir)* to withhold.
retina ➤ *f* retina.
retirada ➤ *f* retreat.
retirado, a ➤ *adj* secluded; *(jubilado)* retired ➤ *mf* retired person.
retirar ➤ *tr* to remove; *(de circulación)* to withdraw; *(retractar)* to retract;

(dinero) to withdraw ➤ *reflex* to withdraw; *(jubilarse)* to retire.

retiro ➤ *m* retreat.

reto ➤ *m* challenge.

retoque ➤ *m* PHOTOG. retouching. SEW. alteration.

retorcer §48 ➤ *tr* to twist ➤ *reflex* to twist; *(de dolor)* to writhe.

retorno ➤ *m* return.

retraído, a ➤ *adj* aloof, withdrawn.

retrasado, a ➤ *adj* *(tardío)* late; *(persona)* retarded; *(país)* backward.

retrasar ➤ *tr* *(demorar)* to delay; *(aplazar)* to postpone; *(un reloj)* to set back ➤ *reflex* to be late *or* delayed.

retraso ➤ *m* delay ■ con r. late.

retratar ➤ *tr* to paint a portrait of; *(describir)* to depict.

retrato ➤ *m* portrait; AMER. photograph.

retrete ➤ *m* toilet.

retribución ➤ *f* retribution.

retroactivo, a ➤ *adj* retroactive.

retroceder ➤ *intr* to step back.

retrospectivo, a ➤ *adj & f* retrospective.

retrovisor ➤ *m* rearview mirror.

reumatismo ➤ *m* rheumatism.

reunión ➤ *f* meeting.

reunir ➤ *tr* to gather; *(requisitos)* to fulfill ➤ *reflex* *(juntarse)* to unite; *(en una reunión)* to meet.

revelación ➤ *f* revelation.

revelar ➤ *tr* to reveal; PHOTOG. to develop.

reventar §33 ➤ *intr* *(globo)* to burst; *(neumático)* to blow ➤ *reflex* to burst; *(cansarse)* to exhaust oneself.

reventón ➤ *m* burst; AUTO. flat tire.

reverencia ➤ *f* reverence; *(saludo)* bow.

reverso, a ➤ *adj & m* reverse.

revés ➤ *m* *(envés)* back; *(desgracia)* setback ■ al r. backwards; *(prenda)* inside out ■ al r. de contrary to.

revisar ➤ *tr* to check.

revisión ➤ *f* revision.

revisor, a ➤ *adj* revising, checking ➤ *mf* inspector ■ r. de cuentas auditor.

revista ➤ *f* magazine.

revivir ➤ *intr* to revive.

revolcarse ➤ *reflex* *(en el suelo)* to roll; *(en el fango)* to wallow.

revoltijo ➤ *m* jumble.

revoltoso, a ➤ *adj* troublemaking ➤ *mf* troublemaker; *(rebelde)* rebel.

revolución ➤ *f* revolution.

revolver §54 ➤ *tr* *(mezclar)* to mix; *(desordenar)* to mix up ➤ *reflex* *(dar vueltas)* to turn around.

revólver ➤ *m* revolver.

revuelo ➤ *m* commotion.

revuelta ➤ *f* revolt; *(riña)* quarrel.

revuelto, a ➤ *adj* jumbled; *(inquieto)* turbulent; *(travieso)* mischievous; *(enrevesado)* complicated ■ huevos revueltos scrambled eggs.

rey ➤ *m* king ■ día de Reyes Epiphany.

rezagar §31 ➤ *tr* to leave behind ➤ *reflex* to lag behind.

rezar §02 ➤ *tr* to say ➤ *intr* to pray.

ribera ➤ *f* shore; *(de río)* bank, shore.

rico, a ➤ *adj* rich, wealthy; *(sabroso)* delicious ➤ *mf* rich person.

ridículo, a ➤ *adj* ridiculous ➤ *m* ridiculous situation ■ hacer el r. to make a fool of oneself.

riego ➤ *m* irrigation.

rienda ➤ *f* rein.

riesgo ➤ *m* risk.

rifa ➤ *f* raffle.

rifle ➤ *m* rifle.

rigidez ➤ *f* rigidity.

rígido, a ➤ *adj* stiff.

rigor ➤ *m* rigor ■ de r. de rigueur.

riguroso, a ➤ *adj* rigorous.

rimar ➤ *intr & tr* to rhyme.

rímel ➤ *m* mascara.

rincón ➤ *m* corner.

rinoceronte ➤ *m* rhinoceros.

riña ➤ *f* quarrel.

riñón ➤ *m* kidney.

río ➤ *m* river ■ r. abajo downstream.

riqueza ➤ *f* wealth.

risa ➤ *f* laugh, laughter ■ ¡qué r.! how funny!

ristra ➤ *f* string.

risueño, a ➤ *adj* smiling.

ritmo ➤ *m* rhythm.

rizado ➤ *m* curling.

rizar §02 ➤ *tr* to curl.

rizo ➤ *m* ringlet.

robar ➤ *tr* to rob; *(saquear)* to burgle.

roble ➤ *m* oak.

robo ➤ *m* robbery.

robusto, a ➤ *adj* robust.

roca ➤ *f* rock.

rociar §18 ➤ *tr* to sprinkle.

rocío ➤ *m* dew; *(llovizna)* sprinkle.

rocoso, a ➤ *adj* rocky.

rodaja ➤ *f* disc; *(de fruta)* slice.

rodaje ➤ *m* CINEM. filming.

rodar §11 ➤ *intr & tr* to roll; CINEM. to shoot, film.

rodear ➤ *tr* to surround ➤ *reflex* ■ r. de to surround oneself with.

rodeo ➤ *m* *(camino indirecto)* round-about way; *(fiesta)* rodeo.

rodilla ➤ *f* knee ■ de rodillas on one's knees.

rodillera ➤ *f* knee pad.

roer ➤ *tr* to gnaw; *(gastar)* to erode.

rogar §08 ➤ *tr* to beg ➤ *intr* to pray.

rojo, a ➤ *adj* red ■ ponerse r. to blush ➤ *m* red.

rollo ➤ *m* roll; *(de cuerda)* coil.

romance ➤ *m* romance.

romano, a ➤ *adj* Roman.

romántico, a ➤ *adj & mf* romantic.

rombo ➤ *m* rhombus.

romero ➤ *m* rosemary.

rompecabezas ➤ *m* jigsaw puzzle; FIG. riddle.

rompeolas ➤ *m* breakwater.

romper §55 ➤ *tr* to break; *(en pedazos)* to tear or rip (up); *(cancelar)* to break off ➤ *intr* to break ■ r. con to break up with • r. en to burst into (tears, etc.) • r. por to break through ➤ *reflex* to break.

ron ➤ *m* rum.

roncar §47 ➤ *intr* to snore.

roncha ➤ *f* welt; *(cardenal)* bruise.

ronco, a ➤ *adj* hoarse; *(áspero)* harsh.

rondar ➤ *intr* *(vigilar)* to patrol; *(vagar)* to prowl around.

ronquera ➤ *f* hoarseness.

ronquido ➤ *m* snore.

ronronear ➤ *intr* to purr.

roñoso, a ➤ *adj* *(sucio)* filthy; *(tacaño)* stingy.

ropa ➤ *f* clothes, clothing ■ r. interior underwear.

ropero ➤ *m* closet.

rosa ➤ *f* rose; *(color)* pink ➤ *adj* pink.

rosado, a ➤ *adj* pink; *(vino)* rosé.

rosal ➤ *m* rosebush.

rosario ➤ *m* rosary.

rosbif ➤ *m* roast beef.

rostro ➤ *m* face.

roto, a ➤ *adj* broken; *(quebrado)* smashed; *(papel, tela)* torn, ripped.

rótula ➤ *f* kneecap; MECH. rounded joint.

rotulador, a ➤ *adj* labeling ➤ *m* felt-tipped pen.

rotular ➤ *tr* to label.

rótulo ➤ *m* label.

rotundo, a ➤ *adj* *(sonoro)* resounding; *(definitivo)* categorical.

rotura ➤ *f* break; *(en papel, tela)* tear.

rozar §02 ➤ *tr* to brush against ➤ *intr* to touch lightly.

rubí ➤ *m* ruby.

rubio, a ➤ *adj & mf* blond(e).

ruborizarse §02 ➤ *reflex* to blush.

rudo, a ➤ *adj* rough.

rueda ➤ *f* wheel.

ruedo ➤ *m* bullring.

ruego ➤ *m* request.

rugido ➤ *m* roar.

rugir §19 ➤ *intr* to roar.

ruido ➤ *m* noise; *(alboroto)* din.

ruidoso, a ➤ *adj* noisy, loud; FIG. smashing.

ruin ➤ *adj* mean, despicable; *(avaro)* stingy; *(animales)* vicious.

ruina ➤ *f* ruin; FIG. fall, downfall.

ruiseñor ➤ *m* nightingale.

ruleta ➤ *f* roulette.

rulo ➤ *m* roller.

rumbo ➤ *m* direction; AER., MARIT. course ■ con r. a bound for.

rumor ➤ *m* murmur; *(chismes)* rumor.

rumorearse ➤ *reflex* to be rumored.

ruptura ➤ *f* *(acción)* breaking; MED. fracture; *(de relaciones)* breakup.

rural ➤ *adj* rural.

rústico, a ➤ *adj* rustic ➤ *mf* hick.

ruta ➤ *f* route.

rutina ➤ *f* routine.

S

sábado ➤ *m* Saturday; RELIG. Sabbath.

sabana ➤ *f* AMER. savanna(h).

sábana ➤ *f* bed sheet.

saber¹ ➤ *m* knowledge.

saber² §40 ➤ *tr* to know; *(cocinar, etc.)* to know how; *(noticia)* to learn ▪ hacer a. to inform • ¿qué sé yo? how should I know? • que yo sepa as far as I know • s. de memoria to know by heart ➤ *intr* to know ▪ s.a to taste like.

sabiduría ➤ *f (prudencia)* wisdom; *(conocimiento)* knowledge.

sabio, a ➤ *adj* wise ➤ *mf* wise person; *(instruido)* learned person, scholar.

sable ➤ *m* saber.

sabor ➤ *m* taste, flavor ▪ con s. a limón lemon-flavored.

saborear ➤ *tr* to taste; FIG. to relish.

sabroso, a ➤ *adj* delicious, tasty; *(agradable)* delightful.

sacacorchos ➤ *m* corkscrew.

sacapuntas ➤ *m* pencil sharpener.

sacar §47 ➤ *tr* to take out; *(quitar)* to remove; *(arrancar)* to pull out; *(de un apuro)* to bail out; *(información)* to get out; *(ganar)* to win; *(fotografiar)* to take; SPORT. to serve; CHEM. to extract.

sacarina ➤ *f* saccharin.

sacerdote ➤ *m* priest.

saciar ➤ *tr* to satiate.

saco ➤ *m (bolsa)* bag; AMER. *(chaqueta)* jacket ▪ s. de dormir sleeping bag.

sacramento ➤ *m* sacrament.

sacrificar §47 ➤ *tr* to sacrifice; *(ganado)* to slaughter ➤ *reflex* to sacrifice oneself.

sacrificio ➤ *m* sacrifice.

sacrosanto, a ➤ *adj* sacrosanct.

sacudida ➤ *f (acción)* shake; *(sismo)* tremor; *(de explosión)* blast; *(emoción)* jolt ▪ s. eléctrica electric shock.

sacudir ➤ *tr (agitar)* to shake; *(quitar el polvo)* to dust; *(un ala)* to flap; *(alterar)* to jolt ➤ *reflex (la ropa)* to shake or brush off.

sagaz ➤ *adj* sagacious, astute.

sagrado, a ➤ *adj* sacred.

sal ➤ *f* salt.

sala ➤ *f* living room; MED. hospital ward ▪ s. de charla chat room • s. de clase classroom • s. de espectáculos theater, hall • s. de espera waiting room.

salado, a ➤ *adj* salt, salty; *(plato)* salted.

salar ➤ *tr* to salt; *(curar)* to cure.

salario ➤ *m* wage.

salchicha ➤ *f* sausage.

saldar ➤ *tr* COM. to pay off.

saldo ➤ *m (cifra)* balance; *(mercancías)* remnants.

salero ➤ *m* saltshaker; *(gracia)* wit.

salida ➤ *f (acción)* departure; *(abertura)* exit; *(escapatoria)* way out; *(ocurrencia)* witty remark ▪ dar s. a to vent • s. del sol sunrise.

salir §41 ➤ *intr* to leave; *(a la calle)* to go out; *(aparecer)* to come out; *(el sol)* to rise; *(libro)* to come out; *(oportunidad)* to come or turn up; *(cálculo)* to work out; COMPUT. to log off or out ▪ s. bien, mal to turn out well, badly • s. con to go out with, date ➤ *reflex (derramarse)* to leak; *(rebosar)* to boil over ▪ s. con la suya to get one's own way • s. del tema to digress.

saliva ➤ *f* saliva, spit.

salmón ➤ *m* salmon.

salobre ➤ *adj* briny.

salón ➤ *m (sala grande)* hall ▪ s. de conferencias lecture hall ▪ s. de belleza beauty parlor ▪ s. de té tearoom.

salpicar §47 ➤ *tr* to splash, splatter; *(rociar)* to sprinkle; *(motear)* to fleck.

salsa ➤ *f* sauce, gravy.

saltamontes ➤ *m* grasshopper.

saltar ➤ *intr (brincar)* to jump; *(levantarse)* to jump up; *(dar saltitos)* to hop; *(lanzarse)* to jump (a into); *(salir con ímpetu)* to bound ▪ s. sobre to pounce on ➤ *tr (atravesar)* to jump over; *(omitir)* to skip over.

salto ➤ *m* jump, leap ▪ a saltos by leaps and bounds.

salud ➤ *f* health, well-being ▪ estar bien, mal de s. to be in good, bad health ➤ *interj* COLL. *(al estornudar)* (God) bless you!; *(brindis)* cheers!

saludable ➤ *adj* healthy.

saludar ➤ *tr* to greet; *(honrar)* to salute ▪ Le saluda atentamente Yours truly.

saludo ➤ *m* greeting ▪ pl regards.

salvación ➤ *f* salvation.

salvadoreño, a ➤ *adj & mf* Salvadoran.

salvaguardar ➤ *tr* to safeguard.

salvaje ➤ *adj (planta, animal)* wild;

(feroz) savage; *(primitivo)* uncivilized ➤ *mf* savage.

salvamento ➤ *m* rescue.

salvapantallas ➤ *m* screen saver.

salvar ➤ *tr (librar)* to save; *(resolver)* to overcome; *(recorrer)* to cover ➤ *reflex* to escape.

salvavidas ➤ *m* life preserver ➤ *mf* lifeguard.

salvia ➤ *f* BOT. sage.

salvo, a ➤ *adj* safe ■ a s. safe (and sound) • a s. de safe from ➤ *adv* except (for), save ■ s. que unless.

san ➤ *adj contr of* **santo.**

sanar ➤ *tr* to heal ➤ *intr* to recover *(from illness)*; *(herida)* to heal.

sanción ➤ *f* sanction.

sancionar ➤ *tr* to sanction.

sandalia ➤ *f* sandal.

sándalo ➤ *m* sandalwood.

sandía ➤ *f* watermelon.

sangrar ➤ *tr & intr* to bleed.

sangre ➤ *f* blood ■ a s. fría in cold blood • pura s. thoroughbred.

sangría ➤ *f (bebida)* sangria.

sangriento, a ➤ *adj* bloody; *(manchado)* blood-stained; *(cruel)* cruel.

sanguinario, a ➤ *adj* bloodthirsty.

sanguíneo, a ➤ *adj* blood ■ grupo s. blood group.

sanitario, a ➤ *adj* sanitary.

sano, a ➤ *adj* healthy ■ s. y salvo safe and sound.

santidad ➤ *f* sanctity, holiness.

santo, a ➤ *adj* holy ➤ *mf* saint ➤ *m (imagen)* image of a saint; *(festividad)* saint's day.

santuario ➤ *m* sanctuary; *(intimidad)* privacy.

sapo ➤ *m* toad.

saque ➤ *m (tenis)* serve; *(fútbol)* kick ■ s. de banda throw-in.

saquear ➤ *tr* to plunder.

sarampión ➤ *m* measles.

sarcasmo ➤ *m* sarcasm.

sardina ➤ *f* sardine.

sargento ➤ *m* sergeant.

sarpullido ➤ *m* rash.

sarro ➤ *m* crust; DENT. tartar.

sartén ➤ *f* frying pan.

sastre ➤ *m* tailor.

satélite ➤ *adj & m* satellite.

satén *or* **satín** ➤ *m* satin.

sátira ➤ *f* satire.

satisfacción ➤ *f* satisfaction.

satisfacer §24 ➤ *tr* to satisfy; *(deuda)* to pay.

satisfecho, a ➤ *adj* satisfied.

sauce ➤ *m* willow ■ s. llorón weeping willow.

sazón ➤ *f* CUL. seasoning ■ en s. *(fruta)* in season; FIG. at the right moment.

sazonar ➤ *tr* to season.

se ➤ *reflex pron* himself, herself, etc. ■ se están mirando en el espejo they're looking at themselves in the mirror • se aman they love each other ➤ *indef pron* one, they ■ se dice que they say that ➤ *aux pron* a se venden libros aquí books are sold here ➤ *pers pron* ■ se lo dijo a él she said it to him • él se lo robó a ellos he stole it from them.

secador ➤ *m* hair dryer.

secadora ➤ *f* clothes dryer.

secar §47 ➤ *tr* to dry ➤ *reflex* to dry (out); *(persona)* to dry oneself, dry off; *(río)* to dry up, run dry; BOT. to wither.

sección ➤ *f* section.

seco, a ➤ *adj* dry; *(desecado)* dried; *(corto y brusco)* sharp ■ limpiar en s. to dry-clean.

secretaria ➤ *f* secretary.

secretario ➤ *m* secretary.

secreto, a ➤ *adj & m* secret ■ en s. secretly • guardar un s. to keep a secret.

secta ➤ *f* sect.

sector ➤ *m* sector.

secuencia ➤ *f* sequence.

secuestrar ➤ *tr (personas)* to kidnap; *(vehículos)* to hijack.

secuestro ➤ *m (de personas)* kidnapping; *(de vehículos)* hijacking.

secundario, a ➤ *adj & m* secondary ■ escuela s. high school.

sed ➤ *f* thirst.

seda ➤ *f* silk.

sedal ➤ *m* fishing line.

sedativo, a ➤ *adj & m* sedative.

sede ➤ *f (del gobierno)* seat; *(de organi-*

zación) headquarters.
sedentario, a ➤ *adj* sedentary.
sedimento ➤ *m* sediment.
sedoso, a ➤ *adj* silky.
seducir §14 ➤ *tr* to seduce.
segar §35 ➤ *tr* to harvest.
seglar ➤ *adj* secular ➤ *mf* layman/ woman.
segmento ➤ *m* segment.
seguibola ➤ *f* COMPUT. trackball.
seguidamente ➤ *adv* next.
seguido, a ➤ *adj* consecutive ➤ *adv* often ■ en seguida immediately, right away.
seguidor, a ➤ *mf* follower.
seguir §42 ➤ *tr* to follow; *(venir después)* to come after; *(continuar)* to keep or go on ➤ *intr* to continue.
según ➤ *prep* according to ➤ *adv* depending on.
segundero ➤ *m* second hand.
segundo, a ➤ *adj* second ■ de s. clase second-class • s. enseñanza secondary education ➤ *m* second.
seguramente ➤ *adv (ciertamente)* certainly; *(probablemente)* probably.
seguridad ➤ *f* security, safety ■ con toda s. with absolute certainty • de s. safety.
seguro, a ➤ *adj* safe; *(cierto)* certain, sure; *(confiable)* trustworthy; *(firme)* stable ➤ *m* insurance; *(dispositivo)* safety catch ■ s. de vida life insurance ➤ *adv* certainly, for sure.
seis ➤ *adj & m* six ■ las s. six o'clock.
selección ➤ *f* selection.
seleccionar ➤ *tr* to select.
selecto, a ➤ *adj* select.
sello ➤ *m* stamp; *(de documento)* seal.
selva ➤ *f* woods; *(jungla)* jungle.
semáforo ➤ *m* traffic light.
semana ➤ *f* week ■ entre s. during the week • s. laboral working week.
semanal ➤ *adj* weekly.
semanario ➤ *m* weekly publication.
sembrar §33 ➤ *tr* to sow.
semejante ➤ *adj* similar ➤ *mf* fellow man.
semestre ➤ *m* six months, semester.
semilla ➤ *f* seed.
seminario ➤ *m* seminary.

sémola ➤ *f* semolina.
sencillez ➤ *f* simplicity.
sencillo, a ➤ *adj* simple, easy; *(sin adorno)* plain; *(ingenuo)* naive.
senda ➤ *f or* **sendero** ➤ *m* path.
seno ➤ *m (pecho)* breast; FIG. bosom.
sensación ➤ *f* sensation; *(impresión)* feeling.
sensacional ➤ *adj* sensational.
sensato, a ➤ *adj* sensible.
sensibilidad ➤ *f* sensibility; *(emotividad, susceptibilidad)* sensitivity.
sensible ➤ *adj* sensitive.
sensitivo, a ➤ *adj* sensitive.
sensualidad ➤ *f* sensuality.
sentar §33 ➤ *tr* to seat; *(establecer)* to set ➤ *intr (la comida)* to agree with; *(la ropa)* to fit ➤ *reflex* to sit (down).
sentencia ➤ *f* LAW *(juicio)* sentence.
sentido ➤ *m* sense; *(conciencia)* consciousness; *(dirección)* direction ■ doble s. double meaning • tener s. to make sense.
sentimental ➤ *adj* sentimental.
sentimiento ➤ *m (emoción)* sentiment; *(pesar)* sorrow.
sentir[1] ➤ *m (sentimiento)* feeling; *(opinión)* opinion.
sentir[2] §43 ➤ *tr* to feel; *(experimentar)* to experience; *(lamentar)* to regret ■ lo siento I'm sorry ➤ *intr* to feel ➤ *reflex* to feel ■ s. como en (su) casa to feel at home.
seña ➤ *f (indicio)* sign; *(marca)* mark ■ hacer señas to signal.
señal ➤ *f (marca)* sign; *(seña)* reminder; *(vestigio)* trace; *(aviso)* signal.
señalar ➤ *tr* to mark; *(indicar)* to point (at); FIG. to signal, announce.
señor, a ➤ *m (dueño, noble)* lord; *(caballero)* gentleman ■ (el) S. Márquez Mr. Márquez • sientese, s. sit down, sir ➤ *f (dueña, noble)* lady; *(esposa)* wife ■ (la) s. Pérez Mrs. Pérez • buenos días, s. good morning, ma'am.
señorita ➤ *f* young lady ■ (la) s. García Miss García.
señorito ➤ *m* young man.
separación ➤ *f* separation.

separar ➤ *tr* to separate; *(partir)* to divide ➤ *reflex* to separate.

septentrional ➤ *adj* northern(ly).

septiembre ➤ *m* September.

séptimo, a ➤ *adj & m* seventh.

sepulcro ➤ *m* sepulcher.

sepultura ➤ *f* grave.

sequía ➤ *f* drought.

séquito ➤ *m* entourage.

ser¹ ➤ *m* being ■ s. humano human being ▪ s. vivo living creature.

ser² §44 ➤ *aux* to be ➤ *intr* to be ■ a or de no s. por if it were not for • a no s. que unless • así sea so be it • no sea que lest • o sea or esto es that is to say • o sea que in other words • sea como sea one way or the other • sea lo que sea be that as it may • s. de to be made of; *(tener origen)* to be or come from; *(suceder)* to become of; *(corresponder)* to be suitable for ■ ya sea . . . ya sea either . . . or.

sereno, a ➤ *adj* calm.

serial ➤ *adj & m* serial.

serie ➤ *f* series ■ fabricar or producir en s. to mass-produce.

seriedad ➤ *f* seriousness; *(comportamiento)* dependability.

serio, a ➤ *adj* serious.

sermón ➤ *m* sermon.

serpiente ➤ *f* snake ■ s. de cascabel rattlesnake.

serranía ➤ *f* mountains.

serrano, a ➤ *adj* mountain ➤ *mf* mountain-dweller, highlander.

serrucho ➤ *m* saw.

servicio ➤ *m* service; *(retrete)* bathroom ■ al s. de in the service of • prestar un s. to perform a service.

servidor, a ➤ *mf* servant ➤ *m* COMPUT. server.

servidumbre ➤ *f* staff of servants; *(esclavitud)* slavery.

servilleta ➤ *f* napkin.

servir §32 ➤ *intr* to serve ■ no s. para nada to be useless • s. de to act or serve as • s. para to be used for ➤ *tr* to serve ➤ *reflex* to make use of.

sesenta ➤ *adj & m* sixty.

sesión ➤ *f* session, meeting.

seso ➤ *m* brain; FIG. sense.

setenta ➤ *adj & m* seventy.

seto ➤ *m* fence ■ s. vivo hedge.

seudónimo ➤ *m* pseudonym.

severidad ➤ *f* severity, harshness.

severo, a ➤ *adj* severe.

sexo ➤ *m* sex; *(órganos)* genitals.

sexto, a ➤ *adj & m* sixth.

sexual ➤ *adj* sexual.

si ➤ *conj* if, whether ■ como si as if • por si acaso just in case • si bien although • si no if not, otherwise.

sí¹ ➤ *pron* himself, herself, etc. ■ dar de sí to give of oneself • de sí or en sí in itself • fuera de sí beside oneself • para sí to oneself • sí mismo oneself.

sí² ➤ *adv* yes; *(en votación)* aye; *(ciertamente)* certainly ■ creo que sí I think so ➤ *m* yes; *(consentimiento)* consent, permission ■ dar el sí to say yes.

sico- *see* **psico-.**

SIDA ➤ *m* AIDS.

siderurgia ➤ *f* iron and steel industry.

sidra ➤ *f* alcoholic cider.

siempre ➤ *adv* always ■ como s. as always • de s. usual • para or por s. forever • s. jamás forever and ever • s. que every time; *(a condición de)* provided that • s. y cuando provided that.

sien ➤ *f* temple.

sierra ➤ *f* saw; GEOL. mountain range.

siesta ➤ *f* afternoon nap.

siete ➤ *adj & m* seven ■ las s. seven o'clock.

sigiloso, a ➤ *adj* *(secreto)* secretive; *(prudente)* discreet.

sigla ➤ *f* acronym.

siglo ➤ *m* century.

significado ➤ *m* meaning.

significar §47 ➤ *tr* to mean.

significativo, a ➤ *adj* significant.

signo ➤ *m* sign; *(de puntuación)* mark ■ s. de admiración exclamation point • s. de interrogación question mark.

siguiente ➤ *adj* following, next.

sílaba ➤ *f* syllable.

silba ➤ *f* hissing, booing.

silbar ➤ *intr* to whistle; *(sisear)* to hiss.

silbato or **silbido** ➤ *m* whistle.

silencio ➤ *m* silence.

silencioso, a ➤ *adj* quiet, silent.

silicona ➤ *f* silicone.

silla ➤ *f (asiento)* chair; *(para montar)* saddle ■ **s. de ruedas** wheelchair.

sillón ➤ *m* armchair.

silueta ➤ *f* outline.

silvestre ➤ *adj (planta, animal)* wild.

simbólico, a ➤ *adj* symbolic(al).

símbolo ➤ *m* symbol.

simetría ➤ *f* symmetry.

simétrico, a ➤ *adj* symmetric(al).

simiente ➤ *f* seed.

similar ➤ *adj* similar.

similitud ➤ *f* similarity.

simpatía ➤ *f (afecto)* liking; *(afinidad)* sympathy, affinity; *(amabilidad)* congeniality ■ **tener s. a** or **por** to like.

simpático, a ➤ *adj* nice, likable.

simpatizar §02 ➤ *intr* to get along *(together)*.

simple ➤ *adj* simple; *(fácil)* easy ➤ *mf* simpleton.

simulacro ➤ *m* pretense.

simular ➤ *tr* to feign.

simultáneo, a ➤ *adj* simultaneous.

sin ➤ *prep* without; *(fuera de)* not including.

sinagoga ➤ *f* synagogue.

sinceridad ➤ *f* sincerity.

sincero, a ➤ *adj* sincere.

sincronizar §02 ➤ *tr* to synchronize.

sindicato ➤ *m* labor or trade union.

sinfonía ➤ *f* symphony.

singular ➤ *adj* single; *(excepcional)* unique; *(peculiar)* peculiar ➤ *m* GRAM. singular.

siniestro, a ➤ *adj (izquierdo)* left, left-hand; *(perverso)* wicked; *(funesto)* fateful ➤ *m* disaster.

sino¹ ➤ *m* fate.

sino² ➤ *conj* but; *(excepto)* except ■ **no sólo . . . s.** not only . . . but also.

sinónimo, a ➤ *adj* synonymous ➤ *m* synonym.

sinsabor ➤ *m* discontent; *(pena)* grief.

sintético, a ➤ *adj* synthetic.

sintetizador ➤ *m* synthesizer.

síntoma ➤ *m* symptom.

sintonía ➤ *f* tuning (in).

sintonizador ➤ *m* tuner.

sintonizar §02 ➤ *tr* to tune (in) ■ **s. con** to be tuned to.

sinvergüenza ➤ *adj & mf* shameless or brazen (person).

siquiera ➤ *conj* even though, if only ➤ *adv* at least ■ **ni s.** not even.

sirena ➤ *f* siren; MYTH. mermaid ■ **s. de niebla** foghorn.

sirvienta ➤ *f* maid.

sirviente ➤ *m* servant.

sismógrafo ➤ *m* seismograph.

sistema ➤ *m* system ■ **con s.** systematically • **s. métrico** metric system • **s. nervioso** nervous system.

sitio ➤ *m (localidad)* site; *(lugar)* place; MIL. siege ■ **s. web** website.

situación ➤ *f* situation; *(estado)* position.

situar §45 ➤ *tr* to place.

smoking ➤ *m* tuxedo.

snob ➤ *adj* snobbish ➤ *mf* snob.

sobaco ➤ *m* armpit.

soberanía ➤ *f* sovereignty.

soberano, a ➤ *adj & mf* sovereign.

soberbio, a ➤ *adj (orgulloso)* arrogant; *(magnífico)* superb ➤ *f* arrogance.

sobornar ➤ *tr* to bribe.

sobra ➤ *f* excess ■ **de s.** superfluous, extra ■ *pl* leftovers.

sobrante ➤ *adj* remaining ➤ *m* surplus.

sobrar ➤ *intr (estar de más)* to be more than enough; *(quedar)* to remain; *(ser inútil)* to be superfluous.

sobre¹ ➤ *m* envelope.

sobre² ➤ *prep (encima)* above, over; *(en)* on, on top of; *(superior a)* above, over; *(acerca de)* about, on; *(además de)* on top of, over.

sobrecoger §20 ➤ *tr* to scare ➤ *reflex* to be scared.

sobreentendido, a ➤ *adj* understood.

sobrehumano, a ➤ *adj* superhuman.

sobremesa ➤ *f* after-dinner conversation.

sobrenatural ➤ *adj* supernatural.

sobrepasar ➤ *intr* to surpass.

sobreponer §37 ➤ *tr* to superimpose ➤ *reflex* to control oneself; *(vencer)* to triumph.

sobresaliente ➤ *adj* outstanding ➤ *m* highest mark.

sobresalir §41 ➤ *intr (resaltar)* to project; *(sobrepujar)* to be outstanding.

sobresalto ➤ *m* fright.

sobrevenir §52 ➤ *intr* to occur unexpectedly.

sobreviviente ➤ *adj* surviving ➤ *mf* survivor.

sobrevivir ➤ *intr* to survive.

sobrino, a ➤ *m* nephew ➤ *f* niece.

sobrio, a ➤ *adj* (*sin beber*) sober; (*conservador*) moderate.

socavón ➤ *m* cave-in.

socorrer ➤ *tr* to aid.

sociable ➤ *adj* sociable.

social ➤ *adj* social.

socialista ➤ *adj & mf* socialist.

sociedad ➤ *f* society ■ s. anónima corporation.

socio, a ➤ *mf* (*asociado*) member; (*accionista*) business associate.

sociología ➤ *f* sociology.

socorrer ➤ *tr* to aid.

socorro ➤ *m* (*apoyo*) aid; (*provisiones*) supplies ➤ *interj* help!

sofá ➤ *m* sofa.

sofisticado, a ➤ *adj* sophisticated.

sofocar §47 ➤ *tr* (*asfixiar*) to suffocate; (*un fuego*) to put out ➤ *reflex* to suffocate; FIG. to get embarrassed.

sofreír §39 ➤ *tr* to fry lightly.

sofrito ➤ *m* lightly-fried mixture of seasonings.

soga ➤ *f* rope.

sol ➤ *m* sun, sunlight ■ al ponerse el s. at sunset • al salir el s. at sunrise • hacer s. to be sunny • tomar el s. to sunbathe.

solamente ➤ *adv* only.

solapa ➤ *f* flap; (*de chaqueta*) lapel.

solar[1] ➤ *adj* solar.

solar[2] ➤ *m* (*terreno*) lot; (*bajo construcción*) building site.

soldado ➤ *mf* soldier.

soldar §11 ➤ *tr* to solder, weld.

soleado ➤ *adj* sunny.

soledad ➤ *f* (*aislamiento*) solitude; (*sentirse solo*) loneliness.

solemne ➤ *adj* solemn.

soler §54 ➤ *intr* to be in the habit of; (*ser frecuente*) to tend to ■ suelo llegar tarde I usually arrive late.

solicitante ➤ *mf* petitioner.

solicitar ➤ *tr* to request; (*gestionar*) to apply for; (*atraer*) to attract.

solicitud ➤ *f* application; (*petición*)

request ■ a s. de at the request of.

solidaridad ➤ *f* solidarity.

sólido, a ➤ *adj* solid.

solitario, a ➤ *adj* lone, solitary.

sollozar §02 ➤ *intr* to sob.

sollozo ➤ *m* sob.

solo, a ➤ *adj* alone; (*único*) sole; (*aislado*) lonely ■ a solas alone.

sólo ➤ *adv* only.

solomillo ➤ *m* sirloin.

soltar §11 ➤ *tr* to let go of; (*liberar*) to free; (*irrumpir*) to let out; (*decir*) to blurt out ➤ *reflex* to become proficient; (*relajarse*) to loosen up.

soltero, a ➤ *adj* single ➤ *m* bachelor ➤ *f* unmarried woman.

solterón, ona ➤ *adj* old and unmarried ➤ *m* confirmed bachelor ➤ *f* spinster; COLL. old maid.

soluble ➤ *adj* CHEM. soluble.

solución ➤ *f* solution; (*desenlace*) ending.

solucionar ➤ *tr* to solve.

sombra ➤ *f* shade; (*imagen*) shadow ■ dar s. to cast a shadow.

sombrero ➤ *m* hat.

sombrilla ➤ *f* parasol.

sombrío, a ➤ *adj* (*lugar*) gloomy; (*persona*) sullen.

someter ➤ *tr* to subjugate; (*subordinar*) to subordinate; (*entregar*) to submit ■ s. a prueba to test • s. a tratamiento to put under treatment ➤ *reflex* to surrender ■ s. a to undergo.

somnífero ➤ *m* sleeping pill.

sonajero ➤ *m* rattle.

sonar[1] ➤ *m* TECH. sonar.

sonar[2] §11 ➤ *intr* (*producir sonido*) to sound; (*tintinear*) to ring; (*parecer*) to sound like ➤ *reflex* to blow.

sondeo ➤ *m* (*encuesta*) poll.

sonido ➤ *m* sound.

sonoro, a ➤ *adj* (*sonido*) sound; (*resonante*) deep, sonorous.

sonreír §39 ➤ *intr & reflex* to smile.

sonrisa ➤ *f* smile.

sonrojarse ➤ *reflex* to blush.

soñador, a ➤ *adj* dreamy ➤ *mf* dreamer.

soñar §11 ➤ *tr & intr* to dream ■ ¡ni soñarlo! not on your life! • s. con to dream of or about.

sopa ➤ f soup.

sopero, a ➤ adj soup ■ f soup tureen.

soplar ➤ intr to blow ➤ tr (mover el viento) to blow (away); (velas) to blow out; (globos) to blow up.

soplo ➤ m blow; FIG. instant.

soportar ➤ tr (sostener) to support; (sufrir) to bear.

soporte ➤ m support; (base) stand.

sorber ➤ tr (beber) to sip; (absorber) to absorb.

sorbete ➤ m sherbet.

sorbo ➤ m sip; (trago) swallow, gulp.

sordo, a ➤ adj deaf; (silencioso) muffled ■ mf deaf person.

sordomudo, a ➤ adj & mf deaf-mute.

sorprendente ➤ adj surprising.

sorprender ➤ tr to take by surprise; (asombrar) to surprise.

sorpresa ➤ f surprise.

sorpresivo, a ➤ adj unexpected.

sortear ➤ tr to draw lots for; (rifar) to raffle; (evitar) to avoid.

sorteo ➤ m drawing; (rifa) raffle.

sortija ➤ f (anillo) ring.

sosegar §35 ➤ tr & intr to calm (down) ➤ reflex to calm down.

sosiego ➤ m tranquility, quiet.

soso, a ➤ adj (de poco sabor) tasteless; (sin sal) unsalted.

sospecha ➤ f suspicion.

sospechar ➤ tr to suspect ➤ intr to be suspicious.

sospechoso, a ➤ adj suspicious.

sostén ➤ m (apoyo) support; (prenda) bra ■ s. de familia breadwinner.

sostener §46 ➤ tr (sustentar) to support; (sujetar) to hold (up); (defender) to uphold ➤ reflex to hold oneself up; (mantenerse) to support oneself.

sótano ➤ m basement.

Sr. ➤ m Mr.

Sra. ➤ f Mrs.

standard ➤ adj & m standard ■ s. de vida standard of living.

su, sus ➤ adj one's, his, her, your, its, their.

suave ➤ adj soft; (liso) smooth; (dulce) sweet; (tranquilo) gentle.

suavizar §02 ➤ tr to soften; (hacer plano) to smooth; (moderar) to temper ➤ reflex to soften; (volver plano) to become smooth.

subalterno, a ➤ adj & mf subordinate.

subasta ➤ f auction.

subconsciente ➤ adj & m subconscious (mind).

subdesarrollado, a ➤ adj underdeveloped.

subdirector, a ➤ mf assistant manager.

súbdito, a ➤ mf (de un monarca) subject; (ciudadano) citizen.

subestimar ➤ tr to underestimate.

subir ➤ tr to climb, go up; (llevar arriba) to take or carry up; (levantar, aumentar) to raise; COMPUT. to upload ➤ intr to rise; (ascender) to go up ■ s. a (montar) to get on or into; (alcanzar) to come or amount to ➤ reflex to go up ■ s. a to get on or into.

súbito, a ➤ adj sudden ■ de s. suddenly.

sublevarse ➤ reflex to revolt.

sublime ➤ adj sublime.

submarinismo ➤ m scuba diving.

submarino, a ➤ adj & m submarine.

subordinado, a ➤ adj & mf subordinate.

subrayar ➤ tr (señalar) to underline; (poner énfasis) to emphasize.

subscri- see suscri-.

subsecretario, a ➤ mf assistant secretary; POL. undersecretary.

subsidiario, a ➤ adj subsidiary.

subsidio ➤ m subsidy; (ayuda) aid.

subsistencia ➤ f subsistence.

subsistir ➤ intr to subsist.

substan-, substi- see sustan-, susti-.

subterráneo, a ➤ adj underground ➤ m (tren) subway.

suburbano, a ➤ adj suburban.

suburbio ➤ m (arrabal) suburb; (barrio pobre) slum, shantytown.

subvención ➤ f subsidy.

suceder ➤ intr to follow; (ocurrir) to occur ➤ reflex to follow one another.

sucesión ➤ f succession.

sucesivamente ➤ adv successively.

sucesivo, a ➤ adj consecutive ■ en lo s. in the future.

suceso ➤ m event; (transcurso) course; (resultado) outcome.

sucesor, a ➤ *mf* successor.
suciedad ➤ *f* dirt, filth.
sucio, a ➤ *adj* dirty.
suculento, a ➤ *adj* succulent.
sucumbir ➤ *intr* to succumb.
sucursal ➤ *f* branch (office); *(de empresa)* subsidiary.
Sudamérica ➤ *f* South America.
sudamericano, a ➤ *adj & mf* South American.
sudar ➤ *intr* to sweat.
sudeste ➤ *adj* southeastern ➤ *m* southeast.
sudoeste ➤ *adj* southwestern ➤ *m* southwest.
sudor ➤ *m* sweat.
suegra ➤ *f* mother-in-law.
suegro ➤ *m* father-in-law ➤ *pl* in-laws.
suela ➤ *f* sole.
sueldo ➤ *m* salary ■ a s. on a salary.
suelo ➤ *m (tierra)* ground; *(piso)* floor.
suelto, a ➤ *adj* loose; *(desatado)* untied; *(sin pareja)* odd ■ **venderse s.** *(por peso)* to be sold in bulk; *(por separado)* to be sold singly ➤ *m (dinero)* loose change.
sueño ➤ *m* sleep; *(representación)* dream ■ quitar el s. to keep awake • tener s. to be sleepy.
suerte ➤ *f (destino)* fate; *(fortuna)* luck ■ buena, mala s. good, bad luck • tener s. to be lucky.
suéter ➤ *m* sweater.
suficiente ➤ *adj* sufficient.
sufrimiento ➤ *m* suffering.
sufrir ➤ *tr (padecer)* to suffer; *(experimentar)* to undergo; *(soportar)* to endure ➤ *intr (padecer)* to suffer; *(preocuparse)* to worry.
sugerencia ➤ *f* suggestion.
sugerir §43 ➤ *tr* to suggest.
sugestión ➤ *f* suggestion.
sugestionar ➤ *tr (influenciar)* to influence; *(hipnotizar)* to hypnotize.
suicida ➤ *adj* suicidal ➤ *mf* suicide.
suicidarse ➤ *reflex* to commit suicide.
suicidio ➤ *m* suicide.
sujetador, a ➤ *adj* fastening ➤ *m (sostén)* bra.
sujetapapeles ➤ *m* paper clip.
sujetar ➤ *tr* to fasten; *(agarrar)* to

grasp; *(dominar)* to subject.
sujeto, a ➤ *adj* fastened ➤ *m* subject.
suma ➤ *f* sum; MATH. *(adición)* addition; *(cantidad)* amount of money.
sumamente ➤ *adv* extremely.
sumar ➤ *tr* to add (up); to add up to ➤ *reflex* ■ s. a to be added to.
sumergible ➤ *adj & m* submersible.
sumergir §19 ➤ *tr* to submerge ➤ *reflex* to dive, submerge ■ s. en to become immersed or absorbed in.
suministrar ➤ *tr* to supply.
suministro ➤ *m* supply ■ s. a domicilio home delivery.
sumiso, a ➤ *adj (sometido)* submissive; *(obediente)* obedient.
sumo, a ➤ *adj* greatest ■ a lo sumo at (the) most.
suntuoso, a ➤ *adj* sumptuous.
superar ➤ *tr (sobrepujar)* to surpass; *(dificultades)* to overcome.
superdotado, a ➤ *adj & mf* exceptionally gifted (child).
superficial ➤ *adj* superficial.
superficie ➤ *f* surface; GEOM. area.
superfino, a ➤ *adj* extra fine.
superfluo, a ➤ *adj* superfluous.
superior ➤ *m* superior ➤ *adj (de más altura)* upper; *(más alto)* higher; *(excelente)* superior.
superioridad ➤ *f (calidad)* superiority; *(autoridad)* higher authority.
supermercado ➤ *m* supermarket.
supersónico, a ➤ *adj* supersonic.
supersticioso, a ➤ *adj* superstitious.
supervisar ➤ *tr* to supervise.
supervivencia ➤ *f* survival.
suplantar ➤ *tr* to supplant.
suplementario, a *or* **suplemental** ➤ *adj* supplemental, supplementary.
suplemento ➤ *m* supplement.
suplencia ➤ *f* replacement.
suplente ➤ *adj* substitute; SPORT. reserve ➤ *mf* replacement; SPORT. reserve player; THEAT. understudy.
suplicar §47 ➤ *tr* to implore.
suplicio ➤ *m (tortura)* torture; *(castigo corporal)* corporal punishment.
suplir ➤ *tr (compensar)* to make up for; *(reemplazar)* to replace.
suponer §37 ➤ *tr* to suppose; *(imagi-*

nar) to imagine; *(traer consigo)* to entail ▪ **ser de** s. to be likely.

supositorio ➤ *m* suppository.

supremo, a ➤ *adj* supreme; *(definitivo)* final.

suprimir ➤ *tr* to eliminate.

supuesto, a ➤ *adj (fingido)* assumed; *(que se supone)* supposed; *(imaginario)* imaginary; *(hipotético)* hypothetical ▪ **por** s. of course ➤ *m* supposition.

sur ➤ *adj* southern, southerly ➤ *m* south.

surco ➤ *m* trench; AGR. furrow.

surgir §19 ➤ *intr (surtir)* to shoot up; *(aparecer)* to arise.

surtido, a ➤ *adj* assorted ➤ *m* selection.

surtidor ➤ *m (chorro)* spout; *(fuente)* fountain ▪ s. **de gasolina** filling station.

susceptible *or* **susceptivo, a** ➤ *adj* susceptible; *(quisquilloso)* sensitive.

suscitar ➤ *tr* to stir up.

suscribir §55 ➤ *tr & reflex* to subscribe (to).

suscripción ➤ *f* subscription.

suspender ➤ *tr* to suspend; *(colgar)* to hang; *(interrumpir)* to interrupt; *(un estudiante)* to fail.

suspensión ➤ *f* suspension.

suspenso ➤ *m* EDUC. failing mark ▪ **de** s. suspense ▪ **en** s. pending, outstanding.

suspicacia ➤ *f* distrust.

suspicaz ➤ *adj* distrustful.

suspirar ➤ *intr* to sigh.

suspiro ➤ *m* sigh.

sustancia ➤ *f* substance.

sustantivo, a ➤ *adj* substantive ➤ *m* noun.

sustento ➤ *m (alimento)* sustenance; *(medios)* livelihood.

sustitución ➤ *f* substitution.

sustituir §10 ➤ *tr* to substitute.

sustituto, a ➤ *adj & mf* substitute.

susto ➤ *m* fright, scare.

sustracción ➤ *f* subtraction.

sustraer §49 ➤ *tr* to subtract.

susurrar ➤ *intr* to whisper.

susurro ➤ *m* whisper.

sutil ➤ *adj* subtle; *(perspicaz)* sharp.

suyo, a ➤ *adj* his, her, your, their; of his,

hers, yours, *or* theirs ➤ *pron* his, hers, yours, theirs ▪ **lo** s. one's share • **los suyos** one's friends *or* family • **salirse con la** s. COLL. to get one's way.

T

tabaco ➤ *m* tobacco.

taberna ➤ *f* tavern.

tabique ➤ *m* partition.

tabla ➤ *f (de madera)* board; *(lista)* table ▪ t. **de planchar** ironing board • t. **de surf** surfboard.

tablero ➤ *m* board ▪ t. **de ajedrez** chess board • t. **de dibujo** drawing board • t. **de instrumentos** instrument panel; AUTO. dashboard.

tablón ➤ *m* thick plank.

taburete ➤ *m* stool.

tacaño, a ➤ *adj* stingy ➤ *mf* miser.

tachar ➤ *tr* to cross out.

tacón ➤ *m* heel.

táctico, a ➤ *adj* tactical ➤ *f* tactics.

tacto ➤ *m (sentido)* (sense of) touch; *(delicadeza)* tact.

tajada ➤ *f* CUL. slice.

tajo ➤ *m (corte)* cut, slash.

tal ➤ *adj* such (a); *(cierto)* certain ▪ t. **cual** such as • t. **vez** perhaps, maybe ➤ *pron* such a thing; *(alguno)* some, someone ▪ **fulano de** t. so-and-so • t. **para cual** COLL. two of a kind ➤ *adv* thus, so ▪ **con** t. **que** provided that • **¿qué t.?** COLL. how goes it?

tala ➤ *f (de árboles)* felling.

talante ➤ *m* mood ▪ **hacer algo de buen, mal** t. to do something willingly, unwillingly.

talar ➤ *tr (un árbol)* to fell, cut down.

talco ➤ *m* talc; PHARM. talcum powder.

talega ➤ *f* sack.

talento ➤ *m* talent.

talla ➤ *f (estatura)* height; *(medida)* size; *(escultura)* wood carving.

tallar ➤ *tr* to carve; *(en metal)* to engrave; JEWEL. to cut; ARTS to sculpt.

tallarín ➤ *m* noodle.

talle ➤ *m* waist.

taller ➤ *m (de obreros)* shop; *(de artistas)* studio ▪ t. **de reparaciones** AUTO. body shop.

tallo ➤ *m* stem.

talón ➤ m heel; *(comprobante)* receipt; *(de cheque)* stub.

talonario ➤ m *(de recibos)* receipt book; *(de cheques)* checkbook.

tamaño ➤ m *(dimensión)* size; *(volumen)* volume ▪ del t. de as large as • t. natural life-size.

tambalear ➤ intr to stagger.

también ➤ adv also, too; *(asimismo)* likewise.

tambor ➤ m drum.

tamiz ➤ m sieve.

tampoco ➤ adv neither, nor.

tampón ➤ m ink pad; PHARM. tampon.

tan ➤ adv so, as ▪ t. pronto como as soon as • t. siquiera at least • t. sólo only.

tanque ➤ m tank; *(barco)* tanker.

tanto, a ➤ adj so much, so many ➤ pron that ▪ por (lo) t. therefore • t. como or cuanto as much as ➤ m *(cantidad)* certain amount; *(en deportes)* point ▪ entre t. in the meantime • no ser para t. not to be so bad • otro t. the same thing • t. por ciento per cent • y tantos and some, odd ➤ adv ▪ t. como as much as • t. más all the more • t. mejor all the better • t. que so much that.

tapa ➤ f *(de olla)* lid; *(de libro)* cover; *(bocado)* hors d'oeuvre.

tapar ➤ tr to cover (up); *(cerrar)* to plug up ➤ reflex to cover oneself up.

tapete ➤ m table runner.

tapia ➤ f mud or adobe wall; *(cerca)* (adjoining) wall.

tapiz ➤ m tapestry.

tapizar §02 ➤ tr *(muebles)* to upholster.

tapón ➤ m *(de botellas)* cork; *(de tonel)* plug.

taponar ➤ tr to plug.

taquilla ➤ f THEAT. *(ventanilla)* box office; *(cantidad)* receipts.

tardanza ➤ f delay.

tardar ➤ intr *(demorarse)* to delay; *(durar)* to take; *(tomar tiempo)* to take a long time; *(llegar tarde)* to be late.

tarde ➤ f afternoon, (early) evening ▪ buenas tardes good afternoon ➤ adv *(a hora avanzada)* late ▪ lo más t. at the latest.

tarea ➤ f task ▪ pl homework.

tarifa ➤ f *(tasa)* tariff; *(precio)* fare.

tarjeta ➤ f card ▪ t. de crédito credit card • t. de identidad identity card • t. postal post card.

tarro ➤ m *(vasija)* jar; *(de lata)* tin can.

tarta ➤ f pie, tart.

tartamudear ➤ intr to stammer.

tartamudo, a ➤ mf stammerer.

tartera ➤ f baking pan.

tasa ➤ f rate ▪ t. aduanera customs duty.

tasar ➤ tr *(poner precio)* to set the price of; *(valorar)* to appraise.

tatuaje ➤ m tattoo.

taurino, a ➤ adj taurine, of bulls.

tautología ➤ f tautology.

taxi ➤ m taxi.

taxista ➤ mf taxi driver.

taza ➤ f cup; *(contenido)* cupful; *(de fuente)* basin; *(de retrete)* bowl.

tazón ➤ m large cup; *(cuenco)* bowl.

te ➤ pron [informal] you; to, for, or from you ▪ cálmate calm yourself.

té ➤ m tea.

teatro ➤ m theater.

techo ➤ m roof; *(cielo raso)* ceiling.

tecla ➤ f key.

teclado ➤ m keyboard.

técnico, a ➤ adj technical ➤ mf technician ➤ f technique.

tecnología ➤ f technology.

tedio ➤ m tedium.

teja ➤ f *(mosaico)* tile; *(de techo)* slate.

tejado ➤ m roof.

tejer ➤ intr *(con telar)* to weave; *(hacer punto)* to knit.

tejido ➤ m fabric.

tela ➤ f *(paño)* fabric; *(de araña)* web.

telar ➤ m *(para tejer)* loom.

telaraña ➤ f spider web.

telefonear ➤ tr to phone.

teléfono ➤ m telephone ▪ t. celular cellular telephone, cell phone.

telegrama ➤ m telegram.

teleobjetivo ➤ m telephoto lens.

telescopio ➤ m telescope.

televisión ➤ f television.

televisor ➤ m television (set).

telex ➤ m telex.

telón ➤ m THEAT. curtain.

tema ➤ m subject.

temblar §33 ➤ *intr* to tremble; *(de frío)* to shiver; *(de miedo)* to quiver.

temblor ➤ *m* tremor; AMER. earthquake.

temer ➤ *tr & intr* to fear ▪ **t. a** to be afraid of.

temerario, a ➤ *adj* reckless.

temor ➤ *m* fear; *(recelo)* foreboding.

temperamento ➤ *m* temperament.

temperatura ➤ *f* temperature.

tempestad ➤ *f* storm.

templado, a ➤ *adj (moderado)* moderate; *(tibio)* lukewarm; *(el clima)* mild.

templo ➤ *m* temple.

temporada ➤ *f (del año)* season; *(período)* period ▪ **fuera de t.** off-season • **t. baja** off season, slow season.

temporal ➤ *adj* temporary ➤ *m* storm.

temprano, a ➤ *adj & adv* early.

tenaz ➤ *f* tenacious.

tenaza(s) ➤ *f(pl)* pliers.

tendencia ➤ *f* tendency.

tender §34 ➤ *tr (extender)* to spread (out); *(alargar)* to stretch out; *(ropa)* to hang out; *(cable)* to lay; *(puente)* to build ➤ *intr* to tend *(a* to) ➤ *reflex* to lie down.

tendero, a ➤ *mf* shopkeeper.

tendón ➤ *m* tendon.

tenebroso, a ➤ *adj (sombrío)* dark; *(secreto)* shady; *(oscuro)* obscure.

tenedor ➤ *m* fork.

tener §46 ➤ *tr* to have; *(contener)* to contain; *(edad)* to be; *(cumplir)* to keep, fulfill ▪ **t. calor, frío** to be hot, cold • **t. celos** to be jealous • **t. cuidado** to be careful • **t. en cuenta** to take into account • **t. éxito** to succeed • **t. ganas de** to feel like • **t. hambre, sed** to be hungry, thirsty • **t. miedo** to be afraid • **t. presente** to bear in mind • **t. prisa** to be in a hurry • **t. que** to have to • **t. razón** to be right • **t. sueño** to be sleepy • **t. suerte** to be lucky ➤ *reflex* to steady oneself ▪ **t. de pie** to stand up • **t. por** to consider oneself.

teniente ➤ *mf* lieutenant.

tenis ➤ *m* tennis ▪ **t. de mesa** table tennis.

tenista ➤ *mf* tennis player.

tenor ➤ *m* MUS. tenor.

tensar ➤ *tr* to stretch.

tensión ➤ *f* tension; *(emocional)* stress ▪ **t. arterial** blood pressure.

tenso, a ➤ *adj* tense; *(nervios, relaciones)* strained; *(emocionalmente)* stressed.

tentación ➤ *f* temptation.

tentar §33 ➤ *tr (seducir)* to tempt; *(intentar)* to try.

tenue ➤ *adj (delgado)* thin; *(luz)* soft.

teñir ➤ *tr* to dye; FIG. to imbue.

teoría ➤ *f* theory.

terapia ➤ *f* therapy.

tercer ➤ *adj contr* of **tercero**.

tercero, a ➤ *adj & m* third.

tercio, a ➤ *adj & m* third.

terciopelo ➤ *m* velvet.

terco, a ➤ *adj* stubborn.

tergiversar ➤ *tr* to distort.

terminal ➤ *adj & m* terminal.

terminar ➤ *tr* to end ➤ *intr* to come to an end ▪ **t. de** *(acabar de)* to have just; *(concluir)* to finish • **t. en** to end up in • **t. por** to end up ➤ *reflex* to come to an end.

término ➤ *m* end; *(palabra, tiempo)* term ▪ **en buenos términos con** on good terms with • **t. medio** MATH. average; *(compromiso)* middle ground.

termómetro ➤ *m* thermometer.

termostato ➤ *m* thermostat.

ternera ➤ *f* female calf; CUL. veal.

ternero ➤ *m* male calf.

ternura ➤ *f* tenderness.

terquedad ➤ *f* stubbornness.

terracota ➤ *f* terra cotta.

terraza ➤ *f* terrace; veranda.

terremoto ➤ *m* earthquake.

terreno, a ➤ *adj* earthly; *(terrenal)* worldly ➤ *m (tierra)* land; *(campo)* piece of land, ground.

terrestre ➤ *adj* terrestrial.

terrible ➤ *adj* terrible.

territorial ➤ *adj* territorial.

territorio ➤ *m* territory; *(comarca)* zone.

terrón ➤ *m* clod; *(de azúcar)* lump.

terror ➤ *m* terror.

terrorista ➤ *adj & mf* terrorist.

terso, a ➤ *adj* clear; *(estilo)* smooth.

tertulia ➤ *f* social gathering ∎ t. litera-ria literary circle.

tesis ➤ *f* thesis; *(opinión)* theory.

tesoro ➤ *m (dinero)* treasure; *(fondos públicos)* treasury.

testamento ➤ *m* will, testament.

testarudo, a ➤ *adj* stubborn.

testificar §47 ➤ *tr* to testify (to).

testigo ➤ *mf* witness.

testimonio ➤ *m* testimony.

tétano(s) ➤ *m* tetanus.

tetera ➤ *f* teapot.

textil ➤ *adj & m* textile.

texto ➤ *m* text; *(libro)* textbook.

tez ➤ *f* complexion.

ti ➤ *pron* you, yourself (informal).

tía ➤ *f* aunt ∎ t. abuela great-aunt.

tibio, a ➤ *adj* lukewarm.

tiburón ➤ *m* shark.

tic ➤ *m* tic.

tiempo ➤ *m* time; *(época)* times; *(ocasión)* moment; *(estación)* season; METEOROL. weather ∎ a t. in *or* on time • con t. *(por adelantado)* in advance; *(en el momento oportuno)* in good time • de t. en t. from time to time • fuera de t. at the wrong time • ganar t. to save time • perder el t. to waste time • t. atrás some time ago.

tienda ➤ *f* shop ∎ ir de tiendas to go shopping • t. de campaña tent.

tienta ➤ *f* ∎ a tientas gropingly.

tierno, a ➤ *adj (afectuoso)* loving; *(blando)* soft; *(carne)* tender.

tierra ➤ *f* land; *(suelo)* ground; *(patria)* country ∎ t. adentro inland • t. de nadie no man's land

tieso, a ➤ *adj* stiff, rigid; *(terco)* stub-born.

tigre ➤ *m* tiger ∎ t. americano jaguar.

tijera(s) ➤ *f(pl)* scissors.

tilo ➤ *m* linden.

timar ➤ *tr* to cheat.

timbre ➤ *m* buzzer; *(sonido)* ring; *(sonoridad)* timbre.

timidez ➤ *f* timidity.

tímido, a ➤ *adj* timid.

timo ➤ *m* swindle.

timón ➤ *m* MARIT. rudder.

tímpano ➤ *m* MUS. kettledrum; ANAT. eardrum.

tina ➤ *f* bathtub.

tinieblas ➤ *fpl* darkness.

tinta ➤ *f* ink.

tinte ➤ *m (colorante)* dye; *(color)* tint.

tinto ➤ *m* red wine; AMER. black coffee.

tintorería ➤ *f* dry cleaner's shop.

tío ➤ *m* uncle ∎ t. abuelo great-uncle ∎ *pl* aunt and uncle.

tiovivo ➤ *m* merry-go-round.

típico, a ➤ *adj* typical.

tiple ➤ *mf* MUS. soprano.

tipo ➤ *m (clase)* kind; *(modelo)* type; *(figura)* figure; *(persona)* guy; PRINT. type; COM. rate.

tira ➤ *f* strip.

tiranía ➤ *f* tyranny.

tirante ➤ *adj (tenso)* tight; *(relaciones)* strained ➤ *m (correa)* strap; ARCHIT. tie beam; TECH. brace ∎ *pl* suspenders.

tirar ➤ *tr* to throw; *(desechar)* to throw away; *(derribar)* to knock down; *(dis-parar)* to fire; *(trazar)* to draw ➤ *intr (hacia sí)* to pull, draw; *(chimenea)* to draw; *(torcer)* to turn, go ∎ t. de to pull (at), tug (on) ➤ *reflex* to throw one-self; *(tenderse)* to lie down.

tiritar ➤ *intr* to shiver.

tiro ➤ *m (lanzada)* throw; *(disparo)* shot; *(caballos)* team (of horses); *(de chimenea)* draft.

tisana ➤ *f* infusion.

títere ➤ *m* puppet.

titubear ➤ *intr* to hesitate.

titular¹ ➤ *m* PRINT. headline ➤ *mf* holder of a passport, office).

titular² ➤ *tr* to entitle ➤ *intr* to receive a title ➤ *reflex* EDUC. to receive one's degree.

título ➤ *m* title; *(encabezado)* heading; *(diploma)* degree ∎ a t. de by way of.

tiza ➤ *f* chalk.

tiznar ➤ *tr* to smudge; FIG. to stain.

toalla ➤ *f* towel.

toallero ➤ *m* towel rack.

tobillo ➤ *m* ankle.

tobogán ➤ *m (para niños)* slide; *(para mercancías)* chute; *(trineo)* sled.

tocado ➤ *m* hairdo.

tocador ➤ *m* dressing room ∎ artículos de t. toiletries.

tocar §47 ➤ *tr* to touch; *(palpar)* to feel;

tocino ► *m* bacon; *(cerdo)* salt pork.

todavía ► *adv* still; *(sin embargo)* nevertheless; *(aún)* even ■ t. no not yet.

todo, a ► *adj* all; *(cada)* each, every; *(entero)* whole, entire ■ t. el mundo everybody ► *m* whole, all ■ ante t. first of all • con t. still • sobre t. above all ■ t. está listo everything is ready ■ *pl* everybody, everyone ► *adv* all.

toldo ► *m* awning.

tolerancia ► *f* tolerance.

tolerar ► *tr* to tolerate.

toma ► *f (acción)* taking; *(captura)* capture; *(dosis)* dose; *(entrada)* intake; ELEC. plug.

tomar ► *tr* to take; *(capturar)* to capture; *(comer, beber)* to eat, drink, have ■ t. en cuenta to take into account ■ t. parte to participate • t. partido to take sides • t. prestado to borrow.

tomate ► *m* tomato.

tomillo ► *m* thyme.

tonel ► *m* barrel.

tonelada ► *f* ton.

tonelaje ► *m* tonnage.

tónico, a ► *adj & m* MED. tonic ► *f* MUS. tonic ■ dar la t. to set the tone.

tono ► *m* tone.

tontería ► *f* foolishness; *(acción)* foolish action; *(dicho)* stupid remark ■ decir tonterías to talk nonsense.

tonto, a ► *adj* foolish ► *mf* fool.

topar ► *tr* to bump (into).

tope ► *m (extremo)* butt, end; MECH. catch, stop; AUTO. bumper; *(choque)* collision.

tópico ► *m* topic.

topo ► *m* ZOOL. mole.

torbellino ► *m* whirlwind.

torcer §48 ► *tr* to twist; *(doblar)* to bend; *(la cara)* to contort; MED. to sprain ► *intr* to turn.

torear ► *tr & intr* to fight (bulls).

toreo ► *m* bullfighting.

torero ► *m* bullfighter.

tormenta ► *f* storm.

tormento ► *m* torment.

tormentoso, a ► *adj* stormy.

tornillo ► *m* screw.

torno ► *m* lathe ■ en t. a around • t. de alfarero potter's wheel.

toro ► *m* bull ■ *pl* bullfight.

torpe ► *adj* clumsy; *(necio)* stupid.

torre ► *f* tower; *(de petróleo)* oil derrick; *(de ajedrez)* rook, castle.

torrente ► *m* torrent.

torso ► *m* torso.

torta ► *f* cake; COLL. *(bofetada)* slap.

tortazo ► *m* COLL. blow.

tortícolis(s) ► *m* stiff neck.

tortilla ► *f* CUL. omelet; AMER. tortilla.

tortuga ► *f* turtle.

tortura ► *f* torture.

tos ► *f* cough, coughing ■ acceso de t. coughing fit.

tosco, a ► *adj* crude, coarse.

toser ► *intr* to cough.

tostada ► *f* toast.

tostador, a ► *m or f* toaster.

tostar §11 ► *tr (pan)* to toast; *(café)* to roast.

total ► *adj & m* total ► *adv* so, in short.

tótem ► *m* totem.

tóxico, a ► *adj* toxic ► *m* poison.

tozudo, a ► *adj* stubborn.

traba ► *f* obstacle.

trabajador, a ► *adj* hard-working ► *mf* worker.

trabajar ► *intr* to work ■ t. de to work as ► *tr* to work; AGR. to till.

trabajo ► *m* work; *(labor)* labor; *(tarea)* job; *(esfuerzo)* trouble ■ costar t. to be hard • t. a destajo piecework.

trabalenguas ► *m* tongue twister.

trabar ► *tr* to start up ► *reflex* to get tangled up ■ trabársele a uno la lengua to get tongue-tied.

tracción ► *f* traction ■ t. delantera front-wheel drive.

tractor ► *m* tractor.

tradición ► *f* tradition.

tradicional ► *adj* traditional.

traducción ► *f* translation.

traducir §14 ► *tr* to translate.

traductor, a ➤ *mf* translator.

traer §49 ➤ *tr* to bring; *(causar)* to bring about; *(llevar)* to wear.

traficante ➤ *adj* dealing ➤ *mf* dealer.

tráfico ➤ *m* traffic.

tragaluz ➤ *m* skylight.

tragar §31 ➤ *intr & tr* to swallow.

tragedia ➤ *f* tragedy.

trágico, a ➤ *adj* tragic.

trago ➤ *m (bebida)* drink; *(porción)* gulp ∎ de un t. in one shot.

traición ➤ *f* treason.

traicionar ➤ *tr* to betray.

traidor, a ➤ *adj* traitorous ➤ *mf* traitor.

traje ➤ *m (vestido)* dress; *(conjunto)* suit; THEAT. costume ∎ t. de baño bathing suit • t. de luces bullfighter's costume.

trama ➤ *f (de novela)* plot.

trámite ➤ *m* procedure ➤ *pl* formalities.

tramo ➤ *m (de terreno)* stretch; *(de una escalera)* flight.

trampa ➤ *f* trap ∎ hacer trampas to cheat.

trampolín ➤ *m (del gimnasta)* trampoline; *(del nadador)* diving board.

tramposo, a ➤ *adj* cheating ➤ *mf* swindler.

tranquilidad ➤ *f* tranquility.

tranquilizante ➤ *adj* tranquilizing ➤ *m* tranquilizer.

tranquilizar §02 ➤ *tr* to quiet ➤ *reflex* to be quieted.

tranquilo, a ➤ *adj* tranquil ∎ ¡déjame t.! leave me alone!

transacción ➤ *f* COM. transaction; *(acuerdo)* settlement.

transatlántico, a ➤ *adj* transatlantic ➤ *m* ocean liner.

transbordador ➤ *m* ferry ∎ t. espacial space shuttle.

transbordo ➤ *m* transshipment.

transcontinental ➤ *adj* transcontinental.

transcurrir ➤ *intr* to elapse.

transcurso ➤ *m* course.

transeúnte ➤ *mf* passerby.

transferencia ➤ *f* transfer(ence).

transferir §43 ➤ *tr* to transfer.

transformación ➤ *f* transformation.

transformador, a ➤ *adj* transforming

➤ *m* ELEC. transformer.

transformar ➤ *tr* to transform; SPORT. to convert ➤ *reflex* to be transformed.

transfusión ➤ *f* transfusion.

transición ➤ *f* transition.

transistor ➤ *m* transistor.

transitable ➤ *adj* passable.

transitivo, a ➤ *adj* transitive.

tránsito ➤ *m* traffic ∎ de t. in transit.

transitorio, a ➤ *adj* temporary.

transmisión ➤ *f* transmission; RAD., TELEV. broadcast.

transmisor ➤ *m* ELEC. transmitter.

transmitir ➤ *tr* to transmit; RAD., TELEV. to broadcast.

transoceánico, a ➤ *adj* transoceanic.

transparente ➤ *adj (un objeto)* transparent; *(evidente)* obvious.

transpiración ➤ *f* perspiration.

transplantar ➤ *tr* to transplant.

transportar ➤ *tr* to transport.

transporte ➤ *m* transport.

transversal ➤ *adj* transverse ➤ *f* side street.

tranvía ➤ *m* streetcar.

trapo ➤ *m* rag ∎ pl clothing.

tráquea ➤ *f* trachea.

tras ➤ *prep (después de)* after; *(detrás de)* behind.

trasatlántico, a ➤ *adj* transatlantic.

trascendencia ➤ *f* PHILOS. transcendence; *(importancia)* significance.

trascendental ➤ *adj* PHILOS. transcendental; *(importante)* very significant.

trasero, a ➤ *adj* back, rear ➤ *m* ANAT. bottom; ZOOL. rump ➤ *f* back, rear.

trasladar ➤ *tr (mover)* to move; *(a un empleado)* to transfer ➤ *reflex* to change residence, move.

traslado ➤ *m (de un empleado)* transfer; *(mudanza)* change of residence.

trasnochar ➤ *intr* to stay up all night.

traspasar ➤ *tr (perforar)* to pierce; *(atravesar)* to cross.

traspié ➤ *m* stumble.

trasplantar ➤ *tr* to transplant ➤ *reflex* to uproot oneself.

trasplante ➤ *m* transplant.

trastienda ➤ *f* stock room.

trasto ➤ *m* piece of junk.

trastornar ➤ *tr (perturbar)* to disrupt;

(inquietar) to worry; *(enloquecer)* to drive mad ▸ *reflex* to go mad.

trastorno ➤ *m* upset.

tratado ➤ *m* treatise; POL. treaty.

tratamiento ➤ *m* treatment.

tratar ➤ *tr* to treat; *(manejar)* to handle; *(dar el tratamiento de)* to address as; *(comerciar)* to manage; CHEM. to process; MED. to treat ▪ *intr* t. con to have dealings with ▪ t. de *(discutir)* to be about; *(procurar)* to try to ▸ *reflex* to treat each other.

trato ➤ *m* treatment; *(título)* form of address; *(relaciones)* dealings; *(negocio)* trade; *(convenio)* agreement ▪ ¡t. hecho! COLL. it's a deal!

trauma ➤ *m* trauma.

traumático, a ➤ *adj* traumatic.

través ➤ *m* slant; *(torcimiento)* bend ▪ a t. de across, through • al *or* de t. across, crosswise.

travesía ➤ *f (distancia)* distance across; *(viaje)* crossing; *(viento)* crosswind.

travesura ➤ *f* mischief.

travieso, a ➤ *adj* mischievous.

trayecto ➤ *m (distancia)* distance; *(recorrido)* route, way.

trazar §02 ➤ *tr (diseñar)* to design; *(bosquejar)* to outline, trace; *(discurrir)* to draw up (plans).

trébol ➤ *m* BOT. clover; ARCHIT. trefoil ▪ *pl (naipes)* clubs.

trece ➤ *adj & m* thirteen.

trecho ➤ *m* distance, stretch; *(de tiempo)* spell ▪ de t. en t. at intervals.

treinta ➤ *adj & m* thirty.

tremendo, a ➤ *adj* tremendous; *(horrendo)* horrible.

tren ➤ *m* train.

trenza *or* **trencilla** ➤ *f* braid.

trepar ➤ *intr* to climb.

tres ➤ *adj & m* three ▪ las t. three o'clock.

treta ➤ *f* trick, ruse; SPORT. feint.

triángulo ➤ *m* triangle.

tribu ➤ *f* tribe.

tribuna ➤ *f* rostrum; SPORT. bleachers.

tribunal ➤ *m (lugar)* court; *(magistrados)* bench ▪ t. de menores juvenile court.

tributo ➤ *m* tribute; *(impuesto)* tax.

tríceps ➤ *adj & m* triceps.

triciclo ➤ *m* tricycle.

tricolor ➤ *adj* tricolor.

tridimensional ➤ *adj* three-dimensional.

trigo ➤ *m* wheat.

trillizo, a ➤ *adj* triple ▪ *mf* triplet.

trimestral ➤ *adj* quarterly.

trimestre ➤ *m (tres meses)* quarter; *(pago)* quarterly payment; *(revista)* quarterly.

trinchar ➤ *tr* to carve.

trinchera ➤ *f* MIL. trench.

trineo ➤ *m* sled, sleigh.

trío ➤ *m* trio.

tripa ➤ *f* intestine; *(panza)* belly, tummy ▪ *pl* innards.

triple ➤ *adj & m* triple.

trípode ➤ *m* tripod ▸ *adj* three-legged.

tripulación ➤ *f* crew.

tripulante ➤ *mf* crew member.

tripular ➤ *tr* AVIA., MARIT. to man.

triquiñuela ➤ *f* COLL. trick, ruse.

triste ➤ *adj* sad; *(melancólico)* melancholy, gloomy.

tristeza ➤ *f* sadness.

triturar ➤ *tr* to crush.

triunfador, a ➤ *adj* triumphant ▸ *mf* winner.

triunfar ➤ *intr* to win; FIG. to succeed.

triunfo ➤ *m* triumph; FIG. success.

trivial ➤ *adj* trivial.

triza ➤ *f* piece, shred ▪ hacer trizas to tear to pieces.

trocear ➤ *tr* to divide into pieces.

trofeo ➤ *m* trophy.

trole ➤ *m* trolley.

tromba ➤ *f* waterspout.

trombón ➤ *m* trombone.

trompa ➤ *f* MUS. horn; ZOOL. trunk.

trompeta ➤ *f* trumpet.

tronchar ➤ *tr (un árbol)* to fell; *(romper)* to split.

tronco ➤ *m* ANAT., BOT. trunk ▪ dormir como un t. COLL. to sleep like a log.

trono ➤ *m* throne.

tropa(s) ➤ *f(pl)* troops.

tropel ➤ *m* confusion ▪ en t. in a mad rush.

tropezar §17 ➤ *intr* to stumble, trip;

(cometer un error) to slip up ∎ t. con COLL. to bump into.

tropezón ➤ *m* stumble; *(desliz)* slip ∎ **a tropezones** by fits and starts.

tropical ➤ *adj* tropical.

trópico, a ➤ *adj* tropical ➤ *m* tropic ∎ t. de Cáncer, Capricornio Tropic of Cancer, Capricorn.

tropiezo ➤ *m (obstáculo)* stumbling block; *(traspiés)* stumble; *(desliz)* slip.

trozo ➤ *m* piece, chunk.

trucha ➤ *f* trout.

truco ➤ *m* trick.

trueno ➤ *m* thunder.

trufa ➤ *f* truffle.

tú ➤ *pron* you *(informal)*.

tu, tus ➤ *adj* your *(informal)*.

tubería ➤ *f (serie)* pipes; *(tubo)* pipe; *(instalación)* plumbing.

tubo ➤ *m* tube ∎ t. de desagüe drainpipe • t. de escape exhaust pipe.

tuerca ➤ *f* MECH. nut.

tufo ➤ *m* fume.

tulipán ➤ *m* tulip.

tullido, a ➤ *adj* crippled.

tumba ➤ *f* tomb, grave.

tumbar ➤ *tr (derribar)* to knock down; COMPUT. to crash ➤ *reflex* to lie down.

tumbona ➤ *f* deck chair.

tumor ➤ *m* tumor.

tumulto ➤ *m* tumult.

tunante ➤ *adj* crooked ➤ *mf* rascal.

túnel ➤ *m* tunnel.

túnica ➤ *f* tunic.

tupé ➤ *m* toupee.

tupido, a ➤ *adj* thick, dense.

turbar ➤ *tr* to upset; *(desconcertar)* to embarrass ➤ *reflex* to be upset.

turbiedad ➤ *f* muddiness.

turbina ➤ *f* turbine.

turbio, a ➤ *adj* muddy ➤ *mpl* sediment.

turbulencia ➤ *f* turbulence.

turbulento, a ➤ *adj* turbulent.

turismo ➤ *m* tourism.

turista ➤ *mf* tourist.

turístico, a ➤ *adj* tourist.

turnar ➤ *intr & reflex* to take turns.

turno ➤ *m (vez)* turn; *(de obreros)* shift ∎ t. on duty • t. de día *or* de noche day *or* night shift.

turquesa ➤ *f* turquoise.

turrón ➤ *m* nougat.

tutear ➤ *tr* to address as *tú*.

tutela ➤ *f (de personas)* guardianship; *(dirección)* guidance.

tuteo ➤ *m* addressing as *tú*.

tutor, a ➤ *mf* guardian.

tuyo, a ➤ *adj & pron* yours *(informal)* ∎ lo t. your affair • los tuyos your people • un pariente t. a relative of yours.

U

u ➤ *conj var of* o used before *(h)o*.

ubicación ➤ *f* location.

ubicar §47 ➤ *tr* AMER. to locate ➤ *reflex* to be located.

úlcera ➤ *f* ulcer.

últimamente ➤ *adv* ultimately; *(recientemente)* lately.

último, a ➤ *adj (final)* last; *(de dos)* latter; *(más reciente)* latest, most recent; *(mejor)* finest; *(definitivo)* last; COM. lowest ∎ estar a lo ú. to be nearly at the end of • por ú. lastly.

ultraje ➤ *m* insult, outrage.

ultramar ➤ *m* overseas country.

ultramarino ➤ *mpl* imported foods; *(tienda)* grocery store.

ultrasonido ➤ *m* ultrasound.

ultratumba ➤ *f* otherworld.

ultravioleta ➤ *adj* ultraviolet.

ulular ➤ *intr* to howl.

umbilical ➤ *adj* umbilical.

umbral ➤ *m* threshold.

un ➤ *contr of* uno.

unánime ➤ *adj* unanimous.

unanimidad ➤ *f* unanimity ∎ por u. unanimously.

undécimo, a ➤ *adj & m* eleventh.

único, a ➤ *adj (solo)* only, sole; *(sin igual)* unique ➤ *mf* only one ∎ lo ú. only thing.

unidad ➤ *f (acuerdo)* unity; *(armonía)* harmony; MATH., MIL., TECH. unit ∎ u. de disco COMPUT. disk drive.

unido, a ➤ *adj (juntos)* united, joined; *(familia)* close, tight.

unificar ➤ *tr* to unify.

uniforme ➤ *adj & m* uniform.

unilateral ➤ *adj* unilateral.

unión ➤ *f* union.

unir ➤ *tr* to unite ➤ *reflex* to join.

unísono ➤ *m* unison ■ al u. in unison.

universal ➤ *adj* universal.

universidad ➤ *f* university.

universitario, a ➤ *adj* university ➤ *mf* university student.

universo ➤ *m* universe.

uno, a ➤ *m* one ➤ *adj* one ■ la u. one o'clock • u. que otro a few ■ *pl* some, a few • u. diez horas about ten hours ➤ *indef pron* one, you; (*alguien*) somebody • cada u. each one, every one • u. a otro *or* con otro each other, one another • u. a *or* por u. one at a time • u. y otro both • u. tras otro one after another ■ *pl* u. a otros one another • u. cuantos a few, some ➤ *indef art* a, an.

untar ➤ *tr* (*engrasar*) to grease; (*manchar*) to smear; to spread; MED. to rub.

uña ➤ *f* fingernail; (*del pie*) toenail ■ comerse las uñas to bite one's nails.

urbanización ➤ *f* urbanization, city planning; (*desarrollo*) development.

urbano, a ➤ *adj* urban.

urbe ➤ *f* large city.

urgencia ➤ *f* urgency ■ con u. urgently.

urgente ➤ *adj* urgent.

urgir §19 ➤ *intr* to be urgent.

urna ➤ *f* urn; (*arca*) ballot box ■ acudir *or* ir a las urnas to go to the polls.

urraca ➤ *f* magpie.

urticaria ➤ *f* MED. hives.

uruguayo, a ➤ *adj & mf* Uruguayan.

usado, a ➤ *adj* (*deteriorado*) worn-out; (*de segunda mano*) secondhand.

usar ➤ *tr* (*emplear*) to use; (*ropa*) to wear ➤ *reflex* to be used.

uso ➤ *m* use; (*costumbre*) custom.

usted ➤ *pron* you (formal) ■ de u. yours • hablar *or* tratar de u. to use the polite form of address ■ *pl* you, all of you.

usual ➤ *adj* usual.

usuario, a ➤ *mf* user.

utensilio ➤ *m* utensil.

útil ➤ *adj* useful ➤ *m* tool, utensil ■ *pl* implements • ú. de pesca fishing tackle.

utilidad ➤ *f* usefulness.

utilizar §02 ➤ *tr* to utilize.

uva ➤ *f* grape ■ u. pasa raisin.

V

vaca ➤ *f* cow; CUL. beef.

vacaciones ➤ *fpl* ■ estar de v. to be on vacation.

vacante ➤ *adj* vacant ➤ *f* vacancy.

vaciar §18 ➤ *tr & reflex* to empty.

vacilación ➤ *f* hesitation.

vacilar ➤ *intr* to hesitate.

vacío, a ➤ *adj* empty; (*desocupado*) vacant; (*hueco*) hollow ➤ *m* emptiness; (*hueco*) hollow; PHYS. vacuum ■ envasado al v. vacuum-packed.

vacuna ➤ *f* vaccine.

vacunar ➤ *tr* to vaccinate.

vacuo, a ➤ *adj* vacuous, empty.

vadear ➤ *tr* (*un río*) to ford; (*a pie*) to wade across; FIG. to overcome.

vado ➤ *m* (*de un río*) ford.

vagabundo, a ➤ *adj & mf* vagabond.

vagar §31 ➤ *intr* to wander.

vago, a ➤ *adj* vague; (*holgazán*) lazy ➤ *m* loafer, idler.

vagón ➤ *m* RAIL. car, coach ■ v. cama sleeping car.

vaho ➤ *m* steam.

vaina ➤ *f* BOT. pod; (*molestia*) nuisance.

vainilla ➤ *f* vanilla.

vajilla ➤ *f* tableware.

vale ➤ *m* voucher; (*recibo*) receipt; (*bueno*) all right, OK.

valentía ➤ *f* bravery.

valer §50 ➤ *intr* to be of value; (*ser válido*) to be valid; (*servir*) to be useful ■ más vale it is better ➤ *tr* (*tener un valor de*) to be worth; (*costar*) to cost ■ v. la pena to be worthwhile ➤ *reflex* to manage for oneself ■ v. de to make use of ➤ *m* worth.

valeroso, a ➤ *adj* courageous, brave.

validación ➤ *f* validation.

validar ➤ *tr* to validate.

valiente ➤ *adj* courageous, brave.

valioso, a ➤ *adj* valuable.

valla ➤ *f* fence.

valle ➤ *m* valley.

valor ➤ *m* (*cualidad*) worth; (*precio*) price; (*importancia*) importance; (*coraje*) valor ■ *pl* COM. securities • v. inmuebles real estate.

valoración ➤ *f* appraisal.

vals ➤ *m* waltz.

válvula ➤ *f* valve; RAD. tube.

vampiro ➤ *m* vampire.

vandalismo ➤ *m* vandalism.

vanguardia ➤ *f* MIL. vanguard; ARTS, LIT. avant-garde.

vanidad ➤ *f* vanity.

vanidoso, a ➤ *adj* vain, conceited.

vano, a ➤ *adj* vain; *(frívolo)* frivolous; *(vanidoso)* conceited ∎ en v. in vain.

vapor ➤ *m (gas)* steam; *(vaho)* vapor; *(buque)* steamship ∎ al v. CUL. steamed.

vaporizador ➤ *m* vaporizer.

vaquero, a ➤ *m* cowboy *f* cowgirl.

vara ➤ *f (palo)* stick; *(rama)* rod; *(bastón)* staff.

variable ➤ *adj & f* variable.

variación ➤ *f* variation.

variado, a ➤ *adj* varied.

variante ➤ *adj* varying ➤ *f* variant.

variar §18 ➤ *tr & intr* to vary.

varicela ➤ *f* chicken pox.

variedad ➤ *f* variety ∎ *pl (cosas diversas)* miscellany; THEAT. variety show.

varilla ➤ *f* rod ∎ v. mágica magic wand.

vario, a ➤ *adj* varied; *(cambiadizo)* varying ∎ *pl* several ➤ *mf* ∎ *pl* several.

varón ➤ *m (hombre)* male; *(niño)* boy.

vasectomía ➤ *f* vasectomy.

vasija ➤ *f* container.

vaso ➤ *m* glass.

vasto, a ➤ *adj* vast, immense.

vaticinar ➤ *tr* to predict.

vatio ➤ *m* watt.

vecindad ➤ *f (vecindario)* neighbors; *(cercanías)* neighborhood, vicinity.

vecindario ➤ *m* neighborhood.

vecino, a ➤ *adj* next ➤ *mf* neighbor.

veda ➤ *f* prohibition; HUNT. closed season.

vedado, a ➤ *adj* prohibited ➤ *m* game preserve.

vegetación ➤ *f* vegetation.

vegetal ➤ *adj & m* vegetable.

vegetariano, a ➤ *adj & mf* vegetarian.

vehemente ➤ *adj* vehement.

vehículo ➤ *m* vehicle; MED. carrier.

veinte ➤ *adj & m* twenty.

vejez ➤ *f* old age.

vejiga ➤ *f* ANAT. bladder.

vela[1] ➤ *f (vigilia)* vigil; *(luz)* candle ∎ en v. awake.

vela[2] ➤ *f* MARIT. sail ∎ barco de v. sailboat.

velar ➤ *tr* to keep watch over ➤ *intr* to stay awake ➤ *reflex* PHOTOG. to blur.

velero ➤ *m* sailboat.

veleta ➤ *f* weather vane.

vello ➤ *m (pelo)* hair; *(pelusilla)* fuzz.

velo ➤ *m* veil.

velocidad ➤ *f* velocity, speed; AUTO. gear ∎ v. máxima *or* límite de v. speed limit.

velocímetro ➤ *m* speedometer.

veloz ➤ *adj* swift.

vena ➤ *f* vein.

venado ➤ *m* stag, deer; CUL. venison.

vencedor, a ➤ *adj* winning ➤ *mf* winner.

vencer §51 ➤ *tr* to defeat; *(aventajar)* to overcome ➤ *intr (ganar)* to win; COM. *(cumplirse un plazo)* to expire; *(una deuda)* to fall due.

vencido, a ➤ *adj* defeated; COM. *(una deuda)* due; *(cumplido)* expired.

venda ➤ *f or* **vendaje** ➤ *m* bandage.

vendar ➤ *tr* to bandage.

vendaval ➤ *m* gale.

vendedor, a ➤ *mf* vendor, seller; *(de tienda)* salesperson.

vender ➤ *tr & reflex* to sell ∎ se vende for sale.

vendimia ➤ *f* grape harvest.

veneno ➤ *m* poison.

venenoso, a ➤ *adj* poisonous.

venezolano, a ➤ *adj & mf* Venezuelan.

venganza ➤ *f* vengeance.

vengar §31 ➤ *tr & reflex* to avenge (oneself) ∎ v. de alguien to take revenge on someone.

venir §52 ➤ *intr* to come; *(llegar)* to arrive; *(ropa)* to fit ∎ el año que viene next year ➤ *reflex* ∎ v. abajo *or* por tierra *or* al suelo to collapse, fall down.

venta ➤ *f* sale.

ventaja ➤ *f* advantage; *(en una carrera)* head start, lead.

ventana ➤ *f* window.

ventanal ➤ *m* large window.

ventanilla ➤ *f (de vehículo)* window; *(taquilla)* box office.
ventilación ➤ *f* ventilation.
ventilador ➤ *m* fan.
ventilar ➤ *tr (un lugar)* to air out.
ventisca ➤ *f* blizzard.
ventolera ➤ *f* gust of wind.
ver §53 ➤ *tr* to see; *(mirar)* to look at; *(televisión, películas)* to watch; *(visitar)* to visit; *(examinar)* to examine; *(observar)* to observe ■ a v. let's see ▪ tener que v. con to have to do with • veremos we'll see ➤ *reflex (ser visto)* to be seen; *(ser obvio)* to be obvious or clear; *(visitarse)* to see one another; *(encontrarse)* to meet ▪ estar por v. to remain to be seen • véase see.
veracidad ➤ *f* veracity.
veraneante ➤ *mf* summer resident.
veranear ➤ *intr* to spend the summer.
veraneo ➤ *m* vacationing ■ ir de v. to go on vacation • lugar de v. summer resort.
veraniego, a ➤ *adj (del verano)* summer; *(ligero)* light, flimsy.
verano ➤ *m* summer.
verbo ➤ *m* GRAM. verb.
verdad ➤ *f* truth; *(veracidad)* truthfulness ■ de v. truly; *(verdadero)* real • ¿de v.? really? • ¿v.? is that so?
verdadero, a ➤ *adj* true, real.
verde ➤ *adj* green; *(inmaduro)* unripe; ➤ *m* green.
verdura ➤ *f (legumbre)* vegetable; *(follaje)* greenery.
vereda ➤ *f* trail, path; AMER. sidewalk.
veredicto ➤ *m* verdict.
vergonzoso, a ➤ *adj* shameful; *(tímido)* shy ➤ *mf* shy person.
vergüenza ➤ *f* shame; *(timidez)* shyness ■ darle v. a uno to embarrass • tener v. to be ashamed.
verificar §47 ➤ *tr (la verdad)* to verify; *(una máquina)* to check.
verja ➤ *f (de cerca)* railings; *(de ventana)* grating.
vermut or **vermú** ➤ *m* vermouth.
verosímil ➤ *adj* probable.
verruga ➤ *f* wart.
versión ➤ *f* version.
verso ➤ *m* verse.

vértebra ➤ *f* vertebra.
vertebrado, a ➤ *adj & m* vertebrate.
vertedero ➤ *m (desaguadero)* drain; *(de basura)* garbage dump.
verter §34 ➤ *tr (derramar)* to spill; *(lágrimas, sangre)* to shed; *(vaciar)* to empty out ➤ *intr* to flow.
vertical ➤ *adj & f* vertical.
vértice ➤ *m* apex.
vertiente ➤ *f (declive)* slope; *(manantial)* spring.
vertiginoso, a ➤ *adj* dizzying, giddy.
vértigo ➤ *m* vertigo ■ tener v. to feel dizzy.
vestíbulo ➤ *m* vestibule; THEAT. lobby.
vestido ➤ *m* dress ■ v. de noche evening gown.
vestigio ➤ *m* vestige.
vestir §32 ➤ *tr* to dress; *(llevar)* to wear ➤ *intr (ir vestido)* to dress ➤ *reflex* to get dressed; *(ir vestido)* to dress.
vestuario ➤ *m* wardrobe; *(cuarto)* dressing room; SPORT. locker room.
veterano, a ➤ *adj & mf* veteran.
veterinario, a ➤ *adj* veterinary ➤ *mf* veterinarian ➤ *f* veterinary medicine.
veto ➤ *m* veto ■ poner el v. a to veto.
vez ➤ *f* time; *(turno)* turn ■ a la v. at the same time • algunas veces sometimes • a veces at times • cada v. every time • cada v. que whenever • de una v. all at once • de v. en cuando from time to time • en v. de instead of • muchas veces often • otra v. again • tal v. perhaps.
vía ➤ *f (camino)* road; *(ruta)* route; RAIL. *(carril)* track ■ en vías de in the process of • v. aérea airway.
viajar ➤ *intr* to travel.
viaje ➤ *m* trip ■ ¡buen v.! bon voyage! • ir de v. to go on a trip • v. de ida y vuelta round trip.
viajero, a ➤ *adj* traveling ➤ *mf* traveler.
víbora ➤ *f* viper.
vibración ➤ *f* vibration.
vibrar ➤ *intr* to vibrate.
vicepresidente, a ➤ *mf* vice president; *(en reunión)* vice chairman/woman.
viceversa ➤ *adv* vice versa.
vicio ➤ *m* vice; *(fumar, etc.)* bad habit.
vicioso, a ➤ *adj* depraved.

víctima ➤ *f* victim.

victoria ➤ *f* victory; *(éxito)* success.

vid ➤ *f* grapevine.

vida ➤ *f* life; *(duración)* lifetime; *(sustento)* living ■ así es la v. such is life.

video *or* **vídeo** ➤ *m* video ■ v. juego video game.

videocámara ➤ *f* videocamera, camcorder.

videocasete ➤ *m* videocassette.

vidriera ➤ *f* window; *(de colores)* stained-glass window.

vidrio ➤ *m* glass.

viejo, a ➤ *adj* old ➤ *m* old man ■ *pl* old folks ➤ *f* old woman.

viento ➤ *m* wind ■ hacer v. to be windy.

vientre ➤ *m (abdomen)* belly; *(matriz)* womb; *(intestino)* bowels.

viernes ➤ *m* Friday.

viga ➤ *f (madero)* beam; *(de metal)* girder ■ v. transversal crossbeam.

vigencia ➤ *f* force ■ en v. in force.

vigésimo, a ➤ *adj & m* twentieth.

vigilante ➤ *mf* guard, watchman.

vigilar ➤ *tr* to watch over.

vigor ➤ *m* vigor ■ en v. in force or effect.

vil ➤ *adj* vile, base.

villa ➤ *f (pueblo)* village; *(casa)* villa.

vinagre ➤ *m* vinegar.

vinagrera ➤ *f* vinegar bottle ■ *pl* cruets.

vinagreta ➤ *f* vinaigrette.

vinatero, a ➤ *mf* wine merchant.

vínculo ➤ *m* link.

vino ➤ *m* wine ■ v. tinto red wine.

viña ➤ *f or* **viñedo** ➤ *m* vineyard.

viñeta ➤ *f* vignette.

violación ➤ *f* violation; *(sexualmente)* rape.

violar ➤ *tr* to violate; *(sexualmente)* to rape.

violencia ➤ *f* violence.

violento, a ➤ *adj* violent.

violeta ➤ *f & adj* violet.

violín ➤ *m* violin ➤ *mf* violinist.

violinista ➤ *mf* violinist.

violón ➤ *m* double bass, bass viol ➤ *mf* double bass player.

violonc(h)elo ➤ *m* cello.

virar ➤ *tr* MARIT. *(de rumbo)* to turn ➤ *intr* to swerve.

viril ➤ *adj* virile.

virtud ➤ *f* virtue; *(eficacia)* ability.

virtuoso, a ➤ *adj* virtuous ➤ *mf* virtuoso.

viruela ➤ *f* smallpox.

virus ➤ *m* virus.

visa ➤ *f* AMER. visa.

visera ➤ *f* visor.

visibilidad ➤ *f* visibility.

visible ➤ *adj* visible; COLL. decent.

visillo ➤ *m* window curtain.

visión ➤ *f* vision; *(vista)* eyesight.

visita ➤ *f* visit; *(persona)* visitor ■ hacer una v. or ir de v. to pay a visit.

visitar ➤ *tr & reflex* to visit (one another).

vislumbrar ➤ *tr* to glimpse.

visón ➤ *m* mink.

víspera ➤ *f* eve ■ en v. de on the eve of ■ *pl* RELIG. vespers.

vistazo ➤ *m* glance ■ dar un v. a to take a glance at.

visto, a ➤ *adj* ■ bien, mal v. proper, improper • por lo v. apparently ➤ *f (visión)* sight; *(buena, mala)* eyesight; *(panorama)* view; *(cuadro)* scene; *(vistazo)* look, glance ■ corto de v. nearsighted ■ hasta la v. so long.

vistoso, a ➤ *adj* colorful.

vitalicio, a ➤ *adj* life ■ miembro v. member for life.

vitalidad ➤ *f* vitality.

vitamina ➤ *f* vitamin.

vitorear ➤ *tr* to cheer.

vítreo, a ➤ *adj* vitreous.

vitrina ➤ *f (caja)* display case; *(de tienda)* window.

viudo, a ➤ *m* widower ➤ *f* widow.

vivaracho, a ➤ *adj* COLL. lively.

vivaz ➤ *adj* quick-witted; BOT. perennial.

víveres ➤ *mpl* provisions.

vivero ➤ *m* BOT. nursery; *(de peces)* fish hatchery; *(de moluscos)* farm.

vivienda ➤ *f* housing; *(casa)* house.

vivir ➤ *intr* to live ■ ¡viva! hurrah! ➤ *tr* to live; *(experimentar)* to go through.

vivo, a ➤ *adj (con vida)* alive; *(brillante)* vivid; *(listo)* sharp ■ al rojo v. red-hot • en v. TELEC. live.

vocabulario ➤ *m* vocabulary.

vocación ➤ *f* vocation.

vocal ➤ *adj* vocal ➤ *mf* board *or* committee member ➤ *f* vowel.

vocalista ➤ *mf* vocalist.

vocero, a ➤ *mf* spokesman/woman.

vociferar ➤ *tr & intr* to shout.

volante ➤ *adj* flying ➤ *m* AUTO. steering wheel; *(papel)* flier; *(juego)* badminton.

volar §11 ➤ *intr* to fly; *(irse volando)* to fly away; *(desaparecer)* to disappear; *(divulgarse)* to spread quickly ➤ *tr* to blow up.

volcán ➤ *m* volcano.

volcar ➤ *tr* to dump ➤ *intr* to overturn ➤ *reflex (derribarse)* to tip over; *(entregarse)* to do one's utmost.

voltaje ➤ *m* voltage.

voltear ➤ *tr* to turn over; *(dar la vuelta)* to turn around.

voltio ➤ *m* volt.

volumen ➤ *m* volume.

voluminoso, a ➤ *adj* voluminous.

voluntad ➤ *f (facultad)* will; *(firmeza)* willpower ■ fuerza de v. willpower.

voluntario, a ➤ *adj* voluntary ➤ *mf* volunteer.

volver §54 ➤ *tr* to turn; *(dar vuelta)* to turn around; *(colchón, etc.)* to turn over; *(prenda)* to turn inside out; *(al propio sitio)* to return; *(restablecer)* to restore ■ v. la espalda a alguien to turn one's back on someone ➤ *intr* to return; *(reanudar)* to get back ■ v. a to . . . again ➤ *reflex (darse vuelta)* to turn around; *(hacerse)* to become ■ v. atrás *(desdecirse)* to back down; *(no cumplir)* to back out • v. loco to go crazy.

vomitar ➤ *tr* to vomit; *(decir)* to spew; *(un secreto)* to spill ➤ *intr* to vomit.

vómito ➤ *m* vomit.

voraz ➤ *adj* voracious.

vos ➤ *pron* you, thou, ye; S. AMER. you (singular, informal).

vosotros, as ➤ *pron* you, yourselves (plural, informal).

votación ➤ *f* voting; *(voto)* vote.

votante ➤ *adj* voting ➤ *mf* voter.

votar ➤ *intr* to vote; RELIG. to make a vow ➤ *tr* to vote.

voto ➤ *m* vote.

voz ➤ *f* voice; *(rumor)* rumor ■ a media v. in a low voice • a una v. unanimously • a voces shouting • dar voces to shout • en v. alta *(al leer)* aloud; *(a gritos)* in a loud voice • tener la v. ronca to be hoarse.

vuelo ➤ *m* flight.

vuelta ➤ *f (giro)* turn; *(regreso)* return; *(repetición)* recurrence; SPORT. lap ■ a la v. on the way back • a la v. de la esquina around the corner • a v. de correo by return mail ■ dar una v. to take a walk • de ida y v. round-trip • estar de v. to be back.

vuestro, a ➤ *poss adj* [informal] *(su)* your; *(suyo)* (of) yours ■ los vuestros *or* las vuestras yours.

vulgar ➤ *adj* common; *(grosero)* vulgar.

vulgaridad ➤ *f* vulgarity.

vulnerable ➤ *adj* vulnerable.

W

wat ➤ *m* watt.

web ➤ *m or f* COMPUT. Web.

whisky ➤ *m* whiskey.

X

xenofobia ➤ *f* xenophobia.

xilófono ➤ *m* xylophone.

Y

y ➤ *conj* and ■ ¿y bien? and then? • y eso que even though • ¿y qué? so what?

ya ■ *adv (finalmente)* already; *(ahora)* now; *(pronto)* soon; *(en seguida)* right away; *(por último)* now ■ ya no no longer • ya que since ➤ *conj* now, at times ➤ *interj* I see!

yacer ➤ *intr* to lie.

yacimiento ➤ *m* GEOL. deposit y. petrolífero oil field.

yarda ➤ *f* yard.

yate ➤ *m* yacht.

yegua ➤ *f* mare.

yema ➤ *f* yolk; BOT. bud ■ y. del dedo finger tip.

yerba ➤ *f* grass; *(droga)* marijuana.

yermo, a ➤ *adj* barren ➤ *m* desert.

yerno ➤ *m* son-in-law.

yeso ➤ *m* GEOL. gypsum; ARTS, CONSTR. plaster; ARTS, MED. plaster cast.

yo ➤ *pron* I ∎ **soy yo** it's I *or* me • **yo mismo** I myself ➤ *m* ego.
yodo ➤ *m* iodine.
yoga ➤ *m* yoga.
yogur(t) ➤ *m* yogurt.
yuca ➤ *f* AMER., CUL. manioc; BOT. yucca.
yugo ➤ *m* *(arreo)* yoke; *(opresión)* oppression; *(carga pesada)* burden; MARIT. transom.
yugular ➤ *adj & f* jugular.

Z

zafar ➤ *tr reflex* to escape *(de* from).
zaguán ➤ *m* front hall, vestibule.
zalamería ➤ *f* flattery.
zalamero, a ➤ *adj* flattering ➤ *mf* flatterer.
zamarra ➤ *f* sheepskin; *(chaqueta)* sheepskin jacket.
zambo, a ➤ *adj & mf* bowlegged (person).
zambullir ➤ *reflex* (*en el agua)* to dive; *(esconderse)* to duck out of sight.
zanahoria ➤ *f* carrot.
zancada ➤ *f* stride.
zancadilla ➤ *f* *(caida)* tripping; COLL. *(engaño)* trick; *(trampa)* trap.
zanco ➤ *m* stilt.
zancón, ona ➤ *adj* COLL. long-legged.
zancudo, a ➤ *adj* long-legged; ORNITH. wading ➤ *fpl* wading birds ➤ *m* AMER. mosquito.
zanja ➤ *f* ditch, trench.
zapatear ➤ *tr* *(golpear)* to hit with the shoe; *(bailar)* to tap-dance ➤ *intr* to tap one's feet.
zapatería ➤ *f* shoe store.
zapatero, a ➤ *mf* shoemaker, cobbler; *(venta)* shoe seller.
zapatilla ➤ *f* *(pantufla)* slipper; *(de baile)* dancing shoe.
zapato ➤ *m* shoe.
zar ➤ *m* czar.
zarandear ➤ *tr* to shake ➤ *reflex* to be on the go.
zarcillo ➤ *m* earring; BOT. tendril.
zarina ➤ *f* czarina.
zarpa ➤ *f* claw, paw.
zarpar ➤ *tr* to weigh ➤ *intr* to set sail.
zarpazo ➤ *m* scratch, lash of a paw.
zarza ➤ *f* bramble.
zarzamora ➤ *f* blackberry.
zarzuela ➤ *f* Spanish comic opera.
zenit ➤ *m* zenith.
zigzag ➤ *m* zigzag.
zócalo ➤ *m* *(de pared)* baseboard; ARCHIT. plinth; AMER. public square.
zodiaco ➤ *m* zodiac.
zona ➤ *f* zone; *(distrito)* district.
zonificar §47 ➤ *tr* to zone.
zoo ➤ *m* zoo.
zoológico, a ➤ *adj* zoological ∎ **jardín z.** zoo.
zoom ➤ *m* zoom lens.
zopilote ➤ *m* buzzard.
zoquete ➤ *m* chunk of wood; *(tonto)* dummy, blockhead.
zorra ➤ *f* fox; *(hembra)* vixen.
zorro ➤ *m* fox.
zozobra ➤ *f* capsizing, sinking.
zueco ➤ *m* clog, wooden shoe.
zumbar ➤ *intr* *(un insecto)* to buzz; *(los oídos)* to ring.
zumbido ➤ *m* *(de insecto)* buzzing; *(de los oídos)* ringing.
zumo ➤ *m* juice.
zurdo, a ➤ *adj & mf* left-handed (person).
zurra ➤ *f* tanning; *(paliza)* thrashing.
zurrar ➤ *tr* to tan; *(pegar)* to beat, thrash.

Inglés/Español

A

a ➤ *art indef* un, una ∎ **a cat** un gato.

aback ➤ *adv* ∎ **to be taken a.** quedar desconcertado.

abandon ➤ *tr* abandonar; *(to desert)* desertar, dejar.

abbey ➤ *s* abadía, convento.

abbreviation ➤ *s (act)* abreviación *f*; *(form)* abreviatura.

abdomen ➤ *s* abdomen *m*, vientre *m*.

abide◇ ➤ *tr* tolerar, soportar ➤ *intr* permanecer, continuar ∎ **to a. by** cumplir con, acatar.

ability ➤ *s (skill)* capacidad *f*, habilidad *f*; *(talent)* aptitud *f*; *(power)* facultad *f*.

able ➤ *adj* capaz, hábil ∎ **to be a. to** poder, ser capaz (de).

abnormal ➤ *adj* anormal.

abnormality ➤ *s* anormalidad *f*.

aboard ➤ *adv & prep* a bordo (de) ∎ **all a.!** ¡pasajeros al tren!

abolish ➤ *tr* abolir, eliminar.

abolition ➤ *s* abolición *f*.

abortion ➤ *s* aborto.

about ➤ *prep (concerning)* acerca de, sobre; *(with regard to)* con respecto a ∎ **a. two o'clock** alrededor de las dos • **to be a. to** estar al punto de ➤ *adv* casi.

above ➤ *adv* encima; *(in a text)* más arriba ∎ **a. all** sobre todo • **from a.** desde lo alto ➤ *prep (over)* sobre, por encima de; *(greater than)* superior a.

abreast ➤ *adv* en una línea ∎ **to keep a. of** mantenerse al corriente de.

abroad ➤ *adv* en el extranjero ∎ **to go a.** ir al extranjero.

abrupt ➤ *adj (curt)* brusco; *(sudden)* repentino.

abscess ➤ *s* absceso.

absence ➤ *s* ausencia, falta.

absent ➤ *adj* ausente; *(lacking)* que falta; *(distracted)* abstraído ➤ *tr* ∎ **to a. oneself from** ausentarse de.

absent-minded ➤ *adj* distraído.

absolute ➤ *adj* absoluto; *(unconditional)* total.

absorb ➤ *tr* absorber; *(shock)* amortiguar.

abstinence ➤ *s* abstinencia.

abstract ➤ *adj* abstracto.

absurd ➤ *adj* absurdo, ridículo.

abundant ➤ *adj* abundante.

abuse ➤ *tr* abusar de; *(to hurt)* maltratar; *(to berate)* insultar ➤ *s* abuso; *(injury)* maltrato; *(sexual)* violación *f*.

abusive ➤ *adj (abusing)* abusivo; *(insulting)* injurioso, insultante.

abyss ➤ *s* abismo.

academic ➤ *adj* académico, universitario ➤ *s* catedrático/a.

academy ➤ *s* academia.

accelerate ➤ *tr* acelerar.

accelerator ➤ *s* acelerador *m*.

accent ➤ *s* acento.

accept ➤ *tr* aceptar; *(to admit)* admitir.

acceptable ➤ *adj* aceptable, admisible.

access ➤ *s* acceso, entrada.

accessible ➤ *adj* accesible.

accessory ➤ *s* accesorio; DER. cómplice *mf* ➤ *adj* accesorio, adjunto.

accident ➤ *s* accidente *m*; *(chance)* casualidad *f* ∎ **by a.** por casualidad.

accommodate ➤ *tr* hacer un favor a, complacer ➤ *intr* adaptarse.

accommodations ➤ *spl* alojamiento.

accompany ➤ *tr & intr* acompañar(se).

accomplice ➤ *s* cómplice *mf*.

accomplish ➤ *tr* lograr, realizar.

accord ➤ *s* acuerdo, convenio ∎ **in a. with** de acuerdo con • **of one's own a.** de propia voluntad.

accordance ➤ *s* acuerdo *f*, conformidad *f* ∎ **in a. with** de conformidad con.

according to ➤ *prep* conforme a, según.

accordion ➤ *s* acordeón *m*.

account ➤ *s (report)* relato, informe *m*; *(explanation)* explicación *f*, motivo; COM. cuenta ∎ **to give an a. of** *(oneself)* dar buena cuenta de (sí) • **to take into a.** tomar en cuenta ➤ *intr* ∎ **to a. for** dar razón de.

accountant ➤ *s* contador/a, contable *mf*.

accumulate ➤ *tr & intr* acumular(se), amontonar(se).

accuracy ➤ *s* exactitud *f*, precisión *f*.

accurate ➤ *adj* exacto, preciso.

accuse ➤ *tr* acusar.

accustom ➤ *tr* acostumbrar *(to a)*.

accustomed ➤ *adj* acostumbrado, habitual ∎ a. to acostumbrado a.

ace ➤ *s* as *m.*

ache ➤ *intr* doler ∎ to a. for anhelar, ansiar ➤ *s* dolor *m.*

achieve ➤ *tr* llevar a cabo, lograr.

achievement ➤ *s* logro, hazaña.

acid ➤ *s & adj* ácido.

acknowledge ➤ *tr* admitir; *(to recognize)* reconocer; *(a gift)* agradecer ∎ to a. receipt of acusar recibo de.

acne ➤ *s* acné *m.*

acorn ➤ *s* bellota.

acoustic(al) ➤ *adj* acústico ∎ acoustics *ssg* acústica.

acquaint ➤ *tr* familiarizar, poner al corriente ∎ to be acquainted conocerse • to be acquainted with conocer, estar al corriente de.

acquaintance ➤ *s (knowledge)* conocimiento; *(person)* conocido/a.

acquire ➤ *tr* adquirir, obtener.

acre ➤ *s* acre *m.*

acrobatic ➤ *adj* acrobático.

acronym ➤ *s* siglas.

across ➤ *prep (through)* por, a través de; *(on the other side of)* al *o* en el otro lado de ➤ *adv (on the other side)* a través, del otro lado; *(crosswise)* en cruz ∎ to be ten feet a. tener diez pies de ancho • to come *o* run a. encontrarse con • to go a. atravesar, cruzar.

acrylic ➤ *adj* acrílico.

act ➤ *intr* actuar, hacer algo; *(to behave)* conducirse, comportarse; *(to perform)* hacer un papel, actuar ∎ to a. like *o* as if hacer como que • to a. on *o* upon influir en, obrar sobre ➤ *tr* representar, hacer el papel de ➤ *s* acto, hecho; TEAT. acto; *(a law)* ley *f,* decreto.

action ➤ *s* acción *f; (act)* acto, hecho; *(motion)* movimiento; *(activity)* actividad *f; (effect)* influencia, efecto ∎ to put out of a. inutilizar • to take a. tomar medidas ∎ *pl* conducta.

activate ➤ *tr* activar, agitar.

active ➤ *adj* activo, en movimiento; *(energetic)* enérgico, vigoroso.

activity ➤ *s* actividad *f.*

actor ➤ *s* actor/a.

actress ➤ *s* actriz *f.*

actual ➤ *adj* real, verdadero.

actually ➤ *adv* en realidad.

acute ➤ *adj* agudo; *(sensitive)* sagaz, perspicaz; *(critical)* grave.

ad ➤ *s* FAM. anuncio, publicidad *f.*

adage ➤ *s* adagio, proverbio.

adapt ➤ *tr & intr* adaptar(se).

adaptable ➤ *adj* adaptable.

adaptation ➤ *s* adaptación *f.*

adapter ➤ *s* adaptador *m.*

add ➤ *tr* añadir, agregar; MAT. sumar ∎ to a. up sumar.

addict ➤ *tr* ∎ addicted to adicto a; FAM. entregado a ➤ *s* adicto/a; FAM. fanático/a.

addiction ➤ *s* vicio; FAM. afición *f.*

addictive ➤ *adj* que forma hábito.

addition ➤ *s* adición *f;* MAT. suma ∎ in a. además, también.

additional ➤ *adj* adicional.

additive ➤ *adj & s* aditivo.

address ➤ *s (postal)* dirección *f,* señas; *(lecture)* discurso ∎ home a. (dirección de) domicilio ➤ *tr (a person)* dirigirse a; *(a group)* dar un discurso a; *(a letter)* dirigir.

adequate ➤ *adj* adecuado.

adhesion ➤ *s* adhesión *f.*

adhesive ➤ *adj & s* adhesivo.

adjective ➤ *s* adjetivo.

adjoining ➤ *adj* contiguo.

adjust ➤ *tr* ajustar; *(to fix)* arreglar; *(to adapt)* adaptar ➤ *intr* ajustarse.

adjustable ➤ *adj* ajustable.

adjustment ➤ *s* ajuste *m; (fixing)* arreglo; COM. liquidación *f* (de una cuenta).

administer ➤ *tr* administrar; *(to manage)* dirigir, manejar.

administration ➤ *s* administración *f,* manejo; POL. gobierno.

admiral ➤ *s* almirante *mf.*

admiration ➤ *s* admiración *f.*

admire ➤ *tr* admirar.

admission ➤ *s* admisión *f; (fee)* entrada; *(acceptance)* ingreso (al foro, universidad).

admit ➤ *tr (to let in)* admitir, dar

entrada a; *(to confess)* confesar.
admittance ➤ s acceso, entrada.
adolescent ➤ s & adj adolescente mf.
adopt ➤ tr adoptar.
adopted ➤ adj *(a child)* adoptivo; *(assumed)* adoptado.
adoption ➤ s adopción f.
adorable ➤ adj adorable.
adore ➤ tr adorar.
adult ➤ s adulto/a ■ pl mayores.
adulthood ➤ s edad adulta.
advance ➤ tr avanzar, adelantar; *(to propose)* proponer ➤ intr avanzar; *(to improve)* hacer progresos ➤ s avance m, adelanto; *(progress)* progreso ➤ adj adelantado, anticipado.
advanced ➤ adj *(in level, degree)* avanzado, superior; *(in time, ability)* adelantado.
advantage ➤ s ventaja ■ to take a. of *(to make use of)* aprovechar, valerse de.
adventure ➤ s aventura.
adventurous ➤ adj aventurero.
adverb ➤ s adverbio.
adversity ➤ s adversidad f.
advertise ➤ tr anunciar ■ to a. for buscar por medio de avisos ➤ intr hacer publicidad.
advertisement ➤ s anuncio, publicidad f.
advice ➤ s consejo.
advisable ➤ adj prudente.
advise ➤ tr dar consejo a, aconsejar.
adviser ➤ s consejero/a, asesor/a.
aerial ➤ s antena.
aerie ➤ s aguilera.
aerobic ➤ adj aeróbico.
aerosol ➤ s aerosol m.
affair ➤ s *(business)* asunto; *(liaison)* amorío.
affect[1] ➤ tr afectar, influir en.
affect[2] ➤ tr fingir, simular.
affection ➤ s afecto, cariño.
affectionate ➤ adj afectuoso, cariñoso.
affinity ➤ s afinidad f, semejanza.
affirm ➤ tr afirmar, aseverar.
affix ➤ tr pegar, adherir.
afflict ➤ tr afligir, acongojar ■ to be afflicted with padecer de, sufrir de.
affluence ➤ s riqueza, opulencia.
affluent ➤ adj rico, opulento.

afford ➤ tr *(to spare)* poder disponer de; *(to risk)* afrontar.
affordable ➤ adj que se puede comprar o dar.
affront ➤ tr afrentar, insultar ➤ s afrenta, insulto.
afloat ➤ adj & adv a flote, flotando.
afraid ➤ adj asustado, atemorizado ■ to be a. (of) tener miedo (de o a) • to be a. that temer que.
Africa ➤ s África.
African ➤ adj & s africano/a.
African-American ➤ adj & s afroamericano/a.
after ➤ prep *(in place, order)* después de, detrás de; *(in time)* después de; *(in pursuit of)* en pos, tras; *(at the end of)* al cabo de ■ a. all al fin y al cabo • day a. day día tras día ➤ conj después (de) que ➤ adv después; *(behind)* atrás.
aftereffect ➤ s consecuencia.
afternoon ➤ s tarde f ■ good a.! ¡buenas tardes!
afterward(s) ➤ adv después, luego.
again ➤ adv otra vez, de nuevo ■ a. and a. una y otra vez • and then a. por otra parte • as much a. otro tanto más • never a. nunca más • now and a. de vez en cuando.
against ➤ prep contra.
age ➤ s edad f; *(era)* época, era ■ middle a. edad mediana • of a. mayor de edad • old a. vejez • under a. menor de edad ➤ tr & intr envejecer(se).
agency ➤ s *(means)* medio; *(business)* agencia; POL. ministerio.
agenda ➤ s agenda, temario.
agent ➤ s agente mf, representante mf.
aggravate ➤ tr *(to worsen)* agravar, empeorar; *(to annoy)* irritar.
aggression ➤ s agresión f.
aggressive ➤ adj agresivo.
agile ➤ adj ágil, ligero.
agility ➤ s agilidad f, ligereza.
aging ➤ s añejamiento.
agitated ➤ adj agitado, inquieto.
ago ➤ adj & adv hace ■ how long a.? ¿cuánto tiempo hace? • two years a. hace dos años.
agony ➤ s *(pain)* dolor m, tortura; *(anguish)* angustia, tormento.

agree ➤ *intr (to consent)* consentir, acceder a; *(to concur)* estar de acuerdo, coincidir; *(to match)* corresponder a; GRAM. concordar ■ **don't you a.?** ¿no le parece? • **to a. on** ponerse de acuerdo con • **to a. that** quedar en • **to a. with** one sentarle bien.

agreeable ➤ *adj (pleasant)* agradable; *(willing to agree)* complaciente.

agreed ➤ *adj* convenido, entendido.

agreement ➤ *s (accord)* conformidad *f; (contract)* acuerdo, pacto ■ **in a. with** de acuerdo con • **to enter into an a.** firmar un contrato.

agricultural ➤ *adj* agrícola.

agriculture ➤ *s* agricultura.

ahead ➤ *adv* delante, al frente, adelante; *(in advance)* por adelantado ■ **a. of** antes que • **go a.!** ¡adelante! • **to be a. of** llevar ventaja a • **to get a.** progresar.

aid ➤ *tr & intr* ayudar ➤ *s* ayuda, auxilio ■ **first a.** primeros auxilios.

AIDS ➤ *s* SIDA.

ailment ➤ *s* dolencia, enfermedad *f.*

aim ➤ *tr (a weapon)* apuntar ➤ *intr (to aspire)* aspirar ➤ *s (of a weapon)* puntería; *(goal)* meta.

air ➤ *s* aire *m* ■ **a. conditioning** aire acondicionado • **a. letter** carta aérea ➤ *tr* orear, ventilar.

aircraft ➤ *s* nave aérea ■ **a. carrier** portaaviones.

airfare ➤ *s* tarifa aérea.

airfield ➤ *s* campo de aviación.

airlift ➤ *s* puente aéreo ➤ *tr* transportar por vía aérea.

airline ➤ *s* aerolínea.

airliner ➤ *s* avión *m* de pasajeros.

airmail ➤ *s* ■ **by a.** por vía aérea.

airplane ➤ *s* avión *m,* aeroplano.

airport ➤ *s* aeropuerto, aeródromo.

airsick ➤ *adj* mareado (en avión).

airtight ➤ *adj* hermético.

aisle ➤ *s* pasillo; *(of church)* nave *f.*

ajar ➤ *adv & adj* entreabierto.

alarm ➤ *s* alarma, temor *m* ■ **a. clock** despertador ➤ *tr* alarmar.

album ➤ *s* álbum *m; (record)* elepé *m.*

alcohol ➤ *s* alcohol *m.*

alcoholic ➤ *adj & s* alcohólico/a.

alert ➤ *adj* alerta ➤ *s* alarma ■ **to be on**

the a. estar sobre aviso ➤ *tr (to warn)* alertar; *(to inform)* poner sobre aviso.

algebra ➤ *s* álgebra.

alias ➤ *s* alias *m.*

alibi ➤ *s* DER. coartada, alibí *m.*

alien ➤ *adj (foreign)* extranjero; *(unfamiliar)* extraño ➤ *s* extranjero/a; CIENC. FIC. ser *m* de otro planeta.

alight ➤ *intr (bird)* posarse; *(from a vehicle)* bajar, apearse.

alike ➤ *adj* semejante, parecido ➤ *adv* igualmente, de la misma manera.

alive ➤ *adj* vivo ■ **to come a.** FIG. cobrar vida.

all ➤ *adj* todo ➤ *pron* todo(s), todo el mundo ■ **above a.** sobre todo • **after a.** al fin y al cabo • **a. in a.** en resumen • **not at a.** en absoluto; *(you're welcome)* no hay de qué ➤ *s* todo ■ **that's a.** eso es todo ➤ *adv* completamente ■ **a. along** siempre • **a. around** por todas partes • **a. at once** de repente • **a. but** casi • **a. of a sudden** de repente • **a. over** *(finished)* terminado; *(everywhere)* por todas partes • **a. right** bueno; *(uninjured)* ileso, sin daño; *(very well)* muy bien; *(yes)* sí.

all-around ➤ *adj* completo.

allergic ➤ *adj* alérgico.

allergy ➤ *s* alergia.

alley ➤ *s* callejón *m.*

allied ➤ *adj* aliado.

alligator ➤ *s* caimán *m.*

allocate ➤ *tr* destinar, asignar.

allotment ➤ *s* lote *m,* porción *f.*

all-out ➤ *adj* extremo, máximo.

allow ➤ *tr (to permit)* dejar, permitir; *(to give)* conceder, dar; *(to admit)* confesar, admitir; *(to discount)* deducir ■ **a. me** permítame • **to a. for** tener en cuenta • **to a. oneself** darse el gusto de.

allowance ➤ *s* permiso; *(rebate)* rebaja; *(money)* dinero de bolsillo ■ **to make a. for** tener en cuenta.

all-purpose ➤ *adj* de uso múltiple.

all-right ➤ *adj* bueno, excelente.

allusion ➤ *s* alusión *f.*

ally ➤ *tr & intr* unir(se), aliar(se) ➤ *s* aliado/a.

almond ➤ *s* almendra.

almost ➤ *adv* casi, por poco.

alone ➤ *adj* solo; *(with nothing added)* solamente ▪ **let a.** sin mencionar • **to leave** *o* **let a.** no molestar, dejar en paz • **to stand a.** ser único ➤ *adv (only)* sólo, solamente; *(by oneself)* a solas.

along ➤ *adv (in line with)* a lo largo de; *(forward)* adelante; *(with one)* consigo ▪ **all a.** desde el principio • **a. with** junto con • **to get a. with someone** llevarse bien con alguien • **to go a. with** aceptar ➤ *prep* a lo largo de, por.

alongside ➤ *adv & prep* a lo largo (de), junto (a).

aloud ➤ *adv* en voz alta.

alphabet ➤ *s* alfabeto.

alphabetic(al) ➤ *adj* alfabético.

alpine ➤ *adj* alpino.

already ➤ *adv* ya.

also ➤ *adv* también, además.

altar ➤ *s* altar *m* ▪ **a. boy** monaguillo.

alter ➤ *tr* alterar, cambiar; COST. arreglar ➤ *intr* transformarse.

alteration ➤ *s* alteración *f*; COST. arreglo.

altercation ➤ *s* altercado, disputa.

alternate ➤ *tr & intr* alternar ➤ *adj* alterno ➤ *s* sustituto, suplente *mf*.

alternately ➤ *adv* alternativamente, por turno.

alternative ➤ *s* alternativa ➤ *adj* alternativo.

although ➤ *conj* aunque, si bien.

altitude ➤ *s* altitud *f*.

altogether ➤ *adv (entirely)* enteramente, del todo; *(all told)* en total.

aluminum ➤ *s* aluminio.

always ➤ *adv* siempre.

am ➤ *vea* **be** en tabla de verbos.

amateur ➤ *adj & s* amateur *mf*.

amaze ➤ *tr* asombrar, sorprender.

amazing ➤ *adj* asombroso.

ambassador ➤ *s* embajador/a.

amber ➤ *s* ámbar *m* ➤ *adj* ambarino.

ambient ➤ *adj* ambiente.

ambition ➤ *s* ambición *f*, afán *m*.

ambitious ➤ *adj* ambicioso.

ambulance ➤ *s* ambulancia.

America ➤ *s* América; *(U.S.A.)* Norteamérica.

American ➤ *adj* americano/a; *(of U.S.A.)* norteamericano/a.

amicable ➤ *adj* amigable.

ammunition ➤ *s* municiones *f*.

among(st) ➤ *prep* entre, en medio de.

amorous ➤ *adj* amativo.

amount ➤ *s* cantidad *f* ➤ *intr* ▪ **to a. to** subir a.

ample ➤ *adj* extenso, amplio.

amplifier ➤ *s* amplificador *m*.

amplify ➤ *tr* amplificar.

amputate ➤ *tr* amputar.

amuse ➤ *tr* entretener, divertir ▪ **to a. oneself** divertirse, entretenerse.

amusement ➤ *s (pastime)* entretenimiento; *(laughter)* risa.

amusing ➤ *adj* entretenido, divertido.

an ➤ *art indef* un, una ▪ **an eye** un ojo.

analysis ➤ *s* análisis *m*.

analyst ➤ *s* analista *mf*.

analyze ➤ *tr* analizar; PSIC. psicoanalizar.

anarchy ➤ *s* anarquía.

anatomic(al) ➤ *adj* anatómico.

anatomize ➤ *tr* anatomizar.

anatomy ➤ *s* anatomía.

ancestor ➤ *s* antepasado/a.

ancestral ➤ *adj* ancestral.

ancestry ➤ *s* linaje *m*, abolengo.

anchor ➤ *s* ancla; TELEV. anunciador/a ➤ *intr* anclar ➤ *tr* sujetar, asegurar.

anchovy ➤ *s* anchoa.

ancient ➤ *adj* antiguo.

and ➤ *conj* y, e ▪ **try a. come** trata de venir • **go a. see** anda a ver.

anesthesia ➤ *s* anestesia.

anesthetic ➤ *s & adj* anestésico.

anew ➤ *adv* nuevamente, de nuevo.

angel ➤ *s* ángel *m*.

anger ➤ *s* ira, enojo ➤ *tr & intr* enojar(se).

angle ➤ *s* ángulo.

angler ➤ *s* pescador/a (de caña).

angrily ➤ *adv* con enojo, con ira.

angry ➤ *adj* enojado, enfadado ▪ **to make (someone) a.** enojar (a alguien).

anguish ➤ *s* angustia, congoja.

animal ➤ *adj & s* animal *m*.

ankle ➤ *s* tobillo.

annex ➤ *s* anexo.

anniversary ➤ *s* aniversario.

announce ➤ *tr* anunciar, declarar.

announcement ➤ *s* anuncio, declaración *f*.

announcer ➤ *s* anunciador/a, locutor/a.

annoy ➤ *tr* molestar, fastidiar.

annoying ➤ *adj* molesto, irritante.

annual ➤ *adj* anual ➤ *s* (*yearbook*) anuario; BOT. planta anual.

anomaly ➤ *s* anomalía.

anonymity ➤ *s* anonimato.

anonymous ➤ *adj* anónimo.

another ➤ *adj* otro; (*different*) (otro) distinto; (*additional*) más ∎ a. one otro más • a. time otro día ➤ *pron* otro ∎ one a. uno(s) a otro(s).

answer ➤ *s* respuesta, contestación *f*; (*solution*) solución *f* ➤ *intr* responder ∎ answering machine contestador automático (de teléfono) ➤ *tr* contestar a; (*correctly*) solucionar (problema, enigma) ∎ to a. the telephone contestar el teléfono.

ant ➤ *s* hormiga.

antacid ➤ *adj & s* antiácido.

antelope ➤ *s* antílope *m*.

antenna ➤ *s* RAD., ZOOL. antena.

anthem ➤ *s* RELIG. antífona ∎ national a. himno nacional.

anthology ➤ *s* antología.

antibiotic ➤ *s & adj* antibiótico.

antibody ➤ *s* anticuerpo.

anticipate ➤ *tr* (*to foresee*) anticipar, prever; (*to expect*) esperar, contar con.

anticipation ➤ *s* (*act*) anticipación *f*; (*eagerness*) ilusión *f*.

anticlimactic ➤ *adj* decepcionante.

antifreeze ➤ *s* anticongelante *m*.

antihistamine ➤ *s* antihistamínico.

antique ➤ *adj* antiguo ➤ *s* antigüedad *f*.

antiseptic ➤ *adj & s* antiséptico.

anxiety ➤ *s* ansiedad *f*, ansia; PSIC. angustia.

anxious ➤ *adj* (*worried*) ansioso, inquieto; (*eager*) deseoso, anhelante.

any ➤ *adj* cualquier ∎ a. minute pronto • at a. cost a toda costa • in a. case de todos modos • there isn't a. reason no hay ninguna razón ➤ *pron* alguno, cualquiera; (*negative*) ninguno ∎ if a. si los hay ➤ *adv* algo ∎ a. longer todavía • do you feel a. better? ¿te sientes algo mejor? • I don't feel a. better no me siento nada mejor.

anybody ➤ *pron* cualquiera, cualquier persona ∎ did you see a? ¿viste a alguien? • I didn't see a. no vi a nadie.

anyhow ➤ *adv* (*even so*) de todos modos; (*carelessly*) de cualquier manera.

anymore ➤ *adv* ∎ do you skate a.? ¿patinas todavía? • I don't skate a. ya no patino más.

anyone ➤ *vea* **anybody.**

anyplace ➤ *vea* **anywhere.**

anything ➤ *pron* algo ∎ a. else? ¿algo más? • are you doing a. now? ¿estás haciendo algo ahora? • I can't see a. no veo nada • like a. FAM. a más no poder • take a. you like toma todo lo que quieras.

anytime ➤ *adv* a cualquier hora, en cualquier momento.

anyway ➤ *adv* (*in any case*) de cualquier manera; (*even so*) de todos modos.

anywhere ➤ *adv* (*affirmative*) dondequiera; (*negative*) en, a, *o* por ninguna parte; (*interrogative*) en alguna parte.

apart ➤ *adv* aparte ∎ a. from aparte de • to come a. desprenderse • to fall a. descomponerse • to keep a. apartar, separar • to take a. desarmar.

apartment ➤ *s* departamento, apartamento ∎ a. house casa *o* edificio de departamentos.

ape ➤ *s* mono.

apéritif ➤ *s* aperitivo.

apologetic ➤ *adj* lleno de disculpas.

apologize ➤ *intr* disculparse (*for* por, de) (*to* con).

apology ➤ *s* disculpa.

apostrophe ➤ *s* GRAM. apóstrofo.

appall ➤ *tr* pasmar, horrorizar.

appalling ➤ *adj* pasmoso, horrendo.

apparatus ➤ *s* aparato; (*mechanism*) mecanismo.

apparent ➤ *adj* (*seeming*) aparente; (*perceptible*) evidente, claro.

apparently ➤ *adv* aparentemente, por lo visto.

appeal ➤ *s* (*plea*) súplica; (*a call for*) llamada; (*petition*) petición *f*; (*charm*) atracción *f*, encanto; DER. apelación *f*, recurso ➤ *intr* DER. recurrir a, apelar a; (*to be attractive*) tener atractivo para

➤ *tr* llevar a un tribunal superior.

appealing ➤ *adj* atrayente.

appear ➤ *intr* aparecer; *(to present oneself)* presentarse; *(on the stage)* actuar; *(in court)* comparecer.

appearance ➤ *s (act)* aparición *f;* *(looks)* aspecto, apariencia; *(pretense)* pretensión *f,* simulación *f* ■ to make an a. hacer acto de presencia ■ *pl* apariencias, exterioridad.

appendicitis ➤ *s* apendicitis *f.*

appendix ➤ *s* apéndice *m.*

appetite ➤ *s* apetito, apetencia.

appetizer ➤ *s* aperitivo.

applaud ➤ *tr & intr* aplaudir.

applause ➤ *s* aplauso.

apple ➤ *s* manzana ■ a. tree manzano.

appliance ➤ *s* aparato ■ household a. aparato electrodoméstico.

applicant ➤ *s* aspirante *mf.*

application ➤ *s (act)* aplicación *f;* *(relevance)* correspondencia, pertinencia; *(diligence)* esmero; *(request)* solicitación *f;* *(form)* solicitud *f,* aplicación.

apply ➤ *tr* aplicar; *(to use)* emplear, usar *(to* para) ■ to a. oneself to aplicarse a ➤ *intr* ser pertinente ■ to a. for solicitar (empleo, admisión).

appoint ➤ *tr* nombrar.

appointment ➤ *s (act)* nombramiento, designación *f; (post)* puesto, cargo; *(date)* cita, compromiso.

appreciate ➤ *tr (to recognize)* darse cuenta de; *(to value)* apreciar, estimar; *(to be grateful for)* agradecer ➤ *intr* subir de precio o valor.

appreciation ➤ *s* apreciación *f,* reconocimiento; *(gratitude)* gratitud *f;* COM. valorización *f.*

apprehensive ➤ *adj* aprensivo.

apprentice ➤ *s* aprendiz/a.

apprenticeship ➤ *s* aprendizaje *m.*

approach ➤ *intr* aproximarse, acercarse ➤ *tr* aproximarse a, acercarse a; *(to make overtures to)* abordar ➤ *s (act)* acercamiento; *(access)* acceso.

approaching ➤ *adj (upcoming)* venidero, próximo; *(nearing)* que se acerca.

appropriate ➤ *adj* apropiado.

approval ➤ *s* aprobación *f,* sanción *f* ■ on a. a prueba.

approve ➤ *tr* aprobar.

approximate ➤ *adj* aproximado.

apricot ➤ *s* albaricoque *m.*

April ➤ *s* abril *m.*

apron ➤ *s* delantal *m.*

apt ➤ *adj (suitable)* apropiado, acertado; *(inclined)* propenso; *(bright)* apto, listo.

aptitude ➤ *s* aptitud *f,* capacidad *f.*

aquarium ➤ *s* acuario.

aqueduct ➤ *s* acueducto.

aquifer ➤ *s* acuífero.

Arabic numeral ➤ *s* número arábigo.

arbitration ➤ *s* arbitraje *m.*

arbor ➤ *s* enramada, pérgola.

arc ➤ *s* arco.

arcade ➤ *s* arcada; *(gallery)* galería.

arch ➤ *s* arco ➤ *tr & intr* arquear(se).

archaeology ➤ *s* arqueología.

arched ➤ *adj* arqueado, enarcado.

archer ➤ *s* arquero/a (de arco y flecha).

archery ➤ *s* tiro de arco y flecha.

archetype ➤ *s* arquetipo, prototipo.

archipelago ➤ *s* archipiélago.

architect ➤ *s* arquitecto/a.

architecture ➤ *s* arquitectura.

archway ➤ *s* arcada, arco.

arctic ➤ *adj* frígido, glacial.

are ➤ vea le en tabla de verbos.

area ➤ *s* área; *(region)* zona, región *f* ■ a. code prefijo telefónico.

aren't ➤ *contr de* are not.

Argentine *o* **Argentinian** ➤ *adj & s* argentino/a.

argue ➤ *tr (a case)* argüir, presentar ➤ *intr (to debate)* argumentar, argüir (en favor o en contra de algo); *(to quarrel)* disputar, discutir.

argument ➤ *s* discusión *f,* debate *m;* *(quarrel)* pelea, disputa; *(contention)* razonamiento, argumento.

arid ➤ *adj* árido, seco.

arise ➤ *intr (to get up)* levantarse; *(to originate)* surgir, originarse.

aristocrat ➤ *s* aristócrata *mf.*

arithmetic ➤ *s* aritmética.

arm¹ ➤ *s* ANAT. brazo.

arm² ➤ *s* MIL. arma ➤ *tr* armar.

armband ➤ *s* brazalete *m,* brazal *m.*

armchair ➤ *s* sillón *m,* butaca.

armoire ➤ *s* armario, ropero.

armor ➤ *s* armadura; *(metal plating)* blindaje *m.*

armored ➤ *adj* acorazado, blindado.

armory ➤ *s* armería, arsenal.

armpit ➤ *s* axila.

army ➤ *s* ejército.

aroma ➤ *s* aroma *m,* fragancia.

around ➤ *adv (in all directions)* por todos lados, en derredor; *(in a circle)* alrededor; *(here and there)* por aquí, por allá; *(in circumference)* de circunferencia ■ all a. por todos lados • to get a. *(person)* viajar; *(news)* divulgarse • to have been a. tener experiencia ➤ *prep (about)* cerca de, alrededor de; *(encircling)* alrededor de; *(here and there)* por todos lados, en torno de ■ a. the corner a la vuelta de la esquina.

arrange ➤ *tr* arreglar, ordenar; *(to settle upon)* fijar *(fechas, convenios); (to plan)* preparar; MÚS. arreglar.

arrangement ➤ *s* arreglo; *(order)* disposición *f; (agreement)* convenio ■ *pl* planes, medidas.

arrears ➤ *spl* ■ to be in a. estar atrasado en pagos de deuda.

arrest ➤ *tr (to halt)* detener, parar; *(to seize)* arrestar, detener; *(one's attention)* cautivar ➤ *s* arresto, detención *f* ■ under a. detenido.

arrival ➤ *s* llegada, arribo.

arrive ➤ *intr* llegar.

arrow ➤ *s* flecha.

arson ➤ *s* incendio premeditado.

art ➤ *s* arte *m; (skill)* destreza, técnica ■ fine arts bellas artes.

artery ➤ *s* arteria.

arthritis ➤ *s* artritis *f.*

artichoke ➤ *s* alcachofa.

article ➤ *s* artículo.

articulate ➤ *adj* articulado; *(well-spoken)* claro ➤ *tr (a word)* articular, enunciar; *(to form a joint)* articular.

artifact ➤ *s* artefacto.

artificial ➤ *adj* artificial.

artisan ➤ *s* artesano/a, artífice *mf.*

artist ➤ *s* artista *mf.*

artistic ➤ *adj* artístico.

as ➤ *adv (equally)* así de, tan; *(for example)* (tal) como ■ as . . . as tan

. . . como ➤ *conj* igual que, como; *(while)* mientras; *(because)* ya que ■ as if como si • as if to como para • as it were por así decirlo • as long as *(since)* ya que; *(on the condition that)* siempre y cuando; *(while)* mientras • as to en cuanto a • as yet hasta ahora ➤ *prep* como ■ as a rule por regla general • as for en cuanto a.

ascend ➤ *tr & intr* subir.

ascent ➤ *s (act)* subida, ascensión *f; (in rank)* ascenso; *(upward slope)* cuesta.

ash[1] ➤ *s (from fire)* ceniza.

ash[2] ➤ *s* BOT. fresno.

ashamed ➤ *adj* avergonzado ■ to be a. tener vergüenza.

ashore ➤ *adv* a *o* en tierra ■ to go a. bajar a tierra, desembarcar.

ashtray ➤ *s* cenicero.

Asia ➤ *s* Asia.

Asian ➤ *adj & s* asiático/a.

aside ➤ *adv* al lado, a un lado ■ a. from a no ser por • joking a. bromas aparte.

ask ➤ *tr* preguntar; *(to request)* solicitar, pedir; *(to demand)* exigir; *(to invite)* invitar ■ to a. a favor pedir un favor • to a. a question hacer una pregunta ➤ *intr* preguntar *(about, after* por) ■ to a. for pedir.

asleep ➤ *adj* dormido ■ to fall a. dormirse, quedarse dormido.

asparagus ➤ *s* espárrago.

aspect ➤ *s* aspecto.

aspirin ➤ *s* aspirina.

assassin ➤ *s* asesino/a.

assassinate ➤ *tr* asesinar.

assault ➤ *s* asalto, ataque *m* ➤ *tr & intr* asaltar, atacar.

assemble ➤ *tr* congregar, reunir; MEC. armar, montar ➤ *intr* congregarse.

assembly ➤ *s* asamblea, congreso; MEC. montaje *m* ■ a. line línea de montaje.

assess ➤ *tr (to appraise)* evaluar, tasar *(at* en); *(to levy)* gravar, multar; *(to evaluate)* evaluar, juzgar.

asset ➤ *s (item)* posesión *f,* bien *m; (advantage)* ventaja ■ *pl* bienes, activo.

assign ➤ *tr* asignar.

assignment ➤ *s* tarea, deber *m.*

assist ➤ *tr & intr* asistir, auxiliar ➤ *s* ayuda, auxilio.

assistance ➤ *s* asistencia, ayuda.

assistant ➤ *s & adj* ayudante *mf*, auxiliar *mf*.

associate ➤ *tr & intr* asociar(se) ■ to a. with someone juntarse o tratarse con alguien ➤ *s* socio/a.

association ➤ *s* asociación *f*.

assorted ➤ *adj* surtido, variado.

assortment ➤ *s* surtido.

assume ➤ *tr* asumir; (*to arrogate*) arrogarse (un derecho); (*to presume*) presumir, suponer.

assurance ➤ *s* garantía, promesa; (*self-confidence*) aplomo.

assure ➤ *tr* asegurar.

asterisk ➤ *s* asterisco.

asthma ➤ *s* asma.

asthmatic ➤ *adj & s* asmático/a.

astonish ➤ *tr* asombrar.

astonishing ➤ *adj* asombroso.

astray ➤ *adv* por mal camino ■ to go a. extraviarse • to lead a. descarriar.

astride ➤ *adv* a horcajadas (sobre).

astrology ➤ *s* astrología.

astronaut ➤ *s* astronauta *mf*.

astronomy ➤ *s* astronomía.

astrophysics ➤ *ssg* astrofísica.

at ➤ *prep* en, a, por, de ■ at noon al mediodía • at right angles en ángulo recto • don't laugh at me! ¡no te rías de mí! • to be angry at something estar enfadado por algo.

athlete ➤ *s* atleta *mf* ■ a.'s foot pie de atleta.

athletic ➤ *adj* atlético ■ athletics *ssg o pl* atletismo.

atlas ➤ *s* atlas *m*.

atmosphere ➤ *s* atmósfera.

atom ➤ *s* átomo ■ a. o atomic bomb bomba atómica.

atomic ➤ *adj* atómico.

attach ➤ *tr* (*to fasten*) ligar, sujetar; (*to bond*) unir, pegar; (*to ascribe*) dar, atribuir (importancia, significado).

attaché ➤ *s* agregado/a ■ a. case portafolio, maletín.

attack ➤ *tr* atacar, agredir; FIG. acometer (tarea, problema) ➤ *intr* ir al ataque ➤ *s* ataque *m*, agresión *f*.

attacker ➤ *s* agresor/a, asaltante *mf*.

attain ➤ *tr* lograr, conseguir.

attempt ➤ *tr* intentar, tratar de ➤ *s* (*try*) intento, prueba; (*attack*) atentado.

attend ➤ *tr* (*to go to*) atender, asistir a; (*to take care of*) atender, cuidar ■ to a. to prestar atención a.

attendance ➤ *s* asistencia.

attendant ➤ *s* asistente/a, mozo/a.

attention ➤ *s* atención *f*; (*attentiveness*) cuidado ■ to pay a. (to) prestar atención (a) ■ *pl* cortesías, atenciones.

attentive ➤ *adj* atento.

attic ➤ *s* desván *m*, guardilla.

attitude ➤ *s* actitud *f*.

attorney ➤ *s* abogado/a, apoderado/a ■ a. general fiscal o procurador/a general.

attract ➤ *tr & intr* atraer.

attraction ➤ *s* atracción *f*; (*allure*) atractivo.

attractive ➤ *adj* atractivo, atrayente.

attribute ➤ *tr* atribuir ➤ *s* atributo.

auction ➤ *s* subasta, remate *m* ➤ *tr* subastar, rematar.

auctioneer ➤ *s* subastador/a.

audible ➤ *adj* audible, oíble.

audience ➤ *s* (*public*) auditorio, público; (*formal hearing*) audiencia.

audio ➤ *adj* ■ a. frequency audiofrecuencia ➤ *s* TELEV. transmisión *f* o recepción *f* del sonido.

audio-visual ➤ *adj* audiovisual.

auditorium ➤ *s* auditorio.

August ➤ *s* agosto.

aunt ➤ *s* tía.

Australia ➤ *s* Australia.

Australian ➤ *adj & s* australiano/a.

authentic ➤ *adj* auténtico.

author ➤ *s* autor/a ➤ *tr* escribir.

authoritarian ➤ *adj & s* autoritario/a.

authority ➤ *s* autoridad *f*; (*expert*) experto/a, perito/a ■ on good a. de buena tinta.

authorize ➤ *tr* autorizar.

autobiography ➤ *s* autobiografía.

autograph ➤ *s* autógrafo ➤ *tr* autografiar.

automatic ➤ *adj* automático ■ a. rifle fusil ametrallador ➤ *s* arma automática.

automobile ➤ *s* automóvil *m*.

automotive ➤ *adj* automotor, automotriz; *(industry)* automovilístico.

autonomy ➤ s autonomía.

autopsy ➤ s autopsia.

autumn ➤ s otoño.

auxiliary ➤ adj auxiliar.

available ➤ adj disponible.

avalanche ➤ s avalancha.

avenue ➤ s avenida.

average ➤ s promedio ■ on the a. por término medio ➤ adj *(de término)* medio; *(ordinary)* regular.

aversion ➤ s aversión f.

aviation ➤ s aviación f.

avocado ➤ s aguacate m, palta.

avoid ➤ tr evitar.

await ➤ tr & intr esperar, aguardar.

awake◇ ➤ tr & intr despertar(se) ➤ adj despierto.

award ➤ tr premiar; *(legally)* adjudicar ➤ s *(prize)* premio, recompensa; *(decision)* decisión f, fallo.

aware ➤ adj consciente, percatado ■ to be a. of o that tener conciencia de o que • to become a. of enterarse de.

away ➤ adv lejos de, a ■ **far a.** lejos • **right a.** inmediatamente ➤ adj ausente, fuera; *(at a distance)* lejano.

awesome ➤ adj pasmoso, asombroso.

awful ➤ adj *(terrible)* pavoroso; *(atrocious)* atroz, horrible; *(great)* enorme.

awfully ➤ adv *(atrociously)* muy mal; *(very)* muchísimo, muy.

awhile ➤ adv un rato, algún tiempo.

awkward ➤ adj *(clumsy)* torpe, desmañado; *(embarrassing)* embarazoso; *(shape)* inconveniente.

awning ➤ s toldo.

ax(e) ➤ s hacha.

axis ➤ s eje m.

axle ➤ s eje m, árbol m.

B

baby ➤ s bebé m, nene mf ➤ tr mimar, consentir.

baby-sit ➤ intr cuidar niños.

bachelor ➤ s soltero; EDUC. *(degree)* bachillerato; *(graduate)* bachiller m.

back ➤ s espalda; *(animal)* lomo, espinazo; *(reverse side)* envés m, revés m ➤ adv *(hacia)* atrás ■ **b. and forth** de acá para allá • **in b. of** detrás de, tras de

• **to go** o **come b.** volver, regresar ➤ adj de atrás, posterior ■ **b. talk** impertinencia(s) ➤ tr mover hacia atrás; *(to support)* respaldar, apoyar ■ **to b. up***(vehicle)* dar marcha atrás; *(drain)* atascar(se); COMPUT. hacer una copia de reserva *(de)* ➤ intr moverse hacia atrás ■ **to b. down** echarse atrás • **to b. out** volverse atrás.

backache ➤ s dolor m de espalda.

backfire ➤ s petardeo ➤ intr AUTO. petardear; *(scheme)* salir al revés.

background ➤ s fondo, trasfondo; *(of events)* antecedentes m; *(experience)* experiencia.

backing ➤ s respaldo (moral, económico).

backlash ➤ s FIG. reacción f.

backlog ➤ s acumulación f (de trabajo, pedidos).

backpack ➤ s mochila.

backrest ➤ s respaldo (de un asiento).

backstage ➤ adv entre bastidores.

backup ➤ s reserva; *(support)* respaldo; COMPUT. copia de reserva ➤ adj suplente, de reserva.

backward(s) ➤ adv hacia o para atrás ■ **to do something b.** hacer algo al revés • **to fall b.** caerse de espaldas • **to know backwards and forwards** saberse al dedillo ➤ adj hacia atrás; *(motion)* de retroceso; *(reverse)* al revés; *(place, era)* atrasado.

bacon ➤ s tocino ■ **to bring home the b.** FAM. ganar el pan.

bacteria ➤ spl bacteria.

bad ➤ adj malo; *(check)* sin fondos; *(naughty)* desobediente ■ **a b. cold** un catarro fuerte • **to feel b.** *(ill)* sentirse mal; *(sad)* estar triste • **to go b.** echarse a perder • **too b.!** ¡qué lástima!, ¡mala suerte! ➤ s lo malo ➤ adv ■ **it hurts bad** FAM. me duele mucho ■ **to be b. off** FAM. estar mal.

badge ➤ s distintivo, insignia.

badly ➤ adv mal; *(very much)* mucho, con urgencia ■ **to take something b.** tomar a mal algo.

badminton ➤ s volante m.

baffle ➤ tr confundir ➤ s deflector m.

bag ➤ s bolsa, saco; *(purse)* bolso,

cartera; *(suitcase)* valija, maletín *m* ◼
pl equipaje ➤ *tr* meter en una bolsa;
FAM. *(to capture)* coger, pescar.
baggage ➤ *s* equipaje *m*, maletas; MIL.
bagaje *m*.
baggy ➤ *adj* bombacho.
bagpipe ➤ *s* gaita.
bail ➤ *s* fianza, caución *f* ◼ out on b. en
libertad bajo fianza ➤ *tr* ◼ to b. out
sacar de apuros.
bait ➤ *s* cebo, carnada ➤ *tr* poner el
cebo en (anzuelo, trampa); *(to torment)* atormentar.
bake ➤ *tr* cocer al horno ➤ *intr* cocerse
➤ *s* cocción *f* (al horno).
baker ➤ *s* panadero/a.
bakery ➤ *s* panadería.
baking ➤ *s* cocción *f* ◼ b. powder
levadura en polvo • b. soda bicarbonato de sodio.
balance ➤ *s (scale)* balanza; *(equilibrium)* equilibrio ◼ b. due saldo deudor
• b. sheet balance • off b. en desequilibrio • to throw off b. desconcertar
➤ *tr* balancear, equilibrar; *(to counterbalance)* compensar, contrarrestar ◼
to b. the books pasar balance ➤ *intr*
equilibrarse.
balcony ➤ *s* balcón *m*; TEAT. galería,
paraíso.
bald ➤ *adj* calvo; *(blunt)* categórico, sin
rodeos ◼ to go b. quedarse calvo.
baldness ➤ *s* calvicie *f*.
balk ➤ *intr (to stop)* plantarse; *(to
refuse)* oponerse *(at* a).
ball¹ ➤ *s* bola; DEP. pelota, balón *m* ◼ b.
bearing cojinete de bolas • to be on
the b. JER. estar atento.
ball² ➤ *s* baile *m* de etiqueta ◼ to have a
b. JER. pasarla muy bien.
ballerina ➤ *s* bailarina (de ballet).
ballet ➤ *s* ballet *m*.
balloon ➤ *s* globo ➤ *intr* hincharse,
inflarse.
ballot ➤ *s* papeleta (electoral) ◼ b. box
urna electoral ➤ *intr* votar.
ballpark ➤ *s* estadio ◼ in the b. FAM.
aproximado.
ball-point pen ➤ *s* bolígrafo.
ban ➤ *tr* prohibir, proscribir ➤ *s* pro-
hibición *f*, proscripción *f*.

banana ➤ *s* plátano, banana ◼ b. tree
plátano, banano ◼ *pl* JER. chiflado.
band¹ ➤ *s* banda, faja; *(stripe)* franja;
JOY. anillo (de boda) ➤ *tr* fajar, atar.
band² ➤ *s* banda; *(gang)* cuadrilla; MÚS.
(military) banda; *(jazz)* orquesta;
(rock) conjunto ➤ *tr & intr* ◼ to b.
together agrupar(se), juntar(se).
bandage ➤ *s* venda ➤ *tr* vendar.
bandit ➤ *s* bandido, bandolero/a.
bang ➤ *s (explosion)* estallido; *(loud
slam)* golpe *m*, golpetazo; JER. *(thrill)*
emoción *f*, excitación *f* ➤ *tr* golpear ◼
to b. up estropear ➤ *intr* detonar; *(to
crash)* chocar *(into* con) ➤ *interj
(shot)* ¡pum!; *(blow)* ¡zas!
banister ➤ *s* barandilla, baranda.
bank¹ ➤ *s (of a river)* ribera, orilla; *(of
snow)* montón *m* ➤ *tr (a fire)* cubrir;
(a road) peraltar; AVIA. inclinar.
bank² ➤ *s* COM. banco; *(in gambling)*
banca ◼ b. account cuenta bancaria
• b. note billete de banco ➤ *intr* ◼ to b.
on contar con, confiar en.
banker ➤ *s* banquero/a.
bankrupt ➤ *adj* COM. insolvente ◼ to go
b. declararse en quiebra, quebrar ➤ *tr*
hacer quebrar, arruinar.
bankruptcy ➤ *s* quiebra, bancarrota.
banner ➤ *s* bandera, estandarte *m*;
➤ *adj* sobresaliente.
banquet ➤ *s* banquete *m*.
baptism ➤ *s* bautismo.
baptistery ➤ *s* baptisterio.
baptize ➤ *tr* bautizar.
bar ➤ *s* barra; *(of soap)* pastilla; *(of
chocolate)* tableta; *(obstacle)* obstáculo; *(tavern)* bar *m*; *(counter)* mostrador
m; *(legal profession)* abogacía ➤ *tr (to
fasten)* cerrar con barras; *(to obstruct)*
obstruir; *(to exclude)* excluir; *(to prohibit)* prohibir ➤ *prep* ◼ b. none sin
excepción.
barbaric ➤ *adj* bárbaro.
barbecue ➤ *s* barbacoa, parrillada ➤ *tr*
asar a la parrilla.
barber ➤ *s* barbero, peluquero/a.
barbershop ➤ *s* barbería, peluquería.
bare ➤ *adj* desnudo; *(head)* descubierto; *(feet)* descalzo; *(empty)*
desprovisto, vacío ◼ to lay b. revelar

> *tr* desnudar; *(to reveal)* descubrir.

barefoot(ed) ➤ *adv & adj* descalzo.

barely ➤ *adv* apenas.

bargain ➤ *s (deal)* pacto, convenio; *(good buy)* ganga ∎ into the b. por añadidura ➤ *intr* negociar; *(to haggle)* regatear ∎ to b. for o on esperar.

barge ➤ *s* barcaza, gabarra ➤ *intr* ∎ to b. in entremeterse • to b. into irrumpir en.

bark¹ ➤ *s* ladrido ➤ *tr & intr* ladrar.

bark² ➤ *s* BOT. corteza.

barkeep(er) ➤ *s* barman *m*.

barn ➤ *s (for grain)* granero; *(for live-stock)* establo.

barometer ➤ *s* barómetro.

baroque ➤ *adj & s* barroco.

barracks ➤ *spl* cuartel *m*.

barrage ➤ *s* MIL. bombardeo, cortina de fuego; FIG. *(burst)* andanada.

barrel ➤ *s* barril *m*, tonel *m*; *(of a gun)* cañón *m* ➤ *intr* ir a gran velocidad.

barren ➤ *adj* estéril, infecundo; *(land)* yermo.

barrette ➤ *s* pasador *m*.

barricade ➤ *s* barricada, barrera.

barrier ➤ *s* barrera, valla.

barroom ➤ *s* bar *m*.

bartender ➤ *s* camarero/a, barman *m*.

base ➤ *s* base *f*; ARQ. basa ∎ to be off b. estar equivocado ➤ *adj* de la base ➤ *tr* ∎ to b. (up)on basar en o sobre.

baseball ➤ *s* béisbol *m*; *(ball)* pelota.

basement ➤ *s* sótano.

bash FAM. ➤ *tr* golpear ➤ *s* golpazo, porrazo; *(party)* fiesta, parranda.

basic ➤ *adj* básico ➤ *s* base *f*.

basin ➤ *s* palangana, jofaina; *(wash-bowl)* pila, pileta.

basis ➤ *s* base *f*, fundamento ∎ on the b. of en base a.

bask ➤ *intr* gozar, complacerse.

basket ➤ *s* cesta, canasta; DEP. cesto.

basketball ➤ *s* baloncesto, básquetbol *m*, básquet *m*; *(ball)* pelota, balón *m*.

bas-relief ➤ *s* bajo relieve.

bass¹ ➤ *s (fish)* róbalo.

bass² ➤ *s* MÚS. bajo.

bat ➤ *s* DEP. bate *m*; ZOOL. murciélago ➤ *tr* golpear; DEP. batear ∎ not to b. an eye no pestañear.

batch ➤ *s* CUL. hornada; *(lot)* partida, lote *m*; *(group)* grupo, tanda.

bath ➤ *s* baño; *(bathroom)* cuarto de baño ∎ *pl* casa de baños.

bathe ➤ *intr* bañarse ➤ *tr* bañar; *(to wash)* lavar; *(to flood)* inundar.

bathing suit ➤ *s* traje *m* de baño.

bathrobe ➤ *s* bata, albornoz *m*.

bathroom ➤ *s* cuarto de baño.

bathtub ➤ *s* bañera.

batter¹ ➤ *tr (to beat)* golpear, apalear.

batter² ➤ *s* CUL. pasta; DEP. bateador/a.

battery ➤ *s* ELEC., MIL. batería; *(dry cell)* pila; *(storage)* acumulador *m*; DER. asalto.

battle ➤ *s* batalla ➤ *intr & tr* combatir.

battleship ➤ *s* acorazado.

bawl ➤ *intr* llorar ∎ to b. out regañar.

bay ➤ *s* GEOG. bahía.

be ◇ ➤ *intr (inherent quality, time, possession, passive voice)* ser ∎ ice is cold el hielo es frío • what time is it? ¿qué hora es? • is it yours? ¿es tuyo? ➤ *(location, impermanence)* estar ∎ where are you? ¿dónde estás? • my coffee is cold mi café está frío • *(age, physical sensation)* tener; *(weather)* haber, hacer ∎ as it were por así decirlo • so be it así sea • there is o are hay.

beach ➤ *s* playa ➤ *tr* varar.

beacon ➤ *s* faro; *(radio)* radiofaro.

bead ➤ *s* cuenta, abalorio; *(drop)* gota ∎ *pl* RELIG. rosario.

beak ➤ *s* pico.

beam ➤ *s (of light)* haz *m*, rayo; ARQ. viga; RAD. onda dirigida ➤ *tr* emitir, dirigir ➤ *intr (to smile)* sonreír radiantemente.

bean ➤ *s* habichuela, judía, frijol *m*; *(seed)* haba; *(of coffee)* grano ∎ to spill the beans FAM. descubrir el pastel.

bear¹◇ ➤ *tr (to support)* sostener; *(to carry, display)* llevar; *(to endure)* aguantar; *(a baby)* dar a luz; *(fruit)* producir, dar ∎ to b. in mind tener en cuenta • to b. mention merecer mencionarse • to b. out corroborar • to b. with tener paciencia con ➤ *intr* producir, rendir; *(to pressure)* pesar ∎ to b. on relacionarse con • to b. right girar a la derecha • to b. up resistir • to bring to b. aplicar.

bear² ➤ s ZOOL. oso.

bearable ➤ adj soportable.

beard ➤ s barba.

bearded ➤ adj barbudo.

bearing ➤ s (poise) porte m; AER., MARÍT. rumbo; MEC. cojinete m ■ pl to get one's b. orientarse.

beast ➤ s bestia, bruto ■ b. of burden bestia de carga.

beat◊ ➤ tr (to hit) golpear; (to pound, flap, stir) batir; (to defeat) vencer, derrotar; (to surpass) superar a; (a drum) tocar ■ b. it! ¡lárgate! • to b. back o off repeler ➤ intr latir, pulsar ➤ s latido, pulsación f; (tempo) compás m.

beautiful ➤ adj bello, hermoso.

beauty ➤ s belleza, hermosura.

beaver ➤ s castor m.

because ➤ conj porque ■ b. of a causa de, por.

become ➤ intr (to turn into) llegar a ser, convertirse en; (angry, etc.) hacerse, ponerse, volverse ■ what has b. of George? ¿qué se ha hecho de Jorge?

bed ➤ s cama, lecho; (of flowers) macizo ■ b. and board pensión completa • to go to b. acostarse.

bedbug ➤ s chinche f.

bedding ➤ s ropa de cama.

bedroom ➤ s dormitorio, alcoba.

bedspread ➤ s cubrecama m, colcha.

bedtime ➤ s hora de acostarse.

bee ➤ s abeja; FAM. (contest) concurso.

beef ➤ s carne f de res.

beefsteak ➤ s bistec m, biftec m.

beep ➤ s sonido agudo ➤ intr & tr sonar con sonido agudo.

beeper ➤ s buscapersonas m.

beer ➤ s cerveza ■ dark, light b. cerveza negra, dorada.

beet ➤ s remolacha.

beetle ➤ s escarabajo.

before ➤ adv antes ■ to go b. ir delante (de) ➤ prep (in time) antes de o que; (in space) delante de; (in front of) ante ➤ conj antes de que.

beg ➤ tr & intr (for charity) mendigar, pedir (limosna); (to entreat) suplicar, rogar ■ to b. pardon pedir perdón.

beggar ➤ s mendigo/a, pobre mf.

begin◊ ➤ tr & intr empezar, comenzar ■ to b. by empezar por • to b. with para empezar.

beginner ➤ s principiante/a, novato/a.

beginning ➤ s comienzo, principio; (source) origen m ■ b. with a partir de.

begrudge ➤ tr (to envy) envidiar; (to give reluctantly) dar de mala gana.

behalf ➤ s ■ in b. of para, a favor de • on b. of en nombre de.

behave ➤ tr & intr portarse, comportarse; (properly) portarse bien.

behavior ➤ s comportamiento.

behind ➤ adv (in back) atrás, detrás; (late) atrasado; (slow) con retraso ➤ prep detrás de ■ b. schedule atrasado ➤ s FAM. trasero, nalgas.

being ➤ s existencia; (creature) ser m.

belated ➤ adj atrasado, tardío.

belch ➤ intr & tr eructar; (smoke, fire) arrojar, vomitar ➤ s eructo.

belfry ➤ s campanario.

belief ➤ s creencia, fe f; (conviction) convicción f, opinión f.

believable ➤ adj creíble.

believe ➤ tr creer ■ to make b. fingir.

believer ➤ s creyente mf.

belittle ➤ tr menospreciar.

bell ➤ s campana;; (of a door) timbre m ■ to ring a b. FIG. sonarle a uno

bellboy o **bellhop** ➤ s botones m.

belligerent ➤ adj & s beligerante mf.

belly ➤ s vientre m; FAM. (paunch) panza, barriga ■ b. laugh carcajada.

bellyache ➤ s dolor m de barriga; JER. (gripe) queja ➤ intr JER. quejarse.

bellybutton ➤ s FAM. ombligo.

belong ➤ intr deber estar, corresponder ■ to b. to (as property) pertenecer a, ser de; (as a member) ser miembro de; (as part of) corresponder a.

belongings ➤ spl efectos personales.

below ➤ adv abajo ➤ prep (por) debajo de ■ b. zero bajo cero.

belt ➤ s cinturón m, cinto; TEC. (band) correa.

bench ➤ s banco; DER. tribunal m.

bend◊ ➤ tr (the head) inclinar; (the knee, object) doblar; (one's back) encorvar ➤ intr ■ to b. down o over encorvarse ➤ s curva; (turn) vuelta, recodo.

beneath ➤ *prep* (por) debajo de; *(under)* bajo; *(unworthy)* indigno de ■ *adv* abajo; *(underneath)* debajo.

beneficial ➤ *adj* provechoso.

benefit ➤ *s* beneficio; *(advantage)* ventaja ■ *pl* asistencia ➤ *tr* beneficiar ➤ *intr* ■ **to b. from** sacar provecho de.

bent ➤ *adj* doblado, torcido.

bereavement ➤ *s* luto, duelo.

beret ➤ *s* boina.

berry ➤ *s* baya.

berserk ➤ *adj* frenético, loco ■ **to go b.** volverse loco.

berth ➤ *s (on train)* litera; *(on ship)* camarote *m* ■ **to give a wide b.** evitar.

beside ➤ *prep* junto a, al lado de ■ **to be b. the point** no venir al caso.

besides ➤ *adv* además; *(otherwise)* por otro lado, aparte de eso ➤ *prep* además de; *(except)* aparte de, fuera de.

best ➤ *adj* mejor ■ **b. man** padrino (de una boda) ➤ *adv* mejor ■ **which do you like b.?** ¿cuál te gusta más? ➤ *s* el mejor, lo mejor ■ **at b.** a lo más.

bet◇ ➤ *s* apuesta ■ **to be a sure b.** ser cosa segura ➤ *tr* apostar ■ **I b. . . .** FAM. seguro que . . . ➤ *intr* ■ **I b.!** FAM. ¡ya lo creo! • **you b.!** FAM. ¡claro!

betray ➤ *tr* traicionar; *(to inform on)* delatar; *(a secret)* revelar.

betrayal ➤ *s* traición *f*, delación *f*; *(of a secret)* revelación *f*.

better ➤ *adj* mejor ■ **the b. part of la** mayor parte de • **to be b.** to valer más, ser mejor ➤ *adv* mejor ■ **all the b.** o so much the b. tanto mejor • **b. and b.** cada vez mejor • **b. off** en mejores condiciones • **we had b. go** más vale que nos vayamos • **to get b.** mejorar ➤ *tr & intr* mejorar(se) ➤ *s* el mejor.

between ➤ *prep* entre ■ **b. now and then** de aquí a entonces ➤ *adv* en medio, de por medio ■ **far b.** a grandes intervalos • **in b.** mientras tanto.

beverage ➤ *s* bebida.

beware ➤ *intr* tener cuidado ■ **b. of** cuidado con ➤ *interj* ¡cuidado!

bewilder ➤ *tr* aturdir, dejar perplejo.

beyond➤ *prep* más allá, fuera de ■ **b.** (a) doubt fuera de duda • **b. help** sin

remedio • **it's b. me** no alcanzo a comprender ■ *adv* más lejos, más allá.

bias ➤ *s* inclinación *f*; *(prejudice)* prejuicio ➤ *tr* predisponer, influenciar ■ **to be biased** ser parcial.

bib ➤ *s* babero; *(of an apron)* peto.

Bible ➤ *s* Biblia.

bicycle ➤ *s* bicicleta ➤ *intr* montar or ir en bicicleta.

bid◇ ➤ *tr (to order)* ordenar, mandar; *(in cards)* declarar ■ **to b. goodbye to** decir adiós a ➤ *intr* hacer una oferta ➤ *s (offer)* licitación *f*, oferta.

bifocals ➤ *spl* anteojos bifocales.

big ➤ *adj* gran, grande; *(older)* mayor; *(important)* importante ■ **b. shot** o wheel pez gordo ➤ *adv* ■ **to make it b.** tener gran éxito • **to talk b.** jactarse.

big-hearted ➤ *adj* generoso.

bike ➤ *s* bici *f; (motorcycle)* moto *f.*

biker ➤ *s* motociclista *mf.*

bilingual ➤ *adj* bilingüe.

bill[1] ➤ *s (invoice)* cuenta, factura; *(bank note)* billete *m*; POL. proyecto de ley ■ **b. of exchange** letra de cambio • **b. of fare** carta, menú • **b. of sale** boleto de compra y venta.

bill[2] ➤ *s (beak)* pico; *(visor)* visera.

billboard ➤ *s* cartelera.

billfold ➤ *s* billetera, cartera.

billiards ➤ *ssg* billar *m.*

billing ➤ *s* publicidad *f.*

billion ➤ *s* E.U. [10^9] mil millones *m*; G.B. [10^{12}] billón *m.*

bin ➤ *s (box)* cajón *m; (container)* recipiente *m*, compartimiento.

bind◇ ➤ *tr (to tie)* amarrar, atar; *(a wound)* vendar; *(morally, legally)* obligar, comprometer a ➤ *intr (to be tight)* apretar; *(a mix)* aglutinarse ➤ *s* ■ **to be in a b.** estar en un aprieto.

binder ➤ *s (notebook cover)* carpeta.

binding ➤ *adj* DER. obligatorio; *(promise)* que compromete a uno.

binocular ➤ *adj* binocular ■ **binoculars** *spl* gemelos, prismáticos.

biography ➤ *s* biografía.

biologic(al) ➤ *adj* biológico.

biologist ➤ *s* biólogo/a.

biology ➤ *s* biología.

birch ➤ *s* abedul *m.*

bird ➤ s pájaro; *(large)* ave f ■ **birds of a feather** lobos de la misma camada • **odd b.** bicho raro.

birdcage ➤ s jaula.

birth ➤ s nacimiento; *(ancestry)* linaje m; MED. parto ■ **b. control** control de la natalidad • **by b.** de nacimiento • **to give b.** to dar a luz a.

birthday ➤ s cumpleaños ■ **on one's 15th b.** al cumplir los 15 años.

birthplace ➤ s lugar m de nacimiento.

biscuit ➤ s bizcocho; G.B. galletita.

bishop ➤ s obispo; *(in chess)* alfil m.

bison ➤ s bisonte m.

bit[1] ➤ s pedacito, trocito; *(moment)* ratito ■ **a b. larger** un poco más grande • **a good b.** bastante • **a little b.** un poquito • **b. by b.** poco a poco • **not a b.** en absoluto.

bit[2] ➤ s *(drill)* broca, barrena; *(of a bridle)* freno, bocado.

bit[3] ➤ s COMPUT. bit m, bitio.

bite◇ ➤ tr & intr morder; *(insects, snakes, fish)* picar ➤ s mordisco, dentellada; *(wound)* mordedura; *(sting, in fishing)* picada ■ **a b. to eat** FAM. un piscolabis.

bitter ➤ adj amargo; *(wind, cold)* cortante; *(resentful)* amargado ■ **to the b. end** hasta vencer o morir.

bitterness ➤ s amargura; *(resentment)* rencor m.

bizarre ➤ adj extravagante, extraño.

black ➤ s negro; *(person)* negro/a, persona negra ■ **in b. and white** por escrito ➤ adj negro; *(gloomy)* sombrío ■ **b. eye** ojo a la funerala • **b. market** mercado negro, estraperlo.

blackberry ➤ s zarzamora.

blackbird ➤ s mirlo.

blackboard ➤ s pizarra, pizarrón m.

blacklist ➤ s & tr (poner en la) lista negra.

blackmail ➤ s chantaje m ➤ tr chantajear.

blackout ➤ s *(of a city)* apagón m; MED. desmayo, pérdida de la memoria; *(of news)* supresión f.

blacksmith ➤ s herrero/a.

bladder ➤ s vejiga.

blade ➤ s hoja; *(razor, skate)* cuchilla;

(propeller, fan) aleta; *(grass)* brizna.

blame ➤ tr ■ **to be to b. for** tener la culpa de • **to b.** on echar la culpa a ➤ s culpa ■ **to put the b. on** echar la culpa a.

blameless ➤ adj libre de culpa.

blameworthy ➤ adj censurable.

bland ➤ adj *(mild)* suave; *(dull)* insulso.

blank ➤ adj *(paper, tape)* en blanco; *(wall)* liso; *(look)* vago; *(mind)* vacío ■ **b. check** cheque en blanco; FIG. carta blanca • **to go b.** quedarse en blanco ➤ s *(space)* blanco, vacío; *(form)* formulario (en blanco).

blanket ➤ s manta, frazada ➤ adj general, comprensivo.

blare ➤ intr resonar ➤ s estruendo.

blast ➤ s explosión f; *(shock)* onda de choque ■ **(at) full b.** a todo vapor • **to have a b.** JER. pasarla muy bien ➤ tr *(to blow up)* volar; FAM. *(to criticize)* criticar ■ **to b.** off despegar.

blasted ➤ adj FAM. condenado, maldito.

blastoff o **blast-off** ➤ s lanzamiento.

blaze ➤ s *(glare)* resplandor m; *(fire)* fuego, hoguera ➤ intr arder ■ **blazing with** *(lights, colors)* resplandeciente de (luces, colores).

blazer ➤ s chaqueta deportiva.

bleach ➤ tr blanquear; *(clothes)* colar; *(hair)* des(s)colorar ➤ s de(s)colorante m; *(for clothes)* lejía.

bleachers ➤ spl gradas.

bleak ➤ adj desolado, frío; *(dreary)* sombrío; *(prospect)* poco prometedor.

bleed◇ ➤ intr sangrar, perder sangre; *(colors)* correrse ➤ tr desangrar a.

blemish ➤ tr manchar, mancillar ➤ s mancha; *(flaw)* tacha.

blend◇ ➤ tr & intr mezclar(se) ➤ s mezcla.

blender ➤ s licuadora, batidora.

bless◇ ➤ tr bendecir ■ **b. my soul!** o **b. me!** ¡válgame Dios! • **to b. with** dotar de.

blessed ➤ adj bendito, santo.

blessing ➤ s bendición f; *(benefit)* ventaja; *(approval)* aprobación f.

blind ➤ adj ciego; *(street)* sin salida ■ **b. date, navigation** cita, navegación a ciegas • **b. spot** ángulo muerto; FIG.

punto flaco ➤ s persiana ➤ adv a ciegas ➤ tr cegar; (to dazzle) deslumbrar.

blindfold ➤ tr vendar los ojos a ➤ s venda.

blinding ➤ adj cegador, deslumbrante.

blindly ➤ adv ciegamente, a ciegas.

blindness ➤ s ceguera.

blink ➤ intr parpadear, pestañear; (signal) brillar intermitentemente ➤ tr abrir y cerrar ➤ s parpadeo, pestañeo ■ on the b. JER. descompuesto.

blinker ➤ s intermitente m.

bliss ➤ s dicha, felicidad f.

blister ➤ s ampolla; BOT. verruga ➤ tr & intr ampollar(se).

blizzard ➤ s ventisca; FIG. torrente m.

bloc ➤ s bloque m.

block ➤ s bloque m; (of a city) cuadra, manzana; DEP., MED., PSICOL. bloqueo, obstrucción f ■ b. and tackle aparejo de poleas ➤ tr (to obstruct) bloquear, obstruir (tráfico, avance); MED., PSICOL. obstruir, interrumpir.

blockade ➤ s bloqueo ➤ tr bloquear.

blockage ➤ s obstrucción f.

blond(e) ➤ s & adj rubio/a.

blood ➤ s sangre f; (kinship) parentesco ■ b. count recuento globular • b. relation consanguíneo • b. test análisis de sangre • b. type tipo sanguíneo.

bloodshot ➤ adj inyectado de sangre.

bloody ➤ adj sangriento, G.B., JER. maldito, infame.

bloom ➤ s flor f; (vigor) lozanía ➤ intr florecer.

blossom ➤ s flor f ➤ intr florecer.

blot ➤ s mancha, borrón m ➤ tr ■ to b. out borrar.

blotch ➤ s mancha, manchón m.

blouse ➤ s blusa.

blow¹◇ ➤ intr soplar; (a horn) sonar; (a tire) reventarse ■ to b. over (storm) pasar; (scandal) olvidarse • to b. up (to explode) explotar; (with anger) encolerizarse ➤ tr soplar; (instrument) tocar; (the nose) sonarse; (a fuse) fundir; (a tire) reventar ■ to b. away llevarse • to b. down derribar • to b. out soplar, apagar • to b. up (to destroy) volar; (to inflate) inflar; FOTOG. ampliar ➤ s soplido, soplo.

blow² ➤ s golpe m; (setback) revés m ■ to come to blows agarrarse a puñetazos.

blowdryer ➤ s secador m de cabello.

blowout ➤ s AUTO. reventón m, pinchazo.

blowup ➤ s explosión f; FOTOG. ampliación f.

blue ➤ s azul m ■ out of the b. de repente ➤ pl melancolía; MÚS. jazz melancólico ➤ adj azul; (gloomy) tristón, melancólico ■ b. jeans pantalones vaqueros.

bluff¹ ➤ intr farolear, aparentar ➤ s engaño, farol m ■ to call someone's b. desenmascarar.

bluff² ➤ s (cliff) acantilado; (river bank) ribera escarpada.

blunder ➤ s error craso, metida de pata ➤ intr (to move) andar a tropezones; (to err) cometer un error craso.

blunt ➤ adj desafilado; (frank) franco, brusco ➤ tr desafilar, embotar.

blur ➤ tr empañar, nublar ➤ intr oscurecerse, ponerse borroso ➤ s borrón m, manchón m.

blush ➤ intr ruborizarse, sonrojarse ➤ s rubor m, sonrojo.

board ➤ s madero, tabla; (for games) tablero; (meals) pensión f; (council) junta, consejo ■ above b. honesto • on b. a bordo ➤ tr embarcar(se) en ➤ intr hospedarse con comida.

boarder ➤ s pensionista mf.

boardinghouse ➤ s pensión f.

boast ➤ intr jactarse, alardear ➤ s jactancia.

boat ➤ s (small craft) bote m, barca; (ship) barco, buque m ■ in the same b. en la misma situación.

boating ➤ s paseo en bote.

bodice ➤ s cuerpo, corpiño.

bodily ➤ adj corporal ➤ adv corporalmente.

body ➤ s cuerpo; (corpse) cadáver m; (organization) organismo; (of water) masa; AUTO. carrocería ■ b. and soul completamente, con toda el alma.

bodyguard ➤ s guardaespaldas mf.

bog ➤ s pantano, ciénaga ➤ tr & intr ■ to b. down empantanar(se), atascar(se).

bogus ➤ *adj* falso, fraudulento.

boil ➤ *tr & intr* (hacer) hervir; *(to cook)* cocer ■ **to b. down** (a) • **to b. over** *(pot)* rebosar (al hervir); *(person)* enfurecerse ➤ *s* hervor *m*.

boiler ➤ *s* caldera.

boiling ➤ *adj* hirviente ■ **b. point** FÍS. punto de ebullición.

bold ➤ *adj* intrépido.

Bolivian ➤ *adj & s* boliviano/a.

bolt ➤ *s* MEC. tornillo, perno; *(lock)* cerrojo, pestillo ➤ *tr (to lock)* echar el cerrojo a, cerrar con pestillo; *(to fasten)* sujetar con tornillos o pernos ➤ *intr (to dash off)* fugarse.

bomb ➤ *s* bomba; JER. *(failure)* fracaso, fiasco ➤ *tr* bombardear.

bomber ➤ *s* bombardero.

bombing ➤ *s* bombardeo.

bombshell ➤ *s* MIL., FIG. bomba.

bond ➤ *s* lazo, atadura; DER. fianza, garantía; FIN. bono, obligación *f* ■ **in b. en depósito**, afianzado ■ *pl* cadenas ➤ *tr & intr* unir(se).

bone ➤ *s* hueso; *(of fish)* espina ➤ *tr* deshuesar; *(fish)* quitar las espinas a.

bonfire ➤ *s* fogata, hoguera.

bonnet ➤ *s (hat)* gorra, cofia; G.B., AUTO. capó.

bonus ➤ *s* plus *m*, sobresueldo.

bony ➤ *adj* óseo; *(fish)* espinoso.

boo ➤ *s* abucheo, rechifla ➤ *interj* ¡bú! ➤ *intr & tr* abuchear (a), rechiflar (a).

book ➤ *s* libro ■ **by the b.** según las reglas ➤ *tr (a suspect)* asentar, registrar; *(to reserve)* reservar.

bookcase ➤ *s* estantería para libros.

booking ➤ *s (engagement)* contratación *f*; *(reservation)* reservación *f*, reserva.

bookkeeper ➤ *s* tenedor/a de libros.

bookkeeping ➤ *s* teneduría de libros, contabilidad *f*.

booklet ➤ *s* folleto.

bookshelf ➤ *s* estante *m* para libros.

bookstore ➤ *s* librería.

boom ➤ *s (sound)* estampido, trueno; COM. auge *m* ➤ *intr* tronar, retumbar; COM. estar en auge.

boost ➤ *tr (to lift)* alzar, levantar; *(to increase)* aumentar ➤ *s (push)* impul-

so; *(increase)* aumento.

boot ➤ *s* bota; G.B. *(trunk)* portaequipajes *m* ■ **to b. FAM.** además ➤ *tr (to kick)* patear; COMPUT. iniciar, arrancar.

booth ➤ *s (compartment)* cabina; *(stand)* puesto, quiosco.

booze ➤ *s* FAM. bebida alcohólica.

border ➤ *s* frontera; *(edge)* borde *m*, orilla ➤ *intr* ■ **to b. on** lindar con; FIG. aproximarse a.

borderline ➤ *s* frontera ➤ *adj* dudoso.

bore ➤ *tr* aburrir ➤ *s (person)* pesado/a, pelmazo *mf*; *(thing)* pesadez *f*.

boredom ➤ *s* aburrimiento.

boring ➤ *adj* aburrido, pesado.

born ➤ *adj* nato ■ **a b. fool** un tonto de nacimiento • **a b. liar** un mentiroso innato • **to be b.** nacer.

borough ➤ *s* municipio.

borrow ➤ *tr* tomar prestado.

boss ➤ *s* supervisor/a, capataz *mf* ➤ *tr* dirigir, mandar.

bossy ➤ *adj* mandón.

botanic(al) ➤ *adj* botánico.

botany ➤ *s* botánica.

both ➤ *pron & adj* ambos, los dos ■ **b. of us**, nos nosotros, vosotros dos ➤ *conj* ■ **he is b. strong and healthy** él es fuerte y sano además.

bother ➤ *tr & intr* molestar(se) *(about, with, por)* ➤ *s* molestia, fastidio.

bothersome ➤ *adj* molesto, fastidioso.

bottle ➤ *s* botella; *(baby's)* biberón *m* ■ **to hit the b.** JER. beber ➤ *tr* embotellar.

bottleneck ➤ *s* FIG. embotellamiento.

bottom ➤ *s* fondo; *(of a list)* final *m*; *(foot)* pie *m*; *(of sea, river)* lecho; FAM. *(buttocks)* trasero.

bough ➤ *s* rama.

boulder ➤ *s* canto rodado.

bounce ➤ *intr* rebotar ■ **to b. back** recuperarse ➤ *s* salto, brinco; *(rebound)* rebote *m*; *(springiness)* elasticidad *f*.

bound[1] ➤ *adj (tied)* atado, amarrado; *(obliged)* obligado ■ **it is b. to happen** tiene forzosamente que ocurrir.

bound[2] ➤ *adj* ■ **b. for** con destino a.

boundary ➤ *s* límite *m*, frontera.

bounds ➤ *spl* límite *m* ■ **out of b.** DEP. fuera de la cancha; *(behavior)* fuera de los límites.

bouquet ➤ *s (of flowers)* ramillete *m; (of wine)* buqué *m.*

bow¹ ➤ *s* MARIT. proa.

bow² ➤ *intr (to stoop)* inclinarse, doblegarse; *(to submit)* someterse ■ **to b. out** retirarse, renunciar ➤ *s (obeisance)* reverencia; *(greeting)* saludo.

bow³ ➤ *s* ARM., MÚS. arco; *(knot)* lazo ■ **b. tie** corbata de lazo.

bowel ➤ *s* intestino ■ *pl* entrañas.

bowl¹ ➤ *s (dish)* fuente *f,* cuenco; *(washbasin)* jofaina; *(toilet)* taza, DEP. estadio.

bowl² ➤ *intr* DEP. jugar a los bolos ■ **to b. over** derribar; FIG. pasmar.

bowling ➤ *s* bolos ■ **b. alley** bolera.

box¹ ➤ *s* caja; *(large)* cajón *m; (small)* estuche *m; (pigeonhole)* casilla; TEAT. palco ■ **b. office** taquilla, boletería ■ **b. spring** colchón de resortes ➤ *tr* ■ **to b. in** encerrar.

box² ➤ *s (blow)* bofetada, cachete *m* ➤ *tr* abofetear ➤ *intr* DEP. boxear.

boxer ➤ *s* boxeador/a, púgil *m.*

boxing ➤ *s* boxeo ■ **b. glove** guante de boxeo.

boy ➤ *s* muchacho, chico; *(child)* niño; *(son)* hijo.

boycott ➤ *tr* boicotear ➤ *s* boicot *m.*

boyfriend ➤ *s* FAM. novio.

bra ➤ *s* sostén *m,* corpiño.

bracelet ➤ *s* brazalete *m,* pulsera.

bracket ➤ *s* soporte *m,* escuadra; *(category)* categoría, grupo.

brag ➤ *tr & intr* jactarse (de) ➤ *s* jactancia, alarde *m.*

braid ➤ *tr* trenzar ➤ *s (plait)* trenza; *(trim)* galón *m.*

brain ➤ *s* cerebro ■ **b. child** FAM. invento, creación ■ *pl* CUL. sesos; *(intelligence)* cabeza ■ **to rack one's b.** devanarse los sesos.

brainwash ➤ *tr* lavar el cerebro.

brainy ➤ *adj* FAM. inteligente, listo.

brake ➤ *s* freno ➤ *tr* frenar ➤ *intr* aplicar el freno.

branch ➤ *s* rama; *(division)* ramo, rama; *(of a river)* brazo; F.C. ramal *m* ➤ *intr* ■ **to b. out** extenderse.

brand ➤ *s* COM. marca (de fábrica); *(style)* modo, manera; *(type)* clase *f;* *(on cattle)* marca (de hierro) ➤ *tr (cattle)* marcar, herrar; *(to stigmatize)* calificar de, tildar de.

brand-new ➤ *adj* flamante.

brandy ➤ *s* coñac *m,* aguardiente *m.*

brass ➤ *s* latón *m;* FAM. *(gall)* descaro ■ *pl* MÚS. cobres.

brat ➤ *s* niño/a malcriado/a, mocoso/a.

brave ➤ *adj* valiente, bravo ➤ *s* guerrero indio ➤ *tr* afrontar; *(to defy)* desafiar.

bravery ➤ *s* valentía, valor *m.*

brawl ➤ *s* pelea ➤ *intr* pelear.

Brazilian ➤ *adj & s* brasileño/a.

breach ➤ *s (of law)* violación *f; (of promise)* incumplimiento; *(of relations)* ruptura ➤ *tr* MIL. abrir brecha en; DER. violar.

bread ➤ *s* pan *m;* JER. *(money)* plata.

breadbasket ➤ *s* panera; *(region)* granero.

breadth ➤ *s (width)* anchura; *(scope)* extensión *f.*

breadwinner ➤ *s* sostén *m* de la familia.

break◇ ➤ *tr* romper; *(to damage)* estropear; *(a law)* infringir, violar; *(spirit, will)* quebrantar; *(a record)* batir ➤ *to* **b. off** romper • **to b. open** abrir forzando • **to b. up** *(to put an end to)* acabar, terminar; *(to upset)* quebrantar ➤ *intr* romperse; *(to become unusable)* estropearse; *(the heart)* partirse; *(the voice)* fallar ■ **to b. away** separarse; *(to escape)* escaparse • **to b. down** *(to malfunction)* averiarse; *(physically)* debilitarse; *(emotionally)* abatirse • **to b. even** salir sin ganar o perder • **to b. out** *(to escape)* escaparse; *(to erupt)* estallar • **to b. through** atravesar, abrirse paso ➤ *s* ruptura, rompimiento; *(crack)* grieta, raja; *(gap)* abertura; *(pause)* intervalo, pausa; *(sudden dash)* salida, arrancada; *(escape)* fuga, evasión *f* ■ **at the b. of day** al amanecer • **lucky b.** coyuntura feliz • **to give someone a b.** dar una oportunidad a alguien • **to take a b.** descansar • **without a b.** sin parar.

breakdown ➤ *s* MEC. avería; MED. colapso, depresión *f.*

breakfast ➤ *s* desayuno ➤ *intr* desayunar, tomar el desayuno.

break-in ➤ s *(illegal entry)* entrada forzada; *(testing)* periodo de prueba.

breakthrough ➤ s adelanto, progreso.

breakup ➤ s separación f; *(of marriage, firm)* disolución f, desintegración f.

breast ➤ s pecho; *(of a woman)* pecho, seno; *(of a fowl)* pechuga.

breastbone ➤ s esternón m.

breast-feed ➤ tr amamantar.

breath ➤ s respiración f, aliento; *(of an animal)* hálito ■ out of b. sin aliento • short of b. corto de resuello • under one's b. en voz baja • to waste one's b. gastar saliva en balde.

breathe ➤ tr & intr respirar ■ to b. in, out inhalar, exhalar.

breather ➤ s FAM. respiro, pausa.

breathing ➤ s respiración f.

breathless ➤ adj sin aliento; *(panting)* jadeante; *(amazed)* sin resuello.

breathtaking ➤ adj impresionante.

breech ➤ s ANAT. trasero; ARM. recámara ■ pl calzones; FAM. pantalones.

breed⬦ ➤ tr engendrar; *(to raise, bring up)* criar ➤ intr reproducirse ➤ s *(strain)* raza; *(type)* casta, especie f.

breeder ➤ s criador/a.

breeding ➤ s crianza, educación f.

breeze ➤ s brisa; FAM. *(easy task)* paseo.

brew ➤ tr *(beer)* fabricar; *(tea)* preparar ➤ intr *(to loom)* amenazar ➤ s infusión f; FAM. *(beer)* cerveza.

brewery ➤ s cervecería.

bribe ➤ s soborno ■ to take bribes dejarse sobornar ➤ tr sobornar.

brick ➤ s ladrillo.

bride ➤ s novia, desposada.

bridegroom ➤ s novio, desposado.

bridesmaid ➤ s dama de honor.

bridge ➤ s puente m ■ to burn one's bridges quemar las naves.

bridle ➤ s brida ➤ tr embridar; *(passions)* refrenar, dominar.

brief ➤ adj *(in time)* breve; *(in length)* corto ➤ s sumario, resumen m; DER. escrito ■ in b. en resumen ■ pl calzoncillos ➤ tr informar.

briefcase ➤ s portafolio, cartera.

bright ➤ adj brillante; *(color)* subido; *(smart)* inteligente, despierto

➤ **brights** spl AUTO. luces altas o de carretera.

brighten ➤ tr & intr aclarar(se), iluminar(se); *(with joy)* alegrar(se).

brightness ➤ s claridad f, brillantez f.

brilliant ➤ adj brillante; *(inventive)* genial.

brim ➤ s borde m; *(of a hat)* ala ➤ intr estar lleno hasta el tope ■ to b. over desbordarse.

bring⬦ ➤ tr traer; *(to carry)* llevar ■ to b. about causar, provocar • to b. back *(to return)* devolver; *(a memory)* traer (a la mente) • to b. in *(to harvest)* recoger; *(money)* rendir, producir • to b. off conseguir, lograr hacer • to b. on ocasionar, causar • to b. oneself to resignarse a • to b. up *(children)* criar, educar; *(a topic)* plantear.

brink ➤ s borde m, margen f ■ on the b. of a punto de.

brisk ➤ adj *(energetic)* enérgico, vigoroso; *(invigorating)* estimulante.

bristle ➤ s cerda ➤ intr ■ to b. with estar lleno o erizado de.

britches ➤ spl FAM. pantalones m.

British ➤ adj británico.

brittle ➤ adj quebradizo, frágil.

broad ➤ adj *(wide)* ancho; *(spacious)* extenso, amplio; *(general)* general ■ in b. daylight en pleno día.

broadcast ➤ tr RAD. emitir, radiar; TELEV. transmitir, televisar; *(to make known)* difundir ➤ s transmisión f, emisión f; *(program)* programa m.

broccoli ➤ s brécol m, bróculi m.

brochure ➤ s folleto.

broil ➤ tr asar a la parrilla.

broiler ➤ s parrilla; *(chicken)* pollo para asar.

broken ➤ adj roto, quebrado; *(out of order)* descompuesto; *(health, law)* quebrantado; *(spirit)* sumiso; *(heart)* destrozado.

broker ➤ s agente mf, corredor/a de bolsa.

bronchitis ➤ s bronquitis f.

bronze ➤ s bronce m ➤ adj de bronce; *(color)* bronceado ➤ tr broncear.

brooch ➤ s broche m.

brood ➤ s ORNIT. nidada; FIG. progenie f.

brook ➤ *s* arroyo.

broom ➤ *s* escoba; BOT. retama.

broth ➤ *s* caldo.

brother ➤ *s* hermano; *(fellow member)* compañero; RELIG. hermano.

brother-in-law ➤ *s* cuñado, hermano político.

brow ➤ *s* frente *f*; *(eyebrow)* ceja.

brown ➤ *s* marrón *m*, castaño ➤ *adj* marrón; *(hair)* castaño; *(skin, sugar)* moreno ➤ *tr & intr* CUL. dorar(se).

browse ➤ *intr (shop)* curiosear; *(book)* hojear un libro; *(to graze)* pacer ➤ *tr (Internet)* navegar (por).

browser ➤ *s* COMPUT. navegador *m*, explorador *m*.

bruise ➤ *s (skin)* magulladura, contusión *f*, *(fruit)* daño ➤ *tr* magullar; *(fruit)* dañar; *(feelings)* herir.

brunch ➤ *s* combinación de desayuno y almuerzo.

brunette ➤ *adj & s* morena.

brush ➤ *s* cepillo; *(paintbrush)* brocha; *(artist's)* pincel *m*; *(encounter)* encuentro ➤ *tr* cepillar; *(to graze)* rozar al pasar ∎ to b. up repasar, retocar.

brutal ➤ *adj* brutal, bestial.

brute ➤ *s* bestia ➤ *adj* bruto; *(cruel)* brutal.

bubble ➤ *s* burbuja; *(of soap)* pompa ∎ b. gum chicle de globo ➤ *intr* burbujear ∎ to b. over with rebosar de.

buck[1] ➤ *s* ZOOL. macho; *(deer)* ciervo ➤ *intr (horse)* botar, corcovear.

buck[2] ➤ *s* JER. dólar *m*.

bucket ➤ *s* cubo, balde *m* ∎ to kick the b. FAM. estirar la pata.

buckle[1] ➤ *s (fastener)* hebilla ➤ *tr & intr* abrochar(se) ∎ to b. down to dedicarse con empeño a.

buckle[2] ➤ *tr & intr (to bend)* combar(se).

bud ➤ *s (shoot)* brote *m*, yema; *(flower)* capullo ➤ *intr (plant)* echar brotes; *(flower)* brotar; FIG. estar en cierne.

budge ➤ *tr & intr (object)* mover(se) un poco; *(person)* (hacer) ceder.

budget ➤ *s* presupuesto ➤ *tr* presupuestar.

buffalo ➤ *s* búfalo; *(bison)* bisonte *m*.

buffet ➤ *s (sideboard)* aparador *m*; *(restaurant)* cantina, buffet *m*.

bug ➤ *s* insecto, bicho; FAM. microbio; *(defect)* defecto, falla (en un sistema); JER. *(enthusiast)* entusiasta *mf* ➤ *tr* JER. fastidiar, importunar.

buggy ➤ *s* calesa; *(baby carriage)* coche *m* de niño.

bugle ➤ *s* clarín *m*, corneta.

build◊ ➤ *tr* construir, edificar; *(to make)* hacer ➤ *intr* ∎ to b. up *(to increase)* aumentar; *(to intensify)* intensificarse ➤ *s* talle *m*, figura.

builder ➤ *s* constructor/a.

building ➤ *s* edificio, casa.

built-up ➤ *adj* urbanizado.

bulb ➤ *s* BOT. bulbo; *(lamp)* bombilla.

bulge ➤ *s* protuberancia, bulto ➤ *intr & tr* hinchar(se), abultar.

bulk ➤ *s* volumen *m*, tamaño; *(largest part)* grueso ∎ in b. *(loose)* a granel, suelto; *(in large amounts)* en grandes cantidades.

bulky ➤ *adj (massive)* voluminoso; *(unwieldy)* pesado.

bull ➤ *s* toro; *(elephant, seal)* macho; JER. tontería ∎ b. session FAM. tertulia ➤ *adj* macho ∎ b. market mercado en alza.

bulldog ➤ *s* buldog *m*, dogo.

bulldozer ➤ *s* bulldozer *m*, excavadora.

bullet ➤ *s* bala.

bulletin ➤ *s* boletín *m*; *(report)* comunicado ∎ b. board tablero de anuncios; COMPUT. pizarra (electrónica), tablero.

bulletproof ➤ *adj* a prueba de balas.

bullfight ➤ *s* corrida de toros.

bullfighter ➤ *s* torero.

bullring ➤ *s* plaza de toros.

bull's-eye ➤ *s (target)* blanco; *(shot)* acierto ∎ to hit the b. dar en el blanco.

bully ➤ *s* matón *m*, abusador/a ➤ *tr* intimidar, amedrentar ➤ *intr* abusar.

bum ➤ *s* vagabundo/a; *(loafer)* vago/a, holgazán/ana ➤ *tr & intr* gorronear, sablear ∎ to b. around vagar ➤ *adj* FAM. sin valor, inútil; *(sore)* dolorido.

bumblebee ➤ *s* abejorro.

bump ➤ *tr* topar, chocar contra ∎ to b. into tropezarse con ➤ *s* choque *m*, topetón *m*; *(swelling)* hinchazón *f*,

chichón m; (in a road) bache m.
bumper ➤ s parachoques m.
bumpy ➤ adj (uneven) desigual, accidentado; (jolty) agitado, sacudido.
bun ➤ s bollo, panecillo; (hair) moño.
bunch ➤ s (of grapes) racimo; (of flowers) ramillete m; (group) montón m ➤ tr & intr agrupar(se), juntar(se).
bundle ➤ s bulto, fardo; (papers) fajo ➤ tr (to tie) atar; (to wrap) envolver ➤ intr ■ to b. up arroparse, abrigarse.
bunion ➤ s juanete m.
bunk ➤ s litera.
bunny ➤ s FAM. conejo, conejito.
buoy ➤ s boya.
burden ➤ s carga ➤ tr (to load) cargar; (to oppress) agobiar.
bureau ➤ s (dresser) tocador m; POL. departamento; (business) agencia.
bureaucracy ➤ s burocracia.
burger ➤ s FAM. hamburguesa.
burglar ➤ s ladrón/ona ■ b. alarm alarma antirrobo.
burglarize ➤ tr robar (casa, tienda).
burglary ➤ s robo con allanamiento de morada.
burial ➤ s entierro ■ b. ground cementerio, camposanto.
burn◇ ➤ tr quemar; (a building) incendiar ■ to b. down incendiar • to b. oneself out JER. agotarse • to b. up (to consume) consumir; FAM. (to enrage) enfurecer ➤ intr quemarse, arder; (building) consumirse; (light bulb) estar encendido; (with fever) arder; (with passion) consumirse ■ to b. out (fire) apagarse; (fuse, bulb) quemarse, fundirse ➤ s quemadura.
burner ➤ s quemador m, mechero.
burning ➤ adj (hot) ardiente, abrasador; (passionate) ardiente; (urgent) urgente.
burp ➤ s eructo ➤ intr eructar ➤ tr hacer eructar (a un niño).
burrow ➤ s madriguera.
bursar ➤ s tesorero.
burst ➤ intr (to break open) estallar, reventarse; (to explode) explotar ■ to b. in interrumpir • to b. into flame(s) estallar en llamas • to b. out (to exclaim) exclamar; (crying, laughing)

echarse a ➤ tr reventar ■ to b. into (a room) irrumpir en; (tears, laughter) desatarse en • to b. with rebosar de ➤ s reventón m, explosión f; (of gunfire) ráfaga; (of energy) explosión (of applause) salva.
bury ➤ tr enterrar; FIG. sepultar.
bus ➤ s autobús m, ómnibus m ➤ tr transportar en autobús.
bush ➤ s (shrub) arbusto; (thicket) maleza; (land) matorral m.
business ➤ s (establishment) comercio, negocio; (firma) firma, empresa; (commerce) negocios; (matter, concern) asunto ■ that's none of your b. eso no es cosa tuya • to mean b. no andar con juegos.
businesslike ➤ adj metódico, serio.
businessman ➤ s hombre m de negocios, comerciante m.
businesswoman ➤ s mujer f de negocios, comerciante f.
bust[1] ➤ s ARTE., ANAT. busto.
bust[2] FAM. ➤ tr romper; (to damage) descomponer; (to arrest) arrestar ➤ intr romperse, descomponerse ➤ s (flop) chasco, fracaso; COM. (to quiebra; (arrest) arresto; (raid) redada, batida.
bustle ➤ intr apresurarse ➤ s bullicio, animación f.
busy ➤ adj atareado, ocupado; (place) animado; (telephone) ocupado.
busybody ➤ s entremetido/a.
but ➤ conj pero, mas; (rather) sino; (nevertheless) no obstante, sin embargo; (except) excepto ■ cannot (help) b. no poder menos que • none b. solamente ➤ adv solamente ■ all b. casi • to do nothing b. no hacer más que ➤ prep ■ b. for a no ser por.
butcher ➤ s carnicero/a ■ b. shop carnicería ➤ tr (animals) matar; FAM. (to botch) chapucear.
butler ➤ s mayordomo.
butt[1] ➤ tr & intr topar ■ to b. in(to) FAM. entremeterse en ➤ s topetazo.
butt[2] ➤ s (of a rifle) culata; (cigarette end) colilla; FAM. (buttocks) trasero.
butter ➤ s mantequilla ➤ tr untar con mantequilla ■ to b. up lisonjear.
butterfly ➤ s mariposa ■ to have butter-

flies in one's stomach tener cosquillas en el estómago.

buttock ➤ s nalga ■ *pl* trasero.

button ➤ s botón *m*; *(badge)* insignia ■ on the b. FAM. correcto, exacto ➤ *tr & intr* abotonar(se), abrochar(se).

buttonhole ➤ s ojal *m*.

buy◊ ➤ *tr* comprar ■ to b. off sobornar • to b. up acaparar ➤ *intr* hacer compras ➤ s compra; FAM. *(bargain)* ganga.

buyer ➤ s comprador/a.

buzz ➤ *intr* zumbar; *(buzzer)* sonar; *(to ring)* tocar el timbre ➤ s zumbido; *(murmur)* murmullo; FAM. *(phone call)* telefonazo ■ b. saw sierra circular.

by ➤ *prep* por, de ■ by birth de nacimiento • by mail por correo • by night de noche • by noon para el mediodía • by the bed junto a la cama • by the by de paso, a propósito • by the dozen por docena • by the rules de acuerdo con las reglas • by the way de paso, entre paréntesis • by this time *(hour)* a esta hora; *(point)* a estas alturas • day by day día a día • made by hecho por ➤ *adv (nearby)* cerca, al lado de; *(aside)* a un lado, aparte ■ by and by *(soon)* pronto; *(after a while)* más tarde • by and large en términos generales • by then para entonces.

bye(-bye) ➤ *interj* FAM. ¡adiós!, ¡chau!

by-pass ➤ s carretera de circunvalación ■ coronary b. desviación coronaria ➤ *tr* evitar, pasar por alto.

bystander ➤ s espectador/a, circunstante *mf*.

byte ➤ s byte *m*, octeto.

C

cab ➤ s taxi *m*; *(of vehicle)* cabina.

cabbage ➤ s col *f*, berza.

cabdriver ➤ s taxista *mf*.

cabin ➤ s barraca, choza; *(of ship)* camarote *m*; *(of plane)* cabina.

cabinet ➤ s armario; POL. consejo o gabinete *m* de ministros.

cable ➤ s cable *m*; *(cablegram)* cablegrama *m*; TELEV. televisión *f* por cable ■ c. car funicular ➤ *tr & intr* cablegrafiar.

cablevision ➤ s televisión *f* por cable.

cache ➤ s escondrijo; *(goods)* reserva ➤ *tr* guardar en un escondrijo.

cactus ➤ s cactus *m*, cacto.

cadaver ➤ s cadáver *m*.

cafeteria ➤ s cafetería.

caffeine ➤ s cafeína.

cage ➤ s jaula ➤ *tr* enjaular.

cake ➤ s pastel *m*; *(sponge)* bizcocho; *(of soap)* pastilla ■ to take the c. FAM. ser el colmo ➤ *tr & intr* endurecer(se).

calculate ➤ *tr* calcular ➤ *intr* hacer cálculos.

calculation ➤ s cálculo.

calculator ➤ s calculadora.

calendar ➤ s calendario.

calf¹ ➤ s becerro, ternero; *(of whale, elephant)* cría.

calf² ➤ s ANAT. pantorrilla.

call ➤ *tr* llamar; *(a meeting)* convocar; *(to label)* calificar (de) ■ to c. back hacer volver; TEL. volver a llamar • to c. off cancelar • to c. oneself llamarse • to c. together convocar, reunir • to c. to mind evocar • to c. up telefonear; MIL. llamar a las armas ➤ *intr (to yell)* llamar, gritar; ORNIT., ZOOL. reclamarse ■ to c. for necesitar • to c. on *(to visit)* visitar a; *(to appeal)* recurrir a; *(God)* invocar • to c. out gritar ➤ s llamada; ORNIT., ZOOL. reclamo, canto; *(of bugle)* toque *m*; *(short visit)* visita; *(summons, appeal)* llamamiento ■ on c. de guardia • port of c. puerto de escala.

caller ➤ s visita, visitante *mf*.

calling ➤ s vocación *f* ■ c. card tarjeta de visita.

callus ➤ s callo ■ *intr* encallecerse.

calm ➤ *adj* sereno, tranquilo ➤ s calma ➤ *tr & intr* aplacar(se), calmar(se).

calorie ➤ s caloría.

came ➤ *vea* come en tabla de verbos.

camel ➤ s camello.

camera ➤ s FOTOG. cámara, máquina; CINEM. cámara.

camp ➤ s campo; *(encampment)* campamento ➤ *intr & tr* acampar.

campaign ➤ *intr & s* (hacer una) campaña.

campanile ➤ s campanario.

camper ➤ s campista mf; AUTO. caravana.

campfire ➤ s hoguera de campamento.

campground ➤ s camping m.

campsite ➤ s camping m.

campus ➤ s ciudad universitaria.

can¹ ➤ aux. (to be able to) poder; (to know how to) saber ■ he c. cook él sabe cocinar.

can² ➤ s (tin) lata; (for trash) tacho, cubo ■ c. opener abrelatas ➤ tr enlatar; JER. (to fire) despedir.

Canadian ➤ adj & s canadiense mf.

canal ➤ s canal m.

canary ➤ s canario.

cancel ➤ tr anular, cancelar; (a stamp) matar ➤ s cancelación f, anulación f.

cancellation ➤ s cancelación f; (of stamp) matasellos m.

cancer ➤ s cáncer m.

candid ➤ adj franco; (not posed) espontáneo.

candidate ➤ s candidato/a.

candle ➤ s vela, bujía; (in church) cirio.

candlestick ➤ s candelero.

candy ➤ s caramelo ■ c. store confitería.

cane ➤ s bastón m; (switch) vara; (plant) caña; (wicker) mimbre m ➤ tr golpear con una vara.

canebrake ➤ s cañaveral m.

canned ➤ adj enlatado; FAM. (taped) grabado.

cannery ➤ s fábrica de conservas.

cannibal ➤ s caníbal mf, antropófago/a.

cannon ➤ s cañón m.

canoe ➤ intr & s (ir en) canoa.

canopy ➤ s dosel m; (of leaves, stars) bóveda.

canteen ➤ s (store, cafeteria) cantina; (flask) cantimplora.

canvas ➤ s lona; (painting) lienzo; (sails) velamen m.

canyon ➤ s cañón m.

cap ➤ s gorro, gorra; (cover) tapa; (limit) tope m ➤ tr cubrir; (to complete) terminar ■ to c. off culminar.

capable ➤ adj capaz.

capacity ➤ s capacidad f ■ in the c. of en calidad de.

cape¹ ➤ s GEOG. cabo.

cape² ➤ s (garment) capa.

capital¹ ➤ s (city) capital f; (assets, wealth) capital m; IMPR. (letter) mayúscula ■ c. punishment pena capital o de muerte ➤ adj (foremost) capital; (excellent) excelente.

capital² ➤ s ARQ. capitel m.

capitol ➤ s capitolio.

capsule ➤ s cápsula.

captain ➤ s capitán/ana ➤ tr capitanear.

caption ➤ s leyenda; TELEV. subtítulo.

capture ➤ tr capturar; (a prize) ganar ➤ s captura.

car ➤ s AUTO. coche m, carro; F.C. coche m, vagón m; (tramcar) tranvía m.

caramel ➤ s caramelo.

caravan ➤ s caravana.

carbon ➤ s carbono ■ c. copy copia al carbón • c. dioxide bióxido de carbono • c. paper papel carbón.

carburetor ➤ s carburador m.

card ➤ s (playing) naipe m, carta; (greeting) tarjeta; (post) (tarjeta) postal f; (index) ficha; (ID) carnet m ➤ pl naipes • it's in the c. está escrito.

cardboard ➤ s cartón m.

cardigan ➤ s chaqueta de punto.

cardinal ➤ adj cardinal ➤ s ORNIT., RELIG. cardenal m.

care ➤ s (worry) inquietud f, preocupación f; (grief) pena; (charge) cargo; (caution) cuidado ■ (in) c. of para entregar a • to take c. (not to) tener cuidado (de que no) • to take c. of (person) cuidar de; (thing) (pre)ocuparse de ➤ intr (to be concerned) preocuparse; (to mind) importar ■ I don't c. no me importa • to c. for cuidar • to c. to tener ganas de, querer.

career ➤ s carrera, profesión f.

carefree ➤ adj despreocupado.

careful ➤ adj cauteloso; (thorough) cuidadoso ■ to be c. tener cuidado.

careless ➤ adj descuidado; (unconcerned) indiferente; (offhand) espontáneo.

caress ➤ s caricia ➤ tr acariciar.

cargo ➤ s carga, cargamento.

Caribbean ➤ adj & s caribeño/a.

carnation ➤ s clavel m.

carnival ➤ s (season) carnaval m; (fair) feria, parque m de atracciones.

carol ➤ s villancico.
carpenter ➤ s carpintero/a.
carpentry ➤ s carpintería.
carpet ➤ s alfombra ▪ tr alfombrar.
carriage ➤ s carruaje m, coche m; (posture) porte m ▪ baby c. cochecito de niños.
carrot ➤ s zanahoria.
carry ➤ tr llevar; (a disease) transmitir; MAT. llevarse ▪ to c. on (conversation) mantener; (business) dirigir • to c. out realizar, llevar a cabo • to c. through completar, llevar a cabo.
carsick ➤ adj mareado.
cart ➤ s carro; (handcart) carretilla ▪ tr acarrear; (to lug) arrastrar ▪ to c. away o off llevar.
carton ➤ s caja de cartón.
cartoon ➤ s (political) caricatura; (film) dibujos animados.
cartridge ➤ s cartucho; (cassette) casete m; (ink refill) repuesto ▪ c. belt cartuchera.
carve ➤ tr CUL. trinchar; ARTE. (to sculpt) tallar, cincelar; (to engrave) grabar ▪ to c. out labrar.
carving ➤ s talla, escultura.
cascade ➤ s cascada ➤ intr caer en forma de cascada.
case¹ ➤ s caso; (example) ejemplo; DER. causa, pleito ▪ a c. of honor una cuestión de honor • c. history hoja clínica • in any c. en todo caso • in no c. de ningún modo • in that c. en tal caso • just in c. por si acaso.
case² ➤ s (box) caja; (outer covering) estuche m; (slipcover) funda.
cash ➤ s efectivo ▪ c. register caja registradora • to pay (in) c. pagar al contado ▪ tr hacer efectivo, cobrar ▪ to c. in convertir en efectivo.
cashbox ➤ s caja.
cashier ➤ s cajero/a ▪ c.'s check cheque de caja.
casino ➤ s casino.
cask ➤ s barril m, tonel m.
casserole ➤ s cazuela, cacerola.
cassette ➤ s (film) cartucho; (tape) casete m.
cast◇ ➤ tr (to hurl) tirar, arrojar; (anchor, vote) echar; (glance) volver,

dirigir; (light, shadow) proyectar; CINEM. (roles) repartir; (actor) asignar una parte a; METAL. moldear ▪ to c. aside o away desechar, descartar • to c. doubt (up)on poner en duda ➤ s tirada, lanzamiento; (of dice) tirada; (appearance) apariencia; METAL. molde f, forma; MED. enyesadura; CINEM., TEAT. reparto ▪ c. iron hierro fundido.
castle ➤ s castillo.
casual ➤ adj casual; (occasional) irregular; (indifferent) despreocupado; (informal) informal.
casualty ➤ s accidente m; (victim) accidentado, víctima; MIL. baja.
cat ➤ s gato ▪ to let the c. out of the bag revelar un secreto.
catacombs ➤ spl catacumbas.
catalog(ue) ➤ s catálogo ➤ tr catalogar.
catapult ➤ s catapulta ➤ tr catapultar.
catastrophe ➤ s catástrofe f.
catastrophic ➤ adj catastrófico.
catch◇ ➤ tr coger, agarrar; (to capture) prender, capturar; (animals) atrapar, cazar; (fish) pescar; (bus, train) alcanzar, tomar; (to snag, hook) engancharse (on en); (an illness) coger, contraer; (to surprise) sorprender ▪ to c. up on ponerse al corriente en cuanto a • to c. up with alcanzar ➤ intr (to become hooked) engancharse; (to snag) enredarse ▪ to c. on (to understand) comprender; (a fad) volverse muy popular ▪ s (act) cogida; (lock) cerradura; (in hunting) presa; (in fishing) pesca; (capture) captura.
catcher ➤ s DEP. receptor/a.
catching ➤ adj contagioso.
category ➤ s categoría.
cater ➤ intr abastecer de comida ▪ to c. to intentar satisfacer los deseos de.
caterpillar ➤ s oruga.
cathedral ➤ s catedral f.
catholic ➤ adj general, universal ▪ C. adj & s católico/a.
cattle ➤ s ganado vacuno.
cauliflower ➤ s coliflor f.
cause ➤ s causa; (reason) motivo, razón f ➤ tr causar, provocar.
caution ➤ s cautela, precaución f;

(warning) advertencia ➤ *tr* advertir, amonestar.

cautious ➤ *adj* cauteloso, precavido.

cave ➤ *s* cueva ➤ *intr* ■ **to c. in** *(to collapse)* derrumbarse; *(to yield)* ceder.

cave-in ➤ *s* hundimiento, socavón *m*.

cavern ➤ *s* caverna.

cavity ➤ *s* cavidad *f*; ODONT. caries *f*.

CD ➤ *s* disco compacto, CD *m*.

cease ➤ *tr (to stop)* dejar de; *(to discontinue)* suspender ■ **c. fire!** MIL. ¡alto el fuego! ➤ *intr* cesar ■ **c** cese *m* ■ **without c.** incesantemente.

ceiling ➤ *s* cielo raso, techo.

celebrate ➤ *tr* celebrar; *(an occasion)* festejar, conmemorar ➤ *intr* festejarse.

celebration ➤ *s* celebración *f*.

celebrity ➤ *s* celebridad *f*.

celery ➤ *s* apio.

celestial ➤ *adj (of the sky)* celeste; *(divine)* celestial.

celibacy ➤ *s* celibato.

celibate ➤ *adj & s* célibe *mf*.

cell ➤ *s* celda; BIOL., ELEC., POL. célula ■ **c. phone** celular *m*.

cellar ➤ *s* sótano; *(of wines)* bodega.

cello ➤ *s* violoncelo.

cellular ➤ *adj* celular ■ **c. telephone** teléfono celular, celular *m*.

cement ➤ *s* cemento; *(glue)* pegamento ■ **c. mixer** hormigonera ➤ *tr* unir con cemento; *(to glue)* pegar; FIG. cimentar.

cemetery ➤ *s* cementerio.

censorship ➤ *s* censura.

censure ➤ *s* censura ➤ *tr* censurar.

cent ➤ *s* centavo, céntimo.

center ➤ *s* centro ➤ *tr* centrar.

centigrade ➤ *adj* centígrado.

centimeter ➤ *s* centímetro.

centipede ➤ *s* ciempiés *m*.

central ➤ *adj* central.

Central American ➤ *adj & s* centroamericano/a.

centric ➤ *adj* céntrico, central.

centrifuge ➤ *s* centrifugadora.

century ➤ *s* siglo.

ceramic ➤ *s (clay)* arcilla, barro; *(porcelain)* porcelana ■ **ceramics** *sg* cerámica.

cereal ➤ *s* cereal *m*.

ceremony ➤ *s* ceremonia.

certain ➤ *adj (definite)* cierto; *(sure)* seguro; *(some)* algunos, ciertos ■ **for c.** por cierto • **to make c.** asegurarse.

certainly ➤ *adv* cierto; *(of course)* por supuesto; *(without fail)* seguro.

certainty ➤ *s* certeza; *(fact)* cosa segura.

certificate ➤ *s* certificado, partida.

certify ➤ *tr & intr* certificar.

chain ➤ *s* cadena ■ **c. saw** sierra de cadena • **c. store** sucursal de una cadena de tiendas ➤ *tr* encadenar.

chair ➤ *s* silla; *(chairman/woman)* presidente/a; EDUC. cátedra ■ **c. lift** telesilla ➤ *tr* presidir.

chairman ➤ *s* presidente *m*.

chalk ➤ *s* MIN. creta; *(marker)* tiza ➤ *tr* marcar, escribir (con tiza) ■ **to c. up** apuntarse (tanto, victoria).

challenge ➤ *s* desafío, reto; DER. recusación *f* ➤ *tr* desafiar, retar; *(to contest)* disputar; DER. recusar.

challenging ➤ *adj* arduo, difícil.

chamber ➤ *s* cámara ■ *pl* despacho (de un juez).

champagne ➤ *s* champaña *m*.

champion ➤ *s* campeón/ona ➤ *tr* abogar por.

championship ➤ *s* campeonato.

chance ➤ *s* casualidad *f*; *(luck)* suerte *f*; *(opportunity)* oportunidad *f*; *(possibility)* posibilidad *f*; *(risk)* riesgo ➤ *intr* suceder, acaecer ➤ *tr* arriesgar ➤ *adj* casual, fortuito.

chancellor ➤ *s* canciller *mf*.

chandelier ➤ *s* araña.

change ➤ *tr & intr* cambiar (de); *(clothes, color)* mudar (de); *(to transform)* convertir(se) ➤ *s* cambio; *(substitution)* relevo; *(of clothing)* muda; *(money)* cambio, vuelto; *(coins)* suelto ■ **for a c.** para variar • **keep the c.** quédese con el vuelto.

changeable ➤ *adj* cambiable; *(inconstant)* variable.

changeover ➤ *s* cambio.

channel ➤ *s* canal *m*; *(riverbed)* cauce *m*; *(groove)* ranura ➤ *tr* canalizar.

chant ➤ *s* canto; RELIG. cántico ➤ *tr & intr* cantar, salmodiar.

chaos ➤ s caos m.

chaotic ➤ adj caótico.

chapel ➤ s capilla.

chapter ➤ s capítulo; (of a club) sección f.

character ➤ s carácter m; LIT. (role) personaje m, papel m; FAM. (guy) tipo ■ in c. característico.

characteristic ➤ adj característico ➤ s característica.

charcoal ➤ s carbon m vegetal; DIB. carboncillo.

charge ➤ tr (to entrust) encargar, encomendar; (to accuse) acusar; COM. (a price) pedir, cobrar; (on credit) cargar; MIL. atacar; ELEC. cargar ➤ s (management) cargo; (accusation) acusación f; (burden) carga, peso; (cost) costo; (tax) impuesto; ARM., ELEC., MIL. carga ■ in c. of encargado de • to be in c. ser el encargado • to take c. asumir el mando.

charitable ➤ adj caritativo.

charity ➤ s caridad f, beneficencia; (institution) beneficencia.

charm ➤ s encanto; (amulet) amuleto ➤ tr encantar.

charming ➤ adj encantador.

chart ➤ s MARÍT. carta de navegación ➤ tr trazar.

charter ➤ s POL. carta; (of organization) estatutos ■ c. flight vuelo fletado ➤ tr (to rent) fletar.

chase ➤ tr perseguir (after a) ■ to c. away o off ahuyentar • to c. out echar fuera ➤ s persecución f ■ the c. (sport) la cacería; (quarry) caza, presa.

chasm ➤ s abismo.

chassis ➤ s chasis m.

chat ➤ intr charlar, platicar; COMPUT. charlar, chatear ➤ s charla, plática; COMPUT. charla, chat m ■ c. room sala o canal de charla.

chatter ➤ intr parlotear, chacharear; (teeth) castañetear ➤ s cháchara.

chauffeur ➤ s chófer mf ➤ tr conducir.

chauvinist ➤ s chauvinista mf.

cheap ➤ adj barato; (inferior) de mala calidad; (tawdry) charro; (stingy) tacaño ➤ adv barato.

cheat ➤ tr (to swindle) defraudar, esta-

far; (to deceive) engañar ➤ intr hacer trampa; (on exam) copiar.

check ➤ s (halt) detención f; (restraint) freno; (verification) chequeo; (mark) marca, señal f; (bill) cuenta (de restaurante); (bank draft) cheque m ➤ interj ¡jaque! ➤ tr (to halt) detener; (to restrain) refrenar; (to verify) verificar; (hat, coat) depositar; (luggage) facturar ■ to c. out FAM. comprobar • to c. up on comprobar, verificar • to c. with consultar con ➤ intr ■ to c. in (to) registrarse (en un hotel) • to c. out (of) pagar la cuenta y marcharse (de un hotel).

checkbook ➤ s chequera, talonario.

checkers ➤ spl damas.

checkerboard ➤ s tablero de damas.

checkmate ➤ s jaque y mate m.

check-out ➤ s (exit) salida (de hotel, supermercado); (inspection) inspección f.

checkpoint ➤ s lugar m de inspección.

checkroom ➤ s guardarropa m; (for luggage) consigna.

checkup ➤ s chequeo, reconocimiento médico general.

cheek ➤ s mejilla; (impudence) descaro.

cheeky ➤ adj descarado, caradura.

cheer ➤ tr (to gladden) animar, alegrar; (to encourage) alentar; (to shout) vitorear, ovacionar ■ to c. on animar, alentar ➤ intr aplaudir ■ c. up! ¡ánimo! • to c. up alegrarse ➤ s alegría, ánimo; (shout) viva, hurra ■ pl c.! ¡salud!

cheerful ➤ adj alegre.

cheese ➤ s queso.

cheesecake ➤ s quesadilla.

chef ➤ s cocinero/a, jefe/a de cocina.

chemical ➤ adj químico ➤ s sustancia química.

chemist ➤ s químico/a; G.B. (pharmacist) farmacéutico.

chemistry ➤ s química.

cherry ➤ s cereza ■ c. tree cerezo.

chess ➤ s ajedrez m.

chessboard ➤ s tablero de ajedrez.

chest ➤ s pecho; (box) cofre m, arca m; (dresser) cómoda.

chestnut ➤ s castaña ■ c. tree castaño

➤ adj castaño, marrón.

chew ➤ tr & intr masticar, mascar ■ to c. out regañar • to c. over rumiar.

chewing ➤ s masticación f ■ c. gum chicle, goma de mascar.

chick ➤ s polluelo; JER. (girl) chavala.

chicken ➤ s gallina, pollo ■ c. pox varicela ➤ adj FAM. miedoso, cobarde ➤ intr ■ to c. out acobardarse.

chickpea ➤ s garbanzo.

chief ➤ s jefe/a ■ c. executive primer mandatorio • c. justice presidente del tribunal ➤ adj principal.

chiefly ➤ adv principalmente.

child ➤ s niño/a; (offspring) hijo/a.

childhood ➤ s niñez f, infancia.

childish ➤ adj infantil, pueril.

children ➤ pl de child.

Chilean ➤ adj & s chileno/a.

chili ➤ s chile m, ají m.

chill ➤ s frío; (shiver) escalofrío ■ to catch a c. resfriarse ➤ adj frío ➤ tr enfriar; (food) refrigerar.

chilly ➤ adj frío.

chime ➤ s carillón m; (sound) repique m ■ pl carillón ➤ intr repicar ■ to c. in intervenir (en una conversación).

chimney ➤ s chimenea; (of a lamp) tubo de vidrio.

chimpanzee ➤ s chimpancé m.

chin ➤ s barbilla, mentón m ■ to keep one's c. up no desanimarse.

china ➤ s china, porcelana; (crockery) loza.

chip ➤ s pedacito, trozo; (splinter) astilla; (in china) desportilladura; (in gambling) ficha; ELECTRÓN. placa ■ pl patatas fritas ➤ tr hacer astillas; (to chop) picar ➤ intr ■ to c. in contribuir.

chiropractor ➤ s quiropráctico/a.

chisel ➤ s cincel m ➤ tr cincelar; FAM. (to cheat) estafar.

chlorine ➤ s cloro.

chocolate ➤ adj & s (de) chocolate m.

choice ➤ s elección f, selección f; (option) opción f; (assortment) surtido; (alternative) alternative ■ by c. por gusto ➤ adj escogido, superior.

choir ➤ s coro.

choke ➤ tr estrangular, ahogar; (to suffocate) sofocar ■ to c. back ahogar • to

c. down tragar con asco ➤ intr sofocarse, ahogarse; (on food) atragantarse; (to clog) atorarse ■ to c. up FAM. emocionarse ➤ s sofocación f, ahogo; AUTO. estrangulador m.

cholera ➤ s cólera m.

cholesterol ➤ s colesterol m.

choose◊ ➤ tr elegir, escoger; (to prefer) preferir ➤ intr ■ to do as one chooses hacer lo que quiere.

chop ➤ tr cortar; (to mince) picar ■ to c. down talar • to c. up cortar en trozos ➤ s corte m, tajo; CUL. chuleta.

chopper ➤ s FAM. helicóptero.

choppy ➤ adj picado, agitado.

chopsticks ➤ spl palillos chinos.

chord ➤ s MÚS. acorde m; GEOM. cuerda.

chore ➤ s quehacer m, faena.

choreographer ➤ s coreógrafo/a.

chorus ➤ s coro; (refrain) estribillo ■ in c. al unísono.

chosen ➤ adj & s elegido, escogido.

christen ➤ tr bautizar.

christening ➤ s bautismo, bautizo.

Christian ➤ adj & s cristiano/a ■ C. name nombre de pila.

Christmas ➤ s Navidad f.

chrome ➤ s cromo.

chrysanthemum ➤ s crisantemo.

chubby ➤ adj rechoncho.

chunk ➤ s pedazo, trozo.

church ➤ s iglesia.

churn ➤ s mantequera ➤ tr agitar, revolver ■ to c. out producir en profusión ➤ intr agitarse, revolverse.

chute ➤ s rampa, tobogán m.

cicada ➤ s cigarra.

cider ➤ s sidra.

cigar ➤ s cigarro, puro.

cigarette ➤ s cigarrillo.

cinema ➤ s cine m.

cinematography ➤ s cinematografía.

cinnamon ➤ s canela.

circle ➤ s círculo; (orbit) órbita; (turn) vuelta ■ to come full c. volver al punto de partida ➤ tr (to draw) hacer un círculo alrededor de; (to revolve around) girar alrededor de ➤ intr dar vueltas.

circuit ➤ s circuito ■ c. board placa o tarjeta de circuitos • c. breaker cortacircuitos.

circular ➤ *adj & s* circular *f.*

circulate ➤ *tr & intr* circular.

circulation ➤ *s* circulación *f.*

circumference ➤ *s* circunferencia.

circumstance ➤ *s* circunstancia ■ *pl* situación, posición • **under no c. de** ninguna manera.

circus ➤ *s* circo.

citadel ➤ *s* ciudadela.

cite ➤ *tr* citar.

citizen ➤ *s* ciudadano/a.

citizenship ➤ *s* ciudadanía.

city ➤ *s* ciudad *f* ■ **c. hall** ayuntamiento.

civil ➤ *adj* civil ■ **c. service** administración pública.

civilian ➤ *adj & s* civil *mf.*

civilization ➤ *s* civilización *f.*

civilize ➤ *tr* civilizar.

claim ➤ *tr* reclamar; *(to state)* afirmar ➤ *s* reclamación *f*; *(assertion)* afirmación *f*; *(right)* derecho, título; DER. demanda.

clam ➤ *s* almeja.

clamp ➤ *s* TEC. grapa, abrazadera; CARP. cárcel *f* ➤ *tr* sujetar con abrazadera ■ **to c. down on** FAM. reprimir.

clap ➤ *intr* dar palmadas ➤ *s* aplauso; *(tap)* palmada; *(bang)* estampido.

clapping ➤ *s* aplausos; *(in time)* palmadas.

claret ➤ *s* clarete *m.*

clarinet ➤ *s* clarinete *m.*

clarity ➤ *s* claridad *f.*

clash ➤ *intr* chocar ➤ *s (noise)* estruendo; *(collision)* choque *m*; *(conflict)* desacuerdo.

clasp ➤ *s (device)* cierre *m*, broche *m*; *(hug)* abrazo; *(of the hands)* apretón *m* ➤ *tr (to hug)* abrazar; *(to clutch)* agarrar; *(the hand)* apretar.

class ➤ *s* clase *f* ■ **c. of 2003** promoción de 2003 ➤ *tr* clasificar.

classic ➤ *adj & s* clásico.

classical ➤ *adj* clásico.

classify ➤ *tr* clasificar.

classmate ➤ *s* compañero/a de clase.

classroom ➤ *s* aula, sala de clase.

clause ➤ *s* cláusula *f*; GRAM. oración *f.*

claw ➤ *s* garra; *(of cat)* uña; *(of crab)* tenaza, pinza ➤ *tr & intr* arañar.

clay ➤ *s* arcilla.

clean ➤ *adj* limpio; *(pure)* puro; *(total)* completo, radical ➤ *adv* limpiamente; FAM. completamente ■ **to come c.** confesarlo todo ➤ *tr* limpiar; *(fish)* escamar y abrir ■ **to c. out** *(to empty out)* vaciar; *(to use up)* agotar • **to c. up** acabar con *(un asunto)* ➤ *intr* limpiar(se) ■ **to c. house** FIG. poner las cosas en orden • **to c. up** FAM. ganarse una fortuna.

cleaner ➤ *s* limpiador *m*, quitamanchas *m* ■ **c.'s** tintorería.

cleaning ➤ *s* limpieza.

cleanliness ➤ *s* limpieza, aseo.

clear ➤ *adj* claro; *(sky, view)* despejado; *(air, water)* transparente; *(evident)* evidente; *(conscience)* limpio, tranquilo ■ **c. of** libre de • **c. profit** beneficio neto • **to make oneself c.** explicar claramente ➤ *adv* claro, con claridad ■ **to stand c.** mantenerse aparte ➤ *tr (to make clear)* aclarar; *(to unobstruct)* despejar; *(a path, way)* abrir; *(the table)* levantar; *(to remove)* quitar; *(the throat)* aclararse; *(to exonerate)* limpiar; *(to acquit)* absolver; *(a check)* compensar; *(customs)* sacar de la aduana ■ **to c. up** *(doubt)* disipar; *(mystery)* aclarar ➤ *intr* aclararse; *(sky)* despejarse ■ **to c. out** largarse ➤ *s* ■ **in the c.** fuera de sospecha.

clearance ➤ *s (removal)* despejo; *(sale)* liquidación *f*, saldo; *(leeway)* espacio, margen *m*; *(by customs)* despacho.

clearly ➤ *adv* claramente; *(evidently)* evidentemente; *(of course)* claro.

clench ➤ *tr* apretar ➤ *s* apretón *m.*

clergy ➤ *s* clero.

clergyman ➤ *s* clérigo.

clerical ➤ *adj* de oficina; RELIG. clerical.

clerk ➤ *s (in office)* oficinista *mf*; *(in store)* dependiente *mf*; DER. escribano/a, amanuense *mf.*

clever ➤ *adj (bright)* listo, inteligente; *(witty)* ingenioso; *(skillful)* hábil.

click ➤ *s* chasquido, ruido seco; COMPUT. clic *m*, pinche *m* ➤ *intr* chasquear; COMPUT. pulsar, pinchar ➤ *tr (tongue)* chasquear; *(heels)* taconear.

client ➤ *s* cliente *mf.*

cliff ➤ *s* acantilado, precipicio.

climate ➤ s clima m.

climax ➤ s culminación f; LIT., RET. clímax m ➤ intr culminar.

climb ➤ tr & intr subir; (to scale) escalar, trepar ■ to c. down descender, bajar ➤ s subida, ascenso.

climber ➤ s alpinista mf, andinista mf.

cling◇ ➤ intr (to hold fast) asirse, agarrarse; (to stick) pegarse.

clinic ➤ s clínica.

clip¹ ➤ tr recortar; (to trim) podar.

clip² ➤ s (fastener) sujetador m; (for paper) sujetapapeles m; (for hair) horquilla; (of rifle) cargador m ➤ tr sujetar.

clipper ➤ s (shears) tijeras; MARÍT. clíper m ■ pl tijeras ■ nail c. cortaúñas.

clipping ➤ s recorte m.

cloak ➤ s capa, manto ➤ tr encubrir.

cloakroom ➤ s guardarropa m.

clock ➤ s reloj m (de pie, de mesa); DEP. cronómetro ➤ tr cronometrar.

clockwise ➤ adv & adj en el sentido de las agujas del reloj.

cloister ➤ s claustro; RELIG. monasterio, convento ➤ tr enclaustrar.

clone ➤ s clon m ➤ tr & intr clonar(se), reproducir(se) asexualmente.

close ➤ adj cercano; (relationship) íntimo; (similar) parecido; (contest) reñido; (rigorous) minucioso; (attention) total ■ a c. resemblance un gran parecido ■ at c. range a quemarropa, de cerca • c. call FAM. escape difícil ➤ tr cerrar; (letter) concluir; (session) levantar; (gap, distance) acortar ■ to c. down cerrar definitivamente • to c. in rodear, cercar • to c. up (shop) cerrar; (opening) tapar ➤ intr cerrarse; (shop) cerrar; (story, show) terminarse, concluirse ➤ s final m, conclusión f ■ to bring to a c. terminar ➤ adv cerca ■ c. at hand cerca a mano • c. by muy cerca • c. to muy cerca de, junto a • c. together muy juntos • to come c. acercarse.

closed-circuit television ➤ s televisión f en circuito cerrado.

closet ➤ s armario, ropero.

clot ➤ s coágulo ➤ intr cuajarse.

cloth ➤ s tela, paño; (strip) trapo ■ the c. el clero.

clothes ➤ spl ropa, vestimenta.

clothesline ➤ s cuerda para tender ropa.

clothespin ➤ s pinza para tender ropa.

clothing ➤ s ropa, indumentaria.

cloud ➤ s nube f; (shadow) sombra ■ under a c. bajo sospecha ➤ tr & intr nublar(se), anublar(se) ■ to c. over o up nublarse.

cloudy ➤ adj nublado; (liquid) turbio.

clove ➤ s (spice) clavo de especia; (of garlic) diente m.

clover ➤ s trébol m.

clown ➤ s payaso/a ➤ intr payasear.

club ➤ s (cudgel) porra; (golf) palo; (in cards) trébol m, basto; (association) club m ➤ tr aporrear.

clue ➤ s pista, indicio; (in puzzle) indicación f ■ I haven't a c. no tengo ni idea.

clumsy ➤ adj torpe; (unwieldy) incómodo; (unrefined) crudo.

clutch ➤ tr agarrar, asir ➤ s (grasp) apretón m; MEC. embrague m ■ in the c. en situación crítica ■ pl FIG. garras.

clutter ➤ s desorden m ➤ tr ■ to be cluttered with estar atestado con.

coach ➤ s (carriage) coche m, carruaje m; (bus) ómnibus m; AVIA. clase económica; (trainer) entrenador/a ➤ tr & intr (to tutor) dar lecciones suplementarias; (to train) entrenar.

coal ➤ s carbón m, hulla; (ember) ascua.

coarse ➤ adj (inferior) basto; (uncouth) vulgar; (rough) áspero, tosco; (grainy) granular.

coast ➤ s costa ■ c. guard guardacostas ■ the c. is clear no hay moros en la costa ➤ intr (to slide) deslizarse; (bicycle, car) rodar sin impulso.

coat ➤ s (overcoat) abrigo; (jacket) saco, chaqueta; (of animal) piel f, pelo; (paint) mano f, capa ➤ tr (to cover) revestir; (to paint) dar una capa.

coating ➤ s (layer) capa, mano f; (gold, silver) baño, revestimiento.

cob ➤ s elote m, mazorca.

cobblestone ➤ s piedra redonda ■ c. pavement empedrado.

cobweb ➤ s telaraña.

cocaine ➤ s cocaína.

cock ➤ s *(rooster)* gallo; *(male bird)* macho; *(faucet)* grifo, llave *f*; ARM. martillo ➤ tr ARM. amartillar; *(a hat)* inclinar *(hacia arriba)*.

cockpit ➤ s cancha; AVIA. cabina.

cockroach ➤ s cucaracha.

cocktail ➤ s cóctel *m*.

cocoa ➤ s cacao.

coconut ➤ s coco ■ c. palm cocotero.

cod or **codfish** ➤ s bacalao.

code ➤ s código; *(cipher)* clave *f*, cifra ➤ tr codificar; *(a message)* cifrar.

coed ➤ s FAM. ➤ s alumna de una universidad mixta ➤ adj coeducacional.

coffee ➤ s café *m* ■ c. shop café, cafetería • c. table mesa de café *o* de centro.

coffeepot ➤ s cafetera.

coffin ➤ s ataúd *m*.

cog ➤ s MEC. diente *m*.

cognac ➤ s coñac *m*.

coil ➤ s rollo; *(single)* anillo, vuelta; ELEC. bobina ➤ tr & intr enroscar(se), enroscar(se).

coin ➤ s moneda.

coincide ➤ intr coincidir.

coincidence ➤ s *(identicalness)* coincidencia; *(chance)* casualidad *f*.

cola ➤ s cola *(nuez, bebida)*.

colander ➤ s colador *m*.

cold ➤ adj frío ■ c. cream crema para el cutis • c. cuts fiambres • c. feet JER. miedo • c. sore afta *(labial)* • out c. sin conocimiento • to be c. *(object)* estar frío; *(person)* tener frío; *(weather)* hacer frío ➤ adv *(unprepared)* sin preparación, en seco ■ to know c. saber al dedillo ➤ s frío; MED. catarro, resfriado ■ to catch (a) c. resfriarse.

coldness ➤ s. frío, frialdad *f*.

colic ➤ s cólico.

coliseum ➤ s coliseo.

collaborate ➤ intr colaborar.

collaboration ➤ s colaboración *f*; *(treason)* colaboracionismo.

collage ➤ s collage *m*, montaje *m*.

collapse ➤ intr caerse, derrumbarse; *(person)* desplomarse; *(business)* fracasar; *(to fold)* plegarse ➤ s derrumbe *f*; *(business)* fracaso; MED. colapso.

collar ➤ s collar *m*; *(of shirt)* cuello ➤ tr *(an animal)* poner un collar a; FAM. *(to*

nab) agarrar, detener.

collarbone ➤ s clavícula.

collate ➤ tr *(texts)* colacionar; *(pages)* ordenar.

colleague ➤ s colega *mf*.

collect ➤ tr *(to gather)* juntar, reunir; *(as hobby)* coleccionar; *(payments)* recaudar ➤ adj & adv *(telephone call)* de cobro revertido.

collection ➤ s colección *f*; *(heap)* acumulación *f*; *(of money)* cobro; *(donation)* colecta.

collector ➤ s MEC. colector *m*; *(of taxes)* recaudador/a; *(of bills)* cobrador/a; *(as hobby)* coleccionista *mf*.

college ➤ s universidad *f*; *(department)* facultad *f*; RELIG. colegio.

collide ➤ intr chocar.

collision ➤ s choque *m*.

colloquial ➤ adj familiar.

cologne ➤ s colonia *(perfume)*.

Colombian ➤ adj & s colombiano/a.

colon¹ ➤ s GRAM. dos puntos.

colon² ➤ s ANAT. colon *m*.

colonel ➤ s coronel *mf*.

colonial ➤ adj *(of a colony)* colonial; *(colonizing)* colonizador ➤ s colono/a.

colony ➤ s colonia.

color ➤ s color *m* ■ c. photography cromofotografía • in c. en colores • off c. verde ➤ tr colorear; *(to dye)* teñir; *(to distort)* alterar, embellecer.

colored ➤ adj coloreado, de color; *(person)* de color.

colorful ➤ adj *(vivid)* de gran colorido; *(picturesque)* pintoresco.

colour G.B. ➤ var de **color**.

column ➤ s columna.

coma ➤ s coma *m*.

comb ➤ s peine *m* ➤ tr peinar ■ to c. one's hair peinarse.

combination ➤ s combinación *f*; *(mix)* mezcla.

combine ➤ tr & intr combinar(se); *(to mix)* mezclar.

come◇ ➤ intr venir; *(to arrive at, extend to)* llegar ■ to c. across encontrarse con • to c. along *(to accompany)* acompañar; *(to progress)* progresar • to c. back volver • to c. before preceder • to c. between interponerse entre • to c. by *(to visit)* hacer una visita; *(to obtain)* obtener, lograr • **to c. down** bajar • **to c. in** *(to enter)* entrar; *(to figure into)* figurar, entrar • **to c. of** resultar de, suceder por • **to c. off** *(to detach)* soltarse, separarse; *(to acquit oneself)* salir (bien, mal) • **to c. out** salir; *(book)* publicarse; *(to result)* resultar (bien, mal); *(stain)* quitarse; *(truth)* salir a la luz, revelarse • **to c. to** *(to revive)* recobrar los sentidos, volver en sí; *(to amount to)* reducirse a • **to c. up** subir; *(to arise)* presentarse, surgir; *(to be mentioned)* ser mencionado ▸ *interj* ¡venga!, ¡ven! ■ **c. again?** ¿cómo? • **c.in!** ¡adelante!, ¡pase! • **c.on!** FAM. *(hurry up!)* ¡apúrate!; *(you're kidding!)* ¡no me digas!

comeback ▸ s réplica, respuesta ingeniosa ■ **to make a c.** restablecerse.

comedian ▸ s cómico/a.

comedy ▸ s comedia.

come-on ▸ s aliciente m, incentivo.

comfort ▸ tr confortar, consolar; *(to relieve)* aliviar ▸ s confort m; *(relief)* alivio; *(ease)* comodidad f.

comfortable ▸ adj *(easy)* confortable, cómodo; FAM. *(sufficient)* adecuado.

comforter ▸ s *(person)* consolador/a; *(quilt)* edredón m.

comic ▸ adj & s cómico ■ **c. book** revista de historietas ilustradas • **c. strip** tira cómica.

comical ▸ s cómico.

coming ▸ adj venidero ▸ s venida.

comma ▸ s GRAM. coma.

command ▸ tr mandar; *(to rule)* regir; *(to deserve)* infundir ▸ intr mandar, dar órdenes ▸ s mando; *(order)* orden f; *(mastery)* dominio; MIL. comando ■ **at one's c.** a la disposición de uno • **under the c. of** al mando de.

commemorate ▸ tr conmemorar.

commence ▸ tr & intr comenzar.

comment ▸ s comentario; *(remark)* observación f ▸ intr comentar.

commentary ▸ s comentario.

commentator ▸ s locutor/a.

commerce ▸ s comercio.

commercial ▸ adj comercial ▸ s RAD., TELEV. anuncio.

commission ▸ s comisión f; MIL. nom-

bramiento ■ **out of c.** fuera de servicio ▸ tr MIL. nombrar; *(to order)* encargar, mandar a hacer.

commit ▸ tr cometer; *(to entrust)* encomendar; *(to confine)* internar ■ **to c. oneself** comprometerse.

commitment ▸ s *(pledge)* compromiso; *(institutionalization)* internamiento, reclusión f; *(obligation)* obligación f.

committee ▸ s comité m, comisión f.

commodity ▸ s mercancía.

common ▸ adj común; *(widespread)* general; *(frequent)* usual, frecuente; *(quality)* mediocre, inferior ■ **c. cold** resfriado, catarro • **c. law** derecho consuetudinario • **c. sense** sentido común ▸ s ejido, campo comunal.

commonwealth ▸ s *(people)* comunidad f; *(state)* república.

commotion ▸ s tumulto, alboroto.

communal ▸ adj comunal.

commune ▸ s POL. comuna; *(community)* vivienda colectiva.

communicate ▸ tr & intr comunicar(se).

communication ▸ s comunicación f.

communion ▸ s comunión f.

communism ▸ s comunismo.

communist ▸ s comunista mf.

community ▸ s comunidad f.

commute ▸ tr conmutar ▸ intr viajar diariamente al lugar en que se trabaja ▸ s viaje diario.

commuter ▸ s persona que viaja diariamente *(esp. al trabajo)*.

compact[1] ▸ adj compacto; *(concise)* conciso ■ **c. disk** disco compacto, CD ▸ tr comprimir ▸ s polvera; AUTO. automóvil compacto.

compact[2] ▸ s pacto, convenio.

companion ▸ s compañero/a.

company ▸ s compañía; *(group)* grupo; *(guests)* invitado(s) ■ **to keep c. with** asociarse con.

comparative ▸ adj comparativo; *(relative)* relativo.

compare ▸ tr & intr *(poderse)* comparar ■ **as compared with** comparado con ▸ s **beyond c.** incomparable.

comparison ▸ s comparación f ■ **by c.** en comparación.

compartment ➤ *s* compartimiento.

compass ➤ *s* brújula, compás *m* ■ c. o pl GEOM. compás.

compatible ➤ *adj* compatible.

compel ➤ *tr* compeler, obligar; *(respect, belief)* imponer.

compelling ➤ *adj* obligatorio; *(evidence)* incontestable; *(need)* apremiante.

compensate ➤ *tr* compensar; COM. indemnizar.

compensation ➤ *s* compensación *f*; COM. indemnización *f*.

compete ➤ *intr* competir ■ to c. in concursar *o* tomar parte en.

competent ➤ *adj* competente.

competition ➤ *s* competencia.

competitive ➤ *adj* competitivo; *(person)* competidor.

competitor ➤ *s* competidor/a.

compile ➤ *tr* compilar, recopilar.

complain ➤ *intr* quejarse *(about* de).

complaint ➤ *s* queja; *(protest)* reclamación *f*; DER. querella, demanda.

complete ➤ *adj* completo; *(thorough)* total; *(utter)* verdadero ➤ *tr* completar, llevar a cabo; *(a form)* llenar.

completion ➤ *s* terminación *f*.

complex ➤ *adj (composite)* compuesto; *(intricate)* complejo ➤ *s* complejo.

complexion ➤ *s (skin)* tez *f*; *(character)* aspecto, carácter *m*.

compliance ➤ *s (with an order)* acatamiento; *(acquiescence)* conformidad *f* ■ in c. with conforme a.

complicated ➤ *adj* complicado.

complication ➤ *s* complicación *f*.

compliment ➤ *s (praise)* elogio; *(honor)* honor *m* ■ *pl* saludos • with the c. of obsequio de ➤ *tr* elogiar, felicitar.

comply ➤ *intr (with an order)* acatar, obedecer; *(with a request)* acceder.

component ➤ *s* componente *m*.

compose ➤ *tr & intr* componer ■ to c. oneself tranquilizarse.

composed ➤ *adj* sosegado, tranquilo.

composer ➤ *s* compositor/a.

composition ➤ *s* composición *f*.

compound ➤ *adj* compuesto ■ c. fracture MED. fractura complicada ➤ *s* compuesto.

comprehend ➤ *tr* comprender.

comprehension ➤ *s* comprensión *f*.

comprehensive ➤ *adj (broad)* amplio, general; *(knowledge)* comprensivo.

compress ➤ *tr* comprimir ➤ *s* compresa.

comprise ➤ *tr (to include)* comprender, incluir; *(to consist of)* constar de.

compromise ➤ *s* compromiso, acuerdo ➤ *tr (to endanger)* comprometer ➤ *intr* hacer concesiones.

compulsion ➤ *s* compulsión *f*; *(impulse)* impulso ■ under c. a la fuerza.

compulsive ➤ *adj (desire)* incontrolable; *(person)* obsesivo.

compulsory ➤ *adj (coercive)* compulsorio; *(required)* obligatorio.

compute ➤ *tr* computar, calcular.

computer ➤ *s* computadora, ordenador *m* ■ c. science informática.

comrade ➤ *s* camarada *mf*.

conceal ➤ *tr* ocultar.

concede ➤ *tr* conceder ➤ *intr* hacer una concesión.

conceited ➤ *adj* vanidoso, engreído.

conceivable ➤ *adj* concebible.

concentrate ➤ *tr & intr* concentrar(se) ➤ *s* concentrado.

concentration ➤ *s* concentración *f* ■ c. camp campo de concentración.

concept ➤ *s* concepto.

conception ➤ *s* concepción *f*; *(idea)* concepto.

concern ➤ *tr (to be about)* tratar de; *(to trouble)* preocupar ■ as concerns en lo que concierne a • to c. oneself with ocuparse de, interesarse por ➤ *s (affair)* asunto; *(interest)* interés *m*; *(worry)* preocupación *f* ■ to be of no c. carecer de importancia.

concerned ➤ *adj (interested)* interesado; *(worried)* preocupado.

concert ➤ *s* concierto ■ in c. with de concierto con.

concession ➤ *s* concesión *f*.

concise ➤ *adj* conciso, sucinto.

conclude ➤ *tr & intr* concluir.

conclusion ➤ *s* conclusión *f*.

concrete ➤ *adj* concreto; CONSTR. de hormigón ➤ *s* concreto, hormigón *m*.

condemn ➤ *tr* condenar.

condensation ➤ *s* condensación *f*; LIT. versión condensada.

condense ➤ *tr & intr* condensar(se).

condescension ➤ *s* condescendencia.

condition ➤ *s* condición *f*; *(health)* estado de salud ➤ *tr (to qualify, train)* condicionar; *(to make fit)* poner en condiciones; *(to adapt)* acostumbrar.

conditioner ➤ *s* acondicionador *m*.

condom ➤ *s* preservativo, condón *m*.

condominium ➤ *s* condominio.

conduct ➤ *tr* dirigir (negocio, orquesta); *(to carry out)* llevar a cabo, hacer; FÍS. conducir ▪ to c. oneself conducirse ➤ *s* conducta, comportamiento.

conductor ➤ *s* conductor/a; MÚS. director/a.

cone ➤ *s* cono; CUL. barquillo, cucurucho.

confer ➤ *tr* conferir.

conference ➤ *s (assembly)* conferencia, congreso; *(meeting)* reunión *f*.

confess ➤ *tr* confesar ➤ *intr* confesar; RELIG. confesarse.

confession ➤ *s* confesión *f*.

confetti ➤ *spl* confeti *m*.

confidence ➤ *s* confianza; *(secret)* confidencia.

confident ➤ *s* seguro; *(self-assured)* confiado; *(manner)* de confianza.

confidential ➤ *adj* confidencial.

confine ➤ *tr (person)* confinar, recluir; *(answer)* limitar ➤ *s* ▪ *pl* confines.

confirm ➤ *tr* confirmar; POL. ratificar.

confirmed ➤ *adj* confirmado; POL. ratificado; *(inveterate)* habitual.

confiscate ➤ *tr* confiscar.

conflict ➤ *s* conflicto ➤ *intr* contradecirse.

conflicting ➤ *adj* contradictorio.

conform ➤ *intr* conformarse, concordar; *(to standards, rules)* ajustarse.

confront ➤ *tr (to face)* enfrentar, hacer frente a; *(to encounter)* encontrar.

confuse ➤ *tr* confundir.

confused ➤ *adj* confundido, desconcertado; *(disordered)* confuso.

confusing ➤ *adj* confuso.

confusion ➤ *s* confusión *f*.

congested ➤ *adj (by traffic)* congestionado; *(area)* superpoblado; *(chest, nose)* constipado.

congestion ➤ *s* congestión *f*.

congratulate ➤ *tr* felicitar.

congratulation ➤ *s* felicitación *f*, congratulación *f* ▪ congratulations! ¡felicidades!, ¡enhorabuena!

congregate ➤ *intr & tr* congregar(se).

congress ➤ *s* congreso.

congressman ➤ *s* E.U. diputado de la Cámara de Representantes.

congresswoman ➤ *s* E.U. diputada de la Cámara de Representantes.

conjugate ➤ *tr & intr* conjugar(se).

conjugation ➤ *s* conjugación *f*.

conjunction ➤ *s* conjunción *f* ▪ in c. with conjuntamente con.

conjure ➤ *tr* ▪ to c. up *(a spirit)* invocar; *(to evoke)* evocar.

conjurer or **conjuror** ➤ *s* mago/a.

connect ➤ *tr* conectar; *(to associate)* vincular, relacionar ➤ *intr* unirse; *(rooms)* comunicarse; *(buses, trains)* hacer combinación.

connection ➤ *s* conexión *f*; *(buses, trains)* combinación *f* ▪ in c. with en relación con.

conquer ➤ *tr* conquistar; *(enemy, disease)* vencer ➤ *intr* vencer, triunfar.

conqueror ➤ *s* conquistador/a.

conquest ➤ *s* conquista.

conscience ➤ *s* conciencia.

conscientious ➤ *adj* concienzudo.

conscious ➤ *adj* consciente; *(intentional)* deliberado ▪ to become c. volver en sí • to become c. of darse cuenta de.

consecutive ➤ *adj* consecutivo.

consent ➤ *intr* consentir ➤ *s* consentimiento.

consequence ➤ *s* consecuencia; *(importance)* importancia ▪ in c. por consiguiente.

conservation ➤ *s* conservación *f*.

conservative ➤ *adj* conservador; *(moderate)* moderado; *(cautious)* prudente ➤ *s* conservador/a.

conservatory ➤ *s (for plants)* invernadero; *(school)* conservatorio.

conserve ➤ *tr* conservar.

consider ➤ *tr & intr* considerar ▪ to c. oneself considerarse.

considerable ➤ *adj* considerable.

considerate ➤ *adj* considerado, atento.

consideration ➤ *s* consideración *f* ■ out of c. for por respeto a.

consign ➤ *tr* consignar.

consignment ➤ *s* consignación *f*.

consist ➤ *intr* consistir (*of, in* en).

consistent ➤ *adj* (*in agreement*) coherente; (*uniform*) consistente.

consolation ➤ *s* consolación *f*, consuelo.

console[1] ➤ *tr* consolar.

console[2] ➤ *s* gabinete *m* (de radio o televisor); TEC. tablero de mando.

consonant ➤ *adj & s* consonante *f*.

conspicuous ➤ *adj* destacado, evidente ■ to be c. destacar(se).

constable ➤ *s* alguacil *mf*; G.B. policía *mf*.

constant ➤ *adj & s* constante *f*.

constipation ➤ *s* estreñimiento.

constitute ➤ *tr* constituir.

constitution ➤ *s* constitución *f*.

construct ➤ *tr* construir.

construction ➤ *s* construcción *f*; (*structure*) estructura.

consul ➤ *s* cónsul *mf*.

consulate ➤ *s* consulado.

consult ➤ *tr & intr* consultar.

consultant ➤ *s* consultor/a.

consume ➤ *tr* consumir; (*food*) tragar; (*time, effort*) tomar ■ to be consumed with consumirse de.

consumer ➤ *s* consumidor/a.

consumption ➤ *s* consumo; MED. consunción *f*.

contact ➤ *s* contacto; (*connection*) relación *f* ■ c. lens lente de contacto ➤ *tr* ponerse en contacto con.

contagious ➤ *adj* contagioso.

contain ➤ *tr* contener ■ to c. oneself contenerse.

container ➤ *s* recipiente *m*, envase *m*; COM. contenedor *m*.

contaminate ➤ *tr* contaminar.

contemplate ➤ *tr* contemplar; (*to intend*) pensar, proyectar.

contemporary ➤ *adj & s* contemporáneo, coetáneo.

contempt ➤ *s* desprecio, desdén *m*; DER. desacato.

contend ➤ *intr* contender ➤ *tr* mantener, sostener.

content[1] ➤ *s* contenido; (*meaning*) significado ■ *pl* contenido, materia.

content[2] ➤ *adj* contento, satisfecho ➤ *s* satisfacción *f*.

contented ➤ *adj* contento, satisfecho.

contest ➤ *s* (*struggle*) contienda; (*competition*) competencia, concurso ➤ *tr* cuestionar, impugnar.

contestant ➤ *s* contendiente *mf*.

context ➤ *s* contexto.

continent ➤ *adj & s* continente *m*.

continental ➤ *adj* continental.

contingent ➤ *adj* contingente, eventual ■ to be c. on depender de.

continual ➤ *adj* continuo.

continuation ➤ *s* continuación *f*.

continue ➤ *tr & intr* continuar ■ to be continued continuará.

continuous ➤ *adj* continuo.

contraception ➤ *s* contracepción *f*.

contraceptive ➤ *adj & s* anticonceptivo.

contract ➤ *s* contrato ➤ *tr* (*to agree to*) contratar; (*to acquire*) contraer ➤ *intr* contraerse, encogerse.

contraction ➤ *s* contracción *f*.

contradict ➤ *tr* contradecir.

contradiction ➤ *s* contradicción *f*.

contrary ➤ *adj* contrario; (*ornery*) terco ➤ *s* lo contrario, lo opuesto ➤ *adv* ■ c. to en contra de.

contrast ➤ *tr & intr* (*hacer*) contrastar ➤ *s* contraste *m* ■ in c. por contraste • in c. to a diferencia de.

contribute ➤ *tr & intr* contribuir.

contribution ➤ *s* contribución *f*.

contributor ➤ *s* contribuidor/a.

contrive ➤ *tr* inventar, idear ■ to c. to conseguir (hacer algo).

contrived ➤ *adj* artificial.

control ➤ *tr* controlar, dirigir ■ to c. oneself dominarse ➤ *s* control *m*; (*restraint*) dominio ■ to be in c. tener el mando • to get out of c. desmandarse ■ *pl* mandos, controles.

convalescence ➤ *s* convalecencia.

convenience ➤ *s* (*suitability*) conveniencia; (*comfort*) comodidad *f* ■ at your c. cuando guste.

convenient ➤ *adj (suitable)* conveniente; *(handy)* útil.

convent ➤ *s* convento.

convention ➤ *s* convención *f; (custom)* costumbre *f,* regla convencional.

conversation ➤ *s* conversación *f* ■ **to make c.** dar conversación, platicar.

converse ➤ *intr* conversar.

convert ➤ *tr & intr* convertir(se) ➤ *s* converso/a.

converter ➤ *s* convertidor *m.*

convertible ➤ *adj* convertible ➤ *s* AUTO. descapotable *m.*

convey ➤ *tr* transportar, llevar; *(a meaning)* comunicar, dar a entender.

convict ➤ *tr* condenar ➤ *s* convicto/a.

convince ➤ *tr* convencer.

convoke ➤ *tr* convocar.

convolution ➤ *s* enrollamiento.

convoy ➤ *s* convoy *m.*

cook ➤ *tr* cocinar, guisar ■ **to c. up** FAM. inventar ➤ *intr (food)* cocinarse; *(chef)* cocinar ➤ *s* cocinero/a.

cookbook ➤ *s* libro de cocina.

cookie *or* **cooky** ➤ *s* galleta *(dulce).*

cooking ➤ *adj & s* (de) cocina.

cool ➤ *adj* fresco; *(calm)* tranquilo; *(unenthusiastic)* frío; JER. fenomenal ■ **to keep c. no** perder la calma ➤ *tr & intr* refrescar(se), enfriar(se); *(passions)* entibiar(se) ■ **c. it!** JER. ¡cálmate! ➤ *s* frescor *m* ■ **to keep c., lose one's c.** conservar, perder la serenidad.

coolant ➤ *s* líquido refrigerante.

cooler ➤ *s* enfriador *m.*

coolness ➤ *s* frescor *m,* fresco; *(calmness)* calma; *(indifference)* frialdad *f.*

coop ➤ *s* gallinero ➤ *tr* ■ **to c. up** enjaular.

cooperate ➤ *intr* cooperar.

cooperative ➤ *adj (joint)* cooperativo; *(helpful)* servicial ➤ *s* cooperativa.

cop ➤ *s* FAM. policía *mf.*

cope ➤ *intr* FAM. arreglárselas *(with para); (to face up)* hacer frente *(with* a).

copier ➤ *s* copiadora.

copper ➤ *s* cobre *m* ➤ *adj* (de) cobre; *(color)* cobrizo.

copy ➤ *s* copia; *(book, magazine)* ejemplar *m* ➤ *tr* copiar, sacar en limpio; *(to imitate)* imitar.

coral ➤ *adj & s* (de) coral *m.*

cord ➤ *s* cuerda; ELEC. cordón *m.*

cordial ➤ *adj* amable ➤ *s* cordial *m.*

cordless ➤ *adj* inalámbrico, sin cable.

cordon ➤ *s* cordón *m* ➤ *tr* ■ **to c. off** acordonar.

corduroy ➤ *s* pana ■ *pl* pantalones de pana.

core ➤ *s (essence)* corazón *m,* médula; *(center)* núcleo, foco; *(of fruit)* corazón ➤ *tr* quitar el corazón de.

cork ➤ *s* corcho ➤ *tr* encorchar.

corkscrew ➤ *s* sacacorchos *m.*

corn[1] ➤ *s* maíz *m* ■ **c. flakes** copos de maíz.

corn[2] ➤ *s* MED. callo, callosidad *f.*

corner ➤ *s* esquina; *(inside)* rincón *m; (of eye)* rabillo; *(of mouth)* comisura ■ **to cut corners** hacer economías • **to turn the c.** doblar la esquina; FIG. pasar el punto crítico ➤ *tr (to trap)* arrinconar; COM. monopolizar.

cornice ➤ *s* cornisa.

cornmeal ➤ *s* harina de maíz.

corny ➤ *adj (mawkish)* sensiblero; *(joke)* demasiado obvio.

corporal[1] ➤ *adj* corporal ■ **c. punishment** castigo corporal.

corporal[2] ➤ *s* MIL. cabo *mf.*

corps ➤ *s* cuerpo.

corpse ➤ *s* cuerpo, cadáver *m.*

correct ➤ *tr* corregir; *(to remedy)* remediar; *(to adjust)* ajustar ➤ *adj* correcto ■ **to be c.** tener razón.

correction ➤ *s* corrección *f; (punishment)* castigo; *(adjustment)* ajuste *m.*

correspond ➤ *intr* corresponder; *(to write)* escribirse.

correspondence ➤ *s* correspondencia ■ **c. course** curso por correspondencia.

correspondent ➤ *s* correspondiente *mf;* PERIOD. corresponsal *mf* ➤ *adj* correspondiente.

corridor ➤ *s* pasillo, corredor *m.*

corrugated ➤ *adj (cardboard)* corrugado, ondulado; *(metal)* acanalado.

corrupt ➤ *adj* corrompido; *(dishonest)* corrupto ➤ *tr & intr* corromper(se).

corruption ➤ *s* corrupción *f.*

cosmetic ➤ *s & adj* cosmético.

cost◇ ➤ *s* costo, coste *m; (in time,*

effort) costa ■ **at all costs** *o* **at any c.** cueste lo que cueste ■ *pl* gastos; *(risks)* riesgos ➤ *intr* costar.

Costa Rican ➤ *adj & s* costarricense *mf*, costarriqueño/a.

costly ➤ *adj* caro; FIG. costoso.

costume ➤ *s (dress)* traje *m*; *(disguise)* máscara, disfraz *m* ■ *pl* TEAT. vestuario ■ ➤ *tr* vestir, disfrazar.

cot ➤ *s* catre *m*.

cottage ➤ *s* casa de campo, chalet *m* ■ **c. cheese** requesón *m*, cuajada.

cotton ➤ *s* algodón *m*.

couch ➤ *s* sofá *m* ■ ➤ *tr* expresar.

cough ➤ *intr* toser ➤ *tr* ■ **to c. up** escupir; JER. *(money)* soltar ➤ *s* tos *f* ■ **c. drop** pastilla para la tos.

could ➤ *vea* **can** *en* tabla de verbos.

council ➤ *s* consejo, junta; RELIG. concilio ■ **city c.** concejo municipal.

council(l)or ➤ *s* consejero/a.

counsel(l)or ➤ *s (adviser)* consejero/a; *(lawyer)* abogado/a.

count ➤ *tr* contar; *(to deem)* considerar ■ **to c. against** pesar contra • **to c. for** valer por • **to c. in** incluir • **to c. on** contar con • **to c. out** excluir ➤ *intr* contar; *(to matter)* valer ➤ *s (act)* cuenta; *(number)* cómputo, cálculo.

countdown ➤ *s* cuenta atrás.

counter ➤ *s* mostrador *m*; *(of a kitchen)* tablero; *(chip, token)* ficha.

counteract ➤ *tr* contrarrestar.

counterclockwise ➤ *adv & adj* en sentido contrario de las agujas del reloj.

counterfeit ➤ *tr* falsificar ➤ *adj* contrahecho, falso ➤ *s* falsificación *f*, imitación *f*; *(money)* moneda falsa.

counterproductive ➤ *adj* contraproducente.

counting ➤ *s* cuenta, contaje *m*.

country ➤ *s* país *m*; *(rural area)* campo; *(homeland)* patria ■ **c. house** casa de campo, quinta.

countryside ➤ *s* campo, paisaje *m*.

county ➤ *s* condado, distrito.

couple ➤ *s* par *m*; *(of people)* pareja; *(several)* unos cuantos ➤ *tr* juntar; TEC. acoplar.

coupon ➤ *s* cupón *m*.

courage ➤ *s* coraje *m*, valor *m* ■ **to take c.** animarse.

courageous ➤ *adj* valiente.

courier ➤ *s* correo, mensajero/a.

course ➤ *s (flow, path)* curso; *(duration)* transcurso; *(of a meal)* plato; *(of studies)* programa *m*; *(subject)* curso ■ **in due c.** a su debido tiempo • **of c. (not)** claro (que no) • **to change c.** cambiar de rumbo ➤ *intr* correr.

court ➤ *s (royal)* corte *f*; *(of law)* tribunal *m*; DEP. cancha ■ **c. order** orden judicial ➤ *tr (to curry favor)* cortejar; *(to woo)* enamorar.

courteous ➤ *adj* cortés, atento.

courthouse ➤ *s* palacio de justicia.

courtroom ➤ *s* sala de justicia.

courtship ➤ *s* corte *f*; *(period)* noviazgo.

courtyard ➤ *s* patio.

cousin ➤ *s* primo/a ■ **first, second c.** primo/a hermano/a, segundo/a.

cover ➤ *tr* cubrir; *(with a lid)* tapar; *(a subject)* tratar; *(to encompass)* abarcar; *(to insure)* asegurar ■ **to c. up** disimular, encubrir ➤ *s* cubierta; *(lid)* tapa; *(of a magazine)* portada; *(bedspread)* sobrecama; *(shelter)* refugio; *(table setting)* cubierto ■ **c. charge** precio del cubierto • **to take c.** refugiarse, ponerse a cubierto • **under c.** clandestinamente ■ *pl* ropa de cama.

coveralls ➤ *spl* mono.

cow ➤ *s* vaca; *(whale, elephant)* hembra.

coward ➤ *s* cobarde *mf*.

cowardice ➤ *s* cobardía.

cowardly ➤ *adj* cobarde ➤ *adv* cobardemente.

cowboy ➤ *s* vaquero.

cozy ➤ *adj* cómodo, calentito.

crab ➤ *s* cangrejo; *(louse)* ladilla.

crabby ➤ *adj* de malas pulgas.

crack ➤ *intr (to break)* romperse; *(to snap)* chasquear; *(bones, knuckles)* crujir; *(to split)* rajarse, agrietarse ■ **to c. down** tomar medidas represivas ■ **to c. up** *(to wreck)* estrellarse; *(mentally)* chiflarse; *(to laugh)* morirse de risa ➤ *tr* romper; *(to break open)* partir; *(eggs, nuts)* cascar; *(to solve)* solucionar; FAM. *(a joke)* contar ► s *(snap)* chasquido; *(of a whip)* restallido; *(split)* rajadura, grieta; *(slit)* rendija ► adj experto; *(marksman)* certero.

cracker ► s galleta (salada).

crackpot ► s chiflado/a, excéntrico/a.

cradle ► s cuna ► tr mecer en los brazos.

craft ► s habilidad f, arte m; *(guile)* astucia; *(trade)* oficio; *(boat)* embarcación f; *(airplane)* avión m.

craftsman ► s artesano/a.

craftsmanship ► s arte m, destreza.

cram ► tr *(to force)* meter a la fuerza; *(to stuff)* abarrotar, rellenar.

cramp MED. ► s calambre m ■ pl retortijones ► intr ■ to c. up acalambrarse.

cramped ► adj apretado, apiñado.

crane ► s ORNIT. grulla; TEC. grúa ► tr estirar (el cuello).

crash ► intr estrellarse, chocar; *(to break)* hacerse pedazos; *(to resound)* retumbar; COMPUT. colgar, caer ► tr estrellar; COMPUT. tumbar ► s *(noise)* estrépito; *(collision)* choque m, colisión f; AVIA. caída; COM. *(failure)* ruina; COMPUT. fallo (de sistema).

crash-land ► intr hacer un aterrizaje forzoso.

crate ► s cajón m ► tr encajonar.

crave ► tr ansiar, morirse por.

craving ► s anhelo, antojo.

crawl ► intr arrastrarse, reptar; *(baby)* gatear; *(skin)* erizarse ► s gateado; DEP. crol m ■ at a c. a paso de tortuga.

crayon ► s & tr (dibujar al) crayón m.

craze ► tr enloquecer ► s moda.

crazy ► adj loco; *(foolish)* de locos, disparatado ■ to be c. about *(person)* estar loco por; *(fad)* estar loco con • to go c. volverse loco.

creak ► intr crujir, chirriar ► s crujido, chirrido.

cream ► s crema ■ c. cheese queso crema • whipped c. nata montada.

crease ► s pliegue m; *(of trousers)* filo, raya ► tr plegar.

create ► tr crear; *(to cause)* producir.

creation ► s creación f.

creator ► s creador/a.

creature ► s criatura; *(being)* ente m, ser m; *(animal)* bestia, bicho.

credentials ► s credenciales f.

credible ► adj creíble.

credit ► s crédito; *(merit)* mérito; *(recognition)* reconocimiento; TEN. haber m ■ c. card, line tarjeta, límite de crédito • on c. a crédito ► pl títulos de crédito ► tr *(to recognize)* otorgar reconocimiento; *(to attribute)* atribuir.

creek ► s riachuelo, arroyo ■ up the c. FAM. en apuros.

creep◇ ► intr arrastrarse, deslizarse; *(to crawl)* gatear; BOT. trepar ■ to c. by pasar lentamente ► s gateado; *(pace)* paso lento; JER. desgraciado/a, cretino/a ■ pl FAM. escalofrío, pavor.

creepy ► adj horripilante.

cremate ► tr incinerar.

crematorium ► s crematorio.

crepe o **crêpe** ► s crepé m; CUL. panqueque m ■ c. paper papel crepé.

crest ► s cresta; *(on a helmet)* penacho, cimera; HER. timbre m.

crew ► s AVIA., MARÍT. tripulación f; MIL. dotación f; *(of workers)* equipo ■ c. cut pelado al cepillo.

crib ► s cuna ► tr FAM. plagiar ► intr usar una chuleta.

cricket ► s ENTOM. grillo.

crime ► s crimen m ■ c. rate criminalidad.

criminal ► adj & s criminal mf ■ c. record antecedentes penales.

crimson ► s carmesí m.

cripple ► s lisiado/a, cojo/a ► tr lisiar, tullir; FIG. inutilizar, estropear.

crisis ► s crisis f.

crisp ► adj *(crunchy)* tostado, crujiente; *(fresh)* fresco; *(precise)* preciso, claro.

critic ► s crítico/a.

critical ► adj crítico; *(carping)* criticón ■ in c. condition grave • to be c. of criticar.

critically ► adv gravemente.

criticism ► s crítica.

criticize ► tr & intr criticar.

crockery ► s vajilla de barro, loza.

crocodile ► s cocodrilo.

crocus ► s azafrán m.

crook ➤ s ángulo; FAM. *(thief)* tramposo/a, ladrón/ona.

crooked ➤ adj *(road, thief)* torcido; *(nose)* corvo; *(back)* encorvado.

crop ➤ s cosecha; *(variety)* cultivo ➤ tr cortar, recortar ∎ to c. up surgir.

cross ➤ s cruz f; *(mixture)* mezcla ➤ tr cruzar; FAM. *(to oppose)* contrariar ∎ to c. off o out tachar ∎ to c. one's arms cruzarse de brazos ∎ to c. oneself santiguarse ∎ to c. over atravesar ➤ intr cruzarse ➤ adj transversal; *(angry)* de mal humor ∎ c. section sección transversal; FIG. muestra representativa.

cross-country ➤ adj a campo traviesa; *(flight, drive)* a través del país.

cross-eyed ➤ adj bizco.

crossing ➤ s cruce m; *(ford)* vado; F.C. paso a nivel.

cross-reference ➤ s remisión f.

crossroad ➤ s vía transversal f ∎ pl encrucijada.

crossword puzzle ➤ s crucigrama m.

crotch ➤ s *(of tree)* horquilla; ANAT. entrepiernas.

crouch ➤ intr agacharse, acuclillarse.

crow[1] ➤ s ORNIT. cuervo.

crow[2]◇ ➤ intr cantar, cacarear ➤ s canto, cacareo.

crowbar ➤ s pata de cabra, palanca.

crowd ➤ s multitud f, muchedumbre f; *(spectators)* público; *(clique)* gente f ➤ intr apiñarse, amontonarse.

crowded ➤ adj lleno, concurrido; *(cramped)* apiñado.

crown ➤ s corona; *(of a hat, tree)* copa; *(summit, honor)* cima ➤ tr coronar ∎ to c. it all para rematar.

crucial ➤ adj crucial, decisivo.

crude ➤ adj *(vulgar)* ordinario, grosero; *(rough)* tosco, basto; *(raw)* crudo, bruto ➤ s *(oil)* (petróleo) crudo.

cruel ➤ adj cruel, despiadado.

cruelty ➤ s crueldad f.

cruet ➤ s vinagrera, aceitera.

cruise ➤ intr *(to sail)* navegar; *(car)* circular; *(to patrol)* patrullar ➤ s crucero.

crumb ➤ s miga, migaja.

crumble ➤ tr & intr desmigajar(se); FIG. desmoronar(se).

crummy o **crumby** ➤ adj *(miserable)* malísimo; *(cheap)* de mala muerte.

crumple ➤ tr & intr *(to crush)* arrugar(se); *(to collapse)* derribar(se).

crunch ➤ tr triturar ➤ intr crujir ➤ s crujido; FAM. *(crisis)* aprieto, crisis f.

crunchy ➤ adj crujiente.

crusade ➤ s & intr (hacer una) cruzada.

crush ➤ tr *(to squash, defeat)* aplastar; *(to squeeze)* exprimir; *(to grind)* triturar, moler ➤ s aplastamiento; *(infatuation)* enamoramiento.

crust ➤ s *(bread, pie)* corteza; *(coating, scab)* costra; *(layer)* capa.

crutch ➤ s muleta; FIG. sostén m.

cry ➤ intr llorar; *(to shout)* gritar; *(animals)* aullar ∎ to c. for clamar por ∎ to c. over lamentarse por ➤ s grito; *(weeping)* llanto; *(entreaty)* petición f; *(peddler's call)* pregón m.

crystal ➤ s cristal m ➤ adj de cristal; *(transparent)* cristalino.

cub ➤ s cachorro; *(novice)* novato/a.

Cuban ➤ adj & s cubano/a.

cube ➤ s cubo; *(of sugar)* terrón m.

cubicle ➤ s compartimiento.

cuckoo ➤ s *(bird)* cuco, cuclillo; *(call)* cucú m ➤ adj loco, chiflado.

cucumber ➤ s pepino.

cuddle ➤ tr & intr acurrucar(se).

cuddly ➤ adj mimoso.

cue[1] ➤ s *(stick)* taco.

cue[2] ➤ s TEAT. pie m, señal f.

cuff ➤ s *(shirt)* puño; *(pant)* bajos, vuelta ∎ c. links gemelos, yugos • off the c. FAM. de improviso.

cuisine ➤ s cocina, arte culinario.

culinary ➤ adj culinario.

culprit ➤ s culpable mf.

cult ➤ s culto; *(sect)* secta.

cultivate ➤ tr cultivar.

cultural ➤ adj cultural.

culture ➤ s cultura; AGR., BIOL. cultivo.

cultured ➤ adj culto; *(pearl)* de cultivo.

cumbersome ➤ adj incómodo.

cunning ➤ adj astuto, taimado ➤ s astucia, habilidad f.

cup ➤ s taza; DEP. copa ➤ tr ahuecar.

cupboard ➤ s *(cabinet)* aparador m; *(closet)* alacena.

curb ➤ s *(of a street)* bordillo; *(restraint)* freno ➤ tr refrenar.

cure ➤ *s* cura *f.* ➤ *tr & intr* curar(se).

curiosity ➤ *s* curiosidad *f.*

curious ➤ *adj* curioso ■ to be c. to tener deseos de.

curl ➤ *tr & intr* rizar(se), ensortijar(se); ■ to c. up acurrucarse ➤ *s* riza, crespo; *(of smoke)* voluta.

curly ➤ *adj* rizado, crespo.

currency ➤ *s* moneda, dinero (corriente) ■ foreign c. divisas.

current ➤ *adj (present-day)* actual; *(in progress)* corriente, en curso; *(edition)* último ■ c. events actualidades ➤ *s* corriente *f.* ■ alternating, direct c. corriente alterna, continua.

currently ➤ *adv* actualmente.

curriculum ➤ *s* programa *m* de estudios ■ c. vitae historial profesional.

curry ➤ *s* CUL. (salsa de) cari *m.*

curse◇ ➤ *s* maldición *f;* (scourge) desgracia, calamidad *f* ➤ *tr* maldecir; *(to afflict)* desgraciar, afligir; *(to swear at)* insultar a ➤ *intr* decir malas palabras.

cursor ➤ *s* cursor *m.*

curtain ➤ *s* cortina; TEAT. telón *m.*

curve ➤ *s* curva ➤ *intr* curvear; *(surface)* doblarse.

cushion ➤ *s* cojín *m,* almohadilla ➤ *tr (to pad)* acolchar; *(a blow)* amortiguar.

custard ➤ *s* natilla ■ caramel c. flan *m.*

custom ➤ *s* costumbre *f* ■ *pl* aduana ■ to go through c. pasar la aduana ➤ *adj* hecho a la medida.

customary ➤ *adj* acostumbrado, usual.

customer ➤ *s* cliente *mf.*

cut◇ ➤ *tr* cortar; *(to divide)* dividir, repartir; *(to omit)* omitir, excluir; *(to fell)* talar; *(to carve)* tallar; *(the size of)* reducir, acortar; *(time)* abreviar; *(prices)* rebajar; FAM. *(classes)* faltar a ■ c. it out! ¡basta ya! ■ to c. back reducir, disminuir ■ to c. off *(to sever)* cortar; *(to shut off)* parar ■ to c. out *(to remove)* cortar; *(designs)* recortar; *(to delete)* suprimir ■ to c. up partir ➤ *intr* cortar ■ to be c. out for estar hecho para ■ to c. down on reducir ➤ *s* aminorar ■ to c. in *(a line of people)* colarse; *(to interrupt)* interrumpir ■ to c. loose JER. hablar *o* actuar sin

cuidarse ➤ *s* corte *m;* (reduction) reducción *f;* (discount) rebaja; FAM. *(share)* tajada, parte *f;* CINEM. corte ■ a c. above mejor que.

cutback ➤ *s* reducción *f.*

cute ➤ *adj* mono; *(contrived)* afectado ■ to get c. with hacerse el listo con.

cuticle ➤ *s* cutícula.

cutlery ➤ *s* cubiertos.

cutlet ➤ *s* chuleta.

cutting ➤ *s* recorte *m* ➤ *adj* cortante; *(remark)* mordaz.

cyberspace ➤ *s* ciberespacio.

cycle ➤ *s* ciclo ➤ *intr* ocurrir cíclicamente; *(to bicycle)* ir en bicicleta.

cyclist ➤ *s (bicycle)* ciclista *mf;* (motorcycle) motociclista *mf.*

cylinder ➤ *s* cilindro.

cynic ➤ *adj & s* cínico/a.

cyst ➤ *s* quiste *m.*

D

dad ➤ *s* FAM. papá *m.*

daddy ➤ *s* FAM. papacito, papito.

daffodil ➤ *s* narciso.

daily ➤ *adj & s* diario ➤ *adv* diariamente, cada día.

dairy ➤ *s* lechería ■ d. farm granja lechera.

daisy ➤ *s* margarita.

dam ➤ *s (barrier)* presa; *(reservoir)* embalse *m* ➤ *tr* embalsar, represar.

damage ➤ *s* daño; *(mechanical)* avería; FIG. perjuicio ■ *pl* daños y perjuicios ➤ *tr & intr* dañar(se), estropear(se).

damn ➤ *tr* condenar; *(to swear at)* maldecir ➤ *interj* ■ d. (it)! ¡maldito sea!, ¡maldición! ➤ *s* ■ I don't give a d. no me importa un comino ➤ *adj* maldito ➤ *adv* FAM. muy.

damnation ➤ *s* condenación *f* ➤ *interj* ¡maldición!

damned ➤ *adj* condenado, maldito ➤ *adv* FAM. muy, sumamente ➤ *s* ■ the d. los condenados.

damp ➤ *adj* húmedo ➤ *s* humedad *f;* (gas) mofeta ➤ *tr* humedecer; *(a fire)* apagar; *(to discourage)* desanimar.

dampen ➤ *tr* humedecer; *(spirit, zeal)* deprimir, disminuir.

dampness ➤ *s* humedad *f.*

dance ➤ *tr & intr* bailar ➤ *s* baile *m*.

dancer ➤ *s* bailador/a; *(ballet)* bailarín/ina.

dandelion ➤ *s* diente *m* de león.

dandruff ➤ *s* caspa.

danger ➤ *s* peligro.

dangerous ➤ *adj* peligroso.

dare ➤ *intr* osar, atreverse ➤ *tr* retar, desafiar ▪ I d. say me parece probable ➤ *s* desafío, reto.

daring ➤ *adj* temerario, audaz ➤ *s* audacia, atrevimiento.

dark ➤ *adj* oscuro; *(skin)* moreno, morocho; *(dismal)* triste; *(evil)* siniestro; *(unknown)* misterioso ➤ *s* oscuridad *f*; *(nightfall)* anochecer *m*, noche *f* ▪ to be in the d. no estar informado.

darkness ➤ *s* oscuridad *f*.

darling ➤ *s* querido/a, amado/a; *(favorite)* predilecto/a ➤ *adj* querido, amado; FAM. adorable.

dart ➤ *intr* correr, lanzarse ➤ *tr* lanzar, arrojar ➤ *s* dardo, saeta.

dash ➤ *tr (to smash)* estrellar, romper; *(to spoil)* arruinar, frustrar ▪ to d. off hacer rápidamente ➤ *intr* correr, lanzarse ▪ to d. in, out entrar, salir corriendo ➤ *s (bit)* pizca; *(rush)* prisa; *(race)* carrera corta; AUTO. salpicadero.

dashboard ➤ *s* salpicadero.

data ➤ *spl o sg* información *f*, datos ▪ d. bank base *o* banco de datos • d. processing procesamiento de datos • d. processor ordenador, computadora.

database ➤ *s* base *f* de datos.

date¹ ➤ *s* fecha; *(appointment)* cita, compromiso; *(companion)* acompañante *mf* ➤ *tr & intr* fechar; *(socially)* salir (con) ▪ to d. from datar de.

date² ➤ *s (fruit)* dátil *m* ▪ d. palm datilero.

daughter ➤ *s* hija.

daughter-in-law ➤ *s* nuera, hija política.

dawdle ➤ *intr* demorarse.

dawn ➤ *s* amanecer *m*, alba ➤ *intr* amanecer ▪ it dawned on me caí en la cuenta.

day ➤ *s* día *m*; *(workday)* jornada; *(epoch)* época ▪ day-care center guardería • d. in, d. out día tras día • the d. after al día siguiente • the d. before . . . la víspera de . . . • these days hoy en día.

daybreak ➤ *s* amanecer *m*, alba.

daylight ➤ *s* luz *f* del día; *(dawn)* amanecer *m*; *(daytime)* día *m*.

daytime ➤ *s* día *m*.

dead ➤ *adj* muerto; *(dull)* triste, aburrido; ELEC. sin corriente; *(battery)* descargado ▪ d. center, weight punto, peso muerto • d. end callejón sin salida ➤ *s* muerto ▪ the d. los muertos • the d. of night, winter plena noche, pleno invierno.

dead-end ➤ *adj* sin salida.

deadline ➤ *s* fecha tope, plazo.

deadly ➤ *adj* mortífero, mortal; *(dull)* pesado.

deaf ➤ *adj* sordo.

deafness ➤ *s* sordera.

deal◊ ➤ *tr* repartir, distribuir ➤ *intr* comerciar *(in* en) ▪ to d. with COM. tratar con; *(a situation)* enfrentarse con; *(to treat)* tratar de *o* sobre ➤ *s (agreement)* arreglo, convenio; *(in cards)* reparto; FAM. *(dealings)* trato ▪ a good *o* great d. mucho • big d.! ¡gran cosa! • it's a d.! ¡trato hecho!

dealer ➤ *s* negociante *mf*, traficante *mf*.

dealings ➤ *spl (business)* negocios; *(relations)* trato.

dean ➤ *s* EDUC. decano/a; RELIG. deán *m*.

dear ➤ *adj* querido; *(esteemed)* estimado; *(precious)* valioso; *(costly)* caro ▪ D. Sir Estimado señor mío ➤ *adv* caro ➤ *s* querido/a.

death ➤ *s* muerte *f* ▪ d. certificate partida de defunción • d. penalty pena de muerte • d. rate índice de mortalidad • to put to d. ejecutar.

debate ➤ *tr & intr* discutir, debatir ➤ *s* discusión *f*, debate *m*.

debit ➤ *s* débito, debe *m* ▪ d. balance saldo deudor ➤ *tr* cargar en cuenta.

debt ➤ *s* deuda.

debtor ➤ *s* deudor/a.

decade ➤ *s* decenio, década.

decay ➤ *intr* pudrirse, descomponerse; *(a tooth)* cariarse; FÍS. desintegrarse; FIG. decaer ➤ *s* descomposición *f*; *(of a* *tooth)* caries *f*; FIS. desintegración *f*; *(of morals)* decadencia.

deceased ➤ *adj & s* difunto/a.

deceit ➤ *s* engaño, fraude *m*.

deceive ➤ *tr & intr* engañar.

December ➤ *s* diciembre *m*.

decent ➤ *adj* decente; *(kind)* bueno.

decide ➤ *tr & intr* decidir.

decimal ➤ *s & adj* decimal *m* ■ d. point coma.

decision ➤ *s* decisión *f*.

decisive ➤ *adj* decisivo.

deck ➤ *s* cubierta; *(of cards)* baraja ■ to clear the d. prepararse para la acción.

declaration ➤ *s* declaración *f*.

declare ➤ *tr* declarar ➤ *intr* hacer una declaración.

decline ➤ *tr* rehusar ➤ *intr (to slope)* inclinarse; *(health)* deteriorarse.

decongestant ➤ *s* descongestionante *m*.

decorate ➤ *tr* decorar; *(with medals)* condecorar.

decoration ➤ *s* decoración *f*; *(medal)* condecoración *f*.

decorative ➤ *adj* decorativo.

decorator ➤ *s* decorador/a.

decrease ➤ *intr & tr* disminuir, reducir ➤ *s* disminución *f*.

dedicate ➤ *tr* dedicar.

dedication ➤ *s* dedicación *f*; *(inscription)* dedicatoria.

deduct ➤ *tr* restar, substraer.

deduction ➤ *s* deducción *f*.

deed ➤ *s* acto, hecho; *(feat)* proeza; DER. *(title)* escritura (de propiedad) ➤ *tr* traspasar por escritura.

deem ➤ *tr* considerar, juzgar.

deep ➤ *adj* profundo; *(colors)* subido; MÚS. bajo, grave ■ d. down en el fondo • to go off the d. end ponerse histérico • two meters d. dos metros de profundidad ➤ *adv* profundamente, en lo más hondo ➤ *s* profundidad *f*; *(of night, winter)* lo más profundo.

deer ➤ *s* ciervo, venado. .

defeat ➤ *tr* derrotar, vencer ➤ *s (loss)* derrota; *(failure)* fracaso.

defect ➤ *s* defecto ➤ *intr* desertar.

defective ➤ *adj* defectuoso; *(subnormal)* deficiente; GRAM. defectivo.

defend ➤ *tr* defender; *(to justify)* justi-

ficar ➤ *intr* hacer una defensa.

defendant ➤ *s* acusado/a.

defender ➤ *s* defensor/a.

defense ➤ *s* defensa.

defiant ➤ *adj* provocador, desafiante.

deficient ➤ *adj* deficiente, carente.

deficit ➤ *s* déficit *f*.

define ➤ *tr* definir.

definite ➤ *adj* definido; *(certain)* definitivo; *(explicit)* claro, explícito.

definitely ➤ *adv* definitivamente.

definition ➤ *s* definición *f*; *(of power, authority)* limitación *f*.

deformed ➤ *adj* deforme, desfigurado.

defrost ➤ *tr & intr* descongelar(se).

defy ➤ *tr* desafiar; *(to resist)* resistir.

degenerate ➤ *adj & s* degenerado/a ➤ *intr* degenerar.

degree ➤ *s* grado; EDUC. título ■ by degrees gradualmente, poco a poco • to a certain d. hasta cierto punto • to take a d. in licenciarse en.

dejected ➤ *adj* desanimado.

delay ➤ *tr (to postpone)* postergar; *(to make late)* retrasar, demorar ➤ *intr* demorarse, tardar ➤ *s* demora, retraso.

delegate ➤ *s* delegado/a ➤ *tr* delegar.

delegation ➤ *s* delegación *f*.

delete ➤ *tr* tachar, suprimir.

deliberate ➤ *adj* deliberado; *(slow)* pausado ➤ *intr & tr* deliberar.

delicacy ➤ *s* delicadeza; *(fine food)* manjar *m*, golleria.

delicate ➤ *adj* delicado.

delicatessen ➤ *s* fiambrería.

delicious ➤ *adj* delicioso.

delight ➤ *s* deleite *m*; *(person, thing)* encanto ➤ *tr* deleitar, encantar.

delighted ➤ *adj* encantado.

delightful ➤ *adj* delicioso, encantador.

delinquent ➤ *adj* delincuente; *(in payment)* moroso ➤ *s* delincuente *mf*.

deliver ➤ *tr (to free)* liberar; *(to hand over)* entregar; *(a blow, speech)* dar; *(baby)* asistir al parto de ➤ *intr* cumplir *(on con)*; *(to give birth)* alumbrar ■ we d. entregamos a domicilio.

delivery ➤ *s* entrega; *(release)* liberación *f*; *(birth)* parto; *(style)* elocución *f*.

delude ➤ *tr* engañar, despistar.

delusion ➤ *s* engaño, ilusión *f*.

deluxe *o* **luxe** ➤ *adj* de lujo, lujoso.

demand ➤ *tr (to ask for)* demandar; *(to claim, require)* reclamar, exigir ➤ *s (request)* solicitud *f; (claim)* reclamación *f; (requirement)* necesidad *f;* COM. demanda ■ on d. COM. a la vista • to be in d. ser popular.

demanding ➤ *adj* exigente.

democracy ➤ *s* democracia.

democrat ➤ *s* demócrata *mf.*

democratic ➤ *adj* democrático.

demolish ➤ *tr* demoler, derribar.

demolition ➤ *s* demolición *f.*

demonstrate ➤ *tr* demostrar ➤ *intr* protestar, manifestarse.

demonstration ➤ *s* demostración *f; (rally)* manifestación *f.*

demonstrative ➤ *adj* demostrativo; *(expressive)* expresivo, efusivo.

demonstrator ➤ *s* manifestante *mf.*

demoralize ➤ *tr* desmoralizar.

den ➤ *s (lair)* cubil *m; (study)* estudio.

denial ➤ *s* negativa; *(disavowal)* repudio; DER. denegación *f.*

denim ➤ *s* denim *m,* dril *m* de algodón.

denomination ➤ *s* denominación *f; (sect)* secta.

denounce ➤ *tr* denunciar.

dense ➤ *adj* denso.

dent ➤ *s* abolladura, mella ➤ *tr & intr* abollar(se), mellar(se).

dental ➤ *adj* dental.

dentist ➤ *s* dentista *mf.*

denture ➤ *s* dentadura postiza.

deny ➤ *tr* negar; *(to withhold)* rehusar; *(to repudiate)* repudiar ■ to d. oneself privarse de.

deodorant ➤ *s* desodorante *m.*

depart ➤ *intr* marcharse, irse; *(train, bus)* salir ➤ *tr* partir de.

department ➤ *s* departamento; POL. ministerio ■ d. store gran almacén.

departure ➤ *s* partida, salida; *(deviation)* desviación *f.*

depend ➤ *intr* ■ to d. (up)on *(as a dependent, consequence)* depender de; *(to trust)* confiar en, fiar; *(to count on)* contar con.

dependable ➤ *adj (trustworthy)* (digno) de confianza; *(reliable)* seguro.

dependent ➤ *adj* ■ d. (up)on depen-

diente de ➤ *s* persona a cargo.

depict ➤ *tr* representar, pintar.

deplorable ➤ *adj* deplorable.

deplore ➤ *tr* deplorar, desaprobar.

deposit ➤ *tr* depositar; COM. *(down payment)* dar de señal ➤ *s* depósito; *(down payment)* señal *f,* entrada.

depot ➤ *s (bus, train)* estación *f; (warehouse)* almacén *m,* depósito.

depress ➤ *tr* deprimir, desanimar; *(button)* presionar; *(prices)* bajar.

depressed ➤ *adj* deprimido; *(economy)* deprimido.

depression ➤ *s (a hollow)* cavidad *f,* hueco; ECON., MED. depresión *f.*

deprive ➤ *tr* privar *(of de).*

deprived ➤ *adj* pobre, necesitado.

depth ➤ *s* profundidad *f; (most intense part)* lo más profundo; *(color)* intensidad *f* ■ in d. a fondo.

deputy ➤ *s* delegado/a; POL. diputado/a.

derail ➤ *tr & intr* (hacer) descarrilar.

derelict ➤ *s (person)* vago/a; *(ship)* derrelicto ➤ *adj (remiss)* remiso; *(property)* abandonado.

derive ➤ *tr & intr* derivar *(from de).*

descend ➤ *tr & intr* descender.

descendant ➤ *s* descendiente *mf.*

descent ➤ *s* descenso; *(slope)* declive *m; (lineage)* descendencia.

describe ➤ *tr* describir.

description ➤ *s* descripción *f.*

desert[1] ➤ *s* desierto ➤ *adj* desértico.

desert[2] ➤ *tr* abandonar; MIL. desertar de ➤ *intr* desertar.

deserve ➤ *tr & intr* merecer(se).

design ➤ *tr (to invent)* idear; *(a plan)* diseñar; *(pattern)* dibujar ➤ *intr* hacer diseños ➤ *s* diseño; ARQ. plano; *(intention)* propósito ■ by d. intencionalmente • to have designs on poner las miras en.

designer ➤ *s* diseñador/a.

desirable ➤ *adj* deseable.

desire ➤ *tr & tr* desear ➤ *s* deseo.

desk ➤ *s* escritorio; *(at school)* pupitre *m; (in hotel)* recepción *f; (counter, booth)* mesa.

desktop publishing ➤ *s* autoedición *f.*

despair ➤ *s* desesperación *f* ➤ *intr* desesperar(se).

desperation ➤ s desesperación f.

despicable ➤ adj odioso, vil.

despise ➤ tr despreciar.

despite ➤ prep a pesar de, no obstante.

dessert ➤ s CUL. postre m.

destination ➤ s destino.

destine ➤ tr destinar.

destiny ➤ s destino.

destitute ➤ adj indigente.

destroy ➤ tr destruir.

destruction ➤ s destrucción f.

destructive ➤ adj destructivo, destructor ■ d. of o to perjudicial para.

detach ➤ tr separar, desprender.

detachable ➤ adj desmontable.

detached ➤ adj separado; (aloof) indiferente, despreocupado.

detachment ➤ s separación f; (impartiality) objetividad f.

detail ➤ s detalle m, pormenor m; MIL. destacamento ➤ tr detallar.

detailed ➤ adj detallado, minucioso.

detain ➤ tr (to delay) retardar, demorar; (in custody) detener.

detect ➤ tr percibir, detectar.

detective ➤ s detective mf.

detector ➤ s detector m.

detention ➤ s detención f.

deter ➤ tr impedir.

detergent ➤ s detergente m.

deteriorate ➤ intr empeorar, degenerar.

determination ➤ s determinación f; (resolve) resolución f; DER. decisión f.

determine ➤ tr determinar ➤ intr decidir.

determined ➤ adj determinado.

deterrent ➤ s agente disuasivo ➤ adj impeditivo.

detour ➤ s desvío ➤ tr & intr desviar(se).

develop ➤ tr desarrollar; (the body) fortalecer; (an ability) formar; (land) urbanizar; FOTOG. revelar ➤ intr desarrollarse; (to advance) progresar.

development ➤ s desarrollo; (event) suceso; FOTOG. revelado.

deviate ➤ intr desviarse.

device ➤ s dispositivo, aparato.

devil ➤ s diablo ■ d.'s advocate abogado del diablo.

devise ➤ tr (to conceive) idear, conce-

bir; (to contrive) trazar, tramar.

devote ➤ tr dedicar, consagrar.

devoted ➤ adj (loving) afectuoso; (dedicated) devoto; (ardent) fervoroso.

devotion ➤ s devoción f.

devour ➤ tr devorar.

dew ➤ s rocío ■ d. point punto de condensación.

diabetes ➤ s diabetes f.

diabetic ➤ adj & s diabético/a.

diagnosis ➤ s diagnóstico.

diagonal ➤ adj & s diagonal f.

diagram ➤ s diagrama m ➤ tr representar con un diagrama.

dial ➤ s (scale, clock) esfera, cuadrante m; RAD., TELEV. dial m, botón m selector ■ d. tone TEL. tono para marcar ➤ tr TEL. marcar (un número).

dialect ➤ s dialecto.

dialogue ➤ s diálogo.

diameter ➤ s diámetro.

diamond ➤ s (jewel, cards) diamante m; (shape) rombo.

diaper ➤ s pañal m ➤ tr poner el pañal a.

diarrhea ➤ s diarrea.

diary ➤ s diario.

dice ➤ spl dados ➤ tr picar en cubitos.

dictate ➤ tr (letter) dictar; (policy) imponer ➤ intr mandar ➤ s mandato ■ pl dictados.

dictation ➤ s dictado.

dictator ➤ s dictador/a.

dictionary ➤ s diccionario.

did ➤ vea do en la tabla de verbos.

didn't ➤ contr de did not.

die ➤ intr morir; (to lose force) apagarse, disminuir; (to become extinct) extinguirse, desaparecer.

diesel engine ➤ s motor m diesel.

diet ➤ s & intr (estar a) dieta.

differ ➤ intr disentir, diferenciar (with de) ■ to d. from diferenciarse de.

difference ➤ s diferencia ■ it makes no d. da lo mismo • what d. does it make? ¿qué más da?

different ➤ adj diferente, distinto.

difficult ➤ adj difícil.

difficulty ➤ s dificultad f ■ pl apuros.

dig◊ ➤ tr cavar, excavar; (well, tunnel) hacer, abrir ■ to d. in(to) hincar, hundir en • **to d. out** *(hole)* excavar; *(object)* extraer • **to d. up** *(object)* extraer, desenterrar; *(facts)* descubrir ➤ *intr* cavar ■ **to d. for** buscar • **to d. in** atrincherarse; FAM. *(to eat)* atacar ➤ *s (with the elbow)* codazo; *(gibe)* pulla; ARQUEOL. excavación *f.*

digest ➤ *tr & intr* digerir(se) ➤ *s* compendio, sinopsis *f.*

digestion ➤ *s* digestión *f.*

digit ➤ *s* ANAT. dedo; MAT. dígito.

digital ➤ *adj* digital.

dignity ➤ *s* dignidad *f.*

dilapidated ➤ *adj* desvencijado.

dilute ➤ *tr* diluir, desleír ➤ *adj* diluido.

dim ➤ *adj (dark)* oscuro; *(lights)* bajo, débil; *(outline)* borroso; *(memory)* vago; *(person)* de pocas luces ■ **to take a d. view of** ver de modo poco favorable ➤ *tr* oscurecer; *(lights)* bajar ➤ *intr* oscurecerse; *(lights)* perder intensidad; *(outline, memory)* borrarse.

dime ➤ *s* E.U. moneda de diez centavos.

dimension ➤ *s* dimensión *f.*

diminish ➤ *tr & intr* disminuir(se).

din ➤ *s* estrépito; *(of a crowd)* clamoreo.

dine ➤ *intr* cenar.

diner ➤ *s* comensal *mf*; F.C. vagón *m* restaurante; *(restaurant)* restaurante *m* popular.

dinghy ➤ *s* bote *m* (de remo).

dingy ➤ *adj* sórdido, sucio.

dining ➤ *adj* ■ **d. car** vagón restaurante • **d. hall** refectorio • **d. room** comedor *m.*

dinner ➤ *s* cena; *(at noon)* comida (principal); *(formal)* banquete *m* ■ **d. jacket** smoking.

dinosaur ➤ *s* dinosaurio.

dip ➤ *tr (to immerse)* sumergir, meter; *(to lower)* inclinar, bajar ➤ *intr (to plunge)* sumergirse; *(prices, road)* bajar ■ **to d. into** *(a subject)* meterse en; *(a book)* hojear; *(savings)* echar mano a ➤ *s* inmersión *f*; *(swim)* chapuzón *m*; *(slope, drop)* bajada; *(hollow)* depresión *f*; CUL. salsa.

diphtheria ➤ *s* difteria.

diploma ➤ *s* diploma *m.*

diplomacy ➤ *s* diplomacia.

diplomat ➤ *s* diplomático/a.

direct ➤ *tr* dirigir; *(to order)* ordenar ➤ *adj* directo; *(candid)* franco ➤ *adv* directamente.

direction ➤ *s* dirección *f*; *(order)* orden *f* ■ *pl* instrucciones.

directly ➤ *adv* directamente; *(immediately)* inmediatamente.

director ➤ *s* director/a.

directory ➤ *s* directorio ■ **telephone d.** guía telefónica • **d. assistance** información telefónica.

dirt ➤ *s* tierra; *(grime)* mugre *f*; *(filth)* suciedad; *(smut)* porquería.

dirty ➤ *adj* sucio; *(joke)* verde; *(language)* grosero ■ **d. language** groserías • **d. trick** mala jugada • **d. work** trabajo pesado ➤ *tr & intr* ensuciar(se).

disability ➤ *s* discapacidad *f*, incapacidad *f*, invalidez *f.*

disable ➤ *tr* discapacitar, incapacitar; *(vehicle)* averiar.

disabled ➤ *adj* discapacitado, incapacitado; *(vehicle)* averiado.

disadvantage ➤ *s* desventaja, inconveniente *m.*

disagree ➤ *intr* no estar de acuerdo, estar en desacuerdo; *(food)* sentar mal; *(to quarrel)* reñir.

disagreeable ➤ *adj* desagradable.

disagreement ➤ *s* desacuerdo; *(quarrel)* riña.

disappear ➤ *intr* desaparecer.

disappearance ➤ *s* desaparición *f.*

disappoint ➤ *tr* decepcionar, desilusionar; *(to fail to please)* defraudar.

disappointing ➤ *adj* decepcionante.

disappointment ➤ *s* desilusión *f*, decepción *f*; *(in love)* desengaño.

disapproval ➤ *s* desaprobación *f.*

disapprove ➤ *tr* desaprobar.

disarm ➤ *tr & intr* desarmar(se).

disaster ➤ *s* desastre *m.*

disc ➤ *s* disco ■ **d. jockey** animador/a.

discard ➤ *tr (cards)* descartar; *(clothing, books)* desechar ➤ *intr* descartarse ➤ *s* descarte *m.*

discharge ➤ *tr* descargar; *(soldiers)* licenciar; *(patients)* dar de alta; *(pus)* arrojar; *(duty)* desempeñar, ejecutar ➤ *s* descarga; *(emission)* escape *m*;

(secretion) secreción *f; (flow)* flujo; *(from hospital)* alta; *(of soldiers)* licenciamiento.

disciple ➤ *s* discípulo/a.

discipline ➤ *s* disciplina; *(punishment)* castigo ➤ *tr* disciplinar; *(to punish)* castigar.

disclose ➤ *tr* divulgar, revelar.

disco ➤ *s* (baile *m* de) discoteca.

discomfort ➤ *s* molestia, malestar *m*.

disconnected ➤ *adj* desconectado; *(unrelated)* sin relación; *(illogical)* inconexo.

discontented ➤ *adj* descontento.

discontinue ➤ *tr* discontinuar.

discount ➤ *tr* descontar ➤ *s* descuento, rebaja ■ **d. rate** tasa de descuento.

discourage ➤ *tr* desanimar, desalentar; *(to hinder)* no fomentar ■ **to d. from** disuadir o recomendar que no.

discourse ➤ *s* discurso ➤ *intr* conversar *(on* sobre*)*.

discover ➤ *tr* descubrir.

discovery ➤ *s* descubrimiento.

discreet ➤ *adj* discreto.

discretion ➤ *s* discreción *f* ■ **at the d. of** a juicio de, según el deseo de.

discrimination ➤ *s (prejudice)* discriminación *f; (perception)* discernimiento; *(distinction)* distinción *f*.

discuss ➤ *tr (to talk over)* hablar de *o* sobre; *(formally)* discutir, tratar.

discussion ➤ *s (conversation)* discusión *f; (discourse)* disertación *f*.

disease ➤ *s* enfermedad *f*.

disembark ➤ *tr & intr* desembarcar.

disfigure ➤ *tr* desfigurar, afear.

disgrace ➤ *s* deshonra; *(ignominy)* ignominia ➤ *tr* deshonrar.

disgraceful ➤ *adj* vergonzoso.

disguise ➤ *s* disfraz *m* ➤ *tr* disfrazar.

disgust ➤ *tr* repugnar, asquear ➤ *s* repugnancia, asco.

disgusted ➤ *adj* asqueado, repugnado.

disgusting ➤ *adj* repugnante, asqueroso.

dish ➤ *s* plato; RAD., TELEV. disco (de antena) ➤ *tr* ■ **to d. out** *(food)* servir; *(advice, abuse)* repartir, dar.

dishonest ➤ *adj* deshonesto, deshonrado; *(dealings)* fraudulento.

dishonor ➤ *s* deshonra; *(shame)* vergüenza ➤ *tr* deshonrar.

dishwasher ➤ *s* lavaplatos *m*.

disillusion ➤ *tr* desilusionar.

disillusionment ➤ *s* desilusión *f*.

disincentive ➤ *s* falta de incentivo.

disinfect ➤ *tr* desinfectar.

disinfectant ➤ *s & adj* desinfectante *m*.

disk ➤ *s* disco ■ **d. drive** COMPUT. unidad de disco • **d. jockey** animador/a.

diskette ➤ *s* disco, diskette *m*.

dislike ➤ *tr* tener aversión a, no gustarle a uno ➤ *s* antipatía, aversión *f*.

dislocate ➤ *tr* dislocar.

dismal ➤ *adj* triste, deprimente.

dismantle ➤ *tr (to tear down)* desmantelar; *(to disassemble)* desarmar.

dismay ➤ *tr (to upset)* consternar; *(to dishearten)* desalentar ➤ *s* consternación *f*, desaliento.

dismiss ➤ *tr* dar permiso para salir; *(employee)* despedir; *(officials)* destituir.

dismissal ➤ *s* despido; *(official)* destitución *f*; DER. desestimación *f*.

disobedient ➤ *adj* desobediente.

disobey ➤ *tr & intr* desobedecer.

disorder ➤ *s* desorden *m;* MED. trastorno ➤ *tr* desordenar.

disorganize ➤ *tr* desorganizar.

dispatch ➤ *tr* despachar ➤ *s* despacho; *(speed)* diligencia.

dispel ➤ *tr* disipar.

disperse ➤ *tr & intr* dispersar(se).

displace ➤ *tr* desplazar; *(to supplant)* substituir, suplantar ■ **displaced person** persona expatriada.

display ➤ *tr* exhibir, mostrar; *(to show off)* ostentar ➤ *s* exhibición *f; (ostentation)* ostentación *f;* COMPUT. representación *f* visual.

displease ➤ *tr & intr* desagradar.

disposal ➤ *s* disposición *f; (of waste)* eliminación *f* ■ **at your d.** a su disposición.

dispose ➤ *tr* disponer ■ **to d. of** *(property, business)* despachar; *(waste)* eliminar, desechar.

disposed ➤ *adj* dispuesto.

disposition ➤ *s* disposición *f*.

dispute ➤ *tr* disputar; *(to doubt)* cuestionar; *(in court)* litigar, contender ➤ *intr* disputar, discutir; *(to quarrel)* pelear ➤ *s (debate)* disputa; *(conflict)* conflicto; *(quarrel)* pelea, riña.

disqualify ➤ *tr* descalificar.

disregard ➤ *tr* no hacer caso de, desatender ➤ *s* desatención *f*, negligencia.

disrespect ➤ *s* falta de respeto, descortesía ➤ *tr* faltar el respeto.

disrupt ➤ *tr* interrumpir.

disruption ➤ *s* interrupción *f.*

dissatisfaction ➤ *s* descontento.

dissertation ➤ *s (discourse)* disertación *f; (thesis)* tesis *f.*

dissolve ➤ *tr & intr* disolver(se).

dissuade ➤ *tr* disuadir.

distance ➤ *s* distancia; *(stretch)* trecho, tirada; *(coolness)* reserva ■ at *o* from a d. a (la) distancia • in the d. a lo lejos ➤ *tr* alejar, distanciar.

distant ➤ *adj* distante, alejado; *(in relationship)* lejano; *(aloof)* reservado.

distasteful ➤ *adj* desagradable.

distinct ➤ *adj* distinto, claro; *(clear)* claro; *(unquestionable)* marcado, indudable.

distinction ➤ *s* distinción *f.*

distinctive ➤ *adj* distintivo.

distinguish ➤ *tr & intr* distinguir.

distort ➤ *tr* distorsionar; *(to misrepresent)* tergiversar, alterar.

distortion ➤ *s* distorsión *f; (misrepresentation)* tergiversación *f.*

distract ➤ *tr* distraer.

distraction ➤ *s* distracción *f.*

distraught ➤ *adj* aturdido, turbado.

distress ➤ *s (suffering)* aflicción *f*, pena; *(anxiety)* ansiedad *f* ➤ *tr* afligir.

distribute ➤ *tr* distribuir.

distribution ➤ *s* distribución *f*, reparto.

distributor ➤ *s* distribuidor/a.

district ➤ *s* región *f*, comarca; *(of a city)* zona, barrio; POL. distrito ■ d. attorney fiscal • d. court tribunal federal.

distrust ➤ *s* desconfianza, recelo ➤ *tr* desconfiar de, sospechar.

disturb ➤ *tr (to alter)* perturbar; *(to upset)* turbar, trastornar; *(to interrupt)* interrumpir; *(to bother)* molestar ■ do not d. no molestar.

disturbance ➤ *s* perturbación *f; (worry)* trastorno; *(interruption)*

interrupción *f; (bother)* molestia; *(disorder)* desorden *m; (riot)* disturbio.

ditch ➤ *s* zanja; *(irrigation)* acequia; *(drainage)* canal *m; (of a road)* cuneta ➤ *tr* FAM. abandonar.

dive◊ ➤ *intr (headfirst)* zambullirse de cabeza; DEP. saltar; *(scuba)* bucear; *(to plummet)* caer a plomo ➤ *s (headfirst)* zambullida; DEP. salto; *(plane)* picado; *(submarine)* sumersión *f.*

diver ➤ *s* DEP. saltador/a; *(underwater)* buzo, buceador/a.

diversion ➤ *s* diversión *f.*

diversity ➤ *s* diversidad *f*, variedad *f.*

divert ➤ *tr* divertir; *(to turn aside)* desviar.

divide ➤ *tr & intr* dividir(se) ■ to d. up *(to apportion)* repartir.

dividend ➤ *s* dividendo.

divine ➤ *adj* divino.

diving ➤ *s* DEP. salto; *(scuba)* buceo ■ d. board trampolín • d. suit escafandra.

division ➤ *s* división *f; (section)* sección *f*, departamento.

divorce ➤ *s* divorcio ➤ *tr & intr* divorciarse (de).

divorcé ➤ *s* divorciado ■ **divorcée** divorciada.

dizziness ➤ *s* vértigo, mareo.

dizzy ➤ *adj* mareado; *(speed, height)* vertiginoso ➤ *tr* marear, dar vértigo.

do◊ ➤ *tr* hacer; *(dishes)* fregar; *(justice, homage)* rendir, tributar; *(to work on)* trabajar en; JER. *(drugs)* tomar, usar ■ to do again *o* over volver a hacer, hacer de nuevo • to do away with eliminar • to do in JER. *(to kill)* liquidar; *(to exhaust)* agotar, cansar • what can I do for you? ¿en qué puedo servirle? ➤ *intr (to perform)* obrar, actuar; *(to get along)* andar, irle a uno; *(to serve the purpose)* servir ■ how do you do? ¿cómo está usted? • that will do! ¡basta ya! ➤ *s (hairdo)* peinado.

dock ➤ *s* muelle *m*, embarcadero ➤ *tr & intr (ship)* (hacer) atracar al muelle; *(spacecraft)* acoplar(se).

doctor ➤ *s* médico, doctor/a; EDUC. doctor/a ➤ *tr (to treat)* tratar, atender; *(to falsify)* adulterar.

doctorate ➤ *s* doctorado.

document ➤ *s* documento ➤ *tr* documentar, probar con documentos.

documentary ➤ *adj & s* documental *m*.

dodge ➤ *tr* esquivar ➤ *intr* echarse a un lado ➤ *s* regate *m*.

does ➤ *vea* **do** *en tabla de verbos*.

dog ➤ *s* perro; *(scoundrel)* canalla *mf* ➤ *tr* perseguir, seguir.

doll ➤ *s* muñeca.

dollar ➤ *s* dólar *m*.

dolphin ➤ *s* ZOOL. delfín *m*; *(fish)* dorado.

domain ➤ *s* dominio; FIG. campo.

dome ➤ *s* cúpula, domo.

domestic ➤ *adj* doméstico; *(home-loving)* casero; ECON. nacional.

dominant ➤ *adj & s* dominante *f*.

dominate ➤ *tr & intr* dominar.

Dominican ➤ *adj & s* dominicano/a.

dominion ➤ *s* dominio.

domino ➤ *s* *(game piece)* ficha ■ *pl* *(game)* dominó.

donate ➤ *tr* donar.

donation ➤ *s* *(act)* donación *f*; *(gift)* donativo.

done ➤ *adj* terminado, hecho; CUL. cocido, hecho ■ d. for FAM. vencido • well d.! ¡muy bien!

donkey ➤ *s* burro, asno.

donor ➤ *s* donador/a, donante *mf*.

don't ➤ *contr* de **do not**.

door ➤ *s* puerta; AUTO. portezuela.

doorbell ➤ *s* timbre *m*.

doorknob ➤ *s* perilla.

doorman ➤ *s* portero.

doormat ➤ *s* felpudo, estera.

doorway ➤ *s* puerta, entrada.

dope ➤ *s* FAM. narcótico, droga; JER. *(dolt)* tonto/a; *(information)* datos.

dorm ➤ *s* FAM. *(room)* dormitorio; *(building)* residencia para estudiantes.

dormitory ➤ *s* *(room)* dormitorio; *(building)* residencia.

dosage ➤ *s* dosificación *f*; *(amount)* dosis *f*.

dose ➤ *s* dosis *f* ➤ *tr* medicinar.

dot ➤ *s* punto ■ d. matrix matriz de puntos ■ **on the d.** FAM. *(on time)* a la hora; *(o'clock)* en punto ➤ *tr* poner el punto a; *(to scatter)* salpicar ■ **dotted line** línea de puntos.

double ➤ *adj* doble ■ d. take reacción tardía • d. talk lenguaje ambiguo ➤ *s* doble *m* ■ **on the d.** FAM. con toda rapidez ➤ *tr* doblar; *(to repeat)* redoblar ➤ *intr* doblarse, duplicarse ■ **to d. as** servir también como • **to d. back** volver uno sobre sus pasos ➤ *adv* doble, doblemente.

doublebreasted ➤ *adj* cruzado.

doubt ➤ *tr* dudar; *(to distrust)* desconfiar de ➤ *intr* dudar ➤ *s* duda ■ **beyond d.** fuera de duda • **in d.** dudoso • **no d.** sin duda.

doubtful ➤ *adj* dudoso.

doubtless ➤ *adv* sin duda.

dough ➤ *s* masa, pasta; JER. *(money)* plata.

doughnut ➤ *s* buñuelo.

dove ➤ *s* paloma; FIG. pacifista *mf*.

down[1] ➤ *adv* *(downward)* *(hacia)* abajo; *(in writing)* por escrito; COM. *(in advance)* como adelanto ■ d. and out pobrísimo • d. with . . . ! ¡abajo . . . ! ➤ *adj* que va hacia abajo; *(depressed)* deprimido; COM. inicial, a cuenta ■ to be d. on tenerle inquina a ➤ *prep* abajo ■ d. the centuries a través de los siglos ➤ *s* descenso, caída.

down[2] ➤ *s* *(feathers)* plumón *m*.

downhill ➤ *adv* cuesta abajo ■ to go d. deteriorarse; *(health)* debilitarse.

download ➤ *tr* bajar, descargar.

downpour ➤ *s* chaparrón *m*, aguacero.

downright ➤ *adj* absoluto, completo ➤ *adv* completamente, categóricamente.

downstairs ➤ *adv & adj* en o del piso de abajo ■ to go d. bajar (de un piso a otro) ➤ *spl* planta baja.

downtown ➤ *adv & s* *(hacia o en el)* centro de una ciudad ➤ *adj* del centro.

downward(s) ➤ *adv* hacia abajo ➤ *adj* descendente.

doze ➤ *intr* dormitar ➤ *s* sueño ligero.

dozen ➤ *s & adj* docena (de).

drab ➤ *adj* ordinario, monótono.

draft ➤ *s* corriente *f* de aire; *(of a chimney)* tiro; *(sketch)* bosquejo; *(written)* borrador *m*, versión *f*; MIL. conscripción *f*, quinta; COM. giro ■ **on d. de barril** ➤ *tr* *(a bill)* hacer un anteproyecto de; *(a writing)* hacer un borrador de; MIL. quintar, reclutar ➤ *adj (horse)* de tiro; *(beer)* de barril.

drag ➤ *tr* arrastrar; *(river, lake)* dragar ∎ **to d. out** alargar interminablemente ➤ *intr* arrastrar(se) ∎ *s (act)* arrastre *m*; *(hindrance)* estorbo; JER. *(bore)* pesado; *(puff)* chupada, pitada ∎ **in d.** JER. vestido de mujer (un hombre, o vice versa) • **main d.** JER. calle principal.

dragon ➤ *s* dragón *m*.

dragonfly ➤ *s* libélula.

drain ➤ *tr* drenar, desaguar; *(to drink)* beber; *(to empty)* vaciar ➤ *intr* desaguarse, vaciarse ➤ *s* desagüe *m*, desaguadero.

drama ➤ *s* drama *m*.

dramatic ➤ *adj* dramático.

drape ➤ *tr (to cover)* cubrir; *(to hang)* colgar; *(arms, legs)* echar ➤ *spl* cortinas.

drastic ➤ *adj* drástico.

draw◇ ➤ *tr (to pull)* tirar de, halar; *(to lead)* llevar; *(to attract)* atraer; *(liquid, gun, conclusion)* sacar; *(fire, criticism)* provocar; *(cards)* robar; ARTE. dibujar ∎ **to d. attention** llamar la atención • **to d. out** *(information)* sonsacar; *(to prolong)* prolongar • **to d. up** preparar ➤ *intr (to take in air)* tirar; DEP. *(to tie)* empatar; ARTE. dibujar ∎ **to d. back** echarse para atrás ➤ *s (attraction)* atracción *f*; *(air intake)* tiro; *(tie)* empate *m*.

drawback ➤ *s* desventaja.

drawer ➤ *s* cajón *m*, gaveta.

drawing ➤ *s* dibujo; *(lottery)* sorteo.

dread ➤ *s* pavor *m*, terror *m*; *(anticipation)* aprensión *f* ➤ *tr* temer ➤ *adj* espantoso, terrible.

dreadful ➤ *adj* espantoso, terrible.

dream◇ ➤ *s* sueño; *(daydream)* ensueño ➤ *tr & intr* soñar *(of, about* con); *(to daydream)* soñar despierto ∎ **to d. up** inventar.

dreary ➤ *adj (bleak)* deprimente, sombrío; *(dull)* monótono, aburrido.

drench ➤ *tr* empapar.

dress ➤ *s (garment)* vestido, traje *m*; *(apparel)* vestimenta, ropa ➤ *tr* vestir;

(to decorate) decorar; *(hair)* peinar, arreglar; *(wounds)* curar ➤ *intr* vestirse ∎ **to d. up** vestirse de etiqueta.

dresser ➤ *s* cómoda, tocador *m*.

dressing ➤ *s* MED. vendaje *m*; *(sauce)* aliño, salsa; *(stuffing)* relleno ∎ **d. gown** bata.

dressy ➤ *adj* elegante.

dribble ➤ *intr (to trickle)* gotear; *(to drool)* babear; DEP. *(soccer)* gambetear; *(basketball)* driblar ➤ *tr* echar a gotas; DEP. gambetear, driblar.

drift ➤ *intr* ser arrastrado por la corriente; *(to roam)* vagar, vagabundear; *(snow, sand)* amontonarse ➤ *s (of sand, snow)* pila, montón *m*; *(general idea)* dirección *f*, rumbo ∎ **to get the d.** FAM. caer en la cuenta.

drill ➤ *s (tool)* torno, taladro; *(oil rig)* perforadora; *(machine)* taladradora; *(exercises)* ejercicios repetitivos ➤ *intr & tr* taladrar, perforar; *(to teach)* enseñar por medio de repetición.

drink◇ ➤ *tr & intr* beber, tomar ∎ **to d. to** brindar por • **to d. up** FAM. bebérselo todo ➤ *s* bebida; *(swallow)* trago.

drinkable ➤ *adj* potable.

drinking ➤ *s* beber *m*; *(habit)* bebida.

drip ➤ *tr* echar (a gotas) ➤ *intr* gotear ➤ *s* gota; *(sound)* goteo, goteadero.

drive◇ ➤ *tr (a vehicle)* conducir, guiar; *(passengers)* llevar; *(to compel)* forzar, obligar; *(a nail)* clavar ∎ **to d. away** *o* **off** alejar, apartar • **to d. out** echar ➤ *intr* ir en coche ➤ *s (ride)* vuelta en coche; *(journey)* viaje *m*; *(road)* carretera, camino; *(vigor)* vigor *m*, energía; MEC. transmisión *f*; AUTO. tracción *f*; COMPUT. unidad *f* de disco.

driver ➤ *s* chofer *mf*, conductor/a; COMPUT. controlador *m*.

driveway ➤ *s* camino de entrada.

driving ➤ *adj (impelling)* impulsor, motriz; *(rain)* torrencial; AUTO. de conducción ➤ *s* acción *f* de conducir.

drizzle ➤ *intr* lloviznar, garuar ➤ *s* llovizna, garúa.

droop ➤ *intr* inclinarse; *(trees, eyelids)* caerse; *(shoulders)* encorvarse; *(spir-*

its) desanimarse.

drop ➤ *s* gota; *(trace)* poco, pizca; *(lozenge)* pastilla; *(fall)* bajada, caída; *(height of fall)* altura; *(in prices)* baja; *(in value, quality)* disminución *f*; *(abyss)* precipicio; *(by parachute)* lanzamiento ➤ *intr (to fall)* caer a tierra, desplomarse; *(temperature, prices)* bajar; *(value, quality)* disminuir ■ to d. behind quedarse atrás • to d. in o by pasar (por casa de alguien) • to d. out dejar de participar ➤ *tr (to let fall)* dejar caer, soltar; *(to let go of)* soltar; *(plan)* abandonar; *(habit)* dejar de; *(hint)* soltar; *(voice, prices)* bajar; *(bombs)* lanzar.

dropout ➤ *s* estudiante *mf* que abandona sus estudios; *(from society)* persona que rechaza a la sociedad.

dropper ➤ *s* gotero, cuentagotas *m*.

drought ➤ *s* sequía, seca.

drown ➤ *tr & intr* ahogar(se).

drowsy ➤ *adj* soñoliento.

drug ➤ *s* droga; MED. medicamento; *(narcotic)* narcótico ■ d. addict drogadicto ➤ *tr* MED. dar medicamento; *(with a narcotic)* drogar, narcotizar; *(food, drink)* poner una droga en.

druggist ➤ *s* farmacéutico/a, boticario/a.

drugstore ➤ *s* farmacia, botica.

drum ➤ *s* cilindro, tambor *m*; *(barrel)* tonel *m*; MÚS. tambor ■ *pl* MÚS. batería ➤ *intr & tr* tocar (el tambor); *(fingers)* tamborilear (con) ■ to d. up conseguir.

drummer ➤ *s* baterista *mf*, tambor *mf*.

drunk ➤ *adj* ebrio, borracho ■ to get d. emborracharse ➤ *s (drunkard)* borracho/a; *(bout)* juerga.

dry ➤ *adj* seco; *(arid)* árido; *(thirsty)* sediento; *(boring)* pesado; *(wit, style)* agudo, satírico ■ d. cleaner's tintorería, tinte • to run d. secarse, agotarse ➤ *tr & intr* secar(se), desecar(se).

dry-clean ➤ *tr* limpiar en seco.

dryer ➤ *s (clothes)* secador *m*; *(hair)* secadora.

dual ➤ *adj* dual, doble.

dub ➤ *tr* MÚS. mezclar; CINEM. doblar.

dubious ➤ *adj (doubtful)* dudoso, incierto; *(questionable)* sospechoso.

duck[1] ➤ *s* pato; *(female)* pata.

duck[2] ➤ *tr (head)* agachar; *(to dodge)* eludir, evadir ➤ *intr* agacharse.

due ➤ *adj (payable)* pagadero; *(amount)* sin pagar; *(just)* debido, merecido; *(sufficient)* suficiente ■ d. date vencimiento • d. process proceso legal correspondiente • d. to debido a ➤ *s (comeuppance)* merecido; *(reward)* recompensa ■ *pl* cuota ➤ *adv* ■ d. north derecho hacia el norte.

duel ➤ *s (batirse en)* duelo.

duet ➤ *s* dueto, dúo.

dull ➤ *adj (stupid)* torpe; *(blunt)* desafilado, romo; *(sound, pain)* sordo; *(boring)* aburrido; *(color, sound)* apagado ➤ *tr & intr* desafilar(se), enromar(se); *(pain)* aliviar(se).

duly ➤ *adv* debidamente.

dumb ➤ *adj (mute)* mudo, FAM. *(stupid)* tonto, estúpido.

dump ➤ *tr* tirar, deshacerse de; *(to empty)* vaciar, descargar ➤ *intr* caerse, desplomarse ➤ *s* vertedero, muladar *m*; *(depot)* depósito; JER. *(unkept place)* pocilga ■ d. truck volquete ■ *pl* FAM. abatimiento.

dune ➤ *s* duna.

duplex ➤ *s* apartamento de dos pisos; *(house)* casa de dos viviendas.

duplicate ➤ *s* duplicado, copia ■ in d. por duplicado ➤ *tr* copiar, duplicar; *(on a machine)* multicopiar.

durable ➤ *adj* duradero ■ d. goods productos no perecederos.

duration ➤ *s* duración *f*.

during ➤ *prep* durante.

dusk ➤ *s* crepúsculo ■ at d. al atardecer.

dust ➤ *s* polvo ➤ *intr* limpiar el polvo.

dusty ➤ *adj* polvoriento.

duty ➤ *s* deber *m*, obligación *f*; *(task)* función *f*; *(tax)* impuesto, arancel *m* ■ in the line of d. en cumplimiento del deber • to be on (off) d. (no) estar de servicio.

duty-free ➤ *adj & adv* exento de derechos de aduana.

dwarf ➤ *s* enano/a ➤ *tr* achicar.

dwell◇ ➤ *intr* morar ■ to d. on detenerse en.

dwelling ➤ *s* residencia, morada.

dye ➤ s tintura, tinte m ➤ tr teñir, colorar.

dynamic ➤ adj dinámico ■ **dynamics** ➤ s dinámica.

dynamite ➤ s dinamita.

dynamo ➤ s dínamo f.

E

each ➤ adj cada ➤ pron cada uno ■ **e. other** uno a otro • **to e. his own** cada uno con su gusto ➤ adv por persona, cada uno.

eager ➤ adj (avid) ansioso, ávido; (desirous) deseoso, ardiente.

eagle ➤ s águila.

ear¹ ➤ s oreja; (organ of hearing) oído ■ • **to give** o **lend an e. to** prestar atención a.

ear² ➤ s BOT. espiga, mazorca.

earache ➤ s dolor m de oído.

early ➤ adj temprano; (near the beginning) primero; (premature) prematuro; (primitive) primitivo ■ **e. bird** FAM. (riser) madrugador; (arrival) persona que llega temprano ➤ adv (soon) temprano, pronto; (before) antes; (in advance) con anticipación; (prematurely) prematuramente ■ **bright and e.** muy temprano.

earmuff ➤ s orejera.

earn ➤ tr ganar; (to deserve) merecer; (to acquire) obtener; (interest) devengar.

earnest ➤ adj sincero, serio ■ **en e.** en serio.

earnings ➤ spl (salary) sueldo; (income) ingresos; (profits) utilidades f.

earphone ➤ s auricular m.

earring ➤ s pendiente m, arete m.

earth ➤ s tierra; (world) mundo ■ **down to e.** sensato, realista • **E. Tierra.**

earthquake ➤ s terremoto, temblor m.

ease ➤ s (comfort) comodidad f; (relief) alivio; (naturalness) desenvoltura; (facility) facilidad f ■ **at e.** cómodo, MIL. en posición de descanso • **to put at e.** poner cómodo • **with e.** fácilmente ➤ tr & intr (pain) aliviar(se); (pressure) descargar(se); (tension) relajar(se); (to loosen) aflojar(se) ■ **to e. in(to)** (hacer) entrar con cuidado • **to e. up on** tratar con menos rigor.

easel ➤ s caballete m.

easily ➤ adv fácilmente; (possibly) muy probablemente.

east ➤ s este m, oriente m ➤ adj del este, oriental ➤ adv al este, hacia el este.

Easter ➤ s Pascua de Resurrección; (period) Semana Santa ■ **E. Sunday** domingo de Pascua.

eastern ➤ adj oriental, del este.

easterner ➤ s habitante mf del este.

eastward ➤ adv hacia el este.

easy ➤ adj fácil; (free from worry) tranquilo; (comfortable) cómodo; (simple) sencillo; (unhurried) lento, pausado ■ **e. chair** sillón • **to be on e. street** vivir acomodado ➤ adv fácilmente ■ **e. does it** con calma • **to come e.** costar poco esfuerzo • **to go e. on** FAM. (to use moderately) usar con moderación; (to be lenient to) no tratar con mucha severidad • **to take it e.** FAM. (to relax) descansar; (to stay calm) no agitarse.

easygoing ➤ adj despreocupado, descuidado; (tolerant) tolerante.

eat◇ ➤ tr comer; (lunch, dinner) tomar (el almuerzo, la cena); JER. (to annoy) molestar, fastidiar ■ **to e. away** corroer, carcomer • **to e. up** (to devour) comérselo todo; (to use up) gastar; (to enjoy) deleitarse en ➤ intr comer, alimentarse ■ **to e. (away)** ro roer, corroer • **to e. out** comer fuera (de casa).

ebb ➤ s menguante f ➤ intr menguar.

eccentric ➤ adj & s excéntrico/a.

echo ➤ s eco m ➤ tr repetir; (to imitate) imitar ➤ intr producir eco, resonar.

eclipse ➤ s eclipse m ➤ tr eclipsar.

ecological ➤ adj ecológico.

ecology ➤ s ecología.

economic ➤ adj económico ■ **economics** ssg economía.

economical ➤ adj económico.

economize ➤ intr economizar (on en).

economy ➤ s economía f ■ **e. car** automóvil económico.

ecosystem ➤ s ecosistema m.

Ecuadorian ➤ adj & s ecuatoriano/a.

edge ➤ s (cutting side) filo, corte m; (border, rim) borde m; (boundary) límite m; (of table, coin) canto; (farthest part) extremidad f; FAM. (advan-

tage) ventaja ∎ **to be on e.** tener los nervios de punta • **to be on the e. of** estar al borde *o* al punto de ➤ *tr (to border)* bordear ∎ **to e. out** vencer por un margen pequeño ➤ *intr* andar *o* moverse cautelosamente.

edible ➤ *adj & s* comestible *m.*

edict ➤ *s* edicto.

edit ➤ *tr (to draft)* redactar; *(to correct)* corregir, editar; *(edition)* preparar; *(a publication)* dirigir; CINEM. montar.

editing ➤ *s (of text)* redacción *f; (correction)* corrección *f,* revisión *f; (of a publication)* dirección *f; (of film)* montaje *m.*

edition ➤ *s* edición *f; (number of copies)* tiraje *m,* tirada; FIG. versión *f.*

editor ➤ *s* editor/a; *(supervisor)* redactor/a jefe; CINEM. montador/a ∎ **e. in chief** jefe/a de redacción, redactor/a en jefe.

editorial ➤ *adj & s* editorial *m.*

educate ➤ *tr* educar.

educated ➤ *adj (cultured)* culto; *(schooled)* educado.

education ➤ *s* educación *f.*

educational ➤ *adj (institution, staff)* docente; *(instructive)* educativo.

eel ➤ *s* anguila.

effect ➤ *s* efecto; *(result)* resultado ∎ **for e.** para impresionar • **in e.** *(in fact)* efectivamente; *(virtually)* casi • **to be in e.** estar vigente • **to go into e.** entrar en vigor • **to take e.** *(medication)* surtir efecto; *(laws, schedule)* entrar en vigor ∎ *pl* bienes, pertenencias ➤ *tr* efectuar, realizar.

effective ➤ *adj* efectivo; *(striking)* impresionante; *(operative)* vigente.

efficiency ➤ *s* eficiencia; FAM. *(apartment)* apartamento de un cuarto con cocina y baño; MEC. rendimiento.

efficient ➤ *adj* eficaz, eficiente.

effort ➤ *s* esfuerzo; *(achievement)* obra ∎ **to spare no e.** hacer todo lo posible.

egg ➤ *s* huevo; BIOL. óvulo ∎ **bad e.** JER. calavera • **good e.** JER. buen tipo • **to put all one's eggs in one basket** jugárselo todo en una carta ➤ *tr* ∎ **to e. on** incitar.

eggplant ➤ *s* berenjena.

eggshell ➤ *s* cascarón *m.*

eight ➤ *s & adj* ocho ∎ **e. hundred** ochocientos • **e. o'clock** las ocho.

eighteen ➤ *s & adj* dieciocho.

eighth ➤ *s & adj* octavo.

eighty ➤ *s & adj* ochenta *m.*

either ➤ *pron & adj* uno u otro, cualquiera de los dos; *(negative)* ni uno ni otro, ninguno de los dos ➤ *conj* ∎ **e. we go now, or we stay** o nos vamos ahora *o* nos quedamos ➤ *adv* tampoco.

elastic ➤ *adj & m* elástico.

elbow ➤ *s* codo ∎ **e. grease** FAM. energía física ➤ *tr* dar un codazo.

elder ➤ *adj* mayor ➤ *s (old person)* mayor *mf; (leader)* anciano/a.

elderly ➤ *adj* mayor (de edad).

eldest ➤ *adj* mayor ∎ **the e.** el mayor.

elect ➤ *tr & intr* elegir ➤ *adj* electo ∎ **the e. los** elegidos.

election ➤ *s (choice)* elección *f;* POL. elecciones.

electric(al) ➤ *adj* eléctrico.

electrician ➤ *s* electricista *mf.*

electricity ➤ *s* electricidad *f.*

electrify ➤ *tr* electrizar; *(a building, town)* electrificar.

electrocute ➤ *tr* electrocutar.

electron ➤ *s* electrón *m.*

electronic ➤ *adj* electrónico ∎ **electronics** *ssg* electrónica.

elegance ➤ *s* elegancia.

elegant ➤ *adj* elegante.

element ➤ *s* elemento ∎ *pl (weather)* los elementos.

elemental ➤ *adj* elemental.

elementary ➤ *adj* elemental ∎ **e. school** escuela primaria.

elephant ➤ *s* elefante *m.*

elevation ➤ *s* elevación *f;* GEOG. altitud *f.*

elevator ➤ *s* ascensor *m.*

eleven ➤ *s & adj* once *m* ∎ **e. o'clock** las once.

eleventh ➤ *s & adj* undécimo; *(part)* onzavo.

eligible ➤ *adj* elegible.

eliminate ➤ *tr* eliminar.

else ➤ *adj & adv* ∎ **all** *o* **everything e.** todo lo demás • **anybody** *o* **anyone e.**

cualquier otro; *(negative)* ningún otro • **anything** e. algo más; *(negative)* nada más • **anywhere** e. *(place)* en cualquier otra parte; *(direction)* a cualquier otra parte; *(negative) (place)* a ningún otro lugar; *(in existence)* en ningún otro lugar • **everyone** e. todos los demás • **how** e.? ¿de qué otro modo? • **nobody** o **no one** e. nadie más • **nothing** e. nada más • **nowhere** e. en o a ninguna otra parte • **or** e. si no • **what** e. ¿qué más? • **where** e.? ¿en o a qué otro sitio? • **who** e? ¿quién más?

elude ➤ *tr* eludir, esquivar.

e-mail ➤ *s* correo electrónico, e-mail *m* ➤ *tr* enviar o mandar por e-mail.

emancipate ➤ *tr* emancipar.

embark ➤ *tr & intr* embarcar(se) ▪ **to e. on** lanzarse a.

embarrass ➤ *tr (to disconcert)* desconcertar, turbar; *(to shame)* avergonzar.

embarrassing ➤ *adj* desconcertante.

embarrassment ➤ *s (shame)* vergüenza, turbación *f*; *(trouble)* embarazo; *(confusion)* desconcierto.

embassy ➤ *s* embajada.

embrace ➤ *tr* abrazar; *(to accept eagerly)* aprovecharse de ➤ *intr* abrazarse ➤ *s* abrazo.

embroider ➤ *tr* bordar; *(a story)* exagerar ➤ *intr* hacer bordado.

embroidery ➤ *s* bordado.

emerald ➤ *s* esmeralda.

emerge ➤ *intr* emerger, surgir.

emergency ➤ *s* emergencia; MED. caso de urgencia; *(need)* necesidad *f* urgente ▪ **e. landing** aterrizaje forzoso.

emigrant ➤ *s* emigrante *mf*.

emigrate ➤ *intr* emigrar.

emit ➤ *tr* emitir.

emotion ➤ *s* emoción *f*.

emotional ➤ *adj* emocional; *(scene, person)* emotivo.

emperor ➤ *s* emperador *m*.

emphasis ➤ *s* énfasis *m*.

emphasize ➤ *tr* enfatizar, hacer hincapié en.

empire ➤ *s* imperio.

employ ➤ *tr* emplear ▪ **to be employed** tener empleo ➤ *s* empleo.

employee ➤ *s* empleado/a.

employer ➤ *s* empleador/a.

employment ➤ *s* empleo.

empower ➤ *tr* autorizar.

emptiness ➤ *s* vacío; *(of a person, words)* vacuidad *f*.

empty ➤ *adj* vacío; *(place)* desierto; *(devoid)* falto ➤ *tr* vaciar; *(to vacate)* dejar vacío, desalojar; *(to unload)* descargar ➤ *intr* vaciarse ▪ **to e. into** desembocar en ➤ *s* envase vacío.

enable ➤ *tr* capacitar; *(to make possible)* posibilitar; DER. autorizar.

enact ➤ *tr* promulgar; TEAT. representar.

enamel ➤ *s* esmalte *m* ➤ *tr* esmaltar.

encase ➤ *tr* encerrar, encajonar.

enchanting ➤ *adj* encantador.

encircle ➤ *tr* rodear, circundar.

enclose ➤ *tr* encerrar; *(a document)* adjuntar; *(to fence in)* cercar ▪ **enclosed herewith** encontrará adjunto.

enclosure ➤ *s* encierro; *(land)* cercado; *(document)* adjunto, documento; *(fence)* cerco, valla.

encounter ➤ *s* encuentro; *(clash)* choque *m* ➤ *tr* encontrar.

encourage ➤ *tr* animar, alentar; *(to embolden)* fortalecer; *(to foster)* fomentar.

encouragement ➤ *s* ánimo, aliento; *(incentive)* incentivo.

encyclopedia ➤ *s* enciclopedia.

end ➤ *s (tip)* extremo, punta; *(boundary)* límite *m*; *(conclusion)* fin *m*, final *m*; *(outcome)* desenlace *m*; *(goal)* propósito ▪ **at the e.** al cabo de • **e. to e.** punta con punta • **in the e.** al fin, al final • **on e.** *(upright)* de pie, derecho; *(nonstop)* sin parar; *(hair)* de punta • **to bring** *(come)* **to an e.** terminar(se), acabar(se) ➤ *tr* acabar, concluir; *(to destroy)* destruir ➤ *intr* terminar(se), acabar(se) ▪ **to e. up** ir a parar.

endanger ➤ *tr* poner en peligro.

endeavor ➤ *s (effort)* esfuerzo, empeño; *(attempt)* intento ➤ *intr* intentar.

ending ➤ *s* conclusión *f*, fin *m*; *(of a story)* desenlace *m*, final *m*.

endive ➤ *s* escarola, endibia.

endless ➤ *adj* interminable; *(infinite)* infinito; *(continuous)* continuo.

endorse ➤ *tr* endosar; *(to support)* apoyar; *(to approve)* sancionar.

endorsement ➤ *s* endoso; *(approval)* aprobación *f*; *(support)* apoyo.

endow ➤ *tr* dotar.

endowment ➤ *s* dotación *f*.

endurance ➤ *s* resistencia, aguante *m*.

endure ➤ *tr* resistir, aguantar; *(to tolerate)* tolerar ➤ *intr* aguantarse, resistir; *(to last)* durar.

enemy ➤ *s & adj* enemigo/a.

energetic ➤ *adj* enérgico.

energy ➤ *s* energía.

enforce ➤ *tr (a law)* hacer cumplir *o* respetar; *(to impose)* imponer.

engage ➤ *tr (to hire)* emplear; *(to reserve)* contratar; *(to engross)* cautivar ➤ *intr* ▪ to e. in ocuparse en.

engaged ➤ *adj (employed)* empleado; *(busy)* ocupado; *(reserved)* contratado; *(betrothed)* comprometido; MEC. engranado ▪ to be e. *(busy)* estar ocupado; *(betrothed)* estar comprometido • to get e. prometerse.

engagement ➤ *s* compromiso; *(appointment)* cita; MIL. batalla, combate *m*.

engine ➤ *s* máquina, motor *m*; F.C. locomotora.

engineer ➤ *s* ingeniero/a; F.C. maquinista *mf* ➤ *tr* maniobrar, maquinar.

engineering ➤ *s* ingeniería.

English ➤ *adj* inglés ➤ *s (idioma)* inglés *m* ▪ the E. los ingleses.

Englishman/woman ➤ *s* inglés/esa.

engrave ➤ *tr* grabar; *(on stone)* tallar.

engraving ➤ *s* grabado.

enjoy ➤ *tr* gozar (de), disfrutar (de) ▪ I e. swimming me gusta nadar • to e. oneself divertirse, pasarlo bien.

enjoyable ➤ *adj* agradable, encantador; *(fun)* divertido.

enjoyment ➤ *s* placer *m*, goce *m*; disfrute *m*.

enlarge ➤ *tr* agrandar, aumentar; *(to magnify)* magnificar; FOTOG. ampliar ➤ *intr* agrandarse.

enlighten ➤ *tr* iluminar, ilustrar; *(to inform)* aclarar.

enormous ➤ *adj* enorme.

enough ➤ *adj* bastante, suficiente ▪ to be e. bastar ➤ *adv* bastante ▪ sure e. en

efecto ➤ *s* lo bastante, lo suficiente ▪ e. is e. basta y sobra • to have had e. *(to be satisfied)* estar satisfecho; *(to be tired of)* estar harto ➤ *interj* ¡basta! ▪ e. of this! ¡basta ya!

enrich ➤ *tr* enriquecer; AGR. abonar.

enrol(l) ➤ *tr & intr* registrar(se), inscribir(se); *(a student)* matricular(se).

enrol(l)ment ➤ *s* inscripción *f*; *(in school)* matriculación *f*; *(record)* registro.

ensure ➤ *tr* asegurar, garantizar.

entail ➤ *tr* implicar, comportar; DER. vincular.

enter ➤ *tr* entrar en; *(to penetrate)* penetrar en; *(to participate in)* participar en; *(to embark upon)* emprender; *(to obtain admission to)* ingresar, entrar a; *(in a register)* asentar, anotar ➤ *intr* entrar; *(to register)* inscribirse, matricularse ▪ to e. into *(a contract)* celebrar, concertar; *(to begin)* iniciar.

enterprise ➤ *s* empresa; *(initiative)* iniciativa.

entertain ➤ *tr* divertir, entretener; *(an idea)* considerar ▪ to e. oneself divertirse ➤ *intr* recibir invitados.

entertainer ➤ *s* artista *mf*.

entertaining ➤ *adj* entretenido, divertido.

entertainment ➤ *s* entretenimiento, diversion *f*; *(show)* espectáculo.

enthusiasm ➤ *s* entusiasmo.

enthusiast ➤ *s* entusiasta *mf*.

enthusiastic ➤ *adj* entusiástico.

entire ➤ *adj* entero, total; *(in one piece)* intacto.

entirety ➤ *s* totalidad *f*.

entitle ➤ *tr* titular; *(to give a right)* dar derecho a ▪ to be entitled to tener derecho a.

entrance ➤ *s* entrada.

entrée or **entree** ➤ *s (admittance)* entrada; CUL. plato principal.

entrepreneur ➤ *s* empresario/a.

entry ➤ *s* entrada; *(in a register)* registro; DEP. competidor *m*; *(teneduría)* asiento.

enumerate ➤ *tr* enumerar.

envelop ➤ *tr* envolver.

envelope ➤ *s* sobre *m*; *(wrapping)* envoltura; (cover) cobertura.

envious ➤ adj envidioso.

environment ➤ s medio ambiente; (atmosphere) ambiente m.

envy ➤ s envidia; (object) cosa o persona envidiada ➤ tr envidiar, tener envidia de ➤ intr sentir envidia.

epidemic ➤ adj epidémico ➤ s MED. epidemia; FIG. ola.

episode ➤ s episodio.

epoch ➤ s época.

equal ➤ adj igual; (evenhanded) equitativo ■ all things being e. si todo sigue igual • to be e. to ser igual que; (capable) ser apto para ➤ s igual mf ■ e. sign signo de igualdad • without e. sin par ➤ tr ser igual a; (to match) igualar.

equality ➤ s igualdad f.

equalize ➤ tr & intr igualar.

equally ➤ adj igualmente, por igual.

equation ➤ s ecuación f.

equator ➤ s ecuador m.

equip ➤ tr equipar; FIG. preparar.

equipment ➤ s equipo; (tools) avíos.

equivalent ➤ adj & s equivalente m.

erase ➤ tr borrar.

eraser ➤ s goma, borrador m.

erect ➤ adj erecto, erguido; (hair) erizado ➤ tr (to construct) erigir, construir; (to raise, establish) levantar.

erode ➤ tr & intr erosionar(se), desgastar(se); (to corrode) corroer(se).

erosion ➤ s erosión f.

erotic ➤ adj erótico.

err ➤ intr errar, equivocarse.

errand ➤ s mandado, recado.

erratic ➤ adj irregular; (eccentric) excéntrico, extravagante.

error ➤ s error m.

escalator ➤ s escalera mecánica.

escape ➤ intr escaparse ➤ s escapatoria.

escort ➤ s escolta; (companion) acompañante m ➤ tr acompañar, escoltar.

especially ➤ adv especialmente.

essay ➤ tr ensayar ➤ s ensayo.

essence ➤ s esencia ■ in e. esencialmente.

essential ➤ adj & s (element) esencial.

establish ➤ tr establecer; (to prove) demostrar; (facts) verificar.

establishment ➤ s establecimiento ■ E.

iglesia oficial; POL. clase dirigente.

estate ➤ s (land) hacienda, finca; (property) propiedad f; DER. testamentaría ■ real e. bienes raíces.

esteem ➤ tr estimar ➤ s estimación f, aprecio.

estimate ➤ tr estimar ➤ s estimación f; (of costs) presupuesto ■ rough e. cálculo aproximado.

eternal ➤ adj eterno.

eternity ➤ s eternidad f.

ethical ➤ adj ético, moral.

ethnic ➤ adj étnico.

etiquette ➤ s etiqueta, protocolo.

Europe ➤ s Europa.

European ➤ adj & s europeo/a.

evacuate ➤ tr evacuar ➤ intr retirarse.

evade ➤ tr evitar, evadir.

evaluate ➤ tr evaluar; (to appraise) tasar, valorar.

evaluation ➤ s evaluación f, valoración f; (judgment) opinión f.

evaporate ➤ tr & intr evaporar(se).

evaporation ➤ s evaporación f.

eve ➤ s víspera; (before a feast) vigilia ■ on the e. of en vísperas de.

even ➤ adj (flat) plano, llano; (level) a nivel; (uniform) regular; (score) empatado; MAT. par ■ to get e. desquitarse • to break e. cubrir los gastos ➤ adv todavía, aun ■ e. as justo cuando • e. if o though aunque • e. so aun así • I didn't e. cry ni siquiera lloré ➤ tr (to level) emparejar, nivelar; (to make equal) igualar.

evening ➤ s tarde f; (dusk) anochecer m, noche f ■ e. class clase nocturna • e. dress (for men) traje de etiqueta; (for women) traje de noche • good e.! ¡buenas noches!

event ➤ s suceso, acontecimiento; (outcome) resultado; DEP. evento ■ in any e. en todo caso • in the e. of en caso de (que).

eventual ➤ adj final.

eventually ➤ adv con el tiempo, a la larga.

ever ➤ adv siempre; (at any time) alguna vez; (at all) jamás ■ as e. como siempre • better than e. mejor que nunca • e. since (from the time) desde que; *(since then)* desde entonces • **for e. and e.** por siempre jamás • **hardly e.** casi nunca • **not e.** nunca.

every ➤ *adj* cada; *(all)* todo(s) ■ **e. day** todos los días • **e. other day** cada dos días.

everyday ➤ *adj* diario, cotidiano; *(usual)* común; *(clothes)* de todos los días.

everyone *o* **everybody** ➤ *pron* cada uno, cada cual; *(all)* todos, todo el mundo ■ **e. for himself** cada cual por su cuenta.

everything ➤ *pron* todo.

everywhere ➤ *adv* en, a *o* por todas partes; *(wherever)* dondequiera que.

evidence ➤ *s* prueba; *(data)* hechos, datos; *(testimony)* declaración *f* ■ **to be in e.** estar a la vista • **to give e.** declarar como testigo • **to show e. of** presentar señales de ➤ *tr* evidenciar, probar.

evident ➤ *adj* evidente.

evil ➤ *adj* malo, malvado; *(harmful)* nocivo, perjudicial; *(influence)* pernicioso ➤ *s* mal, maldad *f*; *(harm)* perjuicio; *(immorality)* perversidad *f*.

evolution ➤ *s* evolución *f*.

ewe ➤ *s* oveja hembra.

exact ➤ *adj* exacto.

exactly ➤ *adv* exactamente; *(wholly)* precisamente; *(time)* en punto; *(quite true)* es verdad, así es.

exaggerate ➤ *tr & intr* exagerar.

exaggeration ➤ *s* exageración *f*.

exam ➤ *s* FAM. examen *m*.

examination ➤ *s* examen *m*; DER. interrogatorio; *(inquiry)* investigación *f* ■ **to take an e.** sufrir un examen.

examine ➤ *tr* examinar; *(to scrutinize)* escudriñar; DER. interrogar.

example ➤ *s* ejemplo ■ **to set an e.** dar ejemplo.

excavate ➤ *tr* excavar; *(ruins)* desenterrar.

exceed ➤ *tr* exceder; *(limits, authority)* propasarse en, excederse en.

exceedingly ➤ *adv* extremadamente.

excel ➤ *tr* superar, aventajar ➤ *intr* distinguirse.

excellent ➤ *adj* excelente.

except ➤ *prep* excepto, menos ■ **e. for** *(were it not for)* a no ser por; *(apart*

from) aparte de ➤ *conj (only)* sólo que; *(otherwise than)* sino ■ **e. that** salvo *o* excepto que ➤ *tr* exceptuar, excluir.

exception ➤ *s* excepción *f*.

exceptional ➤ *adj* excepcional.

excerpt ➤ *s* extracto ➤ *tr* extractar ■ **to e. from** citar de.

excess ➤ *s* exceso ➤ *adj* excesivo.

excessive ➤ *adj* excesivo.

exchange ➤ *tr* cambiar, intercambiar; *(glances, words)* cruzar; *(prisoners, goods)* canjear ➤ *s* cambio, intercambio; *(of prisoners, goods)* canje *m*; COM. bolsa ■ **e. rate** tipo de cambio • **in e. for** a cambio de.

excise tax ➤ *s* impuesto indirecto.

excite ➤ *tr* excitar; *(to thrill)* entusiasmar, emocionar.

excited ➤ *adj* excitado; *(emotions)* agitado; *(thrilled)* entusiasmado.

excitement ➤ *s* emoción *f*, agitación *f*; *(enthusiasm)* entusiasmo.

exciting ➤ *adj* emocionante.

exclaim ➤ *intr* exclamar ➤ *tr* gritar.

exclamation ➤ *s* exclamación *f* ■ **e. point** signo de admiración.

exclude ➤ *tr* excluir.

exclusive ➤ *adj* exclusivo; *(select)* selecto ■ **e. rights** exclusividad *f*.

excursion ➤ *s* excursión *f*, paseo.

excuse ➤ *tr* excusar, disculpar; *(to exempt)* dispensar *(from* de) ■ **e. me** *(I'm sorry!)* ¡discúlpeme!; *(pardon me)* con permiso ■ **to make excuses (for)** dar excusas (por).

execute ➤ *tr* ejecutar; *(to do)* hacer; *(to validate)* formalizar.

execution ➤ *s* ejecución *f*; *(validation)* legalización *f*.

executive ➤ *s* ejecutivo/a; POL. presidente/a, jefe/a de estado; *(branch)* poder ejecutivo ➤ *adj* ejecutivo.

exempt ➤ *tr* eximir *(from* de) ➤ *adj* exento.

exemption ➤ *s* exención *f*.

exercise ➤ *s* ejercicio ■ *pl (ceremony)* ceremonia ➤ *tr (to use)* usar de, proceder con; *(to drill)* ejercitar, entrenar; *(rights)* ejercer ➤ *intr* ejercitarse.

exert ➤ *tr (strength)* emplear; *(influence)* ejercer.

exertion ➤ s (of strength) empleo; (of influence) ejercicio; (effort) esfuerzo.

exhaust ➤ tr agotar; (to tire) cansar ➤ s AUTO. escape m; (fumes) gases m de escape ■ e. pipe tubo de escape.

exhaustion ➤ s agotamiento.

exhibit ➤ tr exhibir; (at a show) exponer; (emotion, trait) manifestar ➤ intr exponer ➤ s (display) exhibición f; (object) objeto exhibido.

exhibition ➤ s exhibición f.

exhibitor ➤ s expositor/a.

exile ➤ s exilio, destierro; (persona) desterrado/a ➤ tr exiliar, desterrar.

exist ➤ intr existir, ser; (to live) vivir.

existence ➤ s existencia; (life) vida f.

existing ➤ adj existente.

exit ➤ s salida ➤ intr salir.

exorbitant ➤ adj exorbitante.

expand ➤ tr & intr extender(se); (to enlarge) expandir(se); FÍS. dilatar(se).

expanse ➤ s extensión f.

expansion ➤ s expansión f; FÍS. dilatación f; (of a town) ensanche m; (of an idea) ampliación.

expect ➤ tr (to await) esperar; (to require) contar con.

expectation ➤ s expectación f, expectativa; (prospect) esperanza.

expedition ➤ s expedición f.

expel ➤ tr expeler; (to dismiss) echar, expulsar.

expenditure ➤ s desembolso, gasto.

expense ➤ s gasto ■ at the e. of a expensas de ■ pl expensas.

expensive ➤ adj costoso, caro.

experience ➤ s experiencia ➤ tr (to undergo) experimentar; (to feel) sentir.

experienced ➤ adj experimentado.

experiment ➤ s experimento ➤ intr experimentar (on en).

expert ➤ s & adj experto/a, perito/a.

expertise ➤ s pericia.

expiration ➤ s (end, death) expiración f; (lapse) caducidad f; (breath) espiración f; COM. vencimiento.

expire ➤ intr expirar; (to lapse) vencer, caducar; (to exhale) espirar.

explain ➤ tr explicar ➤ intr dar explicaciones.

explanation ➤ s explicación f.

explode ➤ intr explotar, estallar ➤ tr hacer explotar; (to detonate) detonar; (to disprove) desbaratar.

exploit ➤ s hazaña, proeza ➤ tr explotar.

exploration ➤ s exploración f.

explore ➤ tr explorar; FIG. investigar.

explorer ➤ s explorador/a.

explosion ➤ s explosión f.

explosive ➤ adj & s explosivo.

export ➤ tr exportar ➤ s exportación f.

expose ➤ tr exponer; (to reveal) revelar; (to unmask) desenmascarar.

express ➤ tr expresar; (to show) manifestar ➤ adj expreso; (explicit) explícito; (mail) de entrega inmediata ➤ adv por expreso ➤ s transporte rápido; (train) expreso, rápido.

expression ➤ s expresión f; (sign) señal f; (gesture) gesto.

expressway ➤ s autopista.

extend ➤ tr extender; (road, visit) prolongar; (hand, arm) alargar; (to enlarge) agrandar, ampliar ■ to e. an invitation invitar ➤ intr extenderse; (to reach) alcanzar.

extension ➤ s extensión f; (expansion) ampliación f; (annex) anexo; (continuation) prolongación f; FIN. prórroga.

extensive ➤ adj extensivo, extenso.

extent ➤ s extensión f; (degree) grado ■ to a certain e. hasta cierto punto.

exterior ➤ adj (outer) exterior; (external) externo ➤ s exterior m.

external ➤ adj externo; (exterior, foreign) exterior.

extinct ➤ adj extinto, desaparecido; (inactive) inactivo.

extra ➤ adj extra; (additional) adicional ➤ s extra m ➤ adv excepcionalmente.

extract ➤ tr extraer; (to excerpt) extractar ➤ s extracto.

extraordinary ➤ adj extraordinario.

extravagant ➤ adj pródigo; (wasteful) derrochador; (exorbitant) costoso.

extreme ➤ adj extremo; (extraordinary) excepcional; (drastic) drástico ➤ s extremo ■ to go to extremes tomar medidas extremas.

extremely ➤ adv extremadamente.

eye ➤ s ojo ■ e. **shadow** sombreador • **to catch someone's e.** llamar la atención de alguien • **to keep an e. on** vigilar • **to roll one's eyes** poner los ojos en blanco • **to see e. to e.** estar de acuerdo ➤ tr ojear, mirar.

eyeball ➤ s globo ocular.

eyebrow ➤ s ceja.

eyeglasses ➤ spl lentes m.

eyelash ➤ s pestaña.

eyelid ➤ s párpado.

eyesight ➤ s vista ■ **within e.** al alcance de la vista.

F

fable ➤ s fábula.

fabric ➤ s tela.

fabulous ➤ adj fabuloso.

face ➤ s cara; (façade) frente m; (of a clock) esfera ■ **f. down,** up boca abajo, arriba • **f. value** FIN. valor nominal • **in the f. of** frente a • **to lose f.** desprestigiarse • **to save f.** salvar las apariencias ➤ tr mirar hacia; (building, window) dar a; (to confront) hacer frente a ■ **to be faced with** enfrentarse con • **to f. up to** encararse con, enfrentarse a.

facility ➤ s facilidad f ■ pl COM. facilidades; (buildings) instalaciones; (public toilet) servicio, baño.

fact ➤ s hecho ■ **in fact** en realidad ■ pl datos, información.

factor ➤ s factor m.

factory ➤ s fábrica.

faculty ➤ s (ability) facultad f; EDUC. profesorado.

fade ➤ intr (light) palidecer; (flower) marchitarse; (color) desteñirse.

fail ➤ intr fracasar; (motor, health, support) fallar; (to be inadequate) faltar; (in school) aplazarse; COM. quebrar ■ **to f. to** (to be unsuccessful in) no alcanzar a; (to neglect to) dejar de ➤ tr fallar, frustrar; (course, exam) salir mal en ➤ s **without f.** sin falta.

failing ➤ s falla, defecto.

failure ➤ s fracaso; (person) fracasado/a; (weakening) deterioro; ELEC. apagón m; COM. quiebra.

faint ➤ adj (indistinct) borroso; (slight) vago, ligero; (dizzy) mareado; (weak)

débil ➤ s desmayo ➤ intr desmayarse.

fair[1] ➤ adj imparcial; (just) justo; (mediocre) regular; (weather) bueno; (sky) despejado ■ **f. enough!** ¡vale! • **f. play** juego limpio ➤ adv honrado.

fair[2] ➤ s (exhibition) exposición f, feria.

fairly ➤ adv (justly) justamente, equitativamente; (moderately) bastante.

fairy ➤ s hada ■ **f. tale** cuento de hadas.

faith ➤ s (confidence) confianza; (belief) fe f ■ **in good, bad f.** de buena, mala fe.

faithful ➤ adj fiel.

fake ➤ adj falso, fraudulento ➤ s impostor/a; (fraud) engaño; (forgery) falsificación f ➤ tr falsificar; (to feign) fingir.

fall◊ ➤ intr caer(se); (prices, temperature) bajar ■ **to f. behind** quedarse atrás • **to f. down o over** caer(se) • **to f. for** FAM. (person) volverse loco por; (trick) tragarse • **to f. off** (to come loose) desprenderse; (to decrease) disminuir, decaer • **to f. through** fracasar ➤ s caída; (autumn) otoño; (reduction) bajada, descenso; (decline) decadencia, ruina ■ pl catarata, cascada.

fallout ➤ s lluvia radioactiva; (side effects) consecuencias.

false ➤ adj falso; (hope) infundado; (teeth) postizo ■ **f. pretense** intención fraudulenta • **f. start** salida mala o nula • **f. step** paso en falso ➤ adv falsamente, con falsedad; (wrong) mal.

fame ➤ s fama, renombre m.

familiar ➤ adj familiar, conocido; (intimate) de confianza; (forward) confianzudo ■ **to be f. with** conocer.

familiarity ➤ s familiaridad f; (impropriety) atrevimiento ■ pl libertades.

familiarize ➤ tr familiarizar.

family ➤ s familia ■ **f. name** apellido.

famine ➤ s hambre f.

famous ➤ adj famoso.

fan[1] ➤ s (hand) abanico; (electric) ventilador m ➤ tr abanicar.

fan[2] ➤ s FAM. (enthusiast) aficionado/a.

fanatic ➤ s & adj fanático/a.

fancy ➤ s fantasía; (whim) capricho ➤ adj adornado; (superior) fino ➤ tr imaginar; (to like) gustarle a uno; (to suppose) suponer.

fantastic ➤ *adj* fantástico.

fantasy ➤ *s* fantasía.

far ➤ *adv* lejos ▪ **as f. as I am concerned** por mi parte • **f. away** *o* **f. off** (a lo) lejos • **f. different** muy diferente • **f. from** de lejos de • **f. from it** al contrario • **f. more** mucho más • **how f.?** ¿a qué distancia? • **to go f.** realizar mucho • **to go too f.** pasarse de la raya ➤ *adj* lejano; POL. extremo ▪ **a f. cry** una gran diferencia.

faraway ➤ *adj* lejano.

farce ➤ *s* farsa.

fare ➤ *s* pasaje *m*; *(food)* comida.

farewell ➤ *s & interj* adiós *m*.

farm ➤ *s* granja, finca ➤ *tr* cultivar ➤ *intr* labrar la tierra, ser agricultor.

farmer ➤ *s* granjero/a.

farmhouse ➤ *s* granja, cortijo.

farmyard ➤ *s* corral *m*.

farther ➤ *adv* (in space) más lejos; *(in time)* más adelante; *(degree)* más.

farthest ➤ *adj* más remoto ➤ *adv* más lejos.

fascinate ➤ *tr* fascinar.

fascination ➤ *s* fascinación *f*.

fashion ➤ *s* manera; *(style)* moda ▪ **in f.** de moda • **to go out of f.** pasar de moda.

fashionable ➤ *adj* de moda; *(elegant)* elegante.

fast[1] ➤ *adj* rápido; *(clock)* adelantado ➤ *adv* rápidamente; *(securely)* firmemente.

fast[2] ➤ *s* ayuno ➤ *intr* ayunar.

fasten ➤ *tr* fijar; *(to tie)* atar; *(to close)* cerrar.

fastener ➤ *s* sujetador *m*, cierre *m*.

fat ➤ *s* grasa; CUL. manteca ➤ *adj* gordo; *(thick)* grueso; *(large)* grande ▪ **to get f.** ponerse gordo, engordar.

fatal ➤ *adj* fatal, mortal.

fate ➤ *s* destino.

father ➤ *s* padre *m* ➤ *tr* engendrar.

father-in-law ➤ *s* suegro.

fatigue ➤ *s* fatiga ➤ *tr* fatigar.

fattening ➤ *adj* que engorda.

fatty ➤ *adj* graso, adiposo.

fatuous ➤ *adj* fatuo.

faucet ➤ *s* grifo, llave *f*.

fault ➤ *s* culpa; *(shortcoming)* defecto;

ELEC., GEOL. falla ▪ **to be at f.** tener la culpa • **to find f.** criticar.

faulty ➤ *adj* defectuoso.

favor ➤ *s* favor *mf* ▪ **to be in f. of** estar a favor de ➤ *tr* favorecer; *(to be partial to)* preferir.

favorable ➤ *adj* favorable.

favorite ➤ *adj & s* favorito/a.

fear ➤ *s* miedo ➤ *tr & intr* tener miedo (de), temer.

fearful ➤ *adj* temeroso; FAM. *(dreadful)* tremendo.

fearless ➤ *adj* intrépido, audaz.

feast ➤ *s* banquete *m* ➤ *tr & intr* banquetear.

feat ➤ *s* proeza, hazaña.

feather ➤ *s* pluma ▪ *pl* plumaje *m*.

feature ➤ *s* característica, rasgo; CINEM. película principal ▪ *pl* facciones, rasgos ➤ *tr* presentar.

February ➤ *s* febrero.

fed ➤ *adj* ▪ **f. up with** harto de.

federation ➤ *s* federación *f*.

fee ➤ *s* honorarios; *(fixed)* cuota.

feeble◇ ➤ *adj* débil.

feed◇ ➤ *tr* dar de comer a; *(to nourish, supply)* alimentar ➤ *intr* comer.

feedback ➤ *s* información *f*; ELECTRÓN. realimentación *f*, retroacción *f*.

feel◇ ➤ *tr* sentir; *(to touch)* tocar; *(to sense)* percibir ➤ *intr* sentir (por tacto); *(emotionally)* sentirse, estar; *(to seem)* parecer ▪ **f. like** FAM. *(to want to)* tener ganas de; *(to touch)* parecer (como) • **to f. smooth, rough** ser suave, áspero al tacto • **to f. up to** FAM. sentirse con ánimos para ➤ *s* *(touch)* tacto; *(perception)* sensación *f*; *(atmosphere)* atmósfera.

feeling ➤ *s* *(touch)* tacto; *(sensation)* sensación *f*; *(emotion)* emoción *f*; *(impression)* impresión *f*; *(premonition)* presentimiento ▪ *pl* sensibilidades • **ill f.** malos sentimientos.

fellow ➤ *s* compañero; *(guy)* tipo ➤ *adj* ▪ **f. citizens** (con)ciudadanos • **f. worker** compañero de trabajo.

fellowship ➤ *s* comunidad *f* (de intereses, ideas); EDUC. beca.

felt ➤ *adj & s* (de) fieltro.

female ➤ *adj* del sexo femenino; BIOL.,

MEC. hembra ➤ s mujer f; BIOL. hembra.

feminine ➤ adj & s femenino.

fence ➤ s cerca, valla, empalizada ➤ tr cercar, vallar; (to close off) encerrar.

fend ➤ tr ■ to f. off (blow) parar; (attack) repeler ➤ intr ■ to f. for oneself valerse por sí mismo.

fender ➤ s AUTO. guardafango.

ferocious ➤ adj feroz.

ferry ➤ tr transportar en barco o avión ➤ s transbordador m.

fertile ➤ adj fértil; BIOL. fecundo.

fertilize ➤ tr abonar; BIOL. fecundar.

fertilizer ➤ s fertilizante m, abono.

festival ➤ s fiesta; (art, film) festival m.

festive ➤ adj festivo, de fiesta.

festivity ➤ s festividad f ■ pl diversiones.

fetch ➤ tr ir a buscar.

fever ➤ s fiebre f.

feverish ➤ adj febril.

few ➤ adj pocos ■ a f. unos • every f. cada dos o tres ➤ s & pron pocos ■ a f. unos cuantos • quite a f. muchos.

fiancé ➤ s novio, prometido ■ fiancée novia, prometida.

fiber ➤ s fibra.

fiction ➤ s ficción f.

fiddle FAM. ➤ s violín m ➤ intr tocar el violín ■ to f. around perder el tiempo • to f. with juguetear con.

fidget ➤ intr moverse, no estarse quieto.

field ➤ s campo; (profession) profesión f ■ f. glasses gemelos • f. of view campo visual • f. trip excursión.

fieldwork ➤ s trabajo en el terreno.

fierce ➤ adj feroz; (hard-fought) reñido; (ardent) furioso.

fiery ➤ adj (blazing) llameante; (hot) abrasador; FIG. enardecido.

fifteen ➤ s & adj quince m.

fifth ➤ adj & s quinto.

fifty ➤ adj & s cincuenta m.

fig ➤ s higo ■ f. tree higuera.

fight◇ ➤ intr luchar, pelear; (to box) boxear; (to argue) reñir ■ to f. back defenderse ➤ tr luchar con o contra; (to resist) combatir; (a battle) dar ➤ s lucha; (combat) combate m; (quarrel) riña; (brawl, boxing) pelea.

fighter ➤ s luchador/a, combatiente mf; (boxer) boxeador m.

figure ➤ s figura; (number) cifra; (price) precio; (illustration) dibujo; (silhouette) silueta ■ f. of speech figura, tropo ■ pl cálculos ➤ tr computar, calcular; (to depict) figurar ■ to f. out (to solve) resolver ➤ intr hacer cálculos; (to appear) figurar.

file[1] ➤ s archivo; (for cards) fichero; COMPUT. archivo, fichero; (folder) carpeta; MIL. fila ■ f. server servidor de archivos • to be on f. estar archivado ➤ tr archivar; (to put in order) clasificar ➤ intr marchar en fila.

file[2] ➤ s (tool) lima ➤ tr limar.

filet ➤ s filete m.

fill ➤ tr llenar; (a tooth) empastar ■ to f. in o out (a form) llenar; (to complete) completar con (información, detalles).

fillet ➤ s filete m.

filling ➤ s relleno; ODONT. empaste m ■ f. station gasolinera.

film ➤ s película ➤ tr (an event) filmar; (a scene) rodar ➤ intr rodar.

filter ➤ s filtro ➤ tr & intr filtrar(se).

filth ➤ s mugre f, suciedad f.

filthy ➤ adj sucio, mugriento.

fin ➤ s aleta.

final ➤ adj último, final ➤ s DEP. final f; EDUC. examen m final.

finally ➤ adv finalmente, por último.

finance ➤ s finanzas ■ pl finanzas, fondos ➤ tr financiar.

financial ➤ adj financiero.

find◇ ➤ tr encontrar; (to notice) hallar; (to discover) descubrir ■ to f. out averiguar, descubrir ➤ intr ■ to f. out about informarse sobre ➤ s descubrimiento, hallazgo.

fine[1] ➤ adj fino; (skillful) excelente; (weather) bueno ■ f. arts bellas artes • that's f.! ¡está bien! ➤ adv FAM. muy bien.

fine[2] ➤ s multa ➤ tr multar.

finger ➤ s dedo ■ index f. (dedo) índice • little f. (dedo) meñique • not to lift a f. no mover un dedo • ring f. (dedo) anular ➤ tr (to handle, play) tocar.

fingernail ➤ s uña.

fingerprint ➤ *s* huella digital ➤ *tr* tomar las huellas digitales.

fingertip ➤ *s* punta *o* yema del dedo.

finish ➤ *tr* acabar (con); *(to terminate)* terminar ■ **to f. up** acabar, terminar ➤ *intr* acabar, terminar ➤ *s* final *m*, fin *m*; *(substance)* pulimento; *(perfection)* perfección *f*.

fir ➤ *s* abeto.

fire ➤ *s* fuego; *(destructive)* incendio *m*. **f. department, engine** cuerpo, camión de bomberos • **f. escape** salida de urgencia • **to be on f.** estar en llamas • **to set on f.** prenderle fuego a ➤ *tr* encender; *(to arouse)* enardecer; FAM. *(to hurl)* tirar, arrojar; *(from a job)* despedir ➤ *intr* disparar *(on* contra).

firearm ➤ *s* arma de fuego.

firecracker ➤ *s* cohete *m*, petardo.

fireman *o* **firefighter** ➤ *s* bombero/a.

fireplace ➤ *s* hogar *m*, chimenea *m*.

firewood ➤ *s* leña.

fireworks ➤ *spl* fuegos artificiales.

firm[1] ➤ *adj & adv* firme.

firm[2] ➤ *s* COM. firma, casa.

firmament ➤ *s* firmamento.

firmness ➤ *s* firmeza.

first ➤ *adj* primero; *(elementary)* primario; *(outstanding)* sobresaliente; *(principal)* principal ■ **f. aid** primeros auxilios • **f. name** nombre de pila ➤ *adv* primero; *(before anything else)* antes; *(firstly)* en primer lugar ■ **at f.** en un principio ➤ *s* primero; *(beginning)* principio.

first-class ➤ *adj* de primera clase; *(first-rate)* de primera categoría ➤ *adv* en primera.

fish ➤ *s* pez *m*; *(food)* pescado ➤ *intr* pescar ■ **to go fishing** ir de pesca.

fisherman ➤ *s* pescador *m*.

fishhook ➤ *s* anzuelo.

fishing ➤ *s* pesca ■ **f. ground** zona de pesca • **f. rod** caña de pescar.

fist ➤ *s* puño.

fit[1] ➤ *tr* *(to go on, in)* entrar en; *(to put on, in)* colocar, meter; *(to alter, adjust, match)* ajustar; *(to suit)* sentar bien ➤ *intr* caber; *(part, piece)* ajustar, encajar; *(clothes)* sentar bien ■ **to f. in with** *(people)* congeniar con; *(things)*

cuadrar con ➤ *adj* *(healthy)* sano; *(competent)* idóneo ■ **to keep f.** mantenerse en buen estado físico • **to see f.** juzgar conveniente ➤ *s* ajuste *m*, encaje *m*; *(clothes)* corte *m*, entalladura.

fit[2] ➤ *s* ataque *m*; MED. convulsión *f*.

fitting ➤ *adj* apropiado, oportuno; *(proper)* justo.

five ➤ *s & adj* cinco ■ **f. hundred** quinientos • **f. o'clock** las cinco.

fix ➤ *tr* fijar; *(to repair)* componer; *(hair)* arreglar; *(meal)* preparar ➤ *s* apuro, aprieto.

flag ➤ *s* bandera ➤ *tr* *(taxi, bus)* hacer parar con señales a.

flake ➤ *s* escama, hojuela; *(snowflake)* copo ➤ *intr* *(skin)* descamarse; *(paint)* desprenderse en escamillas.

flame ➤ *s* llama; FAM. *(sweetheart)* novio/a ➤ *intr* arder, llamear.

flammable ➤ *adj* inflamable.

flank ➤ *s* costado ➤ *tr* flanquear.

flannel ➤ *s* franela.

flap ➤ *s* *(of wings)* aleteo; *(of flags)* ondulación *f*; *(of envelopes)* solapa ➤ *tr & intr* *(wings)* aletear; *(arms)* agitar.

flare ➤ *intr* llamear; *(to glow)* brillar; *(in anger)* encolerizarse; *(conflict)* estallar ➤ *s* llamarada; *(signal)* señal luminosa.

flare-up ➤ *s* llamarada repentina; *(outburst)* estallido.

flash ➤ *tr* *(to emit)* lanzar, despedir ➤ *intr* *(to sparkle)* brillar, destellar ➤ *s* destello, resplandor *m*; FOTOG. flash *m*; *(of lightning)* relámpago *m* ■ **f. bulb** lámpara de flash.

flashlight ➤ *s* linterna eléctrica.

flask ➤ *s* frasco.

flat[1] ➤ *adj* *(level)* plano, llano; *(smooth)* liso, raso; *(tasteless)* soso; *(tire)* desinflado; *(color)* sin brillo; MÚS. *(key)* bemol ➤ *s* plano, superficie *f*; *(tire)* pinchazo; MÚS. bemol *m*.

flat[2] ➤ *s* *(apartment)* apartamento.

flatten ➤ *tr* allanar ➤ *intr* achatarse.

flatter ➤ *tr* adular; *(to suit)* favorecer.

flattery ➤ *s* lisonja, halago.

flavor ➤ *s* gusto, sabor *m* ➤ *tr* condimentar, aderezar.

flavoring ➤ *s* condimento, aderezo.

flaw ➤ *s* imperfección *f*, defecto.

flea ➤ s pulga ▪ f. market mercado de pulgas, mercado de artículos usados.

flee◊ ➤ intr huir, escaparse.

fleet ➤ s (of ships) flota.

flesh ➤ s carne f; (of fruits) pulpa.

flex ➤ tr & intr doblar(se).

flick ➤ s golpecito; (of tail) coleada; (of fingers) capirotazo; FAM. (film) película ➤ tr golpear rápida y ligeramente.

flight[1] ➤ s vuelo; (of stairs) tramo ▪ f. attendant aeromozo/a • to take f. alzar el vuelo.

flight[2] ➤ s huida, fuga.

flimsy ➤ adj insubstancial, endeble; (excuse) flojo.

fling◊ ➤ tr arrojar, tirar.

flint ➤ s pedernal m.

flip ➤ tr lanzar, tirar; (coin) echar (a cara o cruz) ▪ to f. over dar la vuelta a.

flirt ➤ intr flirtear, coquetear ➤ s (man) galanteador m; (woman) coqueta.

float ➤ tr hacer flotar, poner a flote ➤ intr flotar ➤ s flotador m; (buoy) boya.

flock ➤ s (of birds) bandada; ZOOL., RELIG. rebaño ➤ intr congregarse ▪ to f. to llegar en tropel a.

flood ➤ s inundación f; (torrent) torrente m ➤ tr & intr inundar(se).

floodlight ➤ s luz f de proyector.

floor ➤ s piso; (of dance hall) pista.

flop ➤ s FAM. fracaso ➤ tr dejar caer (pesadamente) ➤ intr dejarse caer; (to move about) agitarse; FAM. fracasar.

floppy ➤ adj flojo, blando ▪ f. disk disco flexible (de memoria auxiliar).

florist ➤ s florista mf.

flour ➤ s harina ➤ tr enharinar.

flourish ➤ intr florecer ➤ s floreo.

flow ➤ intr fluir; ELEC., FIG. correr; (to gush) manar ➤ s flujo.

flower ➤ s flor f ▪ f. shop florería ➤ intr florecer, dar flor.

flu ➤ s FAM. gripe f.

fluent ➤ adj perfecto; (fluid) fluyente ▪ to be f. in dominar.

fluently ➤ adv con soltura.

fluff ➤ s (down) pelusa; FIG. nadería.

fluid ➤ s & adj fluido, líquido ▪ f. ounce onza líquida.

flunk ➤ intr FAM. sacar suspenso.

fluorescent ➤ adj fluorescente.

flush[1] ➤ intr (to blush) ruborizarse ➤ tr limpiar con agua ➤ s (gush) chorro; (blush) rubor m.

flush[2] ➤ tr (toilet) hacer funcionar.

flute ➤ s MÚS flauta.

flutter ➤ intr revolotear, aletear; (heart) palpitar ➤ tr agitar, mover ➤ s revoloteo, aleteo; MED. palpitación f.

fly[1]◊ ➤ intr volar; (hair, flag) ondular; (to flee) huir; (sparks, chips) saltar ➤ tr hacer volar; (to pilot) pilotear ➤ s (of trousers) bragueta.

fly[2] ➤ s mosca.

foam ➤ s espuma ➤ intr hacer espuma.

foamy ➤ adj espumoso.

focus ➤ s foco ▪ in f. enfocado • out of f. desenfocado ➤ tr enfocar.

fog ➤ s neblina, niebla.

foggy ➤ adj neblinoso; FIG. ofuscado.

foghorn ➤ s sirena de niebla.

foil[1] ➤ tr frustrar, hacer fracasar.

foil[2] ➤ s (sheet) lámina fina de metal.

fold ➤ tr doblar, plegar; (arms) cruzar ➤ intr plegarse ➤ s pliegue m.

folder ➤ s carpeta.

folding ➤ adj plegable.

foliage ➤ s follaje m.

folk ➤ s pueblo f ▪ pl folks gente; FAM. (relatives) familia.

follow ➤ tr seguir; (rules) observar; (to understand) comprender ▪ to f. through llevar a cabo ➤ intr seguir.

follower ➤ s (disciple) discípulo/a; (supporter) partidario/a.

following ➤ adj siguiente ➤ s adherentes mf.

folly ➤ s tontería.

fond ➤ adj cariñoso ▪ to be f. of (person) tener cariño a; (thing) ser aficionado a.

font ➤ s fuente f; RELIG. pila bautismal.

food ➤ s comida; (nourishment) alimento ▪ f. poisoning intoxicación alimenticia.

fool ➤ s tonto/a, necio/a ➤ tr engañar ➤ intr ▪ to f. around jugar (sin propósito).

foolish ➤ adj tonto, absurdo.

foot ➤ s pie m; ZOOL. pata; (base) base f ▪ by o on f. a pie • to put one's f. down ponerse firme • to put one's f. in one's

mouth meter la pata.
football ➤ s fútbol americano; *(ball)* pelota; G.B. fútbol; *(ball)* balón *m*.
footprint ➤ s huella.
footstep ➤ s pisada.
for ➤ prep para, por; *(destination)* para, hacia; *(beneficiary)* para; *(exchange)* por; *(duration)* por; *(on account of)* de, por ▪ as f. en cuanto a • f. all that con todo • to be f. estar de parte de ➤ conj ya que, pues, porque.
forbid ➤ tr prohibir.
forbidden ➤ adj prohibido.
force ➤ s fuerza ▪ by f. por la fuerza • in f. DER. vigente, en vigor ➤ tr compeler, obligar; *(to impose)* imponer ▪ to f. back *(to repel)* rechazar.
fore ➤ adj delantero.
forearm ➤ s antebrazo.
foreboding ➤ s presentimiento.
forecast ➤ tr & intr pronosticar ➤ s pronóstico.
forecaster ➤ s pronosticador/a.
forefather ➤ s antepasado.
forefront ➤ s vanguardia.
foreground ➤ s primer plano.
forehead ➤ s frente *f*.
foreign ➤ adj extranjero; *(trade)* exterior.
foreigner ➤ s extranjero/a, forastero/a.
foreman ➤ s capataz *m*; DER. presidente *m* de un jurado.
foremost ➤ adj primero.
forensic ➤ adj forense.
forerunner ➤ s precursor/a.
foresee ➤ tr prever, anticipar.
foresight ➤ s previsión *f*.
forest ➤ s bosque *m*, selva.
foretell ➤ tr predecir.
forever ➤ adv por o para siempre, eternamente.
foreword ➤ s prólogo, prefacio.
forge ➤ s forja, fragua ➤ tr fraguar, forjar; *(to counterfeit)* falsificar.
forgery ➤ s falsificación *f*.
forget ➤ tr & intr olvidar, olvidarse de ▪ f. to olvidarse de.
forgetful ➤ adj olvidadizo.
forgive ➤ tr & intr perdonar.
forgotten ➤ adj olvidado.
fork ➤ s tenedor *m*; *(of a road)* bifur-

cación *f* ➤ intr bifurcarse.
form ➤ s forma; *(figure)* figura; *(type)* clase *f*, tipo; *(document)* formulario ▪ f. letter circular ➤ tr formar; *(to model)* moldear ➤ intr formarse.
formal ➤ adj formal; *(official)* oficial; *(dress)* de etiqueta ➤ s ceremonia de etiqueta; *(attire)* traje *m* de etiqueta.
formality ➤ s formalidad *f*.
formally ➤ adv formalmente; *(officially)* oficialmente.
format ➤ s formato ➤ tr COMPUT. *(a diskette)* formatear.
formation ➤ s formación *f*.
former ➤ adj *(earlier)* antiguo; *(of two)* anterior.
formerly ➤ adv anteriormente, antes.
formula ➤ s fórmula.
fort ➤ s fuerte *m*.
fortify ➤ tr fortificar.
fortress ➤ s fortaleza.
fortunate ➤ adj afortunado ▪ to be f. *(person)* tener suerte.
fortunately ➤ adv afortunadamente.
fortune ➤ s fortuna; *(good luck)* suerte *f*.
forty ➤ adj & s cuarenta *m*.
forward ➤ adj *(bold)* descarado; *(progressive)* avanzado ➤ adv hacia adelante ▪ to look f. to anticipar ➤ s DEP. delantero ➤ tr *(mail)* reexpedir.
fossil ➤ s & adj fósil *m*.
foul ➤ adj *(revolting)* asqueroso; *(polluted)* contaminado; *(obscene)* obsceno, grosero ➤ s DEP. falta.
found ➤ tr *(to establish)* fundar.
foundation ➤ s fundación *f*; *(base)* fundamento; CONSTR. cimientos.
founder ➤ s fundador/a.
fountain ➤ s fuente *f*; *(for drinking)* surtidor *m*.
four ➤ s & adj cuatro ▪ f. hundred cuatrocientos • f. o'clock las cuatro.
fourteen ➤ s & adj catorce *m*.
fourth ➤ adj & s cuarto.
fowl ➤ s aves *f* (en general); *(domesticated)* ave de corral.
fox ➤ s zorra, zorro ➤ tr embaucar.
fraction ➤ s MAT. fracción *f*, quebrado; *(bit)* porción minúscula, pizca.
fracture ➤ s fractura ➤ tr & intr fracturar(se).

fragile ➤ *adj* frágil.

fragment ➤ *s* fragmento.

fragrance ➤ *s* fragancia, perfume *m*.

fragrant ➤ *adj* fragante.

frail ➤ *adj* débil.

frame ➤ *s* armadura, armazón *f*; *(border)* cerco, marco; *(glasses)* montura ■ **f. of mind** estado de ánimo *f* ➤ *tr (picture)* enmarcar, encuadrar.

framework ➤ *s* armadura, esquéleto; *(system)* sistema *m*.

frank ➤ *adj* franco, sincero.

frantic ➤ *adj* desesperado; *(pace)* frenético.

fraternity ➤ *s* (con)fraternidad *f*; *(organization)* asociación estudiantil masculina.

fraud ➤ *s* fraude *m*; *(person)* impostor/a.

fray ➤ *tr & intr* desgastar(se).

freckle ➤ *s* peca.

freckled ➤ *adj* pecoso.

free ➤ *adj* libre; *(gratis)* gratis, gratuito ➤ *adv* libremente; *(gratis)* gratis ➤ *tr* libertar, poner en libertad.

freedom ➤ *s* libertad *f*.

freeway ➤ *s* autopista.

freeze◇ ➤ *intr* helarse, congelarse ■ **to f. over** helarse ➤ *tr* helar; *(food, assets)* congelar ➤ *s* congelación *f*.

freezer ➤ *s* congelador *m*.

freezing ➤ *adj* glacial ■ **it's f. cold** hace un frío tremendo ➤ *s* congelación *f*.

freight ➤ *s* carga, flete *m*.

French ➤ *adj & s* francés *m* ■ **F. fries** papas fritas.

frequent ➤ *adj* frecuente ➤ *tr* frecuentar.

frequently ➤ *adv* frecuentemente.

fresco ➤ *s* fresco.

fresh ➤ *adj* fresco; *(new)* nuevo.

freshen ➤ *tr & intr* refrescar ■ **to f. up** refrescarse, asearse.

freshman ➤ *s* estudiante *mf* de primer año; *(novice)* novato.

fret ➤ *intr (to worry)* preocuparse.

friction ➤ *s* fricción *f*.

Friday ➤ *s* viernes *m*.

fridge ➤ *s* FAM. refrigerador *m*, nevera.

fried ➤ *adj* frito.

friend ➤ *s* amigo/a.

friendly ➤ *adj* amable, simpático.

friendship ➤ *s* amistad *f*.

fright ➤ *s* miedo, susto.

frighten ➤ *tr & intr* asustar(se).

frightening ➤ *adj* espantoso.

frill ➤ *s* faralá *m* ■ *pl* FAM. adornos.

fringe ➤ *s (trim)* franja; *(flounce)* fleco ■ **f. benefits** beneficios suplementarios.

frog ➤ *s* rana.

from ➤ *prep* de, desde.

frond ➤ *s* fronda.

front ➤ *s* frente *m* ■ **from the f.** por delante, de frente ■ **in f. of** delante de, frente a, en frente de ➤ *adj* delantero, frontal ■ **f. door** puerta de entrada • **f. page** primera plana ➤ *tr (to face)* dar frente a; *(to confront)* hacer frente a ➤ *intr* ■ **to f. on(to)** dar frente a.

frontier ➤ *s* frontera.

frost ➤ *s* escarcha; *(freezing weather)* helada.

frostbite ➤ *s* congelación *f*.

frosty ➤ *adj* muy frío, de helada; *(welcome)* frío, glacial.

froth ➤ *s* espuma.

frown ➤ *s* ceño, entrecejo ➤ *intr* fruncir el entrecejo.

frozen ➤ *adj* helado; *(food, assets)* congelado.

fruit ➤ *s* fruta; BOT. fruto.

fruitcake ➤ *s* torta de frutas.

fruitful ➤ *adj* fructuoso, fructífero.

frustrate ➤ *tr* frustrar.

fry ➤ *tr & intr* freir(se) ■ **frying pan** sartén.

fuel ➤ *s* combustible *m* ■ **f. oil** aceite fuel *o* combustible.

fugitive ➤ *adj & s* fugitivo/a.

fulfill ➤ *tr (requirements)* llenar; *(contract, promise)* cumplir (con); *(ambition)* realizar.

full ➤ *adj* lleno; *(complete)* completo; *(maximum)* máximo; *(entire)* entero; *(total)* total ■ **to be f.** *(person)* estar satisfecho; *(hotel)* no tener lugar ➤ *adv* muy ➤ *s* **in f.** completamente • **to pay in f.** pagar íntegramente.

full-scale ➤ *adj* de tamaño natural; *(all-out)* en gran escala, a todo dar.

full-size(d) ➤ *adj* de tamaño natural.

full-time ➤ *adj* de jornada completa.

fully ➤ *adv* completamente.

fume ➤ *s* humo, tufo ■ *pl* gases, humo ■ *intr* enfurecerse.

fun ➤ *s* diversión *f* ■ **for f.** *(as a joke)* en broma, bromeando; *(to have fun)* para divertirse • **in f.** en broma, bromeando • **to be f.** ser divertido • **to have f.** divertirse • **to make f. of** burlarse de.

function ➤ *s* función *f*; *(ceremony)* acto, ceremonia ➤ *intr* funcionar.

fund ➤ *s* fondo ■ *pl* fondos ➤ *tr* *(to finance)* costear.

funeral ➤ *s* funeral(es).

funnel ➤ *s* embudo; *(stack)* chimenea.

funny ➤ *adj (amusing)* divertido, cómico, gracioso; *(odd)* raro, extraño ■ **funnies** *spl* tiras cómicas.

fur ➤ *s* pelo, pelaje *m*; *(pelt)* piel *f.*

furious ➤ *adj* furioso.

furnace ➤ *s* horno.

furnish ➤ *tr (room, house)* amueblar; *(supplies)* suministrar.

furnishings ➤ *spl* mobiliario.

furniture ➤ *s* muebles *m* ■ **a piece of f.** un mueble.

further ➤ *adj (more distant)* más lejano *o* alejado; *(additional)* más ➤ *adv (extent, degree)* más; *(distance)* más lejos ■ **f. back** *(space)* más atrás.

furthermore ➤ *adv* además.

furthest ➤ *adj* más lejano.

fury ➤ *s* furia.

fuse¹ ➤ *s (wick)* mecha.

fuse² ➤ *tr & intr* fundir(se) ➤ *s* ELEC. fusible *m*, plomo ■ **f. box** caja de fusibles *o* plomos • **to blow a f.** ELEC. fundir(se) un plomo.

fuss ➤ *s (commotion)* alboroto ■ **to kick up** *o* **to make a f.** armar un lío ➤ *intr* inquietarse *(over por).*

fussy ➤ *adj* irritable; *(baby)* llorición; *(fastidious)* quisquilloso, melindroso; *(meticulous)* concienzudo.

future ➤ *s* futuro, porvenir *m.*

fuzzy ➤ *adj* velloso, velludo; *(indistinct)* borroso; *(confused)* confuso.

G

gabardine ➤ *s* gabardina.

gadget ➤ *s* FAM. artilugio, dispositivo.

gaffe ➤ *s* metida de pata.

gag ➤ *s* mordaza; FAM. *(joke)* chiste *m.*

gain ➤ *tr* ganar; *(strength, momentum)* cobrar ➤ *intr* aumentar ➤ *s* ganancia; *(increase)* aumento.

gait ➤ *s* paso.

gala ➤ *adj & s* (de) gala, (de) fiesta.

galaxy ➤ *s* galaxia.

gale ➤ *s* vendaval *m.*

gallant ➤ *adj* galante.

gallery ➤ *s* galería.

gallon ➤ *s* galón *m.*

gallop ➤ *s* galope *m* ➤ *intr* galopar.

gambit ➤ *s* estratagema, maniobra.

gamble ➤ *intr* jugar ➤ *tr (to bet)* jugar, apostar; *(to risk)* arriesgar ➤ *s (bet)* jugada; *(risk)* riesgo.

gambler ➤ *s* jugador/a.

gambling ➤ *s* juego.

game ➤ *s* juego; *(of checkers, etc.)* partida; *(of baseball, etc.)* partido ➤ *adj (plucky)* valeroso; *(willing)* listo.

gang ➤ *s* pandilla; *(laborers)* cuadrilla ➤ *intr* ■ **to g. up on** atacar en grupo.

gangster ➤ *s* gángster *mf.*

gap ➤ *s* boquete *m*, hueco; *(blank)* espacio; *(of time)* intervalo.

garage ➤ *s* garaje *m.*

garbage ➤ *s* basura; FIG. porquería.

garden ➤ *s* jardín *m*; *(for vegetables)* huerto ➤ *intr* cultivar el huerto.

gardener ➤ *s* jardinero/a.

gardening ➤ *s* jardinería.

gargle ➤ *intr* hacer gárgaras.

garland ➤ *s* guirnalda.

garlic ➤ *s* ajo.

garment ➤ *s* prenda de vestir.

gas ➤ *s* gas *m*; *(gasoline)* gasolina ■ **g. mask** máscara antigás • **g. station** gasolinera ➤ *tr* asfixiar con gas.

gash ➤ *s* cuchillada, tajo.

gasoline ➤ *s* gasolina, nafta.

gasp ➤ *intr (in surprise)* quedar boquiabierto; *(to pant)* jadear ➤ *s* jadeo; *(surprise)* grito ahogado.

gate ➤ *s* puerta; *(of iron)* verja.

gateway ➤ *s* pórtico; FIG. camino.

gather ➤ *tr* reunir, juntar; *(to amass)* acumular ➤ *intr* reunirse, congregarse; *(to accumulate)* amontonarse.

gathering ➤ *s* asamblea, reunión *f.*

gaudy ➤ *adj* llamativo, chillón.

gauge ➤ s TEC. calibrador m; ARM. calibre m ■ tr evaluar; (to determine) determinar.

gaunt ➤ adj macilento, demacrado.

gauze ➤ s gasa.

gay ➤ adj alegre; (sexually) gay, homosexual ■ s homosexual mf.

gaze ➤ intr mirar con fijeza, contemplar ■ s mirada fija.

gazette ➤ s gaceta.

gear ➤ s MEC. engranaje m; AUTO. marcha; (assembly) tren m; (equipment) equipo, aparejos; FAM. (belongings) cosas ■ in g. engranado.

geese ➤ pl de **goose**.

gel ➤ s gel m.

gem ➤ s piedra preciosa.

gender ➤ s GRAM. género; (sex) sexo.

general ➤ adj general ■ in g. por lo general ■ s MIL. general mf.

generally ➤ adv generalmente.

generation ➤ s generación f.

generator ➤ s generador m.

generosity ➤ s generosidad f.

generous ➤ adj generoso.

genius ➤ s genio.

gentle ➤ adj amable; (tender) dulce; (mild) suave.

gentleman ➤ s caballero.

gentleness ➤ s (mildness) suavidad f; (tameness) mansedumbre f.

genuine ➤ adj (authentic) genuino; (sincere) sincero.

geographic(al) ➤ adj geográfico.

geography ➤ s geografía.

geology ➤ s geología.

geometric(al) ➤ adj geométrico.

geometry ➤ s geometría.

germ ➤ s BIOL., FIG. germen m; MED. (microbe) microbio.

gesticulate ➤ intr gesticular.

gesture ➤ s gesto.

get◇ ➤ tr (to obtain) obtener, conseguir; (to receive) recibir; (to seize) agarrar; (flu, cold) coger, contraer; (to bring) traer; (to understand) comprender ■ to g. back recobrar • to g. down poner por escrito • to g. out of (information) sonsacar de; (pleasure, benefit) sacar o obtener de • to g. over (with) acabar con ➤ intr (to become) ponerse, hacer

■ to g. along (in years) ponerse viejo; (to be friendly) llevarse bien (with con) • to g. around to encontrar tiempo para • to g. back volver • to g. back at vengarse de • to g. into (car) subir a; (bed, trouble) meterse en; (a habit) adquirir • to g. off (train, horse) apearse; (work) salir (del trabajo); (to escape punishment) librarse • to g. on (train, horse) montar en • to g. out of (bed, chair) levantarse de; (town) alejarse de; (obligation) librarse de; (trouble) sacarse de; (the way) quitarse (de en medio) • to g. through (exam) aprobar; (to finish) terminar; (to arrive) llegar a su destino (provisiones, mensaje) • to g. up (to stand up) levantarse, ponerse de pie; (out of bed) levantarse (de la cama).

geyser ➤ s geiser m.

ghastly ➤ adj horrible, horroroso.

ghetto ➤ s ghetto.

ghost ➤ s fantasma m ■ g. town pueblo desierto.

giant ➤ adj & s gigante m.

giddy ➤ adj mareado; (causing dizziness) vertiginoso; (frivolous) frívolo.

gift ➤ s regalo, obsequio; (talent) talento, aptitud f.

gifted ➤ adj dotado.

gigantic ➤ adj gigantesco.

giggle ➤ intr reírse tontamente.

gimmick ➤ s truco.

gin ➤ s ginebra.

ginger ➤ s jengibre m.

giraffe ➤ s jirafa.

girdle ➤ s faja.

girl ➤ s muchacha, chica; (child) niña; (daughter) hija.

girlfriend ➤ s amiga; (sweetheart) novia.

give◇ ➤ tr dar; (a gift) regalar; (an illness) transmitir, contagiar; (medicine, sacraments) administrar; (to yield) ceder; (dance, party) dar ■ to g. away (secret, plot) contar, revelar; (to sell cheaply) regalar • to g. back devolver • to g. up abandonar, renunciar a (intento, tarea); (to hand over) entregar; (to stop) dejar de; (to consider as lost) dar por perdido • to g. in (to col-

lapse) ceder, caerse; *(to accede)* acceder; *(to admit defeat)* darse por vencido.

given ➤ *adj* dado ■ **g. name** nombre de pila • **g. that** dado que.

glacier ➤ *s* glaciar *m.*

glad ➤ *adj* alegre, contento.

glamour ➤ *s* encanto, hechizo.

glamourous ➤ *adj* elegante, hechicero.

glance ➤ *intr* echar un vistazo *o* una mirada *(at* a) ➤ *s* vistazo, mirada.

gland ➤ *s* glándula.

glaring ➤ *adj (light)* deslumbrador; *(error)* patente, manifiesto.

glass ➤ *s* vidrio, cristal *m; (drinking vessel)* vaso; *(mirror)* espejo ■ *pl (eyeglasses)* lentes, anteojos; *(binoculars)* gemelos • **dark g.** lentes oscuros.

gleam ➤ *s* destello ➤ *intr* destellar.

glee ➤ *s* regocijo, alegría • **g. club** orfeón.

glide ➤ *intr* deslizarse; AVIA. planear.

glider ➤ *s* planeador *m.*

glimmer ➤ *s & intr* (lucir con) luz trémula.

glimpse ➤ *s* ojeada ➤ *tr* vislumbrar.

glitter ➤ *s* centello ➤ *intr* centellear.

gloat ➤ *intr* regodearse.

global ➤ *adj* mundial; *(total)* global.

globe ➤ *s* globo (terrestre).

gloom ➤ *s (partial)* penumbra; *(total)* tinieblas *f; (melancholy)* melancolía.

gloomy ➤ *adj (dark)* oscuro; *(melancholy)* triste; *(pessimistic)* pesimista.

glorious ➤ *adj* glorioso; *(magnificent)* esplendoroso; FAM. magnífico.

glory ➤ *s* gloria.

gloss ➤ *s* lustre *m,* brillo.

glossy ➤ *adj* lustroso, brillante.

glove ➤ *s* guante *m* ■ **g. compartment** guantera.

glow ➤ *intr* resplandecer, brillar ➤ *s* resplandor *m,* brillo.

glue ➤ *s* pegamento ➤ *tr* pegar.

glutton ➤ *s* glotón/ona.

gnat ➤ *s* jején *m.*

gnaw ➤ *tr & intr* roer.

go◇ ➤ *intr* ir; *(to proceed)* seguir adelante; *(to leave)* irse, marcharse; *(to function)* funcionar, andar ■ **to go after** seguir a • **to go before** preceder,

ir antes • **to go by** *(to pass by)* pasar por; *(time)* pasar • **to go down** *(to descend)* bajar; *(the sun)* ponerse; *(a ship)* hundirse; *(airplane)* caerse • **to go into** *(to enter)* entrar en; *(to fit)* caber *o* encajar en; *(a profession)* dedicarse a • **to go off** *(gun)* dispararse; *(bomb)* hacer explosión; *(to sound)* sonar • **to go on** continuar, seguir • **to go out** *(to exit, socially)* salir; *(light)* apagarse • **to go over** *(to rehearse)* ensayar; *(to review)* repasar • **to go under** *(to fail)* fracasar ➤ *s (try)* intento; *(energy)* energía ■ **on the go** en actividad.

goal ➤ *s* meta; *(score)* gol *m,* tanto ■ **g. line** línea de gol • **g. post** poste.

goalkeeper *o* **goalie** ➤ *s* portero/a.

goat ➤ *s* cabra, macho cabrío ■ **to get someone's g.** molestar a alguien.

god ➤ *s* dios; *(idol)* ídolo ■ **G. Dios.**

goddaughter ➤ *s* ahijada.

goddess ➤ *s* diosa.

godfather ➤ *s* padrino.

godmother ➤ *s* madrina.

godson ➤ *s* ahijado.

goggles ➤ *spl* gafas, anteojos.

going ➤ *s* ida, partida ➤ *adj* actual.

goings-on ➤ *spl* actividades *f.*

gold ➤ *s* oro ➤ *adj (made of gold)* de oro; *(golden)* dorado.

golden ➤ *adj* dorado; *(voice, epoch)* de oro; *(hair)* rubio; *(opportunity)* excelente • **g. mean** justo medio.

goldfish ➤ *s* pez *m* de colores.

golf ➤ *s* golf *m* ➤ *intr* jugar al golf.

golfer ➤ *s* golfista *mf.*

gone ➤ *vea* **go** *en* tabla de verbos ➤ *adj (past)* pasado, ido.

good ➤ *adj* bueno; *(beneficial)* beneficioso; *(valid)* válido; *(pleasant)* agradable; *(favorable)* favorable ■ **to be g. at** tener capacidad *o* talento para • **to be no g.** ser inútil • **to have a g. time** pasarlo bien ➤ *s* bien *m; (goodness)* bondad *f* ■ **for g.** para siempre ■ *pl (wares)* bienes; *(merchandise)* mercancías, géneros ➤ *adv* FAM. **bien** ■ **to feel g.** *(satisfied)* estar satisfecho; *(well)* sentirse bien ➤ *interj* ¡bueno!, ¡muy bien!

goodby(e) ➤ *interj* ¡adiós!, ¡hasta luego! ➤ *s* adiós, despedida.

good-looking ➤ *adj* bien parecido.

goodness ➤ *s* bondad *f.*

goose ➤ *s* ganso.

gorge ➤ *s* (*ravine*) desfiladero ➤ *tr* ■ to g. oneself hartarse a atiborrarse.

gorgeous ➤ *adj* hermosísimo.

gorilla ➤ *s* gorila *m.*

gospel ➤ *s* evangelio.

gossip ➤ *s* chismes *m;* (*gossiper*) chismoso/a ■ g. column noticias sociales.

got, gotten ➤ *vea* got en tabla de verbos.

Gothic ➤ *adj* gótico.

gourmet ➤ *s* gastrónomo/a.

govern ➤ *tr* gobernar; (*to determine*) determinar ➤ *intr* gobernar.

government ➤ *s & adj* (del) gobierno.

governor ➤ *s* gobernador/a; MEC. (*regulator*) regulador automático.

gown ➤ *s* vestido (de etiqueta); (*nightgown*) camisón *m;* (*judge, etc.*) toga.

grab ➤ *tr* (*to seize*) agarrar, coger ➤ *intr* ■ to g. at tratar de arrebatar ➤ *s* ■ to make a g. at tratar de agarrar • up for grabs disponible.

grace ➤ *s* gracia; (*at table*) bendición *f* de la mesa ➤ *tr* adornar, embellecer.

graceful ➤ *adj* agraciado, elegante.

gracious ➤ *adj* amable, cortés *m.*

grade ➤ *s* (*degree, rank*) grado; EDUC. (*class*) año, curso; (*mark*) nota ➤ *tr* clasificar; (*an exam*) calificar.

gradual ➤ *adj* gradual.

graduate ➤ *tr & intr* graduar(se) ■ to g. as recibirse de ➤ *adj & s* graduado/a, diplomado/a.

graduation ➤ *s* graduación *f;* (*commencement*) entrega de diplomas.

graffiti ➤ *spl* graffiti *m.*

graft¹ AGR., MED. ➤ *tr & intr* injertar(se) ➤ *s* injerto.

graft² ➤ *s* (*crime*) concusión *f,* extorsión *f.*

grain ➤ *s* grano; (*cereals*) cereales *m.*

gram ➤ *s* gramo.

grammar ➤ *s* gramática ■ g. school escuela primaria.

grand ➤ *adj* grandioso, magnífico ■ g. jury jurado de acusación • g. piano piano de cola.

grandaunt ➤ *s* tía abuela.

grandchild ➤ *s* nieto/a.

granddaughter ➤ *s* nieta.

grandfather ➤ *s* abuelo ■ g. clock reloj de pie *o* de caja.

grandma ➤ *s* FAM. abuelita.

grandmother ➤ *s* abuela.

grandpa ➤ *s* FAM. abuelito.

grandson ➤ *s* nieto.

grant ➤ *tr* conceder; (*to bestow*) otorgar; (*to admit*) admitir ■ to take it for granted dar por sentado ➤ *s* (*funding*) subvención *f;* (*scholarship*) beca; DER. (*transfer*) cesión *f.*

grape ➤ *s* uva.

grapefruit ➤ *s* toronja, pomelo.

graph ➤ *s* gráfico, diagrama *m.*

graphic ➤ *adj* gráfico ➤ *spl* (*drawing*) dibujo lineal; ARTE. artes gráficas; COMPUT. gráficos.

grasp ➤ *tr* (*to seize*) agarrar, asir; (*to comprehend*) captar ➤ *s* (*grip*) apretón *m;* FIG. comprensión *f.*

grass ➤ *s* hierba; (*lawn*) césped *m;* JER. (*marijuana*) yerba.

grasshopper ➤ *s* saltamontes *m.*

grate¹ ➤ *tr* CUL. rallar; FIG. irritar ➤ *intr* (*teeth, hinge*) rechinar.

grate² ➤ *s* reja, verja; (*for coals*) parrilla.

grateful ➤ *adj* agradecido.

grater ➤ *s* rallador *m.*

gratitude ➤ *s* gratitud *f.*

grave¹ ➤ *s* tumba.

grave² ➤ *adj* grave, serio.

gravel ➤ *s* grava.

graveyard ➤ *s* cementerio.

gravity ➤ *s* gravedad *f;* (*solemnity*) solemnidad *f.*

gravy ➤ *s* (*sauce*) salsa.

gray ➤ *s* gris *m* ➤ *adj* gris; (*hair*) cano.

graze¹ ➤ *intr* (*to feed*) pacer, pastar ➤ *tr* apacentar.

graze² ➤ *tr & intr* (*to touch*) rozar.

grease ➤ *s* grasa ➤ *tr* engrasar.

greasy ➤ *adj* (*coated*) engrasado; (*fatty*) grasoso; (*dirty*) grasiento.

great ➤ *adj* grande; FAM. magnífico ■ a great *m* ➤ *adv* FAM. muy bien.

great-grandchild ➤ *s* bisnieto/a.

great-grandfather ➤ *s* bisabuelo.

great-grandmother ➤ *s* bisabuela.

greatly ➤ *adv* muy, mucho.

greed ➤ *s (for wealth)* codicia, avaricia; *(for food)* gula, glotonería.

greedy ➤ *adj (avaricious)* codicioso; *(gluttonous)* glotón *m; (eager)* ávido.

green ➤ *s* verde *m* ■ *pl* verduras ➤ *adj* verde; *(raw)* inexperto.

greenhouse ➤ *s* invernadero.

greet ➤ *tr* dar la bienvenida, saludar.

greeting ➤ *s* saludo.

greyhound ➤ *s* galgo.

grief ➤ *s* pena; *(trouble)* desgracia.

grieve ➤ *tr* dar pena, afligir ➤ *intr* apenarse; *(to mourn)* lamentarse.

grill ➤ *tr* asar a la parrilla ■ *s (rack)* parrilla; *(food)* asado.

grim ➤ *adj (forbidding)* imponente; *(ghastly)* macabro; *(gloomy)* lúgubre.

grime ➤ *s* mugre *f.*

grimy ➤ *adj* mugriento.

grin ➤ *intr* sonreír ■ *s* sonrisa abierta.

grind◇ ➤ *tr (to crush)* triturar, pulverizar; *(coffee, wheat)* moler; *(teeth)* hacer rechinar ■ **to g. down** *(to wear away)* desgastar; *(to oppress)* oprimir.

grip ➤ *s (of hands)* apretón *m; (control)* control *m; (handle)* asidero ■ **to have a good g. on** tener un buen dominio de ➤ *tr (to seize)* agarrar; *(to clasp)* apretar ➤ *intr* agarrarse.

groan ➤ *intr* gemir ■ *s* gemido.

grocer ➤ *s* tendero/a, almacenero/a.

grocery ➤ *s* tienda de comestibles, almacén *m.*

groin ➤ *s* ANAT. ingle *f.*

groom ➤ *s* mozo de caballos; *(bridegroom)* novio ➤ *tr (horses)* cuidar; *(oneself)* arreglarse, acicalarse.

groove ➤ *s* ranura; *(of a record)* surco.

gross ➤ *adj (income, weight)* bruto; *(error, ignorance)* craso; *(vulgar)* grosero ■ *s* total *m; (12 dozen)* gruesa.

grotesque ➤ *adj* grotesco.

grotto ➤ *s* gruta.

ground ➤ *s* tierra, suelo; *(area)* terreno, campo ■ **g. floor** planta baja • **to break new g.** marcar nuevos rumbos • **to give, gain g.** ceder, ganar terreno ➤ *pl (land)* terreno; *(basis)* base; *(cause)* motivo ➤ *adj* triturado; *(coffee, wheat)* molido.

groundwork ➤ *s* fundamento, base *f.*

group ➤ *s* grupo ➤ *tr & intr* agrupar(se).

grow◇ ➤ *tr* cultivar; *(beard, hair)* dejar(se) crecer ➤ *intr (business, industry)* expandirse, agrandarse; *(to increase)* aumentar; *(person)* madurar ■ **to g. dark** oscurecerse • **to g. old** envejecer • **to g. up** crecer.

growl ➤ *s* gruñido ➤ *intr* gruñir.

grown ➤ *adj* mayor, adulto.

grown-up ➤ *adj & s* adulto/a.

growth ➤ *s* crecimiento; *(development)* desarrollo; *(increase)* aumento.

grubby ➤ *adj* sucio.

grudge ➤ *tr* escatimar, dar a regañadientes ➤ *s* rencor *m.*

gruel(l)ing ➤ *adj* abrumador.

gruesome ➤ *adj* horrible, horrendo.

grumble ➤ *intr* quejarse, gruñir.

grumpy ➤ *adj* malhumorado.

grunt ➤ *intr* gruñir ➤ *s* gruñido.

guarantee ➤ *s* garantía ➤ *tr* garantizar; *(to promise)* prometer.

guard ➤ *tr* guardar; *(to protect)* proteger; *(to watch over)* custodiar ➤ *s (sentinel, soldier)* guardia *mf; (troops)* guardia *f; (escort)* escolta; DEP. defensa *mf* ■ **off g.** desprevenido • **to be on g.** MIL. estar de guardia.

guardian ➤ *s* guardián/ana; *(of an orphan)* tutor/a, curador/a.

Guatemalan ➤ *adj & s* guatemalteco/a.

guess ➤ *tr & intr (to suppose)* suponer; *(correctly)* adivinar ■ **I g. so** supongo que sí ➤ *s* conjetura, suposición *f.*

guest ➤ *s (at home)* invitado/a; *(at hotel)* huésped/a.

guidance ➤ *s (direction)* dirección ■ **under the g. of** guiado por.

guide ➤ *s* guía *mf; (book, device)* guía *f* ➤ *tr* guiar.

guidebook ➤ *s* guía.

guilty ➤ *adj* culpable.

guinea pig ➤ *s* conejillo de Indias, cui *m.*

guitar ➤ *s* guitarra.

gulf ➤ *s* golfo; *(abyss)* abismo.

gulp ➤ *tr* tragar, engullir ➤ *s* trago.

gum¹ ➤ *s (sap, glue)* goma; *(for chewing)* chicle *m* ➤ *tr* engomar.

gum² ➤ s ODONT. encía.

gun ➤ s arma de fuego; *(cannon)* cañón *m*; *(handgun)* pistola; *(rifle)* fusil *m*.

gunshot ➤ s tiro.

gush ➤ *intr* brotar, chorrear.

gust ➤ s ventolera, ráfaga ➤ *intr* soplar.

gutter ➤ s *(street)* cuneta; *(roof)* canalón *m*.

guy ➤ s FAM. tipo, tío ∎ *pl* muchachos.

gym ➤ s FAM. gimnasio.

Gypsy ➤ *adj & s* gitano/a.

H

habit ➤ s costumbre *f*; *(addiction)* dependencia ∎ to be in the h. of acostumbrarse de.

habitat ➤ s hábitat *m*.

hack ➤ *tr* cortar; COMPUT. hackear ∎ h. into COMPUT. sabotear ➤ s tos seca.

hacker ➤ s hacker *mf*, pirata *mf*.

had ➤ *vea* have en tabla de verbos.

haddock ➤ s abadejo.

haggle ➤ *intr* regatear.

hail ➤ s *(ice)* granizo; *(barrage)* lluvia, andanada ➤ *intr* granizar.

hailstone ➤ s granizo.

hair ➤ s pelo, cabello ∎ gray h. canas • h. style peinado.

hairbrush ➤ s cepillo (para el pelo).

haircut ➤ s corte *m* de pelo.

hairdresser ➤ s peluquero/a.

hairpin ➤ s horquilla.

hairy ➤ *adj* peludo; JER. *(hazardous)* espinoso.

half ➤ s mitad *f*; DEP. tiempo ∎ and a h. y medio • in h. por la mitad • h. brother, sister hermanastro/a ➤ *adj & adv* medio, a medias.

halfway ➤ *adv (partially)* a medias ∎ to meet h. hacer concesiones.

hall ➤ s corredor *m*; *(lobby)* vestíbulo; *(auditorium)* sala.

hallway ➤ s pasillo, corredor *m*.

halt ➤ s *(stop)* alto, parada; *(pause)* interrupción *f* ➤ *tr & intr* parar(se) ∎ halt! ¡alto!

halve ➤ *tr* partir *o* reducir a la mitad; *(a number)* dividir por dos.

ham ➤ s jamón *m*.

hamburger ➤ s hamburguesa.

hammer ➤ s martillo ➤ *tr* martillar.

hammock ➤ s hamaca.

hamster ➤ s hámster *m*.

hand ➤ s mano *f*; *(of clock, gauge)* aguja, manecilla ∎ by h. a mano • *(close)* at h. muy cerca, a mano • on h. disponible • on the one (other) h. por una (otra) parte • to be an old h. at tener mucha experiencia en • to clap one's hands batir palmas • to give *o* lend a h. (with) echar una mano (a) • to have a h. in tener parte en • to shake hands darse la mano ➤ *tr* entregar, dar ∎ to h. down transmitir; *(verdict)* dictar • to h. in presentar • to h. out *(to administer)* dar; *(to distribute)* repartir.

handbag ➤ s cartera, bolso.

handbook ➤ s manual *m*.

handcuff ➤ s esposas ➤ *tr* esposar.

handful ➤ s puñado.

handicap ➤ s DEP. hándicap *m*; *(hindrance)* obstáculo; *(physical, mental)* discapacidad *f*, minusvalía ➤ *tr (to impede)* poner en desventaja.

handicapped ➤ *adj* discapacitado, minusválido; *(hindered)* obstaculizado.

handicraft ➤ s destreza manual; *(occupation, product)* (artículo de) artesanía.

handkerchief ➤ s pañuelo.

handle ➤ *tr* tocar, andar con; *(conveyance)* manejar, dirigir; *(to deal with)* encargarse de; *(to cope with)* poder con ➤ s mango; *(of door)* manija; *(grip)* asa, asidero.

handmade ➤ *adj* hecho a mano.

handout ➤ s limosna; *(leaflet)* folleto.

handrail ➤ s pasamano, barandilla.

handshake ➤ s apretón *m* de manos.

handsome ➤ *adj* guapo, bien parecido; FIG. liberal, generoso.

handwriting ➤ s escritura; *(style)* letra.

handy ➤ *adj* mañoso; *(accessible)* a mano; *(useful)* conveniente.

hang◇ ➤ *tr* suspender, colgar; *(one's head)* bajar, inclinar ∎ to h. up *(to delay)* demorar; *(telephone)* colgar ➤ *intr* colgar; *(to be executed)* ser ahorcado; *(in air)* flotar ∎ to h. around *o* out FAM. haraganear • to h. on *(to wait)* esperar; *(to persevere)* persistir.

hanger ➤ s colgadero, percha.

hangout ➤ s guarida, punto de reunión.

hangover ➤ s resaca.

hang-up ➤ s FAM. complejo, problema m.

happen ➤ intr (to come to pass) pasar, suceder; (to take place) producirse, ocurrir ■ to h. to be dar la casualidad de ser o estar.

happiness ➤ s felicidad f, dicha.

happy ➤ adj feliz, dichoso ■ h. birthday! ¡feliz cumpleaños!, ¡felicidades!

harass ➤ tr acosar; (to annoy) molestar.

harbor ➤ s puerto, bahía ➤ tr (hopes) abrigar; (doubt) guardar.

hard ➤ adj duro, sólido; (firm) firme; (resistant) resistente; (difficult) difícil, arduo; (robust) fuerte ■ h. cash metálico • h. line postura firme • h. luck mala suerte ➤ adv (intensely) mucho; (vigorously) con fuerza.

hard-boiled ➤ adj (egg) duro.

hard disk ➤ s disco rígido o duro.

harden ➤ tr & intr endurecer(se).

hardly ➤ adv apenas ■ h. ever casi nunca.

hardship ➤ s sufrimiento; (privation) penuria.

hardware ➤ s (artículos de) ferretería; COMPUT. equipo, maquinaria, hardware m ■ h. store ferretería.

hare ➤ s liebre f.

harm ➤ s daño, perjuicio ➤ tr hacer daño.

harmful ➤ adj perjudicial.

harmless ➤ adj inocuo.

harmonica ➤ s armónica.

harmonious ➤ adj armonioso.

harmony ➤ s armonía.

harness ➤ s arreos ➤ tr (horse) enjaezar; (energy) aprovechar, utilizar.

harp ➤ s arpa ■ to h. on machacar.

harsh ➤ adj áspero; (stern) severo.

harvest ➤ s cosecha; (of grapes) vendimia ➤ tr & intr cosechar.

has ➤ vea **have** en tabla de verbos.

hassle FAM. ➤ s jaleo ➤ tr fastidiar, molestar.

haste ➤ s prisa.

hasty ➤ adj apresurado; (rash) precipitado.

hat ➤ s sombrero.

hatch¹ ➤ s trampa; MARÍT. escotilla.

hatch² ➤ intr salir del cascarón ➤ tr (a plot) tramar.

hatchet ➤ s hacha.

hate ➤ tr odiar ➤ intr sentir odio ➤ s odio.

hatred ➤ s odio.

haul ➤ intr & tr halar, tirar (de) ➤ s ■ over the long h. a la larga.

have◇ ➤ tr tener; (to possess) poseer; (in mind) retener; (disease) sufrir de; (good time) pasar; (baby) dar a luz ■ to be had JER. ser engañado • to h. to do with tener que ver con ➤ aux haber.

havoc ➤ s estragos.

hawk ➤ s halcón m.

hay ➤ s heno ■ h. fever fiebre del heno.

hazard ➤ s riesgo, peligro; (chance) azar m ➤ tr arriesgar; (a guess) aventurar.

haze ➤ s niebla ligera.

hazelnut ➤ s avellana.

hazy ➤ adj nebuloso.

he ➤ pron él ➤ s varón m.

head ➤ s cabeza; (sense) inteligencia; (chief) jefe m ■ h. start ventaja • to be over one's h. estar (algo) fuera de la capacidad de uno • to go to one's h. subírsele a la cabeza ■ pl cara (de moneda) ■ h. or tails cara o cruz ➤ tr encabezar ➤ intr dirigirse ■ to h. back regresar • to h. for ir con rumbo a ➤ adj principal, central.

headache ➤ s dolor m de cabeza.

headlight ➤ s faro, luz delantera.

headline ➤ s titular m.

headmaster ➤ s EDUC. director m.

headmistress ➤ s EDUC. directora.

headphones ➤ spl auriculares m.

headquarters ➤ spl cuartel m general; (police) jefatura; COM. oficina central.

headwaiter ➤ s jefe m de comedor.

headway ➤ s ■ to make h. avanzar, progresar.

heal ➤ tr curar ➤ intr sanar.

health ➤ s salud f ■ h. food alimentos naturales ■ h. insurance seguro médico.

healthy ➤ adj sano; (air, place) saludable, salubre.

heap ➤ s montón ➤ tr amontonar.

hear◇ ➤ tr oír; *(to listen to)* escuchar; *(to know)* enterarse de ➤ intr oír ■ to h. from tener noticias de.

hearing ➤ s oído; DER. audiencia ■ h. aid audífono.

hearse ➤ s carroza fúnebre.

heart ➤ s corazón m; *(in cards)* corazón, copa ■ at h. en el fondo ■ h. failure colapso (cardiaco) • to lose it descorazonarse • to one's h.'s content hasta saciarse • to take it cobrar ánimo • with all o from one's h. de todo corazón.

heartbeat ➤ s latido.

heartbreak ➤ s angustia, pena.

heartburn ➤ s acedía.

hearth ➤ s hogar m.

hearty ➤ adj cordial, sincero; *(robust)* robusto; *(appetite)* bueno; *(meal)* abundante.

heat ➤ s calor m; DEP. carrera; *(for building)* calefacción f ■ h. rash miliaria • h. stroke insolación ➤ tr & intr calentar(se); *(to excite)* acalorar(se) ■ to h. up recalentarse.

heater ➤ s estufa, calentador m.

heating calefacción f.

heave ➤ tr alzar (con esfuerzo); *(to hurl)* arrojar; *(sigh)* exhalar.

heaven ➤ s cielo ■ for h.'s sake! ¡por Diós! ■ spl cielo • good h.! ¡cielos!

heavy ➤ adj pesado; *(rain)* fuerte; *(grave)* serio; *(heart)* oprimido.

hectic ➤ adj ajetreado.

hedge ➤ s seto (vivo) ➤ tr encerrar (con us seto) ■ to h. against cubrirse contra.

heed ➤ tr hacer caso (a, de) ➤ s ■ to pay h. to prestar atención a.

heedless ➤ adj descuidado, incauto.

heel ➤ s talón m; *(of shoe)* tacón m.

hefty ➤ adj pesado; *(strong)* robusto.

height ➤ s altura, alto; *(summit)* cumbre f; *(of folly)* colmo; *(of person)* estatura.

heir ➤ s heredero/a.

heiress ➤ s heredera (de una fortuna).

helicopter ➤ s helicóptero.

hell ➤ s infierno ■ to h. with it! ¡al diablo! • to raise h. armar una de todos los diablos • what, who the h. . . .?

¿qué, quién diablos . . .?

hello ➤ interj ¡hola!

helm ➤ s timón m.

helmet ➤ s casco.

help ➤ tr ayudar; *(to relieve)* aliviar ■ to h. oneself to *(food)* servirse ➤ intr ser útil ■ to h. out dar una mano ➤ s ayuda.

helper ➤ s ayudante mf.

helpful ➤ adj útil; *(kind)* amable.

helping ➤ s ración f.

helpless ➤ adj indefenso; *(powerless)* incapaz.

hem ➤ s dobladillo.

hemorrhage ➤ s & intr *(sufrir una)* hemorragia.

hen ➤ s gallina.

hepatitis ➤ s hepatitis f.

her ➤ pron la, le, ella ■ I saw h. la vi • for h. para ella ➤ adj su, de ella.

herb ➤ s hierba ■ pl finas hierbas.

herd ➤ s & tr (reunir en) manada.

here ➤ adv aquí; *(to this place)* acá ■ that's neither h. nor there eso no viene al caso.

heredity ➤ s herencia.

heritage ➤ s herencia.

hermit ➤ s ermitaño/a.

hero ➤ s héroe m; LIT. protagonista mf.

heroic ➤ adj heróico.

heroine ➤ s heroína; LIT. protagonista.

herpes ➤ s herpes m,

herring ➤ s arenque m.

hers ➤ pron (el) suyo, el de ella.

herself ➤ pron ■ by h. sola • she h. ella misma • she hurt h. se lastimó.

hesitant ➤ adj vacilante.

hesitate ➤ intr vacilar; *(not to dare)* no atreverse.

hesitation ➤ s indecisión f; *(vacillation)* titubeo.

hey ➤ interj ¡eh!, ¡oiga!

hi ➤ interj ¡hola!

hiccup ➤ s hipo ➤ intr tener hipo, hipar.

hide[1]◇ ➤ tr ocultar, esconder; *(to conceal)* disimular; *(to cover up)* tapar ➤ intr esconderse; *(to seek refuge)* refugiarse.

hide[2] ➤ s cuero.

hideaway ➤ s escondite m; *(retreat)* retiro.

hideous ➤ *adj* espantoso; *(atrocious)* atroz.

hide-out ➤ *s* escondite *m.*

hiding ➤ ■ in h. escondido.

high ➤ *adj* alto; *(wind, fever)* fuerte; *(voice)* agudo; *(advanced)* avanzado; *(crime)* grave; JER. drogado ■ h. jump salto de altura • h. priority primera importancia • h. school escuela secundaria • h. tide pleamar • two feet h. dos pies de altura ➤ *adv* en lo alto, alto ■ to look h. and low buscar por todas partes ➤ *s* altura; *(gear)* directa.

highchair ➤ *s* silla alta para niños.

higher ➤ *adj* más alto; *(greater)* mayor; *(advanced)* superior.

highlands ➤ *spl* tierras altas, sierra.

highlight ➤ *s* toque *m* de luz; *(event)* suceso *o* atracción *f* principal ➤ *tr* iluminar; *(to emphasize)* destacar.

highly ➤ *adv* altamente; *(extremely)* extremadamente; *(well)* muy bien.

high-pitched ➤ *adj* agudo; *(voice)* chillón.

high-rise ➤ *s* edificio de muchos pisos.

high-tech ➤ *adj* de tecnología avanzada.

highway ➤ *s* carretera, autopista.

hijack ➤ *tr* secuestrar.

hijacker ➤ *s* secuestrador/a; *(of plane)* pirata *mf* aéreo.

hijacking ➤ *s* secuestro; *(of plane)* piratería aérea.

hike ➤ *intr* caminar ➤ *s* caminata.

hiker ➤ *s* excursionista *mf.*

hill ➤ *s* colina; *(heap)* montón *m.*

hilly ➤ *adj* montuoso.

him ➤ *pron* le, lo, él ■ I know h. lo conozco • to h. a él.

himself ➤ *pron* ■ by h. solo • he h. él mismo • he hit h. se golpeó.

hinder ➤ *tr* impedir, obstaculizar.

hinge ➤ *s* bisagra.

hint ➤ *s* insinuación *f*; *(tip)* sugerencia ➤ *tr & intr* ■ to h. (at) insinuar.

hip ➤ *s* ANAT. cadera.

hippopotamus ➤ *s* hipopótamo.

hire ➤ *tr* emplear; *(to rent)* alquilar ➤ *s* ■ for h. se alquila.

his ➤ *adj* su, de él ➤ *pron* (el) suyo, el de él.

Hispanic ➤ *adj & s* hispano/a.

hiss ➤ *s* siseo ➤ *tr & intr* silbar.

historic(al) ➤ *adj* histórico.

history ➤ *s* historia.

hit◇ ➤ *tr* golpear; *(to collide with)* chocar contra *o* con ➤ *s* golpe *m*; *(collision)* choque *m*; *(success)* éxito.

hitch ➤ *tr* enganchar ■ to h. a ride FAM. hacerse llevar en automovil ➤ *intr* FAM. *(to hitchhike)* hacer autostop.

hitchhike ➤ *intr* hacer autostop.

hitchhiker ➤ *s* autostopista *mf.*

hive ➤ *s* colmena; *(colony)* enjambre *m.*

hoarse ➤ *adj* ronco.

hoax ➤ *s* engaño, trampa.

hobby ➤ *s* pasatiempo, afición *f.*

hobo ➤ *s* vago, vagabundo.

hockey ➤ *s* hockey *m.*

hoe ➤ *s* azada ➤ *tr & intr* azadonar.

hog ➤ *s* cerdo, puerco ➤ *tr* acaparar.

hold◇ ➤ *tr* asir, agarrar; *(to take)* tener; *(to support)* sostener; *(to secure)* sujetar; *(for questioning)* tener bajo custodia; *(to keep)* retener; *(to control)* contener; *(to occupy)* ocupar; *(meeting)* celebrar; *(elections)* convocar ■ to h. back *(to repress)* reprimir, contener • to h. down a job mantener un trabajo • to h. off alejar • to h. one's own defenderse • to h. to hacer cumplir • to h. up FAM. *(to delay)* atrasar; *(to rob)* atracar; *(to stop)* detener ➤ *intr* asirse, agarrarse; *(to be firm)* sostenerse; *(to be valid)* seguir en vigor ■ to h. off demorarse • to h. on *(to grip)* agarrarse bien; *(to wait)* aguardar, esperar • to h. out *o* up *(to last)* durar; *(to resist)* aguantar ➤ *s* *(grip)* asidero; *(influence)* influencia ■ to get h. of *(to grasp)* coger; *(to obtain)* conseguir • to get h. of oneself dominarse.

holdup ➤ *s* *(delay)* demora; *(robbery)* asalto, atraco (a mano armada).

hole ➤ *s* hueco; *(in ground)* hoyo; *(in road)* bache *m*; *(small)* agujero.

holiday ➤ *s* día feriado; RELIG. día de fiesta.

hollow ➤ *adj* hueco; *(empty)* vacío ➤ *s* hueco; FIG. vacío.

holly ➤ *s* acebo.

holy ➤ *adj* sacro; *(revered)* venerable;

(saintly) santo, pío ■ **h. day** fiesta de guardar.

home ➤ *s* casa; *(residence)* domicilio; *(household)* hogar *m* ■ **to feel at h.** sentirse a gusto ➤ *adj* casero; *(native)* natal; *(team)* de casa ■ **h. page** página inicial • **h. run** DEP. jonrón ➤ *adv* ■ **at h.** en casa • **to be h.** estar (en casa).

homeless ➤ *adj* sin hogar.

homely ➤ *adj* sin atractivo; *(plain)* sencillo, rústico.

homemade ➤ *adj* hecho en casa.

homesick ➤ *adj* nostálgico.

hometown ➤ *s* ciudad *f* de origen.

homeward ➤ *adj* de vuelto, de regreso ➤ *adv* hacia casa.

homework ➤ *s* deberes *m*, tareas escolares.

homosexual ➤ *adj & s* homosexual *mf*.

Honduran ➤ *adj & s* hondureño/a.

honest ➤ *adj* honesto; *(sincere)* franco.

honesty ➤ *s* honestidad *f*; *(integrity)* honradez *f*; *(truthfulness)* veracidad *f*.

honey ➤ *s* miel *f*; *(darling)* tesoro.

honeymoon ➤ *s & intr* (pasar la) luna de miel.

honk ➤ *tr & intr* tocar (la bocina) ➤ *s* bocinazo; *(goose)* graznido.

honor ➤ *s* honor ➤ *tr* honrar; *(check)* aceptar; *(contract)* cumplir.

honorable ➤ *adj* honorable; *(praiseworthy)* honroso; *(honest)* honrado.

hood ➤ *s* capucha; *(of car)* capó.

hoof ➤ *s* pezuña.

hook ➤ *s* gancho; *(for fishing)* anzuelo ■ **off the h.** *(telephone)* descolgado ➤ *tr* enganchar ■ **to get hooked on** enviciarse con.

hooked ➤ *adj* ganchudo; *(addicted)* adicto.

hop ➤ *intr* brincar; *(to skip)* saltar con un pie ➤ *s* brinco.

hope ➤ *intr* esperar ➤ *s* esperanza.

hopeful ➤ *adj* esperanzado; *(promising)* prometedor.

hopeless ➤ *adj* desesperado.

horizon ➤ *s* horizonte *m*.

horizontal ➤ *adj & s* horizontal *f*.

hormonal ➤ *adj* hormonal.

hormone ➤ *s* hormona.

horn ➤ *s* cuerno; AUTO., TEC. bocina.

horrible ➤ *adj* horrible.

horrify ➤ *tr* horrorizar.

horror ➤ *s* horror *m* ■ **h. film** película de miedo.

horse ➤ *s* caballo.

horseback ➤ *adv* a caballo.

hose ➤ *s* medias; *(for water)* manguera.

hospitable ➤ *adj* hospitalario; *(receptive)* receptivo.

hospital ➤ *s* hospital *m*.

hospitality ➤ *s* hospitalidad *f*.

hospitalize ➤ *tr* hospitalizar.

host ➤ *s* *(at a meal)* anfitrión *m*; *(of inn)* mesonero/a; TELEV. presentador/a.

hostage ➤ *s* rehén *mf*.

hostel ➤ *s* albergue *m* (para jóvenes).

hostess ➤ *s* *(host)* anfitriona; *(waitress)* camarera; *(stewardess)* azafata.

hostile ➤ *adj* hostil.

hostility ➤ *s* hostilidad.

hot ➤ *adj* caliente; *(climate)* cálido; *(spicy)* picante; *(temper)* vivo ■ **h. line** línea de emergencia.

hotel ➤ *s* hotel *m*.

hound ➤ *s* podenco ➤ *tr* acosar.

hour ➤ *s* hora.

hourly ➤ *adj* por hora ➤ *adv* a cada hora.

house ➤ *s* casa ➤ *tr* alojar; *(to shelter)* proteger; *(to contain)* contener.

household ➤ *s* casa.

housekeeping ➤ *s* manejo de una casa.

housewarming ➤ *s* fiesta para el estreno de una casa.

housewife ➤ *s* ama de casa.

housework ➤ *s* quehaceres domésticos.

housing ➤ *s* vivienda.

how ➤ *adv* cómo; *(in what condition)* qué tal; *(to what extent)* cuánto, qué ■ **h. about . . .?** ¿qué te parece . . .? • **h. do you do?** ¿cómo está usted? • **h. old are you?** ¿cuántos años tienes? ➤ *conj* cómo; *(that)* que.

however ➤ *adv* de cualquier modo; *(to whatever degree)* por . . . que ■ **h. much** por más *o* por mucho que ➤ *conj* no obstante.

howl ➤ *intr* aullar ➤ *tr* gritar ➤ *s* aullido.

huddle ➤ *intr* apiñarse ➤ *s* grupo.

hug ➤ *tr* abrazar ➤ *s* abrazo.

huge ➤ *adj* enorme.
hull ➤ *s (shell)* cáscara; MARÍT. casco.
hum ➤ *tr & intr* tararear ➤ *s* zumbido.
human ➤ *adj & s (ser)* humano ■ h. being ser humano.
humanity ➤ *s* humanidad *f; (humanness)* naturaleza humana.
humble ➤ *adj* humilde.
humid ➤ *adj* húmedo.
humidity ➤ *s* humedad *f.*
humiliate ➤ *tr* humillar.
humiliation ➤ *s* humillación *f.*
humor ➤ *s* humor *m.*
humorous ➤ *adj* cómico.
hunch ➤ *s (feeling)* corazonada.
hundred ➤ *s & adj* cien, ciento; MAT. centena ➤ *pl* centenares.
hunger ➤ *s* hambre *f* ➤ *intr* tener hambre *(for, after* de).
hungry ➤ *adj* hambriento.
hunt ➤ *tr* cazar ➤ *s* caza.
hunter ➤ *s* cazador/a.
hunting ➤ *s* cacería ➤ *adj* de caza.
hurdle ➤ *s* valla; FIG. barrera.
hurl ➤ *tr* lanzar.
hurricane ➤ *s* huracán *m.*
hurry ➤ *intr* darse prisa ■ to h. up apresurarse ➤ *tr* apurar; *(to rush)* dar prisa a ➤ *s* prisa; *(urgency)* apuro ■ to be in a h. (to) tener prisa (por).
hurt◇ ➤ *tr* hacer daño ➤ *intr* doler ➤ *s (harm)* daño; *(anguish)* angustia.
husband ➤ *s* marido.
hush ➤ *tr & intr* callar(se) ➤ *s* silencio.
hustle ➤ *tr* empujar; FAM. *(to hurry)* apurar ➤ *s* FAM. ajetreo.
hut ➤ *s* choza.
hydrant ➤ *s* boca de agua.
hydrogen ➤ *s* hidrógeno.
hygiene ➤ *s* higiene *f.*
hygienic ➤ *adj* higiénico.
hymn ➤ *s* himno.
hyphen ➤ *s* guión *m.*
hypocrisy ➤ *s* hipocresía.
hypocrite ➤ *s* hipócrita *mf.*
hysteric ➤ *s* histérico.
hysterical ➤ *adj* histérico.

I

I ➤ *pron* yo ➤ *s* yo, ego.
ice ➤ *s* hielo ■ i. cream helado • i.-cream cone helado de cucurucho • i. cube cubito de hielo ➤ *tr* helar; *(a cake)* escarchar.
iceberg ➤ *s* iceberg *m.*
ice-skate ➤ *intr* patinar sobre hielo.
icicle ➤ *s* carámbano.
icing ➤ *s* alcorza, escarchado.
icon ➤ *s* icono.
icy ➤ *adj* helado; *(person, look)* glacial.
idea ➤ *s* idea.
ideal ➤ *adj & s* ideal *m.*
identical ➤ *adj* idéntico.
identification ➤ *s* identificación *f* ■ i. card, papers carnet, documentos de identidad.
identify ➤ *tr & intr* identificar(se).
identity ➤ *s* identidad *f* ■ i. card, papers tarjeta, documentos de identidad.
idiom ➤ *s* modismo.
idiot ➤ *s* idiota *mf.*
idiotic ➤ *adj* idiota.
idle ➤ *adj* ocioso; *(threat)* vano.
idol ➤ *s* ídolo.
idolize ➤ *tr* idolatrar.
if ➤ *conj* si ■ if and when siempre y cuando • if at all si es que.
ignite ➤ *tr & intr* encender(se).
ignition ➤ *s* AUTO. encendido.
ignorance ➤ *s* ignorancia.
ignorant ➤ *adj* ignorante.
ignore ➤ *tr (to disregard)* no hacer caso de; *(to leave out)* pasar por alto.
ill ➤ *adj* enfermo, malo ➤ *s* mal *m.*
illegal ➤ *adj* ilegal ➤ *s* inmigrante *mf* ilegal.
illegible ➤ *adj* ilegible.
illiterate ➤ *s & adj* analfabeto/a.
illness ➤ *s* enfermedad *f.*
illuminate ➤ *tr* iluminar.
illusion ➤ *s* ilusión *f.*
illustrate ➤ *tr & intr* ilustrar.
illustration ➤ *s* ilustración *f.*
image ➤ *s* imagen *f.*
imagination ➤ *s* imaginación *f.*
imagine ➤ *tr* imaginar; *(to suppose)* imaginarse.
imbecile ➤ *adj & s* imbécil *mf.*
imitate ➤ *tr* imitar.
imitation ➤ *s* imitación *f.*
immature ➤ *adj* inmaduro.
immediate ➤ *adj* inmediato.

immense ➤ *adj* inmenso, enorme.

immigrant ➤ *s* inmigrante *mf.*

immigration ➤ *s* inmigración *f.*

immortal ➤ *adj & s* inmortal *mf.*

immune ➤ *adj* inmune *(from* de).

immunize ➤ *tr* inmunizar.

impact ➤ *s* impacto, choque *m; (influence)* efecto.

impatience ➤ *s* impaciencia.

impatient ➤ *adj* impaciente.

impel ➤ *tr* impeler, impulsar.

imperial ➤ *adj* imperial.

imperative ➤ *adj* imperioso.

impersonate ➤ *tr* hacerse pasar por.

impersonator ➤ *s* imitador/a.

impertinent ➤ *adj* impertinente.

impetus ➤ *s* ímpetu *m,* impulso.

implant   ➤ *tr* implantar   ➤ *s* MED. injerto.

implement ➤ *s* utensilio, instrumento ➤ *tr* poner en práctica.

implication ➤ *s* implicación *f; (inference)* inferencia.

implied ➤ *adj* implícito.

imply ➤ *tr (to entail)* implicar; *(to hint)* dar a entender, insinuar.

impolite ➤ *adj* descortés.

import   ➤ *tr* importar   ➤ *s* artículo importado; *(business)* importación *f.*

importance ➤ *s* importancia.

important ➤ *adj* importante.

importer ➤ *s* importador/a.

impose ➤ *tr* imponer ➤ *intr* ■ to i. (up)on abusar de.

imposing ➤ *adj* imponente.

imposition ➤ *s (act)* imposición *f; (unfair demand)* abuso.

impossibility ➤ *s* imposibilidad *f.*

impossible ➤ *adj* imposible.

impostor ➤ *s* impostor/a.

impractical ➤ *adj* poco práctico.

impress ➤ *tr* impresionar ■ I was not impressed no me pareció gran cosa.

impression ➤ *s* impresión *f; (memory)* idea ■ to be under the i. that tener la impresión de que.

impressive ➤ *adj* impresionante.

imprison ➤ *tr* aprisionar.

improbable ➤ *adj* improbable.

improper ➤ *adj* impropio; *(indecorous)* incorrecto, indebido.

improve ➤ *tr & intr* mejorar(se).

improvement ➤ *s* mejora; *(in school)* progreso; *(in health)* mejoría.

improvise ➤ *tr & intr* improvisar.

impudent ➤ *adj* impudente, descarado.

impulse ➤ *s* impulso.

impulsive ➤ *adj* impetuoso.

impurity ➤ *s* impureza.

in ➤ *prep* en, dentro de, por; *(time)* a, por, durante, de; *(arrival)* a; *(method)* a, en, por; *(with verbs)* al, mientras ➤ *adv (inside)* (a)dentro ■ is the doctor in? ¿está el médico? • to be in on tomar parte en; *(to know)* estar enterado de • to have it in for someone FAM. tenerle antipatía a alguien ➤ *adj* FAM. *(fashionable)* de moda.

inability ➤ *s* incapacidad *f.*

inaccessible ➤ *adj* inaccesible.

inaccuracy ➤ *s* inexactitud *f.*

inaccurate ➤ *adj* inexacto.

inadequacy ➤ *s* inadecuación *f; (insufficiency)* insuficiencia.

inadequate ➤ *adj* inadecuado; *(insufficient)* insuficiente.

inappropriate ➤ *adj* impropio.

inaugurate ➤ *tr* inaugurar.

inauguration ➤ *s* inauguración *f.*

incapable ➤ *adj* incapaz; *(incompetent)* incompetente.

incentive ➤ *s* incentivo.

inch ➤ *s* pulgada ■ i. by i. poco a poco ➤ *intr* avanzar poco a poco.

incident ➤ *adj & s* incidente *m.*

incite ➤ *tr* incitar.

incitement ➤ *s* incitación *f.*

inclination ➤ *s* inclinación *f; (tendency)* tendencia; *(preference)* gusto.

incline ➤ *tr & intr* inclinar(se) ■ to be inclined to estar dispuesto a.

include ➤ *tr* incluir, abarcar.

inclusive ➤ *adj (including)* inclusive; *(comprehensive)* inclusivo.

income ➤ *s* ingresos *m; (on investments)* renta; *(profit)* utilidades *f* ■ i. tax impuesto sobre la renta.

incompatible ➤ *adj* incompatible.

incompetent ➤ *adj & s* (persona) incompetente.

incomplete ➤ *adj* incompleto.

inconceivable ➤ *adj* inconcebible.

inconsiderate ➤ *adj* desconsiderado.
inconsistency ➤ *s* inconsecuencia.
inconsistent ➤ *adj* inconsecuente.
inconspicuous ➤ *adj* no conspicuo.
inconvenience ➤ *s* inconveniencia; *(bother)* molestia ➤ *tr* incomodar.
inconvenient ➤ *adj* inconveniente; *(bothersome)* molesto.
incorporate ➤ *tr* incorporar, incluir.
incorrect ➤ *adj* incorrecto.
increase ➤ *tr & intr* aumentar ➤ *s* aumento; *(in prices)* subida, alza; *(in production)* incremento.
increasing ➤ *adj* creciente.
increasingly ➤ *adv* cada vez más.
incredible ➤ *adj* increíble.
incurable ➤ *adj* incurable.
indecent ➤ *adj* indecente.
indecisive ➤ *adj (inconclusive)* dudoso; *(irresolute)* indeciso, irresoluto.
indeed ➤ *adv (truly)* verdaderamente; *(in fact)* en efecto; *(of course)* claro ∎ i.? ¿de verdad? • that is i. a luxury eso sí que es lujo ➤ *interj* de veras, verdad.
indefinite ➤ *adj* indefinido.
Indian ➤ *adj & s* indio/a.
independence ➤ *s* independencia.
independent ➤ *adj & s* independiente *mf*.
index ➤ *s* índice *m* ∎ i. card ficha, tarjeta.
indicate ➤ *tr* indicar.
indication ➤ *s* indicación *f; (sign)* indicio.
indicator ➤ *s* indicador *m*.
indifference ➤ *s* indiferencia.
indifferent ➤ *adj* indiferente.
indigestion ➤ *s* indigestión *f*.
indignant ➤ *adj* indignado.
indirect ➤ *adj* indirecto.
indiscreet ➤ *adj* indiscreto.
indiscriminate ➤ *adj* sin criterio; *(random)* al azar.
indisposed ➤ *adj (slightly ill)* indispuesto; *(averse)* averso.
indistinguishable ➤ *adj* indistinguible.
individual ➤ *adj* individual; *(style, manner)* particular ➤ *s* individuo.
individuality ➤ *s* individualidad *f*, particularidad *f*.
indoor ➤ *adj* interior, interno.

indoors ➤ *adv* dentro, bajo techo.
induce ➤ *tr* ocasionar; *(childbirth)* provocar.
indulge ➤ *tr (to pamper)* consentir, mimar; *(to gratify)* satisfacer.
indulgent ➤ *adj* indulgente.
industrial ➤ *adj* industrial.
industry ➤ *s* industria; *(diligence)* diligencia.
inedible ➤ *adj* incomestible.
ineffective ➤ *adj* ineficaz.
inefficient ➤ *adj* ineficiente, ineficaz.
inept ➤ *adj* inepto, incapaz.
inequality ➤ *s* desigualdad *f*.
inevitable ➤ *adj* inevitable.
inexcusable ➤ *adj* inexcusable.
inexpensive ➤ *adj* barato.
inexperienced ➤ *adj* inexperto.
inexplicable ➤ *adj* inexplicable.
infallible ➤ *adj* infalible.
infamous ➤ *adj* infame.
infancy ➤ *s* infancia.
infant ➤ *s* infante *mf*, niño/a.
infantry ➤ *s* infantería.
infatuated ➤ *adj* locamente enamorado; *(foolish)* encaprichado.
infatuation ➤ *s* encaprichamiento.
infect ➤ *tr* infectar.
infection ➤ *s* infección *f*.
infectious ➤ *adj* infeccioso.
inferior ➤ *adj & s* inferior *mf*.
inferiority ➤ *s* inferioridad *f*.
infest ➤ *tr* infestar, plagar.
infinite ➤ *adj & s* infinito.
infinitive ➤ *s* infinitivo.
infinity ➤ *s* infinidad *f;* MAT. infinito.
infirm ➤ *adj* débil, enfermizo.
infirmary ➤ *s* enfermería.
inflame ➤ *tr* inflamar.
inflammable ➤ *adj* inflamable.
inflammation ➤ *s* inflamación *f*.
inflate ➤ *tr* inflar.
inflation ➤ *s* inflación *f*.
inflexible ➤ *adj* inflexible.
inflict ➤ *tr* infligir, causar.
influence ➤ *s* influencia, influjo ➤ *tr* influir en, ejercer influencia sobre.
influential ➤ *adj* influyente.
influenza ➤ *s* influenza.
influx ➤ *s* afluencia, entrada.
inform ➤ *tr* informar, avisar.

informal ➤ *adj (casual)* familiar, llano; *(unofficial)* extraoficial; *(agreement)* no legalizado.

information ➤ *s* información *f; (data)* datos ▪ **for your i.** para su conocimiento.

informative ➤ *adj* informativo.

infuriate ➤ *tr* enfurecer.

infusion ➤ *s* infusión *f.*

ingenious ➤ *adj* ingenioso.

ingenuity ➤ *s* ingenio.

ingest ➤ *tr* ingerir.

ingratitude ➤ *s* ingratitud *f.*

ingredient ➤ *s* ingrediente *m.*

inhabit ➤ *tr* habitar, vivir en.

inhabitant ➤ *s* habitante *mf.*

inhale ➤ *tr* aspirar; *(smoke)* tragar; MED. inhalar ➤ *intr* aspirar aire.

inherit ➤ *tr* heredar.

inheritance ➤ *s* herencia.

inhibit ➤ *tr* inhibir; *(to prevent)* impedir; *(to prohibit)* prohibir.

inhibition ➤ *s* inhibición *f.*

inhospitable ➤ *adj* inhospitalario; *(barren)* inhóspito.

initial ➤ *adj & s* inicial *f* ▪ *spl (person)* iniciales; *(organization)* siglas.

initiative ➤ *s* iniciativa.

inject ➤ *tr* inyectar.

injection ➤ *s* inyección *f.*

injure ➤ *tr* lastimar, herir.

injury ➤ *s* herida.

injustice ➤ *s* injusticia.

ink ➤ *s* tinta.

inland ➤ *adj (del) interior* ➤ *adv* tierra adentro.

in-law ➤ *s* pariente político.

inmate ➤ *s (of asylum)* asilado/a; *(prisoner)* preso/a.

inn ➤ *s* posada, hostería.

inner ➤ *adj* interior ▪ **i. tube** cámara.

innocence ➤ *s* inocencia.

innocent ➤ *adj & s* inocente *mf.*

inoculate ➤ *tr* inocular.

inoculation ➤ *s* inoculación *f.*

inpatient ➤ *s* paciente *mf* internado en un hospital.

input ➤ *s* COMPUT., ELEC. entrada ➤ *tr* COMPUT. entrar, ingresar.

inquire ➤ *tr & intr* preguntar (por).

inquiry ➤ *s* pregunta; *(investigation)* investigación *f,* inquisición *f.*

inquisitive ➤ *adj (prying)* preguntón, inquisitivo; *(curious)* curioso.

insane ➤ *adj* loco.

insanity ➤ *s* locura.

inscribe ➤ *tr* inscribir.

inscription ➤ *s* inscripción *f.*

insect ➤ *s* insecto.

insecticide ➤ *s* insecticida *m.*

insecure ➤ *adj* inseguro.

insensitive ➤ *adj* insensible.

insert ➤ *tr (into)* insertar, introducir; *(between)* intercalar.

inside ➤ *s* interior *m,* parte *f* de adentro ▪ **i. out** al revés ▪ *pl* FAM. entrañas ➤ *adj (inner)* interior, interno ▪ *adv (within)* dentro, adentro; *(on the inner side)* por dentro ➤ *prep* dentro de.

insight ➤ *s* perspicacia.

insignificant ➤ *adj* insignificante.

insincere ➤ *adj* insincero.

insist ➤ *intr* insistir.

insistence ➤ *s* insistencia.

insistent ➤ *adj* insistente.

insolence ➤ *s* insolencia, descaro.

insolent ➤ *adj* insolente, descarado.

insomnia ➤ *s* insomnio.

inspect ➤ *tr* inspeccionar.

inspection ➤ *s* inspección *f.*

inspector ➤ *s* inspector/a.

inspiration ➤ *s* inspiración *f.*

inspire ➤ *tr* inspirar, motivar; *(emotion)* infundir ▪ **to i. with** llenar de.

install ➤ *tr* instalar.

installment ➤ *s* plazo, pago ▪ **i. plan** pago a plazos.

instance ➤ *s (example)* ejemplo, muestra; *(case)* caso ▪ **for i.** por ejemplo.

instant ➤ *s* instante *m,* momento ➤ *adj* inmediato; *(success)* instantáneo.

instantly ➤ *adv* inmediatamente.

instead ➤ *adv* en su lugar; *(rather than)* en cambio ▪ **i. of** en vez de.

instinct ➤ *s* instinto.

instinctive ➤ *adj* instintivo.

institute ➤ *tr* instituir ➤ *s* instituto.

institution ➤ *s* institución *f.*

instruct ➤ *tr* instruir; *(to order)* dar instrucciones, mandar.

instruction ➤ *s* instrucción *f.*

instructor ➤ *s* instructor/a.

instrument ➤ *s* instrumento.

insufficient ➤ *adj* insuficiente.

insulate ➤ *tr* aislar.

insulation ➤ *s* aislamiento.

insulin ➤ *s* insulina.

insult ➤ *tr* insultar; ➤ *s* insulto.

insurance ➤ *s* seguro; FIG. seguridad *f.*

insure ➤ *tr* asegurar.

insured ➤ *s* asegurado.

intact ➤ *adj* intacto.

integral ➤ *adj & s* integral *f.*

intellect ➤ *s* intelecto.

intellectual ➤ *adj & s* intelectual *mf.*

intelligence ➤ *s* inteligencia.

intelligent ➤ *adj* inteligente.

intelligible ➤ *adj* inteligible.

intend ➤ *tr (to plan)* proponerse; *(to mean)* pensar, tener intención de.

intense ➤ *adj* intenso.

intensify ➤ *tr & intr* intensificar(se).

intensity ➤ *s* intensidad *f.*

intensive ➤ *adj* intensivo.

intent ➤ *s* intención *f,* propósito.

intention ➤ *s* intención *f.*

intentional ➤ *adj* intencional.

intercept ➤ *tr* interceptar.

interchange ➤ *s* intercambio; *(highway junction)* empalme *m.*

interchangeable ➤ *adj* intercambiable.

intercom ➤ *s* sistema *m* de intercomunicación.

interest ➤ *s* interés *m* ■ in one's own i. en beneficio propio • to be of i. ser interesante ➤ *tr* interesar.

interesting ➤ *adj* interesante.

interfere ➤ *intr* interferir; *(to meddle)* entrometerse ■ to i. with obstruir.

interference ➤ *s* interferencia.

interior ➤ *adj & s* interior *m.*

intermediary ➤ *s* intermediario/a.

intermediate ➤ *adj* intermedio.

intermission ➤ *s* intermisión *f;* TEAT. intermedio, entreacto.

intern ➤ *s* interno/a, médico/a residente.

internal ➤ *adj* interno; *(domestic)* interior, nacional.

international ➤ *adj* internacional.

Internet ➤ *s* Internet *m,* Red *f.*

interpret ➤ *tr* interpretar.

interpreter ➤ *s* intérprete *mf.*

interrogate ➤ *tr* interrogar.

interrogation ➤ *s* interrogación *f.*

interrupt ➤ *tr* interrumpir.

interruption ➤ *s* interrupción *f.*

intersect ➤ *tr & intr* cruzarse.

intersection ➤ *s* intersección *f.*

interval ➤ *s* intervalo.

intervene ➤ *intr* intervenir.

intervention ➤ *s* intervención *f.*

interview ➤ *s* entrevista ➤ *tr & intr* entrevistar(se).

interviewer ➤ *s* entrevistador/a.

intimate ➤ *adj & s* íntimo/a.

into ➤ *prep* en, a, dentro de, contra.

intolerable ➤ *adj* intolerable.

intoxicate ➤ *tr* embriagar.

intransitive ➤ *adj & s* (verbo) intransitivo.

intricate ➤ *adj* complejo, intrincado.

intrigue ➤ *s* intriga ➤ *intr & tr* intrigar.

introduce ➤ *tr* presentar; *(to bring into use)* introducir.

introduction ➤ *s* introducción *f; (of people)* presentación *f.*

intrude ➤ *tr* meter por fuerza (en) ➤ *intr (to meddle)* inmiscuirse, entrometerse; *(to interrupt)* molestar.

intruder ➤ *s* intruso/a.

intrusion ➤ *s* intrusión *f.*

intuition ➤ *s* intuición *f.*

inundate ➤ *tr* inundar.

inundation ➤ *s* inundación *f.*

invade ➤ *tr* invadir.

invader ➤ *s* invasor/a.

invalid[1] ➤ *adj & s* inválido/a.

invalid[2] ➤ *adj* nulo.

invaluable ➤ *adj* inestimable.

invariable ➤ *adj* invariable.

invent ➤ *tr* inventar.

invention ➤ *s* invención *f; (new device)* invento; *(skill)* inventiva.

inventor ➤ *s* inventor/a.

inventory ➤ *s* inventario.

inversion ➤ *s* inversión *f.*

invest ➤ *tr (money)* invertir; *(effort)* dedicar.

investigate ➤ *tr* investigar.

investigation ➤ *s* investigación *f.*

investigator ➤ *s* investigador/a.

investment ➤ *s* inversión *f.*

investor ➤ *s* inversionista *mf.*

invisible ➤ *adj* invisible.
invitation ➤ *s* invitación *f.*
invite ➤ *tr* invitar; *(for food, drink)* convidar; *(a response)* solicitar; *(trouble)* provocar, buscar.
inviting ➤ *adj* atrayente, tentador.
invoice ➤ *s* factura ➤ *tr* facturar.
involve ➤ *tr (to include)* comprender, incluir; *(to entail)* implicar.
involved ➤ *adj* complicado, enredado.
involvement ➤ *s* participación *f.*
inward(s) ➤ *adj* interior, interno ➤ *adv* hacia adentro.
iodine ➤ *s* yodo.
iris ➤ *s (of the eye)* iris *m;* BOT. lirio.
iron ➤ *s* hierro; *(for clothes)* plancha ➤ *tr & intr* planchar ■ **to i. out** allanar.
ironic(al) ➤ *adj* irónico.
ironing ➤ *s* planchado ■ **i. board** tabla de planchar.
irony ➤ *s* ironía.
irrational ➤ *adj* irracional.
irregular ➤ *adj* irregular.
irrelevance *or* **irrelevancy** ➤ *s* improcedencia, falta de pertinencia.
irrelevant ➤ *adj* inaplicable, improcedente ■ **to be i.** no venir al caso.
irrespective ➤ *adj* ■ **i. of** sin tener en cuenta, no obstante.
irretrievable ➤ *adj (not recoverable)* irrecuperable; *(mistake)* irreparable.
irrigate ➤ *tr* irrigar.
irritable ➤ *adj* irritable.
irritate ➤ *tr* irritar.
irritating ➤ *adj* irritante, molesto.
irritation ➤ *s* irritación *f.*
is ➤ *vea* **be** *en* tabla de verbos.
island ➤ *s* isla; *(in a street)* isleta.
isolate ➤ *tr* aislar.
isolation ➤ *s* aislamiento.
issue ➤ *(magazine)* edición *f; (result)* consecuencia; *(matter)* cuestión *f* ➤ *intr* salir ➤ *tr (magazine)* publicar; *(stamps, money)* emitir.
it ➤ *pron* lo, la, le ■ **it's cold** hace frío • **it is good** es bueno • **it is raining** llueve, está lloviendo.
italic ➤ *s & adj* cursiva.
itch ➤ *s* picazón *f* ➤ *intr* picar ➤ *tr* dar picazón; *(to scratch)* rascarse.
itchy ➤ *adj* que da picazón.

item ➤ *s* artículo; *(on an agenda)* punto; *(of a document)* item *m.*
its ➤ *adj* su ■ **its flavor** su sabor.
it's ➤ *contr de* **it is.**
itself ➤ *pron* ■ (all) **by i.** solo • **it turns i. off automatically** se apaga automáticamente • *of o* in **i.** de sí • **the book i.** el libro mismo.
ivory ➤ *s* marfil *m.*
ivy ➤ *s* hiedra, yedra.

J

jab ➤ *tr* golpear ➤ *s* pinchazo; *(with elbow)* codazo; *(punch)* golpe corto.
jack ➤ *s (in cards)* sota; MEC. gato, cric *m* ➤ *tr* ■ **to j. up** alzar con el gato; *(prices)* aumentar.
jacket ➤ *s* saco, chaqueta.
jade ➤ *s* MIN. jade *m.*
jagged ➤ *adj* dentado.
jail ➤ *s* cárcel *f* ➤ *tr* encarcelar.
jam¹ ➤ *tr & intr (to lock)* atascar(se), trabar(se) ■ **jammed with** atestado de ➤ *s (blockage)* atasco; FIG. aprieto.
jam² ➤ *s* CUL. mermelada.
January ➤ *s* enero.
jar¹ ➤ *s (jug)* jarra; *(pot)* tarro, pote *m.*
jar² ➤ *tr & intr* sacudir(se) ■ **to j. with** no concordar con ➤ *s* choque *m.*
jaundice ➤ *s* ictericia.
jaw ➤ *s* mandíbula.
jazz ➤ *s* jazz *m.*
jealous ➤ *adj* celoso; *(suspicious)* receloso; *(envious)* envidioso ■ **to be j. of** tener celos de.
jealousy ➤ *s* celos *m,* envidia.
jeans ➤ *s* jeans *m,* pantalones vaqueros.
jeer ➤ *intr (to mock)* burlarse *(at* de); *(to boo)* abuchear ➤ *s (mockery)* mofa, burla; *(boo)* abucheo.
jelly ➤ *s* jalea.
jeopardize ➤ *tr* poner en peligro.
jerk ➤ *tr* dar un tirón a, tironear ➤ *s* tirón *m,* sacudida; FAM. pelmazo *mf.*
jet ➤ *s (spurt)* chorro; *(airplane)* jet *m; (engine)* reactor *m.*
Jew ➤ *s* judío/a.
jewel ➤ *s* joya.
jewel(l)er ➤ *s* joyero.
jewelry ➤ *s* joyas, alhajas.
Jewish ➤ *adj* judío.

jingle ➤ *tr & intr* (hacer) cascabelear o tintinear.

jitters ➤ *spl* ■ to give someone the j. poner nervioso a alguien.

job ➤ *s (task)* tarea; *(work)* trabajo; *(employment)* empleo.

jobless ➤ *adj* sin trabajo.

jog ➤ *tr (to push)* empujar levemente; *(the memory)* refrescar ➤ *intr* correr despacio ➤ *s* paso lento.

jogger ➤ *s* persona que corre despacio para hacer ejercicio.

join ➤ *tr* juntar, unir; *(a cause)* abrazar; *(political party)* afiliarse a ➤ *intr* juntarse, unirse ■ to j. in participar en.

joint ➤ *s* junta, unión *f*; JER. cigarrillo de marihuana ➤ *adj* (en) común; *(collective)* mutuo ■ j. ownership propiedad en común.

joke ➤ *s* chiste *m*; *(amusing remark)* gracia; *(prank)* broma ➤ *intr* contar chistes ■ to j. around bromear.

joker ➤ *s* bromista *mf*; *(cards)* comodín *m*.

jolly ➤ *adj* alegre.

jolt ➤ *tr & intr* sacudir(se) ➤ *s* sacudida.

jostle ➤ *intr & tr* empujar, dar empellones ➤ *s* empujón *m*, empellón *m*.

jot ➤ *tr* ■ to j. down anotar, apuntar.

journal ➤ *s* diario; *(periodical)* revista.

journalist ➤ *s* periodista *mf*.

journey ➤ *s* viaje *m*; *(distance)* jornada.

joy ➤ *s* alegría.

joyful ➤ *adj* alegre, jubiloso.

joystick ➤ *s* AVIA. palanca de mando; *(game)* palanca de juego, joystick *m*.

judge ➤ *tr & intr* juzgar ➤ *s* juez *mf*; *(in a contest)* árbitro/a.

judg(e)ment ➤ *s (good sense)* juicio; *(ruling)* opinión *f*; DER. decisión *f*.

jug ➤ *s (jar)* jarra, cántaro.

juggle ➤ *tr* hacer malabares con ➤ *intr* hacer juego de manos.

juggler ➤ *s* malabarista *mf*.

juice ➤ *s* jugo, zumo *f*.

juicy ➤ *adj* jugoso.

July ➤ *s* julio.

jumble ➤ *tr* mezclar ➤ *s* revoltijo.

jumbo ➤ *s* coloso ➤ *adj* enorme.

jump ➤ *intr* saltar; *(to be startled)* sobresaltarse ■ to j. at *(a chance)* aprovechar ➤ *tr* saltar *(por encima de)* ➤ *s* salto; *(leap)* brinco ■ to get o have a j. on adelantarse a.

jumpy ➤ *adj* nervioso.

junction ➤ *s* juntura; F.C., ELEC. empalme *m*.

June ➤ *s* junio.

jungle ➤ *s* selva, jungla.

junior ➤ *adj* más joven; *(for children)* juvenil; *(in rank)* subalterno ➤ *s* joven *mf*, menor *mf*; *(rank)* subordinado.

junk ➤ *s* FAM. trastos viejos, cachivaches *m* ➤ *tr* desechar.

juror ➤ *s* jurado, miembro *mf* del jurado.

jury ➤ *s* jurado, tribunal *m*.

just ➤ *adj (fair, right)* justo ➤ *adv (recently)* recién ■ j. about *(not quite)* casi • j. about to a punto de • j. as if lo mismo que si • j. in case por si acaso • j. in time to o for justo a tiempo para • j. so a su gusto, ni más ni menos • not j. yet todavía no • to have j. acabar de.

justice ➤ *s* justicia.

justify ➤ *tr* justificar.

juvenile ➤ *adj* joven, juvenil; *(immature)* infantil ➤ *s* joven *mf* ■ j. court tribunal de menores.

K

kangaroo ➤ *s* canguro ■ k. court tribunal desautorizado.

karat ➤ *s* quilate *m*.

kayak ➤ *s* kayac *m*, kayak *m*.

keel ➤ *s* quilla.

keen ➤ *adj* agudo; *(interest)* vivo ■ to be k. on tener entusiasmo por.

keep◇ ➤ *tr* quedarse con; *(to put aside)* guardar; *(a family)* sostener; *(in a place)* guardar; *(order, tradition)* mantener; *(diary, accounts)* llevar ■ to k. away mantener alejado • to k. from *(to prevent)* impedir; *(to conceal)* ocultar • to k. out no dejar entrar ■ to k. up *(to continue)* proseguir; *(to maintain)* mantener ➤ *intr (food)* conservarse ■ k. off prohibido pasar • to k. on continuar • to k. quiet quedarse callado ➤ *s (care)* custodia.

kennel ➤ *tr & s* (meter en la) perrera.

kernel ➤ *s* grano.

kerosene *o* **kerosine** ➤ *s* queroseno.

ketchup ➤ *s* salsa de tomate.

kettle ➤ *s* marmita; *(teakettle)* tetera.

key[1] ➤ *s* llave *f*; *(code, solution)* clave *f*; *(of a piano, keyboard)* tecla ■ **off k.** desafinado ➤ *adj* clave, importante.

key[2] ➤ *s* GEOG. cayo.

keyboard ➤ *s* teclado.

khaki ➤ *s* caqui *m*.

kick ➤ *tr* patear, dar un puntapié a; *(animals)* dar coces a; DEP. patear; *(a goal)* marcar, meter ■ **to k. out** echar a patadas ➤ *s* patada, puntapié *m*; *(animal)* coz *f* ■ *pl* sensación *f* ■ **for k.** por diversión.

kickoff ➤ *s* DEP. saque *m* inicial; FIG. comienzo.

kid ➤ *s* *(goat)* cabrito; FAM. niño ➤ *tr & intr* FAM. bromear *o* jugar (con).

kidnap ➤ *tr* secuestrar, raptar.

kidnapper ➤ *s* secuestrador/a, raptor/a.

kidnapping ➤ *s* secuestro, rapto.

kidney ➤ *s* riñón *m*.

kill ➤ *tr* matar ➤ *s* *(hunting)* cacería; *(final blow)* acabamiento.

killer ➤ *s* asesino/a.

kilo ➤ *s* kilo.

kilogram ➤ *s* kilogramo, kilo.

kilometer ➤ *s* kilómetro.

kind[1] ➤ *adj* bueno, afable; *(thoughtful)* amable.

kind[2] ➤ *s* tipo, clase *f* ■ **in k.** del mismo modo • **k. of** FAM. un poco.

kindergarten ➤ *s* jardín *m* de infantes.

kindly ➤ *adj* bondadoso ➤ *adv* bondadosamente.

kindness ➤ *s* bondad *f*; *(favor)* favor *m*.

king ➤ *s* rey *m*.

kingdom ➤ *s* reino.

kiosk ➤ *s* quiosco.

kiss ➤ *tr* besar, dar un beso a ➤ *intr* besarse ➤ *s* beso.

kit ➤ *s* *(set of tools)* equipo, conjunto ■ **first-aid k.** botiquín *m*.

kitchen ➤ *s* cocina.

kitchenette ➤ *s* cocina pequeña.

kite ➤ *s* *(toy)* cometa.

kitten ➤ *s* gatito.

knapsack ➤ *s* mochila.

knee ➤ *s* rodilla.

kneel◇ ➤ *intr* arrodillarse.

knife ➤ *s* cuchillo ➤ *tr* apuñalar.

knife-edge ➤ *s* filo.

knight ➤ *s* caballero; *(in chess)* caballo.

knit◇ ➤ *tr & intr* tejer, hacer punto ➤ *s* prenda de punto.

knitting ➤ *s* tejido, labor *f* de punto.

knitwear ➤ *s* artículos de punto.

knob ➤ *s* tirador *m*; *(dial)* botón *m*.

knock ➤ *tr* *(to hit)* golpear, pegar ■ **to k. down** derribar, tumbar • **to k. out** *(a person)* dejar sin sentido; *(in boxing)* poner fuera de combate; *(power)* cortar • **to k. over** tirar (vasa, lámpara) ➤ *intr* *(at the door)* golpear, llamar ■ **to k. against** chocar contra ➤ *s* *(blow)* golpe *m*; *(rap)* toque *m*, llamada.

knocker ➤ *s* aldaba, picaporte.

knot ➤ *s* nudo ➤ *tr & intr* anudar(se).

know◇ ➤ *tr* saber; *(a person, place)* conocer ■ **to get to k.** someone llegar a conocer a alguien • **to let someone k.** hacer saber a alguien • **to k. how to** saber ➤ *intr* saber.

know-how ➤ *s* habilidad *f*.

knowledge ➤ *s* *(understanding)* conocimiento; *(information)* conocimientos ■ **without my k.** sin saberlo yo.

known ➤ *adj* conocido.

knuckle ➤ *s* nudillo.

L

lab ➤ *s* laboratorio.

label ➤ *s* rótulo, etiqueta ➤ *tr* rotular, marcar; *(to describe)* describir.

labor ➤ *s* trabajo, labor *f*; *(task)* tarea, faena; *(workers)* mano *f* de obra ■ **l. union** sindicato • **to be in l.** estar de parto ➤ *intr* trabajar.

laboratory ➤ *s* laboratorio.

laborer ➤ *s* trabajador/a, obrero/a; *(unskilled)* peón *m*, jornalero/a.

lace ➤ *s* encaje *m*; *(trim)* puntilla; *(shoelace)* cordón *m* ➤ *tr* encordonar.

lack ➤ *s* *(deficiency)* falta, carencia; *(need)* escasez *f* ➤ *tr* carecer de, faltar.

lad ➤ *s* joven *m*, muchacho.

ladder ➤ *s* escalera.

ladle ➤ *s & tr* (servir con) cucharón *m*.

lady ➤ *s* dama; *(married)* señora.

ladybug ➤ s mariquita.

lake ➤ s lago.

lamb ➤ s cordero; *(dear)* amor m.

lame ➤ adj cojo; *(excuse)* débil.

lamp ➤ s lámpara.

lamppost ➤ s poste m de farol.

land ➤ s tierra; *(tract)* campo, terreno; *(country)* tierra, país m ■ pl tierras, posesiones ➤ intr *(boat)* arribar ➤ tr & intr *(to unload, disembark)* desembarcar; *(plane)* aterrizar.

landing ➤ s *(plane)* aterrizaje m; *(of a staircase)* descanso.

landlord/lady ➤ s propietario/a.

landscape ➤ s paisaje m.

landslide ➤ s derrumbe m (de tierra).

lane ➤ s *(path)* senda, vereda; *(road)* camino; *(of a highway)* vía, carril m.

language ➤ s lenguaje m; *(tongue)* lengua, idioma m.

lantern ➤ s linterna.

lap¹ ➤ s *(of body)* falda, regazo.

lap² ➤ s *(of a race)* vuelta a la pista; *(swimming)* largo; *(segment)* etapa.

lapel ➤ s solapa.

laptop ➤ s *(computadora)* portátil.

large ➤ adj & adv grande ■ by and l. por lo general.

largely ➤ adv en gran parte.

lark ➤ s ORNIT. alondra.

laser ➤ s láser m.

last¹ ➤ adj *(final, newest)* último; *(past)* pasado ■ l. name apellido • l. night anoche ➤ adv el último, en último lugar; *(most recently)* la última vez; *(finally)* por último, finalmente ➤ s el último; *(the end)* final m.

last² ➤ intr durar; *(to survive)* sobrevivir.

last-minute ➤ adj de última hora.

latch ➤ s & tr *(cerrar con)* pestillo.

late ➤ adj *(behind schedule)* atrasado; *(former)* antiguo; *(dead)* fallecido ■ to get l. hacerse tarde ➤ adv tarde.

latecomer ➤ s rezagado/a.

lately ➤ adv últimamente.

later ➤ adj posterior ➤ adv más tarde ■ l. on luego, después.

latest ➤ adj & s (lo) último ■ at the l. a más tardar.

Latin America ➤ s Latinoamérica.

Latin American ➤ adj & s Latinoamericano/a.

latter ➤ adj último.

laugh ➤ intr reír(se) ■ to l. at *(with amusement)* reírse con; *(to ridicule)* reírse de ➤ s risa.

laughter ➤ s risa(s).

launch ➤ tr lanzar; *(a ship)* botar ➤ s lanzamiento; *(of ship)* botadura.

laundry ➤ s *(soiled)* ropa sucia; *(clean)* ropa limpia; *(place)* lavandería.

lavatory ➤ s servicios, baño.

law ➤ s ley f; *(code)* fuero, código; *(study)* derecho.

lawful ➤ adj legal, lícito.

lawn ➤ s césped m ■ l. mower cortacéspedes.

lawsuit ➤ s pleito, juicio.

lawyer ➤ s abogado/a.

lay◇ ➤ tr poner; *(to cause to lie)* acostar; *(eggs)* poner ■ to be laid up guardar cama • to l. down dictar, establecer • to l. off despedir • to l. out *(to plan)* proyectar; *(to spread out)* preparar ➤ intr poner huevos ■ to l. over pararse.

layer ➤ s capa.

layman/woman ➤ s lego/a, seglar mf.

layoff ➤ s despido.

layover ➤ s escala, parada.

lazy ➤ adj perezoso.

lead¹◇ ➤ tr *(to guide)* guiar, conducir; *(to command)* dirigir, mandar ➤ intr estar a la cabeza; *(to go first)* enseñar el camino; *(to command)* mandar ➤ s *(position)* primer lugar m, delantera; *(margin)* ventaja; *(clue)* pista ■ in the l. a la cabeza, primero • to take the l. tomar la delantera ➤ adj principal.

lead² ➤ s plomo.

leader ➤ s jefe/a, líder mf.

leading ➤ adj primero; *(main)* principal.

leaf ➤ s hoja ■ gold l. pan de oro.

leaflet ➤ s folleto, panfleto.

league ➤ s liga.

leak ➤ intr *(container)* salirse; *(roof, faucet)* gotear ➤ tr divulgar ➤ s *(faucet, roof)* gotera; *(gas)* salida, escape; *(disclosure)* divulgación f.

lean¹◇ ➤ intr inclinarse; *(to rest on)*

apoyarse, reclinarse ▪ to l. back recostarse ➤ tr (to rest) apoyar, recostar.

lean² ➤ adj (thin) flaco; (meat) magro.

leap◇ ➤ intr & tr saltar (por encima de) ➤ s salto, brinco.

learn◇ ➤ tr aprender; (to find out) saber, enterarse de ➤ intr aprender; (from mistakes) escarmentar ▪ to l. how to aprender a.

learner ➤ s principiante/a.

learning ➤ s aprendizaje m; (knowledge) saber m, erudición f.

leash ➤ s correa ➤ tr atraillar.

least ➤ adj menor; (smallest) mínimo ➤ adv & s (lo) menos ▪ at l. por lo menos ▪ not in the l. en absoluto.

leather ➤ s cuero, piel f.

leave◇ ➤ tr salir de; (to forget, let stay, result in) dejar ▪ to l. alone dejar en paz • to l. out omitir ➤ intr irse, marcharse; (to depart) salir, partir.

lecture ➤ s conferencia; (class) curso, clase f ➤ intr dictar conferencia ➤ tr dar una conferencia a; (to scold) sermonear.

lecturer ➤ s conferenciante mf, conferencista mf.

leek ➤ s puerro.

left ➤ adj izquierdo ➤ s izquierda ➤ adv a o hacia la izquierda.

left-hand ➤ adj a la izquierda.

left-handed ➤ adj zurdo.

leftover ➤ adj sobrante ▪ leftovers spl sobras, restos.

leg ➤ s pierna; (of animal, chair) pata.

legal ➤ adj legal; (relating to the law) jurídico; (statutory) legítimo.

legend ➤ s leyenda.

legible ➤ adj legible.

legitimate ➤ adj legítimo; (lawful) lícito.

leisure ➤ s ocio ▪ l. time tiempo libre.

lemon ➤ s limón m ▪ l. tree limonero.

lemonade ➤ s limonada.

lend◇ ➤ tr prestar.

length ➤ s largo; (piece) pedazo, tramo; (duration) duración f.

lengthen ➤ tr & intr alargar(se), estirar(se); (time) prolongar(se).

lenient ➤ adj indulgente.

lens ➤ s lente m o f.

lentil ➤ s lenteja.

leopard ➤ s leopardo.

leotard ➤ s malla de bailarines.

less ➤ adj menos ▪ l. than menos de (lo que) ➤ prep menos ➤ adv menos ▪ l. and l. cada vez menos ➤ s menos m.

lesson ➤ s lección f ▪ to take lessons tomar clases.

let◇ ➤ tr permitir; (to allow) dejar ▪ to l. down bajar; (to disappoint) fallar ▪ to l. go (to fire) despedir; (to set free) dejar en libertad; (to release) soltar • to l. in dejar entrar • to l. out dejar salir ➤ intr ▪ to l. up FAM. (to cease) cesar; (to slacken) disminuirse ➤ conj ▪ l. alone y mucho menos.

letter ➤ s carta; (of alphabet) letra.

lettuce ➤ s lechuga.

level ➤ s nivel m; (height) altura; (flat land) llano, llanura ▪ at ground l. a ras de tierra ➤ adj plano, llano; (horizontal) a nivel; (even) parejo, igual ➤ tr nivelar; (to make flat) allanar.

lever ➤ s palanca.

liability ➤ s responsabilidad f; (hindrance) desventaja.

liable ➤ adj responsable; (obligated) obligado; (subject) sujeto; (tending to) susceptible.

liar ➤ s mentiroso/a.

liberal ➤ adj & s liberal mf.

liberty ➤ s libertad f ▪ at l. libre, en libertad.

librarian ➤ s bibliotecario/a.

library ➤ s biblioteca.

license ➤ s licencia, permiso; (card) carnet m ▪ l. plate patente, placa (de matrícula) ➤ tr licenciar, autorizar.

lick ➤ tr lamer.

licorice ➤ s regaliz m.

lid ➤ s tapa; (eyelid) párpado.

lie¹◇ ➤ intr (to recline) tenderse, acostarse; (to be stretched out) yacer.

lie² ➤ s mentira ➤ intr mentir.

lieutenant ➤ s teniente mf.

life ➤ s vida ▪ l. jacket chaleco salvavidas • l. preserver salvavidas • true to l. verosímil.

lifeboat ➤ s bote m salvavidas.

lifeguard ➤ s salvavidas mf.

lifetime ➤ s vida.

lift ➤ *tr* alzar, levantar; *(to revoke)* revocar ➤ *s* G.B. ascensor *m* ■ **to give someone a l.** llevar a alguien en un vehículo.

liftoff ➤ *s* despegue *m*.

light[1◇] ➤ *s* luz *f* ■ **l.** bulb bombilla • **to bring to l.** sacar a luz, revelar • **to see the l.** comprender, darse cuenta ➤ *tr* encender; *(to illuminate)* alumbrar, iluminar ➤ *intr* encenderse ■ **to l. up** iluminarse ➤ *adj (colors)* claro; *(hair)* rubio; *(bright)* bien iluminado.

light[2] ➤ *adj (not heavy)* ligero, liviano; *(rain)* fino; *(food)* ligero ➤ *adv* ligeramente.

lighthouse ➤ *s* faro.

lighting ➤ *s* iluminación *f*, alumbrado.

lighter ➤ *s* encendedor *m*.

lightning ➤ *s* rayo, relámpago.

likable ➤ *adj* agradable, grato.

like[1] ➤ *tr* ■ **I l.** to read me gusta leer • **do you l.** to cook? ¿te gusta cocinar? ➤ *intr* querer ■ **as you l.** como usted quiera.

like[2] ➤ *prep* como ■ **l.** this *o* that así ➤ *adj* similar, parecido.

likelihood ➤ *s* probabilidad *f*.

likely ➤ *adj* probable; *(plausible)* verosímil ➤ *adv* probablemente.

likeness ➤ *s* semejanza.

likewise ➤ *adv* del mismo modo, lo mismo; *(also)* además.

liking ➤ *s* afición *f*; *(taste)* gusto.

lily ➤ *s* lirio ■ **l.** pad hoja de nenúfar.

limb ➤ *s* BOT. rama; ANAT. miembro, extremidad *f*.

lime[1] ➤ *s (tree, fruit)* lima.

lime[2] ➤ *s* MIN. cal *f*.

limit ➤ *s* límite *m*; *(maximum)* máximo ■ *pl* límites, confines ➤ *tr* limitar.

limited ➤ *adj* limitado ■ **l.** company sociedad anónima ➤ *s (tren)* expreso.

limousine ➤ *s* limosina.

limp ➤ *intr* cojear ➤ *s* cojera.

line[1] ➤ *s* línea; *(mark)* raya; *(row)* hilera, fila; *(queue)* cola; *(verse)* verso; *(brief letter)* letras, líneas ■ **down the l.** en el futuro • **to draw the l.** fijar límites ➤ *tr* rayar, trazar líneas en ➤ *intr* ■ **to l. up** hacer cola.

line[2] ➤ *tr* COST. forrar; TEC. revestir.

linen ➤ *s* lino, hilo; *(goods)* lencería ■ *pl* ropa de cama.

liner ➤ *s* transatlántico.

lineup ➤ *s* fila (de personas); DEP. alineación *f*.

lining ➤ *s* forro.

link ➤ *s (chain)* eslabón *m*; FIG., COMPUT. enlace *m* ➤ *tr* & *intr (to unite)* unir(se); *(to connect)* conectar(se).

links ➤ *spl* campo de golf.

lion ➤ *s* león *m*.

lioness ➤ *s* leona.

lip ➤ *s* labio.

lipstick ➤ *s* lápiz *m* labial.

liqueur ➤ *s* licor *m*.

liquid ➤ *s* & *adj* líquido.

liquor ➤ *s* licor *m*.

list ➤ *s* lista ➤ *tr* enumerar; *(to register)* poner en una lista.

listen ➤ *intr* escuchar; *(to heed advice)* prestar atención.

listener ➤ *s* oyente *mf*.

literary ➤ *adj* literario.

literature ➤ *s* literatura; *(printed material)* folletos, impresos.

litter ➤ *s* ZOOL. camada, cría; *(trash)* basura ➤ *tr* & *intr* tirar basura (en).

little ➤ *adj (small)* pequeño; *(not much)* poco ➤ *adv (not much)* poco; *(somewhat)* un poco, algo ■ **l.** by **l.** poco a poco • **l. did I know** that no me imaginé que ➤ *s* poco; *(short time)* momento.

live ➤ *intr* & *tr* vivir ■ **to l. it up** FAM. vivir la vida • **to l. off** *(someone)* vivir a expensas de; *(the land)* vivir de • **to l. through** sobrevivir • **to l. with** tolerar ➤ *adj* vivo; RAD., TELEV. en directo.

lively ➤ *adj* vivaz; *(spirited)* alegre; *(keen)* vivo, grande.

liver ➤ *s* ANAT., CUL. hígado.

living ➤ *adj* vivo ■ **l.** expenses gastos de manutención • **l.** room sala de estar ➤ *s* vida ■ **to earn a l.** ganarse la vida.

lizard ➤ *s* lagarto.

load ➤ *s (weight)* peso; *(cargo)* carga ■ *pl* FAM. un montón, muchísimo ➤ *tr* & *intr* cargar(se).

loaf[1] ➤ *s* pan *m*.

loaf[2] ➤ *intr* haraganear, holgazanear.

loafer ➤ *s* holgazán/ana; *(shoe)* mocasín *m*.

loan ➤ s préstamo ∎ on l. prestado ➤ tr prestar.

lobby ➤ s vestíbulo ➤ intr POL. ejercer presiones.

lobster ➤ s langosta, bogavante.

local ➤ adj local ∎ l. call TEL. llamada urbana.

locate ➤ tr localizar; (to place) ubicar.

location ➤ s lugar m, sitio.

lock[1] ➤ s cerradura; (of a canal) esclusa ➤ tr cerrar con llave ➤ intr cerrarse.

lock[2] ➤ s (of hair) mecha.

locker ➤ s armario ∎ l. room vestuario (de un gimnasio, club).

locksmith ➤ s cerrajero/a.

lodge ➤ s (inn) posada ➤ tr & intr alojar(se).

lodger ➤ s inquilino/a.

lodging ➤ s alojamiento.

log ➤ s leño, tronco; para AVIA., MARÍT. diario ∎ l. cabin cabaña de troncos.

logic ➤ s lógica.

logical ➤ adj lógico.

loin ➤ s lomo.

lollipop ➤ s pirulí m.

loneliness ➤ s soledad f.

lonely ➤ adj solo; (isolated) solitario.

long[1] ➤ adj largo ∎ l. jump salto de longitud • six feet l. seis pies de largo • to take a l. time tardar mucho ➤ adv mucho tiempo ∎ as l. as (while) mientras; (if) si, siempre y cuando • how l.? (time) ¿cuánto tiempo?; (length) ¿qué largo? • no longer ya no ➤ s mucho tiempo ∎ before l. dentro de poco.

long[2] ➤ intr ∎ to l. for añorar • to l. to anhelar.

long-distance ➤ adj & adv de larga distancia.

long-term ➤ adj a largo plazo.

look ➤ intr mirar; (to seem) parecer ∎ l. out! ¡cuidado! ➤ tr mirar ∎ to l. after (someone) cuidar a, ocuparse de; (something) ocuparse de, encargarse de • to l. for buscar; (to expect) esperar • to l. forward to anticipar ➤ s (quick glance) ojeada, vistazo; (gaze) mirada; (aspect) aspecto ∎ pl aspecto.

lookout ➤ s (watch) vigilancia; (vantage point) mirador m ∎ to be on the l. for estar al acecho de.

loose ➤ adj (unfastened) suelto; (slack) flojo; (not tight) holgado; (not packaged) a granel ∎ to tie up l. ends FIG. atar cabos ➤ adv ∎ to come l. aflojarse, desatarse • to turn l. soltar, libertar ➤ s ∎ on the l. FAM. suelto, en libertad.

loosen ➤ tr aflojar; (to untie) desatar.

lord ➤ s señor m.

lose[◊] ➤ tr perder.

loser ➤ s perdedor/a.

loss ➤ s pérdida.

lost ➤ adj perdido; (engrossed) absorto ∎ l. and found oficina de objetos perdidos • to get l. perderse.

lot ➤ s (articles for sale) lote m; (large amount) gran cantidad f, mucho; (land) solar m, lote ∎ lots of cantidades de, mucho.

lotion ➤ s loción f.

lottery ➤ s lotería.

loud ➤ adj alto, fuerte; (noisy) ruidoso, bullicioso.

loudspeaker ➤ s altavoz m.

love ➤ s amor m, cariño; (lover) amor; DEP. cero (en tenis) ∎ l. un cariñoso saludo • to fall in l. enamorarse ➤ tr amar, querer ∎ I l. to travel me encanta viajar.

lovely ➤ adj precioso, bonito.

lover ➤ s amante mf; (devotee) aficionado/a.

low ➤ adj bajo; (in quality) inferior; (humble) humilde ∎ l. tide bajamar ➤ adv bajo • s punto más bajo.

lower ➤ adj más bajo, inferior ➤ tr & intr bajar; (to diminish) disminuir.

lowercase ➤ adj minúsculo.

lowlands ➤ spl tierras bajas.

loyal ➤ adj leal.

loyalty ➤ s lealtad f.

lozenge ➤ s (cough drop) pastilla.

luck ➤ s suerte f ∎ good l.! ¡buena suerte! • to be in l. estar de suerte ➤ intr ∎ to l. out FAM. tener suerte.

lucky ➤ adj afortunado; (fortuitous) fortuito, oportuno.

ludicrous ➤ adj absurdo, ridículo.

luggage ➤ s equipaje m.

lukewarm ➤ adj tibio.

lullaby ➤ s canción f de cuna, nana.

lump ➤ s montón m, masa; (of soil,

sugar) terrón *m* ➤ *tr* amontonar ■ **to l. together** juntar.

lunatic ➤ *adj* loco ➤ *s* lunático/a.

lunch ➤ *s* almuerzo ➤ *intr* almorzar.

luncheon ➤ *s* almuerzo.

lung ➤ *s* pulmón *m.*

luxurious ➤ *adj* lujoso; *(lush)* suntuoso.

luxury ➤ *s* lujo.

lyric ➤ *adj* lírico ■ **lyrics** *spl* MÚS. letra.

M

macaroni ➤ *spl* macarrones *m.*

machine ➤ *s* máquina ■ **m. gun** ametralladora.

machinery ➤ *s* maquinaria; *(working parts)* mecanismo.

mackerel ➤ *s* caballa.

mad ➤ *adj* enojado; *(insane)* loco; *(frantic)* frenético; *(rabid)* rabioso ■ **to be m. at** estar enojado con • **to get m.** enfadarse.

Madam ➤ *s* señora.

made ➤ *adj* hecho.

madness ➤ *s* locura; *(fury)* rabia.

magazine ➤ *s* revista.

magic ➤ *s* magia ➤ *adj* mágico.

magical ➤ *adj* mágico.

magician ➤ *s* mago/a.

magistrate ➤ *s* magistrado/a.

magnet ➤ *s* FÍS. imán *m.*

magnetic ➤ *adj* magnético.

magnificent ➤ *adj* magnífico.

magnify ➤ *tr* aumentar ■ **magnifying glass** lupa.

mahogany ➤ *s* caoba.

maid ➤ *s (servant)* criada; *(maiden)* doncella ■ **m. of honor** dama de honor.

maiden ➤ *s* doncella ■ **m. name** apellido de soltera.

mail ➤ *s* correo ■ **air m.** vía aérea • **m. carrier** cartero/a ➤ *tr* enviar por correo; *(to post)* echar al correo.

mailbox ➤ *s* buzón *m.*

mailman ➤ *s* cartero.

main ➤ *adj* principal; *(office)* central ■ **the m. thing** lo principal.

mainframe ➤ *s* elaborador *m* central.

maintain ➤ *tr* mantener; *(to repair)* cuidar.

maintenance ➤ *s* mantenimiento; *(upkeep)* cuidado.

majestic ➤ *adj* majestuoso.

majesty ➤ *s* majestad *f; (splendor)* majestuosidad *f.*

major ➤ *adj* mayor; *(chief)* principal ➤ *s* EDUC. especialidad *f* ➤ *intr* ■ **to m. in** EDUC. especializarse en.

majority ➤ *s* mayoría.

make◇ ➤ *tr* hacer; *(to build)* construir; *(to manufacture)* fabricar; *(decision)* tomar; *(food)* preparar; *(to earn)* ganar; *(to compel)* obligar a ■ **to m. clear** poner en claro • **to m. easy** facilitar • **to m. into** convertir en • **to m. up** preparar; *(story)* inventar; *(to constitute)* integrar ➤ *s* fabricación *f; (style)* corte *m; (brand)* marca.

maker ➤ *s* fabricante *mf.*

make-up o **makeup** *s* maquillaje *m.*

malaria ➤ *s* malaria, paludismo.

male ➤ *adj* del sexo masculino; BIOL., MEC. macho ➤ *s* varón *m;* BIOL. macho.

malice ➤ *s* malicia.

malicious ➤ *adj* malicioso.

malignant ➤ *adj* maligno.

mall ➤ *s* paseo, alameda; *(for shopping)* galería.

malnutrition ➤ *s* desnutrición *f.*

malt ➤ *s* malta; *(beer)* cerveza de malta.

mammal ➤ *s* mamífero.

man ➤ *s* hombre *m; (male)* varón *m; (mankind)* el hombre.

manage ➤ *tr* controlar; *(business)* dirigir; *(to handle)* poder con ➤ *intr* arreglárselas.

manageable ➤ *adj* manejable; *(tame)* dócil; *(task)* realizable.

management ➤ *s* gerencia; *(directors)* gerentes *mf; (skill)* habilidad directiva.

manager ➤ *s* gerente *mf; (agent)* apoderado/a.

mandatory ➤ *adj* obligatorio.

mane ➤ *s (of horse)* crin *f; (of lion)* melena.

maneuver ➤ *s* maniobra ➤ *intr* maniobrar; *(to manipulate)* manipular.

mangrove ➤ *s* mangle *m.*

mania ➤ *s* manía.

maniac ➤ *s & adj* maníaco/a.

manicure ➤ *s* manicura.

manipulate ➤ *tr* manipular.

mankind ➤ *s* género humano.

manmade ➤ *adj* artificial.

manner ➤ *s* manera, modo; *(bearing)* comportamiento ▪ *pl* modales; *(politeness)* educación.

manor ➤ *s (estate)* finca.

mantel *o* **mantelpiece** ➤ *s* repisa de la chimenea.

manual ➤ *adj & s* manual *m*.

manufacture ➤ *tr* fabricar ➤ *s* fabricación *f*; *(product)* producto manufacturado.

manufacturer ➤ *s* fabricante *mf*.

manufacturing ➤ *adj* manufacturero ➤ *s* manufactura.

manure ➤ *s* estiércol *m*.

manuscript ➤ *s* manuscrito.

many ➤ *adj* muchos ▪ **how m.?** ¿cuántos? • **too m.** demasiados ➤ *s & pron* muchos ▪ **as m. as** *(the same number)* tantos como; *(up to)* hasta.

map ➤ *s* mapa *m*.

marathon ➤ *s* maratón *m*.

marble ➤ *s* mármol *m*; *(glass ball)* canica, bola.

march ➤ *intr* MIL. marchar ➤ *s* marcha.

March ➤ *s* marzo.

mare ➤ *s* yegua.

margarine ➤ *s* margarina.

margin ➤ *s* margen *mf*.

marine ➤ *adj* marítimo; BIOL. marino ➤ *s* soldado *mf* de marina.

marital ➤ *adj* matrimonial, marital.

maritime ➤ *adj* marítimo.

mark ➤ *s* marca; *(grade)* nota; *(indication)* signo; *(reference point)* señal *f* ▪ **to hit the m.** dar en el clavo ➤ *tr* marcar; *(a spot)* señalar; *(to grade)* calificar ▪ **to m. down** *(prices)* rebajar.

markdown ➤ *s* rebaja.

marker ➤ *s* marcador *m*.

market ➤ *s* mercado; *(stock market)* bolsa ▪ **m. price** precio corriente ➤ *tr* vender.

marketing ➤ *s* comercio; *(of new products)* mercadeo, marketing *m*.

marmalade ➤ *s* mermelada.

maroon ➤ *s & adj (color)* marrón *m*, castaño ➤ *tr* abandonar.

marriage ➤ *s* matrimonio; *(wedding)* boda ▪ **m. certificate** partida de matrimonio.

married ➤ *adj* casado.

marrow ➤ *s* médula.

marry ➤ *tr (to join in marriage)* casar; *(to take in marriage)* casarse con.

marsh ➤ *s* pantano; *(salt)* marisma.

marshal ➤ *s* mariscal *m*.

marvel ➤ *s* maravilla ➤ *intr* maravillarse.

marvellous ➤ *adj* maravilloso.

mascara ➤ *s* rimel *m*.

masculine ➤ *adj & s* masculino.

mask ➤ *s* máscara ➤ *tr* enmascarar.

masking tape ➤ *s* cinta adhesiva opaca.

masonry ➤ *s* obra de albañilería.

mass ➤ *s* masa; *(large amount)* montón *m* ➤ *adj* de las masas • **m.** media medios de comunicación de masa.

Mass *o* **mass** ➤ *s* RELIG. misa.

massacre ➤ *s* masacre *f* ➤ *tr* masacrar.

massage ➤ *s* masaje *m* ➤ *tr* dar masajes a.

masseur ➤ *s* masajista *m*.

masseuse ➤ *s* masajista *f*.

massive ➤ *adj* masivo; *(huge)* monumental.

mast ➤ *s* mástil *m*; *(pole)* palo.

master ➤ *s* maestro; *(degree)* maestría (título académico entre la licenciatura y el doctorado); *(owner)* amo; *(of household)* señor *m* ➤ *adj* maestro; *(main)* principal ➤ *tr* lograr dominar; *(to overcome)* superar.

masterpiece ➤ *s* obra maestra.

mat ➤ *s* estera; *(doormat)* esterilla; DEP. colchoneta; *(tangled mass)* maraña.

match[1] ➤ *s* par *m*; DEP. partido ▪ **to be a m. for** poder competir con ➤ *tr* corresponder a; *(to go with)* hacer juego con; *(to equal)* igualar ➤ *intr* hacer juego.

match[2] ➤ *s (for lighting)* fósforo.

mate ➤ *s* compañero; *(spouse)* cónyuge *mf* ➤ *intr (to breed)* aparearse.

material ➤ *s* material *m*; *(cloth)* tela ➤ *adj* material; *(noticeable)* notable.

maternal ➤ *adj* maternal; *(of one's mother)* materno.

maternity ➤ *s* maternidad *f*.

math ➤ *s* matemática(s).

mathematics ➤ *ssg* matemática(s).

matinée ➤ *s* matinée *f.*

matrimonial ➤ *adj* matrimonial.

matrimony ➤ *s* matrimonio.

matter ➤ *s* materia; *(concern)* cuestión *f* ■ as a m. of fact de hecho • for that m. en cuanto a eso • what's the m.? ¿qué pasa? ➤ *intr* importar.

mattress ➤ *s* colchón *m.*

mature ➤ *adj* maduro ➤ *tr & intr* madurar.

maturity ➤ *s* madurez *f.*

maximum ➤ *adj & s* máximo.

may ➤ *aux (permission)* poder; *(possibility)* ser posible (que) ■ come what m. pase lo que pase • it m. rain es posible que llueva • m. I? ¿me permite?

May ➤ *s* mayo.

maybe ➤ *adj (perhaps)* quizá(s); *(possibly)* tal vez.

mayonnaise ➤ *s* mayonesa.

mayor ➤ *s* alcalde *m*, alcaldesa.

maze ➤ *s* laberinto.

me ➤ *pron* me; *(after preposition)* mí ■ with m. conmigo.

meadow ➤ *s* pradera.

meal[1] ➤ *s (ground grain)* harina.

meal[2] ➤ *s* comida.

mean[1]◇ ➤ *tr (to signify)* querer decir; *(to intend)* tener la intención de; *(to allude to)* referirse a; *(to entail)* implicar ➤ *intr* ■ to m. well tener buenas intenciones.

mean[2] ➤ *adj (stingy)* tacaño; *(malicious)* mal intencionado.

mean[3] ➤ *s* punto medio; MAT. *(average)* promedio ■ *pl* medios • by m. of por medio de • by no m. de ningún modo.

meaning ➤ *s* sentido; *(intent)* significado.

meaningful ➤ *adj* significativo.

meaningless ➤ *adj* insignificante; *(senseless)* sin sentido.

meanwhile *o* **meantime** ➤ *adv* entretanto, mientras tanto.

measure ➤ *s* medida ■ beyond m. sin límite • for good m. por añadidura ➤ *tr* medir.

measurement ➤ *s* medición *f;* *(unit)* medida.

meat ➤ *s* carne *f.*

meatless ➤ *adj* sin carne.

mechanic ➤ *s* mecánico/a ■ *pl* mecánica.

mechanical ➤ *adj* mecánico.

mechanism ➤ *s* mecanismo.

medal ➤ *s* medalla.

medalist ➤ *s* DEP. ganador/a.

media ➤ *spl* medios.

medical ➤ *adj* médico.

medication ➤ *s* medicamento.

medicine ➤ *s* medicina.

medieval ➤ *adj* medieval.

mediocre ➤ *adj* mediocre.

meditate ➤ *tr & intr* meditar.

medium ➤ *s* medio ➤ *adj* mediano.

meet◇ ➤ *tr (to encounter)* con; *(an arrival)* recibir; *(to be introduced)* conocer; *(to confer with)* entrevistarse con; *(to confront)* hacer frente a; *(requirements)* satisfacer ➤ *intr* encontrarse, verse; *(to join)* unirse; *(to assemble)* reunirse ➤ DEP. encuentro.

meeting ➤ *s* reunión *f;* *(rally)* mitin *m.*

melody ➤ *s* melodía.

melon ➤ *s* melón *m.*

melt ➤ *tr & intr* derretir(se); *(to dissolve)* disolver(se); FIG. ablandar(se).

member ➤ *s* miembro.

membrane ➤ *s* membrana.

memo ➤ *s* memorándum *m.*

memorial ➤ *s & adj (monument)* conmemorativo.

memory ➤ *s* memoria; *(recollection)* recuerdo.

men ➤ *pl de* **man.**

mend ➤ *tr* remendar ➤ *intr* curar, sanar.

menswear ➤ *s* ropa para hombres.

mental ➤ *adj* mental; *(hospital)* psiquiátrico.

mentality ➤ *s* mentalidad *f.*

mention ➤ *tr* mencionar ➤ *s* mención *f.*

menu ➤ *s* menú *m*, carta.

merchandise ➤ *s* mercancía.

merchant ➤ *s* comerciante *mf;* *(shopkeeper)* tendero/a.

mercy ➤ *s* clemencia; *(compassion)* misericordia.

mere ➤ *adj (simple)* puro; *(no more than)* no más que.

merely ➤ *adv* simplemente; *(no more*

than) no más que.
merge ➤ *tr & intr* unir(se); COM. fusionar(se).
merger ➤ *s* unión *f*; COM. fusión *f*.
meridian ➤ *s* meridiano.
merit ➤ mérito ➤ *tr & intr* merecer.
merry ➤ *adj* alegre ■ M. Christmas Feliz Navidad.
mesh ➤ *s* TEJ. malla ➤ *intr* enredarse; *(to harmonize)* encajar; MEC. engranar.
mess ➤ *s* desorden *m*; *(dirty condition)* asquerosidad *f*; *(difficulty)* lío ■ m. hall comedor ➤ *tr* ■ to m. up *o* make a m. of desarreglar; *(to spoil)* echar a perder ➤ *intr* ■ to m. around FAM. entretenerse • to m. with FAM. molestar.
message ➤ *s* mensaje *m*.
messenger ➤ *s* mensajero/a.
messy ➤ *adj* desordenado; *(slovenly)* desaseado.
metal ➤ *s* metal *m*.
metallic ➤ *adj* metálico.
meter ➤ *s* *(measurement, verse)* metro; *(device)* contador *m*.
method ➤ *s* método.
methodic(al) ➤ *adj* metódico.
meticulous ➤ *adj* meticuloso; *(overscrupulous)* minucioso.
metric ➤ *adj* métrico.
metropolis ➤ *s* metrópoli *f*.
metropolitan ➤ *adj* metropolitano.
Mexican ➤ *adj & s* Mexicano/a.
mice ➤ *pl de* mouse.
microbe ➤ *s* microbio.
microchip ➤ *s* microchip *m*.
microphone ➤ *s* micrófono.
microprocessor ➤ *s* microprocesador *m*.
microscope ➤ *s* microscopio.
microwave ➤ *s* microonda; *(oven)* (horno) microondas *m*.
mid ➤ *adj* medio ■ in mid-May a mediados de mayo.
midday ➤ *s* mediodía *m*.
middle ➤ *adj* medio; *(intermediate)* intermedio ➤ *s* medio ■ in the m. of en medio de.
middle-class ➤ *adj* de la clase media.
midnight ➤ *s* medianoche *f*.
midwife ➤ *s* comadrona.

might¹ ➤ poder, fuerzas.
might² ➤ *aux* ■ it m. rain es posible que llueva.
migrant ➤ *adj* migratorio ➤ *s* emigrante *mf*; *(worker)* trabajador/a ambulante.
migrate ➤ *intr* emigrar.
mild ➤ *adj* suave; *(climate)* templado; *(cold, cough)* leve.
mile ➤ *s* milla.
mileage ➤ *s* distancia en millas.
military ➤ *adj* militar ➤ *s* las fuerzas armadas.
milk ➤ *s* leche *f* ■ m. shake batido de leche • skim m. leche desnatada.
mill ➤ *s* molino; *(for spices, coffee)* molinillo; *(factory)* fábrica.
millimeter ➤ *s* milímetro.
million ➤ *s* millón *m*.
millionaire ➤ *s* millonario/a.
mimic ➤ *tr* remedar; *(resemble)* simular ➤ *s* imitador/a.
mind ➤ *s* mente *f* ■ to bring to m. recordar • to change one's m. cambiar de opinión • to come to m. venir a la memoria • to have in m. planear ➤ *tr* *(to heed)* prestar atención a; *(to obey)* obedecer; *(to look after)* cuidar ■ he does not m. the cold no le molesta el frío ➤ *intr* ■ never m. no importa.
mine¹ ➤ *s* mina ■ land m. mina terrestre ➤ *tr* extraer.
mine² ➤ *pron* (el) mío, (la) mía, etc.
miner ➤ *s* minero/a.
mineral ➤ *s & adj* mineral *m*.
miniature ➤ *adj & s* (en) miniatura.
minicomputer ➤ *s* minicomputadora.
minimum ➤ *s & adj* mínimo ■ m. wage salario vital.
minister ➤ *s* POL. ministro/a; RELIG. pastor/a, clérigo/a ➤ *intr* cuidar.
ministry ➤ *s* POL. ministerio; RELIG. sacerdocio.
minor ➤ *adj* menor; *(secondary)* de poca importancia ➤ *s* menor *mf* de edad.
minority ➤ *s* minoría.
mint¹ ➤ *s* casa de moneda ➤ *tr* acuñar.
mint² ➤ *s* BOT. menta, hierbabuena; *(candy)* (pastilla de) menta.
minus ➤ *prep* MAT. menos; FAM. *(with-*

out) sin ➤ *adj* MAT. negativo.

minute¹ ➤ *s* minuto; *(moment)* momento.

minute² ➤ *adj* diminuto; *(insignificant)* insignificante; *(thorough)* minucioso.

miracle ➤ *s* milagro; FIG. maravilla.

mirror ➤ *s* espejo ➤ *tr* reflejar.

misbehave ➤ *intr* portarse mal.

miscarriage ➤ *s* MED. aborto.

miscellaneous ➤ *adj* misceláneo.

mischief ➤ *s (prank)* travesura; *(perverseness)* malicia.

mischievous ➤ *adj* malicioso; *(playful)* travieso; *(troublesome)* molesto.

miser ➤ *s* avaro/a.

miserable ➤ *adj (unhappy)* desdichado; *(inadequate)* miserable.

misery ➤ *s* miseria; *(unhappiness)* desdicha.

misfortune ➤ *s* mala suerte.

misgiving ➤ *s* duda.

mishandle ➤ *tr (to botch)* manejar mal; *(to maltreat)* maltratar.

mishap ➤ *s* desgracia.

mislead ➤ *tr* descaminar; *(to deceive)* engañar.

misleading ➤ *adj* engañoso.

misplace ➤ *tr (to lose)* extraviar.

misprint ➤ *s* error *m* de imprenta.

miss¹ ➤ *tr* perder; *(not to achieve)* no conseguir; *(a person, place)* echar de menos, extrañar ■ to m. the point no comprender ➤ *intr* fallar ■ to be missing faltar ➤ *s* fallo; *(failure)* fracaso.

miss² ➤ *s* señorita.

missile ➤ *s (rock, spear)* proyectil *m*; MIL. misil *m*.

missing ➤ *adj (lost)* perdido; *(absent)* ausente; *(lacking)* que falta.

mission ➤ *s* misión *f*; DIPL. embajada.

misspell ➤ *tr* escribir mal.

mist ➤ *s* neblina.

mistake ➤ *s* error *m* ➤ *tr* interpretar *o* entender mal ■ to m. . . . for confundir . . . con.

mistaken ➤ *adj (wrong)* equivocado, errado; *(inexact)* erróneo ■ to be m. equivocarse.

Mister ➤ *s* señor *m*.

mistreat ➤ *tr* maltratar.

mistress ➤ *s (of household)* señora;

(lover) amante *f*; *(owner)* ama.

mistrust ➤ *s* desconfianza ➤ *tr & intr* desconfiar (de).

misty ➤ *adj* nebuloso; *(glass)* empañado.

misunderstand ➤ *tr* entender *o* interpretar mal.

misunderstanding ➤ *s* malentendido; *(disagreement)* desacuerdo.

misuse ➤ *s* mal empleo; *(mistreatment)* maltrato ➤ *tr* emplear mal; *(to mistreat)* maltratar.

mitten ➤ *s* mitón *m*, manopla.

mix ➤ *tr* mezclar; *(a drink)* preparar ■ to m. up *(to confuse)* confundir; *(to jumble)* mezclar ➤ *intr* mezclarse; *(to go together)* pegar ➤ *s* mezcla.

mixed ➤ *adj* mezclado; *(conflicting)* contradictorio; *(composite)* mixto.

mixed-up ➤ *adj* FAM. confundido, que no sabe lo que quiere.

mixer ➤ *s (appliance)* batidora.

mixture ➤ *s* mezcla.

mix-up ➤ *s* confusión *f*, lío.

moat ➤ *s* foso (de un castillo).

mob ➤ *s* turba.

mobile ➤ *adj* móvil.

mobility ➤ *s* movilidad *f*.

mock ➤ *tr* mofarse de ➤ *adj* simulado.

mockingbird ➤ *s* sinsonte *m*.

model ➤ *s & adj* modelo *mf*.

moderate ➤ *adj* moderado; *(price)* módico ➤ *s* moderado/a.

moderation ➤ *s* moderación *f*.

modern ➤ *adj & s* moderno.

modernize ➤ *tr & intr* modernizar(se).

modest ➤ *adj* modesto; *(reserved)* recatado; *(in price)* módico.

modesty ➤ *s* modestia; *(decency)* pudor *m*; *(in price)* modicidad *f*.

modification ➤ *s* modificación *f*.

modify ➤ *tr* modificar.

moist ➤ *adj* húmedo.

moisten ➤ *tr & intr* humedecer(se).

moisture ➤ *s* humedad *f*.

mold¹ ➤ *s* molde *m* ➤ *tr* moldear.

mold² BIOL. ➤ *s* moho.

moldy ➤ *adj* mohoso; *(musty)* enmohecido.

mole¹ ➤ *s* ANAT. lunar *m*.

mole² ➤ *s* ZOOL. topo.

mom ➤ *s* FAM. mamá.

moment ➤ *s* momento.

monarch ➤ *s* monarca *mf.*

monarchy ➤ *s* monarquía.

monastery ➤ *s* monasterio.

Monday ➤ *s* lunes *m.*

monetary ➤ *adj* monetario.

money ➤ *s* dinero; *(currency)* moneda ■ m. order giro postal.

monitor ➤ *s* monitor/a; COMPUT., TEC. monitor *m* ➤ *tr (signal, quality)* comprobar.

monk ➤ *s* monje *m.*

monkey ➤ *s* mono.

monologue ➤ *s* monólogo.

monopolize ➤ *tr* monopolizar.

monopoly ➤ *s* monopolio.

monorail ➤ *s* monocarril *m.*

monotonous ➤ *adj* monótono.

monotony ➤ *s* monotonía.

monster ➤ *s* monstruo.

month ➤ *s* mes *m.*

monthly ➤ *adj* mensual ➤ *adv* mensualmente.

monument ➤ *s* monumento.

mood ➤ *s* humor *m* ■ to be in the m. for tener ganas de.

moody ➤ *adj* malhumorado.

moon ➤ *s* luna.

moor¹ ➤ *tr* MARÍT. amarrar.

moor² ➤ *s* GEOG. terreno pantanoso.

mooring ➤ *s (cable)* amarra.

moose ➤ *s* alce.

mop ➤ *s* fregona; *(of hair)* greña ➤ *tr* fregar.

moped ➤ *s* ciclomotor *m.*

moral ➤ *adj* moral ➤ *s* moraleja ■ *pl* principios morales.

morale ➤ *s* moral *f.*

more ➤ *adj* más; *(greater in quantity)* superior ➤ *s* más ■ the m. . . . the m. . . . cuanto más . . . más . . . ➤ *pron* más ➤ *adv* más ■ m. and m. cada vez más • m. or less más o menos.

moreover ➤ *adv* además.

morning ➤ *s* mañana ■ good m.! ¡buenos días! • in the m. por la mañana.

mortal ➤ *adj & s* mortal *mf.*

mortality ➤ *s* mortalidad *f.*

mortgage ➤ *s* hipoteca ➤ *tr* hipotecar.

mosaic ➤ *s* mosaico.

mosque ➤ *s* mezquita.

mosquito ➤ *s* mosquito ■ m. net mosquitero, toldillo.

moss ➤ *s* musgo.

most ➤ *adj (in quantity)* más . . . que todos los demás; *(in measure)* mayor; *(almost all)* la mayoría de ➤ *s* la mayor parte; *(the majority)* la mayoría ■ at (the) m. a lo sumo • to make the m. of aprovechar al máximo ➤ *s* la mayor parte ➤ *adv* más . . . que todos los demás; *(superlative)* más; *(very)* muy ■ m. of all sobre todo.

mostly ➤ *adv* en su mayor parte.

motel ➤ *s* motel *m.*

moth ➤ *s* mariposa nocturna; *(clothes moth)* polilla.

mother ➤ *s* madre *f.*

motherhood ➤ *s* maternidad *f.*

mother-in-law ➤ *s* suegra.

motion ➤ *s* movimiento; *(gesture)* ademán *m; (proposal)* moción *f* ■ m. picture película • m. sickness mareo ➤ *intr* hacer señas.

motivation ➤ *s* motivación *f.*

motive ➤ *s* motivo; DER. móvil *m.*

motor ➤ *s* motor *m.*

motorboat lancha motora.

motorcycle ➤ *s* motocicleta, moto *f.*

motorist ➤ *s* automovilista *mf.*

mound ➤ *s* montículo; *(heap)* montón *m.*

mount¹ ➤ *tr* subir (a); *(a horse)* montar ➤ *s* montura; *(base)* soporte *m.*

mount² ➤ *s (hill)* monte *m.*

mountain ➤ *s* montaña ■ m. range cordillera.

mountaineer ➤ *s* montañero/a.

mountainous ➤ *adj* montañoso.

mourn ➤ *intr & tr* llorar; *(a death)* lamentar(se).

mourning ➤ *s* duelo; *(period)* luto.

mouse ➤ *s* ZOOL., COMPUT. ratón *m.*

mousepad ➤ *s* alfombrilla de ratón.

mouth ➤ *s* boca.

mouthwash ➤ *s* enjuague *m* bucal.

move ➤ *intr* moverse; *(to change position)* cambiar de postura; *(to relocate)* mudarse; *(in a game)* jugar ■ to m. away alejarse • to m. in instalarse ➤ *tr* mover; *(to reposition)* trasladar; *(to prompt)* impulsar ➤ s movimiento; *(change of residence)* mudanza; *(of a piece)* jugada; *(player's turn)* turno; *(step)* paso ■ on the m. andando de acá para allá; *(active)* activo.

movement ➤ s movimiento.

mover ➤ s persona que hace mudanzas ■ pl agencia de mudanzas.

movie ➤ s película.

moving ➤ adj móvil; *(in motion)* en marcha; *(touching)* conmovedor.

mow◇ ➤ tr segar.

mower ➤ s segador/a; *(machine)* segadora; *(for lawn)* cortacéspedes m.

Mr. ➤ s Sr.

Mrs. ➤ s Sra.

much ➤ adj mucho ■ as m. . . . as tanto . . . como • too m. demasiado ➤ s mucho ■ as m. again otro tanto • as m. as tanto como • not so m. as ni siquiera • so m. the better tanto mejor • to make m. of dar mucha importancia a ➤ adv mucho ■ however m. por mucho que • how m.? ¿cuánto?

mud ➤ s barro.

muddle ➤ tr *(to befuddle)* atontar; *(to bungle)* chapucear.

muddy ➤ adj fangoso; *(liquid)* turbio ➤ tr enfangar; *(liquid)* enturbiar.

mug ➤ s *(cup)* jarra.

mugger ➤ s asaltante mf.

mugging ➤ s asalto (con intento de robo).

muggy ➤ adj bochornoso.

mule ➤ s mulo.

multimedia ➤ adj multimedia.

multiple ➤ adj múltiple; MAT. múltiplo ➤ s múltiplo.

multiplication ➤ s multiplicación f.

multiply ➤ tr & intr multiplicar(se).

mumble ➤ tr mascullar ➤ intr balbucir ➤ s refunfuño.

mummy ➤ s *(corpse)* momia.

mumps ➤ spl paperas f.

mural ➤ s pintura mural.

murder ➤ s asesinato ➤ tr asesinar.

murderer ➤ s asesino/a.

murmur ➤ s murmullo; MED. soplo cardíaco ➤ tr & intr murmurar.

muscle ➤ s ANAT. músculo.

muscular ➤ adj muscular; *(strong)* musculoso.

museum ➤ s museo.

mushroom ➤ s BOT. hongo; CUL. champiñón m ➤ intr crecer rápidamente.

music ➤ s música.

musical ➤ adj de música; *(like music)* musical ➤ s comedia musical.

musician ➤ s músico/a.

mussel ➤ s mejillón m.

must ➤ aux deber, tener que; *(indicating probability)* deber de.

mustache ➤ s bigote(s) m.

mustard ➤ s mostaza.

musty ➤ adj mohoso.

mute ➤ adj & s mudo.

mutter ➤ intr & tr murmurar.

mutual ➤ adj mutuo ■ m. fund fondo mutualista (de inversión).

muzzle ➤ s *(snout)* hocico; *(restraint)* bozal m; *(gun)* boca ➤ tr abozalar; *(to restrain)* amordazar.

my ➤ adj pos mi, mis.

myself ➤ pron yo mismo; *(reflexive)* me; *(after preposition)* mí (mismo).

mysterious ➤ adj misterioso.

mystery ➤ s misterio; LIT. novela policíaca.

myth ➤ s mito.

mythology ➤ s mitología.

N

nail ➤ s clavo; *(finger, toe)* uña ➤ tr clavar.

naive ➤ adj cándido, ingenuo.

naked ➤ adj desnudo.

name ➤ s nombre m; *(surname)* apellido; *(reputation)* fama ■ full n. nombre y apellido • my n. is me llamo ➤ tr llamar; *(to mention)* nombrar.

namely ➤ adv es decir, a saber.

nanny ➤ s niñera.

nap ➤ s siesta ➤ intr dormir la siesta.

napkin ➤ s servilleta.

narrow ➤ adj angosto, estrecho ➤ tr & intr estrechar(se).

nasal ➤ adj nasal.

nasty ➤ adj *(filthy)* sucio; *(malicious)* malicioso; *(cough, cold)* molesto.

nation ➤ s nación f.

national ➤ *adj & s* nacional.
nationality ➤ *s* nacionalidad *f*.
native ➤ *adj* nativo, indígeno; *(country, town)* natal; *(language)* materno; *(product)* del país ➤ *s* nativo/a, indígena *mf*.
natural ➤ *adj* natural; *(one's own)* propio ■ n. **resource** recurso natural.
naturally ➤ *adv* naturalmente; *(by nature)* por naturaleza; *(of course)* por supuesto, claro.
nature ➤ *s* (la) naturaleza; *(temperament)* natural *m*.
naughty ➤ *adj* travieso, desobediente.
nausea ➤ *s* náusea; *(disgust)* asco.
nauseate ➤ *tr* dar náuseas a; *(to disgust)* dar asco a.
naval ➤ *adj* naval.
navel ➤ *s* ombligo.
navigate ➤ *intr & tr* navegar.
navigation ➤ *s* navegación *f*.
navy ➤ *s* marina, flota; *(color)* azul marino ■ the N. la marina, la armada.
near ➤ *adv* cerca, próximo; *(almost)* casi; *(closely related)* íntimo, cercano ■ to come n. acercarse ➤ *adj* próximo; *(relation)* allegado; *(direct)* directo, corto ➤ *prep (close to)* cerca de; *(almost)* casi ➤ *tr & intr* acercarse (a).
nearby ➤ *adj* cercano, próximo ➤ *adv* cerca.
nearly ➤ *adv* casi.
nearsighted ➤ *adj* miope.
neat ➤ *adj (orderly)* ordenado; *(work)* esmerado, bien hecho; *(writing)* claro.
necessary ➤ *adj* necesario.
necessity ➤ *s* necesidad *f*.
neck ➤ *s* cuello; *(of animals)* pescuezo.
necklace ➤ *s* collar *m*.
necktie ➤ *s* corbata.
nectarine ➤ *s* griñón *m*, pelón *m*.
need ➤ *s* necesidad *f*; *(trouble)* apuro ■ if n. be si fuera necesario • to be in n. of necesitar ➤ *tr* necesitar ➤ *intr* ■ to n. to *(to have to)* deber, tener que; *(to be necessary)* ser necesario.
needle ➤ *s* aguja.
needless ➤ *adj* innecesario ■ n. to say huelga decir que.
negative ➤ *adj* negativo ➤ *s* negativa; GRAM. negación *f*; FOTOG. negativo.

neglect ➤ *tr* descuidar ■ to n. to olvidarse de ➤ *s* descuido, negligencia.
negligence ➤ *s* negligencia.
negligent ➤ *adj* negligente, descuidado.
negotiate ➤ *intr* negociar.
negotiation ➤ *s* negociación *f*.
neigh ➤ *intr* relinchar.
neighbor ➤ *s* vecino/a.
neighborhood ➤ *s* barrio; *(people)* vecindario.
neighboring ➤ *adj* vecino.
neither ➤ *adj* ninguno (de los dos) ➤ *pron* ninguno (de dos), ni uno ni otro ➤ *conj & adv* (ni . . .) tampoco ■ n. . . . nor ni . . . ni.
nephew ➤ *s* sobrino.
nerve ➤ *s* nervio; *(courage)* valor *m* ■ to get on one's nerves crispar los nervios a uno • to lose one's n. acobardarse ■ *pl* nerviosidad.
nervous ➤ *adj* nervioso; *(high-strung)* irritable, excitable.
nest ➤ *s* nido ➤ *intr* anidar.
net[1] ➤ *s* red *f* ■ N. Red, Internet.
net[2] ➤ *adj (after deductions)* neto.
netting ➤ *s* red *f*.
network ➤ *s* red *f*.
neutral ➤ *adj* neutral; FÍS., QUÍM. neutro ➤ *s* neutral *mf*; AUTO. punto muerto.
never ➤ *adv* nunca, jamás ■ n. **again** nunca más • n. **ever** nunca jamás.
nevertheless ➤ *adv* sin embargo, no obstante.
new ➤ *adj* nuevo.
newborn ➤ *adj & s* (niño/a) recién nacido/a.
newcomer ➤ *s* recién llegado/a.
news ➤ *s* noticia; *(current events)* noticias, actualidades *f*; *(broadcast)* noticiario.
newscast ➤ *s* noticiario.
newscaster ➤ *s* locutor/a.
newsletter ➤ *s* hoja informativa.
newspaper ➤ *s* periódico, diario.
next ➤ *adj (in time)* próximo; *(adjacent)* de al lado; *(following)* siguiente ➤ *adv* después, luego ■ n. **door** al lado • n. **to** *(beside)* junto a; *(almost)* casi.
nibble ➤ *tr* mordiscar ➤ *s* mordisco.
Nicaraguan ➤ *adj & s* nicaragüense *mf*.
nice ➤ *adj (friendly)* amable, bueno;

(pleasant) agradable; *(dress, looks)* bonito, lindo ■ to be n. to ser amable con • to have a n. time pasarlo bien.

nickel ➤ s QUÍM. níquel m; *(U.S. coin)* moneda de cinco centavos.

nickname ➤ s apodo.

niece ➤ s sobrina.

night ➤ s noche f; *(nightfall)* anochecer m ■ at o by n. de noche • good n.! ¡buenas noches! • last n. anoche • n. school escuela nocturna.

nightclub ➤ s club nocturno.

nightgown ➤ s camisa de dormir, camisón m.

nightingale ➤ s ruiseñor m.

nightmare ➤ s pesadilla.

nighttime ➤ s noche f.

nine ➤ s & adj nueve m ■ n. hundred novecientos • n. o'clock las nueve.

nineteen ➤ s & adj diecinueve m.

ninety ➤ s & adj noventa.

ninth ➤ s & adj noveno.

nip ➤ tr *(to pinch)* pellizcar; *(to bite)* morder.

nipple ➤ s pezón m; *(on bottle)* tetilla.

nitrogen ➤ s nitrógeno.

no ➤ adv no ■ no longer ya no ➤ adj no ■ by no means de ninguna manera • no smoking prohibido fumar • no way! ¡nunca!, ¡jamás! • to have no hope no tener ninguna esperanza.

nobility ➤ s nobleza.

noble ➤ adj & s noble mf.

nobody ➤ pron nadie ➤ s don nadie m.

nod ➤ intr *(sleepily)* dar cabezadas; *(in agreement)* asentir con la cabeza; *(in greeting)* saludar con la cabeza ■ to n. off dormirse ➤ tr inclinar (la cabeza) ➤ s inclinación f de la cabeza.

noise ➤ s ruido.

noisy ➤ adj ruidoso.

nominate ➤ tr nombrar.

nominee ➤ s candidato/a.

none ➤ pron nadie, ninguno.

nonetheless ➤ adv sin embargo.

nonfat ➤ adj sin grasa.

nonfiction ➤ s literatura no ficción.

nonnegotiable ➤ adj no negociable.

nonresident ➤ adj & s no residente mf, transeúnte mf.

nonsense ➤ s disparate(s) m ■ n.! ton-

terías. • to talk n. decir tonterías.

nonstop ➤ adv sin parar ➤ adj *(train)* directo; *(plane)* sin escalas.

nontransferable ➤ adj intransferible.

noodle ➤ s CUL. tallarín m, fideo.

noon ➤ s mediodía m.

nor ➤ conj ni ■ neither rain n. snow ni lluvia ni nieve.

normal ➤ adj normal.

north ➤ s norte m ➤ adj del norte ➤ adv al norte, hacia el norte.

North America ➤ s Norteamérica.

North American ➤ adj & s norteamericano/a.

northeast ➤ adj & s (del) nordeste m.

northeastern ➤ adj del nordeste.

northern ➤ adj septentrional, del norte ■ n. lights aurora boreal.

northerner ➤ s norteño/a.

North Pole ➤ s Polo Norte.

northwest ➤ adj & s (del) noroeste m.

northwestern ➤ adj del noroeste.

nose ➤ s nariz f ■ on the n. exacto • to blow one's n. sonarse la nariz.

nosebleed ➤ s hemorragia nasal.

nostril ➤ s ventana ■ pl narices.

nosy ➤ adj entrometido.

not ➤ adv no ■ n. even ni siquiera • n. yet ya no, todavía no.

notable ➤ adj & s notable mf.

note ➤ s nota; FIN. billete m ■ to make a n. of tomar nota de ■ pl notas, apuntes • to compare n. cambiar impresiones ➤ tr *(to notice)* notar, advertir; *(to mention)* señalar.

notebook ➤ s cuaderno.

notepaper ➤ s papel m de escribir.

nothing ➤ pron nada ■ for n. *(for free)* por nada; *(in vain)* para nada • n. but sólo • to have n. to do with no tener nada que ver con • s nada ■ to believe in n. no creer en nada.

notice ➤ s atención f; *(warning)* aviso; *(announcement)* anuncio; *(sign)* letrero ■ at a moment's n. sin previo aviso • to give n. *(to resign)* renunciar ➤ tr darse cuenta de.

noticeable ➤ adj evidente.

notification ➤ s notificación f, aviso.

notify ➤ tr notificar, avisar.

notion ➤ s noción f, idea.

noun ➤ s sustantivo, nombre m.

nourish ➤ tr nutrir, alimentar.

novel ➤ s novela ➤ adj nuevo, original.

novelist ➤ s novelista mf.

novelty ➤ s novedad f.

November ➤ s noviembre m.

now ➤ adv ahora; (immediately) ahora mismo ■ **right n.!** ¡ahora mismo! ➤ conj ■ n. that ya que ➤ s ■ by n. ya.

nowadays ➤ adv hoy (en) día.

nowhere ➤ adv en, por, o a ninguna parte ■ n. near muy lejos de ➤ s ■ out of n. de la nada.

nozzle ➤ s boquilla.

nuclear ➤ adj nuclear.

nude ➤ s & adj desnudo.

nuisance ➤ s (person) pesado/a; (thing) fastidio, molestia.

numb ➤ adj entumecido ➤ tr entumecer.

number ➤ s número ■ a n. of varios ■ pl (many) muchos; MAT. números ➤ tr numerar.

numeral ➤ s número.

numerous ➤ adj numeroso.

nun ➤ s monja, religiosa.

nurse ➤ s enfermero/a ➤ tr (infant) criar; (patient) cuidar.

nursery ➤ s cuarto de los niños; (center) guardería infantil; AGR. vivero ■ n. school escuela de párvulos.

nut ➤ s nuez f; MEC. (for bolts) tuerca; JER. (crazy person) chiflado/a.

nutcracker ➤ s cascanueces m.

nutmeg ➤ s nuez moscada.

nutrition ➤ s nutrición f.

nylon ➤ s nilón m ■ pl medias de nilón.

O

oak ➤ s roble m.

oar ➤ s remo.

oath ➤ s juramento.

oatmeal CUL. gachas de avena.

obedience ➤ s obediencia.

obedient ➤ adj obediente.

obese ➤ adj obeso.

obey ➤ tr & intr obedecer.

object¹ ➤ intr hacer objeciones; (to disapprove) oponerse (to a).

object² ➤ s objeto; (purpose) propósito; (goal) fin m; GRAM. complemento.

objection ➤ s objeción f, reparo.

objective ➤ adj & s objetivo.

obligation ➤ s obligación f.

oblige ➤ tr obligar; (to do a favor for) hacer un favor a ■ **to be obliged to** verse obligado a.

obliging ➤ adj complaciente.

oblique ➤ adj oblicuo.

oblong ➤ adj oblongo, rectangular.

obscene ➤ adj obsceno.

obscure ➤ adj oscuro; (meaning) oculto ➤ tr ocultar; (view) tapar.

observant ➤ adj observador.

observation ➤ s observación f.

observatory ➤ s observatorio.

observe ➤ tr observar; (to say) decir.

observer ➤ s observador/a.

obsession ➤ s obsesión f.

obstacle ➤ s obstáculo.

obstinate ➤ adj obstinado.

obstruct ➤ tr obstruir.

obtain ➤ tr obtener.

obvious ➤ adj obvio, patente.

obviously ➤ adv evidentemente.

occasion ➤ s ocasión f; (event) acontecimiento ■ on o. ocasionalmente.

occasional ➤ adj ocasional.

occupant ➤ s (tenant) inquilino/a; (guest) huésped mf; (passenger) pasajero/a.

occupation ➤ s ocupación f.

occupy ➤ tr (space) ocupar; (time) emplear ■ **to o. oneself with** entretenerse con.

occur ➤ intr ocurrir, suceder; (to be found) encontrarse.

occurrence ➤ s (incident) suceso.

ocean ➤ s océano.

o'clock ➤ adv ■ one o. la una ■ it's ten o. son las diez.

October ➤ s octubre m.

octopus ➤ s pulpo.

odd ➤ adj (unusual) raro, extraño; (strange) curioso; MAT. impar, non ■ o. jobs chapuces ■ o. or even? ¿pares o nones? ● thirty-o. treinta y pico.

odds ➤ spl ventaja; (chances) probabilidades f ■ o. and ends retazos ● the o. are against it no es muy probable.

odor ➤ s olor m.

of ➤ prep de ■ a friend of mine un

amigo mío • **all of them** todos ellos.

off ➤ *adv* lejos, a distancia ■ **o. and on** de vez en cuando • **ten per cent** o. diez por ciento de descuento ➤ *adj (lights)* apagado; *(not operating)* desconectado; *(canceled)* cancelado ■ **in the o. position** en posición de cerrado • **o. chance** posibilidad remota ➤ *prep (from)* de; *(near)* frente a; *(away from)* lejos de; *(down from)* desde, por.

offend ➤ *tr* ofender.

offender ➤ *s* ofensor/a; *(criminal)* infractor/a.

offense ➤ *s* ofensa; *(crime)* delito ■ **no o. (intended)** sin intención de ofender • **to take o. at** ofenderse por.

offensive ➤ *adj* ofensivo ➤ *s* ofensiva.

offer ➤ *tr* ofrecer; *(to propose)* proponer; *(to provide)* proporcionar; *(to present)* presentar ➤ *s* oferta.

offhand ➤ *adv* sin pensarlo ➤ *adj* improvisado; *(manner)* desenvuelto.

office ➤ *s* oficina.

officer ➤ *s* oficial *mf*; *(police)* agente *mf* de policía.

official ➤ *adj* oficial ➤ *s* oficial *mf*, funcionario/a.

often ➤ *adv* frecuentemente, a menudo ■ **every so o.** alguna que otra vez • **not very o.** pocas veces.

oil ➤ *s* aceite *m*; *(fuel)* petróleo; *(lubricant)* aceite lubricante ➤ *tr* aceitar, lubricar.

ointment ➤ *s* ungüento, pomada.

O.K. *o* **okay** ➤ *s* autorización *f* ➤ *tr* autorizar ➤ *interj* ¡muy bien!

old ➤ *adj* viejo; *(elderly)* mayor, anciano; *(ancient, former)* antiguo ■ **older mayor** • **oldest** (el, la) mayor.

old-fashioned ➤ *adj* anticuado; *(person)* chapado a la antigua.

olive ➤ *s* oliva, aceituna ■ **o. tree** olivo.

Olympic ➤ *adj* olímpico ■ **Olympics** *spl* juegos olímpicos.

omelet(te) ➤ *s* tortilla.

omit ➤ *tr* omitir.

on ➤ *prep (general)* en; *(on top of)* sobre ➤ *adv* ■ **on and off** de vez en cuando • **on and on** sin parar ➤ *adj (appliance, lights, gas)* encendido; *(faucet)* abierto; *(brakes, alarms)* puesto.

once ➤ *adv (one time)* una vez; *(formerly)* en otro tiempo, antes ■ **at o.** inmediatamente; *(at the same time)* al mismo tiempo • **o. again** otra vez • **o. and for all** de una vez para siempre • **o. in a while** de vez en cuando ➤ *s* una vez ■ **for o.** una vez siquiera.

one ➤ *adj* un, uno ➤ *s* uno; *(unit)* unidad *f* ■ **o. and all** todos • **o. never knows** nunca se sabe • **o. o'clock** la una ➤ *pron* uno ■ **that o.** aquél • **this o.** éste • **which o.?** ¿cuál?

oneself ➤ *pron* sí (mismo), uno (mismo); *(reflexively)* se ■ **by o. solo** • **to be o.** comportarse con naturalidad • **to wash o.** lavarse.

one-way ➤ *adj (street)* de sentido único; *(ticket)* de ida solamente.

onion ➤ *s* cebolla.

online ➤ *adj* en línea, conectado.

onlooker ➤ *s* espectador/a.

only ➤ *adj (sole)* único, solo ➤ *adv (merely)* sólo; *(solely)* únicamente ■ **not o. . . . but also** no sólo . . . sino también.

onward(s) ➤ *adv* hacia adelante.

opaque ➤ *adj* opaco.

open ➤ *adj* abierto; *(uncovered)* descubierto; *(uncapped)* destapado ■ **o. for business** abierto al público • **o. house** recepción general ➤ *tr* abrir; *(to uncover)* destapar ➤ *intr* abrirse; *(to come undone)* desatarse; TEAT. estrenarse ➤ *s* ■ **in the o.** al aire libre • **to bring, come into the o.** sacar, salir a la luz.

open-air ➤ *adj* al aire libre.

opener ➤ *s* abridor *m*.

opening ➤ *s* abertura, orificio; *(breach)* grieta; *(clearing)* claro; *(of a store)* inauguración *f*; *(job)* puesto.

opera ➤ *s* ópera.

operate ➤ *intr* funcionar; *(to have an effect)* actuar; CIR., MIL. operar ➤ *tr (to drive)* manejar; *(tool)* usar; *(appliance)* accionar; *(business)* manejar.

operation ➤ *s* operación *f*; *(condition)* funcionamiento.

operative ➤ *adj* operativo; *(law)* en vigor; MED. operatorio.

operator ➤ *s (of a machine)* operario;

TEL. telefonista *mf*; *(of a vehicle)* conductor/a.
opinion ➤ *s* opinión *f.*
opponent ➤ *s* adversario/a.
opportunity ➤ *s* oportunidad *f.*
oppose ➤ *tr* oponerse a.
opposite ➤ *adj* opuesto; *(direction)* contrario; *(across from)* de enfrente; *(opinions)* contrario ■ **on the o. side of** del otro lado de ➤ *s* contrario ➤ *adv* enfrente ➤ *prep* enfrente de, frente a.
opposition ➤ *s* oposición *f; (resistance)* resistencia ■ **to be in o.** to estar en contra de.
oppress ➤ *tr* oprimir; FIG. agobiar.
opt ➤ *intr* optar *(for, to* por).
oppression ➤ *s* opresión *f.*
optician ➤ *s* óptico/a.
optimist ➤ *s* optimista *mf.*
optimistic ➤ *adj* optimista ■ **to feel o.** tener optimismo.
option ➤ *s* opción *f.*
optional ➤ *adj* opcional.
optometrist ➤ *s* optómetra *mf.*
or ➤ *conj* o, u; *(after negative)* ni.
oral ➤ *adj* oral ➤ *s* examen *m* oral.
orange ➤ *s* naranja; *(tree)* naranjo ➤ *adj* anaranjado.
orbit ➤ *s* órbita ➤ *tr* girar alrededor de ➤ *intr* estar en órbita.
orchard ➤ *s* huerto.
orchestra ➤ *s* orquesta.
ordeal ➤ *s* prueba dura.
order ➤ *s* orden *m;* COM. pedido; *(organization)* orden *f* ■ **out of o.** descompuesto ➤ *tr (to command, arrange)* ordenar; *(to request)* pedir ➤ *intr (command)* dar una orden; *(request)* hacer un pedido.
ordinary ➤ *adj* ordinario; *(plain)* corriente, cualquiera; *(average)* medio ■ **out of the o.** fuera de lo común.
ore ➤ *s* mineral *m,* mena.
oregano ➤ *s* orégano.
organ ➤ *s* órgano; *(agency)* organismo.
organic ➤ *adj* orgánico.
organism ➤ *s* organismo.
organization ➤ *s* organización *f.*
organize ➤ *tr & intr* organizar(se).
organizer ➤ *s* organizador/a.
Oriental ➤ *adj & s* oriental *mf.*

origin ➤ *s* origen *m.*
original ➤ *adj & s* original *m.*
originality ➤ *s* originalidad *f.*
ornament ➤ *s* ornamento.
orphan ➤ *s & adj* huérfano/a.
orphanage ➤ *s* orfanato, orfelinato.
ostrich ➤ *s* avestruz *m.*
other ➤ *adj* otro ➤ *s* otro ■ **no o.** ningún otro ➤ *pron* otro ➤ *adv* ■ **o. than** *(differently)* de otro modo; *(anything but)* otra cosa que.
otherwise ➤ *adv (differently)* de otro modo; *(under other circumstances)* de lo contrario, si no; *(in other respects)* por lo demás, a no ser por eso.
ought ➤ *aux (to be obliged)* deber; *(to be wise)* convenir; *(to be likely)* deber de.
ounce ➤ *s* onza.
our ➤ *adj* nuestro, nuestra, etc.
ours ➤ *pron* (el) nuestro, (la) nuestra, etc.
ourselves ➤ *pron* nos ■ **we did it o.** lo hicimos nosotros mismos.
oust ➤ *tr* expulsar.
ouster ➤ *s* expulsión *f.*
out ➤ *adv (away from)* fuera; *(outside)* afuera ■ **all o.** con tesón • **o. and o.** completamente • **to be o.** *(not at home)* no estar en casa; *(sun, moon)* haber salido; *(eliminated)* quedar excluido ➤ *adj* exterior; *(absent)* ausente; *(used up)* agotado; *(extinguished)* apagado; *(not in fashion)* fuera de moda ➤ *prep (through)* por; *(beyond)* fuera de, al otro lado de ■ **o. of** de • **o. of curiosity** por curiosidad • **o. of money** sin dinero • **three o. of four times** tres veces de cada cuatro.
outbreak ➤ *s* brote *m.*
outburst ➤ *s* arranque *m,* estallido.
outcome ➤ *s* resultado, consecuencia.
outdated ➤ *adj* obsoleto, anticuado.
outdo ➤ *tr* superar.
outdoor ➤ *adj* al aire libre.
outdoors ➤ *adv* al aire libre; *(outside)* (a)fuera ➤ *s* el aire libre.
outer ➤ *adj* exterior, externo.
outfit ➤ *s (clothing)* conjunto; *(business)* empresa ➤ *tr* equipar.
outgoing ➤ *adj* sociable.

outing ➤ s excursión f.

outlast ➤ tr durar más que.

outlet ➤ s salida; *(socket)* tomacorriente m; *(drain)* desagüe m; *(store)* distribuidor m.

outline ➤ s *(contour)* contorno; *(profile)* perfil m; *(shape)* silueta; *(summary)* resumen.

outlook ➤ s punto de vista; *(attitude)* actitud f; *(prospect)* posibilidades f.

outnumber ➤ tr superar en número.

outpatient ➤ s paciente externo/a.

output ➤ s producción f; *(yield)* rendimiento; COMPUT. salida ➤ tr COMPUT. imprimir.

outright ➤ adv *(frankly)* sin reservas; *(straightway)* en el acto ➤ adj *(unqualified)* sin reservas.

outside ➤ s exterior m ■ from, on the o. desde, por fuera ➤ adj exterior; *(influence)* de afuera ➤ adv (a)fuera; *(outdoors)* en o a la calle ➤ prep fuera de ■ o. of fuera de; *(except)* excepto.

outskirts ➤ spl afueras.

outstanding ➤ adj sobresaliente; *(superior)* excelente; *(unresolved)* pendiente.

outward ➤ adj exterior, externo; *(direction)* hacia afuera; *(journey)* de ida ➤ adv hacia afuera.

oval ➤ adj ovalado, oval ➤ s óvalo.

oven ➤ s horno.

over ➤ prep sobre; *(above)* encima de; *(across, on, higher than)* por encima de; *(more than)* más de o que ■ o. the border al otro lado de la frontera • o. the past two years durante los dos últimos años • o. the phone por teléfono • to stumble o. tropezar con ➤ adv *(above)* (por) encima; *(across)* al otro lado, enfrente; allá; *(again)* otra vez, de nuevo ■ o. again otra vez • o. and above además de • o. and o. una y otra vez • o. here, there aquí, allá • o. with FAM. acabado, overol m.

overall ➤ adj total ➤ adv en general.

overalls ➤ spl mono, overol m.

overboard ➤ adv por la borda ■ man o.! ¡hombre al agua!

overcast ➤ adj nublado.

overcharge ➤ tr & intr cobrar demasiado ➤ s precio excesivo.

overcoat ➤ s sobretodo, abrigo.

overcome ➤ tr *(to defeat)* derrotar, conquistar; *(to overwhelm)* abrumar; *(obstacle, difficulty)* superar.

overdo ➤ tr hacer demasiado; *(diet, exercise)* exagerar.

overdraft ➤ s giro en descubierto.

overdraw ➤ tr girar en descubierto.

overdue ➤ adj *(delayed)* retrasado.

overeat ➤ intr comer demasiado.

overflow ➤ intr desbordarse ■ to o. with rebosar de ➤ tr desbordar, salirse de; *(to flood)* inundar.

overhead ➤ adj de arriba; *(light)* del techo; *(railway)* elevado ➤ s COM. gastos generales.

overhear ➤ tr oír por casualidad.

overheat ➤ tr & intr recalentar(se).

overlap ➤ tr & intr superponerse (a).

overload ➤ tr sobrecargar.

overlook ➤ tr mirar desde lo alto; *(view, window)* dar a, tener vista a; *(to disregard)* pasar por alto.

overnight ➤ adj *(guests)* por la noche; *(sudden)* repentino ➤ adv durante o por la noche; *(suddenly)* de la noche a la mañana ■ to stay o. pasar la noche.

overpass ➤ s paso superior, puente m.

overpay ➤ tr & intr pagar demasiado.

overpower ➤ tr abrumar.

overrate ➤ tr sobrestimar.

overreact ➤ intr reaccionar de modo exagerado.

overrun ➤ tr invadir.

overseas ➤ adv en el o al extranjero ➤ adj extranjero; *(trade)* exterior.

oversee ➤ tr supervisar.

oversight ➤ s descuido, omisión f.

oversleep ➤ intr quedarse dormido.

overtake ➤ tr *(to catch up with)* alcanzar; *(to pass)* pasar.

overtime ➤ s & adv horas extras.

overturn ➤ tr volcar.

overwhelming ➤ adj *(staggering)* abrumador; *(victory)* arrollador; *(majority)* inmenso; *(passion)* irresistible.

overwork ➤ tr & intr (hacer) trabajar demasiado.

owe ➤ tr deber.

owing ➤ *adj* por pagarse ■ **o. to** debido a.

owl ➤ *s* lechuza, búho.

own ➤ *adj* propio ➤ *s* lo mío, lo tuyo, etc. ■ **on one's o.** *(unaided)* sin ayuda de nadie; *(independently)* por cuenta propia ➤ *tr* ser dueño de, tener ➤ *intr* ■ **to o. up** confesar.

owner ➤ *s* dueño/a, propietario/a.

ox ➤ *s* buey *m*.

oxygen ➤ *s* oxígeno.

oyster ➤ *s* ostra.

P

pace ➤ *s* paso; *(speed)* ritmo ➤ *tr* pasearse por ➤ *intr* pasear.

pacific ➤ *adj* pacífico.

pacifier ➤ *s* chupete *m*.

pack ➤ *s* paquete *m*; *(knapsack)* mochila; *(of cigarettes)* cajetilla; *(of cards)* baraja; *(of dogs)* jauría ➤ *tr* *(to wrap up)* envolver; *(for shipping)* embalar; *(to put)* poner; *(to package)* empaquetar; *(to cram)* apiñar ➤ *intr* hacer las maletas; *(people)* apiñarse *(into* en).

package ➤ *s* paquete *m* ➤ *tr* empaquetar.

packed ➤ *adj* *(crowded)* atestado; *(suitcase)* hecho ■ **p. with** lleno de.

packet ➤ *s* paquete pequeño.

packing ➤ *s* embalaje *m*, envase *m*.

pact ➤ *s* pacto, convenio.

pad ➤ *s* *(cushion)* almohadilla, cojín *m*; *(stuffing)* relleno; *(of paper)* bloc *m*.

paddle ➤ *s* pala, remo ➤ *intr* remar con pala.

padlock ➤ *s & tr* (cerrar con) candado.

page¹ ➤ *s* HIST. paje *m* ➤ *tr* llamar.

page² ➤ *s* *(of book)* página.

paid ➤ *adj* pagado.

pail ➤ *s* cubo, balde *m*.

pain ➤ *s* dolor *m*; *(distress)* pena.

painful ➤ *adj* doloroso.

painkiller ➤ *s* calmante *m*.

paint ➤ *s* pintura ➤ *tr & intr* pintar.

paintbrush ➤ *s* brocha; ARTE. pincel *m*.

painter ➤ *s* pintor/a.

painting ➤ *s* pintura, cuadro.

pair ➤ *s* par *m*; *(persons, animals)* pareja.

pajamas ➤ *spl* piyama *m*.

palace ➤ *s* palacio.

palate ➤ *s* paladar *m*.

pale ➤ *adj* *(complexion)* pálido; *(color)* claro.

palm¹ ➤ *s* *(of a hand)* palma.

palm² ➤ *s* BOT. palma, palmera.

pamphlet ➤ *s* folleto.

pan ➤ *s* cacerola; *(frying pan)* sartén *f*.

pancake ➤ *s* panqueque *m*.

pane ➤ *s* hoja de vidrio.

panel ➤ *s* panel *m*; *(jury)* jurado; *(group)* grupo.

panic ➤ *s* pánico ➤ *tr & intr* aterrar(se).

panorama ➤ *s* panorama *m*.

pansy ➤ *s* pensamiento.

pant ➤ *intr* jadear.

pantheon ➤ *s* panteón *m*.

panther ➤ *s* pantera.

panties ➤ *spl* bragas, calzones.

pantry ➤ *s* despensa.

pants ➤ *spl* pantalones *m*.

pantyhose ➤ *s* pantimedia.

paper ➤ *s* papel *m*; *(composition)* trabajo escrito; *(newspaper)* periódico ■ **on p.** por escrito • **p. clip** sujetapapeles ■ *pl* papeles ➤ *tr* empapelar.

paperback ➤ *s* libro de bolsillo.

paprika ➤ *s* paprika, pimentón *m*.

parachute ➤ *s & intr* (saltar en) paracaídas *m*.

parade ➤ *s* desfile *m* ➤ *intr* desfilar.

paradise ➤ *s* paraíso.

paragraph ➤ *s* párrafo.

Paraguayan ➤ *adj & s* paraguayo/a.

parallel ➤ *adj* paralelo; FIG. análogo.

paralyze ➤ *tr* paralizar.

parasite ➤ *s* parásito.

parcel ➤ *s* paquete *m*.

parchment ➤ *s* pergamino.

pardon ➤ *tr* perdonar; *(an offense)* disculpar ■ **p. me** perdóneme ➤ *s* perdón *m*; *(exemption)* indulto ■ **I beg your p.?** ¿cómo?, ¿cómo dijo?

parent ➤ *s* *(father)* padre *m*; *(mother)* madre *f* ■ *pl* padres.

parish ➤ *s* parroquia.

park ➤ *s* parque *m* ➤ *tr & intr* *(a vehicle)* estacionar(se).

parking ➤ *s* aparcamiento, estacionamiento ■ **p. lot** aparcamiento • **p.**

meter parquímetro.

parliament ➤ s parlamento.

parliamentary ➤ adj parlamentario.

parlor ➤ s salón m ■ funeral p. funeraria • ice-cream p. heladería.

parquet ➤ s parqué m.

parrot ➤ s papagayo, loro.

parsley ➤ s perejil m.

part ➤ s parte f; (of a machine) pieza; (role) papel m ■ for the most p. generalmente, por lo general ➤ tr dividir; (to break) partir, romper; (to come between) apartar ■ to p. with deshacerse de ➤ intr separarse, apartarse; (to leave) irse ➤ adv en parte.

partake ➤ intr participar (in, de).

partial ➤ adj parcial ■ p. to partidario de, aficionado a.

participant ➤ s & adj participante mf.

participate ➤ intr participar.

participation ➤ s participación f.

participle ➤ s participio.

particular ➤ adj particular; (fussy) exigente, minucioso ➤ s particularidad f, detalle m ■ pl pormenores.

particularly ➤ adv especialmente.

partition ➤ s partición f; (wall) tabique m.

partly ➤ adv en parte.

partner ➤ s socio/a; (in a dance, games) pareja.

partnership ➤ s sociedad f.

partridge ➤ s perdiz f.

part-time ➤ adj & adv por horas.

party ➤ s fiesta; POL. partido; (group) grupo.

pass ➤ intr pasar; (to cross) cruzarse; EDUC. aprobar ■ in passing de paso • to p. away fallecer • to p. out desmayarse ➤ tr pasar; (to exceed) sobrepasar, superar ■ to p. on pasar, transmitir • p. out repartir, distribuir • to p. over pasar por alto • to p. up (opportunity) dejar pasar; (offer) rechazar ➤ s paso; (permit, free ticket) pase m; (authorization) permiso, licencia ■ to make a p. at hacer insinuaciones amorosas a.

passable ➤ adj (road) transitable; (work) aceptable; (satisfactory) pasable.

passage ➤ s paso; (journey, ticket)

pasaje m; (corridor) pasillo.

passenger ➤ s pasajero/a, viajero/a.

passing ➤ adj (transitory) pasajero, transitorio ■ p. grade EDUC. calificación aprobatoria.

passion ➤ s pasión f.

passionate ➤ adj apasionado.

passive ➤ adj pasivo.

passport ➤ s pasaporte m.

password ➤ s MIL. contraseña; COMPUT. clave f, contraseña.

past ➤ adj pasado; (former) anterior, último; GRAM. pretérito, pasado ➤ s pasado; (background) historia; GRAM. pretérito, pasado ➤ prep (by) por delante de; (on the far side of) más allá de; (beyond) ya no ■ it's ten p. two son las dos y diez.

pasta ➤ s (plato de) pasta.

paste ➤ s engrudo ➤ tr (to stick) pegar.

pasteurize ➤ tr paste(u)rizar.

pastime ➤ s pasatiempo.

pastry ➤ s pasteles m.

pasture ➤ s pastura.

pat ➤ tr (to tap) dar palmaditas o golpecitos a ➤ s palmada, golpecito.

patch ➤ s parche m ➤ tr remendar.

patent ➤ s patente f ➤ tr patentar.

paternal ➤ adj (fatherly) paternal; (on the father's side) paterno.

path ➤ s (trail) sendero, senda; (track) camino, pista.

pathetic ➤ adj patético.

pathway ➤ s sendero.

patience ➤ s paciencia.

patient ➤ adj & s paciente mf.

patio ➤ s patio, terraza.

patriot ➤ s patriota mf.

patriotic ➤ adj patriótico.

patrol ➤ s patrulla ➤ tr & intr rondar.

patron ➤ s benefactor/a; (customer) cliente mf.

pattern ➤ s (for sewing) patrón m; (design) diseño, dibujo.

pause ➤ intr (mentally) hacer una pausa; (physically) pararse, detenerse; (to hesitate) vacilar ➤ s pausa; (rest) descanso.

pavement ➤ s pavimento.

paving ➤ s pavimentación f.

paw ➤ s pata.

pawn¹ ➤ s (object) prenda; (hostage) rehén mf ➤ tr empeñar.

pawn² ➤ s (in chess) peón m; FIG. pelele m.

pay◇ ➤ tr pagar; (to profit) compensar; (visit, compliment) hacer; (attention) prestar ■ to p. back (money) devolver, reembolsar • to p. off (debts) liquidar ➤ intr pagar; (to be profitable) ser rentable ■ it pays vale la pena • to p. off merecer la pena ➤ s paga, pago ➤ adj de pago ■ p. telephone teléfono público.

payable ➤ adj pagable.

paycheck ➤ s cheque m de pago de sueldo.

payment ➤ s pago.

payoff ➤ s pago; FAM. resultado final.

payroll ➤ s nómina o planilla de pagos.

pea ➤ s guisante m.

peace ➤ s paz f ■ at p. (serene) en calma, tranquilo.

peaceful ➤ adj pacífico; (tranquil) apacible, tranquilo.

peach ➤ s melocotón m, durazno.

peacock ➤ s pavo real.

peak ➤ s punta; (of a mountain) cima, cumbre f; (mountain) pico; (maximum) tope m ➤ intr culminar.

peanut ➤ s cacahuate m, maní m.

pear ➤ s (tree) peral m; (fruit) pera.

pearl ➤ s perla.

peasant ➤ s campesino/a.

pebble ➤ s guijarro, canto rodado.

pecan ➤ s pacana.

peck ➤ tr & intr (bird) picotear ➤ s picotazo.

peculiar ➤ adj peculiar; (odd) raro, extraño; (special) especial, singular.

pedal ➤ s pedal m ➤ intr pedalear.

pedestrian ➤ s peatón/ona.

peek ➤ intr echar una ojeada; (furtively) atisbar ➤ s atisbo, ojeada.

peel ➤ s cáscara, mondadura ➤ tr & intr pelar(se).

peer ➤ intr mirar curiosamente, mirar con atención.

peg ➤ s (plug, spike) clavija; (clothes hook) percha, gancho.

pen¹ ➤ s pluma; (ballpoint) bolígrafo.

pen² ➤ s corral m; (sty) pocilga ➤ tr acorralar.

penalty ➤ s pena; (fine) multa; (consequences) consecuencias; FIN. descuento; DEP. castigo, penalty m.

pencil ➤ s lápiz m ■ p. sharpener sacapuntas.

pendulum ➤ s péndulo.

penetrate ➤ tr penetrar.

penguin ➤ s pingüino.

penicillin ➤ s penicilina.

peninsula ➤ s península.

penniless ➤ adj sin dinero.

penny ➤ s centavo; G.B. penique m.

pension ➤ s pensión f ➤ tr pensionar.

people ➤ spl gente f; (nation) pueblo ■ thirteen p. trece personas ➤ ssg (ethnic group) pueblo.

pepper ➤ s (seasoning) pimienta; (fruit) pimiento, chile m ■ black p. pimienta negra • green, red p. pimiento verde, rojo.

peppermint ➤ s hierbabuena, menta; (candy) pastilla de menta.

per ➤ prep por; (according to) según ■ p. capita por cabeza • p. se por sí mismo.

perceive ➤ tr percibir.

percent ➤ adv & ssg por ciento.

percentage ➤ s porcentaje m.

perch¹ ➤ s percha ➤ intr (to roost) posarse.

perch² ➤ s (fish) perca.

percolator ➤ s cafetera de filtro.

perfect ➤ adj perfecto; (ideal) ideal ➤ tr perfeccionar.

perfection ➤ s perfección f.

perfectly ➤ adv perfectamente; (completely) completamente; (utterly) absolutamente.

perforate ➤ tr perforar.

perform ➤ tr (to do) ejecutar, hacer; (a function) desempeñar; TEAT. representar ➤ intr funcionar; (to act) actuar.

performance ➤ s (doing) ejecución f; (of a play) representación f; (of a role, musical composition) interpretación f; (in a competition) actuación f; (functioning) funcionamiento.

performer ➤ s (actor) artista mf; (musician) músico/a; (dancer) bailarín/ina.

perfume ➤ s perfume m.

perhaps ➤ adv quizá(s).

peril ➤ s peligro.

period ➤ s período, periodo; *(term)* plazo; *(age, stage)* época; *(class)* hora, clase f; DEP. tiempo; *(menstruation)* período, regla; GRAM. punto.

periodical ➤ adj periódico ➤ s publicación periódica, revista.

peripheral ➤ adj & s periférico.

perish ➤ intr perecer.

perishable ➤ adj perecedero.

perk ➤ intr ■ to p. up (re)animarse.

perm ➤ s permanente f.

permanent ➤ adj & s permanente f.

permission ➤ s permiso.

permit ➤ tr permitir; *(to give consent to)* dar permiso a, dejar ➤ s permiso.

perpendicular ➤ adj & s perpendicular f.

perpetual ➤ adj perpetuo.

persecute ➤ tr perseguir.

persecution ➤ s persecución f.

perseverance ➤ s perseverancia.

persevere ➤ intr perseverar.

persist ➤ intr persistir.

persistent ➤ adj persistente.

person ➤ s persona.

personal ➤ adj personal; *(private)* particular; *(in person)* en persona; *(for one's use)* de uso personal ■ p. property bienes muebles.

personality ➤ s personalidad f; *(celebrity)* personaje m, figura.

personnel ➤ s personal m.

perspiration ➤ s sudor m.

perspire ➤ intr sudar, transpirar.

persuade ➤ tr persuadir.

persuasion ➤ s persuasión f.

Peruvian ➤ adj & s peruano/a.

pessimism ➤ s pesimismo.

pessimist ➤ s pesimista mf.

pest ➤ s *(insect)* insecto; *(person)* pelmazo, persona molesta; *(plant, animal)* plaga, peste f.

pester ➤ tr molestar, fastidiar.

pet ➤ s mascota, animal domesticado ➤ tr acariciar.

petal ➤ s pétalo.

petition ➤ s petición f.

petroleum ➤ s petróleo.

petticoat ➤ s enaguas f.

petty ➤ adj insignificante, trivial; *(self-ish)* mezquino ■ p. cash caja chica.

pharmacist ➤ s farmacéutico/a.

pharmacy ➤ s farmacia.

phase ➤ s fase f ■ out of p. desfasado ➤ tr ■ to p. in, out introducir, eliminar progresivamente.

pheasant ➤ s faisán m.

phenomenal ➤ adj fenomenal.

phenomenon ➤ s fenómeno.

philanthropy ➤ s filantropía.

philosopher ➤ s filósofo/a.

philosophic(al) ➤ adj filosófico.

philosophy ➤ s filosofía.

phlegm ➤ s flema.

phone FAM. ➤ s teléfono ➤ tr & intr telefonear, llamar por teléfono.

phonetic ➤ adj fonético.

phosphorus ➤ s fósforo.

photo ➤ s foto f, fotografía.

photocopier ➤ s fotocopiadora.

photocopy ➤ tr fotocopiar ➤ s fotocopia.

photograph ➤ s fotografía, foto f ➤ tr fotografiar.

photographer ➤ s fotógrafo/a.

photography ➤ s fotografía.

phrase ➤ s frase f.

physical ➤ adj físico.

physician ➤ s médico/a, facultativo/a.

physicist ➤ s físico/a.

physics ➤ ssg física.

pianist ➤ s pianista mf.

piano ➤ s piano.

pick ➤ tr escoger, elegir; *(to gather)* recoger ■ to p. apart destrozar, despedazar • to p. oneself up levantarse • to p. out escoger • to p. up *(to lift)* coger; *(fallen object, mess)* recoger; *(to buy)* comprar; *(to learn)* aprender; *(a habit)* adquirir ➤ intr ■ to p. at *(food)* picar, picotear • to p. on atormentar ➤ s elección f, selección f.

pickle ➤ s encurtido ➤ tr encurtir.

pickpocket ➤ s carterista mf.

pickup ➤ s *(collection)* recogida; *(truck)* camioneta, FAM. *(increase)* aumento.

picnic ➤ s picnic m ➤ intr comer al aire libre.

picture ➤ s *(painting)* cuadro, pintura; *(illustration)* ilustración f; *(photograph)* fotografía; *(mental image)* imagen f ➤ tr *(to visualize)* imaginar.

picturesque ➤ *adj* pintoresco.
pie ➤ *s* (*with meat*) empanada; (*with fruit*) pastel *m*.
piece ➤ *s* pedazo; (*in a set*) pieza ■ in one p. en buen estado; (*person*) sano y salvo ■ *pl* • in p. (*unassembled*) desarmado; (*shattered*) hecho añicos.
pier ➤ *s* muelle *m*, embarcadero.
pierce ➤ *tr* traspasar, perforar.
piercing ➤ *adj* (*sharp*) agudo; (*look*) penetrante.
piety ➤ *s* piedad *f*.
pig ➤ *s* cerdo, puerco; FAM. glotón/ona.
pigeon ➤ *s* paloma.
piggyback ➤ *adv* a cuestas.
pigtail ➤ *s* coleta, trenza.
pile ➤ *s* pila, montón *m* ➤ *tr* apilar, amontar ➤ *intr* ■ to p. up acumularse.
pilgrim ➤ *s* peregrino/a.
pill ➤ *s* píldora.
pillar ➤ *s* pilar *m*.
pillow ➤ *s* almohada.
pillowcase ➤ *s* funda de almohada.
pilot ➤ *s* AVIA. piloto *mf*.
pimple ➤ *s* grano.
pin ➤ *s* alfiler *m*; (*brooch*) broche *m* ➤ *tr* prender con alfileres.
pinball ➤ *s* pinball *m*, millón *m*.
pincer ➤ *s* pinza ■ *pl* pinzas, tenazas.
pinch ➤ *tr* pellizcar ➤ *intr* (*shoes*) apretar ➤ *s* pellizco ■ in a p. en caso de apuro.
pine ➤ *s* pino ■ p. cone piña.
pineapple ➤ *s* piña, ananás *m*.
pink ➤ *s* & *adj* (*color*) rosado, rosa.
pinkie ➤ *s* FAM. dedo meñique.
pint ➤ *s* pinta.
pioneer ➤ *s* pionero/a.
pipe ➤ *s* (*for liquids, gas*) tubería, cañería; (*for tobacco*) pipa.
pipeline ➤ *s* (*gas*) gasoducto; (*oil*) oleoducto.
pirate ➤ *s* pirata *mf* ➤ *tr* (*book, software*) piratear.
pistachio ➤ *s* (*nut*) pistacho.
pit[1] ➤ *s* (*hole*) hoyo, pozo.
pit[2] ➤ *s* hueso (de frutas) ➤ *tr* deshuesar.
pitch[1] ➤ *s* MIN. alquitrán *m*, brea.
pitch[2] ➤ *tr* (*to throw*) lanzar, tirar; (*hay*) echar; (*tent*) montar, armar ➤ *s*

(*throw*) lanzamiento; (*of a roof*) pendiente *f*; MÚS. tono; (*intensity*) grado.
pitcher[1] ➤ *s* DEP. lanzador/a.
pitcher[2] ➤ *s* jarra, cántaro.
pitiful ➤ *adj* lastimoso.
pity ➤ *s* (*compassion*) piedad *f*; (*regrettable fact*) lástima, pena ➤ *intr* & *tr* compadecer(se de).
pizza ➤ *s* pizza.
placard ➤ *s* cartel *m*, letrero.
place ➤ *s* lugar *m*; (*locale*) sitio, local *m*; (*house*) casa; (*seat*) asiento ■ all over the p. por todas partes • in p. en orden • in p. of en vez de • out of p. fuera de lugar • p. setting cubierto • to take p. tener lugar ➤ *tr* colocar, poner; (*to situate*) situar, ubicar; (*an order, bet*) hacer.
plague ➤ *s* peste *f*.
plain ➤ *adj* (*obvious*) claro, evidente; (*simple*) sencillo; (*unattractive*) nada atractivo ■ in p. sight a la vista de todos • the p. truth la pura verdad ➤ *s* llanura, llano ■ *pl* praderas.
plan ➤ *s* plan *m*; (*schedule*) programa *m* ➤ *tr* planear, proyectar; (*to project*) planificar ■ to p. to o *on* pensar.
plane[1] ➤ *s* MAT. plano; AVIA. avión *m*.
planet ➤ *s* planeta *m*.
planetarium ➤ *s* planetario.
plank ➤ *s* tablón *m*.
plant ➤ *s* planta; (*factory*) fábrica ➤ *tr* plantar.
plantain ➤ *s* BOT., CUL. plátano.
plantation ➤ *s* plantación *f*.
plaster ➤ *s* yeso; (*of a cast*) escayola.
plastic ➤ *adj* & *s* plástico.
plate ➤ *s* (*dish*) plato; (*plaque*) placa; (*of metal*) plancha, lámina.
platform ➤ *s* plataforma; (*railroad*) andén *m*; POL. programa político.
platinum ➤ *s* platino.
platter ➤ *s* fuente *f*.
play ➤ *intr* jugar; (*to pretend*) fingirse ■ to p. along cooperar • to p. around bromear, tomar el pelo • to p. fair jugar limpio ➤ *tr* jugar (a); TEAT. (*a role*) desempeñar; (*to act as*) hacer de; DEP. jugar contra; MÚS. tocar ■ to p. back volver a poner (algo grabado) • to p. down quitar importancia a ➤ *s*

juego; *(drama)* obra ▪ **to bring into p.** poner en juego • **p. on words** juego de palabras.

playback ➤ *s* reproducción *f*.

playbill ➤ *s (poster)* cartel *m*; *(program)* programa *m*.

player ➤ *s* jugador/a; *(actor)* actor *m*; *(actress)* actriz *f*; *(musician)* ejecutante *mf*, músico/a.

playground ➤ *s* parque *m* infantil.

play-off ➤ *s* DEP. partido de desempate.

playwright ➤ *s* dramaturgo/a.

plead ➤ *intr* suplicar ▪ **to p. guilty, innocent** declararse culpable, inocente.

pleasant ➤ *adj* agradable.

please ➤ *adv* por favor ➤ *tr* agradar, gustar; *(to satisfy)* contentar, complacer ▪ **to be pleased with** estar contento con.

pleasing ➤ *adj* agradable.

pleasure ➤ *s* placer *m* ▪ **with p.** con gusto.

pleat ➤ *s* pliegue *m*.

plentiful ➤ *adj* abundante, copioso.

plenty ➤ *s* abundancia ➤ *adj* abundante; *(sufficient)* suficiente, bastante ▪ **p. of** bastante; *(more than enough)* de sobra ➤ *adv* FAM. muy.

pliers ➤ *s* alicates *m*, tenazas.

plot ➤ *s (of land)* parcela; *(story line)* trama; *(conspiracy)* complot *m* ➤ *tr (a chart, curve)* trazar; *(to scheme)* tramar.

plow ➤ *s* arado; *(snowplow)* quitanieves *m* ➤ *tr (a field)* arar.

pluck ➤ *tr (to pick)* coger; *(a chicken)* desplumar; *(to pull out)* arrancar.

plug ➤ *s* tapón *m*; ELEC. enchufe *m*; *(spark plug)* bujía ➤ *tr* tapar ▪ **to p. in** enchufar ➤ *intr* ▪ **p. away at** perseverar en.

plum ➤ *s (tree)* ciruelo; *(fruit)* ciruela; FIG. breva, chollo.

plumber ➤ *s* plomero/a, fontanero/a.

plumbing ➤ *s (pipes)* cañería, tubería; *(trade)* plomería.

plump ➤ *adj* rechoncho, regordete.

plunge ➤ *tr & intr* hundir(se) ➤ *s (dive)* zambullida; *(in prices)* baja vertiginosa.

plunger ➤ *s* desatascador *m*.

plural ➤ *adj & s* plural *m*.

plus ➤ *prep* más ➤ *s* ventaja ➤ *conj* y además.

pneumatic ➤ *adj* neumático.

poach[1] ➤ *tr* cocer a fuego lento, escalfar.

poach[2] ➤ *intr* cazar en vedado.

pocket ➤ *s* bolsillo ➤ *adj* de bolsillo.

pocketknife ➤ *s* navaja, cortaplumas *m*.

poem ➤ *s* poema *m*.

poet ➤ *s* poeta *mf*.

poetic ➤ *adj* poético.

poetry ➤ *s* poesía.

point ➤ *s* punto; *(sharp tip)* punta; *(place)* lugar *m*; *(reason)* motivo, razón *f*; DEP. punto, tanto; GEOG. punta ▪ **at this p.** a estas alturas ▪ **to miss the p.** no comprender • **to the p.** pertinente • **what's the p.?** ¿para qué? ➤ *tr (to aim)* apuntar; *(to show)* indicar ▪ **to p. out** señalar ➤ *intr* apuntar.

pointed ➤ *adj* puntiagudo.

pointless ➤ *adj (meaningless)* sin sentido; *(useless)* inútil.

poison ➤ *s* veneno ➤ *tr* envenenar; *(to pollute)* contaminar.

poisonous ➤ *adj* venenoso.

poke ➤ *tr (with elbow)* dar codazo; *(with finger)* dar con la punta del dedo.

poker[1] ➤ *s* atizador *m*, hurgón *m*.

poker[2] ➤ *s (game)* póker *m*, póquer *m*.

polar ➤ *adj* polar ▪ **p. bear** oso blanco.

pole[1] ➤ *s (axis)* polo.

pole[2] ➤ *s (post)* poste *m*, palo.

police ➤ *s* policía ▪ **p. force** fuerza pública • **p. station** jefatura de policía.

policeman ➤ *s* policía *m*.

policewoman ➤ *s* mujer *f* policía.

policy[1] ➤ *s* POL. política.

policy[2] ➤ *s (written contract)* póliza.

policyholder ➤ *s* asegurado/a.

polish ➤ *tr (to wax)* encerar; *(metals)* bruñir; *(nails)* pintar; *(to refine)* pulir ➤ *s (wax)* cera; *(for metals)* líquido de bruñir; *(for nails)* esmalte *m* ▪ **shoe p.** betún.

polite ➤ *adj* cortés; *(refined)* educado.

politeness ➤ *s* cortesía.

political ➤ *adj* político.
politician ➤ *s* político/a.
politics ➤ *ssg* política.
poll ➤ *s* (*votes*) votación *f*; (*survey*) encuesta ■ *pl* urnas, centro electoral.
pollen ➤ *s* polen *m*.
pollutant ➤ *s* agente *m* contaminador.
pollute ➤ *tr* (*to corrupt*) corromper; (*to contaminate*) contaminar.
pollution ➤ *s* contaminación *f*.
polo ➤ *s* polo ■ p. shirt polo.
polyester ➤ *s* poliéster *m*.
polytechnic ➤ *adj & s* (*instituto*) politécnico.
pomegranate ➤ *s* granada.
pond ➤ *s* estanque *m*.
pony ➤ *s* poney *m*, jaca.
ponytail ➤ *s* cola de caballo.
poodle ➤ *s* perro de lanas, caniche *m*.
pool[1] ➤ *s* (*small pond*) charca; (*puddle*) charco; (*for swimming*) piscina.
pool[2]. ➤ *s* (*in betting*) banco, bolsa; (*game*) billar americano.
poor ➤ *adj* pobre; (*mediocre*) malo, mediocre.
pop ➤ *intr* (*to explode*) estallar; (*eyes*) abrirse ■ to p. up aparecer de repente ➤ *tr* hacer estallar ■ to p. open abrir haciendo sonar • to p. out asomar ➤ *s* estallido; (*of a cork*) taponazo; (*soda pop*) gaseosa.
popcorn ➤ *s* rosetas o palomitas de maíz.
pope o **Pope** ➤ *s* papa *m*.
poppy ➤ *s* amapola.
popular ➤ *adj* popular; (*in vogue*) de moda.
popularity ➤ *s* popularidad *f*.
population ➤ *s* población *f*.
porch ➤ *s* porche *m*.
pore ➤ *s* ANAT. poro.
pork ➤ *s* (*carne f*) de cerdo.
port[1] ➤ *s* puerto ■ p. of call puerto de escala.
port[2] ➤ *s & adj* (*de o a*) babor *m*.
port[3] ➤ *s* (*wine*) oporto.
portable ➤ *adj & s* (*máquina*) portátil.
porter ➤ *s* mozo.
portfolio ➤ *s* cartera.
portion ➤ *s* porción *f*, parte *f* ➤ *tr* dividir ■ to p. out repartir.

portrait ➤ *s* retrato.
pose ➤ *intr* posar ■ to p. as hacerse pasar por ➤ *tr* (*question*) plantear; (*threat*) representar ➤ *s* pose *f*.
position ➤ *s* posición *f*; (*post, job*) puesto; (*point of view*) postura, actitud *f* ➤ *tr* colocar, poner.
positive ➤ *adj* positivo; (*sure*) seguro, cierto ■ *s* positivo; FOTOG. positiva.
possess ➤ *tr* poseer.
possession ➤ *s* posesión *f* ■ to get o take p. of apoderarse de ■ *pl* posesiones.
possessive ➤ *adj* posesivo.
possibility ➤ *s* posibilidad *f*.
possible ➤ *adj* posible ■ as much as p. todo lo posible • as soon as p. lo antes posible.
post[1] ➤ *s* (*pole*) poste *m*; (*stake*) palo, estaca; COMPUT. mensaje *m*, nota ➤ *tr* (*poster*) pegar, fijar; COMPUT. enviar.
post[2] ➤ *s* MIL. base *f*; (*job*) puesto, cargo.
post[3] ➤ *s* G.B. (*mail*) correo ■ p. card tarjeta postal • p. office correos ➤ *tr* echar al correo.
postage ➤ *s* franqueo ■ p. stamp sello (postal), estampilla.
postal ➤ *adj & s* postal *f*.
poster ➤ *s* cartel *m*, afiche *m*, póster *m*.
posterity ➤ *s* posteridad *f*.
postgraduate ➤ *adj & s* postgraduado/a.
postmark ➤ *s* matasellos ➤ *tr* matasellar.
postpone ➤ *tr* (*to delay*) posponer; (*to put off*) aplazar.
postponement ➤ *s* aplazamiento.
postscript ➤ *s* posdata.
posture ➤ *s* postura ➤ *intr* posar, asumir una pose.
pot ➤ *s* CUL. cazuela, olla; (*flowerpot*) maceta; FAM. (*marijuana*) yerba.
potato ➤ *s* patata, papa ■ p. chips papas fritas.
potential ➤ *adj* potencial, posible ➤ *s* posibilidad *f*.
pothole ➤ *s* bache *m*.
potter ➤ *s* alfarero/a.
pottery ➤ *s* alfarería.
potty ➤ *s* FAM. orinal *m* para niños.
pouch ➤ *s* bolsa pequeña, valija.
poultry ➤ *s* aves *f* de corral.

pounce ➤ *intr (to spring)* saltar sobre; *(to attack)* abalanzarse sobre.

pound¹ ➤ s FIN., FÍS. libra.

pound² ➤ *tr* golpear; *(to grind)* moler; *(to crush)* machacar.

pound³ ➤ s *(for dogs)* perrera.

pour ➤ *tr* verter, derramar ➤ *intr* manar; *(to rain)* llover a cántaros.

poverty ➤ s pobreza.

powder ➤ s polvo; *(cosmetic, medicinal)* polvos ■ **p. room** tocador, servicios.

power ➤ s poder *m; (capacity)* capacidad *f; (strength)* fuerza; *(nation)* potencia; *(energy)* energía; *(electricity)* corriente *f* ■ **p. brake** servofreno • **p. line** línea de transmisión eléctrica • **p. steering** servodirección ■ *pl* poder, capacidad.

powerful ➤ *adj* poderoso; *(strong)* fuerte; *(convincing)* convincente.

practical ➤ *adj* práctico ■ **p. joke** broma pesada.

practically ➤ *adv* de modo práctico; *(almost)* prácticamente, casi.

practice ➤ *tr* practicar; *(to train in)* ejercitarse o entrenarse en; *(a profession)* ejercer ➤ *intr* hacer prácticas ➤ s práctica; *(custom)* costumbre *f; (of a profession)* ejercicio; *(of a doctor)* clientela; *(of a lawyer)* bufete *m.*

prairie ➤ s llanura, planicie *f.*

praise ➤ s alabanza *f* ➤ *tr* alabar.

prank ➤ s jugarreta, travesura.

prawn ➤ s camarón *m*, gamba.

pray ➤ *intr* rezar, orar.

prayer ➤ s oración *f.*

preach ➤ *tr & intr* predicar.

precaution ➤ s precaución *f.*

precede ➤ *tr & intr* preceder.

preceding ➤ *adj* precedente.

precept ➤ s precepto.

precious ➤ *adj* precioso.

precipice ➤ s precipicio.

precise ➤ *adj* preciso.

precision ➤ s precisión *f.*

precocious ➤ *adj* precoz.

predecessor ➤ s predecesor/a; *(ancestor)* antepasado/a.

predicament ➤ s apuro.

predict ➤ *tr* predecir; *(to forecast)* pronosticar.

predictable ➤ *adj* previsible; *(behav-*

ior) invariable, constante.

prediction ➤ s predicción *f; (forecast)* pronóstico.

prefabricate ➤ *tr* prefabricar.

preface ➤ s prefacio, prólogo.

prefer ➤ *tr* preferir.

preferable ➤ *adj* preferible.

preference ➤ s preferencia.

prefix ➤ s prefijo.

pregnancy ➤ s embarazo.

pregnant ➤ *adj* encinta, embarazada.

prehistoric(al) ➤ *adj* prehistórico.

prejudice ➤ s prejuicio.

preliminary ➤ *adj & s* preliminar *m.*

premature ➤ *adj* prematuro.

première ➤ s estreno ➤ *tr & intr* estrenar ➤ *adj* primero.

premise ➤ s premisa ■ *pl* local *m.*

premium ➤ s *(prize)* premio, recompensa; *(fee)* prima; *(installment)* prima (de un seguro).

preparation ➤ s preparación *f; (medicine)* preparado ■ *pl* preparativos.

prepare ➤ *tr & intr* preparar(se).

prepay ➤ *tr* pagar por adelantado.

preposition ➤ s preposición *f.*

prescribe ➤ *tr* prescribir; MED. recetar.

prescription ➤ s prescripción *f; MED.* receta.

presence ➤ s presencia; *(bearing)* porte *m*, talle *m; (confidence)* seguridad *f.*

present¹ ➤ s presente *m* ■ **for the p.** por ahora ➤ *adj* presente; *(month)* corriente; *(year)* en curso ■ **to be p.** asistir.

present² ➤ *tr* presentar; *(a gift)* regalar, obsequiar; *(a case)* exponer; *(a problem)* plantear; *(charges)* formular ➤ s presente *m*, regalo.

presentation ➤ s presentación *f; (of a play)* representación *f; (of a case, argument)* exposición *f.*

presently ➤ *adv (soon)* dentro de poco; *(now)* actualmente.

preservation ➤ s preservación *f; (of customs, food)* conservación *f.*

preservative ➤ *adj* preservativo ➤ s conservante *m*, preservador *m.*

preserve ➤ *tr* preservar; *(to maintain)* conservar; *(food)* conservar ➤ s coto, vedado ■ *pl* confitura.

preside ➤ *intr* presidir.

presidency ➤ s presidencia.

president ➤ s presidente/a.

presidential ➤ adj presidencial.

press ➤ tr (to bear down on) apretar; (to squeeze) prensar; (to compress) comprimir; (to iron) planchar ■ to be pressed for estar con apuros de • to p. one's luck forzar la suerte ➤ intr apretar, ejercer presión ■ to p. for pedir con insistencia • to p. on seguir adelante ➤ s PERIOD. prensa.

pressure ➤ s presión f; (compression) compresión f ■ blood p. presión arterial • p. cooker olla de presión ➤ tr ejercer presión sobre.

prestige ➤ s prestigio.

presume ➤ tr suponer.

pretend ➤ tr & intr fingir.

pretext ➤ s pretexto.

pretty ➤ adj lindo; FAM. considerable ■ a p. penny mucho dinero ➤ adv bastante ■ p. much más o menos.

prevail ➤ intr prevalecer.

prevent ➤ tr (to avoid) evitar; (to impede) impedir.

prevention ➤ s prevención f.

preview ➤ s exhibición f preliminar; CINEM. avance m.

previous ➤ adj previo.

prey ➤ s presa; FIG. víctima.

price ➤ s precio.

prick ➤ s pinchazo; (of an insect) picadura ➤ tr pinchar.

prickly ➤ adj espinoso.

pride ➤ s orgullo; (self-respect) amor propio ➤ tr ■ to p. oneself on estar orgulloso de.

priest ➤ s sacerdote m, cura m.

primarily ➤ adv principalmente.

primary ➤ adj primario ➤ s lo principal; POL. elección primaria.

prime ➤ adj primero; (main) fundamental ■ p. meridian primer meridiano • p. minister primero/a ministro/a • p. rate tasa preferida.

primitive ➤ adj primitivo.

prince ➤ s príncipe m.

princess ➤ s princesa.

principal ➤ adj principal ➤ s (of a school) director/a; COM., FIN. principal m.

principle ➤ s principio ■ in p. en principio • on p. por principio.

print ➤ s huella; (letters) letra; FOTOG. copia; (engraving) grabado, estampa ■ in p. impreso, publicado • out of p. agotado ➤ tr imprimir; (to publish) publicar; FOTOG. copiar; (to write) escribir con letras de molde.

printer ➤ s (person) impresor/a; (machine) impresora.

printout ➤ s salida impresa.

prior ➤ adj previo ■ p. to antes de.

priority ➤ s prioridad f.

prison ➤ s cárcel f, prisión f.

prisoner ➤ s prisionero/a, preso/a.

privacy ➤ s intimidad f.

private ➤ adj privado; (not public) particular; (secluded) solitario ■ p. enterprise sector privado ➤ s soldado raso.

privilege ➤ s privilegio.

prize ➤ s premio.

prizefighter ➤ s boxeador m profesional.

probable ➤ adj probable.

problem ➤ s problema m.

proceed ➤ intr proceder, continuar ➤ s ■ pl ganancias.

process ➤ s (treatment) procedimiento; (method) proceso ■ in the p. al hacerlo ➤ tr (an application) tramitar; COMPUT., DER. procesar.

processing ➤ s (of food) tratamiento; COMPUT. procesamiento ■ data p. procesamiento de datos; (science) informática.

procession ➤ s procesión f, desfile m.

processor ➤ s procesador m.

proclaim ➤ tr proclamar.

procure ➤ tr obtener.

produce ➤ tr producir; (to manufacture) fabricar; (to give rise to) causar; (to show) exhibir ➤ s producto.

producer ➤ s productor/a.

product ➤ s producto.

production ➤ s producción f.

productive ➤ adj productivo.

profession ➤ s profesión f.

professional ➤ adj & s profesional mf; (expert) perito/a, experto/a.

professor ➤ s profesor/a; (university) catedrático/a.

profile ➤ s perfil m.

profit ➤ s beneficio ■ to make a p. *(person)* ganar dinero; *(business)* rendir ganancias ➤ intr servir ■ to p. by o from COM. sacar dinero de; *(to benefit from)* sacar provecho de.

profitable ➤ adj beneficioso, provechoso; COM. lucrativo.

program ➤ s programa m ➤ tr programar.

program(m)er ➤ s programador/a.

program(m)ing ➤ s programación f.

progress ➤ s progreso ■ in p. en curso ■ to make p. progresar ➤ intr progresar; *(to improve)* mejorar.

prohibit ➤ tr prohibir.

project ➤ s proyecto ➤ tr proyectar ➤ intr sobresalir.

projectile ➤ s proyectil m.

projector ➤ s proyector m.

prolong ➤ tr prolongar.

prominent ➤ adj prominente; *(eminent)* notable.

promise ➤ s promesa ■ to break one's p. faltar a su palabra ➤ tr prometer ➤ intr hacer una promesa.

promising ➤ adj prometedor.

promote ➤ tr *(employee, officer)* ascender; *(to further)* promover; *(to advertise)* promocionar.

promotion ➤ s ascenso; *(furtherance)* fomento.

prompt ➤ adj puntual; *(without delay)* pronto, rápido.

pronoun ➤ s pronombre m.

pronounce ➤ tr pronunciar.

pronunciation ➤ s pronunciación f.

proof ➤ s prueba.

propagate ➤ tr & intr propagar(se).

propeller ➤ s hélice f.

proper ➤ adj apropiado; *(right)* debido; *(correct)* correcto.

properly ➤ adv apropiadamente; *(strictly)* propiamente; *(correctly)* correctamente.

property ➤ s propiedad f; *(possessions)* bienes m; TEAT. accesorio ■ personal p. bienes muebles.

prophecy ➤ s profecía.

prophet ➤ s profeta m, profetisa.

prophylactic ➤ adj & s profiláctico.

proportion ➤ s proporción f ■ out of p. desproporcionado.

proposal ➤ s propuesta.

propose ➤ tr proponer; *(to intend)* tener intención de; *(marriage)* ofrecer ➤ intr ofrecer matrimonio.

proposition ➤ s proposición f; FAM. *(matter)* asunto.

prose ➤ s prosa.

prosecute ➤ tr proseguir; DER. *(a person)* procesar; *(claim, case)* entablar.

prosecutor ➤ s fiscal mf.

prospect ➤ s perspectiva ■ pl perspectivas ➤ tr prospectar.

prospector ➤ s buscador/a.

prospectus ➤ s prospecto.

prosper ➤ intr prosperar.

prosperity ➤ s prosperidad f.

prosperous ➤ adj próspero.

protect ➤ tr proteger.

protection ➤ s protección f.

protective ➤ adj protector.

protest ➤ tr & intr protestar (contra) ➤ s protesta.

Protestant ➤ s & adj protestante mf.

protester ➤ s persona que protesta; *(demonstrator)* manifestante mf.

proud ➤ adj orgulloso, *(arrogant)* soberbio ■ to be p. to tener el honor de.

prove◇ ➤ tr probar; *(to test)* poner a prueba ➤ intr salir, resultar.

proven ➤ adj probado.

proverb ➤ s proverbio.

provide ➤ tr *(to supply)* suministrar; *(to make available)* proveer.

province ➤ s provincia; *(jurisdiction)* competencia.

provincial ➤ adj provincial; *(unsophisticated)* provinciano.

provision ➤ s provisión f ■ pl provisiones.

provoke ➤ tr provocar.

prowl ➤ tr & intr merodear, rondar.

prudent ➤ adj prudente.

prune¹ ➤ s *(fruit)* ciruela pasa.

prune² ➤ tr & intr *(to trim)* podar.

psalm ➤ s salmo.

psychiatrist ➤ s psiquiatra mf.

psychiatry ➤ s psiquiatría.

psychological ➤ adj psicológico.

psychologist ➤ s psicólogo/a.

psychology ➤ *s* psicología.
pub ➤ *s* taberna, cantina.
public ➤ *adj & s* público.
publication ➤ *s* publicación *f.*
publicist ➤ *s* publicista *mf.*
publicity ➤ *s* publicidad *f.*
publish ➤ *tr & intr* publicar.
publisher ➤ *s* editor/a.
puck ➤ *s* DEP. disco.
pudding ➤ *s* budín *m.*
puddle ➤ *s* charco.
Puerto Rican ➤ *s & adj* puertorriqueño/a.
puff ➤ *s (of air)* soplo; *(of smoke, steam)* bocanada ➤ *intr* resoplar, resollar.
pull ➤ *tr* tirar de; *(trigger)* apretar ■ to p. off *(to take off)* quitar; *(to carry out)* llevar a cabo • to p. oneself together componerse, dominarse • to p. out sacar, extraer • to p. strings conseguir algo por influencias ➤ *intr* tirar ■ to p. ahead destacarse • to p. away dejar atrás • to p. over AUTO. parar • to p. through *(to survive)* salir de una enfermedad o apuro ➤ *s (tug)* tirón *m.*
pullout ➤ *s* retirada.
pullover ➤ *s* jersey *m*, suéter *m.*
pulse ➤ *s* pulso.
pump ➤ *s* MEC. bomba; AUTO. surtidor *m* ➤ *tr* bombear; *(blood)* impulsar; *(lever, arm)* mover de arriba abajo.
pumpkin ➤ *s* calabaza.
punch[1] ➤ *s (for paper)* perforadora; *(for tickets)* máquina de picar billetes ➤ *tr (tickets)* picar; *(metal, leather)* taladrar.
punch[2] ➤ *tr (to hit)* dar un puñetazo ➤ *s* puñetazo.
punctual ➤ *adj* puntual.
punctuation ➤ *s* puntuación *f.*
puncture ➤ *tr* perforar; *(a tire)* pinchar ➤ *s* perforación *f*; *(in a tire)* pinchazo.
punish ➤ *tr* castigar.
punishment ➤ *s* castigo.
pupil[1] ➤ *s (student)* alumno/a.
pupil[2] ➤ *s* ANAT. pupila.
puppet ➤ *s* marioneta, títere *m.*
puppy ➤ *s* cachorro ■ p. love amor juvenil.
purchase ➤ *tr* comprar ➤ *s* compra ■ p. order orden de compra.

pure ➤ *adj* puro.
purge ➤ *tr* purgar ➤ *s* purga.
purify ➤ *tr* purificar.
purity ➤ *s* pureza.
purple ➤ *s* violeta, morado ➤ *adj* purpúreo, morado.
purpose ➤ *s* objetivo; *(intention)* propósito.
purposely ➤ *adv* adrede, a propósito.
purse ➤ *s* bolso ➤ *tr (lips)* apretar.
pursue ➤ *tr* perseguir; *(to strive for)* aspirar a; *(to follow)* seguir, continuar; *(a career)* dedicarse a.
pursuit ➤ *s* persecución *f*; *(activity)* pasatiempo.
push ➤ *tr* empujar; *(to press)* apretar, presionar ➤ *intr* empujar ■ to p. ahead avanzar • to p. back retroceder • to p. forward avanzar • to p. on seguir adelante, continuar • to p. on seguir adelante ➤ *s* empujón *m.*
put◇ ➤ *tr* poner; *(to insert)* meter; *(to add)* echar ■ to p. aside poner a un lado; *(to save)* guardar • to p. back volver a poner en su sitio • to p. down *(to let go of)* soltar; *(to suppress)* reprimir; *(to write down)* apuntar; *(to criticize)* poner por los suelos; *(down payment)* hacer un desembolso inicial de • to p. into words expresar • to p. off *(to postpone)* aplazar, diferir; *(to offend)* dar asco, asquear • to p. on TEAT. poner en escena; *(clothes)* ponerse; *(to affect)* afectar • to p. out *(to extinguish)* apagar; *(to inconvenience)* molestar; *(to publish)* publicar • to p. up *(to build)* levantar, construir; *(to offer)* poner; *(to lodge)* hospedar, alojar • to p. up with aguantar.
puzzle ➤ *tr* desconcertar, dejar perplejo ➤ *s* enigma *m*, misterio ■ crossword p. crucigrama • jigsaw p. rompecabezas.
pyramid ➤ *s* pirámide *f.*

Q

quack[1] ➤ *s* graznido ➤ *intr* graznar.
quack[2] ➤ *s (doctor)* curandero/a.
quake ➤ *intr* temblar ➤ *s* temblor *m.*
qualification ➤ *s* calificación *f*; *(requirement)* requisito; *(restriction)* reserva ■ *pl* credenciales.
qualified ➤ *adj (competent)* capaci-

tado; *(certified)* acreditado.

qualify ➤ *intr* tener las capacidades necesarias; DEP. clasificarse ▪ **to q.** as merecer el título de.

quality ➤ *s (nature, excellence)* calidad *f; (attribute)* cualidad *f.*

quantity ➤ *s* cantidad *f.*

quarrel ➤ *s* pelea, discusión *f* ➤ *intr* pelear, discutir.

quarry¹ ➤ *s (prey)* presa.

quarry² ➤ *s (pit)* cantera.

quart ➤ *s* cuarto (de galón).

quarter ➤ *s (fourth part)* cuarto; *(of a dollar)* veinticinco centavos; *(of a year)* trimestre *m; (neighborhood)* barrio ▪ **(a) q. past** y cuarto ▪ **(a) q. to** o **of** menos cuarto ▪ *pl (residence)* residencia; MIL. cuartel *m.*

quarterly ➤ *s & adj* (publicación *f)* trimestral ➤ *adv* trimestralmente.

quartet ➤ *s* cuarteto.

quartz ➤ *s* cuarzo.

queen ➤ *s* reina; *(in cards, chess)* dama.

queer ➤ *adj (strange)* raro; *(odd)* curioso.

quench ➤ *tr (fire)* apagar; *(thirst)* matar.

query ➤ *s* pregunta.

quest ➤ *s* búsqueda.

question ➤ *s* pregunta; *(issue)* cuestión *f* ▪ **beyond o.** fuera de duda ▪ **in q.** en cuestión ▪ **q. mark** signo de interrogación ▪ **to be out of the q.** ser imposible ➤ *tr* preguntar.

questionable ➤ *adj (debatable)* cuestionable; *(dubious)* dudoso.

questionnaire ➤ *s* cuestionario.

quiche ➤ *s* pastel *m* de queso y huevos.

quick ➤ *adj (fast)* rápido; *(bright)* listo.

quiet ➤ *adj (silent)* callado, silencioso; *(calm)* tranquilo ➤ *s (calm)* quietud *f; (silence)* silencio.

quilt ➤ *s* colcha ➤ *tr* acolchar.

quit◊ ➤ *tr (to leave)* salir de; *(a school, job)* abandonar, dejar; *(a habit)* dejar de ➤ *intr (to give up)* desistir; *(to resign)* renunciar.

quite ➤ *adv* totalmente; *(exactly)* exactamente ▪ **q. a bit** bastante ▪ **q. a while** un buen rato ▪ **q. long** bastante largo.

quits ➤ *adj* ▪ **to call it q.** dejarlo así.

quiz ➤ *tr* interrogar; *(to test)* examinar ➤ *s (test)* prueba, examen *m* ▪ **q. show** concurso de televisión.

quota ➤ *s* cuota.

quotation ➤ *s* cita; *(of prices)* cotización *f* ▪ **q. marks** comillas.

quote ➤ *tr (words, source)* citar; *(example, price)* dar; FIN. cotizar ➤ *s* ▪ **in quotes** entre comillas.

R

rabbi ➤ *s* rabino/a.

rabbit ➤ *s* conejo.

rabies ➤ *s* rabia.

race¹ ➤ *s (people)* raza.

race² ➤ *s (contest)* carrera ➤ *intr* correr; *(to compete)* competir; *(engine)* embalarse.

racial ➤ *adj* racial.

racism ➤ *s* racismo.

racist ➤ *adj & s* racista *mf.*

rack ➤ *s (for luggage)* portaequipajes *m; (for hat, coat)* percha.

racket¹ ➤ *s* DEP. raqueta.

racket² ➤ *s (noise)* alboroto; *(crime)* negocio ilegal.

radar ➤ *s* radar *m.*

radial ➤ *adj* radial.

radiate ➤ *intr* radiar ➤ *tr* (ir)radiar.

radiator ➤ *s* radiador *m.*

radio ➤ *s* radio *f* ▪ **r. station** emisora ➤ *tr & intr* transmitir (un mensaje) por radio.

radioactive ➤ *adj* radiactivo.

radish ➤ *s* rábano.

radius ➤ *s* radio.

raffle ➤ *s* rifa ➤ *tr & intr* rifar.

raft ➤ *s* balsa.

rag ➤ *s* trapo ▪ *pl* harapos.

rage ➤ *s* furia ➤ *intr* rabiar; *(storm)* bramar; *(plague, fire)* propagarse.

ragged ➤ *adj (beggar)* andrajoso; *(sleeve)* raído; *(edge)* mellado.

raid ➤ *s* MIL. incursión *f,* ataque sorpresivo; *(by police)* redada ➤ *tr* atacar por sorpresa; *(police)* hacer una redada en.

rail ➤ *s (banister)* barandilla; *(at racetrack)* cerca; F.C. riel *m.*

railing ➤ *s (of balcony)* baranda; *(of stairs)* pasamanos.

railroad ➤ *s* ferrocarril *m* ▪ **r. car** vagón

• r. crossing cruce de ferrocarril • r. station estación ferroviaria.

railway ➤ s ferrocarril m; (track) vía.

rain ➤ s lluvia ∎ r. forest bosque húmedo ➤ intr llover ∎ to r. cats and dogs llover a cántaros.

rainbow ➤ s arco iris.

raincoat ➤ s impermeable m.

raindrop ➤ s gota de lluvia.

rainfall ➤ s (shower) aguacero; (precipitation) precipitación f.

rainstorm ➤ s tempestad f de lluvia.

rainy ➤ adj lluvioso.

raise ➤ tr levantar; (window, prices) subir; (flag) izar; (welt, blister) producir; (voice) alzar; (children, animals) criar; (crop) cultivar; (money) recaudar; (an army) reclutar ➤ s aumento.

raisin ➤ s pasa (de uva).

rake ➤ s rastrillo ➤ tr rastrillar.

rally ➤ intr reunirse; (to recover) recuperarse ∎ to r. round dar apoyo a, adherirse a ➤ s reunión f.

ram ➤ s carnero ➤ tr (to stuff) meter a la fuerza; (to crash into) chocar con.

ramble ➤ intr (to walk) pasear; (to digress) divagar ➤ s paseo.

rampart ➤ s muralla.

ranch ➤ s hacienda ∎ r. house casa de una sola planta ➤ intr llevar una hacienda.

rancher ➤ s estanciero/a, hacendado/a.

random ➤ adj hecho al azar, fortuito.

range ➤ s (reach) alcance m; (variety) gama; (stove) cocina; (of merchandise) surtido ∎ at close r. de cerca.

ranger ➤ s (of a forest) guardabosques mf; (mounted police) policía mf.

rank ➤ s (in society) clase f; (high status) rango; (quality) categoría; MIL. grado ∎ pl filas ∎ to join the r. of unirse con ➤ tr (in rows) alinear; (in order) clasificar.

ransom ➤ s rescate m ➤ tr rescatar.

rap¹ ➤ s golpe seco ➤ tr & intr golpear.

rap² JER. ➤ intr conversar ➤ s conversación f; MÚS. rap m.

rape ➤ s violación f ➤ tr violar.

rapid ➤ adj rápido ∎ r. transit sistema de transporte urbano ∎ rapids spl rápidos.

rapist ➤ s violador m.

rare¹ ➤ adj raro; (special) poco común.

rare² ➤ adj CUL. jugoso, poco hecho.

rascal ➤ s tunante mf, bribón/ona.

rash¹ ➤ adj (act) precipitado; (person) impetuoso.

rash² ➤ s MED. sarpullido; FIG. ola.

raspberry ➤ s (fruit) frambuesa.

rat ➤ s rata; JER. canalla mf.

rate ➤ s (speed) velocidad f; (of change) coeficiente m; (percentage) porcentaje m; FIN. interés m ∎ at any r. de todos modos • at this r. a este paso • postal r. tarifa postal • r. of exchange cambio ➤ tr (to value) valorar; (to classify) clasificar; (to deserve) merecer.

rather ➤ adv (more exactly) mejor dicho; (quite) bastante; (somewhat) un poco ∎ I would r. preferiría • r. than en vez de.

ration ➤ s ración f, porción f.

rational ➤ adj racional.

rationing ➤ s racionamiento.

rattle ➤ intr (vehicle) traquetear; (window, door) golpetear; (teeth) castañetear ➤ tr (to shake) sacudir; FAM. poner nervioso ➤ s traqueteo; (of window) golpe m; (of baby) sonajero.

ravenous ➤ adj hambriento; (voracious) voraz.

ravine ➤ s barranco, quebrada.

ravishing ➤ adj encantador.

raw ➤ adj crudo; (not refined) sin refinar, bruto ∎ r. material materia prima.

rawhide ➤ s cuero sin curtir.

ray¹ ➤ s rayo; MAT., BOT. radio.

ray² (fish) raya.

razor ➤ s navaja de afeitar ∎ r. blade cuchilla u hoja de afeitar.

reach ➤ tr alcanzar; (to arrive at) llegar a ∎ to r. out extender, alargar ➤ intr llegar ∎ to r. for tratar de tomar o agarrar ➤ s alcance m.

react ➤ intr reaccionar.

reaction ➤ s reacción f.

reactor ➤ s reactor m.

read◇ ➤ tr & intr leer ∎ to r. into atribuir (a) ∎ to r. over repasar • to r. up on informarse acerca de.

reader ➤ s lector/a; (schoolbook) libro de lecturas.

readily ➤ *adv (willingly)* de buena gana; *(easily)* con facilidad.

reading ➤ *s* lectura; *(of a text)* versión *f.*

ready ➤ *adj* listo; *(willing)* dispuesto ■ **to get r.** *(to prepare)* preparar(se); *(to fix up)* arreglar(se) ➤ *tr* preparar.

ready-made ➤ *adj* hecho.

ready-to-wear ➤ *adj* hecho, confeccionado ➤ *s* ropa hecha.

real ➤ *adj* real; *(true)* verdadero ■ **r. estate** bienes inmuebles *o* raíces.

realism ➤ *s* realismo.

realistic ➤ *adj* realista.

reality ➤ *s* realidad *f* ■ **virtual r.** COMPUT. realidad virtual.

realize ➤ *tr* darse cuenta de; *(to attain)* realizar; *(a profit)* obtener.

really ➤ *adv (in reality)* en realidad; *(truly)* verdaderamente; *(very)* muy.

realm ➤ *s* reino.

realtor ➤ *s [service mark]* corredor/a *m* de bienes raíces.

realty ➤ *s* bienes *m* raíces.

reap ➤ *tr & intr* cosechar.

reappear ➤ *intr* reaparecer.

rear¹ ➤ *s* parte trasera; *(of a house)* fondo; FAM. *(buttocks)* nalgas ➤ *adj* trasero, de atrás.

rear² ➤ *tr (animals)* criar; *(children)* educar ➤ *intr (horse)* encabritarse.

rearing ➤ *s* crianza, cría.

rearview mirror ➤ *s* retrovisor *m.*

reason ➤ *s* razón *f* ■ **for no r.** sin ningún motivo • **the r. why** el porqué • **to have r. to** tener motivos para ➤ *tr & intr* razonar.

reasonable ➤ *adj* razonable.

reasoning ➤ *s* razonamiento.

reassure ➤ *tr* dar confianza a.

rebel ➤ *intr* rebelarse ➤ *s* rebelde *mf.*

rebellion ➤ *s* rebelión *f.*

reboot ➤ *tr* COMPUT. reiniciar.

rebound ➤ *intr* rebotar ➤ *s* rebote *m.*

rebuild ➤ *tr & intr* reconstruir.

recall ➤ *tr* recordar, acordarse de; *(product)* retirar del mercado.

receipt ➤ *s* recibo ■ **on r. of** al recibir ➤ *pl* ingresos.

receive ➤ *tr* recibir.

receiver ➤ *s* receptor *m;* DER. *(in bankruptcy)* síndico; TEL. auricular *m.*

recent ➤ *adj* reciente.

reception ➤ *s* recepción *f.*

receptionist ➤ *s* recepcionista *mf.*

recharge ➤ *tr* recargar.

recipe ➤ *s* receta.

recite ➤ *tr & intr* recitar.

reckless ➤ *adj (careless)* imprudente; *(rash)* precipitado.

reckon ➤ *tr* calcular; *(to regard)* considerar.

reclaim ➤ *tr (land)* recobrar; *(swamp)* sanear; *(from waste)* recuperar.

recognize ➤ *tr* reconocer.

recollect ➤ *tr & intr* acordarse (de).

recollection ➤ *s* recuerdo.

recommend ➤ *tr* recomendar.

recommendation ➤ *s* recomendación *f.*

reconstruction ➤ *s* reconstrucción *f.*

record ➤ *tr (facts, data)* registrar; *(thoughts)* apuntar; TEC. grabar ➤ *s (tally)* cuenta; *(testimony)* testimonio; *(of conduct, health)* historial *m; (dossier)* expediente *m;* *(for phonograph)* disco; *(recording)* grabación *f;* COMPUT. registro, récord *m* ■ **for the r.** para que así conste • **to break the r.** batir el record ➤ *pl* archivos.

recorder ➤ *s* grabadora; MÚS. flauta dulce.

recording ➤ *s* grabación *f.*

recover ➤ *tr* recuperar; *(damages)* cobrar ➤ *intr* recuperarse.

recreate ➤ *tr* recrear.

recruit ➤ *tr* contratar; MIL. reclutar ➤ *s* MIL. recluta *mf; (new member)* socio/a nuevo/a.

rectangle ➤ *s* rectángulo.

rectangular ➤ *adj* rectangular.

rector ➤ *s (of a parish)* cura párroco; *(of a university)* rector/a.

recur ➤ *intr* repetirse.

recycle ➤ *tr* reciclar.

red ➤ *s* rojo, colorado ■ **be in the r.** tener pérdidas ➤ *adj* rojo, colorado; *(wine)* tinto ■ **r. tape** trámites, papeleo.

redo ➤ *tr* volver a hacer, rehacer.

reduce ➤ *tr* reducir; COM. rebajar.

reduction ➤ *s* reducción *f,* disminución *f; (discount)* descuento.

redundant ➤ *s* superfluo.

reed ➤ *s (plant, stalk)* caña; MÚS.

(instrumento de) lengüeta.

reef ➤ s GEOL. arrecife *m*, escollo.

reel ➤ s *(spool)* carrete *m*; CINEM., FOTOG. rollo ➤ *tr* enrollar en un carrete.

reelect ➤ *tr* reelegir.

refer ➤ *tr (to direct to)* remitir; *(to send to)* enviar; *(to submit to)* someter a ➤ *intr* referirse.

referee ➤ s árbitro/a ➤ *tr & intr* arbitrar.

reference ➤ s referencia; *(allusion)* alusión *f*, mención *f* ■ r. book libro de consulta • r. to en cuanto a.

refill ➤ *tr* rellenar ➤ s recambio.

refine ➤ *tr* refinar.

refinery ➤ s refinería.

reflect ➤ *tr* reflejar ➤ *intr (to think)* reflexionar, meditar.

reflection ➤ s *(image)* reflejo; *(thought)* reflexión *f*.

reflex ➤ *adj & s* reflejo.

reform ➤ *tr & intr* reformar(se) ➤ s reforma.

reformation ➤ s reforma.

refrain¹ ➤ *intr* abstenerse *(from* de).

refrain² ➤ s MÚS., POET. estribillo.

refresh ➤ *tr & intr* refrescar(se).

refreshing ➤ *adj* refrescante.

refreshment ➤ s refresco.

refrigerator ➤ s nevera, frigorífico.

refuge ➤ s refugio ■ to take r. in refugiarse en.

refugee ➤ s refugiado/a.

refund ➤ *tr* reembolsar ➤ s reembolso.

refusal ➤ s negativa.

refuse¹ ➤ *tr (offer)* no aceptar; *(permission)* negar ➤ *intr* negarse *(to* a).

refuse² ➤ s desperdicios, basura.

refute ➤ *tr* refutar.

regain ➤ *tr* recuperar, recobrar.

regard ➤ *tr* considerar ■ regarding o as regards con respecto a ➤ s consideración *f*; *(esteem)* aprecio ■ in o with r. to con respecto a • to send one's regards to dar recuerdos a • without r. to sin tomar en consideración.

regardless ➤ *adv* a pesar de todo; *(come what may)* pase lo que pase.

regime ➤ s régimen *m*.

regiment ➤ s regimiento.

region ➤ s región *f*.

regional ➤ *adj* regional.

register ➤ s registro; *(cash register)* registradora ➤ *tr* registrar; *(students)* matrícular; *(vehicle)* sacar la matrícula de.

registered ➤ *adj (trademark)* registrado; *(student, vehicle)* matriculado; *(certified)* titulado ■ r. mail correo certificado.

registration ➤ s *(of voters)* inscripción *f*; *(of students, cars)* matrícula.

regret ➤ *tr (to be sorry for)* arrepentirse de; *(to be sorry about)* lamentar ➤ s *(sorrow)* pena; *(remorse)* arrepentimiento ■ *pl* excusas.

regular ➤ *adj* regular; *(usual)* normal; *(customary)* habitual, de costumbre; *(work)* fijo.

regularity ➤ s regularidad *f*.

regulate ➤ *tr* regular.

regulation ➤ s *(act)* regulación *f*; *(rule)* regla ■ *pl* reglamento.

rehearsal ➤ s ensayo.

rehearse ➤ *tr & intr* ensayar.

reign ➤ s reinado; *(dominance)* dominio ➤ *intr* reinar.

reimburse ➤ *tr* reembolsar.

rein ➤ s rienda ■ to give free r. to dar rienda suelta a.

reindeer ➤ s reno.

reinforce ➤ *tr* reforzar.

reinforcement ➤ s refuerzo ■ *pl* MIL. refuerzos.

reinstate ➤ *tr (to office)* restituir, reintegrar; *(to reestablish)* restablecer.

reject ➤ *tr* rechazar.

rejection ➤ s rechazo.

rejoice ➤ *tr & intr* regocijar(se).

relate ➤ *tr (to tell)* relatar, contar; *(to associate)* asociar ➤ *intr (to interact)* relacionarse *(with,* to con).

related ➤ *adj* relacionado *(to* con); *(by blood, marriage)* emparentado.

relation ➤ s relación *f*; *(kinship)* parentesco; *(relative)* pariente *mf*.

relationship ➤ s relación *f*; *(kinship)* parentesco; *(tie)* vínculo.

relative ➤ *adj* relativo ➤ s pariente *mf*.

relax ➤ *tr & intr* relajar(se).

relaxation ➤ s relajación *f*.

relaxed ➤ *adj* relajado.

relay ➤ s relevo; *(of messages)* transmisión f ➤ tr transmitir.

release ➤ tr *(to free)* poner en libertad; *(from one's grip)* soltar; *(film)* estrenar; *(record)* sacar ➤ s liberación f; *(of film)* estreno; *(record)* grabación f; *(communiqué)* anuncio.

relevant ➤ adj pertinente.

reliable ➤ adj *(person)* de confianza; *(machine)* fiable; *(data, source)* fidedigno.

relic ➤ s reliquia.

relief ➤ s *(assistance)* ayuda; *(replacement)* relevo ▪ in r. en relieve • what a r.! ¡qué alivio!

religion ➤ s religión f.

religious ➤ adj religioso; *(pious)* devoto.

relish ➤ s entusiasmo; CUL. salsa ➤ tr gustar ▪ I don't r. the idea no me hace ninguna gracia la idea.

reload ➤ tr & intr recargar.

reluctant ➤ adj poco dispuesto.

rely ➤ intr ▪ to r. (up)on *(to depend)* depender de; *(to trust)* contar con.

remain ➤ intr seguir; *(to stay)* quedarse; *(to be left)* quedar.

remainder ➤ s resto, residuo.

remaining ➤ adj restante.

remark ➤ tr & intr comentar *(on sobre)* ➤ s comentario.

remarkable ➤ adj notable; *(admirable)* extraordinario, admirable.

remedy ➤ s remedio ➤ tr remediar.

remember ➤ tr & intr acordarse (de), recordar.

remind ➤ tr recordar.

reminder ➤ s aviso, notificación f.

remit ➤ tr remitir.

remittance ➤ s remesa, envío.

remorse ➤ s remordimiento.

remote ➤ adj remoto; *(relative)* lejano ▪ r. control control a distancia; *(device)* telemando, mando a distancia.

removal ➤ s eliminación f.

remove ➤ tr *(to take off, away)* quitar(se); *(to eliminate)* eliminar.

remunerate ➤ tr remunerar.

render ➤ tr *(help)* dar; *(service)* prestar.

renew ➤ tr renovar; *(to resume)* reanudar.

renounce ➤ tr renunciar a.

rent ➤ s alquiler m, renta ▪ for r. se alquila ➤ tr & intr alquilar(se).

rental ➤ s *(property)* propiedad alquilada ➤ adj de alquiler.

reorganize ➤ tr & intr reorganizar(se).

repair ➤ tr reparar; *(clothes)* remendar ➤ s reparación f ▪ to be beyond r. no tener arreglo.

repairman ➤ s reparador m.

repay ➤ tr *(loan)* pagar; *(favor)* devolver; *(to compensate)* compensar ▪ to r. in kind pagar con la misma moneda.

repayment ➤ s pago, reembolso.

repeat ➤ tr & intr repetir ➤ s repetición f; RAD., TELEV. segunda difusión f.

repeated ➤ adj repetido.

repel ➤ tr repeler.

repent ➤ intr & tr arrepentirse (de).

repetition ➤ s repetición f.

repetitive ➤ adj repetitivo.

replace ➤ tr reponer; *(to substitute)* reemplazar, suplir.

replacement ➤ s reposición f; *(substitution)* reemplazo.

replay ➤ tr volver a jugar; *(videotape)* volver a poner ➤ s repetición f.

replenish ➤ tr volver a llenar.

replica ➤ s copia.

reply ➤ tr & intr contestar, responder ➤ s respuesta, contestación f.

report ➤ s *(account)* relato; *(official account)* informe m; *(of news)* reportaje m ▪ r. card boletín de notas • weather r. boletín meteorológico ➤ tr relatar; *(to denounce)* denunciar.

reporter ➤ s reportero/a, periodista mf.

represent ➤ tr representar.

representation ➤ s representación f; POL. delegación f.

representative ➤ s representante mf ➤ adj representativo; *(typical)* típico.

repression ➤ s represión f.

repressive ➤ adj represivo.

reprieve ➤ tr conmutar la pena de ➤ s conmutación f; FIG. alivio temporal.

reprimand ➤ tr reprender ➤ s reprimenda.

reprint ➤ s *(of book)* reimpresión f; *(of article)* tirada aparte ➤ tr reimprimir.

reproach ➤ *tr* reprochar ➤ *s* reproche *m* ■ above *o* beyond r. intachable.

reproduce ➤ *tr & intr* reproducir(se).

reproduction ➤ *s* reproducción *f.*

reptile ➤ *s* reptil *m;* FIG. canalla *mf.*

republic ➤ *s* república.

republican ➤ *adj & s* republicano/a.

repugnant ➤ *adj* repugnante.

repulsive ➤ *adj* repulsivo.

reputable ➤ *adj* respetable.

reputation ➤ *s* reputación *f.*

request ➤ *tr* solicitar ➤ *s* solicitud *f* ■ available on r. disponible a petición.

require ➤ *tr (to need)* requerir, necesitar; *(to demand)* exigir.

requirement ➤ *s* requisito.

requisite ➤ *adj* necesario, indispensable ➤ *s* requisito.

rerun ➤ *s* CINEM., TELEV. reestreno.

rescue ➤ *tr* rescatar, salvar ➤ *s* rescate *m,* salvamento.

research ➤ *s* investigación *f* ➤ *tr & intr* hacer una investigación (sobre).

researcher ➤ *s* investigador/a.

resemble ➤ *tr* parecerse a.

resent ➤ *tr* resentirse por.

resentful ➤ *adj* resentido.

resentment ➤ *s* resentimiento.

reservation ➤ *s (of room, table)* reservación *f;* *(condition, land)* reserva.

reserve ➤ *tr* reservar ➤ *s* reserva ■ *pl* MIL. reserva ➤ *adj* de reserva.

reserved ➤ *adj* reservado.

reservoir ➤ *s* embalse *m.*

reside ➤ *intr* residir.

residence ➤ *s* residencia.

resident ➤ *s* residente *mf;* MED. interno/a ➤ *adj* residente.

residential ➤ *adj* residencial.

residue ➤ *s* residuo.

resign ➤ *tr* renunciar, dimitir ■ to r. oneself to resignarse a ➤ *intr* dimitir.

resignation ➤ *s (act)* renuncia; *(acceptance)* resignación *f.*

resist ➤ *tr & intr* resistir.

resistance ➤ *s* resistencia.

resolution ➤ *s* resolución *f.*

resolve ➤ *tr* resolver ➤ *intr* decidir ➤ *s* resolución *f.*

resort ➤ *intr* ■ to r. to recurrir a ➤ *s* lugar *m* de temporado ■ as a last r.

como último recurso.

resource ➤ *s* recurso, medio.

respect ➤ *tr* respetar ➤ *s* respeto ■ in that r. en cuanto a eso.

respectable ➤ *adj* respetable.

respiration ➤ *s* respiración *f.*

respirator ➤ *s* respirador *m.*

respond ➤ *intr* responder.

response ➤ *s* respuesta; *(to a proposal)* acogida; *(to a stimulus)* reacción *f.*

responsibility ➤ *s* responsabilidad *f.*

responsible ➤ *adj* responsable *(for de, to ante).*

rest¹ ➤ *s* descanso; *(peace)* tranquilidad *f* ■ r. room baño ■ to come to r. pararse ➤ *intr* descansar.

rest² ➤ *s* ■ the r. *(remainder)* el resto; *(others)* los demás.

restaurant ➤ *s* restaurante *m.*

restful ➤ *adj* quieto, sosegado.

restless ➤ *adj* inquieto, agitado.

restore ➤ *tr (order, relations)* restablecer; *(painting, monarch)* restaurar.

restrict ➤ *tr* restringir, limitar.

restricted ➤ *adj* restringido.

restriction ➤ *s* restricción *f.*

result ➤ *intr* ■ to r. from, in resultar de, en ➤ *s* resultado ■ as a r. of a causa de.

resume ➤ *tr (talking)* reanudar; *(working)* reasumir.

résumé ➤ *s* curriculum vitae *m.*

retail COM. ➤ *s* venta al por menor *o* al detalle ➤ *adj & adv* al por menor, al detalle ➤ *tr & intr* vender(se) al por menor.

retailer ➤ *s* minorista *mf,* detallista *mf.*

retain ➤ *tr* retener; *(lawyer)* contratar; *(sense of humor)* conservar.

retire ➤ *tr (to go to bed)* acostarse; *(to stop working)* jubilarse.

retired ➤ *adj* jubilado.

retirement ➤ *s* jubilación *f.*

retreat ➤ *intr* retirarse ➤ *s* retirada.

retrieve ➤ *tr* recuperar; *(damage)* reparar; *(in hunting)* cobrar.

return ➤ *intr* volver, regresar ➤ *tr* devolver; *(profits, interest)* producir ➤ *s* regreso; *(giving back)* devolución *f;* *(profits)* ganancia ■ r. address dirección *f* del remitente • r. ticket billete *m* de vuelta ■ *pl (income)* ingresos; *(in an*

election) resultados.
reunion ➤ *s* reunión *f.*
reunite ➤ *tr & intr* reunir(se).
reusable ➤ *adj* que puede volverse a usar.
reuse ➤ *tr* volver a usar.
reveal ➤ *tr* revelar.
revenge ➤ *tr* vengar, vengarse de ➤ *s* venganza ■ to take r. on vengarse de.
revenue ➤ *s* ingreso, renta.
reverend ➤ *adj* reverendo ➤ *s* pastor/a.
reverse ➤ *adj* opuesto, contrario ■ the r. side *(of a form)* dorso; *(of a page, coin)* reverso ➤ *s* lo opuesto, lo contrario; AUTO. marcha atrás ➤ *tr (invert-ir; (to transpose)* transponer; *(policy, direction)* cambiar; DER. revocar.
review ➤ *tr (lesson, text)* repasar; *(film, book)* reseñar, criticar ➤ *s* repaso; *(cri-tique)* crítica.
revise ➤ *tr (to correct)* revisar, corregir; *(to modify)* modificar.
revision ➤ *s* corrección *f; (modifica-tion)* modificación *f.*
revive ➤ *tr & intr* resucitar.
revolt ➤ *intr* rebelarse ➤ *s* rebelión *f.*
revolting ➤ *adj* repugnante.
revolution ➤ *s* revolución *f.*
revolutionary ➤ *adj & s* revoluciona-rio/a.
revolve ➤ *tr & intr* (hacer) girar.
revolver ➤ *s* revólver *m.*
reward ➤ *s* recompensa, premio ➤ *tr* recompensar, premiar.
rewrite ➤ *tr* escribir de nuevo.
rheumatism ➤ *s* reumatismo.
rhinestone ➤ *s* diamante falso.
rhinoceros ➤ *s* rinocerante *m.*
rhyme ➤ *s* rima ➤ *intr & tr* rimar.
rhythm ➤ *s* ritmo.
rib ➤ *s* costilla.
ribbon ➤ *s* cinta.
rice ➤ *s* arroz *m.*
rich ➤ *adj* rico; *(color)* vivo, intenso.
riches ➤ *spl* riquezas.
rid◇ ➤ *tr* librar *(of de).*
riddle ➤ *s (puzzle)* acertijo; *(mystery)* enigma *m.*
ride◇ ➤ *intr* montar; *(to travel)* ir, via-jar; *(in a car)* pasearse ➤ *tr (a horse)* montar a; *(a bicycle)* montar en ➤ *s (on*

horse, car) paseo; *(trip)* viaje *m; (tour)* vuelta ■ to give someone a r. llevar a alguien • to go for a r. dar un paseo.
rider ➤ *s (horse)* jinete *mf; (bicycle)* ciclista *mf; (passenger)* viajero/a.
ridiculous ➤ *adj* ridículo.
rifle ➤ *s* rifle *m;* MIL. fusil *m.*
rig ➤ *tr (to equip)* equipar; *(an election)* amañar ➤ *s (gear)* equipo; MARÍT. aparejo ■ oil. r. torre de perforación.
right ➤ *adj (just, fair)* justo; *(ethical, correct)* correcto; *(word, time)* exacto; *(conditions)* favorable; *(opposite the left)* derecho ■ r. angle ángulo recto • to be r. tener razón • to put r. arreglar ➤ *s (justice)* justicia; *(good)* (lo) bueno, bien *m; (side, hand)* derecha; *(claim)* derecho; POL. derecha ■ by rights de derecho • r. of way derecho de paso ➤ *adv (well, correctly)* bien; *(squarely)* en pleno; *(to the right)* a o hacia la derecha ■ r. behind justo detrás • r. now ahora mismo • to come r. home regresar derecho a casa.
right-hand ➤ *adj* a la derecha.
right-handed ➤ *adj* que usa la mano derecha.
rightly ➤ *adj* correctamente; *(properly)* con derecho.
rigid ➤ *adj* rígido.
rim ➤ *s* borde *m; (coin)* canto.
rind ➤ *s (fruits)* cáscara; *(cheese)* corteza.
ring[1] ➤ *s* anillo; *(circle)* círculo; *(on fin-ger)* anillo, sortija; *(for bullfights)* ruedo; *(in boxing)* ring *m* ➤ *tr* rodear.
ring[2]◇ ➤ *intr (bells)* repicar; *(tele-phone, doorbell)* sonar ➤ *tr (a bell, buzzer)* tocar; *(to telephone)* llamar, telefonear ➤ *s (of telephone, buzzer, voice)* timbre *m; (tinkle)* tintineo.
rinse ➤ *tr* enjuagar ➤ *s* enjuague *m.*
riot ➤ *s* motín *m,* disturbio ■ r. police guardia de asalto ➤ *intr* amotinarse.
rip ➤ *tr* rasgar, desgarrar ■ to r. off arrancar, quitar; JER. *(to rob)* timar, limpiar • to r. up desgarrar, destrozar ➤ *intr* rasgarse, desgarrarse ➤ *s* des-garrón *m; (split seam)* descosido ■ r. tide corriente turbulenta.
ripe ➤ *adj* maduro.

ripen ➤ *tr & intr* madurar.

rip-off ➤ *s* FAM. timo.

rise◇ ➤ *intr (person, wind, dough)* levantarse; *(buildings, hills, spirits)* elevarse; *(temperature, prices, land)* subir; *(in rank, position)* ascender; *(water level)* crecer; *(voice)* alzarse; *(sun)* salir ➤ *s* subida, ascensión *f*; *(elevation)* elevación *f*; *(of prices, temperature, land)* subida; *(in rank)* ascenso; *(in pressure, rate, pitch)* elevación; *(of sun)* salida; COM. alza ■ to give r. to ocasionar.

risk ➤ *s* riesgo ➤ *tr* arriesgarse a.

risky ➤ *adj* arriesgado.

rival ➤ *adj & s* rival *mf* ➤ *tr* rivalizar con.

river ➤ *s* río.

road ➤ *s (highway)* carretera; *(street)* calle *f*; *(route, path)* camino.

roam ➤ *intr & tr* vagar (por).

roar ➤ *intr* rugir; *(bull, wind)* bramar ➤ *s* rugido, bramido; *(of the crowd)* clamor *m*; *(of laughter)* carcajada.

roast ➤ *tr (meat)* asar; *(coffee, nuts)* tostar ➤ *s* asado; *(cut)* carne *f* para asar ➤ *adj* asado ■ r. beef rosbif.

rob ➤ *tr & intr* robar.

robber ➤ *s* ladrón/ona.

robbery ➤ *s* robo.

robe ➤ *s (judge)* toga; *(priest)* sotana; *(bathrobe)* bata.

robot ➤ *s* robot *m*, autómata *m*.

rock¹ ➤ *s (stone)* roca; *(stone)* piedra.

rock² ➤ *intr (to sway)* balancearse; *(to shake)* estremecerse ➤ *tr (baby, cradle)* mecer; *(to shake)* sacudir ■ rocking chair mecedora ➤ *s* MÚS. rock *m*.

rocket ➤ *s* cohete *m*.

rocky ➤ *adj* rocoso.

rod ➤ *s (stick)* vara; *(staff)* bastón *m*.

rodent ➤ *adj & s* roedor *m*.

role *o* **rôle** ➤ *s* papel *m*.

roll ➤ *intr* rodar; *(to wallow)* revolcarse; *(thunder)* retumbar; *(drum)* redoblar ■ to r. over dar una vuelta ➤ *tr* rolling pin rodillo • to r. up *(paper, rug)* enrollar; *(sleeves)* arremangar ➤ *s (of paper, film)* rollo; *(bread)* bollo, panecillo.

roller ➤ *s (cylinder)* rodillo; *(small*

wheel) ruedecilla; *(for the hair)* rulo ■ r. coaster montaña rusa • r. skate patín de ruedas.

Roman *adj & s* romano/a ■ R. Catholic católico romano.

romance ➤ *s* romance *m*; *(novel)* novela romántica; *(love affair)* amores *m*; *(adventure)* aventura.

romantic ➤ *adj & s* romántico/a.

roof ➤ *s* techo, tejado.

rook ➤ *s (in chess)* torre *f*.

room ➤ *s* habitación *f*, cuarto; *(space, a spot)* sitio ■ r. and board pensión completa ■ *pl* alojamiento ➤ *intr* alojarse ■ rooming house pensión.

roommate ➤ *s* compañero/a de cuarto.

roomy ➤ *adj* espacioso, amplio.

rooster ➤ *s* gallo.

root ➤ *s* raíz *f* ➤ *intr* echar raíces ➤ *tr* arraigar ■ to r. out extirpar.

rope ➤ *s* soga, cuerda ➤ *tr (to tie)* amarrar, atar; *(horses)* coger con lazo ■ to r. off acordonar.

rose ➤ *s* rosa ■ r. garden rosaleda ➤ *adj (de color)* rosa.

rosebush ➤ *s* rosal *m*.

rosemary ➤ *s* romero.

rot ➤ *tr & intr* pudrir(se) ➤ *s* podredumbre *f*.

rotten ➤ *adj (meat, fruit)* estropeado; *(wood)* carcomido; *(smell, egg)* podrido; *(trick)* malo.

rough ➤ *adj* áspero; *(terrain)* accidentado; *(coarse)* basto, burdo; *(seas)* agitado; *(idea, guess)* aproximado ■ r. draft borrador.

round ➤ *adj* redondo ■ r. trip viaje de ida y vuelta ➤ *s* círculo; *(of talks, drinks)* ronda ■ to make one's rounds *(police, patrol)* hacer la ronda; *(doctor)* hacer las visitas ➤ *tr* ■ to r. off redondear • to r. up acorralar; *(people)* reunir ➤ *adv* ■ all year r. durante todo el año ➤ *prep (the world)* alrededor de; *(the corner)* a la vuelta de.

roundabout ➤ *adj* indirecto.

route ➤ *s (course)* ruta, vía; *(road)* carretera; *(for delivery)* recorrido ➤ *tr* mandar, encaminar.

routine ➤ *s* rutina ➤ *adj* rutinario.

row¹ ➤ *s* línea, fila.

row² ➤ *intr* (*boat*) remar.
row³ ➤ *tr* (*quarrel*) pelea; (*noise*) jaleo.
rowboat ➤ *s* bote *m* de remos.
royal ➤ *adj* real.
royalty ➤ *s* familia real; (*rank, power*) realeza; (*payment*) derechos de autor.
rub ➤ *tr* frotar (*against* contra); (*to massage*) friccionar ■ **to r. in** *u* **on** frotar con ➤ *intr* rozar ➤ *s* fricción *f*.
rubber ➤ *s* caucho; (*synthetic*) goma; (*eraser*) goma de borrar; JER. (*condom*) preservativo ■ **r. band** goma.
rubbish ➤ *s* basura; FIG. tonterías.
rubble ➤ *s* escombros.
ruby ➤ *s* rubí *m*.
rudder ➤ *s* timón *m*.
rude ➤ *adj* (*crude*) crudo, rudo; (*discourteous*) grosero, descortés.
rug ➤ *s* alfombra.
ruin ➤ *s* ruina ➤ *tr* arruinar; (*crops, party*) estropear.
rule ➤ *s* regla; (*control*) dominio, mando; (*reign*) reinado ■ **as a** (*general*) **r.** por lo regular ➤ *s pl* reglamento ➤ *tr* gobernar ■ **to r. out** excluir, descartar ➤ *intr* gobernar; DER. fallar.
ruler ➤ *s* gobernante *mf*; (*strip*) regla.
rum ➤ *s* ron *m*.
rumor ➤ *s* rumor *m*.
run◇ ➤ *intr* correr; (*to function*) andar, marchar; (*color, ink*) correrse; POL. presentarse como candidato ■ **to r. away** fugarse • **to r. in the family** venir de familia • **to r. smoothly** ir sobre ruedas ➤ *tr* (*race, risk*) correr; (*errand, experiment*) hacer; (*to operate*) hacer funcionar; (*household*) llevar; COMPUT. ejecutar ■ **to r. into** (*by chance*) encontrarse con; (*to collide with*) chocar contra • **to r. out of** acabársele a uno • **to r. over** atropellar ➤ *s* (*race*) carrera; (*quick trip*) visita; (*in stockings*) carrera.
runaway ➤ *adj & s* fugitivo/a.
runner ➤ *s* corredor/a.
runner-up ➤ *s* segundo/a.
running ➤ *adj* (*water*) corriente ■ **r. start** salida lanzada ➤ *adv* seguido.
run-off ➤ *s* (*overflow*) derrame *m*; (*competition*) carrera de desempate.
runway ➤ *s* AVIA. pista.

rural ➤ *adj* rural.
ruse ➤ *s* artimaña, treta.
rush ➤ *intr* (*to run*) ir de prisa; (*to hurry*) apresurarse, darse prisa; (*to flow*) correr ➤ *tr* (*a person*) dar prisa, apurar; (*a job*) hacer de prisa; (*an order*) ejecutar urgentemente ➤ *s* (*haste*) prisa; (*bustle*) bullicio, ajetreo; (*of emotion*) arrebato ■ **r. hour** hora punta ➤ *adj* urgente.
rust ➤ *s* herrumbre *f* ➤ *tr & intr* oxidar(se).
rustic ➤ *adj & s* rústico/a.
rusty ➤ *adj* oxidado.
rut ➤ *s* carril *m*; FIG. rutina.
rye ➤ *s* centeno.

S

sabotage ➤ *s* sabotaje *m* ➤ *tr* sabotear.
sack ➤ *s* saco.
sacred ➤ *adj* sacro, sagrado.
sacrifice ➤ *s* sacrificio ➤ *tr* sacrificar.
sad ➤ *adj* triste.
sadden ➤ *tr* entristecer.
saddle ➤ *s* silla de montar; (*bicycle*) sillín *m* ➤ *tr* ensillar.
sadness ➤ *s* tristeza.
safe ➤ *adj* seguro ■ **s. and sound** sano y salvo • **to play it s.** actuar con precaución ➤ *s* caja de caudales.
safely ➤ *adv* (*without harm*) sin accidente; (*driving*) con cuidado.
safety ➤ *s* seguridad *f* ■ **s. belt** cinturón de seguridad • **s. pin** imperdible.
saffron ➤ *s* azafrán *m*.
sag ➤ *intr* (*skin, clothes*) colgar; (*plank*) combarse; (*rope*) aflojarse.
said ➤ *adj* (*ante*)dicho.
sail ➤ *s* vela ➤ *intr* navegar; (*to travel*) ir en barco; (*to set out*) zarpar ➤ *tr* (*a boat*) gobernar.
sailboat ➤ *s* barco de vela.
sailing ➤ *s* navegación *f*; (*sport*) vela.
sailor ➤ *s* marinero/a.
saint ➤ *s* santo/a.
sake ➤ *s* ■ **for God's** *o* **goodness'** *o* **heaven's s.!** ¡por (el amor de) Dios! • **for your own s.** por tu propio bien.
salad ➤ *s* ensalada.
salary ➤ *s* salario.
sale ➤ *s* venta; (*clearance*) liquidación *f*

■ **for** s. se vende • **on** s. *(available)* en venta; *(reduced)* en liquidación ■ *pl* **venta** • **s. tax** impuesto a las ventas.

salesclerk ➤ *s* dependiente/a.

salesperson ➤ *s* vendedor/a.

saliva ➤ *s* saliva.

salmon ➤ *s* salmón *m.*

salt ➤ *s* sal *f* ■ **s. water** agua salada ➤ *tr* echar sal a; *(to preserve)* salar.

saltshaker ➤ *s* salero.

salty ➤ *adj* salado.

salute ➤ *tr* saludar ➤ *intr* hacer un saludo ➤ *s* saludo.

Salvadoran ➤ *adj & s* salvadoreño/a.

salvation ➤ *s* salvación *f.*

same ➤ *adj* mismo; *(similar)* igual ➤ *adv* igual ➤ *pron* el mismo; *(thing)* lo mismo ■ **all the** s. sin embargo.

sample ➤ *s* muestra ➤ *tr* tomar una muestra de.

sand ➤ *s* arena ■ **s. dune** duna, médano ■ *pl* arenales.

sandal ➤ *s* sandalia.

sandalwood ➤ *s* sándalo.

sandbar ➤ *s* arrecife *m* de arena.

sandpaper ➤ *s* papel *m* de lija.

sandwich ➤ *s* emparedado, sandwich *m.*

sane ➤ *adj* cuerdo.

sanitary ➤ *adj* sanitario ■ **s. napkin** paño higiénico.

sanitize ➤ *tr* sanear.

sanity ➤ *s* cordura.

sarcasm ➤ *s* sarcasmo.

sardine ➤ *s* sardina.

satellite ➤ *s* satélite *m.*

satin ➤ *s* raso, satén *m.*

satire ➤ *s* sátira.

satisfaction ➤ *s* satisfacción *f.*

satisfactory ➤ *adj* satisfactorio.

satisfy ➤ *tr* satisfacer; *(requirements)* cumplir con; *(to make do)* contentarse; *(to convince)* convencer ➤ *intr* dar satisfacción.

satisfying ➤ *adj* satisfactorio; *(experience)* agradable; *(food)* sustancioso.

saturate ➤ *tr* saturar.

Saturday ➤ *s* sábado.

sauce ➤ *s* salsa.

saucepan ➤ *s* cacerola.

saucer ➤ *s* platillo.

saucy ➤ *adj* descarado.

sausage ➤ *s* salchicha.

savage ➤ *adj & s* salvaje *mf.*

savanna(h) ➤ *s* sabana.

save ➤ *tr (to rescue)* salvar; *(to keep)* guardar; *(to conserve)* ahorrar; COMPUT. grabar, salvar, guardar ➤ *intr* ahorrar ➤ *s* DEP. parada.

savings ➤ *spl* ahorros ■ **s. account**, **bank** cuenta, caja de ahorros.

saw◇ ➤ *s (handsaw)* serrucho; *(machine)* sierra ➤ *tr* (a)serrar.

saxophone ➤ *s* saxófono.

say◇ ➤ *tr* decir; *(prayer)* rezar ■ **it is said** se dice • **let us** s. digamos • **not to** s. **por no decir** • **that is to** s. o sea, es decir ➤ *s (opinion)* voz *f; (turn to speak)* uso de la palabra.

saying ➤ *s* dicho.

scab ➤ *s* costra, postilla.

scaffolding ➤ *s* andamiaje *m.*

scald ➤ *tr* escaldar.

scale[1] ➤ *s (of fish, skin)* escama ➤ *tr* escamar.

scale[2] ➤ *s* escala ➤ *tr (to climb)* escalar.

scale[3] ➤ *s (balance)* balanza, báscula; *(tray)* platillo *(de balanza).*

scallion ➤ *s* cebollino.

scallop ➤ *s (animal, shell)* venera.

scan ➤ *tr (to examine)* escudriñar; *(the horizon)* recorrer con la mirada; COMPUT. escanear.

scandal ➤ *s* escándalo.

scanner ➤ *s* COMPUT. escáner *m.*

scar ➤ *s* cicatriz *f.*

scarce ➤ *adj* escaso.

scarcely ➤ *adv* apenas.

scarcity ➤ *s* escasez *f.*

scare ➤ *tr & intr* asustar(se) ➤ *s* susto.

scarecrow ➤ *s* espantapájaros *m.*

scarf ➤ *s* bufanda.

scarlet ➤ *s & adj* escarlata ■ **s. fever** escarlatina.

scatter ➤ *tr* dispersar; *(to strew)* esparcir ➤ *intr* dispersarse.

scene ➤ *s* escena; *(place)* lugar ■ **behind the scenes** TEAT. entre bastidores; FIG. en privado.

scenery ➤ *s* paisaje *m;* TEAT. decorado.

scenic ➤ *adj* del paisaje; *(picturesque)* pintoresco; TEAT. escénico.

scent ➤ s olor m; (trail) pista.

schedule ➤ s (timetable) horario; (agenda) calendario ■ to be behind s. (plane) llevar retraso; (work) estar atrasado • on s. a la hora ➤ tr fijar el horario de; (meeting) programar.

scheme ➤ s (plan) proyecto; (plot) ardid m ➤ intr conspirar.

scholar ➤ s erudito/a; (pupil) escolar mf.

scholarship ➤ s erudición f; (financial aid) beca.

school¹ ➤ s escuela; (for teens) colegio; (department) facultad f ■ night s. escuela nocturna • summer s. curso(s) de verano • Sunday s. escuela dominical ➤ tr educar; (to train) disciplinar.

school² ➤ s (fish) cardumen m.

schoolbook ➤ s libro de texto.

schoolhouse ➤ s colegio, escuela.

schoolmate ➤ s compañero/a de clase.

schoolroom ➤ s aula, sala de clase.

schoolteacher ➤ s maestro/a.

science ➤ s ciencia ■ s. fiction ciencia ficción.

scientific ➤ adj científico.

scientist ➤ s científico/a.

scissors ➤ spl tijeras f.

scold ➤ tr regañar ➤ s regañón/a.

scooter ➤ s patineta, monopatín m.

scope ➤ s (reach) alcance m; (freedom) libertad f.

scorch ➤ tr & intr quemar(se) ➤ s quemadura.

score ➤ s DEP. tanteo; EDUC. calificación f; MÚS. partitura ■ final s. DEP. resultado • on that s. en cuanto a eso • to keep s. apuntar los tantos ➤ tr DEP. marcar; FAM. (to get) conseguir; EDUC. sacar ➤ intr FAM. tener éxito; DEP. marcar un tanto; (to keep score) tantear.

scorn ➤ s desprecio ➤ tr despreciar.

scoundrel ➤ s canalla mf.

scout ➤ tr explorar ➤ s explorador/a.

scramble ➤ intr gatear ➤ tr revolver; ELECTRÓN. perturbar ■ scrambled eggs huevos revueltos.

scrap ➤ s (of paper) pedazo; (of fabric) retazo ➤ pl (of food) restos; (waste) desechos ➤ tr desechar.

scrapbook ➤ s álbum m de recortes.

scrape ➤ tr raspar ➤ intr rozar ■ to s. by ir tirando ➤ s (on skin) rasguño; (jam) lío.

scratch ➤ tr & intr rayar(se); (to claw) arañar; (an itch) rascar(se) ➤ s raya; (on skin) arañazo ■ from s. de la nada ➤ adj ■ s. paper papel (de) borrador.

scream ➤ intr chillar ➤ s chillido.

screen ➤ s pantalla; (for privacy) biombo; (for windows) (tela) mosquitera ➤ tr ocultar; CINEM. proyectar.

screen saver ➤ s salvapantallas m.

screw ➤ s CARP. tornillo ➤ tr JER. (to cheat) estafar ■ to s. down o on CARP. atornillar • to s. up FAM. arruinar.

screwdriver ➤ s destornillador m.

scribble ➤ tr & intr garabatear ➤ s garabatos.

script ➤ s letra cursiva; CINEM. guión m.

scroll ➤ s rollo de pergamino ■ s. bar COMPUT. barra de enrollar ➤ intr COMPUT. enrollar.

scrub ➤ tr fregar; (clothes) restregar.

scrutinize ➤ tr escudriñar.

scuba ➤ s submarinismo, escafandra autónoma.

sculpt ➤ tr esculpir.

sculptor ➤ s escultor/a.

sculpture ➤ s escultura ➤ tr esculpir.

scurvy ➤ s escorbuto.

sea ➤ s mar mf ■ at s. en el mar; FIG. confuso ➤ adj marino; (saltwater) de mar.

seafood ➤ s mariscos; (fish) pescado.

seal¹ ➤ s sello; (closure) cierre m ➤ tr sellar; (with wax) lacrar; (envelope) cerrar.

seal² ➤ s ZOOL. foca.

seam ➤ s costura.

seaman ➤ s marinero.

seaport ➤ s puerto marítimo.

search ➤ tr & intr registrar; (conscience) examinar ■ to s. for buscar ➤ s búsqueda; (by police) registro; (of person) cacheo ■ in s. of en busca de • s. engine buscador ■ s. warrant mandamiento de registro.

seashell ➤ s concha marina.

seashore ➤ s playa; (coast) costa.

seasick ➤ adj mareado.

seasickness ➤ s mareo.

seaside ➤ s costa ■ s. resort estación balnearia.

season ➤ s *(of year)* estación f; *(time)* temporada ■ off s. temporada baja • s. ticket abono ➤ tr *(food)* sazonar.

seasoning ➤ s aderezo, condimento.

seat ➤ s asiento; *(for a show, game)* localidad f; *(of bicycle)* sillín m; *(of government)* sede f ■ s. belt cinturón de seguridad ➤ tr sentar; *(to accommodate)* tener sitio para.

seating ➤ s asientos.

seaweed ➤ s alga.

second[1] ➤ s *(time unit)* segundo.

second[2] ➤ adj segundo ■ every s. (uno de) cada dos • s. floor primer piso (en países hispánicos) ➤ s segundo; AUTO. segunda.

secondary ➤ adj secundario ■ s. education enseñanza media.

second-class ➤ adj de segunda clase ➤ adv en segunda (clase).

secret ➤ adj & s secreto.

secretary ➤ s secretario/a.

section ➤ s sección f.

secure ➤ adj seguro; *(stable)* asegurado ➤ tr asegurar; *(to obtain)* conseguir; *(boat)* amarrar.

security ➤ s seguridad f; *(of loan)* garantía ■ s. guard guardia ■ pl FIN. valores.

sedation ➤ s sedación f.

sedative ➤ s & adj sedante m.

seduce ➤ tr seducir.

see◇ ➤ tr ver; *(to understand)* entender; *(socially)* verse; *(to consult)* consultar; *(a place)* conocer ■ s. you later! ¡hasta luego! • to s. off ir a despedirse de • to s. to atender a ➤ intr ver ■ let's s. a ver • to s. fit creer conveniente.

seed ➤ s semilla; *(pip)* pepita ➤ tr sembrar.

seek◇ ➤ tr buscar; *(fame)* anhelar; *(advice)* solicitar ■ to s. out ir en busca de • to s. to tratar de.

seem ➤ intr parecer.

seeming ➤ adj aparente.

seep ➤ intr rezumarse.

see-through ➤ adj transparente.

segment ➤ s segmento.

segregate ➤ tr & intr segregar(se).

segregation ➤ s segregación f.

seize ➤ tr agarrar; *(to possess)* apode-

rarse de; *(to confiscate)* incautarse de.

seizure ➤ s *(of goods)* embargo; *(of power)* toma; MED. ataque m.

seldom ➤ adv rara vez.

select ➤ tr & intr escoger; *(candidate, team)* seleccionar ➤ adj de primera calidad.

selection ➤ s selección f; *(collection)* surtido.

self ➤ s uno mismo; *(ego)* ego.

self-addressed ➤ adj con la dirección del remitente.

self-assured ➤ adj seguro de sí mismo.

self-confidence ➤ s confianza en sí mismo.

self-conscious ➤ adj cohibido.

self-control ➤ s dominio de sí mismo.

self-defense ➤ s autodefensa; DER. legítima defensa ■ in s. en defensa propia.

self-employed ➤ adj que trabaja por cuenta propia.

self-esteem ➤ s amor propio.

self-government ➤ s autonomía.

selfish ➤ adj egoísta.

selfishness ➤ s egoísmo.

self-portrait ➤ s autorretrato.

self-respect ➤ s dignidad f.

self-righteous ➤ adj santurrón.

self-service ➤ adj de autoservicio.

sell◇ ➤ tr vender ■ to s. off COM. liquidar ➤ intr venderse ■ to be sold out estar agotado.

seller ➤ s vendedor/a.

sellout ➤ s COM. liquidación f total; FAM. traidor/a.

semester ➤ s semestre m.

semicircle ➤ s semicírculo.

semicolon ➤ s punto y coma.

semiconductor ➤ s semiconductor m.

semifinal DEP. ➤ s semifinal f ➤ adj semifinalista.

senate ➤ s senado.

senator ➤ s senador/a.

send◇ ➤ tr mandar; *(letter)* enviar ■ to s. away for ordenar por correo • to s. back devolver • to s. off *(letter)* echar al buzón; *(person)* ir a despedir ➤ intr enviar.

sender ➤ s remitente mf.

senior ➤ adj *(partner)* principal; *(senator)* más antiguo; *(officer)* superior ■ s.

citizen anciano/a ➤ s anciano/a; *(student)* estudiante *mf* del último año.

sensational ➤ *adj* sensacional.

sense ➤ *s* sentido; *(feeling)* sensación *f*; *(consciousness)* sentimiento ■ **good s.** sentido común • **in a s.** en cierto sentido • **to come to one's senses** recobrar el juicio • **to make s.** tener sentido ➤ *tr (to perceive)* darse cuenta de; *(to detect)* detectar.

senseless ➤ *adj* sin sentido.

sensible ➤ *adj* sensato; *(perceptible)* sensible.

sensitive ➤ *adj* sensible; *(delicate)* delicado ■ **to be s. to** *o* **about** ser susceptible a.

sensual ➤ *adj* sensual.

sentence ➤ *s* GRAM. oración *f*, frase *f*; DER. sentencia ■ **life s.** condena perpetua • **to pass s. on** sentenciar ➤ *tr* sentenciar.

sentry ➤ *s* centinela *mf*.

separate ➤ *tr & intr* separar(se) ➤ *adj* separado; *(different)* distinto.

separation ➤ *s* separación *f*.

September ➤ *s* septiembre *m*.

sequence ➤ *s* sucesión *f*; *(arrangement)* orden *m*; *(series)* serie *f*.

sergeant ➤ *s* sargento *mf*.

serial ➤ *adj* ■ **s. number** número de serie ➤ *s* serial *m*.

series ➤ *s* serie *f*.

serious ➤ *adj* serio; *(illness)* grave.

servant ➤ *s* sirviente/a; *(civil)* funcionario/a.

serve ➤ *tr* servir; *(to wait on)* atender ■ **to s. as** *o* **for** servir de • **to s. on** ser miembro de ➤ *intr* servir ➤ *s* DEP. saque *m*.

service ➤ *s* servicio; *(set)* juego ■ **at your s.** a sus órdenes • **diplomatic s.** cuerpo diplomático • **s. charge** recargo por servicios • **to be out of s.** no funcionar ➤ *adj* de servicio; *(military)* militar ➤ *tr* mantener, reparar.

serviceman ➤ *s* militar *m*; *(repairman)* mecánico.

session ➤ *s* sesión *f*; *(of legislature)* reunión *f*.

set¹◇ ➤ *tr* poner; *(to locate)* situar; *(date, price)* fijar; *(record)* establecer;

(example) dar ■ **to s. back** atrasar • **to s. free** liberar • **to s. off** *(reaction)* iniciar; *(bomb)* hacer estallar; *(alarm)* hacer sonar • **to s. out** proponerse • **to s. up** *(monument)* levantar; *(machine)* montar; *(business, fund)* crear ➤ *intr (sun)* ponerse ■ **to s. forth** *o* **out** salir, encaminarse ➤ *adj (agreed upon)* señalado; *(price)* fijo; *(opinion)* firme; *(face)* inmóvil; *(determined)* resuelto ■ **all s.** listo • **to be s. on** *(action)* estar empeñado en; *(idea)* estar aferrado a • **to get s.** prepararse.

set² ➤ *s (of items)* juego; *(of rules)* serie *f*; *(people)* grupo; *(works)* colección *f*; TEAT. decorado; RAD. aparato; MAT. conjunto ■ **s. of dishes** vajilla • **television s.** televisor.

setback ➤ *s* revés *m*.

setting ➤ *s (place)* marco; LIT., TEAT. escena, escenario.

settle ➤ *tr (affairs, dispute)* arreglar; *(debt)* saldar; *(territory)* colonizar; *(stomach)* asentar ■ **to s. accounts** ajustar cuentas • **to s. on** decidirse por ➤ *intr (bird, gaze)* posarse; *(dust)* asentarse; *(in a city)* establecerse ■ **to s. down** *(to relax)* calmarse; *(conditions)* normalizarse • **to s. in** instalarse; *(at a job)* acostumbrarse.

settlement ➤ *s (of dispute)* arreglo; *(of problem)* solución *f*; *(agreement)* acuerdo; *(colony)* poblado.

settler ➤ *s* poblador/a.

seven ➤ *s & adj* siete ■ **s. hundred** setecientos • **s. o'clock** las siete.

seventeen ➤ *s & adj* diecisiete *m*.

seventh ➤ *s & adj* séptimo.

seventy ➤ *s & adj* setenta *m*.

several ➤ *adj & s* varios.

severe ➤ *adj* severo.

severity ➤ *s* severidad *f*.

sew◇ ➤ *tr & intr* coser.

sewage ➤ *s* aguas residuales.

sewer ➤ *s* alcantarilla, cloaca.

sewing ➤ *s* costura ■ **s. machine** máquina de coser.

sex ➤ *s* sexo ■ **to have s.** tener relaciones sexuales.

sexual ➤ *adj* sexual.

sexy ➤ *adj* excitante; *(erotic)* erótico.

shabby ➤ *adj (worn)* raído; *(treatment)* malo, mezquino.

shade ➤ *s* sombra; *(for lamp)* pantalla; *(for window)* persiana; *(hue)* tono; *(of meaning)* matiz *m* ➤ *tr (from light)* resguardar; *(to obscure)* dar sombra a.

shadow ➤ *s* sombra.

shady ➤ *adj* sombreado.

shaft ➤ *s (light)* rayo; *(tool)* mango; *(mine)* pozo; *(elevator)* hueco.

shake◇ ➤ *tr* sacudir; *(bottle)* agitar; *(faith)* hacer vacilar ▪ **to s. hands** darse la mano ➤ *intr* temblar.

shall ➤ *aux* ▪ **we s. see** veremos • **s. I call?** ¿quiere que llame por teléfono?

shallow ➤ *adj* poco profundo.

shame ➤ *s* vergüenza; *(pity)* lástima ▪ **s. on you!** ¡qué vergüenza! ➤ *tr* avergonzar; *(to dishonor)* deshonrar.

shameful ➤ *adj* vergonzoso.

shampoo ➤ *s* champú *m* ➤ *intr* lavarse la cabeza con champú.

shape ➤ *s* forma; *(body)* figura; *(guise)* aspecto; *(condition)* estado ▪ **to be in no s.** to no estar en condiciones de o para • **to be out of s.** DEP. no estar en forma ➤ *tr* formar.

share ➤ *s* parte *f*; *(of stock)* acción *f* ➤ *tr & intr* compartir.

shareholder ➤ *s* accionista *mf*.

shark ➤ *s* tiburón *m*; JER. usurero/a.

sharp ➤ *adj (cutting)* afilado; *(pointed)* puntiagudo; *(image)* nítido; *(curve)* cerrado; *(acute)* agudo.

sharpen ➤ *tr* afilar; *(pencil)* sacar punta a; *(appetite)* aguzar.

shatter ➤ *tr & intr* hacer(se) añicos.

shave◇ ➤ *tr & intr* afeitar(se) ➤ *s* afeitado.

shaver ➤ *s* afeitadora.

shawl ➤ *s* chal *m*.

she ➤ *pron* ella ➤ *s* hembra.

shears ➤ *spl* tijeras.

shed¹◇ ➤ *tr (tears)* derramar; *(water)* verter; *(skin)* mudar.

shed² ➤ *s* cobertizo.

sheep ➤ *s* oveja.

sheet ➤ *s (for bed)* sábana; *(paper)* hoja; *(glass)* lámina; *(ice)* capa.

shelf ➤ *s (in closet)* anaquel *m*; *(shelving)* estante *m*.

shell ➤ *s* concha; *(of crab, turtle)* caparazón *m*; *(of nuts, eggs)* cáscara; *(of peas)* vaina; ARM. proyectil *m* ➤ *tr (peas)* desvainar; MIL. bombardear.

shellfish ➤ *s* CUL. mariscos.

shelter ➤ *s* cobertizo; *(refuge)* refugio ▪ **to take s.** ponerse a cubierto ➤ *tr* proteger ➤ *intr* refugiarse.

shelving ➤ *s* estantería.

shepherd/ess ➤ *s* pastor/a.

sheriff ➤ *s* alguacil *m*, sheriff *m*.

sherry ➤ *s* jerez *m*.

shield ➤ *s* escudo ➤ *tr* escudar; *(to conceal)* tapar.

shift ➤ *tr (load)* pasar; *(to switch)* cambiar de ➤ *intr* cambiar; *(person)* moverse; AUTO. cambiar de velocidad ➤ *s* cambio; *(of workers)* turno ▪ **in shifts** por turnos.

shin ➤ *s* espinilla.

shine◇ ➤ *intr* brillar ➤ *tr (to polish)* sacar brillo a; *(light)* dirigir ➤ *s* brillo.

shingle ➤ *s* tablilla ▪ *pl* MED. zona.

shiny ➤ *adj* brillante; *(glossy)* lustroso.

ship ➤ *s* barco ➤ *tr* enviar.

shipment ➤ *s* embarque *m*; *(cargo)* cargamento.

shipping ➤ *s* embarque *m*.

shipwreck ➤ *s* naufragio ➤ *tr* ▪ **to be shipwrecked** naufragar.

shipyard ➤ *s* astillero.

shirt ➤ *s* camisa.

shiver ➤ *intr* tiritar ➤ *s* escalofrío.

shock ➤ *s* choque *m*; *(mental)* golpe *m*; *(of earthquake)* sacudida ▪ **s. absorber** amortiguador ➤ *tr & intr* chocar ▪ **to be shocked at** escandalizarse por.

shocking ➤ *adj (disturbing)* horroroso; *(offensive)* indecente.

shoe◇ ➤ *s* zapato ▪ **s. polish** betún • **s. store** zapatería ➤ *tr (horse)* herrar.

shoelace ➤ *s* cordón *m*.

shoemaker ➤ *s* zapatero/a.

shoot◇ ➤ *tr (gun)* disparar; *(to wound)* herir; *(to kill)* matar a tiros; *(to execute)* fusilar; CINEM. rodar; FOTOG. fotografiar ▪ **to s. down** derribar • **to s. dead** *o* **to death** matar a tiros ➤ *intr (to fire)* disparar; DEP. tirar ▪ **to s. up** *(to grow)* espigar; *(prices)* subir de repente; *(sparks)* brotar ➤ *s* BOT.

retoño ➤ *interj* ¡miércoles!

shooting ➤ *s* tiro; *(murder)* asesinato.

shop ➤ *s* tienda; *(workshop)* taller *m* ■ **s. window** escaparate ➤ *intr* ir de compras ■ **to s. for** ir a comprar.

shopkeeper ➤ *s* tendero/a.

shopping ➤ *s* compras ■ **s. center** centro comercial • **to go s.** ir de compras.

shore ➤ *s (coast)* orilla; *(beach)* playa.

short ➤ *adj* corto; *(in height)* bajo; *(in amount)* poco ■ **a s. distance from a poca distancia de** • **in s. order** sin demora • **s. circuit** ELEC. cortocircuito • **s. story** cuento • **to be s. of** *(money)* tener poco; *(breath)* faltarle a uno ➤ *adv (abruptly)* en seco ■ **to come up s.** quedarse corto • **to fall s.** *(of)* no alcanzar ➤ *s* cortocircuito ■ **in s.** en resumen ■ *pl* pantalones cortos.

shortage ➤ *s* falta.

shortcut ➤ *s* atajo.

shorten ➤ *tr & intr* acortar(se).

shorthand ➤ *s* taquigrafía.

shortly ➤ *adv* dentro de poco.

shortsighted ➤ *adj* corto de vista.

short-term ➤ *adj* a corto plazo.

shot ➤ *s* disparo; *(try)* tiro; CINEM. plano; FOTOG. foto *f*; MED. inyección *f*.

shotgun ➤ *s* escopeta.

should ➤ *aux (obligation)* deber; *(expectation)* deber de.

shoulder ➤ *s* hombro; *(of road)* orilla ■ **s. bag** bolsa *o* bolso bandolera ➤ *tr* echarse al hombro.

shout ➤ *s* grito ➤ *tr & intr* gritar.

shove ➤ *tr* empujar a ➤ *intr* dar empujones ➤ *s* empujón *m*.

shovel ➤ *s* pala ➤ *tr* traspalar.

show◇ ➤ *tr* mostrar; *(to present)* presentar; *(to prove)* demostrar; *(to manifest)* manifestar; *(to exhibit)* exponer ■ **to s. how to** enseñar a • **to s. off** hacer alarde de ➤ *intr* verse; FAM. *(to come)* aparecer ■ **to s. off** alardear • **to s. up** aparecer ➤ *s* demostración *f*; TELEV. programa *m*; TEAT. espectáculo ■ **fashion s.** desfile de modelos • **s. business** mundo del espectáculo • **s. room** sala de exposición.

shower ➤ *s (rain)* chaparrón *m*; *(bath)*

ducha ➤ *intr* ducharse.

showoff ➤ *s* FAM. presumido/a.

showy ➤ *adj* llamativo.

shred ➤ *s* fragmento ➤ *tr* hacer trizas.

shrewd ➤ *adj* astuto.

shrill ➤ *adj* chillón.

shrimp ➤ *s* camarón *m*.

shrine ➤ *s* relicario.

shrink◇ ➤ *tr & intr* encoger(se) ➤ *s* JER. psiquiatra *mf*.

shrivel ➤ *tr & intr* encoger(se).

shrub ➤ *s* matorral *m*.

shrug ➤ *intr* encogerse de hombros.

shudder ➤ *intr* estremecerse.

shuffle ➤ *tr (cards)* barajar.

shut◇ ➤ *tr & intr* cerrar(se) ■ **to s. off** aislar; *(to turn off)* desconectar • **to s. up** encerrar; *(to silence)* hacer callar; *(to be silent)* callarse la boca.

shutdown ➤ *s* cierre *m*.

shutter ➤ *s* contraventana; FOTOG. obturador *m*.

shuttle ➤ *s* lanzadera; *(vehicle)* vehículo de enlace; AVIA. puente aéreo ■ **space s.** transbordador espacial.

shy ➤ *adj* tímido; *(bashful)* vergonzoso; *(wary)* cauteloso.

shyness ➤ *s* timidez *f*.

sibling ➤ *s* hermano/a.

sick ➤ *adj* enfermo; *(disgusted)* asqueado; *(tired)* cansado ■ **to be s.** vomitar • **to get s.** *(seasick)* marearse; *(to take sick)* ponerse enfermo • **to make s.** dar asco a.

sickness ➤ *s* enfermedad *f*; *(nausea)* náusea.

side ➤ *s* lado; *(of hill)* ladera; *(of boat)* costado; *(of coin)* cara; *(edge)* borde *m*; *(team)* facción *f* ■ **by the s. of** al lado de • **on either s. de cada lado** • **s. by s.** juntos • **to take sides** tomar partido ➤ *adj* lateral ■ **s. effect** efecto secundario • **s. view** vista de perfil ➤ *intr* ■ **to s. with** ponerse del lado de.

sidewalk ➤ *s* acera.

sideways ➤ *adv* de lado.

sieve ➤ *s* tamiz *m* ➤ *tr* tamizar.

sift ➤ *tr* cerner; *(to separate)* separar.

sigh ➤ *intr* suspirar ➤ *s* suspiro.

sight ➤ *s* vista; *(vision)* visión *f*; *(thing to see)* lugar *m* de interés; *(of gun)* mira ■ s. unseen sin haberlo visto • to be (with)in s. of estar a la vista de ■ *pl* meta • to set one's s. on tener el ojo puesto en ■ *tr* ver; *(to aim)* apuntar.

sightseeing ➤ *s* excursionismo.

sign ➤ *s* seña, signo; *(gesture)* gesto; *(poster)* letrero; *(symbol)* símbolo; *(trace)* huella ➤ *tr* firmar ➤ *intr* hacer señas; *(to write)* firmar ■ to s. on *o* up alistar(se).

signal ➤ *s* señal *f* ➤ *tr* dar la señal de *o* para; *(to make known)* indicar ➤ *intr* hacer señales.

signature ➤ *s* firma.

significant ➤ *adj* significativo.

signify ➤ *tr* significar.

signpost ➤ *s* poste *m* indicador.

silence ➤ *s* silencio; *tr* hacer callar.

silent ➤ *adj* silencioso; *(mute)* mudo ■ to be s. callar.

silicon ➤ *s* silicio.

silicone ➤ *s* silicona.

silk ➤ *s* seda.

silly ➤ *adj* tonto, bobo; *(ridiculous)* ridículo.

silver ➤ *s* plata; *(color)* plateado ➤ *adj* de plata; *(like silver)* plateado ■ s. plate platería ➤ *tr* platear.

silverware ➤ *s* (vajilla de) plata.

similar ➤ *adj* similar.

similarity ➤ *s* similitud *f*.

simple ➤ *adj* simple, sencillo.

simplify ➤ *tr* simplificar.

simply ➤ *adv* simplemente, sencillamente.

simultaneous ➤ *adj* simultáneo.

sin ➤ *s* pecado ➤ *intr* pecar.

since ➤ *adv* desde entonces; *(ago)* hace ■ long s. hace mucho tiempo ➤ *prep* desde ■ s. that time desde entonces ➤ *conj* desde que; *(inasmuch as)* ya que.

sincere ➤ *adj* sincero.

sincerity ➤ *s* sinceridad *f*.

sinful ➤ *adj* pecaminoso.

sing◇ ➤ *tr & intr* cantar.

singer ➤ *s* cantante *mf*.

single ➤ *adj* solo; *(for one)* individual; *(unmarried)* soltero ■ s. bed cama para una persona • s. file hilera.

singular ➤ *adj & s* singular *m*.

sinister ➤ *adj* siniestro.

sink◇ ➤ *intr* descender; *(ship)* hundirse; ➤ *s (bathroom)* lavabo; *(kitchen)* fregadero.

sip ➤ *tr & intr* sorber ➤ *s* sorbo.

sir ➤ *s* señor *m*.

siren ➤ *s* sirena.

sirloin ➤ *s* solomillo.

sister ➤ *s* hermana.

sister-in-law ➤ *s* cuñada, hermana política.

sit◇ ➤ *intr* sentarse; *(to be at rest)* estar sentado ■ to s. down sentarse • to s. in participar • to s. still no moverse • to s. up incorporarse.

site ➤ *s* sitio ➤ *tr* situar.

sitter ➤ *s* persona que cuida niños.

situation ➤ *s* situación *f*.

six ➤ *s & adj* seis *m* ■ s. hundred seiscientos • s. o'clock las seis.

sixteen ➤ *s & adj* dieciséis *m*.

sixth ➤ *s & adj* sexto.

sixty ➤ *s & adj* sesenta *m*.

size ➤ *s* tamaño; *(of shoes)* número; *(of persons, garments)* talla.

skate ➤ *s* patín *m* ➤ *intr* patinar.

skateboard ➤ *s* monopatín *m*.

skeleton ➤ *s* esqueleto.

sketch ➤ *s* esbozo; *(outline)* bosquejo ➤ *tr* esbozar ➤ *intr* dibujar.

sketchbook ➤ *s* bloc *m* de dibujo.

ski ➤ *s* esquí *m* ■ s. lift telesquí ➤ *intr & tr* esquiar.

skid ➤ *s* patinazo, resbalón *m* ➤ *intr* resbalar (rueda, automóvil).

skier ➤ *s* esquiador/a.

skiing ➤ *s* esquí *m* (deporte).

skill ➤ *s* maña; *(art)* técnica; *(experience)* experiencia.

skilled ➤ *adj* mañoso; *(qualified)* especializado.

skillet ➤ *s* sartén *f*.

skim ➤ *tr (milk)* desnatar; *(book)* hojear ➤ *s* ■ s. milk leche desnatada.

skin ➤ *s* piel *f* ➤ *tr* despellajar.

skinny ➤ *adj* flaco.

skip ➤ *tr & intr* saltar ■ to s. over saltar por encima de ➤ *s* salto.

skirt ➤ *s* falda.

skull ➤ *s* cráneo.

sky ➤ *s* cielo.

skyline ➤ s horizonte m.

skyscraper ➤ s rascacielos m.

slack ➤ adj (loose) flojo ➤ intr aflojarse; (to be remiss) ser negligente ➤ s (of rope) parte floja ∎ pl pantalones.

slam ➤ tr & intr cerrar(se) de golpe ∎ to s. into chocar con ➤ s golpe m fuerte; (of door) portazo.

slander ➤ s calumnia ➤ tr calumniar.

slang ➤ s jerga.

slant ➤ tr & intr inclinar(se) ➤ s inclinación f; FIG. interpretación f.

slap ➤ s palmada; (on face) bofetada ➤ tr dar una palmada; (the face) abofetear.

slash ➤ tr acuchillar; (prices) rebajar ➤ s tajo.

slate ➤ s pizarra.

slaughter ➤ s matanza ➤ tr matar.

slave ➤ s esclavo/a.

slavery ➤ s esclavitud f.

slay◇ ➤ tr matar.

slayer◇ ➤ asesino/a.

sleep◇ ➤ s sueño ∎ go to s. dormirse ➤ intr dormir.

sleeping ➤ adj dormido, durmiendo ∎ s. bag saco de dormir • s. car coche cama • s. pill somnífero.

sleepy ➤ adj soñoliento.

sleet ➤ s aguanieve f ➤ intr cellisquear.

sleeve ➤ s manga.

sleeveless ➤ adj sin mangas.

sleigh ➤ s trineo.

slender ➤ adj delgado; (svelte) esbelto.

slew ➤ s FAM. montón m.

slice ➤ s (of meat) tajada; (of bread) rebanada; (of ham) lonja ➤ tr cortar, tajar; (bread) rebanar.

slide◇ ➤ intr resbalar; (to coast) deslizarse ➤ tr hacer resbalar ➤ s (playground) tobogán m; FOTOG diapositiva.

slight ➤ adj escaso; (trifling) insignificante; (slender) delgado ➤ tr menospreciar; (to shirk) desatender ➤ s desaire m.

slim ➤ adj delgado; (scant) escaso ➤ tr & intr adelgazar.

sling◇ ➤ s (weapon) honda; MED. cabestrillo ➤ tr arrojar; (to hang) colgar.

slip ➤ intr (to slide) deslizarse; (stealth-ily) escabullirse; (to lose one's balance) resbalar ∎ to let s. decir sin querer • to s. by (time) correr; (unnoticed) pasar inadvertido • to s. out salir inadvertido • to s. up FAM. equivocarse ➤ tr librarse (from de) ➤ s resbalón m; (false step) paso en falso; (error) equivocación f; (lapse) desliz m; (undergarment) combinación f.

slipper ➤ s zapatilla.

slippery ➤ adj resbaladizo.

slit◇ ➤ s corte m ➤ tr hender.

slogan ➤ s lema m; COM. slogan m.

slope ➤ tr & intr inclinar(se) ➤ s cuesta; (of roof) vertiente f; (inclination) inclinación f ∎ on a s. en declive.

sloppy ➤ adj (messy) desordenado; (careless) chapucero.

slot ➤ s ranura; (on roster) puesto ∎ s. machine máquina tragaperras.

slow ➤ adj lento; (clock) atrasado; (mentally) torpe ∎ s. motion cámara lenta ∎ to be s. to tardar en ➤ adv lentamente ➤ tr retrasar, retardar ➤ intr ∎ to s. down ir más despacio.

slug ➤ s ZOOL. babosa.

slum ➤ s barrio bajo.

sly ➤ adj astuto.

smack ➤ tr (to strike) dar un palmada ∎ to s. one's lips relamerse ➤ s (sound) chasquido; (blow) golpe m.

small ➤ adj pequeño; (petty) mezquino ∎ s. letters minúsculas • s. talk charloteo.

smallpox ➤ s viruela.

smart ➤ adj listo; (witty) ingenioso; (fashionable) elegante.

smash ➤ tr romper; (to shatter) destrozar ➤ intr romperse ∎ to s. into chocar con • to s. to pieces hacerse pedazos ➤ adj ∎ a s. hit un gran éxito.

smell◇ ➤ tr oler ➤ intr oler; (to stink) apestar ➤ s olor m.

smile ➤ s sonrisa ➤ intr sonreír(se).

smock ➤ s guardapolvo.

smog ➤ s mezcla de humo y niebla.

smoke ➤ s humo ∎ s. detector detector de humo ➤ intr humear; (tobacco) fumar ➤ tr fumar; (to preserve) ahumar ∎ to s. out descubrir.

smooth ➤ adj (fine) liso; (soft) suave;

(calm) tranquilo ➤ *tr (to level)* alisar; *(to polish)* pulir ■ **to s. things over** limar asperezas.

smother ➤ *tr* sofocar ➤ *intr* asfixiarse.

smuggle ➤ *tr* pasar de contrabando.

smuggler ➤ *s* contrabandista *mf.*

snack ➤ *s* bocado.

snail ➤ *s* caracol *m.*

snake ➤ *s* serpiente *f.*

snap ➤ *tr & intr* quebrar(se) ■ **to s. off** desprender(se) • **to s. open, shut** abrir(se), cerrar(se) de golpe ➤ *s (breaking)* rotura; *(clasp)* broche *m* de presión.

snapshot ➤ *s* instantánea.

snarl ➤ *intr* gruñir ➤ *s* gruñido.

snatch ➤ *tr* agarrar, arrebatar; *(purse)* robar ➤ *s (of conversation)* fragmento.

sneaker ➤ *s* zapato de lona.

sneer ➤ *s & intr* (hacer un) gesto de desprecio.

sneeze ➤ *intr* estornudar ➤ *s* estornudo.

sniff ➤ *tr (odor)* olfatear; *(substance)* inhalar ➤ *s* olfateo.

snip ➤ *tr & intr* tijeretear ➤ *s (action)* tijeretazo; *(piece)* recorte *m.*

snore ➤ *intr* roncar ➤ *s* ronquido.

snorkel ➤ *s & intr* bucear con) tubo de respiración.

snout ➤ *s* hocico.

snow ➤ *s* nieve *f; (snowfall)* nevada ➤ *intr* nevar.

snowball ➤ *s* bola de nieve ➤ *intr* aumentar rápidamente.

snowdrift ➤ *s* ventisquero.

snowfall ➤ *s* nevada.

snowplow ➤ *s* quitanieves *m.*

snug ➤ *adj (cozy)* cómodo; *(warm)* calentito; *(tight)* ajustado.

snuggle ➤ *tr & intr* acurrucar(se).

so ➤ *adv (thus)* así; *(to such an extent)* tan; *(consequently)* por eso; *(likewise)* también; *(so much)* tanto; *(then)* así que ■ I hope so espero que sí • not so no es así • **not so much as** ni siquiera • or so más o menos • so far hasta aquí • so far so good por ahora, bien • so long tanto (tiempo); *(goodbye)* hasta luego • so so así, así ➤ *adj* así ➤ *conj* así que ■ **so that** para que.

soak ➤ *tr* empapar; *(to immerse)* remojar ■ **to s. up** absorber ➤ *intr* remojarse; *(to drench)* calar ➤ *s* remojo.

soap ➤ *s* jabón *m* ➤ *tr* (en)jabonar.

soapy ➤ *adj* jabonoso.

sob ➤ *intr* sollozar ➤ *s* sollozo.

sober ➤ *adj* sobrio ➤ *intr* ■ **to s. up** pasársele a uno la embriaguez.

soccer ➤ *s* fútbol *m* ■ **s. ball** balón.

social ➤ *adj* social ■ **s. services** programa de asistencia social • **s. work** asistencia social ➤ *s* reunión *f.*

socialist ➤ *s & adj* socialista *mf.*

society ➤ *s* sociedad *f.*

sock ➤ *s* calcetín *m.*

socket ➤ *s* ELEC. enchufe *m.*

soda ➤ *s* soda, gaseosa.

sodium ➤ *s* sodio.

sofa ➤ *s* sofá *m.*

soft ➤ *adj (not hard)* blando; *(not loud)* bajo; *(gentle, smooth)* suave ■ **s. drink** gaseosa.

soft-boiled ➤ *adj (egg)* pasado por agua.

software ➤ *s* software *m.*

soil ➤ *s (land)* tierra ➤ *tr* ensuciar.

soiled ➤ *adj* sucio.

soldier ➤ *s* soldado *mf.*

sold-out ➤ *adj* agotado.

sole[1] ➤ *s (of foot)* planta; *(of shoe)* suela.

sole[2] ➤ *adj (single)* único; *(rights, ownership)* exclusivo.

sole[3] ➤ *s (fish)* lenguado.

solemn ➤ *adj* solemne.

solicit ➤ *tr* solicitar.

solicitor ➤ *s* G.B. abogado/a.

solid ➤ *adj* sólido; *(not hollow)* macizo; *(line)* continuo ➤ *s* sólido.

solidarity ➤ *s* solidaridad *f.*

solitude ➤ *s* soledad *f.*

solo ➤ *adj & s* solo ➤ *adv* a solas ➤ *intr* volar solo.

solution ➤ *s* solución *f.*

solve ➤ *tr* resolver, solucionar.

solvent ➤ *adj* FIN. solvente ➤ *s (di)*solvente *m.*

some ➤ *adj* alguno(s); *(a little)* un poco de ■ **after s. time** después de cierto tiempo • **s. days ago** hace varios días • **s. other time** otro día ➤ *pron (several)* algunos; *(a little)* un poco, algo ■ **and**

then s. y más todavía.

somebody o **someone** ➤ *pron* alguien.

somehow ➤ *adv* de algún modo; *(for some reason)* por alguna razón.

someplace ➤ *adv* en o a alguna parte.

somersault ➤ *s & intr* (dar un) salto mortal.

something ➤ *pron & s* algo ■ s. or other una cosa u otra • to be s. of a . . . tener algo de . . .

sometime ➤ *adv* alguna vez, algún día.

sometimes ➤ *adv* a veces.

somewhat ➤ *adv* algo.

somewhere ➤ *adv* en o a alguna parte ■ s. around aproximadamente.

son ➤ *s* hijo.

song ➤ *s* canción *f;* *(act)* canto.

son-in-law ➤ *s* yerno, hijo político.

soon ➤ *adv* pronto; *(early)* temprano ■ as s. as en cuanto, tan pronto como • how s.? ¿cuándo? • s. after poco después • sooner or later tarde o temprano.

soothe ➤ *tr* calmar, tranquilizar; *(pain)* aliviar.

sophisticated ➤ *adj* sofisticado.

sophomore ➤ *s* estudiante *mf* de segundo año.

sore ➤ *adj* dolorido ■ s. throat dolor de garganta • to be s. doler ➤ *s (wound)* llaga; *(pain)* dolor *m.*

sorority ➤ *s* asociación estudiantil femenina.

sorrow ➤ *s* pesar.

sorry ➤ *adj (sad)* triste ■ I'm s. lo siento • to be s. sentir • to feel s. for compadecer ➤ *interj* ¡perdón!

sort ➤ *s (class)* clase *f,* tipo ■ s. of *(rather)* más bien; *(somewhat)* algo • out of sorts de mal humor ➤ *tr* clasificar; *(to put in order)* ordenar ■ to s. out *(problems)* resolver.

soul ➤ *s* alma.

sound[1] ➤ *s* sonido ■ from the s. of it al parecer • s. effects efectos sonoros ➤ *intr* sonar; *(to seem)* parecer ➤ *tr (instrument)* tocar; *(alarm)* dar.

sound[2] ➤ *adj* en buenas condiciones; *(healthy)* sano; *(economy)* fuerte; *(sleep)* profundo; *(advice)* razonable; DER. válido ■ to be s. of mind estar uno en su sano juicio.

sound[3] ➤ *s* MARÍT. brazo de mar.

soundproof ➤ *adj* a prueba de sonido.

soundtrack ➤ *s* pista o banda sonora.

soup ➤ *s* sopa ■ s. kitchen comedor de beneficencia.

soupspoon ➤ *s* cuchara de sopa.

sour ➤ *adj* agrio; *(milk)* cortado; *(smell)* acre.

source ➤ *s* origen *m;* *(of river)* manantial *m;* *(of supply, news)* fuente *f.*

south ➤ *s* sur *m* ➤ *adj* del sur ➤ *adv* al sur, hacia el sur.

South America ➤ *s* Sudamérica.

South American ➤ *adj & s* sudamericano/a.

southeast ➤ *adj & s* (del) sudeste *m.*

southeastern ➤ *adj* del sudeste.

southern ➤ *adj* del sur.

southerner ➤ *s* sureño/a.

South Pole ➤ *s* Polo Sur.

southwest ➤ *adj & s* (del) suroeste *m.*

southwestern ➤ *adj* del suroeste.

souvenir ➤ *s* recuerdo.

sovereign ➤ *adj & s* soberano.

sow[1] ➤ *tr* sembrar.

sow[2] ➤ *s (female hog)* cerda.

soy ➤ *s* soja ■ s. sauce salsa de soja.

spa ➤ *s* balneario.

space ➤ *s* espacio; *(place)* sitio, lugar ■ outer s. espacio exterior • s. age era espacial • s. bar espaciador ➤ *tr* espaciar ➤ *intr* ■ to s. out JER. abstraerse.

spaceship ➤ *s* nave *f* espacial.

spacious ➤ *adj* espacioso, amplio.

spade[1] ➤ *s (digging tool)* pala.

spade[2] ➤ *s (in cards)* espada, pico.

spaghetti ➤ *s* espagueti *m.*

Spaniard ➤ *s* español/a.

Spanish ➤ *adj* español ➤ *s (language)* español *m,* castellano.

Spanish-speaking ➤ *adj* hispanohablante.

spank ➤ *tr* dar una zurra a, zurrar.

spare ➤ *tr (expenses, efforts)* escatimar; *(not to kill, destroy)* perdonar; *(to do without)* prescindir de; *(time)* dar, dedicar; *(feelings)* no herir ■ to s. de sobra ➤ *adj (part)* de repuesto, de recambio; *(extra)* sobrante, de sobra; *(unoccupied)* libre ■ s. room cuarto en desuso ➤ *s* pieza de repuesto.

spark ➤ s chispa ➤ intr chispear ➤ tr provocar.

sparkle ➤ intr centellear, brillar.

sparkplug ➤ s AUTO. bujía.

sparrow ➤ s gorrión m.

speak◇ ➤ intr hablar; (in assembly) tomar la palabra ■ to s. out hablar claro • to s. up (louder) hablar más fuerte; (to be heard) decir lo que uno piensa ➤ tr (a language) hablar ■ to s. for (to recommend) hablar en favor de; (on behalf of) hablar en nombre de • to s. for itself ser evidente • to s. the truth decir la verdad.

speaker ➤ s (orator) orador/a; (loudspeaker) altoparlante m, altavoz m.

spear ➤ s lanza.

special ➤ adj especial ■ s. delivery entrega inmediata.

specialist ➤ s especialista mf.

speciality ➤ s especialidad f.

specialize ➤ intr especializarse.

specially ➤ adv especialmente.

specialty ➤ s especialidad f.

species ➤ s especie f.

specific ➤ adj específico.

specify ➤ tr especificar.

specimen ➤ s muestra, ejemplar m.

speck ➤ s mancha, mota.

spectacle ➤ s espectáculo.

spectacular ➤ adj espectacular.

spectator ➤ s espectador/a.

speech◇ ➤ s habla; (address) discurso ■ free s. libertad de expresión.

speed◇ ➤ s velocidad f ■ at full o top s. a toda velocidad • s. limit velocidad máxima ➤ intr ir de prisa, ir corriendo; (to drive fast) conducir con exceso de velocidad ■ to s. up acelerar.

speedboat ➤ s lancha motora.

speedometer ➤ s velocímetro.

spell¹ ➤ tr escribir ■ how do you s....? ¿cómo se escribe...? • to s. out deletrear; (to explain) explicar.

spell² ➤ s encanto, hechizo.

spell³ ➤ s (of time) temporada; (of work) turno.

spelling ➤ s ortografía.

spend◇ ➤ tr (money) gastar; (time) pasar.

sphere ➤ s esfera.

spice ➤ s especia; FIG. sabor m ➤ tr sazonar; FIG. salpimentar.

spicy ➤ adj picante.

spider ➤ s araña.

spike ➤ s (nail) clavo, estaca; (spine) púa; (sharp point) punta.

spill◇ ➤ tr & intr (liquid) derramar(se), verter(se); (a container) volcar(se) ■ to s. over salirse.

spin◇ ➤ tr (thread) hilar; (web) tejer; (to twirl) hacer girar, dar vueltas a ➤ intr (to whirl) girar, dar vueltas ➤ s giro, vuelta; (in a car) vuelta, paseo.

spinach ➤ s espinaca.

spine ➤ s ANAT. espina dorsal; BOT., ZOOL. espina, púa.

spiny ➤ adj espinoso.

spiral ➤ s & intr (moverse en) espiral f.

spirit ➤ s espíritu m; (soul) alma ■ pl alcohol, licor • in high o good s. de buen humor.

spiritual ➤ adj & s espiritual m.

spit◇ ➤ s saliva; (act) escupitajo ➤ tr & intr escupir.

spite ➤ s rencor ■ in s. of a pesar de, no obstante • out of s. por despecho ➤ tr despechar.

splash ➤ tr (to spatter) salpicar (with de); (to wet) chapotear ■ to s. about chapotear • to s. down amerizar.

splendid ➤ adj espléndido.

splinter ➤ s astilla ➤ tr & intr astillar.

split◇ ➤ tr (in two) partir, dividir; (to crack) hender; (to share) compartir ■ to s. off separar • to s. up (to share) repartir; (to separate) separar ➤ intr (in two) partirse; (cloth) desgarrarse ➤ s (crack) grieta.

spoil◇ ➤ tr (to damage) estropear; (child) mimar ➤ intr estropearse ➤ spoils spl botín m.

spoke ➤ s (of a wheel) radio.

spokesperson ➤ s portavoz mf.

sponge ➤ s esponja ➤ tr limpiar con esponja; (money, food) gorronear.

sponsor ➤ s patrocinador m ➤ tr patrocinar.

spontaneous ➤ adj espontáneo.

spool ➤ s carrete m, bobina.

spoon ➤ s & tr (sacar con) cuchara.

sport ➤ s deporte m ■ in s. en broma • s.

shirt camisa de sport • **to be a good s.** ser buen/a perdedor/a.

sports ► *adj* de sport ■ **s.** car automóvil deportivo.

sportsman/woman ► *s* deportista *mf*.

spot ► *s* lugar *m*; *(stain)* mancha; *(dot)* lunar *m*; TELEV. anuncio ■ **in a bad o tight s.** en apuros • **to remove spot-manchas** • **to put on the s.** poner en un aprieto ► *tr* manchar; *(to detect)* notar.

spotless ► *adj* inmaculado.

spotlight ► *s* foco.

spouse ► *s* esposo/a.

spout ► *s (for pouring)* pico; *(tube)* caño; *(stream)* chorro ► *intr* chorrear.

sprain ► *s* torcedura ► *tr* torcer.

spray ► *s* rociada; MARÍT. espuma ■ **s. can** pulverizador ► *tr* rociar.

spread◇ ► *tr* extender; *(to move apart)* separar; *(butter)* untar ► *intr* esparcirse; *(knowledge)* difundirse; *(to move apart)* separarse ■ **to s. out** extenderse; *(to get wider)* ensanchar ► *s* difusión *f*; *(expanse)* extensión *f*.

spreadsheet ► *s* hoja de cálculo.

spring◇ ► *intr (to jump)* saltar ■ **to s. forth** brotar • **to s. up** surgir ► *s (jump)* salto; *(coil)* resorte *m*; *(season)* primavera; *(source)* fuente *f*.

springboard ► *s* trampolín *m*.

springtime ► *s* primavera.

sprinkle ► *tr* rociar ► *intr (rain)* lloviznar ► *s* llovizna.

sprinkler ► *s* regadera; *(fire extinguisher)* extintor *m*.

sprout ► *intr* brotar ► *s* brote *m*.

spur ► *s* espuela; FIG. incentivo ► *tr* espolear; FIG. estimular.

spurt ► *s* chorro ► *intr* salir a chorros.

spy ► *s* espía *mf* ► *intr* ■ **to s. (on)** espiar.

spying ► *s* espionaje *m*.

squander ► *tr* derrochar.

square ► *s* cuadrado; *(in town)* plaza ► *adj* cuadrado ■ **s. dance** baile de figuras • **s. deal** FAM. trato justo.

squash[1] ► *s* BOT. calabaza.

squash[2] ► *tr & intr* aplastar(se).

squat ► *intr* ponerse en cuclillas.

squeak ► *intr* chirriar ► *s* chirrido.

squeal ► *intr* chirriar ► *s* chillido.

squeeze ► *tr* apretar; *(lemon, juice)* exprimir ■ **to s. out** sacar; *(to exclude)* excluir ► *s* presión *f*.

squid ► *s* calamar *m*.

squint ► *intr* entrecerrar los ojos ► *s* mirada bizca.

squirrel ► *s* ardilla.

squirt ► *intr & tr (dejar)* salir a chorros ► *s* chorro.

stab ► *tr* apuñalar ► *s* puñalada; *(wound)* herida; FIG. *(attempt)* intento.

stability ► *s* estabilidad *f*.

stable[1] ► *adj* estable.

stable[2] ► *s (building)* establo.

stack ► *s (pile)* pila; FAM. montón *m* ■ *pl* estantes ► *tr* amontonar.

stadium ► *s* estadio.

staff ► *s (personnel)* personal *m*; *(stick)* báculo, bastón *m*.

stag ► *s* ciervo.

stage ► *s* plataforma; *(phase)* etapa; TEAT. escena ■ **by stages** progresivamente ► *tr* TEAT. representar; *(to arrange)* organizar.

stagger ► *intr* tambalearse ► *tr (to overwhelm)* asombrar; *(to alternate)* escalonar.

stain ► *tr* manchar ► *s* mancha.

stainless ► *adj* inoxidable.

stair ► *s* escalón *m* ■ *pl* escalera.

staircase ► *s* escalera.

stake ► *s (stick)* estaca; *(interest)* intereses *m* ■ **at s.** en juego ■ *pl (bet)* apuesta ► *tr* estacar; *(to risk)* jugarse.

stale ► *adj (food)* rancio; *(bread)* duro; *(news)* viejo.

stalk[1] ► *s (plant stem)* tallo.

stalk[2] ► *tr (to pursue)* acechar.

stall ► *s (in barn)* pesebre *m*; *(booth)* caseta ► *intr (to delay)* andar con rodeos; AUTO. calarse.

stammer ► *intr* tartamudear ► *s* tartamudez *f*, tartamudeo.

stamp ► *tr (to affix stamp)* poner un sello a ■ **to s. on** pisar • **to s. out** sofocar ► *intr* patear ► *s (postage)* sello, estampilla; *(official)* timbre *m*.

stand◇ ► *intr* estar de pie; *(to rise)* ponerse de pie; *(to place oneself)*

ponerse ■ to s. alone ser el único • **to s. aside** retirarse • **to s. by** estar listo; *(to look on)* mirar y no hacer nada • **to s. in** *o* **on line** hacer cola • **to s. out** resaltar • **to s. up** levantarse ➤ *tr (to withstand)* tolerar ■ **to s. for** representar • **to s. up to** hacer frente a; *(to last)* resistir ➤ *s (booth)* quiosco; *(counter)* mostrador *m; (pedestal)* pie *m; (for coats, hats)* perchero ■ **to take a s.** adoptar una actitud.

standard ➤ *s* criterio; *(model)* patrón *m* ■ **s. of living** nivel de vida ■ *pl* normas ➤ *adj* standard; *(accepted)* normal ■ **s. time** hora civil.

standby ➤ *s* persona *o* cosa de confianza ■ **s. list** lista de espera.

standing ➤ *s* reputación *f* ➤ *adj* de pie, parado.

standoff ➤ *s* empate *m.*

standpoint ➤ *s* punto de vista.

standstill ➤ *s* parada.

staple ➤ *s (fastener)* grapa ➤ *tr* sujetar con una grapa.

stapler ➤ *s* grapador *m.*

star ➤ *s* estrella ■ **shooting s.** estrella fugaz ■ *pl* ASTROL. astros ➤ *tr (to feature)* presentar como protagonista ➤ *intr* protagonizar.

starboard ➤ *s & adj* (de) estribor *m.*

starch ➤ *s* CUL. fécula; *(stiffener)* almidón *m* ➤ *tr* almidonar.

stare ➤ *intr* mirar fijamente ➤ *s* mirada fija.

start ➤ *intr* empezar; *(to set out)* salir; *(motor)* arrancar ■ **to s. with** para comenzar ➤ *tr* empezar; *(car, machine)* poner en marcha ➤ *s (beginning)* principio; *(place)* salida, punto de partida ■ **to make a fresh s.** empezar de nuevo.

startle ➤ *tr & intr* sobresaltar(se) ➤ *s* sobresalto.

starvation ➤ *s* hambre *f.*

starve ➤ *intr* morirse de hambre ➤ *tr* matar de hambre.

starving ➤ *adj* hambriento.

state ➤ *s* estado ■ **the States** los Estados Unidos ➤ *tr* declarar.

statement ➤ *s* declaración *f;* COM. *(bill)* cuenta; *(report)* estado de cuenta.

statesman/woman ➤ *s* estadista *mf.*

station ➤ *s* estación *f; (social)* rango ■ **police s.** comisaría • **service s.** estación de servicio ➤ *tr* estacionar; *(to post)* apostar.

stationary ➤ *adj* estacionario; *(fixed)* fijo.

stationery ➤ *s* papel y sobres *m.*

statistic ➤ *s* estadística ■ *pl (science)* estadística.

statistical ➤ *adj* estadístico.

statue ➤ *s* estatua.

stature ➤ *s* estatura.

status ➤ *s* posición *f* social; DER. estado.

statute ➤ *s* estatuto.

stay ➤ *intr* quedarse; *(to sojourn)* alojarse ■ **to s. away** ausentarse • **to s. in** quedarse en casa • **to s. up late** acostarse tarde ➤ *s (visit)* estancia; DER. aplazamiento.

steady ➤ *adj* firme; *(stable)* estable; *(reliable)* seguro ➤ *tr & intr* estabilizar(se).

steak ➤ *s* bistec *m; (fish)* filete *m.*

steal ➤ *tr & intr* robar ■ **to s. away** escabullirse ➤ *s* JER. *(bargain)* ganga.

steam ➤ *s* vapor *m* ■ **s. engine** máquina a vapor ➤ *intr* echar vapor; *(to fog up)* empañarse ➤ *tr* CUL. cocer al vapor.

steamer ➤ *(ship)* vapor *m;* CUL. olla de vapor.

steamroller ➤ *s* apisonadora.

steel ➤ *s & adj* (de) acero.

steep ➤ *adj (high)* empinado; *(price)* excesivo.

steeple ➤ *s* torrecilla; *(spire)* aguja.

steer ➤ *tr (boat)* gobernar; *(car)* conducir; FIG. dirigir, guiar ■ **steering wheel** volante • **to s. clear of** evitar.

stem ➤ *s* BOT. tallo.

step ➤ *s* paso; *(sound)* pisada; *(stair, degree)* escalón *m* ■ **s. by s.** paso a paso ■ *pl* escaleras ➤ *intr* ■ **to s. aside** hacerse a un lado • **to s. down** bajar; *(to resign)* renunciar • **to s. in** entrar; *(to intervene)* intervenir • **to s. on** pisar • **to s. out** salir; *(of car)* apearse • **to s. up** subir; *(to increase)* aumentar.

stepbrother ➤ *s* hermanastro.

stepchild ➤ *s* hijastro/a.

stepfather ➤ *s* padrastro.

stepladder ➤ s escalera de tijera.
stepmother ➤ s madrastra.
stepsister ➤ s hermanastra.
stereo ➤ adj & s estéreo.
stereotype ➤ s estereotipo ➤ tr estereotipar.
sterile ➤ adj estéril.
sterilize ➤ tr esterilizar.
stern¹ ➤ adj severo.
stern² ➤ s MARÍT. popa.
stew ➤ tr guisar ➤ intr cocerse ➤ s guiso ■ in a s. agitado.
steward ➤ s administrador m; (domestic) mayordomo; AVIA. auxiliar m de vuelo, aeromozo.
stewardess ➤ s azafata, aeromoza.
stick◇ ➤ s vara, palo; (of gum) barra ■ s. shift AUTO. cambio manual ➤ tr (to impale) clavar; (to glue) pegar ■ to s. in introducir • to s. out (tongue) mostrar; (head) asomar ➤ intr (to cling) pegarse; (to jam) atascarse ■ to s. around quedarse • to s. out sobresalir • to s. to (promise) cumplir; (friend) ser fiel a; (facts) ceñirse a.
stickup ➤ s JER. atraco.
sticky ➤ adj pegajoso.
stiff ➤ adj rígido; (not limber) tieso; (formal) formal.
stifle ➤ tr & intr sofocar(se).
still ➤ adj (at rest) inmóvil; (tranquil) sosegado; (waters) mansa ■ s. life naturaleza muerta ➤ s foto fija ➤ adv quieto; (nevertheless) sin embargo ■ he's s. awake todavía está despierto • s. more aun más.
stillness ➤ s quietud f; (silence) silencio.
stimulate ➤ tr estimular.
sting◇ ➤ tr & intr picar ➤ s picadura.
stinger ➤ s aguijón m.
stink◇ ➤ intr heder, apestar ➤ s hedor m ■ to make o raise a s. armar un escándulo.
stipulate ➤ tr estipular.
stir ➤ tr (to mix) revolver; (to move) agitar ■ to s. up (memory) despertar; (trouble) provocar ➤ intr moverse.
stirrup ➤ s estribo.
stitch ➤ s COST. puntada; (decorative) punto; MED. punzada.

stock ➤ s (inventory) stock m; (supply) surtido; (livestock) ganado; (shares) acciones f ■ in s. en existencia • out of s. agotado • to take s. of evaluar ➤ tr ■ to s. up on abastecerse de ➤ adj ■ s. exchange o market bolsa.
stockbroker ➤ s corredor/a m de bolsa.
stockholder ➤ s accionista mf.
stocking ➤ s media.
stomach ➤ s estómago.
stomachache ➤ s dolor m de estómago.
stone ➤ s piedra ➤ tr apedrear.
stoned ➤ adj (drunk) borracho; (on drugs) drogado.
stool ➤ s taburete m.
stoop ➤ intr encorvarse; FIG. condescender.
stop ➤ tr (to halt) detener; (to cease) dejar de ■ to s. up taponar ➤ intr detenerse; (to cease) cesar ■ to s. by o in hacer una visita corta ➤ s (place) parada; (en route) escala ■ s. sign señal de alto • to come to a s. pararse • to put a s. to poner fin a.
stoplight ➤ s semáforo.
stopover ➤ s AVIA., MARÍT. escala.
stopwatch ➤ s cronómetro.
storage ➤ s almacenamiento.
store ➤ s tienda; (supply) surtido ■ department s. gran almacén ➤ pl provisiones ➤ tr almacenar ■ to s. up acumular.
storeroom ➤ s despensa, bodega.
stork ➤ s cigüeña.
storm ➤ s tormenta ➤ intr haber tormenta ■ to s. in, out entrar, salir violentamente ➤ tr asaltar, tomar por asalto.
stormy ➤ adj tempestuoso.
story¹ ➤ s cuento, relato; (plot) trama; (article) artículo; (lie) mentira.
story² ➤ s (of a building) piso.
stout ➤ adj (body) fornido, corpulento; (sturdy) fuerte.
stove ➤ s cocina; (heater) estufa.
straight ➤ adj (line) recto; (upright, not bent) derecho; (honest) honrado; (not gay) heterosexual ➤ adv en línea recta; (without delay) directamente ■ s. ahead en frente; (forward) todo seguido • for three days s. durante tres días seguidos.

straighten ➤ *tr & intr* enderezar(se) ∎ **to s. out** ordenar.

straightforward ➤ *adj* (*direct*) directo; (*honest*) sincero.

strain ➤ *tr* (*nerves*) agotar; (*limb*) torcer; (*to sieve*) colar ∎ **to s. one's eyes** cansar la vista ➤ *s* (*effort*) esfuerzo; (*stress*) tensión *f.*

strainer ➤ *s* filtro; CUL. colador *m.*

strait(s) ➤ *s(pl)* GEOG. estrecho(s).

straitjacket ➤ *s* camisa de fuerza.

strange ➤ *adj* desconocido; (*odd*) extraño, raro.

stranger ➤ *s* desconocido/a; (*foreigner*) extranjero/a.

strangle ➤ *tr* estrangular.

strap ➤ *s* (*strip*) tira, correa; (*band*) banda; (*of a dress*) tirante *m.*

strategic ➤ *adj* estratégico.

strategy ➤ *s* estrategia.

straw ➤ *s* paja; (*for drinking*) pajita.

strawberry ➤ *s* fresa.

stray ➤ *intr* errar ➤ *adj* (*pet*) extraviado; (*bullet*) perdido.

streak ➤ *s* raya; (*of lightning*) rayo; (*of luck*) racha ➤ *tr* rayar.

stream ➤ *s* arroyo ➤ *intr* correr ∎ **to s. in, out** entrar, salir en tropel.

street ➤ *s* calle *f.*

streetcar ➤ *s* tranvía *m.*

strength ➤ *s* fuerza; (*of material*) resistencia; (*intensity*) intensidad *f.*

strengthen ➤ *tr* reforzar ➤ *intr* fortalecerse, intensificarse.

stress ➤ *s* (*emphasis*) hincapié *m;* (*tension*) tensión *f;* MED. estrés *m,* fatiga nerviosa; GRAM. énfasis *m.*

stretch ➤ *tr* estirar; (*to extend*) extender; (*wire*) tender ➤ *intr* estirarse; (*shoes*) ensancharse ∎ **to s. out** estirarse; (*to lie down*) tumbarse.

stretcher ➤ *s* camilla.

strew◇ ➤ *tr* esparcir.

strict ➤ *adj* estricto.

strictly ➤ *adv* estrictamente ∎ **s. speaking** en realidad.

stride◇ ➤ *intr* caminar a grandes pasos ➤ *s* zancada.

strident ➤ *adj* estridente.

strike◇ ➤ *tr* golpear; (*a blow*) asestar; (*to crash into*) chocar con ∎ **to s. down**

derribar ∎ **to s. up** (*friendship*) trabar; (*conversation*) entablar ∎ **to s. upon** ocurrírsele a uno ➤ *intr* dar golpes; (*to attack*) atacar; (*bell*) sonar; (*to stop work*) declararse en huelga ∎ **to s. out** (*for*) ponerse en marcha (*hacia*) ➤ *s* (*act*) golpe *m;* (*attack*) ataque *m;* (*labor*) huelga.

striker ➤ *s* huelguista *mf.*

striking ➤ *adj* notable.

string◇ ➤ *s* cuerda; (*series*) serie *f* ➤ *tr* (*to thread*) ensartar.

strip[1] ➤ *tr* desnudar; (*bed*) deshacer ∎ **to s. off** quitar ➤ *intr* desvestirse.

strip[2] ➤ *s* faja; AER. pista de aterrizaje.

stripe ➤ *s* raya.

striped ➤ *adj* a rayas, rayado.

strive◇ ➤ *intr* esforzarse.

stroke ➤ *s* golpe *m;* (*in swimming*) brazada; (*with brush*) pincelada; MED. apoplejía ∎ **s. of luck** suerte ➤ *tr* acariciar.

stroll ➤ *intr* pasearse ➤ *s* paseo.

stroller ➤ *s* cochecito de niño.

strong ➤ *adj* fuerte.

structure ➤ *s* estructura.

struggle ➤ *intr* luchar ➤ *s* lucha; (*effort*) esfuerzo.

strut ➤ *intr* pavonearse.

stub ➤ *s* tocón *m;* (*check*) talón *m* ➤ *tr* (*toe*) tropezar con.

stubborn ➤ *adj* testarudo; (*stain*) duro.

stubbornness ➤ *s* testarudez *f.*

student ➤ *s* estudiante *mf.*

studio ➤ *s* estudio; (*of artist*) taller *m.*

study ➤ *s* estudio ➤ *tr & intr* estudiar.

stuff ➤ *s* material *m;* (*belongings*) cosas ∎ **the same old s.** lo mismo de siempre ➤ *tr* rellenar ∎ **to s. oneself** atiborrarse.

stuffing ➤ *s* relleno.

stuffy ➤ *adj* sofocante, mal ventilado; (*congested*) tupido; FAM. pomposo.

stumble ➤ *intr* tropezar ∎ **to s. across** o **upon** tropezar con.

stump ➤ *s* (*of tree*) tocón *m;* (*limb*) muñón *m* ➤ *tr* dejar perplejo.

stun ➤ *tr* aturdir.

stunning ➤ *adj* (*looks*) imponente.

stunt ➤ *s* (*feat*) proeza ∎ **publicity s.** truco publicitario.

stupefy ➤ *tr* atontar.
stupid ➤ *adj* estúpido, tonto.
stupidity ➤ *s* estupidez *f*, tontería.
sturdy ➤ *adj* robusto; *(shoes)* fuerte.
stutter ➤ *intr* tartamudear ➤ *s* tartamudeo.
sty ➤ *s (for swine)* pocilga.
style ➤ *s* estilo; *(type)* modelo, tipo ■ in s. *(in vogue)* de moda.
stylish ➤ *adj* a la moda.
subconscious ➤ *s* subconsciente *m.*
subdue ➤ *tr* sojuzgar, dominar.
subject ➤ *adj (to a ruler)* sometido ■ s. to sujeto a ➤ *s (topic)* tema *m*; GRAM. sujeto; *(of country)* súbdito/a; *(course)* asignatura ➤ *tr* someter ■ to s. to exponer a.
subjugate ➤ *tr* subyugar.
sublime ➤ *adj* sublime.
submarine ➤ *adj & s* submarino.
submerge ➤ *tr & intr* sumergir(se).
submit ➤ *tr* someter; *(evidence, plan)* presentar ➤ *intr* someterse.
subordinate ➤ *adj & s* subordinado/a ➤ *tr* subordinar.
subscribe ➤ *intr* suscribirse, abonarse *(to* a).
subscriber ➤ *s* suscriptor/a.
subscription ➤ *s* suscripción *f*, abono.
subside ➤ *intr* apaciguarse.
subsidy ➤ *s* subvención *f.*
subsist ➤ *intr* subsistir.
substance ➤ *s* sustancia.
substantial ➤ *adj* sustancial; *(meal)* sustancioso; *(considerable)* considerable; *(well-to-do)* adinerado.
substitute ➤ *s* sustituto/a ➤ *tr & intr* substituir.
subtitle ➤ *s* subtítulo ➤ *tr* subtitular.
subtle ➤ *adj* sutil.
subtract ➤ *tr* sustraer, restar.
subtraction ➤ *s* sustracción *f*, resta.
suburb ➤ *s* suburbio ■ *pl* afueras.
suburban ➤ *adj* suburbano.
subversive ➤ *adj* subversivo.
subway ➤ *s* subterráneo, metro.
succeed ➤ *intr* tener éxito; *(to turn out well)* salir bien; *(to follow)* suceder.
success ➤ *s* éxito.
successful ➤ *adj* de éxito, exitoso.
succession ➤ *s* sucesión *f* ■ in s. seguido.

successive ➤ *adj* sucesivo.
successor ➤ *s* sucesor/a.
such ➤ *adj (of this nature)* tal, semejante; *(so much)* tanto ■ s. and s. tal y cual ■ s. as (tal) como ■ s. as it is tal cual es ➤ *adv* tan ➤ *pron* ■ and s. y cosas por el estilo ■ as s. en sí ■ s. is life así es la vida.
suck ➤ *tr* chupar ➤ *intr* dar chupadas ➤ *s* chupada.
sudden ➤ *adj (unforeseen)* imprevisto; *(abrupt)* brusco; *(swift)* súbito, repentino ■ all of a s. de repente.
suddenly ➤ *adv* de repente.
suds ➤ *s* espuma.
sue ➤ *tr* DER. demandar ➤ *intr* entablar acción judicial.
suede o **suède** ➤ *s* gamuza, ante *m.*
suffer ➤ *tr & intr* sufrir ■ to s. from adolecer de.
sufficient ➤ *adj* bastante, suficiente.
sufficiently ➤ *adv* bastante.
suffix ➤ *s* sufijo.
suffocate ➤ *tr & intr* sofocarse.
suffrage ➤ *s* sufragio.
sugar ➤ *s* azúcar *mf* ➤ *tr* azucarar.
suggest ➤ *tr* sugerir; *(to imply)* insinuar.
suggestion ➤ *s* sugerencia.
suicide ➤ *s* suicidio; *(person)* suicida *mf* ■ to commit s. suicidarse.
suit ➤ *s* traje *m*; *(set)* conjunto; *(cards)* palo ➤ *tr* satisfacer; *(to look good)* quedar bien ■ to s. oneself hacer lo que uno quiere.
suitable ➤ *adj* conveniente; *(compatible)* compatible.
suitcase ➤ *s* maleta.
suite ➤ *s (apartment)* suite *f*; *(furniture)* juego; MÚS. suite.
suitor ➤ *s (wooer)* pretendiente *m*; DER. peticionario/a.
sulfur ➤ *s* azufre *m.*
sulk ➤ *intr* estar de malhumor.
sullen ➤ *adj* resentido.
sum ➤ *s* suma; *(of money)* cantidad *f* ➤ *tr* ■ to s. up sumar, resumir.
summarize ➤ *tr* resumir.
summary ➤ *adj* sumario; *(fast)* rápido ➤ *s* resumen *m.*
summer ➤ *s* verano ➤ *intr* veranear *(at, in* en).

summit ➤ s GEOG., POL. cumbre f.

summon ➤ tr convocar; (person) llamar; DER. citar.

summons ➤ s DER. citación f judicial.

sun ➤ s sol m ■ intr asolearse.

sunbathe ➤ intr tomar el sol.

sunburn ➤ s quemadura de sol.

Sunday ➤ s domingo.

sundown ➤ s ocaso.

sunflower ➤ s girasol m.

sunglasses ➤ spl lentes o gafas de sol.

sunlight ➤ s luz f del sol.

sunny ➤ adj soleado.

sunrise ➤ s amanecer m.

sunset ➤ s ocaso.

sunshine ➤ s luz f del sol.

sunstroke ➤ s insolación f.

suntan ➤ s bronceado.

super ➤ adj FAM. estupendo.

superb ➤ adj soberbio.

superficial ➤ adj superficial.

superfluous ➤ adj superfluo.

superintendent ➤ s superintendente mf.

superior ➤ adj & s superior m.

supermarket ➤ s supermercado.

supernatural ➤ adj sobrenatural.

superstition ➤ s superstición f.

superstitious ➤ adj supersticioso.

supervise ➤ tr supervisar.

supervisor ➤ s supervisor/a.

supper ➤ s cena ■ to have s. cenar.

supplement ➤ s suplemento ➤ tr suplir.

supplementary ➤ adj suplementario.

supplier ➤ s suministrador/a.

supply ➤ tr suministrar; (to satisfy) satisfacer ➤ s suministro; (stock) surtido ■ in short s. escaso ■ pl provisiones.

support ➤ tr sostener; (to bear) soportar; (a child) mantener; (with money) ayudar ■ to s. oneself ganarse la vida ➤ s apoyo; ARQ., TEC. soporte m.

supporter ➤ s TEC. soporte m; (advocate) partidario/a; (fan) hincha mf.

supportive ➤ adj sustentador.

suppose ➤ tr suponer; (to believe) creer ➤ intr imaginarse.

supposed ➤ adj supuesto.

suppository ➤ s supositorio.

suppress ➤ tr suprimir; (to prohibit)

prohibir; (to repress) reprimir; (laughter) contener.

suppurate ➤ intr supurar.

supremacy ➤ s supremacía.

supreme ➤ adj supremo ■ s. court corte supremo.

surcharge ➤ s sobrecarga, recargo ➤ tr sobrecargar, recargar.

sure ➤ adj seguro; (infallible) certero; (hand) firme ■ to make s. asegurarse ➤ adv seguramente; (of course) claro.

surety ➤ s seguridad f; (pledge) garantía; (person) garante mf.

surf ➤ s oleaje m ➤ intr hacer surfing ➤ tr COMPUT. navegar por (Internet).

surface ➤ s superficie f ➤ adj superficial ➤ intr salir a la superficie.

surfboard ➤ s tabla de surf.

surfing ➤ s surfing m.

surge ➤ intr (energy, enthusiasm) subir súbitamente ➤ s (onrush) arranque m; ELEC. sobretensión f.

surgeon ➤ s cirujano/a.

surgery ➤ s intervención quirúrgica; (room) quirófano; (work) cirugía.

surgical ➤ adj quirúrgico.

surname ➤ s apellido.

surpass ➤ tr sobrepasar.

surplus ➤ adj & s excedente m.

surprise ➤ tr sorprender ■ to be surprised at sorprenderse de o con ➤ s sorpresa.

surprising ➤ adj sorprendente.

surrender ➤ tr entregar; (hope) abandonar ➤ intr rendirse ➤ s rendición f.

surround ➤ tr rodear.

surroundings ➤ spl alrededores m.

survey ➤ tr inspeccionar; (land) medir ➤ intr hacer una encuesta ➤ s inspección f; (poll) encuesta; (of land) medición f.

surveyor ➤ s agrimensor/a.

survive ➤ tr & intr sobrevivir.

survivor ➤ s sobreviviente mf.

suspect ➤ tr sospechar ➤ s & adj sospechoso/a.

suspend ➤ tr & intr suspender.

suspenders ➤ spl tirantes m.

suspense ➤ s (doubt) incertidumbre f; CINEM., LIT. suspense, suspenso.

suspension ➤ s suspensión f.

suspicion ➤ s sospecha.

suspicious ➤ adj sospechoso.

sustain ➤ tr sostener.

swallow¹ ➤ tr & intr tragar.

swallow² ➤ s ORNIT. golondrina.

swamp ➤ s pantano ➤ tr inundar.

swan ➤ s cisne m.

swarm ➤ s enjambre ➤ intr pulular, hormiguear; *(bees)* enjambrar.

swat ➤ tr aplastar.

sway ➤ tr influir en, persuadir ➤ intr balancearse ➤ s influencia, dominio.

swear◇ ➤ tr & intr jurar ■ to s. at maldecir.

sweat◇ ➤ intr sudar ➤ s sudor m.

sweater ➤ s suéter m.

sweatshirt ➤ s sudadera.

sweep◇ ➤ tr & intr barrer ➤ ■ to make a clean s. hacer tabla rasa.

sweepstakes ➤ s lotería.

sweet ➤ adj dulce ■ s. pepper pimiento morrón • s. potato batata ➤ s dulce m.

sweeten ➤ tr & intr endulzar(se).

sweetheart ➤ s enamorado/a.

swell◇ ➤ tr & intr hinchar(se); *(to increase)* aumentar.

swelling ➤ s MED. hinchazón f.

swerve ➤ tr & intr desviar(se) ➤ s desviación f.

swift ➤ adj veloz ➤ s ORNIT. vencejo.

swim◇ ➤ intr nadar ■ swimming pool piscina ➤ s ■ to go for o take a s. ir a nadar.

swimsuit ➤ s traje m de baño.

swindle ➤ tr timar ➤ s timo.

swine ➤ s cerdo(s).

swing◇ ➤ intr oscilar; *(on a swing)* columpiarse ➤ tr hacer oscilar; *(on a swing)* columpiar ➤ s *(for children)* columpio; MÚS. ritmo.

switch ➤ s ELEC. interruptor m ➤ tr *(to shift)* cambiar de; *(to exchange)* intercambiar; F.C. desviar ■ to s. off desconectar; *(lights)* apagar • to s. on conectar; *(lights)* encender ➤ intr cambiar.

sword ➤ s espada.

syllable ➤ s sílaba.

syllabus ➤ s programa m de estudios.

symbol ➤ s símbolo.

symbolic(al) ➤ adj simbólico.

symbolism ➤ s simbolismo.

symmetric(al) ➤ adj simétrico.

symmetry ➤ s simetría.

sympathetic ➤ adj compasivo.

sympathize ➤ intr compadecerse; *(to understand)* comprender.

sympathy ➤ s simpatía; *(understanding)* comprensión f; *(condolence)* pésame m.

symphony ➤ s MÚS. sinfonía.

symptom ➤ s MED. síntoma m.

synagogue ➤ s sinagoga.

synchronize ➤ tr sincronizar.

syndicate ➤ s sindicato.

syndrome ➤ s síndrome m.

synonym ➤ s sinónimo.

synthesis ➤ s síntesis f.

synthetic ➤ adj & s *(material)* sintético.

syringe ➤ s jeringa.

syrup ➤ s almíbar m.

system ➤ s sistema m; *(human body)* organismo; ANAT. aparato.

systematic ➤ adj sistemático.

T

tab ➤ s lengüeta; *(bill)* cuenta.

table ➤ s mesa; *(data)* tabla.

tablecloth ➤ s mantel m.

tablespoon ➤ s cuchara de sopa; *(quantity)* cucharada.

tablet ➤ s tableta, tablilla.

taboo ➤ s & adj tabú m.

tack ➤ s *(gear)* tachuela ➤ tr ■ to t. on añadir.

tackle ➤ s *(gear)* equipo, avíos m; MARÍT. aparejo ➤ tr atacar, abordar.

tacky ➤ adj FAM. cursi, vulgar.

tact ➤ s tacto.

tactful ➤ adj discreto.

tactic ➤ s táctica ■ tactics ssg táctica.

tag ➤ s *(label)* etiqueta ➤ intr ■ to t. along seguir, acompañar.

tail ➤ s cola ■ t. pipe tubo de escape ■ pl *(coin)* cruz, reversa.

tailor ➤ s sastre m.

tailored ➤ adj hecho a medida.

taint ➤ tr & intr manchar(se) ➤ s mácula, defecto.

take◇ ➤ tr tomar; *(to a place)* llevar; *(to withstand)* soportar; *(advice)* seguir; *(photo)* sacar ■ to t. along llevarse • to t. apart *(to disassemble)* desarmar • to

t. away *(to remove)* quitar, sacar; *(to subtract)* restar; *(to carry away)* llevarse • to t. back *(to return)* devolver; *(a statement)* retractar • to t. in *(to understand)* comprender; *(to include)* incluir; *(to deceive)* engañar • to t. it out on desahogarse con • to t. off quitar; *(clothes, hat)* quitarse; *(time)* tomarse; *(to deduct)* rebajar • to t. out poner afuera; *(stain, spot)* quitar • to t. up with asociarse con ➤ intr irse; *(aircraft)* despegar • to t. over asumir la autoridad ➤ s *(receipts)* ingresos; *(in hunting)* presa; *(in fishing)* pesca; CINEM. toma.

takeover ➤ s toma de poder.

talc o **talcum** ➤ s talco.

tale ➤ s cuento; *(lie)* mentira.

talent ➤ s talento.

talented ➤ adj talentoso.

talk ➤ tr hablar ■ to t. into persuadir a • to t. nonsense decir tonterías • to t. out of disuadir a ➤ intr hablar; *(to chat)* charlar • to t. back replicar ➤ s conversación f; *(speech)* discurso; *(rumor)* rumor m ■ pl negociaciones.

talkative ➤ adj hablador, locuaz.

tall ➤ adj alto ■ how t. are you? ¿cuánto mides? • six feet t. seis pies de alto.

tambourine ➤ s pandereta.

tame ➤ adj domesticado; *(gentle)* manso; *(docile)* dócil ➤ tr domesticar.

tamper ➤ intr ■ to t. with interferir en.

tampon ➤ s tapón m, tampón m.

tan ➤ tr broncear ➤ intr broncearse, tostarse ➤ adj bronceado.

tangerine ➤ s mandarina.

tangled ➤ adj enredado, embrollado.

tank ➤ s tanque m.

tanker ➤ s *(ship)* buque m tanque; *(truck)* camión m tanque.

tantalize ➤ tr tentar.

tap[1] ➤ tr golpear ligeramente; *(foot, finger)* dar golpecitos con ➤ intr dar golpes ligeros; *(fingers)* tamborilear; *(feet)* zapatear ➤ s golpe ligero ■ t. dance zapateo americano.

tap[2] ➤ s *(faucet)* grifo ■ on t. de barril.

tape ➤ s cinta; *(recording)* grabación f (en cinta magnética) ■ measuring t.

cinta métrica • t. player, t. recorder grabadora ➤ tr *(to stick)* pegar con cinta adhesiva; *(to record)* grabar.

taper ➤ intr ■ to t. off disminuir.

tapestry ➤ s tapiz m.

tar ➤ s alquitrán m.

tardy ➤ adj tardío ■ to be t. llegar tarde.

target ➤ s blanco; *(goal)* meta.

tariff ➤ s tarifa.

tarpaulin o **tarp** ➤ s alquitranado.

tarragon ➤ s estragón m.

tart ➤ s pastelillo.

task ➤ s tarea ■ t. bar COMPUT. barra de tareas • t. force fuerza operante.

taste ➤ tr probar; *(to sample)* catar ➤ intr *(food)* tener sabor ■ to t. like saber a ➤ s gusto.

tasteful ➤ adj de buen gusto.

tasty ➤ adj sabroso.

tattered ➤ adj andrajoso.

tattoo ➤ s tatuaje m ➤ tr tatuar.

tavern ➤ s taberna.

tax ➤ s impuesto ➤ tr gravar.

taxable ➤ adj gravable.

tax-free ➤ adj libre de impuestos.

taxi o **taxicab** ➤ s taxi m.

taxpayer ➤ s contribuyente mf.

tea ➤ s té m.

teach◇ ➤ tr enseñar; *(students)* dar clases a; *(a subject)* dar clases de ➤ intr ser maestro/a.

teacher ➤ s maestro/a, profesor/a.

teaching ➤ s enseñanza.

teacup ➤ s taza (de té).

team ➤ s equipo ➤ intr ■ to t. up with unir fuerzas con.

teammate ➤ s compañero/a de equipo.

teapot ➤ s tetera.

tear[1]◇ ➤ tr desgarrar, rasgar ■ to t. down demoler • to t. off o out arrancar • to t. down *(to demolish)* demoler • to t. in o to pieces despedazar • to t. up hacer pedazos ➤ intr desgarrarse, rasgarse ➤ s desgarradura, rasgadura.

tear[2] ➤ s lágrima ■ pl lágrimas, llanto ■ in t. llorando.

tease ➤ tr *(to annoy)* fastidiar; *(to make fun of)* tomar el pelo a.

teaspoon ➤ s cucharita de té; *(quantity)* cucharadita.

technical ➤ adj técnico.

technician ➤ s técnico/a.

technique ➤ s técnica.

technology ➤ s tecnología.

teddy bear ➤ s osito de juguete.

tedious ➤ adj tedio.

teen o **teenager** ➤ s joven mf, adolescente mf.

telecast ➤ tr & intr televisar ➤ s transmisión f de televisión.

telecommunications ➤ spl telecomunicaciones f.

telegram ➤ s telegrama m.

telegraph ➤ s telégrafo ➤ tr telegrafiar.

telephone ➤ s teléfono ➤ tr telefonear ➤ intr comunicarse por teléfono.

telephoto ➤ adj telefotográfico.

telescope ➤ s telescopio.

televise ➤ tr & intr televisar.

television ➤ s televisión f; (set) televisor m ■ t. screen pantalla (del televisor).

tell◇ ➤ tr decir; (story) contar; (news) comunicar; (future) adivinar ■ all told en total • to t. apart distinguir.

teller ➤ s cajero/a.

temper ➤ s temperamento ■ to keep, lose one's t. dominarse, enfadarse.

temperament ➤ s temperamento.

temperature ➤ s temperatura.

tempest ➤ s tempestad f.

temple[1] ➤ s templo; (synagogue) sinagoga.

temple[2] ➤ s ANAT. sien f.

temporary ➤ adj transitorio; (worker) temporero, temporario; (position) interino ➤ s temporero/a.

tempt ➤ tr tentar.

temptation ➤ s tentación f.

tempting ➤ adj tentador.

ten ➤ s & adj diez m ■ t. o'clock las diez.

tenant ➤ s inquilino/a.

tend[1] ➤ intr (to head) dirigirse; (to be likely) tender; (to be inclined) propender a.

tend[2] ➤ tr (to care for) cuidar, atender.

tendency ➤ s tendencia.

tender ➤ adj (soft) tierno; (delicate) delicado; (affectionate) cariñoso.

tenderloin ➤ s lomo, filete m.

tenderness ➤ s ternura.

tennis ➤ s tenis m.

tense[1] ➤ adj (strained) tenso.

tense[2] ➤ s GRAM. tiempo.

tension ➤ s tensión f.

tent ➤ s tienda.

tentative ➤ adj experimental; (provisional) provisorio; (unsure) indeciso.

tenth ➤ s & adj décimo.

tepid ➤ adj tibio.

term ➤ s (time period) período, plazo; (school year) período académico; (deadline) término, fin m ■ in no uncertain terms muy claramente • in terms of en cuanto a • in the long t. a la larga ■ pl condiciones ■ to be on good t. tener buenas relaciones.

terminal ➤ adj fatal; (final) final ➤ s (bus, train) terminal f; COMPUT., ELEC. terminal m.

terminate ➤ tr & intr terminar.

terrace ➤ s terraza; (balcony) balcón m; (roof) azotea ➤ tr terraplenar.

terrain ➤ s terreno.

terrible ➤ adj terrible; (tremendous) tremendo.

terrific ➤ adj tremendo, bárbaro.

terrify ➤ tr aterrorizar.

territory ➤ s territorio.

terror ➤ s terror m.

terrorism ➤ s terrorismo.

terrorist ➤ s terrorista mf.

terrorize ➤ tr aterrorizar.

test ➤ s examen m, prueba ■ t. tube tubo de ensayo, probeta ➤ tr examinar; (equipment) someter a prueba.

testify ➤ intr declarar ➤ tr ■ to t. that testificar que • to t. to testificar.

testimony ➤ s testimonio.

tetanus ➤ s tétano.

text ➤ s texto.

textbook ➤ s libro de texto.

textile ➤ s & adj textil m.

texture ➤ s textura.

than ➤ conj que ■ more t. half más de la mitad • other t. aparte de • rather t. ántes que.

thank ➤ tr agradecer, dar las gracias a ■ t. you gracias (for por).

thankful ➤ adj agradecido.

thanks ➤ spl gracias; (acknowledgment) reconocimiento; (gratitude) gratitud f.

thanksgiving ➤ *s* acción *f* de gracias.

that ➤ *adj (near)* ese; *(distant)* aquel ■ t. one ése; aquél ➤ *pron* ése; aquél; *(neuter)* eso, aquello ■ like t. así • the dog t. barked el perro que ladró ➤ *adv (so)* tan ■ t. high así de alto • t. many tantos • t. much tanto ➤ *conj* que ■ so t. para que.

thaw ➤ *intr* derretirse ➤ *tr* ■ to t. out *(food)* descongelar ➤ *s* tiempo tibio.

the *art def* el, la, lo, las, los.

theater *o* **theatre** ➤ *s* teatro.

theft ➤ *s* robo.

their ➤ *pron* su, suyo, suya, de ellos, de ellas.

theirs ➤ *pron* (el) suyo, (la) suya, etc.

them ➤ *pron (as direct object)* los, las; *(as indirect object)* les; *(as object of preposition)* ellos, ellas.

theme ➤ *s* tema *m*; *(written)* ensayo.

themselves ➤ *pron (object)* se; *(subject)* mismos, mismas; *(object of preposition)* sí mismos, sí mismas ■ among t. entre ellos.

then ➤ *adv (at that time, in that case)* entonces; *(afterward)* después; *(in addition)* además; *(consequently)* en consecuencia.

theology ➤ *s* teología.

theoretical ➤ *adj* teórico.

theory ➤ *s* teoría.

therapeutic ➤ *s* terapéutico.

therapist ➤ *s* terapeuta *mf*.

therapy ➤ *s* MED. terapia; PSIC. psicoterapia.

there ➤ *adv* allí, allá, ahí; *(in that matter)* en eso ➤ *pron* ■ t. are hay • t. is hay • t. was había, hubo • t. were habían, hubieron • t. will be habrá.

therefore ➤ *adv* por lo tanto.

thermal ➤ *adj* termal.

thermometer ➤ *s* termómetro.

thermostat ➤ *s* termostato.

these ➤ *pl de* **this**.

they ➤ *pron* ellos, ellas ■ t. say se dice.

thick ➤ *adj* grueso; *(not watery)* espeso ■ two meters t. dos metros de grosor.

thicken ➤ *tr & intr* espesar(se).

thickness ➤ *s* grosor *m*, espesor *m*.

thief ➤ *s* ladrón/ona.

thigh ➤ *s* muslo.

thimble ➤ *s* dedal *m*.

thin ➤ *adj* delgado; *(sparse)* escaso; *(hair)* ralo; *(soup)* aguado; *(weak)* débil.

thing ➤ *s* cosa ■ for one t. en primer lugar • it's a good t. that menos mal que ■ *pl (stuff, conditions)* cosas; *(equipment)* equipo.

think◊ ➤ *tr & intr* pensar *(about* en); *(to regard, believe)* creer, parecerle a uno ■ I t. so creo que sí • to t. of pensar; *(to recall)* recordar • to t. over *o* through* pensar bien • to t. up inventar.

third ➤ *s* tercero; *(part)* tercio, tercera parte; MÚS., AUTO. tercera ➤ *adj* tercero.

thirst ➤ *s* sed *f*.

thirsty ➤ *adj* sediento ■ to be t. tener sed.

thirteen ➤ *s & adj* trece *m*.

thirty ➤ *adj & s* treinta *m*.

this ➤ *pron* éste, ésta; *(neuter)* esto ➤ *adj* este, esta ■ t. one éste, ésta ➤ *adv (so)* tan ■ t. long así de largo • t. many tantos • t. much tanto.

thorn ➤ *s* espina.

thorough ➤ *adj* completo; *(detailed)* detallado, minucioso; *(total)* total.

those ➤ *pl de* **that**.

though ➤ *conj* aunque ■ as t. como si • even t. aunque ➤ *adv* sin embargo, no obstante.

thought ➤ *s* pensamiento; *(idea)* idea; *(consideration)* consideración *f*; *(intention, purpose)* intención *f*, propósito ■ on second t. pensándolo bien.

thoughtful ➤ *adj* atento, solícito.

thoughtless ➤ *adj (careless)* descuidado; *(inconsiderate)* falto de consideración.

thousand ➤ *s & adj* mil *m*.

thread ➤ *s* hilo; *(of a screw)* rosca ➤ *tr (needle, beads)* ensartar.

threat ➤ *s* amenaza.

threaten ➤ *tr & intr* amenazar.

three ➤ *s & adj* tres *m* ■ t. hundred trescientos • t. o'clock las tres.

thresh ➤ *tr* trillar.

threshold ➤ *s* umbral *m*.

thrift ➤ *s* economía, ahorro.

thrill ➤ *tr* encantar, deleitar ■ *s* emoción *f*.

thriller ➤ *s* FAM. novela *o* película de suspenso.

thrive◇ ➤ *intr* prosperar; *(to flourish)* crecer.

throat ➤ *s* garganta.

throb ➤ *intr (to beat)* latir; *(pain)* dar punzadas ■ *s (of pain)* punzada.

throne ➤ *s* trono.

throng ➤ *s* muchedumbre *f* ■ *intr* atestar.

through ➤ *prep* por; *(among)* a través de; *(by the agency of)* por medio de, a través de; *(during)* durante; *(between)* entre ■ Monday t. Friday de lunes a viernes ➤ *adv (from one end to another)* de un lado al otro; *(from beginning to end)* hasta el final; *(completely)* completamente ■ to carry something t. llevar algo a cabo ■ to fall t. fracasar ➤ *adj (flight)* directo; *(street)* de paso libre, de vía libre.

throughout ➤ *prep* por todo, en todo; *(during every part of)* durante todo ➤ *adv* por todas partes; *(completely)* completamente ■ *(during the entire time)* todo el tiempo.

throw◇ ➤ *tr* tirar, arrojar; *(punches, party)* dar; *(switch)* echar ■ to t. away tirar, desechar ■ to t. out *(to reject)* rechazar; *(to throw away)* tirar ➤ *intr* ■ to t. up vomitar, devolver ➤ *s* lanzamiento, tiro; *(of dice)* lance *m*; *(coverlet)* colcha, cobertor *m*; *(rug)* alfombra pequeña.

throwaway ➤ *adj* desechable.

thrust◇ ➤ *tr (to push)* empujar; *(knife)* clavar; *(to put in)* meter ➤ *s* empujón *m*; FIS. empuje *m*.

thug ➤ *s* maleante *m*, matón *m*.

thumb ➤ *s* pulgar *m* ➤ *intr* ■ to t. through hojear.

thumbtack ➤ *s* chinche *f*, chincheta.

thunder ➤ *s* trueno ➤ *intr* tronar.

thunderstorm ➤ *s* tronada.

Thursday ➤ *s* jueves *m*.

thus ➤ *adv* así, de esta manera; *(therefore)* por eso ■ t. far hasta ahora.

thyme ➤ *s* tomillo.

tick¹ ➤ *intr & s* (hacer) tictac *m*.

tick² ➤ *s* ENTOM. garrapata.

ticket ➤ *s (for travel)* billete *m*, boleto; *(for movies, theater)* entrada, boleto; *(speeding, parking)* boleta ■ t. office *o* window taquilla ➤ *tr* vender billete a; *(a motorist)* darle una boleta a.

tickle ➤ *tr* cosquillear; *(to delight)* deleitar ■ *s* cosquilleo.

tidbit ➤ *s* bocado.

tide ➤ *s* marea.

tidy ➤ *adj* ordenado, arreglado ➤ *tr & intr* ■ to t. up ordenar.

tie ➤ *tr* atar; *(to knot)* anudar; *(to link)* ligar ■ to t. down atar, sujetar ■ to t. up atar; *(traffic)* obstruir; *(boat)* amarrar ➤ *intr (contestants)* empatar ➤ *s (necktie)* corbata; *(draw)* empate *m*; *(bond)* lazo, vínculo.

tiger ➤ *s* tigre *m*.

tight ➤ *adj (screw, knot)* apretado; *(sealed)* hermético; *(clothes, shoes)* ajustado; *(stingy)* tacaño ➤ *adv (firmly)* bien, fuertemente; *(soundly)* profundamente.

tighten ➤ *tr* apretar; *(a cord)* tensar.

tights ➤ *spl* malla.

tile ➤ *s (of a roof)* teja; *(of a floor)* losa, baldosa; *(of a wall)* azulejo.

till¹ ➤ *tr* AGR. labrar, cultivar

till² ➤ *prep* hasta (donde) ➤ *conj* hasta que.

tilt ➤ *tr & intr* inclinar(se) ➤ *s* inclinación *f*.

timber ➤ *s* árboles maderables; *(lumber)* maderamen *m*; *(beam)* viga.

time ➤ *s* tiempo; *(moment)* momento; *(a specified time)* hora; *(occasion)* ocasión *f*; *(instance)* vez *f* ■ all the t. todo el tiempo; *(always)* siempre • (at) any t. en cualquier momento • at all times en todo momento • at a t. a la vez • at no t. nunca • at times a veces • each *o* every t. cada vez • for the t. being por el momento • in due t. en su día • on t. a tiempo • t. off tiempo libre • t. out DEP. interrupción temporal • t. zone huso horario • to waste t. perder el tiempo • what t. is it? ¿qué hora es? ➤ *tr* fijar la hora *o* el tiempo de; *(to record)* cronometrar.

timely ➤ *adv* oportuno; *(punctual)* puntual.

timer ➤ *s* reloj automático.

times ➤ *prep* multiplicado (por).

timetable ➤ *s* horario.

timid ➤ *adj* tímido.

timing ➤ *s* oportunidad *f;* DEP. coordinación *f.*

tin ➤ *s* estaño; *(container)* lata.

tinfoil *o* **tin foil** ➤ *s* papel *m* de estaño.

tingle ➤ *intr & s* (sentir) picazón *f.*

tinsel ➤ *adj & s* (de) oropel *m.*

tint ➤ *s* matiz *m* ➤ *tr* matizar.

tiny ➤ *adj* minúsculo.

tip¹ ➤ *s (end)* punta, cabo.

tip² ➤ *tr & intr* volcar, derribar; *(to tilt)* inclinar(se) ∎ **to t. over** volcar(se).

tip³ ➤ *s (gratuity)* propina; *(information)* información *f; (advice)* consejo ➤ *tr* dar una propina ∎ **to t. off** dar una información.

tip-off ➤ *s* FAM. información *f,* soplo.

tiptoe ➤ *intr & adv* (andar) de puntillas.

tire¹ ➤ *tr & intr* cansar(se); *(to bore)* aburrir(se).

tire² ➤ *s* AUTO. llanta, neumático.

tired ➤ *adj* cansado; *(hackneyed)* trillado.

tiresome ➤ *s* cansado, tedioso.

tissue ➤ *s* BIOL. tejido; *(for the nose)* pañuelo de papel ∎ **t. paper** papel de seda.

title ➤ *s* título ➤ *tr* titular.

titular ➤ *adj* titular; *(nominal)* nominal.

to ➤ *prep* a; *(direction)* hacia; *(as far as, until)* hasta; *(against)* contra; *(for, of)* de, para ∎ **it's ten to six** son las seis menos diez.

toad ➤ *s* sapo.

toast¹ ➤ *tr & intr* tostar(se) ➤ *s* tostada.

toast² ➤ *s (drink)* brindis *m.*

toaster ➤ *s* tostadora.

tobacco ➤ *s* tabaco.

today ➤ *adv & s* hoy *m.*

toddler ➤ *s* niño que empieza a andar.

toe ➤ *s* dedo del pie; *(of a shoe, sock)* puntera.

toenail ➤ *s* uña del dedo del pie.

toffee ➤ *s* caramelo.

together ➤ *adv* juntos; *(in total)* en total, todos (juntos) ∎ **to come** *o* **get**

t. juntarse, reunirse ∎ **to go t.** *(colors, flavors)* armonizar.

toil ➤ *intr* trabajar duro, afanarse ➤ *s* trabajo, afán *m.*

toilet ➤ *s* retrete *m,* lavabo ∎ **t. paper** papel higiénico.

toiletry ➤ *s* artículo de tocador.

token ➤ *s* señal *f,* prueba; *(coin)* ficha ➤ *adj* simbólico.

tolerance ➤ *s* tolerancia.

tolerant ➤ *adj* tolerante.

tolerate ➤ *tr* tolerar; *(suffering, pain)* sufrir, aguantar.

toll¹ ➤ *s* peaje *m; (on phone call)* tasa.

tollbooth ➤ *s* caseta de peaje.

tomato ➤ *s* tomate *m; (plant)* tomatera.

tomb ➤ *s* tumba; *(place)* sepultura.

tombstone ➤ *s* lápida.

tomorrow ➤ *s & adv* mañana ∎ **the day after t.** pasado mañana.

ton ➤ *s* tonelada ➤ *pl* FAM. montones.

tone ➤ *s* tono.

tongs ➤ *spl* tenacillas.

tongue ➤ *s* lengua.

tonic ➤ *s* tónico; MÚS., FONÉT. tónica; *(quinine water)* agua tónica.

tonight ➤ *adv & s* esta noche.

tonsil ➤ *s* amígdala.

too ➤ *adv (also)* también; *(as well as)* además; *(excessively)* demasiado; *(very)* muy ∎ **not t.** FAM. no muy, nada ∎ **t. many** *o* **much** demasiados.

tool ➤ *s* herramienta; *(utensil)* utensilio, útil *m.*

tooth ➤ *s* diente *m.*

toothache ➤ *s* dolor *m* de muelas.

toothbrush ➤ *s* cepillo de dientes.

toothpaste ➤ *s* pasta dentífrica.

toothpick ➤ *s* mondadientes *m.*

top ➤ *s* parte *f* superior *o* de arriba; *(of the head)* coronilla; *(of a container)* borde *m; (of a mountain)* cumbre *f; (of a tree, hat)* copa; *(of a bottle, pan)* tapa ∎ **from t. to bottom** de arriba abajo ∎ **on t.** encima ∎ **on t. of** además de ➤ *adj* de arriba; *(topmost)* último; *(highest)* más alto; *(great)* de categoría; *(best)* mejor; *(maximum)* máximo ➤ *tr* rematar; *(to surpass)* superar ∎ **to t. it off** por si fuera poco.

topaz ➤ *s* topacio.

topic ➤ s tópico, tema m.

topography ➤ s topografía.

topple ➤ tr derribar; (government) volcar.

torch ➤ s antorcha.

torment ➤ s tormento ➤ tr atormentar; (to pester) molestar.

tornado ➤ s tornado.

torrent ➤ s torrente m.

torrid ➤ adj tórrido.

tortoise ➤ s tortuga de tierra.

torture ➤ s tortura ➤ tr torturar.

torturer ➤ s torturador/a.

toss ➤ tr tirar, lanzar; (one's head, hair) echar hacia atrás; (salad) revolver; (coin) echar a cara o cruz ➤ intr (in bed) revolverse.

total ➤ s total m; (entirety) totalidad f ➤ adj total ➤ tr totalizar ∎ to t. up to ascender a.

totalitarian ➤ adj & s totalitario/a.

touch ➤ tr tocar; (to concern) concernir a; (to move) conmover ➤ to t. off desencadenar, provocar ➤ to t. up retocar ➤ intr tocarse; (to be in contact) estar en contacto ∎ to t. down AVIA. aterrizar ➤ s toque m; (sense) tacto; (mild attack) ataque ligero; (dash) pizca, poquito ∎ by t. al tacto • final of finishing t. último toque • to be out of t. with (people) haber perdido el contacto con; (things) no estar al tanto de • to keep in t. mantenerse en contacto • to lose one's t. perder la mano.

touch-and-go ➤ adj arriesgado.

touched ➤ adj conmovido.

touching ➤ adj conmovedor.

touchup ➤ s retoque m.

touchy ➤ adj (oversensitive) susceptible, quisquilloso; (situation) delicado.

tough ➤ adj duro; (physically hardy) fuerte, robusto; (harsh) severo, áspero; (aggressive) agresivo; (unyielding) inflexible ∎ t. luck! ¡mala suerte! ➤ s matón m.

toughen ➤ tr & intr endurecer(se).

tough-minded ➤ adj duro (de carácter).

toupee ➤ s peluquín m.

tour ➤ s excursión f, viaje m; (visit) visita; TEAT. gira ➤ tr recorrer, hacer un viaje por; TEAT. presentar en gira ➤ intr ir de viaje.

touring ➤ s turismo ➤ adj de turismo; (theatrical company) que está de gira.

tourism ➤ s turismo.

tourist ➤ adj & s (de) turista mf.

tournament ➤ s torneo.

tourniquet ➤ s torniquete m.

tousle ➤ tr desordenar, desarreglar.

tout ➤ tr recomendar.

tow ➤ tr remolcar ➤ s remolque m ∎ t. truck remolcador.

toward(s) ➤ prep hacia.

towel ➤ s toalla, paño ➤ tr & intr secar(se) o frotar(se) con toalla.

tower ➤ s torre f ∎ control t. AER. torre de control ➤ intr elevarse ∎ to t. over o above dominar, destacarse sobre.

town ➤ s (city) ciudad f; (village) pueblo ∎ t. hall ayuntamiento.

township ➤ s municipio.

toxic ➤ adj tóxico.

toxin ➤ s toxino.

toy ➤ adj & s (de) juguete m ➤ intr ∎ to t. with jugar con; (idea) dar vueltas a.

trace ➤ s huella, rastro; (sign) señal f, indicio; (bit) pizca ➤ tr (to copy) dibujar, trazar; (to follow a trail) seguir.

track ➤ s (path) camino, senda; (footprint) huella; (of a person) pista; (of things) vestigio, rastro; (railway) vía (férrea); DEP. (for running) pista; (sport) atletismo en pista ∎ to keep t. of seguir con atención • to lose t. of (person) perder a uno de vista; (time) perder la noción de ➤ tr seguir ∎ to t. down localizar.

trackball ➤ COMPUT. seguibola.

tractor ➤ s tractor m.

trade ➤ s ocupación f; (commerce) comercio, negocio; (exchange) cambio ∎ t. union sindicato, gremio ➤ intr comerciar, negociar ➤ tr cambiar, trocar ∎ to t. off trocar.

trademark ➤ s marca registrada o de fábrica.

trading ➤ s comercio.

tradition ➤ s tradición f.

traditional ➤ adj tradicional.

traditionalist ➤ s & adj tradicionalista mf.

traffic ➤ s tráfico ■ t. jam embotellamiento • t. **light** luz de tráfico, semáforo ➤ intr traficar.

tragedy ➤ s tragedia.

tragic ➤ adj trágico.

trail ➤ tr (to drag) arrastrar; (to track) rastrear; (to follow) seguir ➤ intr arrastrarse; (a plant) trepar ➤ s (trace) huella, rastro; (of a person) pista; (path) camino, sendero.

trailer ➤ s (vehicle) remolque m.

train ➤ tr (to drag) tren m; (of a dress) cola; (of thought) hilo ➤ tr (a person) enseñar; (an animal) amaestrar ➤ intr prepararse; (athlete) entrenarse.

trained ➤ adj entrenado; (physically) preparado; (animals) amaestrado.

trainer ➤ s DEP. entrenador/a; (of animals) amaestrador/a.

training ➤ s adiestramiento; (of animals) amaestramiento; DEP. entrenamiento.

trait ➤ s rasgo.

traitor ➤ s traidor/a.

tram ➤ s (cable car) teleférico; G.B. tranvía m.

tramp ➤ s vagabundo/a.

trample ➤ tr pisotear.

tranquil ➤ adj tranquilo.

tranquilizer ➤ s tranquilizante m.

tranquil(l)ity ➤ s tranquilidad f.

transact ➤ tr tramitar.

transaction ➤ s (act) negociación f; (deal) transacción f ■ pl actas.

transcend ➤ tr & intr transcender.

transfer ➤ tr (to convey) trasladar; (to shift) transferir ➤ intr (to move) trasladarse; (passenger) transbordar ➤ s boleto de transbordo; (of money) transferencia; (of power) transmisión f.

transferal ➤ s transferencia.

transform ➤ tr transformar.

transformation ➤ s transformación f.

transformer ➤ s transformador m.

transfusion ➤ s MED. transfusión f.

transistor ➤ s transistor m.

transit ➤ s tránsito.

transition ➤ s transición f.

transitive ➤ adj & s (verbo) transitivo.

translate ➤ tr traducir.

translation ➤ s traducción f.

translator ➤ s traductor/a.

transmission ➤ s transmisión f ■ automatic t. AUTO. cambio automático.

transmit ➤ tr transmitir.

transmitter ➤ s transmisor m.

transparent ➤ adj transparente.

transplant ➤ tr trasplantar ➤ s trasplante m.

transport ➤ tr transportar ➤ s transporte m.

transportation ➤ s transportación f.

trap ➤ s trampa; (in pipe) sifón m ➤ tr (to ensnare) coger en una trampa; (to catch) atrapar.

trash ➤ s basura, desperdicios ■ t. can cubo de la basura ➤ tr JER. destrozar.

travel ➤ intr viajar; (light, sound) propagarse ➤ tr viajar por ➤ s viajar m ■ pl viajes.

travel(l)er ➤ s viajero/a ■ t.'s check cheque de viajero.

tray ➤ s bandeja.

treacherous ➤ adj traicionero; (dangerous) peligroso.

tread◊ ➤ tr & intr pisar ■ t. water pedalear en el agua ➤ s pisada; (of stair) huella; (of tire) banda de rodadura.

treason ➤ s traición f.

treasure ➤ s tesoro ➤ tr estimar.

treasurer ➤ s tesorero/a.

treasury ➤ s tesorería.

treat ➤ tr tratar; (to invite) convidar, invitar ➤ s (present) regalo; (delight) placer m ■ it's my t. invito yo.

treatment ➤ s tratamiento.

treaty ➤ s convenio, tratado.

tree ➤ s árbol m.

tremble ➤ intr temblar.

tremendous ➤ adj tremendo.

tremor ➤ s temblor m.

trench ➤ s (ditch) foso; MIL. trinchera.

trend ➤ s dirección f; (fashion) moda ➤ intr tender.

trendy ➤ adj FAM. que sigue la última moda.

trespass ➤ intr entrar ilegalmente (on en) ➤ s entrada ilegal ■ pl pecados.

trial ➤ s (test) ensayo; (attempt) tentativa; DER. proceso, juicio ■ on t. enjuiciado, procesado ➤ adj de prueba.

triangle ➤ s triángulo.

tribe ➤ s tribu f.

tribunal ➤ s tribunal m.

tribute ➤ s tributo.

trick ➤ s truco; (swindle) estafa; (prank) travesura; (skill) maña ➤ tr engañar, burlar.

trickle ➤ intr gotear ▪ s goteo.

tricky ➤ adj (wily) astuto; (situation, problem) delicado, complicado.

tricycle ➤ s triciclo.

trifle ➤ s nadería ▪ a t. un poquito ➤ intr jugar (with con).

trigger ➤ s gatillo.

trillion ➤ s E.U. [10^{12}] billón m; G.B. [10^{18}] trillón.

trim ➤ tr (hair, nails) recortar; (branches) podar.

trip ➤ s viaje m ➤ intr (to stumble) dar un traspié ➤ tr (person) hacer tropezar; (alarm) hacer sonar.

triple ➤ adj & s triple m ➤ tr & intr triplicar(se).

tripod ➤ s trípode m.

triumph ➤ intr triunfar ➤ s triunfo.

trivial ➤ adj insignificante, trivial.

trolley ➤ s tranvía m.

trombone ➤ s trombón m.

troop ➤ s grupo ▪ pl MIL. tropas.

trophy ➤ s trofeo.

tropic ➤ s trópico ➤ adj tropical.

tropical ➤ adj tropical.

trot ➤ s trote m ➤ intr trotar.

trouble ➤ s (misfortune) desgracia; (distress) apuro, aprieto; (effort) esfuerzo ▪ to be in t. estar en un aprieto • to get into t. meterse en líos • to start t. dar problemas • to take the t. to tomarse la molestia de ➤ tr (to worry) preocupar; (to afflict) afligir; (to bother) molestar.

troublesome ➤ adj (worrisome) inquietante; (difficult) dificultoso.

trousers ➤ spl pantalones m.

trout ➤ s trucha.

truce ➤ s tregua.

truck ➤ s & tr (transportar en) camión m.

true ➤ adj verdadero; (loyal) leal ▪ to come t. realizarse • t. to life conforme a la realidad.

truly ➤ adv verdaderamente ▪ yours t. suyo atentamente.

trumpet ➤ s trompeta.

trunk ➤ s tronco; (elephant) trompa; (luggage) baúl m; AUTO. maletero ▪ pl swimming t. traje de baño.

trust ➤ s confianza; (charge) custodia; COM., FIN. trust m, consorcio ▪ in t. DER. en depósito ➤ tr tener confianza en, fiarse de.

trustee ➤ s DER. fideicomisario/a; (of a board) síndico.

trusty ➤ adj de confianza.

truth ➤ s verdad f.

try ➤ tr (to test, taste) probar; (to make an effort at) tratar; DER. (case) someter a juicio; (person) procesar ▪ to t. on probarse • to t. out probar ➤ intr esforzarse ▪ s tentativa, intento.

tryout ➤ s prueba de aptitud; (audition) audición f.

T-shirt ➤ s camiseta.

tub ➤ s (vessel) tonel m; (bathtub) bañera.

tuba ➤ s tuba.

tube ➤ s tubo; FAM. (TV) tele f.

tuberculosis ➤ s tuberculosis f.

Tuesday ➤ s martes m.

tuft ➤ s mechón m; (crest) copete m.

tug ➤ tr (to pull) tirar de; (to drag) arrastrar ➤ s tirón m.

tugboat ➤ s remolcador m.

tuition ➤ s matrícula.

tulip ➤ s tulipán m.

tulle ➤ s tul m.

tumble ➤ intr (to roll) rodar; (to fall) caerse ➤ s tumbo, caída.

tumbleweed ➤ s planta rodadora.

tumbling ➤ s acrobacia.

tumescence ➤ s tumescencia.

tummy ➤ s FAM. barriga.

tumor ➤ s tumor m.

tumult ➤ s tumulto.

tumultuous ➤ adj tumultuoso.

tuna ➤ s atún m.

tundra ➤ s tundra.

tune ➤ s melodía ▪ in t. afinado • out of t. desafinado • to carry a t. cantar afinado • to t. in RAD., TELEV. sintonizar • to t. out JER. no prestar atención a.

tuner ➤ s (person) afinador/a; RAD. sintonizador m.

tune-up ➤ s puesta a punto.

tungsten ➤ s tungsteno.

tunic ➤ s túnica.

tunnel ➤ s túnel *m* ➤ tr (*one's way*) cavar ➤ intr hacer un túnel.

turban ➤ s turbante *m*.

turbine ➤ s turbina.

turbojet ➤ s turborreactor *m*.

turboprop ➤ s turbopropulsor *m*.

turbulence ➤ s turbulencia.

turbulent ➤ adj turbulento.

tureen ➤ s sopera.

turf ➤ s (*sod*) césped *m*; JER. territorio.

turkey ➤ s pavo, guajolote *m*.

turmeric ➤ s cúrcuma.

turmoil ➤ s confusión *f*.

turn ➤ tr (*to revolve*) dar vueltas a; (*to flip*) pasar, volver; (*to rotate*) girar; (*corner*) doblar; (*stomach*) revolver; (*to direct*) dirigir ▪ to t. away negar la entrada a; (*to deflect*) rechazar; (*head*) volver; (*eyes*) desviar • to t. back hacer retroceder; (*clock*) retrasar • to t. down (*light, sound*) bajar; (*to reject*) rechazar • to t. into transformar en • to t. off (*radio, light*) apagar; (*tap, gas*) cerrar; (*electricity, water*) cortar; (*engine*) parar • to t. on (*radio*) poner; (*light*) encender; (*engine*) poner en marcha; (*a tap*) abrir; (*stove, fire*) encender, prender • to t. out (*light*) apagar • to t. over (*object*) invertir, volcar; (*idea*) considerar; (*to transfer*) entregar • to t. up (*light, sound*) subir ➤ intr (*to rotate*) girar; (*to change direction*) dar la vuelta; (*to become*) ponerse, volverse ▪ to t. around darse vuelta • to t. away volver la cara *o* la espalda • to t. back retroceder • to t. into volverse • to t. off desviarse • to t. out resultar • to t. over (*car, truck*) volcar; (*in bed*) voltearse • to t. up aparecer ➤ s vuelta; (*rotation*) rotación *f*; (*change*) cambio; (*opportunity*) turno ▪ at every t. a cada instante • by turns por turnos • to take turns turnarse.

turning ➤ s viraje *m* ▪ t. point momento crucial.

turnip ➤ s nabo.

turnoff ➤ s desvío; JER. cosa *o* persona repugnante.

turnout ➤ s (*attendance*) concurrencia.

turnover ➤ s (*pastry*) empanada; (*of staff*) cambio de personal.

turnpike ➤ s autopista de peaje.

turpentine ➤ s trementina.

turquoise ➤ adj & s (de) turquesa.

turtle ➤ s tortuga.

turtleneck ➤ s cuello vuelto *o* alto.

tusk ➤ s colmillo.

tutor ➤ s profesor/a particular; (*in universities*) tutor/a ➤ tr dar clases particulares a.

tuxedo ➤ s smoking *m*.

TV ➤ s televisión *f*; (*set*) televisor *m*.

tweezers ➤ spl pinzas.

twelfth ➤ adj & s duodécimo.

twelve ➤ s & adj doce *m* ▪ t. o'clock las doce.

twenty ➤ adj & s veinte *m*.

twice ➤ adv dos veces, el doble.

twig ➤ s ramita.

twilight ➤ s crepúsculo.

twin ➤ adj & s gemelo/a ▪ t. bed cama separada *o* gemela.

twine ➤ s cordel *m*, bramante *m*.

twinge ➤ s punzada.

twinkle ➤ intr centellear; (*eyes*) brillar ➤ s centelleo.

twinkling ➤ s centelleo; FIG. instante *m*.

twist ➤ tr torcer; (*jar top*) dar vueltas a ➤ s (*of a road, river*) vuelta, recodo; (*of an ankle*) torcedura.

twister ➤ s ciclón *m*, tornado.

two ➤ s & adj dos *m* ▪ t. hundred doscientos • t. o'clock las dos.

twofold ➤ adj doble.

two-way ➤ adj de doble dirección.

type ➤ s tipo ➤ tr & intr escribir a máquina.

typeface ➤ s tipografía.

typesetter ➤ s tipógrafo/a.

typewriter ➤ s máquina de escribir.

typhoid ➤ adj tifoideo ➤ s tifoidea.

typhus ➤ s tifus *m*.

typical ➤ adj típico.

typist ➤ s mecanógrafo/a.

tyranny ➤ s tiranía.

U

udder ➤ s ubre *f*.

UFO ➤ s ovni *m*.

ugliness ➤ s fealdad f.

ugly ➤ adj feo.

ulcer ➤ s úlcera.

ultimate ➤ adj último.

ultrasound ➤ s ultrasonido.

umbrella ➤ s paraguas m.

umpire ➤ s árbitro/a ➤ tr arbitrar.

unable ➤ adj incapaz.

unacceptable ➤ adj inaceptable.

unaccompanied ➤ adj solo.

unaccounted ➤ adj ■ u. for desapare-cido; (unexplained) inexplicado.

unafraid ➤ adj sin temor.

unanimous ➤ adj unánime.

unarmed ➤ adj desarmado; (defense-less) indefenso.

unattractive ➤ adj poco atractivo.

unauthorized ➤ adj desautorizado.

unavailable ➤ adj (not available) no disponible; (busy) ocupado.

unavoidable ➤ adj inevitable.

unaware ➤ adj ignorante ■ to be u. of no darse cuenta de ➤ **unaware(s)** adv de improviso.

unbearable ➤ adj insoportable.

unbelievable ➤ adj increíble.

unbreakable ➤ adj irrompible.

unbutton ➤ tr & intr desabotonar(se).

uncalled-for ➤ adj (undeserved) inme-recido; (out of place) inapropiado.

uncanny ➤ adj inexplicable.

uncertain ➤ adj incierto; (undecided) indeciso.

uncertainty ➤ s incertidumbre f.

unchanged ➤ adj inalterado.

unclaimed ➤ adj no reclamado.

uncle ➤ s tío ■ U. Sam (el) tío Sam.

unclear ➤ adj confuso.

uncomfortable ➤ adj incómodo.

uncommon ➤ adj poco común, raro.

unconditional ➤ adj incondicional.

unconfirmed ➤ adj no confirmado.

unconscious ➤ adj & s inconsciente m.

unconstitutional ➤ adj inconstitu-cional.

uncooked ➤ adj crudo.

uncover ➤ tr destapar, revelar.

undamaged ➤ adj libre de daño.

undecided ➤ adj no resuelto.

undeniable ➤ adj innegable.

under ➤ prep (por) debajo (de); (beneath) bajo; (less than) menos de; (during) durante el reinado de ■ u. the circumstances dadas las circunstan-cias ➤ adv bajo, debajo.

underage ➤ adj menor de edad.

underarm ➤ s axila, sobaco.

undercharge ➤ tr COM. cobrar menos de lo debido.

underclothes ➤ s ropa interior.

undercover ➤ adj clandestino.

underdone ➤ adj poco hecho.

underestimate ➤ tr subestimar ➤ s subestimación f.

undergo ➤ tr (to experience) experi-mentar; (to endure) sufrir.

undergraduate ➤ s & adj (de o para) estudiante mf universitario no gra-duado.

underground ➤ adj subterráneo; (se-cret) clandestino ➤ adv bajo tierra.

underline ➤ tr subrayar ➤ s raya.

underneath ➤ adv (por) debajo; (on the lower part) en la parte inferior ➤ prep bajo, debajo de ➤ s parte f inferior.

underpants ➤ spl calzoncillos.

underpass ➤ s paso por debajo.

underscore ➤ tr subrayar.

undershirt ➤ s camiseta.

understand ➤ tr & intr entender, com-prender.

understandable ➤ adj comprensible.

understanding ➤ s comprensión f; (agreement) acuerdo ➤ adj compren-sivo.

understood ➤ adj entendido; (implied) sobreentendido.

undertake ➤ tr (task) emprender; (duty) encargarse de.

undertaker ➤ s agente mf funerario ➤.

underwater ➤ adj subacuático.

underwear ➤ s ropa interior.

undo ➤ tr anular; (to untie) desatar; (to open) desenvolver; (to ruin) arruinar.

undress ➤ tr & intr desvestir(se) ➤ s desnudez f.

uneasy ➤ adj inquieto.

uneducated ➤ adj inculto.

unemployed ➤ adj desempleado.

unemployment ➤ s desempleo.

unequal ➤ adj desigual.

uneven ➤ *adj* desigual.

uneventful ➤ *adj* sin novedad.

unexpected ➤ *adj* inesperado.

unfair ➤ *adj* injusto.

unfaithful ➤ *adj* infiel; *(adulterous)* adúltero; *(inaccurate)* inexacto.

unfamiliar ➤ *adj* desconocido ▪ u. with no familiarizado con.

unfashionable ➤ *adj* fuera de moda.

unfasten ➤ *tr & intr* desatar(se).

unfavorable ➤ *adj* desfavorable; *(negative)* negativo.

unfinished ➤ *adj* incompleto.

unfit ➤ *adj* incapaz *(for, to de)*; *(unsuitable)* inadecuado; *(unqualified)* incompetente.

unfold ➤ *tr & intr* desdoblar(se); *(plot)* desarrollar(se).

unforgettable ➤ *adj* inolvidable.

unforgivable ➤ *adj* imperdonable.

unformatted ➤ *adj* sin formatear.

unfortunate ➤ *adj* desafortunado ➤ *s* desgraciado.

unfriendly ➤ *adj* hostil.

unfurl ➤ *tr & intr* desplegar(se).

unfurnished ➤ *adj* desamueblado.

ungrateful ➤ *adj* desagradecido.

unhappiness ➤ *s* desgracia.

unhappy ➤ *adj* infeliz; *(unlucky)* desafortunado.

unhealthy ➤ *adj* enfermizo; *(unwholesome)* insalubre.

unhook ➤ *tr* desenganchar.

uniform ➤ *adj & s* uniforme *m.*

unify ➤ *tr & intr* unificar(se).

unilateral ➤ *adj* unilateral.

unimportant ➤ *adj* poco importante.

uninformed ➤ *adj* mal informado.

uninhabited ➤ *adj* inhabitado.

uninterrupted ➤ *adj* ininterrumpido.

union ➤ *s* unión *f*; *(labor)* gremio, sindicato.

unique ➤ *adj* único; *(peerless)* sin igual.

unit ➤ *s* unidad *f*; *(part)* parte *f*; *(device)* aparato.

unite ➤ *tr & intr* unir(se).

unity ➤ *s* unidad *f.*

universal ➤ *adj* universal.

universe ➤ *s* universo.

university ➤ *s* universidad *f.*

unjust ➤ *adj* injusto.

unkind ➤ *adj* poco amable.

unknown ➤ *adj* desconocido.

unlawful ➤ *adj* ilegal.

unleaded ➤ *adj* sin plomo.

unless ➤ *conj* a menos que.

unlike ➤ *prep* diferente de; *(not typical of)* no característico de.

unlikely ➤ *adj* improbable.

unload ➤ *tr & intr* descargar.

unlock ➤ *tr & intr* abrir(se).

unlucky ➤ *adj* desgraciado ▪ to be u. tener mala suerte.

unmarried ➤ *adj* soltero.

unnecessary ➤ *adj* innecesario.

unnoticed ➤ *adj* inadvertido.

unoccupied ➤ *adj* *(vacant)* desocupado; *(idle)* desempleado.

unofficial ➤ *adj* extraoficial.

unpack ➤ *tr* desempacar; *(to unload)* descargar ➤ *intr* deshacer las maletas.

unpaid ➤ *adj* no remunerado.

unpleasant ➤ *adj* desagradable.

unplug ➤ *tr* destapar; ELEC. desenchufar.

unpopular ➤ *adj* impopular.

unpredictable ➤ *adj* que no se puede predecir *o* pronosticar.

unprepared ➤ *adj* desprevenido.

unprejudiced ➤ *adj* imparcial.

unqualified ➤ *adj* incompetente.

unreasonable ➤ *adj* irrazonable.

unrelated ➤ *adj* inconexo.

unreliable ➤ *adj* que no es de fiar.

unrest ➤ *s* desasosiego.

unroll ➤ *tr & intr* desenrollar(se).

unscrew ➤ *tr* destornillar; *(to loosen)* desenroscar.

unselfish ➤ *adj* generoso.

unsettled ➤ *adj* inestable; *(not resolved)* pendiente.

unskilled ➤ *adj* inexperto, sin entrenamiento; *(work)* no especializado.

unsolved ➤ *adj* sin resolver.

unsteady ➤ *adj* inestable; *(hands)* tembloroso.

unsuccessful ➤ *adj* fracasado; *(futile)* infructuoso ▪ to be u. no tener éxito.

unsuitable ➤ *adj* inadecuado; *(inconvenient)* inconveniente; *(unbecoming)* inapropiado.

untangle ➤ *tr* desenredar.

untidy ➤ *adj* desordenado.

untie ➤ *tr & intr* desatar(se).

until ➤ *prep & conj* hasta (que).

untimely ➤ *adj* inoportuno.

untrue ➤ *adj* falso; *(inaccurate)* inexacto.

unused ➤ *adj* sin usar; *(new)* nuevo ■ u. to no acostumbrado a.

unusual ➤ *adj* fuera de lo común; *(exceptional)* extraordinario.

unwell ➤ *adj* enfermo, indispuesto.

unwilling ➤ *adj* no dispuesto.

unworthy ➤ *adj* despreciable ■ u. of no digno de.

unwrap ➤ *tr* desenvolver.

unzip ➤ *tr* bajar la cremallera de.

up ➤ *adv* hacia arriba, en lo alto ■ close up cerca • from ten dollars up de diez dólares para arriba • high up muy arriba • to come *o* go up to acercarse a • to feel up to sentirse capaz de • to get up levantarse • up against junto a • up to hasta • up to date al día ➤ *adj* ■ to be up haberse levantado (de la cama) • to be up against tener que hacer frente a • to be up for *(office)* ser candidato a; *(to feel like)* tener ganas de • to be up on estar bien enterado sobre • to be up to something estar tramando algo • up in arms furioso ➤ *prep* arriba ➤ *s* ■ ups and downs altibajos ➤ *tr (to increase)* aumentar.

upbeat ➤ *adj* FAM. optimista.

upbringing ➤ *s* crianza.

upgrade ➤ *tr* mejorar la calidad de; COMPUT. actualizar ➤ *intr* hacer una actualización ➤ *s* cuesta; COMPUT. actualización *f*, upgrade *m*.

uphill ➤ *adj* ascendente; *(difficult)* arduo ➤ *s* cuesta ➤ *adv* cuesta arriba.

upholster ➤ *tr* tapizar.

upload ➤ *tr* COMPUT. subir, cargar.

upon ➤ *prep* sobre, por.

upper ➤ *adj* superior ■ u. case mayúsculas.

upright ➤ *adj* vertical; *(honorable)* recto ➤ *adv* verticalmente.

uproar ➤ *s* alboroto.

upset ➤ *tr (to tip over)* volcar; *(to throw into disorder)* desordenar; *(physically, mentally)* perturbar; *(the stomach)* caer mal a; *(an opponent)* vencer inesperadamente ➤ *s* vuelco; *(trouble)* molestia; *(defeat)* derrota inesperada ➤ *adj (disordered)* desordenado; *(worried)* preocupado.

upside-down ➤ *adv* al revés ■ to turn u. volcar(se); FIG. trastornar(se).

upstairs ➤ *adv* arriba; *(on upper floor)* en el piso superior ➤ *s* piso de arriba.

upswing ➤ *s* alza.

up-to-date ➤ *adj* al día.

upward ➤ *adj* ascendente ➤ *adv* hacia *o* para arriba.

urge ➤ *tr* incitar; *(to exhort)* exhortar; *(to advocate)* propugnar ➤ *s* impulso; *(desire)* deseo.

urgency ➤ *s* urgencia.

urgent ➤ *adj* urgente.

Uruguayan ➤ *adj & s* uruguayo/a.

us ➤ *pron* ■ she took us downtown nos llevó al centro ■ to us a nosotros.

use ➤ *tr* usar, emplear ■ to be used as, for servir de, para • to u. up agotar ➤ *intr* ■ I used to go. . . yo solía ir. . . ■ to get used to acostumbrarse a ➤ *s* uso; *(usefulness)* utilidad *f*.

used ➤ *adj* usado.

useful ➤ *adj* útil.

usefulness ➤ *s* utilidad *f*.

useless ➤ *adj* ineficaz; *(futile)* inútil.

user ➤ *s* usuario/a; *(addict)* adicto/a.

username ➤ *s* nombre *m* de usuario/a.

usher ➤ *s* acomodador/a.

usual ➤ *adj* usual; *(customary)* acostumbrado ■ as u. como de costumbre.

usually ➤ *adv* usualmente, por lo común.

utensil ➤ *s* utensilio.

utility ➤ *s* utilidad *f*.

utilize ➤ *tr* utilizar.

utmost ➤ *adj* sumo ➤ *s* máximo ■ to do one's u. hacer todo lo posible.

utter[1] ➤ *tr* decir, pronunciar.

utter[2] ➤ *adj* total, absoluto.

U-turn ➤ *s* AUTO. media vuelta.

V

vacancy ➤ *s* vacío; *(unfilled job)* vacante *f*; *(in a hotel)* habitación *f* libre.

vacant ➤ *adj* vacío; *(seat, room)* libre.

vacation ➤ s vacaciones f ➤ intr ir de vacaciones.

vaccinate ➤ tr & intr vacunar.

vaccination ➤ s vacunación f.

vacuum ➤ s vacío ■ v. cleaner aspiradora ➤ tr & intr pasar la aspiradora (por).

vague ➤ adj vago; (shape) borroso.

vain ➤ adj vano, inútil; (conceited) vanidoso.

valid ➤ adj válido.

validity ➤ s validez f.

valley ➤ s valle m.

valuable ➤ adj valioso ➤ valuables spl objetos de valor.

value ➤ s valor m; (importance) importancia ➤ tr estimar, valorar.

valve ➤ s válvula.

van ➤ s (truck) camioneta, furgoneta.

vandalize ➤ tr destrozar, destruir.

vanilla ➤ s vainilla.

vanish ➤ intr desaparecer.

vanity ➤ s vanidad.

vanquish ➤ tr derrotar, vencer.

vapor ➤ s vapor m.

variety ➤ s variedad f; (assortment) surtido.

various ➤ adj (several) varios; (different) diferente.

varnish ➤ s barniz m ➤ tr barnizar.

vary ➤ tr variar ➤ intr variar, cambiar; (to differ) diferir; (to deviate) desviarse.

vase ➤ s jarrón m, florero.

vast ➤ adj vasto, inmenso.

vault ➤ s bóveda.

VCR ➤ s grabadora de video.

veal ➤ s (carne f de) ternera.

vegetable ➤ s verdura, legumbre ➤ adj vegetal.

vegetarian ➤ adj & s vegetariano/a.

vegetation ➤ s vegetación f.

vehicle ➤ s vehículo.

veil ➤ s & tr (cubrir con un) velo.

vein ➤ s vena.

velvet ➤ s terciopelo.

Venetian blind ➤ s persiana veneciana.

vengeance ➤ s venganza.

Venezuelan ➤ adj & s venezolano/a.

venison ➤ s (carne f de) venado.

vent ➤ s respiradero; (hole) abertura.

ventilation ➤ s ventilación f.

verb ➤ s verbo.

verdict ➤ s veredicto; FIG. opinión f.

verge ➤ s borde m.

verify ➤ tr verificar.

vermouth ➤ s vermut m.

verse ➤ s verso; (stanza) estrofa; (of a song) cuplé m; BIBL. versículo.

version ➤ s versión f.

versus ➤ prep contra.

vertical ➤ adj & s vertical f.

very ➤ adv muy ■ at the v. least como mínimo • not v. poco • the v. best el o lo mejor • v. much (so) muchísimo.

vessel ➤ s vaso; MARÍT. nave.

vest ➤ s chaleco.

vestry ➤ s sacristía.

veteran ➤ adj & s veterano/a.

veterinarian ➤ s veterinario/a.

vex ➤ tr fastidiar, molestar.

via ➤ prep vía ■ v. air mail por vía aérea.

vibrate ➤ tr & intr vibrar.

vibration ➤ s vibración f.

vice[1] ➤ s vicio.

vice[2] ➤ s ■ v. president vice presidente ➤ prep ■ v. versa viceversa.

vicinity ➤ s vecindad f, proximidad f.

vicious ➤ adj vicioso, malicioso; (attack) violento, fuerte; (animal) salvaje.

victim ➤ s víctima.

victory ➤ s victoria, triunfo.

video ➤ adj & s video o vídeo.

videocassette ➤ s videocasete m.

videodisc/disk ➤ s videodisco.

video game ➤ s videojuego.

videotape ➤ s & tr (grabar en) videocinta.

view ➤ s (sight, vista) vista; (opinion) opinión f; (approach) enfoque m ➤ tr ver, mirar.

viewer ➤ s espectador/a; (television viewer) televidente mf.

viewpoint ➤ s punto de vista.

vigor ➤ s vigor m.

vigorous ➤ adj vigoroso, fuerte.

vile ➤ adj vil, odioso.

villa ➤ s villa, quinta.

village ➤ s aldea; (town) pueblo.

villager ➤ s aldeano/a.

villain ➤ s villano/a.

vine ➤ *s* parra, vid.
vinegar ➤ *s* vinagre *m*.
vineyard ➤ *s* viñedo, viña.
vinyl ➤ *s* vinilo.
violate ➤ *tr* violar.
violation ➤ *s* violación *f*.
violence ➤ *s* violencia.
violent ➤ *adj* violento.
violet ➤ *s* violeta.
violin ➤ *s* violín *m*.
VIP ➤ *s* FAM. personalidad *f* (importante).
virgin ➤ *s & adj* virgen *mf*.
virtual ➤ *adj* virtual.
virtue ➤ *s* virtud *f*.
virtuous ➤ *adj* virtuoso.
virus ➤ *s* virus *m*.
visa ➤ *s* visa, visado.
visibility ➤ *s* visibilidad *f*.
visible ➤ *adj* visible.
vision ➤ *s* vista, visión *f*; *(foresight)* clarividencia, previsión *f*; *(mental image)* visión, fantasía.
visit ➤ *tr/* visitar ➤ *intr* hacer una visita, ir de visita ➤ *s* visita.
visitor ➤ *s* visitante *mf*, visita.
vitamin ➤ *s* vitamina.
vivid ➤ *adj* vivo.
vocabulary ➤ *s* vocabulario.
vocalist ➤ *s* vocalista *mf*.
vocational ➤ *adj* vocacional.
vogue ➤ *s* moda, boga ■ in v. de moda.
voice ➤ *s* voz *f* ■ at the top of ones' v. a voz en cuello • v. mail correo de voz.
void ➤ *adj* vacío; DER. nulo, inválido ➤ *tr* invalidar ➤ *s* vacío.
volcano ➤ *s* volcán *m*.
volume ➤ *s* volumen *m*.
voluntary ➤ *adj* voluntario.
volunteer ➤ *s & adj* voluntario/a.
vomit ➤ *s & intr* vomitar ➤ *s* vómito.
vote ➤ *s* voto; *(act, result)* votación *f* ➤ *intr & tr* votar.
voter ➤ *s* votante *mf*, elector/a.
voting ➤ *s* votación *f* ➤ *adj* votante; *(campaign)* electoral.
vouch ➤ *intr* ■ to v. for garantizar, responder por.
voucher ➤ *s* comprobante *m*, vale *m*.
vow ➤ *s* promesa; RELIG. voto ➤ *tr* prometer, jurar.

vowel ➤ *s* vocal *f*.
voyage ➤ *s* viaje *m* ➤ *intr* viajar.
vulgar ➤ *adj* vulgar; *(rude)* grosero; *(taste)* cursi.

W

wade ➤ *intr* caminar (por el agua) ■ to w. across vadear.
wafer ➤ *s* oblea; CUL. galleta, barquillo.
wag ➤ *tr & intr* menear(se), sacudir(se) ➤ *s* meneo, sacudida.
wage ➤ *s* pago, sueldo ■ *pl (pay)* salario.
wagon ➤ *s* vagón *m*; *(station wagon)* furgoneta.
waist ➤ *s* cintura; *(of garment)* talle *m*.
wait ➤ *intr* esperar ■ to w. up esperar sin acostarse ➤ *s* espera.
waiter ➤ *s* camarero.
waiting room ➤ *s* sala de espera.
waitress ➤ *s* camarera.
wake◇ ➤ *intr & tr* despertar(se) ➤ *s* velatorio.
walk ➤ *intr* caminar, andar; *(to go on foot)* ir a pie; *(to stroll)* pasear ➤ *tr* caminar por; *(a distance)* caminar, andar ➤ *s* paseo ■ to go for *o* to take a w. dar un paseo.
walk-in ➤ *adj (services)* que no requiere cita previa.
wall ➤ *s* pared *f*; *(around a house)* muro; *(of city)* muralla.
wallet ➤ *s* billetera, cartera.
wallpaper ➤ *s* papel *m* de empapelar ➤ *tr & intr* empapelar.
walnut ➤ *s* nuez *f*; *(tree)* nogal *m*.
walrus ➤ *s* morsa.
waltz ➤ *s & intr* (bailar el) vals *m*.
wander ➤ *intr* vagar.
wane ➤ *intr* disminuir; *(moon)* menguar.
want ➤ *tr* querer; *(to desire)* desear; *(to need)* necesitar.
war ➤ *s & adj* (de) guerra.
ward ➤ *s* distrito; *(of hospital)* sala; *(minor)* pupilo/a ➤ *tr* ■ to w. off prevenir.
wardrobe ➤ *s* armario; *(garments)* vestuario.
wares ➤ *spl* mercancías.
warehouse ➤ *s* almacén *m*.
warm ➤ *adj* tibio, caliente; *(weather)*

cálido, caluroso; *(clothing)* que
mantiene abrigado ■ *tr* calentar ■ to
w. up *(food)* recalentar; DEP. calentarse.
warmth ➤ *s* calor *m;* FIG. afecto.
warm-up ➤ *s* DEP. calentamiento.
warn ➤ *tr & intr* advertir.
warning ➤ *s* advertencia; *(signal)* señal
f; (advice) aviso.
warrant ➤ *s* autorización *f,* orden *f*
judicial ➤ *tr* justificar.
warranty ➤ *s* garantía.
warrior ➤ *s* guerrero/a.
was ➤ *vea* be *en tabla de verbos.*
wash ➤ *tr* lavar ➤ *intr* lavarse; *(clothes)*
lavar ropa ■ to w. up lavarse; *(the
dishes)* lavar los platos ➤ *s* lavado;
(clothes) ropa para lavar.
washable ➤ *adj* lavable.
washbasin ➤ *s* lavabo.
washing machine ➤ *s* lavadora.
washroom ➤ *s* baño.
wasp ➤ *s* avispa.
waste ➤ *tr (money)* despilfarrar; *(time)*
perder; *(talent)* desperdiciar ➤ *s*
despilfarro; *(wastage)* desperdicios;
(of time, energy) pérdida; *(garbage)*
basura ■ to go to w. desperdiciarse.
wastebasket ➤ *s* cesto de papeles.
watch ➤ *intr* mirar ➤ *tr* mirar; *(to pay
attention to)* fijarse en; *(to guard)* vigilar; *(to take care of)* cuidar ➤ *s* reloj *m;*
(act) vigilia, vela.
water ➤ *s* agua *f.* ➤ *tr (a garden)* regar.
watercolor ➤ *adj & s* (de) acuarela.
waterfall ➤ *s* catarata, cascada.
watering can ➤ *s* regadera.
watermelon ➤ *s* sandía.
waterproof ➤ *adj* impermeable.
watt ➤ *s* vatio, watt *m.*
wave ➤ *intr & tr* agitar(se) ■ to w. goodbye decir adiós con la mano ➤ *s* ola;
(surface, hair) ondulación *f.*
wavelength ➤ *s* longitud *f* de onda.
wavy ➤ *adj* ondulante, onduloso;
(curly) ondulado.
wax ➤ *s* cera ➤ *tr* encerar.
way ➤ *s* camino; *(direction)* dirección *f;*
(method) manera, modo ■ all the w.
hasta el final; *(completely)* en todo ■
by the w. a propósito • by w. of vía ■ in
a w. en cierto modo • in every w. en

todos los aspectos • (in) no w. de ninguna manera • on the w. en camino •
right of w. derecho de paso • this, that
w. por aquí, allí; *(manner)* así • which
w? ¿por dónde?
we ➤ *pron* nosotros, nosotras.
weak ➤ *adj* débil; *(fragile)* frágil;
(unconvincing) poco convincente.
weaken ➤ *tr & intr* debilitar(se).
weakness ➤ *s* debilidad *f.*
wealth ➤ *s (riches)* riqueza.
wealthy ➤ *adj* rico.
weapon ➤ *s* arma.
wear◇ ➤ *tr* llevar; *(to damage)* deteriorar; *(to exhaust)* agotar ■ to w. off pasar • to w. out gastar(se) ➤ *s* uso;
(clothing) ropa; *(damage)* desgaste *m.*
weary ➤ *adj* fatigado.
weasel ➤ *s* ZOOL. comadreja.
weather ➤ *s* tiempo.
weave◇ ➤ *tr & intr* tejer; *(to interlace)*
entrelazar(se) ➤ *s* tejido.
web ➤ *s* telaraña; *(net)* red ■ W. web *m.*
webpage ➤ *s* página web.
website ➤ *s* sitio web, website *m.*
wedding ➤ *s* boda.
wedge ➤ *s* cuña; *(slice)* trozo; *(for secur-
ing)* calce *m* ➤ *tr* calzar.
Wednesday ➤ *s* miércoles *m.*
weed ➤ *s* mala hierba.
week ➤ *s* semana.
weekday ➤ *s* día *m* de trabajo.
weekend ➤ *s* fin *m* de semana.
weekly ➤ *adj & adv* semanal(mente)
➤ *s* semanario.
weep◇ ➤ *intr* llorar.
weigh ➤ *tr & intr* pesar.
weight ➤ *s* peso ■ to gain *o* put on w.
engordar • to lose w. adelgazar.
weird ➤ *adj* raro, extraño.
welcome ➤ *adj* bienvenido ■ you're w.!
¡no hay de qué!, ¡de nada! ➤ *tr* dar la
bienvenida a; *(to accept)* aceptar con
beneplácito ➤ *interj* ¡bienvenido!
weld ➤ *tr* soldar.
welfare ➤ *s* bienestar *m; (benefits)* asistencia social.
well¹ ➤ *s* pozo.
well² ➤ *adv* bien ■ as w. también • as w.
as además de; *(just as)* así como • that
is just as w. es mejor así • to do w.

prosperar ➤ *adj* bien ■ **to get w.** mejorar ➤ *interj* ¡bueno!
well-behaved ➤ *adj* bien educado.
well-being ➤ *s* bienestar *m*.
well-done ➤ *adj* (*food*) bien cocido.
well-known ➤ *adj* bien conocido.
well-mannered ➤ *adj* educado.
well-to-do ➤ *adj* próspero.
went ➤ *vea* **go** en tabla de verbos.
were ➤ *vea* **be** en tabla de verbos.
west ➤ *s* oeste *m*, occidente *m* ➤ *adj* del oeste, occidental ➤ *adv* al oeste, hacia el oeste.
western ➤ *adj* occidental, del oeste ➤ *s* película del oeste.
westerner ➤ *s* habitante *mf* del oeste.
westward ➤ *adv* hacia el oeste.
wet◇ ➤ *adj* mojado; (*rainy*) lluvioso; (*paint*) fresco ■ **to get w.** mojarse • **soaking w.** empapado ➤ *tr* mojar.
whale ➤ *s* ZOOL. ballena.
wharf ➤ *s* muelle *m*.
what ➤ *pron* qué; (*which*) cuál ■ **w?** ¿cómo? • **w. for?** ¿para qué? • **w. is that?** ¿qué es eso? • **w. I've learned** lo que he aprendido ➤ *adj* qué; (*which*) cuál ■ **w. music do you like?** ¿qué música te gusta? ➤ *interj* ¡cómo! ■ **w. a pity!** ¡qué lástima!
whatever ➤ *pron* ■ **do w. you want** haz lo que quieras • **w. happens** pase lo que pase ➤ *adj* (*any*) cualquiera que; (*of any kind at all*) de ninguna clase.
wheat ➤ *s* trigo.
wheel ➤ *s* rueda; (*steering*) volante *m*.
wheelbarrow ➤ *s* carretilla.
when ➤ *adv* cuándo ■ **w. will we get there?** ¿a qué hora vamos a llegar? ➤ *conj* cuando; (*as soon as*) al, en cuanto; (*if*) si ➤ *pron* cuándo.
whenever ➤ *adv & conj* cuando quiera (que); (*when*) cuando; (*every time that*) siempre que.
where ➤ *adv* dónde; (*from where*) de dónde; (*to where*) adónde ■ **w. is . . .?** ¿dónde está . . .? ➤ *conj* donde, en dónde; (*to where*) a donde.
whereas ➤ *conj* (*since*) visto que; (*while*) mientras (que).
wherever ➤ *adv & conj* dondequiera que.

whether ➤ *conj* (*if*) si ■ **w. he wins or loses** sea que él gane o pierda.
which ➤ *pron* ■ **my house, w. is small** mi casa, la cual es pequeña • **w. of these . . .?** ¿cuál de éstos . . .? • **w. of you?** ¿quién de ustedes? ➤ *adj* • **for w. reason** por cuya razón • **w. color do you like?** ¿qué color te gusta? • **w. one?** ¿cuál? • **w. way?** ¿por dónde?
whichever ➤ *pron* cualquiera ➤ *adj* cualquier (que sea).
while ➤ *s* rato, tiempo ■ **once in a w.** de vez en cuando • **to be worth (one's) w.** valer la pena ➤ *conj* mientras (que); (*although*) aunque.
whim ➤ *s* capricho, antojo.
whine ➤ *intr* gimotear; (*to complain*) quejarse; (*bullet*) silbar ➤ *s* gimoteo; (*complaint*) quejido; (*bullet*) silbido.
whip ➤ *tr* azotar; (*cream, eggs*) batir ➤ *s* azote *m*, látigo.
whipped cream ➤ *s* nata batida.
whir ➤ *intr* zumbar ➤ *s* zumbido.
whirl ➤ *intr* dar vueltas ➤ *s* giro.
whirlwind ➤ *s* torbellino.
whisk ➤ *tr* CUL. batir ➤ *intr* moverse rápidamente ➤ *s* CUL. batidor *m*.
whiskey ➤ *s* whisky *m*.
whisper ➤ *s* susurro ➤ *intr* susurrar.
whistle ➤ *intr* silbar; (*with a device*) pitar ➤ *tr* silbar ➤ *s* pito, silbato; (*act, sound*) silbido, pitido.
white ➤ *s* blanco; (*of an egg*) clara ➤ *adj* blanco.
who ➤ *pron* quién, quien ■ **it was my sister w. called** fue mi hermana quien llamó • **my sister, w. is sick** mi hermana, que está enferma • **the one(s) w.** el (los) que • **w. knows?** ¿quién sabe?
whoever ➤ *pron* quienquiera que; (*the one who*) el que, quien.
whole ➤ *adj* entero, todo; (*total*) total; (*healthy*) sano; (*undamaged*) intacto ■ **a w. lot of** muchísimo ➤ *s* todo, totalidad *f*; (*complete entity*) suma ■ **as a w.** en conjunto • **on the w.** en general.
wholesale ➤ *adj & adv* al por mayor.
wholesome ➤ *adj* sano.
whole-wheat ➤ *adj* de trigo entero.
whom ➤ *pron* ■ **from w. . . .?** ¿de

quién . . .? • the man with w. . . . el hombre con quien . . . .

whose ➤ *pron & adj* ▪ the girl w. shirt is red la chica cuya camisa es roja • w. shirt is this? ¿de quién es esta camisa?

why ➤ *adv* por qué, para qué ▪ w. not? ¿por qué no? ➤ *conj* por (lo) que.

wick ➤ *s* mecha.

wicked ➤ *adj* malvado; *(mischievous)* travieso.

wicker ➤ *s* mimbre *m.*

wide ➤ *adj* ancho ▪ two feet w. dos pies de ancho • w. open de par en par.

widely ➤ *adv (very)* muy; *(much)* mucho; *(extensively)* extensamente.

widen ➤ *tr & intr* ensanchar(se).

widespread ➤ *adj* extendido; *(prevalent)* general.

widow ➤ *s* viuda.

widower ➤ *s* viudo.

width ➤ *s* anchura, ancho.

wife ➤ *s* esposa, mujer *f.*

wig ➤ *s* peluca.

wild ➤ *adj* salvaje; *(plant)* silvestre; *(crazy)* loco, extraviado; *(frenzied)* frenético; *(guess)* al azar ➤ *adv* alocadamente • *s* ▪ in the w. en estado natural • the w. naturaleza.

wilderness ➤ *s* región *f* sin cultivar.

wildflower ➤ *s* flor *f* silvestre.

wildlife ➤ *s* fauna.

will[1] ➤ *s* voluntad *f*; DER. testamento ➤ *tr* querer; *(to order)* ordenar.

will[2] ➤ *aux* ▪ they w. come vendrán • you w. regret this lo vas a lamentar • w. you help me? ¿quieres ayudarme?

willful ➤ *adj* obstinado.

willing ➤ *adj* de buena voluntad.

willow ➤ *s* sauce *m.*

willpower ➤ *s* fuerza de voluntad.

win◇ ➤ *intr & tr* ganar ➤ *s* victoria, triunfo.

wind[1] ➤ *s* viento; *(air)* aire *m* ▪ pl MÚS. instrumentos de viento.

wind[2]◇ ➤ *tr* envolver; *(to entwine)* enrollar; *(a watch)* dar cuerda a ➤ *intr (road)* serpentear; *(rope)* enrollarse.

windmill ➤ *s* molino de viento.

window ➤ *s* ventana; *(small)* ventanilla; *(of a shop)* escaparate *m.*

windshield ➤ *s* parabrisas *m* ▪ w. wiper limpiaparabrisas.

windy ➤ *adj* ventoso.

wine ➤ *s* vino.

wineglass ➤ *s* copa para vino.

wing ➤ *s* ala ▪ *pl* TEAT. bastidores.

wink ➤ *intr* guiñar ➤ *s* guiño.

winner ➤ *s* ganador/a.

winter ➤ *s* invierno.

wipe ➤ *tr* limpiar; *(to dry)* secar ▪ to w. off quitar • to w. out destruir; *(a debt)* cancelar.

wire ➤ *s* alambre *m*; ELEC. cable *m*; *(telegram)* telegrama.

wireless ➤ *adj* inalámbrico.

wiring ➤ *s* instalación eléctrica.

wisdom ➤ *s* sabiduría.

wise ➤ *adj* sabio; *(judicious)* juicioso; *(sensible)* sensato.

wish ➤ *s* deseo ➤ *tr* querer, desear; *(to like to)* gustar; *(to bid)* dar.

wit ➤ *s* inteligencia; *(cleverness)* ingenio ▪ *pl* juicio.

witch ➤ *s* bruja.

with ➤ *prep* con ▪ to tremble w. fear temblar de miedo • w. me conmigo • w. you contigo, con usted(es).

withdraw ➤ *tr* sacar, quitar; *(to retract)* retractar ➤ *intr (to retreat)* retraerse; *(to draw away)* apartarse.

withdrawn ➤ *adj* remoto; *(shy)* tímido.

wither ➤ *intr* marchitarse.

withhold ➤ *tr* retener, contener.

within ➤ *adv* dentro; *(indoors)* adentro; *(inwardly)* internamente ➤ *prep* dentro de; *(distance)* a menos de; *(time)* antes de; *(not beyond)* dentro de los límites de ➤ *s* adentro.

without ➤ *adv* fuera ➤ *prep* sin; *(on the outside of)* (a)fuera de ▪ it goes w. saying se sobreentiende • to do w. pasar(se) sin.

withstand ➤ *tr* resistir a.

witness ➤ *s* testigo/a ➤ *tr & intr* atestiguar.

witty ➤ *adj* ingenioso, gracioso.

wizard ➤ *s* hechicero.

wobbly ➤ *adj* tembloroso.

wolf ➤ *s* lobo ➤ *tr* ▪ to w. down comer vorazmente.

woman ➤ *s* mujer *f* ▪ women mujeres.

wonder ➤ s maravilla; *(astonishment)* asombro ➤ *intr (to ponder)* pensar; *(to be doubtful)* dudar ➤ *tr* preguntarse.

wonderful ➤ adj maravilloso.

wood ➤ s madera; *(firewood)* leña ■ *pl* bosque.

wooden ➤ adj de madera.

wool ➤ s lana.

woolen ➤ adj de lana.

word ➤ s palabra ■ in other words mejor dicho • take my w. for it se lo aseguro • to keep one's w. cumplir la palabra • w. processing procesamiento de texto • w. processor procesador de texto ■ *pl* MÚS. letra.

work ➤ s trabajo; *(job)* empleo; *(result)* obra ■ the works JER. todo, de todo • w. force mano de obra ➤ *intr* trabajar; *(to operate)* funcionar ➤ *tr (machine)* manejar; *(miracle)* hacer; *(slave)* hacer trabajar ■ to w. out solucionar.

worker ➤ s trabajador/a.

workout ➤ s ejercicio.

workshop ➤ s taller m.

workstation ➤ s consola, estación f de trabajo.

world ➤ s mundo.

worldly ➤ adj secular; *(worldly-wise)* sofisticado.

worldwide ➤ adj mundial.

World Wide Web ➤ s Red f.

worm ➤ s gusano.

worn-out ➤ adj *(used)* gastado; *(exhausted)* agotado.

worry ➤ *intr* & *tr* preocupar(se) ➤ s preocupación f.

worse ➤ adj peor ■ to get w. empeorar ➤ adv peor; *(more severely)* más.

worsen ➤ *tr* & *intr* empeorar(se).

worship ➤ s adoración f; devoción f ➤ *tr* & *intr* venerar.

worst ➤ adj & adv peor ■ s ■ at w. o if w. comes to w. en el peor de los casos.

worth ➤ s valor m; *(wealth)* fortuna; *(merit)* mérito ➤ adj que vale ■ to be w. valer; *(to be the equivalent of)* valer por • to be w. it valer la pena.

worthless ➤ adj sin valor.

worthy ➤ adj meritorio.

would ➤ vea will en tabla de verbos.

wound ➤ s herida ➤ *tr* & *intr* herir.

woven ➤ adj tejido.

wrap◇ ➤ *tr* envolver ■ to be wrapped up in estar absorto en • to w. up *(to end)* cerrar; *(to summarize)* resumir ➤ *intr* enrollarse ➤ s *(cloak)* manto ■ to keep under wraps mantener en secreto.

wrapper ➤ s envoltura.

wrap-up ➤ s resumen m.

wrath ➤ s ira.

wreath ➤ s guirnalda.

wreck ➤ s destrucción f; *(crash)* choque m; *(shipwreck)* naufragio; *(collision remains)* destrozos ➤ *tr* destrozar, arruinar.

wrench ➤ s MEC. llave f ➤ *tr* torcer.

wrestle ➤ *intr* & *tr* luchar (con o contra).

wrestling ➤ s lucha.

wretched ➤ adj desgraciado, miserable.

wring◇ ➤ *tr* escurrir.

wrinkle ➤ s arruga ➤ *tr* arrugar, fruncir.

wrist ➤ s muñeca ■ w. watch reloj de pulsera.

write◇ ➤ *tr* & *intr* escribir.

writer ➤ s escritor/a.

writing ➤ s escritura f; *(handwriting)* letra; *(work)* escrito ■ in w. por escrito.

wrong ➤ adj malo; *(unfair)* injusto; *(incorrect)* erróneo; *(mistaken)* equivocado ■ to be w. hacer mal; *(to be mistaken)* equivocarse; *(to be amiss)* andar mal ➤ adv mal ■ to do, get w. hacer, tener mal • to go w. *(to act mistakenly)* fallar; *(to go amiss)* salir mal ➤ s mal m; *(unjust act)* injusticia; *(bad deed)* maldad f; *(fault)* error m ■ to be in the w. no tener razón ➤ *tr* ser injusto con.

wrought ➤ adj ■ w. iron hierro forjado.

X

X-mas ➤ s FAM. Navidad f.

X-rated ➤ adj no apto para menores de 18 años.

x-ray o **X-ray** ➤ s radiografía; FÍS. rayo X ➤ *tr* radiografiar.

xylophone ➤ s xilófono.

Y

yacht ➤ s yate m.

yak ➤ s ZOOL. yac m.

yam ➤ s ñame f; *(sweet potato)* batata.

Yankee ➤ adj & s yanqui mf.

yard¹ ➤ s *(measure)* yarda.

yard² ➤ s jardín m.

yarn ➤ s hilo.

yawn ➤ intr bostezar ➤ s bostezo.

year ➤ s año ■ school y. año escolar ■ pl *(age)* edad.

yearly ➤ adj anual.

yearn ➤ intr añorar.

yearning ➤ s anhelo, añoranza.

yeast ➤ s levadura.

yell ➤ tr & intr gritar ➤ s grito.

yellow ➤ s & adj amarillo.

yes ➤ adv sí.

yesterday ➤ adv ayer ➤ s (el día de) ayer m ■ the day before y. anteayer.

yet ➤ adv todavía, aún; *(thus far)* ya; *(still more)* aún más; *(eventually)* probablemente ■ as (of) y. hasta ahora • not y. todavía no ➤ conj *(nevertheless)* sin embargo; *(but)* pero.

yield ➤ tr dar, producir ➤ intr rendirse; *(in traffic)* ceder el paso ■ to y. to ceder a ➤ s rendimiento.

yoga ➤ s yoga m.

yogurt ➤ s yogur m.

yolk ➤ s yema.

you ➤ pron [sujeto] *(familiar)* tú, vosotros, vosotras; *(formal)* usted, ustedes; [complemento] *(familiar, direct and indirect)* te, os; *(formal, direct)* lo, la, los, las; *(formal, indirect)* le, les, se; [después de preposición] *(familiar)* ti, vosotros, vosotras; *(formal)* usted, ustedes ■ if I were y. yo que tú • with y. contigo, con usted(es).

young ➤ adj joven ➤ spl jóvenes mf; *(offspring)* cría (de animal).

youngster ➤ s jovencito/a.

your ➤ adj *(familiar, sg.)* tu(s); *(formal, sg.)* su(s), de usted; *(familiar, pl.)* vuestra(s); *(formal, pl.)* su(s), de ustedes.

yours ➤ pron *(familiar, sg.)* (el) tuyo, (la) tuya; *(formal, sg.)* (el o la) de usted, el suyo, la suya; *(familiar, pl.)* (el) vuestro, (la) vuestra; *(formal, pl.)* (el o la) de ustedes, (el) suyo, (la) suya.

yourself ➤ pron *(familiar)* tú (mismo, misma); *(formal)* usted (mismo, misma).

yourselves ➤ pron *(familiar)* vosotros (mismos), vosotras (mismas); *(formal)* ustedes (mismos, mismas).

youth ➤ s juventud f; *(young person)* joven mf.

youthful ➤ adj joven, juvenil.

yo-yo ➤ s yoyó.

Z

zany ➤ adj estrafalario.

zeal ➤ s celo, ahínco.

zealotry ➤ s fanatismo.

zealous ➤ adj fervoroso.

zebra ➤ s cebra.

zenith ➤ s cenit m.

zephyr ➤ s brisa.

zero ➤ s cero; *(nothing)* nada ➤ adj nulo ➤ tr & intr ■ to z. in on apuntar hacia.

zest ➤ s gusto, sabor m; *(enjoyment)* brío.

zigzag ➤ s & adj (en) zigzag m ➤ adv zigzagueando ➤ intr ir zigzagueando.

zillion ➤ s FAM. número astronómico.

zinc ➤ s cinc m.

zip ➤ s vigor m ➤ intr zumbar ■ to z. by pasar como una bala • to z. up subir o cerrar la cremallera.

zip code ➤ s código postal.

zipper ➤ s cremallera.

zodiac ➤ s zodíaco.

zonal ➤ adj zonal.

zone ➤ s zona ➤ tr dividir en zonas.

zoning ➤ s restricciones f para edificar en un barrio urbano.

zoo ➤ s zoo.

zoologist ➤ s zoólogo/a.

zoology ➤ s zoología.

zoom ➤ intr *(to buzz)* zumbar; *(to go fast)* ir zumbando; FOTOG. *(in)* acercarse; *(out)* alejarse ➤ s *(sound)* zumbido; AVIA. subida vertical.

zucchini ➤ s zapallito italiano.

NUMBERS/ NÚMEROS

Cardinal Numbers	Números Cardinales	Ordinal Numbers	Números Ordinales
1	one	uno	first	primero
2	two	dos	second	segundo
3	three	tres	third	tercero
4	four	cuatro	fourth	cuarto
5	five	cinco	fifth	quinto
6	six	seis	sixth	sexto
7	seven	siete	seventh	séptimo
8	eight	ocho	eighth	octavo
9	nine	nueve	ninth	noveno; nono
10	ten	diez	tenth	décimo
11	eleven	once	eleventh	undécimo
12	twelve	doce	twelfth	duodécimo
13	thirteen	trece	thirteenth	decimotercero
14	fourteen	catorce	fourteenth	decimocuarto
15	fifteen	quince	fifteenth	decimoquinto
16	sixteen	dieciséis	sixteenth	decimosexto
17	seventeen	diecisiete	seventeenth	decimoséptimo
18	eighteen	dieciocho	eighteenth	decimoctavo
19	nineteen	diecinueve	nineteenth	decimonoveno; decimonono
20	twenty	veinte	twentieth	vigésimo
21	twenty-one	veintiuno	twenty-first	vigésimo primero
30	thirty	treinta	thirtieth	trigésimo
40	forty	cuarenta	fortieth	cuadragésimo
50	fifty	cincuenta	fiftieth	quincuagésimo
60	sixty	sesenta	sixtieth	sexagésimo
70	seventy	setenta	seventieth	septuagésimo
80	eighty	ochenta	eightieth	octogésimo
90	ninety	noventa	ninetieth	nonagésimo
100	one hundred	cien	(one) hundredth	centésimo
101	one hundred and one	ciento uno	(one) hundred and first	centésimo primero
200	two hundred	doscientos	two-hundredth	ducentésimo
300	three hundred	trescientos	three-hundredth	tricentésimo
400	four hundred	cuatrocientos	four-hundredth	cuadringentésimo
500	five hundred	quinientos	five-hundredth	quingentésimo
600	six hundred	seiscientos	six-hundredth	sexagésimo
700	seven hundred	setecientos	seven-hundredth	septingentésimo
800	eight hundred	ochocientos	eight-hundredth	octingentésimo
900	nine hundred	novecientos	nine-hundredth	noningentésimo
1000	one thousand	mil	(one) thousandth	milésimo
100,000	one hundred thousand	cien mil	(one) hundred thousandth	cienmilésimo
1,000,000	one million	un millón	(one) millionth	millonésimo